THE WARGAMING COMPENDIUM

THE WARGAMING COMPENDIUM

HENRY HYDE

PEN & SWORD
Barnsley

First published in Great Britain in 2013
and reprinted in 2014 by
PEN & SWORD MILITARY
An imprint of
Pen & Sword Books Ltd
47 Church Street
Barnsley
South Yorkshire
S70 2AS

HB ISBN 978 1 84884 221 2
TPB ISBN 978 1 47382 377 8

A CIP catalogue record for this book is
available from the British Library.

Design, typesetting, maps and diagrams by Henry Hyde
Illustrations in Chapter 7 by Bob Marrion
Photography by Henry Hyde except where otherwise credited

Printed and bound in India by Replika Press Pvt. Ltd.

Pen & Sword Books Ltd incorporates the Imprints of Pen & Sword Aviation,
Pen & Sword Family History, Pen & Sword Maritime, Pen & Sword Military,
Pen & Sword Discovery, Wharncliffe Local History, Wharncliffe True Crime,
Wharncliffe Transport, Pen & Sword Select, Pen & Sword Military Classics,
Leo Cooper, The Praetorian Press, Remember When,
Seaforth Publishing and Frontline Publishing

For a complete list of Pen & Sword titles please contact
PEN & SWORD BOOKS LIMITED
47 Church Street, Barnsley, South Yorkshire, S70 2AS, England
E-mail: enquiries@pen-and-sword.co.uk
Website: www.pen-and-sword.co.uk

CONTENTS

To my Annie, for letting me be who I am.

To my late father, Edgar, trusting he would have been proud.

To my mother, Nora, knowing that she will be.

And to my godson Edward, who I hope will remember our games with affection.

ACKNOWLEDGEMENTS

There's a cliché which runs something along the lines of "standing on the shoulders of giants" and it certainly applies here. My wargaming has been inspired most of all by those early British wargame pioneers, some still with us, some now sadly passed on, who wrote with such passion and enthusiasm about the hobby they loved that they inspired a small boy to see his toys in an entirely new way. Their names and works are recorded in this book.

For their practical input into this project, I would first like to thank Phil Sidnell of Pen & Sword whose remarkable stoicism in the face of me requesting yet another extension to my deadline has been inspiring; if ever a man was owed a pint, it's him.

Next, I wish to thank Arthur Harman who threw himself into combing through my first draft with enthusiasm and unerring accuracy. He also gets particular thanks for undertaking the herculean task of creating the index, an act of editorial gallantry indeed. He was joined in proofing the final draft by my dear friend Steve Gill, whose eagle eye and gentle sense of fun have been incredibly helpful. I also want to thank Mike Siggins, veteran campaigner with an encyclopaedic knowledge of the hobby, whose encouragement and approval of this work means a great deal to me.

A number of friends have been involved with play-testing my rules, including Dan Mersey, Will Townshend, Guy Hancock, Graham Knight and, here's that name again, Phil Sidnell, who was professional enough to point out every loophole just when I thought they were finished, prompting me to re-write them entirely! My heartfelt thanks also go to that group of online reprobates on the WD3 forum who gave the *Shot, Steel & Stone* rules a thorough workout accompanied by much laughter and good company at the 2011 and 2012 East Ayton gatherings: Paul Bright, Iain Burt, John Francis, Richard Frost, Tim Hall, Dave Hall, Phil Hope, Dave McClumpha, Ken McGarry, Andy McMaster, Mark Phillips, Peter-Mark Smith, Kerry Thomas, Simon Tonkiss and Mike Whitaker. Any errors or omissions remaining are, of course, entirely my responsibility.

Special thanks are due to Bob Marrion for sourcing a wonderful selection of his marvellous illustrations that enrich Chapter 7.

My magazine has enabled me to meet and engage in conversation with some of the finest minds and brightest talents in the hobby. I thank them all for the inspiration and ideas they have provided, especially Charles Grant, Rick Priestley, Richard Clarke, Nick Skinner, John Drewienkiewicz, Andrew Brentnall, Dave Ryan, Pete Berry and master podcaster Neil Shuck.

And finally, my thanks to the little army of talented miniature sculptors and casters, terrain makers, figure painters, book and magazine publishers, game designers, rules writers, authors, illustrators, show organisers, webmasters, bloggers, podcasters and retailers who make the hobby the thriving and vibrant pursuit that it is today. Truly, we live in a golden age.

A huge game restaging the Battle of Waterloo, 18th June 1815, using 15mm miniatures and played over a weekend by two teams of enthusiastic wargamers. At this point, the French, attacking from the right, have overwhelmed the defences of La Haye Sainte farmhouse and are approaching the British ridge. The game was organised by well-known wargamer Dave Brown, author of the popular *General de Brigade* Napoleonic wargames rules.

FOREWORD

by Brigadier (Retired) Charles S Grant OBE

On the title page of H G Wells' *Little Wars* it says "A game for boys from twelve years of age to a hundred and fifty and for that more intelligent sort of girl who likes boys' games and books." Well, even if the thought police today allowed H G Wells to say such things, the sentiment is dated. Wargaming today embraces the widest possible spectrum of both age and gender. So, what would the pioneer of modern wargaming find in *The Wargame Compendium* for this wide audience?

The Collins Dictionary defines "compendium" as "A book containing a collection of useful hints" and "A selection, especially of different games in one container". Well, *The Wargaming Compendium* does, as they say, "what it says on the tin" – and a great deal more. In producing the *Compendium*, Henry Hyde has boldly gone were no wargamer has gone before. Yes, there have been and are many books on wargaming, but this is truly a *magnum opus*.

The Wargaming Compendium provides a history of the hobby, a step by step beginner's guide, rules and advice on the choice of periods, and an overview of wargaming today. In the latter case, it is a snapshot in time which we may look back on in years to come and compare with what has happened. However, the majority of the content is ageless and I vouch that it can truly boast that there is something for everyone.

This is a labour of love and those that know Henry will know that already. Those that do not will come to understand this as they read the *Compendium*. Whether new to the wargame, in which case the *Compendium* will guide you through the hobby, or a long term wargamer, there is something here for you. It is always fascinating to see how the other chap goes about the hobby and Henry has given us a real and practical insight.

The Wargaming Compendium is a significant contribution to the wargamer's library and can comfortably stand side by side with tomes by the pioneers of the hobby.

Well done Henry.

Charles S Grant
By Bankfoot, April 2012

Warlord Games supremo John Stallard (seated) hosts a *Black Powder* game in his magnificent wargames room. The author (second from left) shares a joke with rules writer Rick Priestley (left), figure sculptor Michael Perry (right) and Games Workshop writer Jervis Johnson (far right). This Crimean War game had the author commanding the British Heavy Brigade and Rick Priestley leading the Light Brigade. We did a lot of charging that day! Photo courtesy of Dan Faulconbridge of *Wargames illustrated*.

The author with a captive audience at the To the Redoubt show in Eastbourne, 2009, waxing lyrical whilst running a simple, fast and furious skirmish game: *The Biebersfurt All-Comers Waxball Competition*. This was an entirely fictitious eighteenth century version of the paintball tournaments of today. Photo courtesy of Nick Elsden.

INTRODUCTION

Wargaming is a fascinating, engrossing and exciting hobby that encompasses many different talents. In the course of pursuing his hobby, the typical wargamer uses the skills of artist, designer, sculptor, illustrator, historian, librarian, researcher, mathematician and creative writer, as well as the more obvious ones of general, admiral or air marshal for large games, or perhaps lieutenant, sergeant or even private soldier for skirmishes. This may seem like an extraordinary statement, but in the course of this book, I hope to show you that this claim is indeed justified.

Not only is wargaming a pursuit which calls upon many skills, but it also covers many aspects of combat of one kind or another, spanning thousands of years of history (and, in the case of science fiction, many thousands of years into the future). A fantasy gamer, of course, deals with eons of *imagined* history, as anyone who has read *The Lord of the Rings* will know. Thus, the wargamer may find himself recreating a skirmish between a handful of adversaries one day, or a massed battle involving perhaps thousands of miniature troops the next. Moreover, it is possible to play wargames that recreate combat on land, on sea, in the air or even in outer space.

Wargaming also takes many forms. Some gamers are perfectly at home with their gaming area represented by a small board, perhaps delineated with hexes or squares, and piles of cardboard or wooden counters. At the time of writing this book, as the 21st century enters its second decade, there are of course millions of gamers worldwide who derive great satisfaction from competing against the Artificial Intelligence offered by modern personal computer software. Such games, whether purchased on CD, DVD or online, are now capable of offering astonishing levels of verisimilitude, with graphic representations of troops from many periods of history obeying the player's electronic orders as they fight across beautifully rendered digital terrain. Nor is this necessarily a solitary pursuit, with Massive Multiplayer Online Games such as *World of Warcraft* pitting literally millions of players worldwide against each other in artificial worlds.

This book, however, will concentrate upon the more, dare I say it, 'traditional' form of wargaming which makes use of small-scale figures and a tabletop decorated with miniature houses, forests, rivers and other scenery that provides the terrain across which our miniature armies will fight. Ranging in size (from the soles of their feet to the tops of their heads) from a tiny 2mm up to 54mm or more, and cast in metal or plastic, our hobby is supplied by an astonishing range of miniatures from which, quite frankly, it is often hard to choose! One of the objectives of this book is to assist you in making informed decisions about the bewildering choice of periods of history, sizes of miniatures and manufacturers there are to select from. I may touch upon the use of miniature aeroplanes in swirling dogfights, and tiny ships that sail upon miniature seas, but this will be only in passing, since their use could justifiably fill additional volumes.

The tabletop battlefield itself varies in aesthetic style from a simple green cloth covering the family dining table, strewn with perhaps a few polystyrene hills and clumps of lichen, to fully dioramic set-ups covering a large, custom-built surface that would easily rival any lovingly created model railway layout. Hills, cliffs, rivers, coastal areas, marshes, forests, farmhouses and full, urban conurbations are the stock in trade of the dedicated (some might say "obsessed"!) wargamer. Model railway enthusiasts have their various gauges, ranging from O, through the popular HO to the smaller N and even the tiny Z; and, in similar fashion, the famous La Haye Sainte farmhouse in the centre of the Battle of Waterloo might occupy a square metre or so in a large-scale 54mm wargame, or merely a few centimetres across in a 6mm game.

It may seem surprising that such a hobby remains so popular today, when there are so many other demands on our time and so many possibilities for instant digital gratification elsewhere. As I hope to demonstrate in this book, it is perhaps the very fact that wargaming with miniatures offers a release from the tyranny of the digital age which makes it so enduringly popular. Moreover, the skills which it encourages and rewards amongst its practitioners provide a refreshing antidote to our growing concerns about attention deficit disorder amongst young people.

I would not wish to give the impression, however, that in order to participate in this wonderful pastime, you must pass some kind of preposterous entrance examination, perhaps taking the form of one of

A game played with just a couple of dozen miniatures on very simple terrain consisting of a painted baseboard with polystyrene hills that have had some cork bark 'rubble' added and have then been painted. The Newline Designs 20mm figures were painted and based by the author. The dice, incidentally, indicate the ammunition remaining to the British as they attempt to escape hordes of Zulus – unsuccessfully, in this instance!

An elaborate 28mm size Peninsular War layout created by talented terrain maker Paul Darnell for the well-known British collector Bill Gaskin, who customised and painted the figures. Few wargamers have the time, space or resources to undertake a project of this kind, which is why such display pieces are often only seen at shows, but they are a spectacular and inspiring insight into just what is possible.

those ghastly 'reality' television shows where ritual humiliation is the order of the day. There is no triumvirate of acid-tongued celebrities waiting to rubbish your first, tentative steps towards tabletop glory, no test that you must pass to grant you some imagined licence to practise. No, on the contrary, this is a hobby in which you will find your own level of satisfaction. There are countless wargamers who sigh and admire the work of master professional painters, sculptors and terrain makers, whilst deriving huge satisfaction from their own hastily-painted armies and convenient, portable terrain pieces laid on their green cloth battlefields. Avid miniaturists may indeed, if they choose, experiment with the latest ultra-realistic techniques for clothing their exquisitely sculpted figures, or cast their own minute bricks from which to build the ruins of Stalingrad, whilst others potter along quite happily daubing old-fashioned enamel paint onto jolly 'toy' soldiers and manoeuvring amongst cardboard buildings with drawn-on windows and doors.

So, what leads a perfectly sane man or woman to take the first steps on this road to becoming a wargamer? Perhaps you might recognise something of your own life story in the journey I have taken to becoming so passionate about this pastime.

I would have been about six years old when my father made me a wooden castle, with towers and a drawbridge. With this, incongruously, came some little plastic British Guards figures in red and blue with black bearskin hats. I remember that, for some reason, the heads were detachable! I also had a Britains WWI cannon that fired matchsticks, as well as those other popular toys of the time, marbles and fivestones, which I used to roll and lob at the hapless defenders.

However, I soon got bored with this and wanted something that felt more like a 'proper' game. I started building a collection of plastic Airfix figures based on what was available in my local toy shop – Ancient Britons and Romans; Union and Confederate American Civil War infantry, cavalry and artillery; and WWII British and German infantry, with Commandos paddling their canoes across our living room carpet.

Naturally, like many boys at the time, I'd also started making Airfix models, encouraged by my father who was creatively very gifted, a fine draughtsman and watercolourist. He had served in the Fleet Air Arm during WWII, and he made all the aircraft kits with me, painted them beautifully with Humbrol enamels and suspended them from my bedroom ceiling with cotton thread. When I went to bed, there were swirling dogfights above my head; a torch made a perfect searchlight, and I'd lie there making machine gun and ack-ack sounds until I fell asleep.

As well as the aircraft, there were the tanks and other Armoured Fighting Vehicles (AFVs) and WWII infantry from Airfix and, later, Matchbox. I have many early memories of conducting enormous battles in our back garden, creating elaborate trench and bunker systems or, with the help of some sand, huge 8th Army versus Afrika Korps desert encounters. Impossible when it rained, of course, but safer than the lounge carpet, where the threat of a careless (perish the thought that it might ever have been deliberate!) foot belonging to another family member was ever-present.

An addition to the armoury at this stage was my Dad's old air rifle. He first taught me how to shoot when I was about seven and, by the age of eight or nine, I could pick off a 1/72 scale Japanese infantryman behind a mud redoubt at 25 yards. There was no safe haven for my plastic opponents!

Unfortunately, my father died in 1971 when I was only ten years old, but it was just after that awful event that during a trip to the local library

I uncovered a real treasure: *The War Game* by Charles Grant, which had just been published. It made a huge impression on me – marching ranks of smartly-painted Spencer Smith 18th century musketeers and grenadiers, squadrons of charging dragoons and hussars, batteries of cannon and howitzers battering the walls of the author's charming balsa wood buildings. And because his wargames were, in fact, based in two completely fictitious nations (the Grand Duchy of Lorraine and Die Vereinigte Freie Städte – the United Free Cities), all his units sported exotic-sounding Germanic and French names, such as the Löwenstein-Oels Grenadiers, the Arquebusiers de Grassin, Brettlach Kürassiere and Mestre de Camp Général. In fact, as I later learned, some of these units were perfectly real, but had been pressed into service with those imagined nations at the whim of the author, who wrote with a wonderful, kindly tone, like a favourite and very wise uncle.

But, as well as the general historical setting, here was a book that answered all my questions: the figures were arranged into battalions, regiments, squadrons, batteries and brigades, all properly organised and using a ground scale, with movement and weapon ranges all prescribed. And here too lay the answers about how casualties were caused, as you will see, using probabilities and that magic ingredient – dice!

Suddenly, I wasn't just playing with toy soldiers any more. I had studied the scriptures.

I was A Wargamer.

This unlocked the flood gates for me, and over the next few years, I read dozens of books: others by Charles Grant, of course, but also Donald Featherstone, Terry Wise, Charlie Wesencraft; and the countless articles in *Airfix Magazine, Military Modelling*, and then its offshoot, *Battle*. And I devoured military history: by the time I was fifteen, I think I could name and give a more or less detailed account of every major war and battle between about 1620 and 1945, as well as quite a lot from the classical ancients period and a fair few in between. I had literally thousands of Airfix figures, all painted to a reasonable and gradually improving standard.

In the mid- to late 1970s I finally saved enough of my pocket money to buy

The magazines I relied upon for inspiration in my youth: *Airfix Magazine, Military Modelling* and then its offshoot, *Battle for Wargamers* (which, in this particular issue, featured the late Peter Gilder on the front cover, promoting the short-lived Tyne Tees TV series *Battleground*).

Encouraging a new generation. The author (centre) watches as a potential convert to the historical wargaming hobby helps with the Imperial attack during a re-staging of the Battle of Sittangbad, a famous encounter from the seminal work *Charge!* by Brigadier Peter Young and Colonel James Lawford. The team formed to stage the game also included John Preece (left, moving troops), Steve Gill (in the blue shirt behind John) and Phil Olley (right), who also provided the lovely scenery.

my first metal miniatures. They were 25mm Minifigs and Hinchliffe – and this was the era of the late Peter Gilder, the man responsible for the highly animated Hinchliffe soldiers, with his immense and gloriously glossy collection at his Wargames Holiday Centre near Scarborough, that became a photographic favourite for all magazine editors of the time. Remarkably, both these companies are still in business, though under new ownership. At that time, I also discovered Bruce Quarrie's *Airfix Guide to Napoleonic Wargaming*, which discussed 'national characteristics' and had fearsome charts and tables with dozens of modifiers for calculating musketry, artillery, movement and morale. Ah, the foibles of youth. And the Wargames Research Group's Ancient rules were on the menu too, the crash of spears and shields drowned out by the scratching of heads stuffed with weapon and troop type statistics! This was perfect for a bright boy in his teens, thirsting for knowledge. All that detail seemed essential. It's only now I'm older that I realise that what I want is the broad brush and the fun of simpler gaming again.

These, then, are some of the things which put me firmly on the road to a lifetime of enjoyment. Along the way, I have learned a great deal and made many firm friends, since wargaming has an undeniably social aspect. But above all, the main reason for getting involved in miniatures wargaming is – it's fun!

Perhaps you are already a seasoned wargamer, but if this is the first book you have read on the subject, it is my earnest hope that you are taking your first steps towards deriving as much enjoyment from the hobby as I have. Wargaming is an adventure of the imagination – so let's get started.

1

BASIC CONCEPTS OF WARGAMING

Understanding Sizes, Scales and Chance

The newcomer to our hobby will require some explanation of how we go about our mysterious battle games. Perhaps he or she will have seen an avid group of enthusiasts moving hundreds of prettily painted models over what appears to be a model railway layout, with no track or trains to be seen, but with dice and tape measures in abundance.

For the purposes of this introduction, I use the horse and musket era of c.1685-1845 as an example, but the principles apply equally to any period.

Miniatures

This is no ordinary game of toy soldiers, using matchstick cannon and plastic men sacrificed on the living room floor. To begin with, the soldiers aren't really toys at all – ask any wargamer who has spent hundreds of hours researching, collecting, painting and basing his or her armies!

The wargamer nowadays has access to miniatures ranging from 2mm size right up to 54mm. You will find figures in this book described as 15 mm, 20mm, 28mm and more besides, but what do we mean by this? Well, quite simply, that is the distance between the soles of the figure's feet and the top of its head – or, at least, it ought to be, but clearly different sculptors interpret these guidelines in different ways. Because of a process we wargamers call 'scale creep', the 28mm miniature has developed from the size that was, a couple of decades ago, known as 25mm, and indeed there are still manufacturers producing models of that size.

From left to right, front row: 3mm (Oddzial Osmy); 6mm (Baccus), 10mm (Pendraken), 15mm (Minifigs), 18mm (AB), 20mm (Newline); back row: 1/72 (Italeri, plastic), 25mm (Minifigs), 28mm (Front Rank), 28mm (Perry plastic), 40mm (Perry). Shown as close to actual size as possible. All those shown are British Napoleonic infantry apart from the Oddzial Osmy, which are American Civil War infantry.

One of the first questions newcomers to the hobby tend to ask is, "why are figures from different manufacturers actually different sizes, when they all claim to be the same size?" There's no easy answer, other than the inevitable variation involved in any artistic endeavour and sculpting wargames figures is an art, not a science. There is no International Wargaming Authority overseeing the process.

20mm can also be expressed as 1/72 scale or, in model railway parlance, HO/OO, and in this form there are huge numbers of figures produced in soft or semi-soft plastic by large manufacturers and sold in hobby and model shops across the globe, as well as via specialist wargaming outlets. I grew up playing with 1/72 Airfix figures, and several notable companies have added greatly to the output of this type of figure, including Revell, Italeri, Esci, HäT and Zvezda. These boxed sets, now covering every conceivable period of history, represent tremendous value and are a great way for the newcomer to get started in an affordable way. More details can be found later in Chapter 5, "Assembling Your Forces".

Another popular size is 15mm, which 'scale creep' has taken up to 18mm in some instances. These little fellows can pack almost as much detail as their larger brethren, are usually cheaper to buy, easier to store and allow the same size wargames table to portray a larger area of battlefield.

Smaller still are the micro-sizes of 6mm (roughly 1/300), 1/285 and 10mm figures. These are incredibly detailed for their size, cast as individuals and allow the average dining room table to portray the largest battlefield. For the truly microscopically-minded, there are even 1/600 (roughly 3mm) figures – an army brigade in a matchbox!

Few manufacturers cast their models to the precise scale they claim, which allows you to mix figures from different sources in your army, reflecting the fact that not all soldiers are exactly six feet tall (and in some historical periods, they have been a great deal shorter). It's a good idea to ask manufacturers for samples or visit their stands at wargaming shows so that you can settle on the most compatible troops from different sources.

The *Shot, Steel & Stone* rules provided in Chapter 7 can be played with whatever size miniatures you like – it really is up to you. Obviously, the larger the figures you use, the fewer you will fit on the standard base size, but you can choose whether to make the base size larger, and adjust the quoted distances for movement and shooting accordingly, or use fewer figures per base to represent the relevant troop type. Conversely, you could use the smaller 15mm, 10mm, 6mm or even 3mm miniatures, and either have more on each base to create a realistic 'mass' effect, or simply reduce the base size and have the standard number of figures, whilst reducing movement and weapon ranges in proportion.

One of the most impressive uses of 6mm miniatures I have seen is a gaming board made by Alan Perry for his twin brother Michael who was hospitalised after losing an arm in a re-enactment accident. The board is divided into squares and all the units have pegs under the bases that locate into holes in the board, just like travel chess!

Distance

Suppose we proceed on the basis that a 28mm miniature soldier represents a fellow some six feet, or 180cm, tall (in other words, about 1/64 scale). Leaving aside the fact that the average soldier in the eighteenth century was considerably smaller than this – perhaps 5 feet 6 inches or less (167cm) – we must deal with our available space. Few beginners in our hobby can command the facilities of a Wargames Holiday Centre with a table some 30 feet by 15 feet. Indeed, nor can many veterans of the hobby! Most of us do battle regularly on surfaces of 8 feet by 6 feet (243cm x 183cm) or less.

You can, of course, conduct fights on a 1:1 scale. These 'skirmish' wargames portray the actions of a company or platoon of men, rather than brigades or divisions. Each figure would represent an individual with his own capabilities. *Dungeons and Dragons* could be described as an elaborate skirmish wargame, and there are many small-scale actions, ambushes and raids throughout history which lend themselves well to this kind of treatment. The point is that if we were to use the same scale as that to which the figures are cast, the average table of 8 feet by 4 feet would represent an area of just 512 feet by 256 feet (156m x 78m). This clearly won't give a satisfactory battle! Most of Frederick the Great's and Napoleon's encounters were fought on a front of several kilometres, so in order to allow us to reproduce battles which are historically correct in scope, we need another scale, called a **ground scale**.

This works on exactly the same principle as a map. A typical Ordnance Survey map might have a scale of one and a quarter inches to the mile. We needn't go that far, or our single model infantryman would be occupying an area some 500 metres square! The choice is really arbitrary, and merely acts as a starting point for convenience.

I'm not this specific in the rules suggested later in this book, because I have no desire to bore you, dear reader, with all manner of arcane calculations, but let's say our scale is 1.5mm = 1 metre; in other words 1:667. This makes our average 6 feet x 4 feet tabletop into an area of ¾ mile x ½ mile (1.2km x 0.8km) – a much more suitable area in which to conduct a battle.

This same scale is used to determine weapon ranges, and the frontage occupied by a body of troops. In conjunction with other scales, it also limits the movement of our troops on the battlefield.

Few battles were fought on totally bare, open desert. Woods, rivers, villages, hills, ditches and other features must be reproduced to occupy our battlefield. I do not intend to discuss their construction in this chapter, but suffice it to say that such terrain is scaled down to fit our table using this same 1.5mm = 1 metre basis. Thus a river 150 metres wide would be 10cm wide on our table, whilst a village 600 metres across will have to cover 40cm.

The reference ruler on the right hand edge of this page will allow you to compare ground scales commonly used in wargames, in this instance 1.5mm = 1 metre, alongside 1mm = 1 yard and 1 inch = 10 yards.

TYPICAL GROUND SCALES

SCALE DISTANCE IN METRES (FOR SHOT, STEEL & STONE)

SCALE DISTANCE IN YARDS

1.5mm = 1m

1mm = 1 yard

1 inch = 10 yards

Height

Height is one of the few things which hamper a wargamer claiming total verisimilitude. Take the above example of our village. Now, let us say you have made a lovely model house, some 4 inches (10cm) square, with plenty of detail. It looks true to the period and very smart. To begin with, its size on the ground (using our 1.5mm = 1metre scale) represents an area 67m square – much bigger than a single house. The compromise is to say that this obviously represents a collection of buildings, gardens and so on. A village could thus be signified by three or four such models clustered together, a small town by perhaps a dozen.

How tall is our model? About 12cm? 80 metres! According to our ground scale, a skyscraper, no less. Come to think about it, our 28mm man towers over 60 feet tall in this land of giants!

This, of course, requires further compromise. The purist's way out is to use the 3mm figures we mentioned earlier, which would fit very closely with our 1.5mm = 1metre ground scale. But unless you are hellbent on letting detail stand in the way of convenience, I suggest you swallow this bitter pill along with veteran wargamers. Besides, do you really have the patience to paint many thousands of figures on a 1:1 basis?

In order to overcome this glaring discrepancy, we must ensure that the effects of height, such as troops on hills overlooking other hills or buildings, are dealt with realistically.

First of all, we need to think things through. Take where I live as an example, in the South Downs of Sussex, on the south coast of England. Now, the South Downs are hardly alpine and these softly rolling hills, though steep enough, I can tell you, to make me puff and pant when I go out for a walk, rarely exceed 200m or so (650 feet).

Now, a little calculation is in order. If we imagine that our miniature

'Dead ground' exists behind obstacles relative to the position of the observer. When adjudicating line of sight, we normally use the base of the miniature, and not its eye level, to calculate Line of Sight, except in skirmish games where the height of the scenery is considered to be 'real' in relation to the miniatures in use. Note how even a small obstacle seriously obstructs vision for troops at ground level.

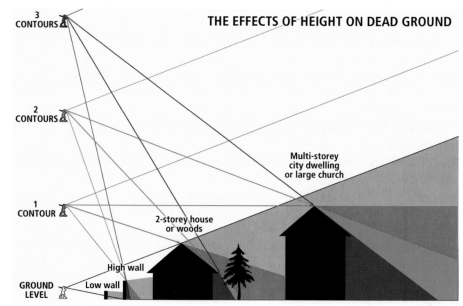

soldier represents a fellow some six feet in height, or perhaps a little less, then we can see that to represent even the lovely South Downs to true scale, we would be looking at constructing a monstrosity standing at least 100 times taller than our miniatures. For a 28mm figure, this would mean building from the floor to the ceiling and beyond – the Devil's Dyke, near Brighton, at 700 feet (215m) would be 3.2m (10' 7") tall!

Clearly, this won't do, in practical terms, so as we have examined earlier in the section discussing scales, we must impose a vertical scale on our games.

For this reason, we use contours to determine whether something is above or below something else, just as on an Ordnance Survey map. The intervals of our contours are entirely arbitrary, but I would suggest that we look in the region of 50 feet, which is somewhat more than 15 metres. To choose a smaller interval would lead to more modelling than required for our games; to go further would reduce some subtleties of line of sight too much.

The average two-storey building stands 30-35 feet (around 10m) tall, which also closely approximates the height of trees in a reasonably well-established wood. Very tall buildings, such as church towers or medieval Italian *campanile*, or ancient trees in a large forest, might rise to double this at perhaps 60-70 feet, or around 20m. Most other linear obstacles are man-height or very close to it.

So, looking again at the hills of my county, the high points around here would require something like twelve to fourteen contours to represent them correctly. If each contour were just 12.5mm (½") thick, then this would give us slopes rising to some 150-180mm (6"-7"), which is perfectly possible. However, most wargamers tend to use dense foam around 1" (25mm) thick, so the model hill would stand a foot or more tall, and in terms of the practical business of moving troops around on the table, this is not feasible.

Therefore, what I recommend is the following. Grade hills into low, medium, high and mountainous. Each grade represents a height increase of one contour above the surrounding countryside (which may already be some way above sea level, of course). The steeper the slope, the closer together the contours should be, just as on an Ordnance Survey map.

The diagram opposite shows the true effect of terrain and scenery on line of sight (abbreviated to LOS in military parlance), creating what is known as 'dead ground' behind them. It is important to understand this concept since, like the Duke of Wellington at Waterloo, it is possible to conceal quite large forces from the enemy in this way – or be ambushed by a clever enemy who has learned this concept better than you.

Simply put, the lower the observer, and the closer he is to an obstacle taller than himself, the more dead ground he has to contend with, whilst troops on higher ground stand a better chance of seeing anything concealed in the lee, or shadow, of a building or hill. No wonder the aeroplane transformed military reconnaissance!

Figures and men

All the aforegoing will have alerted you to the fact that each of our model soldiers represents more than one actual man in all but skirmish wargames.

It is fortunate for us that the horse and musket era saw the apogee of formality in the formations adopted by men in battle. Anyone who has watched the British Household Brigade 'Trooping the Colour' on the Queen's official birthday each year, has seen a live demonstration of the type of linear tactics used by troops of the horse and musket era. Closely packed men in ranks, who, from the mid-1730s onwards, marched in cadenced step, advancing, wheeling and inclining – this was the very lifeblood of the period, requiring tremendous discipline and control.

Fortunate, I say, because drillmasters such as David Dundas[1] of the British Army have left details of the area of ground occupied by a given number of men in various formations. This allows us to replicate lines, columns and squares with some precision, whilst allowing for the fact that a ploughed field is not a parade ground!

Now, we may arbitrarily decide upon a figure scale of, say, 1:33 or 1:20. Thus each and every model soldier would denote 33 or 20 real men. A battalion of 800 men would therefore require 24 figures at the former scale, or 40 at the latter. A squadron of 165 cavalry troopers needs only five miniatures at 1:33, or eight-and-a-bit at 1:20.

Until recently, this kind of literal scaling down was very popular, and indeed many rulesets that you will come across in your gaming career proceed on exactly this basis. However, in recent years a trend has begun to move away from such literal representation, for a number of reasons, and it is a trend that I support.

First of all, imposing such restrictions on the numerical strength of a unit is entirely artificial. You only have to read the history of any unit in any army at any time to realised that the strength of a regiment, battalion, squadron or battery was changing constantly. Men were wounded or fell ill, some recovered, some didn't, reinforcements arrived, some men deserted, horses fell ill leaving their cavalry riders useless, cannon and limbers needed repair or replacement – the list goes on. At the end of a long march, let alone a battle, the strength of a unit would be reduced considerably compared to its 'paper' strength. And don't get me started on corrupt colonels who drew pay for dead men!

Then there is the other question of aesthetics, particularly when it comes to the depth of formations on the wargames table.

The fact is that, like many wargamers, I have carried out endless calculations, based on original drill manuals, concerning the depth of real-life linear formations. As mentioned above, if you have ever watched

---

1 *General Sir David Dundas (1735-1820) served as Commander-in-Chief of the Forces from 1809 to 1811. In the 1780s he became an advocate of officer training and wrote many manuals on the subject, the first being Principles of Military Movements published in 1788.*

The Irish Guards marching past Her Majesty Queen Elizabeth II at 'trooping the colour' during the Queen's Official Birthday Parade which takes place every June in London. The King's Troop Royal Horse Artillery wait in the background. The very 'thin' nature of a two-deep line is plain to see – something hard to achieve in scale on the wargames table. Photo © Andrew Chittock, Dreamstime.com

Trooping the Colour, you will have seen precisely the type of formation that was adopted on the battlefield by troops in the horse and musket era and even the uniforms haven't changed much, certainly since the mid-19th century. Fact: even a three-deep line of men, with officers at their posts, is much, much shallower than it is wide. In fact, the depth of a line is perhaps five metres at the very most.

Now, let's apply that to our ground scale. At 1.5mm = 1 metre, that's 3⅓mm, around an eighth of one inch, whereas the base of an average 28mm miniature is probably 15-20mm deep, the equivalent of 22.5-30 metres. Oops!

So, this is where the compromises start. We can obviously decide, for complete verisimilitude, that we shall play games at 1:1 scale and portray our troops in their realistic ranks. Say hello to a very expensive and frustrating future. On the other hand, we can say, okay, let's reduce the number of ranks of figures to fit. Well, again, unless you are keen to play with 10mm or 6mm figures, you'll be hard pushed to get anywhere near that ideal 3⅓mm depth, and even then you'll only achieve it with a single rank of miniatures. And here, something else comes into play: the 'look' of the thing.

By and large, wargamers like to see their lines portrayed by two ranks of figures, not one. Yes, the single rank is more correct in terms of depth, although still, as we have seen, falling short by some margin. It's just the way things are, and I have to confess that after many years of hand-wringing over this knotty problem, I have fallen firmly into the 'two ranks look better than one' camp, though I wouldn't for one instant denigrate anyone who prefers a single line of miniatures. And on the other side, I have some American friends who use rules that stipulate three or more ranks of miniatures, if that was how their historical counterparts formed up. To my mind, this totally literal approach to formations is illogical (after

A typical 28mm wargame battalion of British infantry in line. These Victrix plastic miniatures were skilfully painted by wargames author Barry Hilton, whose *Republic to Empire* rules were being demonstrated at the Partizan show in Newark in 2009. Even here, the thinness of the 'thin red line' proves elusive, but an attractive compromise has been achieved.

all, if you're going to be literal about the depth, then why not the width too?) and leads not only to units even more grossly out of proportion in terms of their depth compared to frontage, but also saddles the wargamer with the task of painting colossal units of sixty or more miniatures a time. Not for the faint hearted, nor the shallow of pocket, and you need a huge room to play in, but each to their own!

Of course, the problem of depth versus frontage increases when it comes to the cavalry and it is here that, like many gamers, I have stuck with a single rank per squadron, even though historically they were often drawn up in two or even three ranks. Two ranks of cavalry figures just becomes wildly disproportionate, and so one will do and in fact looks fine.

Seen at Salute 2012: Victrix again, but this time a game using their 54mm miniatures! Individually, they look terrific, and there are some serious modelling skills on show here, but in terms of proportion, the lines are way too deep compared to their width for this author's taste. 54mm gaming has a strong following, however, proving yet again that one man's meat...

These solid 'phalanxes' of 15mm cavalry seen during a large recreation of Waterloo look impressive, but give a wildly false impression of cavalry tactics. In reality, attacks were made using waves of successive squadrons with sufficient intervals between them to allow the leading squadrons to retire if necessary. This game used the popular *General de Brigade* rules written by London wargamer Dave Brown.

I'll come to artillery in a little while, as it represents something of a special case, but let's just dwell for a moment on my abandonment of strictly representational ratios between miniature figures and men.

Having seen how the actual numerical strength of a unit could fluctuate from day to day, let alone from campaign to campaign, this led me to realise that the representation of the fighting strength of a wargame unit could also only be said to be approximate. Having spent many years with ferociously detailed rules covering many periods, which tended towards what one might call 'simulation', I realised that hours of pedantic calculation often led to games that not only had outcomes that could not be said to be more plausible or 'realistic' than simpler rules, but also led to hours of tedium rather than fun. Moreover, the advent of more abstract rules such as Phil Barker's *De Bellis Antiquitatis* and Rick Priestley's *Warmaster, Warmaster Ancients* and then *Black Powder* convinced me once and for all that such low-level bayonet- or sabre-counting was entirely unnecessary for a highly enjoyable, thought-provoking, challenging and – there's no other way of saying it – 'realistic', or at least historically plausible, game.

There's another benefit to this. By focusing less on the minutiae and the representation of very small numbers of men, the calculations can be abstracted in some ways and lift the wargamer from the level of the sergeant or second lieutenant, worrying about what individual miniatures are doing, up to the level he should be at of a brigadier or above, making vital command decisions that will affect the lives of thousands, perhaps tens of thousands of his men. This is especially true now, in the early 21st century, when we all seem to have less time for leisure, not more, and often want to fit our games into an extremely busy schedule which allows us mere hours, not days, for play.

Be that as it may, other sets of rules you will come across (and which I encourage you to read and try out) use scales of 1:10, 1:20, 1:50, even 1:100. It is a matter of personal taste, and whatever scale or approach one settles upon, there are advantages and disadvantages to each of them. For example, choosing 1:100 as your ratio will require the purchase of fewer figures to portray your army. However, I would not recommend a scale of less than 1:20, since the cost of purchasing figures becomes prohibitive – quite apart from the time required to paint them. As you will find, the visual impact of your games is by no means an unimportant factor to consider in addition to the factor of cost.

TROUBLESOME ARTILLERY

Moving on, we must tackle the second anomaly – the cannon. It simply will not do to say that every model cannon (or wagon, for that matter) represents 20 or 33 or even 50 real ones. Artillery pieces were divided into batteries of six or eight pieces on average, sometimes less, occasionally more. These batteries were then placed at critical points in the line of battle.

As with our model house, we must compromise. Our model gun will represent an arbitrary number of cannon, let's say perhaps two or three. This also applies should you choose to have models of the limbers, caissons and other paraphernalia of the artillery on the table. For the gunners, a compromise is necessary, in order to help us to gain a visual indication of the battery's effectiveness by the size of the base and the number of gunner figures present. As you will see, I mount gunners on individual stands, and their removal as casualties is then reflected as a loss of effectiveness to the

An impressive French Napoleonic 'grand battery' in action during another *General de Brigade* game using 15mm miniatures. Wargamers commonly use kapok or cotton wool to indicate that a unit has fired – it eliminates record keeping, as well as adding to the spectacle. The *GdB* rules use a ratio of 1 model gun to 2 real ones.

A 28mm wargame recreating the Battle of Chotusitz 1742 seen at Partizan in 2006. Here, batteries of artillery are depicted with just a single gun model and crew, without limbers, and battalions of infantry with just a dozen figures! The figure:man ratio here is around 1:50 or even higher. Clearly, the players are less concerned with realistic proportions, and more with being able to portray the units present using their favourite size of figure on attractive terrain.

guns. You could equally mount your gunner figures permanently around the edge of a base which is also sufficiently large to take a gun model, and denote casualties using some kind of marker or small dice.

A battery of eight guns is therefore shown as three or four gun models with the requisite number of gunner figures. I would recommend that, if you have mixed types in a battery, e.g. howitzers and field guns, you have at least one model of each type in the battery for visual appeal.

Artillery has always been a thorn in the side of the wargamer since, compared to other troop types, it is disproportionately represented. The number of guns in a typical horse and musket army was around one to two guns per battalion, and a battalion is made up of between, say, five hundred and a thousand men. So, when we use even one gun model for every thirty or so infantry figures, we are exaggerating the amount of artillery that would be seen on the battlefield. Planning a successful scenario based on a historical battle is therefore a tricky exercise, and the best way forward is usually to err on the side of reducing the number of batteries that were actually present, as wargame artillery can be excessively powerful if we are not careful.

Time

It slips away, so they say, and certainly in battles of the horse and musket era, time must have seemed variable. Hours of waiting and inactivity would be interspersed with bursts of furious and violent fighting. Only during sieges, with constant bombardment and digging, was there any kind of regularity.

Because battles tended to have variable phases with fighting for some

The US Marshal and his deputies move in for the kill. In a Wild West gunfight game such as this, each turn may represent only a few seconds of actual time but include an enormous range of possible actions for the players — see the rules provided in Chapter 6. These are 32mm Black Scorpion miniatures from the author's collection, with Eric Hotz's 'Whitewash City' PDF buildings printed onto card and resin accessories from Frontline Wargaming.

of the combatants and inactivity for many more, it behoves us to make another arbitrary decision for the sake of convenience, to wit, we must divide our game into 'turns', during which our miniature soldiery may march, shoot or fight hand-to-hand as the situation demands.

Think of it like time-lapse photography. At set intervals, the camera takes a shot and, in due course, the photographer lays out the images one after another, like frames of animation, to build an impression of the complete event. A wargame is like that: we divide our game up into turns and, at set intervals, we stop to check what is going on and make some calculations, which in turn determine much of what happens next,

In a siege game, each move might represent the activity of several hours or even an entire day to depict the measured pace of operations, unless an assault or sortie takes place. Solo wargamers, of course, can take as long as they like to recreate a siege, including the digging of saps and tunnels and the problems of supply. (15mm Heritage miniatures and Starfort fortress.)

until at some point, one side or the other gives way and concedes defeat. The difference is that whilst the photographer just passively records what passes in front of the camera, we as players can influence the outcome via the decisions we make with our troops, for better or for worse.

This decision about the turn length is critical to the 'playability' of the rules. Too short a time lapse, and the game will deteriorate into drudgery as our troops take an interminable number of turns to come into range, and one would be forced to make calculations and dice throws to little effect. Too long a move and disproportionately frantic effects will be the result, with constant backtracking of opposing units that missed each other in the rush.

It is worth considering the actual amount of time taken, historically, to fight a battle. A skirmish between cavalry patrols might be over in seconds, an ambush in minutes. Big battles like Mollwitz, Rossbach or Waterloo lasted many hours, some like Leipzig or Gettysburg even days. Our rules must be able to cover all these eventualities.

It used to be common to set a specific timescale for each turn, such as 1 or 2½ or 5 minutes of 'action' time. However, experience tells me that we really need a more flexible approach – one representing bursts of activity amongst longer periods of inactivity while orders were transmitted and received, formations were dressed and so on. In the long run, what we are interested in is the relative outcome of each turn we play, so whilst I have indeed spent more hours than I would care to remember calculating times and distances and casualty rates for every conceivable situation, it is not necessary to burden you, dear reader, with this level of tiresome minutiae. Suffice it to say that each combined turn (since our rules stipulate players carrying out their turns alternately, without the need for written orders) represents perhaps fifteen to twenty minutes of 'real' time. A typical game of some dozen moves therefore might simulate a 'real' battle of about three to four hours, this being the duration of a pretty standard action of the period.

The unpredictable battlefield

One of the most important differences between chess and wargaming is the part played by chance. Chess, of course, is famously predictable, and those blessed with the powers of analysis of a chess Grand Master or, indeed, a supercomputer, are capable of predicting the outcome of a game many moves ahead. A pawn normally advances one square and attacks diagonally; a knight moves two forward and one to the side; the bishop controls diagonal lines of either black or white and so on. And all this, of course, takes place on a perfectly flat, gridded board of dimensions laid down perhaps more than two millennia ago. No unexpected flank attacks here, no hacking through dense jungle or clambering up steep and rocky slopes. And nor, more to the point, is the chess player ever inconvenienced by his pieces ever displaying signs of disobedience, failing to hit their target or even, perish the thought, turning tail and fleeing.

Of course, chess is a highly abstracted form of wargame. At the other end of the scale are the highly detailed simulation games staged by the military, in which every lump and bump of possibility is factored in, taking advantage of the power of modern supercomputers. And of course the modern video games market is awash with first-person shoot 'em ups and wargames of many kinds, a few of which have guzzled countless hours of this author's time in the past!

Now, computer-driven games have normally been programmed, more or less successfully, to take account of the statistical probability of a range of possible outcomes on a moment-by-moment basis. That's what computers are good at. But even here, as any experienced computer gamer will know, the game usually forces the player down a particular path, with challenges to meet and goals to achieve before moving on to the next level. There are a few Massive Multiplayer Online games such as *World of Warcraft*™ that allow an almost infinite range of possibilities – but that word "almost" is critical.

Miniatures wargames – and, indeed, most board wargames – fall somewhere between the two. Writers such as myself strive to produce rulesets that will provide a game that bears a reasonable resemblance to a real battle of the stipulated historical period, whilst bearing in mind that what we are doing is playing a game. In any case, attempts to create a 100% accurate simulation are doomed to failure, deathly tedium, or both.

Curiously, the one aspect of wargames that has been levelled against the hobby as turning it into a 'mere game' is in fact the very thing which helps us to achieve a surprising degree of realism: our use of dice or, in some systems, playing cards of various kinds, to represent the role played by the imponderable, otherwise known as luck, chance or 'friction'.

Why should we allow such unpredictability into our games at all? A brief consideration of just a few factors should suffice.

Let's start with a subject with which we British are obsessed: the weather. Really, we don't need to be told that the effects of this natural phenomenon can range from the highly positive to the highly negative – and that's just if we're thinking about doing a bit of shopping in town or going on a short trip, or even doing our job, let alone fighting a battle.

Imagine, if you will, a typical musketeer of the eighteenth century. We will see later in more detail that this poor fellow was decked out in a uniform and equipment that were certainly not designed, as we might say nowadays, 'ergonomically'. The uniform itself was woven from a thick woollen material, his boots or shoes were often badly made, and he lugged around a long weapon weighing several pounds and which relied on the vagaries of black powder technology.

The strict discipline of the time meant that the appearance of the unit was paramount, and even in sweltering midsummer heat, the long uniform coat with tails had to be worn, together with the customary felt, tricorne hat or, for grenadiers, a tall mitre cap or fur cap, the latter being the precursor to the British Foot Guards' bearskin. To make matters worse,

Modern re-enactors wearing eighteenth century British uniforms of the Seven Years War era parading at Fort Niagara, New York State, USA. You can tell how warm it is from the sheen on the bald gentleman's head. He has sensibly stripped to his waistcoat and rolled up his sleeves, but for his comrades in the full, long-tailed coat, with haversack, musket, ammunition, tricorne hat, gaiters and ill-fitting shoes, it must have been extremely uncomfortable. Photo © Timothy Boyd.

many regiments stipulated that the men either had to wear powdered wigs, or have their hair long, and then powdered or tied in a queue or pigtail. To add insult to injury, a military fashion of the time was the leather or canvas 'stock', a device bearing an alarming resemblance to a dog's collar, designed to enforce a straight-necked, chin-up bearing, which chafed terribly. And finally, though some armies allowed their men to pile their knapsacks before battle, even this would depend on circumstances, which meant that a typical soldier also went into action with perhaps twenty to thirty pounds of extra weight on their back, and many complained bitterly of the way the straps cut into their shoulders. Having been a reenactor myself, I know that to a certain extent, you get used to it, but the fatigue is undeniable and dehydration can be a real problem.

If, on the other hand, the day was cold and wet, these same items became quickly sodden and even heavier. Greatcoats were not issued in any numbers until the Napoleonic wars, and even then, they were made of poor materials, inefficient for keeping the men either warm *or* dry. Moreover, and more dangerous as far as the soldier was concerned, rain could, and often did, render the flintlock (and its predecessor the matchlock) completely useless as a firearm, because the firing mechanism of cock and priming pan were exposed to the weather.

The point here is that even something as simple as whether the day was dry or wet or cold or hot affected – and still affects – an army in the field, the mood of the men and their ability to fight. Veterans, hardened to the exigencies of campaigning might be better able to tolerate these extremes than raw recruits; indeed, one of the characteristics of veterans is that they have learned a few tricks and techniques to make their burdens more comfortable, adapt their kit and clothing to make it suit the climate better, and find ways of keeping themselves and their equipment ready to fight, whatever the circumstances.

It is possible, of course, to draw up highly detailed rules to cover the effects of weather in our games, and in fact I suggest a few later in this book, but when it comes to the 'sharp end', the ultimate impact of weather is to affect sheer luck. Take the sharpshooter who, taking aim on a hot, sunny day, is disturbed by a bead of sweat running into the corner of his eye. For the officer who was the target, this could make the difference between life and death. Or the battalion of musketeers, in a summer storm, about to open fire on a squadron of onrushing cavalry – if they have not taken care, as the old adage advises, to literally 'keep their powder dry', then the cavalry will smash into their ranks and destroy them where they stand.

What else might we consider as subject to variation beyond the control of the general or, in our games, the player? Again, something we take for granted is the tabletop our miniature troops march across. Some players array their troops on a simple baseboard, either painted green or covered with some kind of cloth, with some representative hills, woods, streams and houses placed on top. Other gamers go to extraordinary lengths to create terrain that would rival an award-winning model railway layout, but even they have to make some compromises, faced by the necessity of their miniature soldiery being able to stand up on it. Either way, it simply

A game taking a very simple approach to the terrain aesthetic: the Battle of Mollwitz 1741, from the late Charles Grant's book *The War Game*, staged by The War Gamers at the Partizan show in 2007 and representative of what has become known as the 'old school' movement. Charles S Grant is on the left in beige trousers, with (l-r) Alan Perry, Phil Olley, Steve Gill, Nick Elsden and Stuart Asquith.

is not possible to represent every single tree, bush, shrub, molehill, rabbit hole, trickling brook, bit of marshy ground or thicket that might, in reality, either impede the steady progress of our troops or provide cover of some kind. Add in the plethora of human constructions, such as walls, ditches, houses, outbuildings, fences, woodpiles, gardens, orchards, dungheaps and so on, and you potentially have an impossible task.

The point about such things is that they have two potential effects: they impede the movement of troops, but some may also provide cover. Let's take the effect on movement first. It is comparatively easy to determine the effects of large objects, such as a hill, a river, a wood or a village. It's easy to go out and experiment yourself: clearly, you can't walk as fast uphill (or, indeed, downhill, especially if the slope is steep) as you can on level ground; forcing your way through a dense wood, especially if the ground is carpeted with ferns and brambles and fallen trees, takes a considerable effort; wading across any watercourse greater than shin-deep and slow-moving can be perilous in the extreme; and moving through any conurbation where you would have to force doors, climb through windows, vault walls or creep down alleyways remains a nightmare for soldiers to this day.

But there are the other, hidden aspects that can add 'friction' for the commander, especially in the pre-modern era. Like many wargamers, whenever I go for a drive into the countryside, I find myself playing 'spot the potential battlefield' – sad, I know, but I can't help it! How often, however, does one find that what looked like a marvellous piece of level, open ground for a cavalry charge from the road turns out to be potted and pricked with gorse and thistles and boggy patches and lumps and bumps of all kinds? It happens all the time. We must ignore, of course, those fields ploughed dead flat by industrial-scale agriculture, though even these, after

At the other end of the scenery scale, we have a scene such as this in a First World War game staged at Partizan by Dave Andrews and Aly Morrison (both of whom do noteworthy work for Games Workshop, as well as being historical wargamers). This kind of museum-quality scenery for demonstration games provides inspiration for us all, whether or not we can achieve the same standards.

RIchard III on the field of Bosworth. "A horse, a horse, my kingdom for a horse!" Well, there's a man who understood precisely what 'friction' is all about and how even a skilful soldier's luck can run out. 28mm Perry Miniatures, beautifully painted by Dave Andrews and seen at Salute 2010 in London. Amazingly, just as this book goes to press, Richard III's remains have been found under a car park in Leicester!

a downpour, can prove a huge obstacle to progress.

One of the ways that chance can assist us here is by representing the little things that a general just can't be entirely aware of and in my own rules, as you'll see, there is the possibility that your troops my not move as far as you would like when you command them. On the other hand, they might actually be able to move a little further, although for the majority of the time, the assumption is that a competent commander who knows his business will have a pretty good idea of what to expect. That same command roll can also represent, for example, the courier carrying orders being delayed or, conversely, making good time to his destination.

In terms of the terrain providing cover, we again factor this into our rules as a modification to the ability of an attacking unit to hit an enemy protected by each category of cover, whether in hand to hand fighting or when shooting, which moves us further along in our discussion of chance.

All weapons used for killing or wounding an enemy beyond arm's reach are inaccurate to a greater or lesser degree. Close in, when the combat is toe-to-toe, the accuracy or otherwise of a blow struck normally comes down to the relative skill of attacker and defender.

Whether we consider the effects of a gust of wind on an arrow, the range to target or the tiny differences in quality of gunpowder in a musket, or the inherent lack of accuracy of smoothbore weapons, or the tendency of later weapons to jam, let alone the skill of the firer and even the fact that the target might be so inconsiderate as to duck at the moment the missile arrives, we can see that the likelihood of hitting the target aimed at is likely to be less than 100% from the moment the missile leaves the firing weapon. Obviously, the greater the range to target, the more imponderables heap upon one another to reduce the chances of hitting. Is the target moving? Is the shooter moving? Is the target in cover of some kind? Is the firer himself under fire, which might upset his concentration?

Looking at melee, as a martial artist, I know full well that whilst the better trained, stronger or more skilful opponent might be expected to win every time, this simply isn't the case. The underdog needs only to land one lucky blow, or the superior fighter to lose his footing on slippery ground or receive an unwelcome shove in the back from his friends behind him at the wrong moment, and probability is stood on its head. For cavalry (and in earlier times, charioteers, camelry and troops on elephants), there is obviously the additional random factor of the very beasts they are riding: anyone who has spent any length of time around horses knows that they can be skittish and wilful beasts even without the clash and clamour of the battlefield. Careful training can help a lot, but can never provide a 100% guarantee of obedience.

And finally, quite apart from the unpredictable nature of the weather, the ground itself, the weapons and the vagaries of hand-to-hand fighting in formations large or small, there are the soldiers themselves and how they feel from moment to moment – what we generically classify as 'morale'.

MORALE

What could be more unpredictable than the state of mind of a group of human beings undergoing the most terrifying ordeal of their lives, knowing that any moment might be their last? Any reasonable person would remove themselves from the source of danger with alacrity, but of course military training throughout the ages has sought to condition individuals into believing that they can overcome, indeed even thrive under, such wholly unreasonable conditions and come to terms with the possibility of severe injury or death on the battlefield.

Morale will crop up again later in this book on several occasions,

A classic example of high morale at work: the defence of Rorke's Drift by the 24th Foot (South Wales Borderers), 22nd-23rd January 1879 during the Zulu Wars. A small force of around 150 British soldiers and allies defeated some 4,000 Zulu warriors who launched repeated – and equally brave – attacks. The men required an exceptional degree of discipline and trust in each other and their weapons in order to survive.

but there simply isn't the space here to explore this subject in the depth it deserves – see the Bibliography for some further reading on this fascinating topic. Suffice it to say that history is littered with examples of units continuing to fight against all the odds, and yet others disintegrating at the first shot, or even before. In recent years, much has been written about the fact that contrary to expectation, 'veteran' troops may not always turn out to be the most effective, because they have lived through several engagements, seeing their friends slaughtered beside them, and consequently can understand the level of danger they are facing with greater acuity than a new recruit. This can lead to a tendency to 'keep their heads down' whilst the rookies expose themselves to greater danger. Many authors have described the 'thousand yard stare' of modern warriors, a sure sign of combat stress, and even though the past is a foreign country, there must have been countless similar examples of men who had decided they had 'done their bit' and just wanted to survive, regardless of the fate of their comrades. Some of them stayed put with their units, some of them deserted, and some of them even resorted to self-harm in order to escape the front line.

There are just so many things that can affect the morale of a unit, besides the physical danger to which it is exposed and the casualties it suffers. Are the men hungry or thirsty? Are they tired? A unit that has had to march many miles to reach the battlefield will certainly not fight as well as if the troops had been rested. Is the unit well-supplied with good footwear or are the men walking on rags and makeshift sandals? Do they like and respect their officers, or do they feel bullied and neglected? When did they last have any leave, or have they been exposed to bombs and bullets for too long? And in the battle itself, are they doing well, or

Another famous incident showing the power of high morale: the charge of the Royal North British Dragoons (Scots Greys) at Waterloo, 1815. After initial success against the French infantry, these magnificent cavalry became literally carried away with their success and ploughed on into the French lines, where they were virtually destroyed by lancers. This colourful 28mm game was staged by Loughton Strike Force at Salute 2008.

badly? Have they suffered many casualties, or just a few? Are they holding exposed ground in isolation, with the enemy looming close, or are they tucked up behind stout walls with lots of friends and allies around them?

All these factors can be represented in our wargame rules to a certain extent, but behind all of these considerations lies what, during the First World War, came to be called 'umpty poo' – that little spark of something that will make one man stand and fight when the rest around have run. And that little flicker of unpredictability which may affect a single man or an entire army can only be represented by the use of chance, luck and fortune.

REPRESENTING CHANCE

Therefore, what we aim to do with wargames rules is to create a set of guidelines that dictate, to the appropriate extent, just what our little soldiers are capable of doing on the wargames table, whilst leaving just a little room for the influence of Lady Luck. Striking this balance is the tricky part: not enough, and our games can feel like the drudge simulationism mentioned earlier; too much, and we start to feel as though we might just as well have had a game of Monopoly or Ludo. The tabletop general needs to feel that with skill and experience, he can learn to factor in the slings and arrows of outrageous fortune without it impeding his ability to command altogether, and indeed, this is what makes a good wargame so entertaining, since it combines the talents of calculating tactician and gambler.

Let's look at an example. Imagine that you are the player commanding an outnumbered defence. Maybe it's a small British force in the Peninsular War, perhaps set in 1809 or thereabouts. Your little force, comprising a handful of British and Portuguese infantry battalions, a battery of guns and a small unit of light dragoons, is atop a ridgeline. Facing you is an entire French division of infantry, with accompanying artillery and a couple of units of dragoons. There is little hope of reinforcement, but you accept the challenge and, as the game progresses, you gamely blast away at the French infantry attempting to climb the slope, push them back, but then they come again and, with their artillery blasting holes in your line, both you and the French commander know you are close to collapse, so he sends forward his dragoons to finish you off.

Now, your light dragoons are your only reserve, and they are less powerful than his dragoons, but you run a quick calculation in your head, bite your lip, look towards heaven, and declare "My light dragoons are charging down the slope into your lead dragoon regiment." Your opponent shrugs, and the tests for morale are duly made. Both sides pass, and the crunch happens halfway up the slope.

Now, the fight is in the balance: your light dragoons are being cheeky, taking on the heavier, stronger opponents, but they have the advantage of being uphill, and there's just a chance...

Your gamble is rewarded. The calculations are done and then the dice roll across the table, showing a little clump of four 6s. The French player grimaces, but confidently picks up the 'hit' dice, now with the chance to 'save' them. Against charging cavalry with swords, he needs 4-6 to save, but to his horror, only one die reaches this target, leaving three casualties,

Now it's the French turn to respond, and they're in trouble. Even though numerically superior, they only manage two hits in return, and you save one of them. So the kills are 3-1, and you've broken through!

Let's draw a veil over the mayhem which follows as your light dragoons career gloriously down the slope, smashing now into the following enemy dragoon regiment and demolishing them too, and concentrate on the point being made – that there must always be a chance, however small, for a gamble to pay off, since this is precisely the kind of leadership quality that has been so prized throughout history. Napoleon is reputed to have asked "Is he lucky?" when promoting generals and in my experience, some of the pivotal moments of the most enjoyable games I have played have see-sawed around the roll of a few dice, regardless of whether I have been the recipient of the subsequent good fortune or have suffered a drubbing as a result.

The fact is that as long as Chance plays a supporting role to the overall attempt at historical accuracy, then there's really nothing to get exercised about and, as has been mentioned, there are countless examples throughout history of the underdog triumphing. From the Spartans at Thermopylae holding up tens of thousands of Persians, through to Frederick the Great's astonishing ability to defeat the larger Austrian forces at Rossbach or Leuthen, Sir Arthur Wellesley's successes in India and the Peninsula, the charge of the Heavy Brigade at Balaclava (yes, the Heavy Brigade, not the heroic foolishness of the Light Brigade), the 24th Foot at Rorke's Drift and so on, the annals of military glory echo down the years showing us that the most skilful generals were also possessed of not a little luck. You may argue that successful people make their own luck, and you may be right, but it is there nonetheless.

Accepting all this, then, let's finally dwell for one moment on the device itself that is chosen to represent the swing of fortune in our games.

DICE

For the purpose the rules found in this book, you will need nothing more arcane than a few ordinary, six-sided dice. These humble objects have been around since before history began, and examples turn up in archaeological finds all the time. Was it not Caesar who declared "Alea iacta est" (the die is cast)?

Of course, the use of a single die gives a range of possibilities of 1 to 6, so each outcome represents an increment of around 16.67% which, for some circumstances, might not be sufficiently precise. The use of two dice increases the fineness of distinction greatly, however, which is why many of the combat tests you will find in the rules in this book are divided into two parts, the 'to hit' and 'to save' sequence. With two dice, we now have 6 x 6 = 36 permutations, and 11 potential outcomes (see the table below).

This also applies to our Command rolls, where it is important that we are able to portray an 'average' commander who stands a reasonable chance of being able to issue orders to his troops, most of the time. In fact, after much experimentation, I decided to make it slightly easier than this, giving a standard, competent commander a rating of 8, not 7, because the enjoyment of the game is no small consideration, and I did not want to feel that players were being stymied and frustrated too often. You are perfectly at liberty, of course, to make the average commander's rating 7 should you so wish, and see how you feel about the resulting games.

Statisticians would tell us that this produces a 'bell shaped curve' on a graph of the results, with the mean result being 7. This is because there are more combinations resulting in a score of 7 than anything else, and because whilst we have 36 permutations for the possible ways the two dice could end up, in fact there are only 11 potential results when they are added together, these being of course between 2 and 12.

This means that whereas with a single die, any result between 1 and 6 was equally probable, with two dice, this changes completely. Now, a score of 2 or 12 at either end have a 2.78% likelihood of coming up, whereas a score of 7 has a 16.67% likelihood.

	Die 1					
	•	••	•.•	::	:.:	::
•	2	3	4	5	6	7
••	3	4	5	6	7	8
•.•	4	5	6	7	8	9
::	5	6	7	8	9	10
:.:	6	7	8	9	10	11
::	7	8	9	10	11	12

(left vertical label: **Die 2**)

Now, it is of course possible to refine this range of possibilities even further by using, say, three dice, but experience tells us that a combination of two ordinary, six-sided dice (known to wargamers, with some affection, as d6s) are perfectly sufficient for our purposes.

Now, in truth, there are lots of other types of 'hedra' that have been recruited to the world of wargaming of the past few decades. Ranging from the pyramidal (d4) tetrahedron, via d8s, d10s, the marvellously-named dodecahedron (d12s) and up to the icosahedron (d20). All these are now commonly available through specialist gaming shops and online.

Most wargamers amass a large collection of dice of various types. Here you can see not only standard d6s, but also d4, dAv, d8, d10, d12, d% (or d100) and d20. The very large dice are especially useful for public display games so that the audience can see what has been rolled; the tiny dice are commonly used to mark casualties or disruption of various kinds on a unit.

There can be no logical objection to their use, and indeed many sets of wargames rules, and particularly role-playing games, prescribe their use in a variety of circumstances.

For example, if it can be shown with some degree of certainty that, say, an eighteenth century musketeer, on a dry and windless day, had a 25% chance of hitting a stationary target at medium range, then it would not be unreasonable to say that a pair of percentage dice (for this is how they tend to appear, with one die marked 0-9 indicating tens, the other often being a different colour, indicating units) could be used, with a roll of 25 or less indicating success. Of course, here, a d4 could also step in, since each face, marked just 1-4, represents a 25% chance.

If this is what a gamer prefers, then that's fine, and I know of many wargamers, especially role-players, who own a bewildering array of multi-sided dice that get used for subtle variations of probability according to the circumstances. For my part, I set out to build a set of rules that are, I hope, reasonably accessible for the newcomer, and therefore I allowed myself the assumption that somewhere in the house, there lurks a backgammon set, or Monopoly, or one of the other popular board games which come with some good, old-fashioned, six-sided dice. In fact, the first dice I ever owned were made of ivory, and passed down to me from my grandfather, who had them since the late nineteenth century.

Having considered the use of dice, let me say something about that other device beloved of gamblers, the playing card.

CARDS

A common set of playing cards numbers 52, divided into four suits (hearts, spades, diamonds and clubs), and numbered 1 (Ace) to 10 and then Jack, Queen, King. In addition, there are commonly two Jokers in a pack. Obviously, this offers a substantial range of possibilities if each card is used to represent a different potential outcome.

One of the simplest ways to use cards is for each player to draw one card from the pack, or 'cut' the pack, and then reveal their card to the opponent, with the highest value card winning. This is the equivalent of two players having a 'dice off', with the highest score winning.

Even as a child, I remember playing games with toy soldiers involving just such mechanisms. My knight attacks your knight. We draw cards. I have the 7 of Clubs, you have the Jack of Diamonds. Argh! I lose!

When it comes to the dice equivalent, Games Workshop's *Lord of the Rings* and Warhammer Historical's *Legends of the Old West* and *Legends of the High Seas* games use the dice-off method to determine combat, followed by a further roll to determine the actual damage inflicted. Simple, but for small-scale games, it's fast and it works.

However, there aren't many wargames I'm aware of that make use of straight-out-of-the-pack playing cards as such. Wargaming doyens Donald Featherstone and Tony Bath recommended them for use in campaigns for determining 'special events' and so on, as indeed do I, but the development of this idea has led to what are known in the hobby as 'card-driven' games.

In this type of game, the manufacturer or publisher (for such games are normally commercially produced, if for no other reason than to be able to produce attractively designed cards) creates a pack of cards, each bearing specific instructions or opportunities for the player. Let's look at a couple of examples.

A popular 'crossover' game, which is to say that it is played by miniatures gamers and boardgamers alike, is *Commands & Colors Ancients* from GMT Games in the USA. They have recently added a Napoleonic variant and, since this present work focuses mostly on the horse and musket era, let's examine some of the cards from that game.

The game itself is played on a board gridded with hexagons, representing the battlefield, on which further hexagonal counters can be overlaid indicating hills, rivers, woods, towns and so on. The publishers

A typical hand of cards in *Commands & Colors Napoleonics*. As described overleaf, some refer to tactical movement, others to special circumstances or abilities. The cards are provided as part of a beautifully-packaged boxed set, together with a battle board, special dice, the rulebook, a scenario book and hundreds of wooden blocks with stickers for units.

supply a booklet of scenarios, which the players use to set up their pieces representing infantry, cavalry and artillery, as well as their generals, in accordance with the scenario instructions for a particular historical battle. The battlefield is divided, for game purposes, into left, centre and right sectors, which are very important, as you will see.

As well as the appropriate playing pieces to represent their army, each player also draws a certain number of 'Command Cards' from a deck of 70 cards. Of these, 48 are 'Section Cards' and 22 are 'Tactical Cards'. Let's look at the difference.

A typical Section Card is "Probe Left Flank". On the face of the card is printed the title of the card, together with a brief description, "Issue an order to 2 units or Leaders on the Left Flank", and an explanatory diagram. Another card is "Assault Right Flank – Order a number of units or Leaders on the Right Flank equal to command (the number of cards held in your hand including this card)."

The Tactical Cards are somewhat different, conferring certain abilities upon your troops. For example, "BAYONET CHARGE – Issue an order to 4 or fewer INFANTRY units. Units may move 2 hexes and still battle in melee. Ordered units may not engage in ranged combat. Guard infantry, when ordered, will melee with 1 additional die. If you do not have any infantry units, issue an order to 1 unit of your choice." And another, "LA GRANDE MANOEUVRE – Issue an order to 4 or fewer units or Leaders. Ordered units or Leaders may make a strategic move up to 4 hexes. An infantry unit in square may not be ordered. Ordered units may not battle. Or, issue an order to 1 unit of your choice."

So, how are they used? Well, at the beginning of the game, all the cards are shuffled together and placed face down on the table. Then, according to the particular scenario, each player is dealt a certain number of these cards. Let's take the Talavera 1809 scenario as an example. Here, the British player, taking the part of Sir Arthur Wellesley (later to become the Duke of Wellington), is dealt six Command Cards, but his opponent, playing the combined leadership of King Joseph Bonaparte, Marshal Jourdan, Marshal Victor and General Sebastiani, is allowed only five. This clever mechanism makes it immediately apparent that the British player has more options to choose from, because each move, players take it in turns to choose a card from their hand, declare it and act upon its instructions before then discarding it and choosing another from the top of the pack, which they may play next move or keep in their hand until later in the game as they see fit.

As we have seen, some of the cards relate only to troops in a particular sector, or tactical possibilities for a particular troop type, and it is of course possible that either all the cards, some or none of them may be of any use to your particular army in its current position or circumstances. Trust me, it can be very frustrating if you pick up a series of cards relating to left flank movements when all your troops are in the centre or right sectors! On the other hand, skilful players can hoard the best cards in their hands to unleash a sustained attack in a particular sector or with, say, their powerful cavalry, that can leave the opponent reeling.

The way combat itself is decided is also interesting, because the rules writers have come up with a clever system of 'Battle Dice', essentially d6s marked with special symbols, which cross-reference with a set of tables to produce a combined action and morale outcome all in one go. I thoroughly recommend that you give the game a try if you have the chance, but for the time being, I want to focus on that use of cards as a way of introducing chance. Of course, as long as the pack is properly shuffled, whilst both players have an idea of the cards that might turn up, there's no way of telling precisely when that might happen, nor when the drawing player might choose to use them. Therefore, *Commands & Colors* is innovative in combining the skills of a poker player with those of a tactician and wargamer, in addition to its dice-based combat system, which it calls 'Battling'.

Now let's look at another card-driven system, this time devised by a popular rules duo Richard Clarke and Nick Skinner, who publish under the name of TooFatLardies and whose rules always display a cheeky sense of fun. Creators of a number of highly innovative and entertaining rulesets, one of their most popular is for small-scale battles set in the Napoleonic Wars, under the title of *Sharp Practice*.

To quote directly from the rulebook,

"The central premise of the rules is that success on the battlefield is generally down to the leadership of a small band of men, of all ranks and social stations, who drive other less dynamic souls forward to achieve their goals. It is these Big Men and their actions that stand tall in the pages of military history and, as with all of our rules, this is reflected here."

A typical *Sharp Practice* scenario, played by the author: French light infantry ambush a British column, somewhere in Spain, 1809. The hectic pace of a small encounter is particularly suited to card-driven rules. The die at the head of the British column represents 'shock' at having received incoming fire. Fortunately, the column recovered and taught the dastardly French a lesson!

Typical cards for use in *Sharp Practice*. The TooFatLardies supply their rules either in printed or PDF format for you to download and print out at home. Some of the cards can be personalised: for example, the "Big Man One" card seen here might be "Captain Richard Sharpe", "Sergeant Hakeswill" or perhaps a tongue-in-cheek character of your own creation.

The way that the rules go about this is very interesting, again combining a uniquely designed set of cards, together with common dice. The latter are used to create random events, determine movement, locate the enemy ('spotting'), resolve shooting and hand-to-hand and so on, generally known as 'Actions'. In addition, they ascribe four levels of Initiative to leaders and heroes, known collectively as 'Big Men', whom they humorously describe as "Cock o' the Walk" at the top, then "Jolly Good Chap" at Level 3, "Fine Fellah" at Level 2 and, bringing up the rear, "Young Buck". As with my own and some other rulesets, as the talent increases, so does the range at which their commands can be applied.

When a Big Man uses his Initiative to activate a Group of up to twelve men, or a larger Formation, it may immediately use its full allocation of Action Dice for that turn. With these it can Spot, Move, Fire, Reload, undertake a task, or any combination of the five.

The cards in *Sharp Practice* determine the sequence of play. The Game Deck contains cards for each of the Big Men and extra cards used to indicate the initiative of combatants. The cards are dealt one at a time, and are acted upon there and then or stored for later use depending on the Initiative Level of the leaders present. Again, quoting from the ruleset, here are a few of the cards:

- **Big Men Cards**
  One card is included in the Game Deck for each Big Man. Upon it being dealt he may take his turn, using his Initiative to influence Groups of men within his influence distance or to simply take his own go.

- **Blinds**

  One Blinds card for each nationality or faction involved in the action. On this card all blinds (literally a blank card representing the area occupied by troops that have not yet been seen or identified) of that force may take their turn, moving or spotting. The troops represented by the blind may fire, but if they do so they will be placed on the table and will remain so for the rest of the game. Troops operate on the Blinds card while they are unspotted or during the turn that they are spotted, after which they will rely on Big Men to influence them.

- **Grasp the Nettle (or *Graspez le Saucisson* for the French)**

  Grasp the Nettle cards are there to vary the level of initiative that a Big Man has. These cards are added to the deck, being force specific and with a status level attached. Once dealt they are left in play, ready to be used by any subsequent Big Men of that Status level or above when his card is dealt. They give that Big Man one additional Initiative Point for each card available to him for that turn. If he uses the card it is returned to the deck to be shuffled in for the next turn, if not it may be left in play for a subsequent Big Man to use.

- **Sharp Practice**

  One card is in the deck for a force highly skilled in musketry. On this card a Group or Formation may fire immediately, or if unloaded it may completely reload. This is the only National Characteristic card in the Game deck, all others will be in the Bonus Deck.

- **Tiffin**

  This card ends the turn. Any Big Man who has not had his card dealt will lose his turn. Any Group of men that has not been activated during the turn may now take its go with two Action dice, spotting, firing or adjusting their position, but not moving (unless they are cavalry attacking). Troops on Blinds may choose to deploy and take their turn on the Tiffin card.

Now, it has to be said that this system is certainly more 'advanced' in some senses than the *Commands & Colors* game we looked at previously, but what it helps the rules writers to achieve is a very detailed representation of warfare in a particular period. By concentrating on small-unit actions of battalion size or even less – what the authors call "large skirmishes" – the use of specific card and dice systems, coupled with clever command and control rules which even cover the use of different musical instruments for signalling on the battlefield, the authors are able to explore many facets of the Napoleonic Wars that, for the sake of brevity, simply have to be excluded in rulesets aimed at representing larger battles. This introduces a level of what wargamers call 'granularity' that is otherwise hard to achieve without a ruleset becoming cumbersome.

Furthermore, it allows nonsequential moves and an almost 1:1 timescale once the players are familiar with the rules and the pace picks up, which can be very exciting.

All rulesets from TooFatLardies are very 'flavoursome', made all the more so when Richard Clarke himself, a true showman, can be found demonstrating them at various wargame events around the country and even overseas.

I have, of course, just plucked two rulesets familiar to me out of the dozens, perhaps hundreds, of card-driven systems out there, but I hope that this at least gives you an idea of the extra nuances that can be added to a wargame by introducing cards as well as dice.

It has to be said that some wargamers dislike such systems intensely, arguing that the prescriptions of cards are too limiting and that they have enough trouble dealing with the tactical challenges of commanding a miniature army as it is, thank you very much! That's fair enough, of course, and I know that I have been left gritting my teeth during games of *Commands & Colors*, for instance, when I have had a handful of cards for commanding cavalry, say, when in fact I am left with only infantry. It just goes to show that wargaming is a very broad church, and one person's innovative game mechanism is another man's idea of spoiling the fun.

2

A History of Wargaming

Just How Did We Get Here?

The birth of the toy warrior

The warrior has been a revered figure in society since time immemorial. In prehistoric societies, it is likely that the role of hunter in hunter-gatherer societies, and then herdsman in nomadic and later agrarian communities, led to that of warrior once it became clear that the spoils of these activities needed to be protected. As communities settled in order to grow crops, raise domestic animals and harvest abundant resources in a particular area, so the need grew to have certain individuals permanently designated to protect these newly-acquired assets.

Maintaining a warrior class is an expensive business. In return for assuming the responsibility for providing protection for the rest of the community, a warrior needs to be fed, clothed, armed, armoured and, in some cases, mounted, and his mount cared for too. A species of contract is formed between the protector and the protected which sets the warrior apart from the rest of society: he trains, at the community's expense, to face a situation that, in truth, everyone hopes he will never actually have to face – to fight, and perhaps to die, to defend his community.

The notion of the warrior as hero reached its apogee in the Middle Ages, fuelled by a heady mix of religion, philosophy and feudal power, and this remains part of our cultural heritage even centuries later. And it is in this fascination with the warrior as a man apart, a symbol of a society's will to defend itself or even to dominate others, that the seeds of wargaming were sown.

We're not entirely certain when the first depictions of warriors were made. We know of many prehistoric wall paintings showing hunting scenes and armed men in places as far-flung as Australia, Africa, the Middle East, China and central Europe. The first three-dimensional representations were made somewhat later, carved in bone, horn, or ivory. It is possible that untold numbers had been carved in wood, but being a perishable material, they have not survived. In due course, we begin to see them in stone, recognisable initially because of the tell-tale helmet, perhaps the first item of equipment to define an individual as a warrior.

Then, from the Middle East and eastern Mediterranean, we see an explosion of objects, small figurines and sculptures in pottery, bone, ivory and stone. We have figurines from grave goods of the Egyptian Pharaohs that tell us that they may well have had armies of miniature warriors, though quite how they might have been used is not certain. They could have been useful in instructing the young kings in basic drill, or the role of different troop types, or battlefield dispositions – we can only speculate, as no written evidence survives.

The Royal Standard of Ur, a Sumerian artifact found in the Royal Cemetery in the ancient city of Ur (south of Baghdad in modern Iraq). It dates to around 2600–2400 BC. It may originally have been in the form of a battle standard. (Wikipedia commons)

In China, of course, there is the spectacular example of the 'Terracotta Warriors', an entire army of military golems, including infantry, cavalry and chariots, rendered life-size. As an impressive statement of an ancient state's power, they are unrivalled; but it is highly unlikely that they were ever intended to be anything other than an Emperor's guard as he travelled to an afterlife, hardly a collection designed for gaming of any kind!

A figurine is an interesting object in itself but, when coupled with the imagination and the power of what the miniature represents, the desire arises to do something with it, rather than just put it on a shelf as an ornament. We have all witnessed young children enter a captivating world of adventure when playing alone with toy soldiers, even if they are simple affairs made by Lego® or Playmobil®. I have fleeting recollections from my early youth of somewhat odd pieces cast in plaster of Paris and a few very old lead figures. Somewhere in the fuzziest recesses of my memory, I remember playing with them, but not in any kind of guided way – they acted as a catalyst, if you will, for my own fantasy journeys in which I *became* those figures: I *was* the British Guardsman fighting, incongruously, some WWI Germans, in the same way as I *was* the digger driver or the farmer ploughing his field when I played with my Dinky®, Corgi® and Matchbox® toys.

This is where the power of toy soldiers lies, in that they are a simplified, almost cartoon-like depiction of the warrior and, like cartoons, they make military subjects accessible to the young by simplifying certain details and conveying the essence of the thing depicted. Such impressions are also reinforced by other cultural inputs, such as comic books, the stories read at bedtime, films, television programmes and even, in the outside world, events attended with the family, such as military shows, local carnival parades with military bands and, in my case at least, a visit to London that included witnessing the changing of the guard at Buckingham Palace.

Toy soldiers have been around for a long time. We know little of what the common man may have had, but famous examples we know of include both Louis XIII and Louis XIV of France, who had substantial collections of miniature soldiers, as did King Frederick IV of Denmark. These royal playthings – or perhaps instructive objects – were made of solid silver.

The Continental Wars Society often stages very attractive games and this Franco-Prussian War encounter seen at Salute 2008 using flat *Zinnfiguren* was no exception. Painting such figures is an art form in itself as almost everything relies upon the skill of the painter to do justice to the fine engraving.

Philip IV of Spain was given a wooden army made by Alberto Struzzi, containing an entire army, its ancillary services such as the pontoon train, armourers and sutlers, and a wide range of terrain pieces. Czar Peter III of Russia made do with less precious metal, his collection of toy soldiers being made of wood, lead, starch, and wax. Even Napoleon I gave a gift of toy soldiers to his son, François Joseph Charles, then styled King of Rome. These included a set of 117 gold figures made by the goldsmith Claude Odinot!

Army officers from the most junior to the most senior also had a use for miniature representations of troops. Examples have survived of wooden blocks onto which have been pasted coloured engravings of British infantry: in 1797, a man called West published a set of paper figures, entitled, somewhat grandly, *Military Figures for the Practice of Tacticks* [sic], *by which the movement of Battalion, or larger body of Troops, may be displayed upon the present improved system. Intended for the instruction of Subalterns of the Army.* A set survives in Stirling Castle, in The Argyll & Sutherland Highlanders Regimental Museum.

Whilst the utility of military figurines for those who might actually be called upon to command troops in the field one day is obvious, toy soldiers for the masses also appeared in the 18th century, inspired by the exploits of Frederick the Great of Prussia during the middle years of the century and then, towards the end, by Napoleon. These took the form of 'flat' figures, pioneered by the Hilperts of Nuremberg in South Germany, with the firm of Ernst Heinrichsen eventually coming to dominate the field of these *Zinnfiguren* (tin figures). The flat figure has persisted as a

Webb's military figures, designed for the instruction of junior officers in various drill manouevres during the late eighteenth and early nineteenth centuries. This set was published in 1797 and depicts blocks of rank-and-file with officers as singles. These pictures were very kindly taken by Mr Rod Mackenzie, Curator of The Argyll and Sutherland Highlanders Museum in Stirling Castle. The main blocks measure 95 x 21 x 21 millimetres, the officers 33 x 8 x 8. The label on the box lid is shown below, with an enlargement of one of the blocks (right) clearly showing the hand-drawn and watercoloured paper covering.

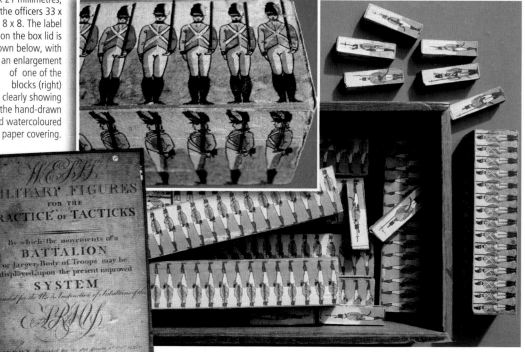

particularly highly-prized branch of the military figurine hobby to this day, requiring a high degree of artistic skill to paint successfully.

It seems that even the great British wartime Prime Minister, Winston Churchill, had a penchant for toy soldiers in his early days. As a boy, he commanded a substantial force of some 1,500 miniature Napoleonic figures imported, somewhat ironically given his later fame, from Germany.

By the end of the 19th century, a number of manufactuers existed, able to supply the mass market with small soldiers not only as 'flats', but also in *demi-ronde* and fully-rounded form. The two most prominent names were Heyde of Germany, producing 45mm tall men, and William Britain, whose 54mm troops were to become the stuff of legend.

So, one thread of the rope which, once entwined, led to the wargaming hobby as we know it, is clearly the development of the toy soldier and its becoming accessible in large quantities at an affordable price. The second strand was the notion of military gaming itself, and here we must look back into ancient times for its origins.

The emergence of military games

The oldest military game was called Wei-Hai and was played in ancient China from around 3,000BC onwards. It survives to this day under the name of *Go*. Chess emerged in India, from around 500AD, under the Sanskrit name of *caturaṅga* meaning the four divisions of the military, in other words infantry, cavalry, elephants, and chariotry or boatmen, which evolved into what we now know as the pawn, knight, bishop, and rook. The piece we now call the queen was, in fact, originally known as the general, which explains why it is the most powerful piece on the board, starting alongside the somewhat feeble and vulnerable king with his retinue around him. Here, we have a recognisable military game, played on a well-defined grid, aping the confines of a formal battlefield, which although highly abstracted, can be seen to have its roots in an understanding of military tactics. *Caturaṅga* was originally a game for four people, and included the rolling of dice to determine movement.

The ancient Greeks and Romans also had their own military games, played on gridded surfaces, such as *Ludus latrunculorum*, but whilst such abstraction provided intellectual stimulation for many centuries, its applicable value was somewhat limited, and it was not until the 19th century that a breakthrough was made in creating a system that was a more accurate representation of the realities faced by army commanders.

'The King's Game' was invented in 1664 by Christopher Weikhmann of Ulm, with 30 pieces per side and 14 distinct moves. It was, in a sense, a variation on chess. This was later developed by Hellwig, Master of the Pages for the Duke of Brunswick, in 1780, whose board contained no less than 1,666 squares, with a variety of terrain, and had units representing infantry, cavalry, and artillery.[1]

---

1 See *www.strategiespielen.de/johann-christian-ludwig-hellwig*

Then, in 1798, Georg Vinturinus created 'Neue Kriegsspiel', featuring a game board of 3,600 squares depicting the 'cockpit of Europe' between France and Belgium, and troop lists containing 1,800 units of various arms. The set was completed by a 60-page rule book which also covered subjects such as reinforcements and logistics.

Part of the driving force behind the search for a game capable of representing military challenges was the growth of the size of armies, which by the end of the Napoleonic Wars had reached hundreds of thousands of men apiece, even half a million, and the increasingly high stakes being played for, both in terms of the lives potentially lost and the catastrophic consequences of both grand tactical and strategic failure. Napoleon I, after all, had dominated mainland Europe for more than a decade and his defeat led to exile and the dissolution of his empire.

It comes as no surprise, perhaps, that the country whose humiliation at the hands of Napoleon had been almost complete was the very place where the science of military planning received the most thoroughgoing overhaul. Prussia, once the most dominant force in central Europe under the command of Frederick the Great, had been crushed in 1806. Set in its rigid ways, it had been utterly overwhelmed by the fervour and flexibility of the French, but this led to an extraordinary catharsis and rebirth that allowed Prussia to eventually tip the balance at Waterloo in 1815 and regain its pride.

We are not sure precisely when he started work on his project, but in 1811, a certain Baron von Reisswitz, a civil administrator with an interest in military history, was brought to the attention of King Friedrich Wilhelm III of Prussia for having invented a sort of war-game to demonstrate the art of military command. After a little delay, von Reisswitz presented an ornate version of his game, incorporating interchangeable terrain pieces and troop counters cast in porcelain, all mounted on a six-foot square table, to the king and his heirs in 1812. This was known as *Kriegsspiel* and is a key moment in our history.[2]

What von Reisswitz had uncovered were a number of the key principles that we examined in the previous chapter: the notions of breaking the game down into moves representing a specific time lapse; basing the battlefield on a realistic map, made to scale; representing the opposing troops with markers occupying a scaled-down 'footprint'; using the same scale to determine weapon ranges; combining the ground and time scales to represent the effect of weapons; and finally introducing the element of chance, coupled with maximum and minimum effects and the personal judgement of an umpire, to adjudicate the outcome of combat.

The game was developed by the Baron's son, Georg Heinrich Leopold

2 *An excellent account of the development of Kriegsspiel by Bill Leeson can be found on the Kriegsspiel website at www.kriegsspiel.org.uk. The Von Reisswitz rules and maps have been republished by TooFatLardies toofatlardies.co.uk and playing pieces are available from Irregular Miniatures: see www.irregularminiatures.co.uk*

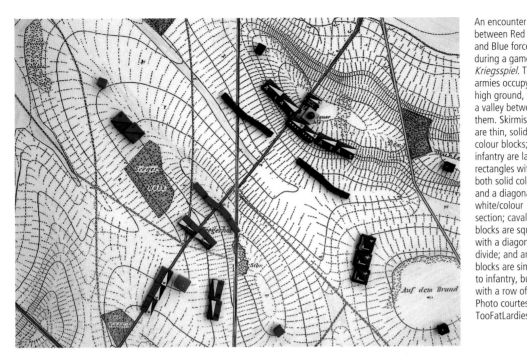

An encounter between Red and Blue forces during a game of *Kriegsspiel*. The armies occupy high ground, with a valley between them. Skirmishers are thin, solid colour blocks; line infantry are larger rectangles with both solid colour and a diagonal white/colour section; cavalry blocks are square, with a diagonal divide; and artillery blocks are similar to infantry, but with a row of dots. Photo courtesy of TooFatLardies.

Freiherrn von Reisswitz, and published in 1824 as *Anleitung zur Darstelling militarische manuver mit dem apparat des Kriegsspiels (Instructions for the Representation of Tactical Maneuvers under the Guise of a Wargame)*. The scale was changed from 1:2373 to 1:8000 and the game was transferred onto duplicate maps for players and umpire, with mechanisms for determining terrain advantage and resolving gunfire. So successful was this game that the king ordered that every regiment of the Prussian army should be issued with a copy, the kind of marketing impetus that a games designer could only dream of today![3]

Other versions of *Kriegsspiel* appeared. In 1880, Charles A Totten published *Strategos: a series of American games of war, based upon military principles and designed for the assistance both of beginners and advanced students in prosecuting the whole study of tactics, grand tactics, strategy, military history, and the various operations of war* and this was followed in 1884 by *The American Kriegsspiel. A game for practicing the art of war upon a topographical map* was published by Captain W R Livermore. This also mentions two more contemporary versions published in the USA, though I have not seen them.

An English version appeared in 1876: *Rules for the Conduct of a War-Game on a Map*[4] prompted, perhaps, by the birth of the very first wargames club at the University of Oxford in 1874 and then, in 1880, the Manchester Tactical Society. As described by John Preece in *Battlegames* issue 13:

---

3   See http://tinyurl.com/8x2zrjw for Bill Leeson's excellent history of Kriegsspiel.

4   Available as a download from www.archive.org/details/rulesforconducto00grearich

"These clubs were usually attached to Officer Training Corps in the Universities or institutions such as The Inns of Court. However, their popularity (Oxford had 50 members) suggests the game was enjoyed for its own sake. Clubs organised competitions against each other, with independent umpiring. In 1911, Oxford played The Bristol Tactical Society, The Inns of Court OTC and Cambridge University under the auspices of a staff officer from HQ Southern Command, and one suspects a rather jolly time was had by all."

Now, the next strand in our rope.

The amateur gamer

The great science fiction novelist H.G. Wells wrote two books of importance to our story: *Floor Games* (1911) and *Little Wars* (1913). Here, the author describes battles fought across his capacious floors using large, 54mm figures, with his friends and literary contemporaries Robert Louis Stevenson[5], Jerome K Jerome and G K Chesterton. The objective here was to actually knock down the opponent's men using the Britains spring-loaded 4.7" Naval Gun model, which fired wooden shells or even brass screws. 'Amateur' wargaming in this period also inspired its first – some might say only – memorable poem, by the author of *Treasure Island*, *Kidnapped* and *The Strange Case of Dr Jekyll and Mr Hyde*:

> For certain soldiers lately dead
> Our reverent dirge shall here be said.
> Them, when their martial leader called,
> No dread preparative appalled;
> But, leaden-hearted, leaden-heeled,
> I marked them steadfast in the field.
> Death grimly sided with the foe,
> And smote each leaden hero low.
> Proudly they perished, one by one:
> The dread Pea-cannon's work was done!
> O not for them the tears we shed,
> Consigned to their congenial lead;
> But while umoved their sleep they take,
> We mourn for their dear Captain's sake,
> For their dear Captain, who shall smart

---

5 *Robert Louis Stevenson, one of the more interesting characters who was gaming at the same time as Wells, featured in a lengthy piece published in Scribner's Magazine (Volume 24, July-December 1898 pp.709-719) entitled "Stevenson at Play". Available online courtesy of the University of Michigan at hdl.handle.net/2027/mdp.39015015393310*

H. G. WELLS, THE ENGLISH NOVELIST, PLAYING AN INDOOR WAR GAME

A spread from the *London Illustrated Gazette* of January 1913, showing H G Wells and friends playing a game.

Both in his pocket and his heart,
Who saw his heroes shed their gore
And lacked a shilling to buy more![6]

Little Wars has an Appendix, which contains an extremely revealing passage which is as relevant to hobby wargamers today in the face of those who scream for 'simulationism' as it was in 1913:

> "This little book has, I hope, been perfectly frank about its intentions. It is not a book upon Kriegspiel [sic]. It gives merely a game that may be played by two or four or six amateurish persons in an afternoon and evening with toy soldiers. But it has a very distinct relation to Kriegspiel; and since the main portion of it was written and published in a magazine[7], I have had quite a considerable correspondence with military people who have been interested by it, and who have shown a very friendly spirit towards it – in spite of the pacific outbreak in its concluding section. They tell me – what I already a little suspected – that Kriegspiel, as it is played by the British Army, is a very dull and unsatisfactory exercise, *lacking in realism, in stir and the unexpected, obsessed by the umpire at every turn, and of very doubtful value in waking up the imagination, which should be its chief function.*" [My italics.]

Now, there's a viewpoint I concur with wholeheartedly!

History intervened just a year after H G Wells penned his seminal work, and the ghastly events of 1914-18 are all too familiar, even to the modern

6 *A Martial Elegy for some Lead Soldiers, ibid, p.719*

7 *Windsor Magazine, December 1912 and January 1913.*

reader. However, wargaming was not completely dormant between the wars, and in 1929 a little book called *Shambattle* was published in America. Written by Lieutenant Harry G Dowdall and Joseph H Gleason, it is firmly aimed at youngsters and cleverly divides the game into three 'levels': the Lieutenant's game (ages 8+); the Captain's game (ages 10+); and the General's game (ages 12+). At each stage some additional rules are added to increase the complexity of the game, which was played with model soldiers but on a map, rather than a terrained board.[8]

One interesting concept in the game, fought between Bluvia and Redina (the notion of having a 'blue' army and a 'red' army had already been introduced with *Kriegsspiel* a century earlier and persisted in *Little Wars*), was the inclusion of hospitals and medical corps men. These chaps have to move 'partial' casualties to the field hospitals, where they may then recover next move.

Another pioneer between the wars was Captain J C Sachs, a member of the British Society of Collectors of Model Soldiers (which later became the influential British Model Soldier Society). Sachs departed from what had already become the traditional form of wargaming with horse, foot and guns by inventing systems suitable for modern warfare, including tanks and machine guns. Fellow Society member W R Gordon had the facilities at home to stage wargames on impressive terrain, and the Society's competitions were held there.[9]

We know that wargaming was practised by professional military men during WWII in order to test the chances of success of various operations. Perhaps the most infamous example is of the Japanese Navy rehearsing for the battle of Midway, during which a scenario arose where an enterprising junior officer, playing the Americans, was able to ambush the Japanese fleet with land-based aircraft and sink two of their carriers. Annoyed by the game's outcome, however, Admiral Ugaki overruled the Lieutenant Commander acting as umpire, and deemed only one of the carriers to have been sunk. History proved, of course, that the umpire and his dice were perfectly correct.

The post-war expansion

Since 1945, the hobby has seen exponential growth, both in terms of the number of participants and the industry that has grown up around it, fuelled by the increasing amount of disposable income and leisure time enjoyed in the West. The fact is that wargaming has not, until comparatively recently, enjoyed any popularity outside the English-speaking world and, in the face of the dominance of electronic and digital entertainment, brought into every home by the Internet, it now struggles

---

8 See *www.nirya.be/snv/shambattle/ for a wonderful account of the book, its rules and a sample game played using them.*

9 See *vintagewargaming.blogspot.com/2009/04/captain-sachs-early-pioneer.html for more details and Sachs' rules published in a 1971 edition of* War Game Digest.

to gain any traction outside those key markets.

Nevertheless, the spread of miniatures wargaming after the mid-1950s was quite remarkable. On the far side of the Atlantic, two names stand out in particular: Jack Scruby and Joseph Morschauser. Scruby began casting inexpensive miniatures using rubber moulds in 1955, and in 1957 started *War Game Digest*, a regular magazine which was snapped up by enthusiasts everywhere. For the first time, here was a forum for wargamers to exchange ideas and learn from others, and even to discover that other gamers lived nearby. In an age before the World Wide Web, one has to bear in mind how exciting and revolutionary such a publication was.

> "...until *WGD* began publication, war gaming was going on in a small, individual way, with little cohesion. During the period from 1952 to 1957 I spent countless hours corresponding with some 30 war gamers and so far as we knew at that time, this was all the players there were in the world!"[10]

Joseph Morschauser published *How to Play War Games in Miniature* in 1962. He created his units with model soldiers stuck onto common-sized bases, together with a system of 'Melee Power' points that would still be recognisable to a modern wargamer.

Here in the UK, however, one of the great names of wargaming began his work. A sports physiotherapist by profession, Don Featherstone had fought with the Royal Tank Regiment in Italy but confesses to having a fascination with toy soldiers since childhood. By the 1960s, he had a fully-formed notion of just how wargames should be played and over the next four decades or so, he became the most prolific wargames writer there has ever been.

His first book, *War Games*, published in 1962, presented rules for ancients, horse and musket and WWII gaming (the latter set actually having been written by Lionel Tarr) and it became an instant best-seller. The full list of Don's works can be found in the Resources chapter, but suffice it to say that this remarkable man – now in his nineties as I write this – produced a host of volumes that were lapped up by at least two generations of wargamers.

The early Featherstone rules considered only movement and fighting – the concept of morale, the state of mind of our miniature troops, had to wait a while yet – but his later works proposed some very sophisticated ways of representing troop quality. His best works, in this author's opinion,

JOSEPH MORSCHAUSER

"Now, toy-soldier battles may seem childish, beneath your dignity. And, indeed, the battles you once fought are; but war gaming in miniature is an entirely different thing. You use the same types of toy soldiers. You use little houses and little trees. But you also use rules, and it is the rules which make the difference."
How to Play War Games in Miniature

---

10   Jack Scruby, *War Games Digest*, Fall 1971. See vintagewargaming.blogspot.com/2009/06/
story-of-war-game-digest-by-jack-scruby.html

are *Advanced War Games* (1969), *War Game Campaigns* (1970), *Solo-Wargaming* (1973), *Skirmish Wargaming* (1975) and, as a primer for newcomers to the hobby, *Battles with Model Soldiers* (1970), a copy of which I was awarded as a school prize in 1974! Alongside these must be placed his magnificent quartet of volumes making up *War Games Through the Ages* (3000BC-1500AD, 1420-1783, 1792-1859 and 1860-1945) published between 1972 and 1976, in which he gives a brief overview of a huge range of combatant nations and their capabilities alongside a summary of the wars and battles fought.

As well as writing books, Don had also taken up editing, creating the UK version of Scruby's *The War Game Digest* in 1960 along with ancients wargaming pioneer Tony Bath. However, in 1962 a schism opened up between Scruby's somewhat scientific approach and Featherstone's more 'gamey' inclinations which led him to establish *Wargamers' Newsletter*, whilst Scruby scrapped *War Games Digest* and started up *Table Top Talk* instead, which also had the commercial purpose of promoting his own miniatures, a trend which continues in some magazines to this day.

Soldiers for the masses

Before we continue, we need to make note of another development, this time in the availability of model soldiers suitable for wargaming, that was to prove pivotal and forms the final strand in our rope making up the growth in wargaming: the availability of suitable miniatures on the mass market.

In 1959, Airfix produced their very first set of OO/HO (20mm) figures, the Guards Band. Suddenly, here was an affordable way for wargamers to collect large armies of miniatures, as long as they were prepared to apply some modelling skills. Following every small boy's favourites the Cowboys and Indians (1961), the most useful sets to arrive were the American Civil War Union Infantry (1962), American Civil War Confederate Infantry (1963), American Civil War Artillery and a Wagon Train (both 1963) and, eventually, the US Cavalry (1966). Meanwhile, useful additions were the French Foreign Legion (1962) who could be easily converted to serve as zouaves in the American Civil War or fight Arab Bedouin Tribesmen (1964), and Robin Hood and the Sheriff of Nottingham (both 1964) kept medieval enthusiasts happy. Fans of ancients were finally addressed with the arrival of the Romans in 1967, followed by some opponents in the form of Ancient Britons (complete with marvellously inaccurate solid-wheeled chariots) in 1969.

World War II gamers were well-served from the beginning, with the Infantry Combat Group (later renamed WWII British Infantry) produced in 1961, followed rapidly by WWII 8th Army, WWII German Infantry and WWII Afrika Korps (1962), WWII Russian Infantry, WWII US Marines and WWII Japanese Infantry (all 1964), WWII British Paratroops (1966) and WWII British Commandos (1968). Coupled with the expanding range of 1/72 plastic kits for armoured vehicles and other transport coming out at the same time, and the support of publications like *Airfix Magazine* which frequently carried articles about painting and converting these models, the possibilities were almost limitless.

After years of having to make do with fiddly conversions from the available types using glue, Plasticene, plastic card, pins, balsa wood and even paper, all sealed with a loving coat of banana oil (isoamyl acetate, another name for what flying model aircraft modellers call 'dope'), Napoleonic wargamers finally had their patience rewarded in 1969 with the arrival of the first 'Waterloo' series troops, the Highland Infantry and French Cavalry (actually cuirassiers). Whilst Waterloo French Artillery arrived in 1970, there was a further wait for British Cavalry (hussars) and French Infantry (1971) and then British Infantry and British Artillery (actually the Royal Horse Artillery) in 1972. Kept firmly in reserve, the Waterloo French Imperial Guard turned up in 1974 and the Waterloo Prussian Infantry, just as in the real battle, arrived in the nick of time in 1978![11]

Meanwhile, there had been a host of others including, from my own perspective, an interesting duo in 1971: British Grenadiers and Washington's Army, both depicting troops from the American War of Independence. My first tricorned troops, before I found out how to get hold of those iconic Spencer Smiths mentioned in the Introduction, were recruited from several boxes of these Airfix marvels.

An important point about the Airfix phenomenon was that the gamer could recruit entire battalions for the price of just a couple of the metal miniatures available at the time. I have a copy of Issue 1 of *Military Modelling*, dated January 1971, which contains a number of small ads for figure manufacturers. Taking Miniature Figurines as an example, one of the popular and least expensive firms of the time, they were advertising 20mm troops at 1/- for infantry, 2/6 for cavalry and 2/6 for artillery guns.[12] Taking inflation into account, that's the equivalent of 57p and £1.42 today,

AIRFIX MAGAZINE

"Because of the relatively recent availability through Airfix of toy figures and lower than pre-war prices, a new craze called war games is gaining hold."
June 1961

MILITARY MODELLING

"While the range of metal figures continues to increase, there will be a large number of the younger enthusiasts and some not so young, who will be unable to afford great numbers of these figures, but have time and ingenuity which can be applied to conversions costing only a penny or two."
Bob O'Brien, "The Plastic Warrior", July 1971 – a series written in the days when if you wanted a troop type not yet available from Airfix, you worked with scalpel, glue, balsa, plasticene and banana oil (a type of varnish) to create whatever you needed.

---

11   See www.vintage-airfix.com for lots of useful information and pack shots.

12   *Those of you born after decimalization will be horrified by these references to 'old money', so let me put you at ease by translating these Shilling prices into 5p and 12.5p respectively.*

BRIGADIER PETER YOUNG & LT COL J P LAWFORD

"War games played with model soldiers and set in previous centuries excite an interest in history and in the pageantry of the past. To understand the course of some historic battle few approaches are better than to war-game it. The study of the setting and the field of battle before actually beginning the game reveal, as nothing else can, the factors governing the tactics of the commanders; the actual course of the game highlights the correctness – or otherwise – of their decision.

But these considerations only partly explain why amateur war-gamers war-game. the real reason is that a war-game can generate an excitement and an emotional tension that must be experienced to be understood. It is a magnificent indoor sport."
Charge! or How to Play War Games

so it's clear that the cost of metal miniatures has outstripped inflation by some 200%, largely due to huge increases in material costs. At the same time, a box of Airfix figures was 3/- – that's just 15p! Thus Charles Grant was moved to write:

> "It would be improper not to mention the products of this firm, whose inexpensive plastic war game figures (20mm to 25mm – they do vary) have started the career of many a junior and not a few senior wargamers. They are quite the cheapest on the market (about 15p for boxes of 20 to 30 figures [they actually contained at least 40 infantry or a dozen cavalry] and the wargaming world owes Airfix a not inconsiderable debt."[13]

He may come across here as slightly patronising about Airfix, the 'poor relation' in comparison to the recently-spawned industry of metal figure manufacture, which was more closely associated with the skills of the craftsman jeweller, perhaps. But the fact is that Airfix's little polythene offerings were often far superior in terms of sculpting, anatomical correctness and casting quality than the somewhat amateurish (though aficionados accord such aesthetics the epithet "charming") output of the wargaming hobby at the time, with a few exceptions. What metal figures certainly *did* allow the wargamer to do was to collect battalions of figures all in the same position (advancing, firing etc) and from a much broader range of historical periods, armies and troop types.

When he wrote *The War Game* in 1971, Charles Grant listed the following companies: Hinton Hunt Figures, Rose Miniatures, Les Higgins Miniatures, 'Willie' Figures, Norman Newton Figures, Douglas Miniatures, 'Garrison' Figures, Miniature Figurines and Airfix. He could also have listed Taylor & McKenna (Warrior Metal Miniatures), Jacklex, Minitanks, Lamming, Scruby Miniatures in the USA and, from July 1971 onwards, Hinchliffe.

And so, by the beginning of the 1970s, the range of miniatures suitable for wargaming had mushroomed, and there can hardly have been a boy in the UK – and beyond – who had not got his hands on at least a couple of boxes of Airfix figures, together with other plastic model kits and, if he was lucky and had saved up his pocket money, perhaps a regiment or two of heavy metal. Almost all my friends from that time were up to their elbows in polystyrene cement and Humbrol enamel paint, high on fumes and the effects of licking paintbrushes to a point after cleaning them in turps or white spirit.

The explosion of wargames literature

The ground was indeed fertile, and a new crop of authors arrived to spread The Word. In 1967, a book appeared that many wargamers still see today as the seminal work that sparked their interest in the hobby: *Charge! Or How to Play Wargames* by Brigadier Peter Young and Lt. Col. J P Lawford.

---

13   *Charles Grant, The War Game, p.185.*

This wonderful work set a tone of playfulness, coupled with an understandable – given its authors – rigour when describing matters of drill and tactics that charmed many a young man into collecting impressive armies and learning how to play with them.

The *Charge!* rules were actually surprisingly comprehensive, containing no less than 42 specific rules with various sub-clauses and some General Points at the end. An interesting aspect is that the good Brigadier (a highly decorated war hero and leader of commandos) decided that whilst the rules are definitely early Napoleonic in character (rules for infantry squares are included), the miniatures on display should sport distinctly 18th century costume, with the glaring exception of the Royal Horse Artillery in their fore-and-aft crested 'Tarleton' helmets, a unit not created until 1793! And finally, this book saw the first appearance of what are now termed imagi-nations (entirely fictitious countries based on historical precedent), with the battles described being fought between the 'Emperor' and the 'Elector' and 'The Action at Blasthof Bridge' remains one of the most iconic wargames ever fought.

Though influential in its way, *Charge!* was the only wargames book that Peter Young wrote, though he wrote introductions for and edited several others. He remains, however, one of the greatest stars in the wargaming firmament, and his giant personality is remembered fondly to this day by those who knew him and encountered him across the wargames table.

Having just discussed the huge growth in the availability of Airfix figures, it is fitting that we should now mention perhaps their greatest cheerleader, Terence (Terry) Wise, whose book *Introduction to Battle Gaming* (1969) championed their use in games from ancient to modern. Terry's rules were straightforward, though they did include simple rules for isolated units, prisoners and morale, and he continued the British gamers' habit of leaving figures as individuals, rather than mounting them on unit or sub-unit bases. You may have noticed the similarity of the title of this book to that of my own magazine, and the fact is that my publication is indeed named in homage to this work, which was one of those I had out on virtually permanent loan from my school library as a boy.

Wise's American Civil War rules appeared later in a stand-alone volume in the *Airfix Magazine Guide* series: number 24, *American Civil War Wargaming* (1977). Again displaying his huge armies of Airfix plastics, this lovely little book reveals that by now, the author had dispensed with the use of dice for musketry and artillery fire, preferring tables and templates

TERRY WISE

"You may have gathered by now that wargaming is a highly individualistic hobby, and there are really no rules except those you make yourself, or those of others which you traditionally accept when playing against them in their home or club, and perhaps use as a basis upon which to create your own rules. It follows therefore that the rules outlined in this book will be *my* rules! You are welcome to accept them, reject them, discard parts, enlarge on other parts; this is how I got mine. I make no excuses for being a wargamer who merely enjoys the game..."
Airfix Magazine Guide 24: American Civil War Wargaming

to create pre-determined outcomes according to circumstances apart from granting a saving throw to officer figures! Curiously, however, hand to hand combat remained affairs of dice rolling. Quite why he imagined that musketry and artillery fire were so much more predictable than melee is not explained.

Charles Grant's first book was not, in fact, *The War Game* (1971), but *Battle: Practical Wargaming*, published in 1970 (and recently re-published and extended by Partizan Press). This little volume had originally appeared as a series of articles in *Meccano Magazine*, in thirty two parts from mid-1968 until December 1970 and in fact, the book was published before the magazine series had finished, omitting several parts[14]. However, it provided an outstanding introduction to WWII gaming, showcasing a host of Airfix figures and kits, along with a number of Roco Minitanks, which were actually made to a slightly smaller scale, but seemed to fit in perfectly well.

One thing that emerged about Charles Grant was his love of 'devices'. *Battle: Practical Wargaming* contained instructions for creating machine gun cones, hand grenade blast area devices and artillery fire devices, a trend that was to continue in his following work *The War Game* (canister cones, howitzer shell burst circles and artillery roundshot bounce sticks) and then *Napoleonic Wargaming* of 1974 (ditto) although by this time, he had revised his ideas about the way roundshot bounced somewhat, advocating the use of a 'sleeve' over the stick, rather than differently-coloured 'zones'.

I shan't dwell on *The War Game* – I think I've made it abundantly clear that it is my favourite wargames book, bar none, which left me with an abiding love of the 18th century – but instead tell you that Charles Grant built up an impressive body of publications before his death in 1979. A long-standing columnist in *Military Modelling* and then its offshoot, *Battle*, he was also sometime Editor of the journal of the Society of Ancients, *Slingshot*, and had a passion for ancient warfare – hence two of the titles to his credit, *The Ancient War Game* (1974) and *Ancient Battles for Wargamers* (1977). As well as providing excellent historical insights, these books, which included entertaining accounts of large wargames he had fought or umpired, also acted as an advertisement for the all-conquering ancients rules of the Wargames Research Group, to whom we shall come shortly.

---

14 See wargaming.info/2011/charles-grant-battle-practical-wargaming/ and download the whole series in PDF from www.hamnavoesolutions.co.uk/BattlebyCharlesGrant.pdf

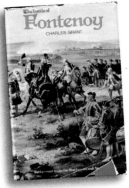

Two other titles by Charles Grant stand out: *The Battle of Fontenoy* (1975), a tremendously in-depth account of the preparation for and refight of this famous mid-18th century battle; and *Wargame Tactics*, which came out in the year of his death (1979), an interestingly Featherstone-esque jaunt through several periods of history, explaining something of each period and recounting large games played in the ancient, medieval, English Civil War, Napoleonic and American Civil War periods.

Ancients wargamer Tony Bath founded the Society of Ancients in 1965 and although his list of publications was rather short – just two, in fact – they deserve an honourable mention[15]. First published by the Wargames Research Group in 1973, his *Setting Up a Wargames Campaign* remains a manual for wargamers interested in more than just tabletop battles to this day.[16] His *Peltast and Pila* wargames rules found favour for a time, until eclipsed by the Wargames Research Group rules discussed later. But most famous of all was Bath's 'Hyborian' campaign, a completely fictitious conflict between a motley collection of ancient armies, fuelled by history, myth and fantasy literature, most particularly the *Conan* novels of Robert Howard. Running for several years, it involved many of the leading wargamers of the time and regular reports were published, first in *Battle* magazine (from January-October 1978) and then in *Military Modelling*, after *Battle* folded, until the last instalment in March 1979.

Sometimes, valuable gems are small, and this is certainly true of the next two little publications. *Discovering Wargames*, by John Tunstill, a book almost unknown amongst modern wargamers, was first published by Shire Publications in 1969. This tiny tome (a mere 64 pages measuring 175mm x 115mm) set a number of trends that were to persist for the next decade or more in some quarters. The first was to create a specific figure:man ratio (in this case 1:33); a specific, but *mixed* metric/Imperial ground scale (1mm = 1 yard); and a game divided into 'bounds' representing 2½ minutes of 'real' time. Moves were to be simultaneous with written orders and, a new departure for British wargaming, miniature troops

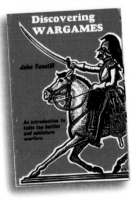

TONY BATH

"I have always maintained that one of the fascinations of our hobby is that it enables us all to participate up to the level we ourselves decide; and as long as we can find a kindred spirit to join us, the results will be stimulating and satisfying regardless of which level we choose."
Setting Up a Wargames Campaign

JOHN TUNSTILL

"The rules for the game should be based always on logic and truth – as far as it is known – and not upon personal preference, whim, legend or biased opinion."
Discovering Wargames

---

15   He was, in fact, a proliic writer of articles for magazines and the SoA journal Slingshot.

16   Bath's work has recently been republished, with extra commentary and including the ancients rules by the History of Wargaming Project: see www.wargames.co.

were to be mounted on card bases cut to sizes representing a scaled-down version of the actual ground occupied by a specific number of real troops.

Compared to what had gone before, the combat systems were fearsomely complex. Weapon ranges were divided into as many as six bands, from close to extreme, with a different effect for each, and these were combined with situational factors to affect the score of another new arrival, the 'average' dice (marked 2, 3, 3, 4, 4, 5, removing the extremes of 1 and 6).

We shall see the Tunstill DNA emerge again shortly.

In 1971, another Shire Publication came to market: *Rules for Wargaming* by Arthur Taylor. Again, we see 1mm = 1 yard as the scale of choice, the 2½ minute bound and simultaneous moves. However, Taylor adds much more sophisticated (some would say "complex", and they might be right) rules for morale, including gradings for troop quaity, confidence in leadership, physical condition and mental condition, as well as a host of situational factors *and* generalship. Whilst the concepts themselves weren't entirely original – Don Featherstone had outlined systems such as this in *Advanced War Games* – it was the first time they had been presented in this way.

But perhaps the most remarkable aspect of Taylor's rules is that they made no use of dice whatsoever: chance was completely eliminated, and casualties determined entirely by cross-referencing a pair of tables at the end of the book. This, of course, leads to a certain predictability much loved, I'm sure, by those with a head for figures, but which, I think it is safe to assume, led to these rules sinking more or less without trace.

Taylor's little book did, however, contain something else of interest: rules for naval (18th century and modern) and WWI aerial combat. Again, Don Featherstone had blazed a trail with *Naval War Games* in 1965 and *Air War Games* in 1966, but Taylor's approach was charming and included diagrams for the construction of wooden model ships and cardboard aircraft.

Let's mention another slender volume before moving on. David Nash's

Wargames, published in 1974, was published by Hamlyn, who were responsible for a number of titles of interest to the wargamer, including *Sailing Ships & Sailing Craft* by George Goldsmith-Carter (1969), *Military Uniforms 1686-1918* by René North (1970) and *Arms and Armour* by Frederick Wilkinson (1971). It seems strange to us now, but these marvellous paperbacks were in full colour throughout, featuring beautiful illustrations of their subject matter. Of course, nowadays, we look at Nash's charming little book and think "If only!" particularly since it includes the first description – as far as I know – of geomorphic terrain squares that I know of. (I talk about terrain squares later in this book). I can remember being extremely frustrated with *Wargames* because it does not provide a set of rules as such, but rather explains what one needs to take into account when devising a set of your own. Nevertheless, it was a coup for the hobby to have such a work published as part of an extremely popular series available in high street bookshops.

1974 turned out to be a vintage year for wargamers, starting with the fourth book in a series produced by Patrick Stephens Ltd for Airfix. Following hard on the heels of the first three *Airfix Magazine Guides* to *Plastic Modelling*, *Aircraft Modelling* and *Military Modelling* came Bruce Quarrie's *Airfix Magazine Guide 4: Napoleonic Wargaming*. Let's not forget that this book came out in the same year as Charles Grant's book on Napoleonics, but their appraches were poles apart.

Contrasting starkly with Grant's fun games with home-made wooden and wire appliances, Quarrie was a disciple of John Tunstill, Steve Tulk and the North London Wargames Group rules, but with added fervour. In addition to the elements mentioned earlier, we now had precise descriptions of wargame unit organisation for specific sub-periods of the era, dual leadership factors for every Napoleonic general according to whether he was in attack or defence, factors for shooting, different factors for melee according to whether it was the initial impact or a subsequent round, the separation of 'control' from general 'morale' to reflect impetuosity and, reflecting a new direction already established by the Wargames Research Group and their Ancients rules that had first been published in 1969, casualties expressed as *men*, instead of whole figures. Couple this complexity with Quarrie's extensive tables of national characteristics, which had different movement rates and fighting factors for hundreds of different troop types and it was clear that, in wargaming terms, we had arrived on a different planet. The formation changes chart alone had seventy (yes, seventy!) permutations and morale checks could take ten minutes a time. I loved them!

Quarrie had hit a rich vein: bright boys now entering their mid-teens, eager for all those charts and statistics, and looking back on their Grantian and Featherstonian origins of just a couple of years before as their 'stone age'. Here, in one volume, were all the facts hungry minds required to outdo their opponent in historical geekiness. The magic, as every young boy knows, was in the minutiae, and in that department, Quarrie did not disappoint – indeed, he followed up in 1977 with the exceptional *Napoleon's Campaigns in Miniature, A Wargamer's*

BRUCE QUARRIE

"Wargaming is many things to many people. For some it is a pure entertainment in which the appearance of the troops on the table is paramount; for others it is a real challenge in which victory is all-important. Of course, we all like to win – but please!: can we have victory without acrimony? The wargamer who argues bitterly the roll of every dice, consistently moves his figures a few millimetres more than he should, contests every arc of fire and orders 'psychic' moves which a real commander on the spot could not possibly do, is very likely to find himself without opponents in extremely short order... In all seriousness, wargaming is a hobby whose principle aim is relaxation. Take it seriously by all means when it comes to studying uniforms, weapons and tactics... But don't approach a battle with a 'win at all costs' attitide."
PSL Guide to Wargaming

CHARLIE WESENCRAFT

"I may be wrong, but I have always thought that a game played with easily understood rules that gave a result, played within a broad outline of a particular period, that gave enjoyment to both the winner and his unfortunate opponent, was to be preferred to one that was so accurate in detail that more often than not no result was achieved apart from one of genuine hostility towards one's enemy of the evening."
Practical Wargaming

G W JEFFREY

"Having read many books on wargaming, I have been struck by their lack of detail with regard to the periods which they cover, brought about most probably by their attempting to cover too many periods in one volume. I most strongly disagree with those who would compress a large part of military history into what they term the 'horse and musket' period..."
The Napoleonic Wargame

guide to the Napoleonic Wars 1796-1815. Packed full of facts and figures concerning not only the battles, but the campaings too and supported by excellent maps and diagrams, this was truly a schoolboy's dream.

Quarrie was also a keen WWII gamer and wrote another book of which I have fond memories: *Airfix Magazine Guide 15, World War 2 Wargaming* (1976) although in fact, he wrote a total of more than forty books (just enter his name in Wikipedia and see what comes up), so I have just 'dipped a toe' into his work, which is well worth exploring.

C F (Charlie) Wesencraft, another retired soldier, made his publication debut in 1974 with *Practical Wargaming*, a book which held my attention because it introduced the concept of changing the figure:men ratio in order to represent bigger battles, in this case shifting from his standard representation of 1:32 to 1:128. If ever there was a case to be made for not judging a book by its cover, this was it, a radical concept being presented in the pages of what seemed to be a slightly old-fashioned tome. One of the most striking paragraphs in the book put clear water between this and other, more literal approaches to the hobby at the time:

> "At the scale at present under discussion, it is impossible to show individual casualties. In fact, it is not even desirable to do so. The only important factor is: how did the regiment perform as a whole? Did it hold its ground or was it forced to fall back or did it merely disintegrate? These are the questions to be answered. No one is interested in the fact that the second man from the left in the front row successfully stopped an arrow with his chest – except his widow. Actually it is barely of consequence as to whether the unit engaged in a fire fight or a mêlée. The two vital points are: did a fight take place? And if so: what was the result?"[17]

The Wesencraft rules in the book covered the ancient, medieval, pike and musket, 18th century (including siege warfare), colonial, Napoleonic (for which he also introduced army corps level gaming, with a single stand representing an entire battalion), American Civil War and Franco-Prussian War eras. He followed this up in 1975 with the superb *With Pike and Musket: Sixteenth- and Seventeenth-Century Battles for the Wargamer*, expanding on his original rules for that period and including no less than twenty seven scenarios based on historical battles.

Also published in 1974 was G W Jeffrey's *The Napoleonic Wargame*, a slender and, it has to be said, largely unloved volume, though notable for being the first to explicly embrace no less than three sizes of miniature: 25mm, 15mm and 5mm. Another wargamer in favour of devices for

---

17   *C F Wesencraft, Practical Wargaming, p.74*

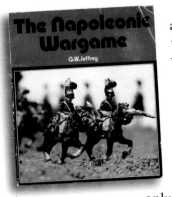

artillery fire, and adding another for wheeling troops, Jeffrey's main contribution to the debate was perhaps in the area of morale, but his rules suffered partly from being buried in the text of the book and hard to find, and so his efforts never gained much traction in the wargames community.

The following year, however, saw another *Airfix Magazine Guide*, this time number 9, *Ancient Wargaming* by Phil Barker, and it is only right that we should spend a moment acknowledging the contribution of yet another of the hobby's doyens, and a towering figure in the field of Ancients. Edited, interestingly enough, by Bruce Quarrie, this little book is a wonderfully compact volume, effectively acting as a shop window for the Wargames Research Group's ancients rules, but also including useful historical background, a discussion of ancient tactics and drill, a number of useful army lists, some tabletop tactics tips and advice on raising a wargames army.

Barker had been introduced to wargaming by his friend Tony Bath and Don Featherstone, and by 1969 his passion for the ancients period was firmly established, forming what was originally known as the Ancient War Games Research Group with "Bob" O'Brien and Ed Smith. Together, they produced the first set of Ancient Wargames Rules for the National Championships that were held in Worthing. Little did they know that they would spawn a little industry all of their own, because the rules were so well received. Ed Smith dropped out of the triumvirate in 1971, but by the end of that year the ancients rules were already in their third edition and a set of rules for 1750-1850 had been added.

The WRG ancients rules were remarkably detailed, and Barker boasted that they were by far the most thoroughly researched of their kind. Using a man:figure ratio of 1:20, combat calculations resulted in actual men killed (like the Quarrie Napoleonic rules) which would be tallied separately until one or more complete figures needed to be removed. Allowance was made for multiple armour and formation types, and of course the ancient period saw a plethora of different weapons facing one another across thousands of years of history, all of which were allowed for. The rules also included a comprehensive system of points, so that balanced games could be fought by utterly dissimilar armies, which soon meant that ancient Greeks were able to face Japanese

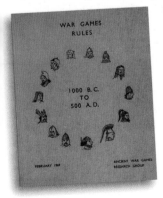

PHIL BARKER

"The crucial test of a good set of wargame rules is whether the tactics and orders that work in real life work equally well under the rules... You should beware on principle of any book calling itself 'A History of the Art of War' or something similar, because it is odds on that the author only knows a period of a hundred years or so in real detail, and is filling in the rest from secondary and often questionable sources."
Airfix Magazine Guide 9: Ancient Wargaming

PHIL BARKER

"What qualities does the perfect umpire need? He should have a deep interest in human nature, a well-developed sense of humour, at least a moderate knowledge of his period, be hard working, literate, hard to bully but easy to convince, and should have plenty of spare time! The best umpires are also very likeable people, this probably helping them survive the occasional wrath of the players."
Alexander the Great's Campaigns

Samurai across the table, which may not have been what the rule writers originally intended but, once begun, could not be prevented. Personally, I still don't see the point of such an encounter, but each to their own!

Further editions and rules for other periods were added to the list, and by now, the vast majority of ancients wargames were being played using the WRG (as they were already known) rules. Achieving this level of universal acceptance was almost unheard of up to this point, and had a great deal to do with the fact that they were used for wargames tournaments both in the UK and overseas, a rare achievement. They also had the backing of other 'big hitters' in the hobby such as Charles Grant and the support of the Society of Ancients.

When, eventually, they were superceded, it was by dint of an act of infanticide by Barker himself, who created entirely new systems in the form of *De Bellis Antiquitatis* (*DBA*), a set of highly abstract, fast-play rules, and *De Bellis Multitudinis* (*DBM*) for larger games, to replace what by then had become a somewhat muddled 7th Edition ancients rules. The latest incarnation is *De Bellis Magistrorum Militum* (*DBMM*). The world of ancients wargames has always seen a certain amount of immodesty, and as Barker himself says on his website, "DBMM is a radical development

of DBM, which had previously been by far the most popular ancient[s] rule[s] around the world."[18]

A last word on Phil Barker: *Alexander the Great's Campaigns, A guide to Ancient political and military wargaming*, published in 1979, in a simliar vein to Quarrie's title on Napoleon's campaigns, remains one of the very best wargaming books ever produced, absolutely choc-a-bloc with fascinating detail, regardless of your primary interests.

The latter part of the 1970s saw a handful of interesting titles, two of which dealt with WWII wargaming.

JOHN SANDARS

"In general, the lower the level at which a game is played the more detail can be included. It is a common mistake to allow for too much detail for its level in a game, and this seldom makes it enjoyable to play."
An Introduction to Wargaming

John Sandars' *An Introduction to Wargaming* incorporated his own highly detailed ideas for wargames in the Western Desert, *Sandskrieg*, together with some discussion of wargames mechanisms in general. The outcome was another frustrating title for wargamers, who craved a definitive set of rules to be included in such a book, but we were only left with hints. The front cover illustration, however, displayed a fearsome array of charts, tape measures

18   See www.wrg.me.uk/ for a full history of Phil Barker and the WRG.

marked with coloured 'zones', burst circles, home-made clock-like devices and more[19]. Sandars had also written a series of articles which appeared in *Airfix Magazine* concerning the British 8th Army that fought against Rommel's Afrikakorps, which became *Airfix Magazine Guide 20: 8th Army in the Desert* in 1976.

Thriller novelist Gavin Lyall, together with his son Bernard, produced a striking book about WWII wargaming in 1976 called *Operation Warboard, Wargaming World War II Battles in 20-25mm scale*. Engagingly written, Lyall's book displayed games played on simple terrain with stepped hills not entirely unlike those used by Charles Grant in *Battle: Practical Wargaming* and even included home-made devices for machine gun and artillery fire. The book incorporated a comprehensive set of highly playable rules, which ought to have made the book more popular than it actually turned out to be – a hidden gem, in my opinion.

A Guide to Wargaming by George Gush and Andrew Finch appeared in 1980. A book which contains a good overview of the birth of the hobby itself, the reader is also treated to an excellent section of advice on writing one's own rules and three useful rulesets for the later 19th century, WWII skirmishes and medieval battles. Gush, an academic and an authority on the subject of Renaissance warfare, was already noteworthy for his contribution to the Wargames Research Group in the form of his rules for the Renaissance period based on the mechanics of their ancients set, *Wargames Rules for Fifteenth to Seventeenth Centuries* (1490-1660, later expanded to 1420-1700). He also wrote a twenty four-part series on Renaissance warfare published in *Airfix Magazine* between June 1973 and May 1975, and a six-part series on the English Civil War published in *Miniature Warfare* magazine in 1970. Another popular credit to his name was *Airfix Magazine Guide 28: The English Civil War*, with Martin Windrow.

Paddy Griffith, who sadly died in 2010, remains a towering figure amongst wargamers although *Napoleonic Wargaming for Fun* (1980) is the only book he has left us directly discussing miniatures wargaming in the style recognisable to most of us. A Sandhurst lecturer, Paddy was most famous

---

GAVIN LYALL

"The object of a game is to learn, as much as to win, and the pleasantest move is the one after the last: when the two generals sit down to discuss what really went on."
Operation Warboard

GEORGE GUSH

"The general nature, many of the problems, and most of the fascination of wargames really lie in this combination of a game of skill and an imaginative reconstruction. It also goes far to explain the great diversity of wargames... both because of the limitless range of actual or imaginary situations which can be reproduced, and because of the infinite number of different ways in which they can be simulated. Hence uniquely, in wargaming there is almost as much interest in the devising of rules and games as there is in the playing of them."
A Guide to Wargaming

---

19   *A version of the Sandskrieg rules can be downloaded from www.battlegames.co.uk/oldschool/ oldschool_rules.html*

PADDY GRIFFITH

"An important point to remember with all types of wargame is that they are fundamentally different from formal games like chess or bridge. With the latter, the fun of the game is derived from the purely abstract competition between the two players. It is the ability to think logically, and almost mathematically, which is most important. In a wargame, on the other hand, the competitive element certainly has a part to play; but it is not really predominant. It is, rather, the sense of re-creating the past which provides the excitement. The wargamer is playing at 'let's pretend' with military history. Some form of realism, or imaginative leap into the Napoleonic era will be essential and anything which helps it along will be good for the wargame."
Napoleonic Wargaming for Fun

for establishing Wargame Developments, a society created for the exploration of alternative forms of wargame, including map *Kriegsspiel* and what might also be termed 'free' *Kriegsspiel* games, often involving many players, divided into teams to explore the possibilities of historical situations. The book itself is fascinating because it was the first time since Wesencraft's *Practical Wargaming* (see above) that anyone had addressed the need for different rules to suit different levels of game, from skirmishes through Brigade and Division up to Army, Generalship and even the Tactical Exercise Without Troops (TEWT) much used by modern armies for training officers.

After the publication of Griffith's book, there was a hiatus in historical wargame publishing that lasted some time, although wargamers had plenty to read on the magazine front. *Battle* magazine had ceased publication as an independent magazine in 1978 and had been taken back into the embrace of *Military Modelling*. In 1983, however, a new magazine emerged under the stewardship of Duncan Macfarlane, a well-known ancients wargamer: *Miniature Wargames*. Leading wargames writers flocked to this publication which was enhanced by a quality of photographs not seen before – hardly surprising, because the editor was an amateur photographer of considerable skill. The images were close-ups of the 'showcase' products of the hobby, including the work of Wargames Holiday Centre owner and Hinchliffe sculptor Peter Gilder, whose enormous layouts frequently featured gargantuan battles from the ancient, Renaissance, Napoleonic and American Civil War periods.

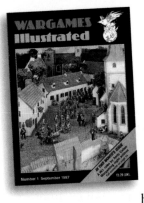

Macfarlane himself has never written a wargaming book which, given that he is an erudite man and a keen wargamer, seems a shame, though the magazine he gave birth to survives, though it has changed hands three times now: first, in 1987, when Macfarlane moved on to establish another title, *Wargames Illustrated*, and new editor Iain Dickie took over the editor's chair; then in 2008 it was bought by owner/editor Andrew Hubback; and then, most recently, it was acquired by Atlantic Publishers early in 2011. Macfarlane eventually bowed out of magazine publishing altogether in February 2009, when he sold the title to Battlefront, who produce the popular WWII gaming system *Flames of War*. *Wargames Illustrated* retains its market-leading position, and has grown under the new owners although inevitably, debate rages about its 'independence'.

Another significant magazine ran from 1987 to its sudden demise in 1999: *Practical Wargamer*. Editor Stuart Asquith had some pedigree as an expert on toy soldiers, as a columnist in *Military Modelling* and

STUART ASQUITH

"It is important to realise that wargaming is, and indeed should be, all things to all men. No one approach to a period, style or type of soldier is necessarily right or wrong. It is, after all, your time and money that are being spent on the hobby so it is important that you 'do your own thing' within the wider framework of wargaming. One of the great strengths of the hobby is that it can contain so many differing approaches and styles."
Military Modelling Guide to Wargaming

a regular contributor to *Wargamers' Newsletter*. Firmly in the 'it's just a game' camp, *Practical Wargamer* garnered a devoted following amongst those who railed against the apparent increase in complexity of wargames rules of the time, and Asquith's editorial style permitted photographs of miniatures that were not painted to award-winning standards, unlike the eye-candy served up by Duncan Macfarlane. By the end of the decade, Asquith had also penned three short works for Argus Books under the *Military Modelling* banner, shown above: the *Guide to Wargaming* (1987); *Guide to Solo Wargaming* (1988), which perhaps remains his best-loved work; and *Guide to Siege Wargaming* (1990). From these, it is abundantly clear that Asquith was as far from the 'simulationist' style of wargaming as it was possible to get.

And finally, in this section, we see the arrival of another soldier and a friend, in fact, of Stuart Asquith, son of the late Charles Grant: Charles Stewart Grant (known as C S Grant) who began his wargame writing career with a series of wargame scenarios that he christened his 'Table Top Teasers'. The first appeared in *Battle* magazine in 1978 and they continued, intermittently, in *Military Modelling* until 1982 before reappearing, after a considerable gap, in my own *Battlegames* magazine, where they ran for twenty-four issues

C S GRANT

"Without wishing to upset chess players, there is none of the mechanical dryness of chess about the wargame. It is fluid and full of surprises. Each game provides a unique challenge to use your miniature troops in a militarily appropriate way to defeat an enemy. My philosophy is that a good game lost is better than a bad game won."
Wargaming in History Volume I

plus a Table Top Teasers special edition. More have subsequently appeared elsewhere, having acquired something of a cult status as intelligently-designed scenarios that can be adapted to any period. As shown here, the Wargames Research Group also published two volumes of them, though under a different name: *Scenarios for Wargames* (1981) and *Programmed Wargames Scenarios*, aimed at solo wargamers (1983). The self-published *Scenarios for All Ages* (1996), co-authored with Stuart Asquith, was in a similar vein.

Grant, now a retired brigadier, writes mostly military history, and he is currently writing an impressive series on

the Peninsular War published by Partizan Press but, as far as wargamers are concerned, it is his contribution of four volumes out of the current five of the *Wargaming in History* series, published by Ken Trotman, that has won the greatest acclaim. So far, Grant's work here has covered the War of the Austrian Succession and the Seven Years War, with a detailed account of key battles accompanied by extensive thought about how to refight them successfully on the tabletop. A volume dealing with the Peninsular War was published in 2012.

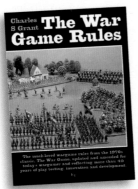

Interestingly, rather than creating his own wargames rules, Grant has essentially built upon those written by his father for *The War Game*. In 2008 he produced *The War Game Companion*, which updated and expanded upon those published in his father's original work, bringing some previously unpublished aspects to the light of day and clarifying others, much to the delight of fans of the original system. And, as I write this in 2012, Ken Trotman has just published *The War Game Rules*, incorporating all the updates and amendments made by the Grant family during what Charles refers to as "forty years of playtesting"!

Taking an honourable place in this pantheon of wargames writers is Neil Thomas, with *Wargaming, an Introduction* (2005), *Ancient & Medieval Wargaming* (2007), *Napoleonic Wargaming* (2009) and now *Wargaming Nineteenth Century Europe 1815-1878*. Thomas is a cerebral wargamer, very much influenced by the simple mechanisms of Phil Barker's *DBA* that have the benefit of proposing easily-attainable wargames armies for beginners. He has some interesting things to say and the Ancient & Medieval volume in particular has attracted a strong following.

The final word in wargames books goes, however, to a title that is more a book about wargamers than about wargaming as such: the marvellous and funny *Achtung Schweinehund!*, subtitled *A Boy's Own Story of Imaginary Combat* by Harry Pearson, published in paperback in 2007. Pearson, a *Guardian* newspaper sports journalist, casts a witty but kindly spotlight on the idiosyncrasies of the hobby and those that share our childlike (but not child*ish*) love of playing with toy soldiers – including himself. An absolute 'must read'.

Some magazines that flourished for a time and then faded away: Don Featherstone's *Wargamer's Newsletter*, John Tunstill's *Miniature Warfare*, Seán C. O'Hogan's *Wargamer's Monthly* and Neil Fawcett's *Wargames Journal*.

The Games Workshop phenomenon

Games Workshop was founded in 1975 and, originally, had nothing whatsoever to do with wargaming – they made boards for playing backgammon, *Go* and other 'standard' games. However, before long they became the import agent for the popular fantasy role-paying system *Dungeons and Dragons* (*D&D*), inspired by J R R Tolkien's *Lord of the Rings* and created by Americans Gary Gygax and Dave Arneson in 1974. These products, and others from TSR (Tactical Studies Rules, Inc.) as well as their own early efforts at rules writing fed a rapidly expanding mail order business, supported by an in-house magazine called, curiously, *Owl and Weasel*, which in June 1977 became *White Dwarf* (still available in high street newsagents in many countries).

The company's first shop opened in Hammersmith, London in 1978, a small beginning which subsequently led, by 2012, to retail outlets in nearly fifty coutries. The company's growth was fuelled by a growing fan base, for whom regular conventions were organised and by 1979, the decision was made to start producing their own range of miniatures for role-playing games and tabletop wargames – and Citadel Miniatures was born, a brand which immediately became synonymous with the parent company, although it was actually spawned from Asgard Miniatures, brainchild of Bryan Ansell, a name that was to become pivotal in the company's history.

Rick Priestley had written a set of fantasy wargames rules called *Reaper* in the late 70s, when he and co-author Richard Halliwell were still at school.[20] The *Reaper* rules were aimed at fighting

---

20 *From a conversation with the author, published in* Battlegames *magazine issue 21.*

RICK PRIESTLEY

"The fantasy genre has never enjoyed such general popularity as it does today. So fantastic are the themes of contemporary books, TV and films that fantasy has become an inseparable part of our everyday lives.

Fantasy is about heroes and monsters, fabulous deeds and fearsome battles, where adventures take place on worlds quite unlike our own. These are realms inhabited by strange and often hostile races as well as daemons, spirits and gods. In short, fantasy is about imagination and not just the imagination of writers and film producers, but of everyone who has ever read a fantasy novel or watched a fantasy film. To this list it is only fair to add the person who takes the process a step further by bringing all this to life in miniature – the fantasy gamer!"
Warhammer Battle Book 1996

fantasy battles, but also allowed for individual miniatures to skirmish under certain circumstances. They made use, however, of percentage dice, a trend which was prevalent in role-playing games of the 1970s. By the early 1980s, however, under the guidance of Bryan Ansell, who now had control of both Games Workshop and Citadel Miniatures and had taken the company to Nottingham, a new rules system was created by Priestley and Halliwell that was to have enormous consequences not just for the company, but for the wargaming hobby as a whole.

Warhammer Fantasy Battles, which first appeared in 1983, was divided into three volumes, *Tabletop Battles*, *Magic* and *Characters*. The rules were built around an imagined world, somewhat Tolkienesque in nature, inhabited by men, elves, dwarves and orcs, endlessly at war. But the project was driven by commercial considerations. The *Warhammer* game was developed to allow people to make use of the collections of Citadel miniatures they already had, and those became the races that were then incorporated into the game.[21]

Considering the fact that *Warhammer* is really just an ancients/medievals ruleset with fantasy aspects like magic bolted on, its success has been remarkable. Effectively, it destroyed the competition and devoured swathes of the market who might otherwise have moved into alternative roleplay systems such as *D&D*, and other fantasy battle systems from competing companies have not reached its dizzying heights of success. Moreover, regular updates to the rules (now in their 8th edition) and ranges of miniatures covering up to a dozen different races have kept at least two generations of young wargamers hooked. This success was boosted by the early adoption of extruded hard plastic miniatures, all manufactured and packaged at the company's headquarters in Lenton, Nottingham and their factory in Memphis, Tennessee.

This was followed by the creation of a science fiction game, *Warhammer 40,000 Rogue Trader*, written by Priestley, which first appeared in 1987. Initially geared towards skirmishes and role-playing, it was with the second and subsequent editions that the system was revised to attract younger players and then really took off, remaining the biggest-selling line in the Games Workshop line-up to this day, having spawned a huge range of figures and equipment and the offshoot company Forgeworld, who create special edition miniatures in resin to complement the main ranges. Coupled with retail outlets on every high street in the land, where the staff are trained to provide a fully rounded hobby

---

21   *ibid.*

support system linked closely to the company's merchandising, this has led to pretty consistent success for what is now a multi-national enterprise.

There have been other games along the way too, such as *Advanced Heroquest, Bloodbowl, Battlefleet Gothic* and *Warmaster*, but the *Warhammer* duo remain the core offering, though both of these have offspring of particular interest to historical gamers.

Perhaps surprisingly, given its sci-fi origins, the *Warhammer 40,000* (also known as *40K*) system came into its own when Games Workshop won the contract to provide the 'official' miniatures and game to accompany director Peter Jackson's *Lord of the Rings* movie trilogy. A great deal of secrecy, both within and outside the company, shrouded this project in mystery until it was launched, to great acclaim, in 2001. Accompanied by a lavish series of books aimed at recreating the action depicted on-screen in the movies, the project also produced some of the company's most beautifully sculpted miniatures, both in metal and hard plastic. A 2009 *War of the Ring* supplement enables players to fight some of the larger battles found in the original books, as well as the films.

The *40K* system was also used to the benefit of historical wargamers under the banner of Warhammer Historical, a purely publishing enterprise, manufacturing no miniatures of its own. This offshoot did not seem to sit entirely comfortably within the Games Workshop armoury, and after an interim phase during which it was controlled by Black Library, the GW publishing arm, and ForgeWorld, with authors coming from both within and outside the company, Warhammer Historical was closed in May 2012. In my view, this is a real shame and a significant loss to the hobby, though the omens were bad for the last couple of years.

Three excellent and beautifully-produced books also made good use of the 40K skirmish approach: *Legends of the Old West*, a Wild West gaming system; *Legends of the High Seas*, for pirate and buccaneer wargames, including ship-to-ship and shipboard action; and *The Great War*, which focuses primarily on trench raid scenarios. One of the last works to emerge was Mark Latham's *Waterloo*, a lavish book dealing with Napoleonic wargames, featuring the not inconsiderable collection of Alan Perry, who sculpts all the Napoleonic figures for Perry Miniatures and who also, coincidentally, works for Games Workshop with his twin brother Michael.[22] The company

RICK PRIESTLEY

"There can be few people who have collected and gamed with armies of model warriors who have not dreamed of recreating the ultimate big battle. Such a battle wouldn't be just a battle – or rather not just the immediate confrontation between rival warriors – but would encompass the manoeuvre and counter-manoeuvre of armies, the disposition of whole brigades and the execution of bold strategies as imaginative as they are ambitious."
Warmaster Rulebook

ALESSIO CAVATORE

"True heroes are recognised not by their medals, but by their scars. So muster your armies and prepare for war - the dark millenium awaits."
Warhammer 40K Rulebook

---

22 *Michael Perry is one of the most remarkable people in wargaming. Having lost his right arm during a medieval re-enactment accident, he re-taught himself to sculpt with his left hand and the aid of an artificial right arm.*

JOHN STALLARD

"I suppose it was Airfix's fault, or maybe Timpo's or Britains', but whoever the villain was, by the age of six my life was destined to be dominated by toy soldiers. Back then I could never have dreamed that my adult career would be similarly dedicated to the wacky world of war games, but I'm happy to say that it has been."
Warhammer English Civil War Rulebook

JERVIS JOHNSON

"When all is said and done [these rules] have been written because I like playing games with model soldiers and they reflect that fact. Put simply, there's nothing I like better than seeing a few hundred well-painted miniatures laid out on nicely made terrain. Or at least, I like nothing better than this except winning a hard fought battle with said miniatures (rare though such victories are!). This is the reason I started wargaming and why I still do today..."
Warhammer Ancient Battles Rulebook (1st Edition)

also addressed World War II with *Kampfgruppe Normandy* by Warwick Kinrade, World War I aerial warfare with *Richthofen's Flying Circus* by Owen Branham, *Over the Top* by Alex Buchel (an extension to *The Great War* WWI rules) and *Gladiator* by Barry Hill.

Warhammer Historical also developed the *Warhammer Fantasy* rules, and it comes as no surprise that the first project was blindingly obvious: remove the magic aspects and you have a very effective ruleset for ancient and medieval wargaming, and thus *Warhammer Ancient Battles* (*WAB*) was born.

WAB, released in 1998 as a part-time project by Rick Priestley, Jervis Johnson and twins Alan and Michael Perry, was based heavily on the fifth edition of *Warhammer Fantasy Battles*, but with extra detail covering ancient weapons and formations. Co-author Johnson was keen to allay the fears of the nervous historical wargames community from the outset, making it clear that the books would never be supported by ranges of Citadel miniatures, nor sold in GW stores – and this turned out to be true[23].

The interesting thing about *WAB* is that in fact it was, in effect, a very 'old' set of rules (or what would now be called 'old school'), harking back to both the mechanisms and the aesthetics of Charles Grant and Don Featherstone, with large units and combat systems promoting the role of the heroic individual.

An update, *WAB2*, was published in 2010, but contained so many errors that the *WAB* gaming community was somewhat stunned and certainly disappointed. Little did we realise at the time that this *faux pas* was the first symptom of the internal strains at Warhammer Historical that were to lead to its ultimate closure.

Nevertheless, *WAB* has been beneficial to the hobby, since many gamers more used to crashing units of orcs and elves into one another found it easy to convert to using Macedonians and Persians or Vikings and Saxons. Some excellent supplements were also spawned by it, with twelve official books ranging from Ancient Egypt to the English Civil War, and a number of unofficial variants proposed by individual wargamers and clubs.

The role of Warhammer Historical will probably remain controversial. Some, like me, have mourned its passing, whilst others have dismissed the part it played as lacking innovation and representing the unattractive side of commercialism. However, what cannot be denied is that for fourteen years, the company produced some of the most attractive publications that the hobby has seen and was responsible for raising the benchmark to that already expected by the fantasy and sci-fi gaming community.

---

23   See 'Informed by History, Warhammer Ancient Battles Design Philosophy', Slingshot, the Journal of the Society of Ancients, July 1998 issue 198, pp.11-14.

The Black Powder controversy

RICK PRIESTLEY
& JERVIS
JOHNSON

One of the interesting developments in recent years has been the exodus of key Games Workshop staff to smaller enterprises of their own devising. Warlord Games is a case in point, based in Nottingham and launched by John Stallard and Paul Sawyer, both previously employees of GW. Leaving aside their excellent and growing range of miniatures, which includes a successful foray into hard plastic, let us concentrate on their publishing venture, which burst onto the scene in 2009 with *Black Powder*, a title co-authored by Rick Priestley (now also a Warlord board member) and Jervis Johnson (still currrently working for GW), in collaboration with Michael and Alan Perry, whose miniatures adorned the pages of the book.

Now, like the works produced by Warhammer Historical, *Black Powder* is really a set of wargames rules for the horse and musket era that also happens to include lots of other useful information about the period in question, as well as inspiring photography of beautifully-painted miniatures. This was followed in 2011 by Priestley's *Hail Caesar*, a work in similar vein dealing with ancient warfare and in 2012 by *Pike & Shotte* written by Steve Morgan, dealing with the period of roughly 1500-1700. Both these are, in essence, extensions of the *Black Powder* core system.

This trio of books are high-quality, hardback publications, written in an enthusiastic, engaging and even somewhat old-fashioned style, with not a little tongue evident in cheek and somewhat self-conscious, ironic 'old school' mannerisms. That they have proved successful is not surprising; that they have been controversial was less expected.

Why should this be? First of all, to some extent, there has always been a section of the wargames community that dismisses anything not period-specific: how on earth, they would argue, can a set of rules cover perhaps 200 years of horse and musket warfare when there were distinct differences between the way the Seven Years War was fought and the Crimean War a hundred years later? Looking at the Ancients period, it's even more potentially problematic – should we really be dealing with Byzantine cataphracts in the same way as Persian cataphracts from a thousand years earlier?

But, leaving aside the wrangling over historicity, much of the kerfuffle about Warlord's publishing output has been to do with aesthetics and

"Black Powder is a game for militarily inclined gentlemen with straight backs, bristling beards and rheumy eyes that have seen a thing or two. If tales of battle and glory in days-gone-by stir nothing in your breast, if the roar of cannon does not quicken the pulse and set a fire in the belly, then stop reading forthwith. Ours is not an adventure to be embarked upon by the faint hearted. Put down this book and be glad that you have spared yourself the discomforting spectacle of grown men attempting to relive the great conflicts of history with armies of toy soldiers."
Black Powder

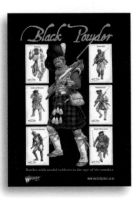

RICHARD BODLEY SCOTT

"The most important lesson that a beginner has to learn is that he should have a plan. Almost any plan is better than no plan at all. A good plan, however, is the first step to victory. It should take into account the layout of the battlefield, the relative strengths and weaknesses of the opposing forces and the enemy's likely actions. If you misjudge, you will find it difficult to change your plan or redeploy, so best get it right first time if possible"
Field of Glory Ancients Rulebook

expense: why should I, goes the argument, have to spend £30 on a book with a lot of (they would argue) unnecessary pretty pictures of miniatures, when all I actually want is the rules? What was wrong, they ask on forums and blogs, with a good, old-fashioned, black and white, stapled pamphlet with a few diagrams, priced at just a couple of pounds?

Perhaps a backlash of this kind was inevitable at some point, but it illustrates the schism between the bibliophiles who enjoy the physical beauty of an attractive book as much as the rules it contains, and the gamers whose interest is purely in the mechanics of the system presented within those pages, and who will probably always see the 'eye candy' as an unnecessary intrusion. Lord help me when this book is published!

Conclusion

Let me finish this section by saying that however detailed it may seem to you, this has been the merest, fleeting overview of the exponential growth of published works dealing with wargaming. Whilst I have managed to include most of the important books written by the doyens of the hobby (though wargamers argue fiercely about that!), I could not possibly cover the hundreds, nay, thousands of magazine articles that have appeared since the 1950s, nor could I hope to successfully list every set of wargames rules published in that time. Besides, hobbyists often quip that there are as many sets of wargame rules as there are wargamers, because we are inveterate tweakers and fiddlers, each of us convinced that this or that set could be improved if only it was +2 for this or -1 for that, or infantry moved slightly further or cavalry were made a bit slower...

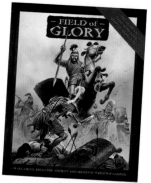

And fashions change. Over the last few years, the

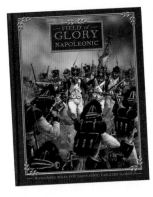

Field of Glory ancients rules by Richard Bodley-Scott, together with its supplements, another lavish line-up produced as a joint venture between Osprey Publishing and Slitherine software, have had a huge surge in popularity in the same way as the WRG rules did in the 1970s and 1980s, and *WAB* did in the 'noughties'. A Renaissance variant by the triumvirate of Richard Bodley Scott, Nik Gaukroger and Charles Masefield, and a Napoleonic version by Terry Shaw and Mike Horah complete the current line-up and I would expect more to follow.

And, as I write this in 2012, there have been perhaps half a dozen different sets of ancients rules released by various publishers in just the last twelve months! Several of these have taken the lavish hardback route, in accordance with the trend set by Warhammer Historical and Warlord.

The most recent to cross my desk has been *War &
Conquest*, written by none other than Rob Broom,
the last person to hold the reins of Warhammer
Historical before it began its descent to dissolution.

Your safest bet, therefore, is to get on your
computer and pop over to the Caliver Books
website at *www.caliverbooks.com*, where you
will find a mind-boggling list of rulesets on sale,
some old, some new, some extremely popular and
others, perhaps the majority, published and then
gathering dust on a shelf somewhere. And of course,
popularity is a fickle friend, sometimes ignoring a ruleset that deserved to
do better, or blessing another set which might, perhaps, have sunk without
trace under different circumstances. You can even go online and find sets
of perfectly good rules for free – see *www.freewargamesrules.co.uk*.

ROB BROOM

"For some, this
will be your
introduction into
the world of
waging war with
armies of model
soldiers. To you,
welcome to an
absorbing and
enjoyable hobby,
where as you
build your armies
and play games
you will develop
a greater
understanding of
history and the
consequences of
war."
*War & Conquest
Rulebook*

And finally, as I said at the outset, this volume cannot possibly cover
the myriad other fantasy and sci-fi, roleplay and boardgame variants that
have developed parallel to, and often hand-in-glove with, miniatures
wargaming. Nor have I mentioned air wargames or naval wargames,
though I shall touch on those subjects later. And lastly, I fully admit that this
work is largely UK-centric, and there have been thousands of wargamers
beavering away elsewhere around the world whose contributions should,
rightfully, be acknowledged. But there simply isn't the space to say more
at this time around and I have a publisher who has been waiting patiently
for this manuscript for far too long!

In conclusion, I hope that I have been able to demonstrate that there
is a fine line between a book about wargaming that happens to include
one or more sets of rules (such as this very volume), but which sets out
to say something about the wider hobby; and what is essentially a set of
wargames rules that has been expanded to incorporate information about
the hobby in general or to include historical background material (such as
Black Powder). There are times when the distinction is a very fine one and,
as we have seen, the hobby's participants can become polarised in the
approach they prefer. Indeed, the same author can write different books,
emphasising one approach or the other: think of Bruce Quarrie, for
example, whose first Airfix Guide was very much really a set of Napoleonic
wargames rules, but who then followed up with *Napoleon's Campaigns
in Miniature* which took a much more comprehensive approach; or Phil
Barker, doyen of ancient wargaming whose WRG rules were a byword for
'bare bones', but who could also pen the magnificent *The Campaigns of
Alexander*.

One thing is certain, however: wargame publishing is in as good health
as it has ever been, with companies better known for their miniatures
joining the traditional publishers in giving us a huge choice of books and
rulesets to choose from.

Duncan Macfarlane, former editor of *Wargames illustrated*, enjoying a 28mm Renaissance era *Warhammer Ancient Battles* competition game. Many wargamers find competitions both a rewarding and sociable way to engage in the hobby, as well as testing their generalship skills in a particular period. This photo was taken at the annual Colours wargames show which takes place every September in Newbury.

At the same show, a 6mm Zulu Wars Battle of Isandlwhana participation game. It's a good idea to visit a couple of shows before deciding on a period because you will find many different eras portrayed in various sizes and scales by enthusiasts happy to offer guidance.

3

Choosing a Period

The Wealth of History – and Beyond

Perhaps the very reason you find yourself interested in this hobby is because you already have a passion for a particular period or style of wargaming. This can be derived from all manner of inspiration, some of which we shall discuss later. A book, a movie, a TV show, a magazine article, a visit to a museum or stately home, perhaps; or even glimpsing a wargame in progress at a convention or a hobby store.

I have made no assumptions whatsoever about how much military history you are familiar with. Indeed, you may not know much at all, beyond what you may have picked up from your history lessons at school and those sources mentioned above. But this should not debar you from taking an interest in historical wargaming and finding a period that suits you, in terms of the uniforms and equipment, tactics and even the most famous commanders from a particular era.

Mankind has not, sadly, spent much of its time on this planet at peace. As a result, from the mists of prehistory right up to the present day, there are countless conflicts that we can call upon as inspiration for our games. All you have to decide is what interests you the most. So, let's spend a little time considering the various periods commonly gamed and show you something of the visual spectacle that each has to offer. Whilst the introductory section preceding the horse and musket era rules in Chapter 7 does indeed contain a more comprehensive essay on the warfare of the time, since it seemed appropriate for me to give you a reasonably solid grounding in that period so that you can make the most of the rules, this is not a comprehensive military history lesson – that would require a mighty tome indeed! But with luck, what I have included here will form a springboard for your own research into military history, a subject which is endlessly fascinating and inspiring.

It is not my intention to seem culturally arrogant by not including much in the way of military developments outside Europe and North America. I have simply had to make this decision for reasons of space and my own ignorance. Whilst I have a deep interest in the martial arts of the Orient, my knowledge of its history is sketchy, and therefore best left to those with expertise in this field, so I have included a number of references in the Bibliography should your interests extend in that direction.

And finally, it would not do to ignore the fact that most wargamers, in fact, either do not play historical games at all, or only some of the time. I mean, of course, the other genres that dominate the hobby: fantasy and science fiction. It would be impossible for me to cover these facets of the hobby in any great depth here, because they have a vast literature all of their own (*The Lord of the Rings* and *Star Wars* are icons in their relative genres, but represent the merest tip of the iceberg), but I felt it only fair to acknowledge their attraction and describe some general themes.

Hoplite phalanxes duel outside the walls of a typical Greek city during the Peloponnesian War of 431 to 404BC. Heavily armoured spearmen with colourful large shields dominated, supported by light troops and relatively few light cavalry. Infantry-based armies such as these are relatively inexpensive and offer the newcomer a solid tactical education.

A Roman legion faces an onrushing Carthaginian force accompanied by terrifying elephants. Roman armies are very popular and, thanks to the advent of hard plastic miniatures, can be collected for relatively little outlay, even in 28mm. Another benefit is that a Roman player never lacks opponents – even including other Romans!

More Romans, this time being massacred by Sassanid Persians in a *Hail Caesar* encounter on John Stallard's wargames table. The author managed to catch the dismayed Roman cohorts both in front and flank simultaneously, an opportunity which delighted his cataphracts in particular. 28mm miniatures painted by Dr Phil Hendry.

The Ancient era

This covers a period from the very dawn of recorded history, roughly 2000BC, through to what we commonly call the Dark Ages, with 1000AD being a convenient cut-off date, though it depends on which part of the world you're interested in as to where you draw the line.

The Ancient era is by far the longest time span during which weapons, armour and tactics changed comparatively little. From the deserts of Egypt to the Russian steppes to the wild fringes of northern Britain and Scandinavia, across the jungles of the Far East and South America, to the searing heat of India and the heart of Africa, civilizations rose and fell, powerful dynasties flourished and then wasted away, leaving us either with monuments that stand to this very day or that vanished from the face of the planet as if they were never there. Many aspects of our ancient ancestors still remain a mystery to us, but a combination of archaeology and historical research has uncovered a rich tapestry of the past that we can draw upon for our own pleasure and excitement.

In essence, warfare of old relied on just three things: the strength of a man's arm, the speed and power of a beast that could be ridden, and the protection afforded by wooden or mud-brick walls. Castles were still largely undreamt-of creations of a later era, but battering rams and other contraptions of the engineer's art were relatively commonplace when a defended town was attacked.

Whether from reading books or watching the latest Hollywood offerings, almost everyone will be aware that the Mediterranean Sea and the land surrounding it became the cradle of Western civilization and a vast stage for the wars that arose as one people sought to impose their will upon another. From the Egypt of the Pharaohs with their massed chariots of war, to Classical Greece with its citizen armies of spear and shield armed hoplites, through the seemingly unstoppable, short-sword-stabbing legions of Imperial Rome, up to the roaring charge of axe-wielding Vikings

Ancient Chinese armies face one another in a 28mm *Warhammer Ancient Battles* demonstration game staged at Partizan. The armies of the Orient make a fascinating change from those of the Western World and John Kersey's *WAB* supplement *The Art of War* is a highly regarded source book whatever ruleset you decide to use.

A Dark Ages game staged at Salute by the Newark Irregulars, showing the considerable modelling and painting skills of James Morris and Steve Jones in particular. The plundering of this delightful settlement was taking place alongside a major battle outside the walls to the right of this picture, and could easily be played as a stand-alone game.

and Saxons leaping from their longships, these are images that are familiar and that are reproduced on countless wargame tables. Recent research has also uncovered the panoply of colour that graced the battlefields of ancient China and Japan, and the ongoing struggles of Byzantium (the Rome of the East, modern Istanbul) against the rise of Islam in the south and many other belligerent, barbarian opponents to the north and east.

If you are excited by the Ancient era, then, you will never tire nor lose inspiration. There is the glint of sunlight on armour of bronze and, later, iron mail, with costumes, cloaks and shields of many colours. Wars raged across some of the greatest empires the world has ever known, led by perhaps the greatest generals and emperors of history, such as Alexander the Great and Julius Caesar. Many wargamers see 'Ancients' as the purest form of contest, the most classic challenge, perhaps closest in character to chess, unsullied by firearms and long-range artillery, where the bow and the spear and the sword wielded on foot or on horseback or from a swaying chariot provided a true test of courage for our ancestors and challenge the mental agility of the wargamer.

The Medieval era

The transition from 'Ancient' to 'Medieval' has as much to do with the politics of the time as it did with methods of making war. After all, a Norman knight at Hastings in 1066 would be almost indistinguishable from a Byzantine cavalryman facing the Muslim incursions in 600AD. Protection came from a shield, a padded garment, boots, gauntlets, and perhaps some highly-prized (and expensive) mail armour or a brigandine. So what had changed?

A key factor of the medieval age is feudalism, whereby a monarch granted a large area of land to a tenant in chief – a nobleman – who became the monarch's vassal; the latter was then obliged to provide troops to serve the monarch, and did so by making smaller grants of land to

Everybody's idea of the medieval period: beautiful Kingmaker Miniatures 28mm knights of the Hussite Wars, as splendid an example of miniature chivalry as you are likely to see. The same game featured an impressive central European castle, as well as war wagons commanded by Jan Žižka.

An impressive array of 28mm Perry Miniatures, both plastic and metal, seen engaging in the Battle of Tewkesbury, 1471. Nowadays, the availability of printed paper flags and banners and water-slide transfers has made the whole business of applying heraldic designs to miniatures much less terrifying!

The battle of Wakefield 1460 in 10mm using the *Warmaster Ancients* Medieval supplement, seen at the Games Workshop Games Day, which briefly flirted with historical games as well as fantasy and sci-fi during the lifetime of Warhammer Historical. Author Rick Priestley can be seen chatting in the background with Philip Mackie of the Devizes club.

knights, who would actually do the military service. The knight, in turn, used the peasants to farm his land in order to provide the wherewithal for him to do the king's bidding. The income generated would pay for horses, arms and armour and the peasants would become, more or less, slaves to make this possible.

In addition, with the Normans there arrived another manifestation of the era: the castle. Built both to house the new landowners and protect them in times of trouble, they were also mighty instruments of power over the land. These colossal and imposing structures would, quite literally, overawe the local population and make them compliant.

In terms of warfare, many aspects of medieval conflict seemed brutal, blunt and unsophisticated compared to the ancient period that had preceded it, but there was a quiet revolution taking place in arms and armour, an arms race, in fact. The immense wealth of certain monarchs and landowners funded an upsurge in metallurgical research, particularly in Augsburg in Germany, Milan in Italy and Toledo in Spain, leading to greatly improved smithing of swords and edged weapons and a dramatic leap forward in the production of sheet steel. The rich would happily spend the equivalent of the price of a modern supercar or family home for a hand-crafted suit of armour, individually tailored for their needs. And of course, many great nobles had several sets, some for the battlefield, some for parade, and more still for tournaments. It was no longer enough to be seen on the field of battle; it was important to look good while you were about it, too.

In Japan, great sword-smiths created the beautiful single-edged and curved blade known as the *katana*, the classic weapon of the samurai. Warfare in the east became curiously stylised, dominated by the leading clans who ruled the Japanese islands, and can reward the wargamer with some of the most dramatic and colourful gaming. Likewise, the rise of China as a great power can form the basis of fascinating and colourful

Arsuf 1191, where Richard the Lion heart faced Saladin, staged by the Crawley Wargames Club using 15mm miniatures. The use of smaller figures can really help to recreate the sweeping spectacle of a large battle and, of course, helps to reduce costs, especially when large numbers of cavalry are required, such as for Saladin's army here.

The medieval period is particularly suited to small, skirmish-level games such as this raid from the sea spotted at a show in Rheindahlen, Germany. The players have obviously invested a lot of time and effort creating suitable scenery, customising miniatures and building the wonderful boats!

battles. Both, of course, have inspired some of the most remarkable cinema to come from Asia in recent years.

The net result of the feudal system was the emergence of a distinct warrior class in both East and West. The knight – and in the East, the samurai – gained in status and privilege on the field of battle and in court. By the beginning of the fifteenth century and the wars fought against France by Henry V, the charge of the mounted knights, in their gaudy heraldic tabards on caparisoned warhorses, had become the apogee of glory and honour, whilst the footsoldier slogged along in the mud in their wake, armed with what were, in effect, adapted farmyard implements like bills and glaives, hacking and stabbing at their opposite number in ill-disciplined mass formations. Nasty, brutal and short would be an apt description of the life of a peasant soldier.

But the horsemen wouldn't have it all their own way, and there were already signs of their potential demise. At Crécy and Agincourt, well-deployed English longbow men defeated the flower of French chivalry, crossbows were capable of penetrating plate armour and at the end of the period, a new power made an ominous appearance.

Gunpowder.

The Renaissance era

The Renaissance is usually taken to have begun in Florence, Italy in the early fifteenth century, and was characterized by an increase in religious, scientific, artistic and philosophical enquiry. However, human beings being what they are, there was also conflict, and the couple of hundred years from roughly 1425 to 1685 were peppered with armed disputes.

At the same time as the cavalryman's armour reached its apogee – some of the harnesses for both man and horse from this period have to

Flamboyant 28mm opponents for the Swiss: German *Landsknechts* advancing in their colourful 'puff and slash' outfits, preceded by men wielding double-handed swords known as *Doppelsöldner* because they received double pay for bravely charging enemy pike formations to disrupt them. Seen at Cavalier in Tonbridge.

28mm Polish winged hussars from Phil Olley's stunning recreation of the Cossack Rebellion, 1648, featuring hand-painted linen flags. Phil is something of a scenery making wizard too and we'll see his work again later in this book.

Fighting on the borders: a 28mm Reiver raid during the Elizabethan period, staged by the Crawley Wargames Club. Like many club games, this toured the shows for a season.

The siege of Vienna 1520 seen at the Rheindahlen show in Germany, using 15mm miniatures and played with an adaptation of the *Warmaster Ancients* rules. The lovingly-recreated city walls and entrenchments are a miniature masterpiece. The art of sieges developed apace during the Renaissance era, both in terms of attack and defence, and can form the focal point for extremely satisfying wargames.

be seen to be believed – the common foot soldier was being issued with two, very different, weapons that would prove to be their undoing. The first was actually a reincarnation of a weapon dating back to the time of Alexander the Great, some 1,800 years earlier: the pike. Essentially a long pole, up to 16 feet (5 metres) long, with a pointy end, it demanded great physical strength and excellent unit discipline to wield properly, but when this was achieved, it made a formation virtually impregnable to cavalry, a veritable porcupine of war. And the second weapon of note, often found sheltering beneath or beside the outstretched hedge of pike-points, was the handgun.

'Handgun' is actually something of a misnomer, because the last thing you'd be able to do with the early version was wield it single-handed. A heavy metal tube bound to a crude wooden stock, the weapon required some dexterity and not a little luck to use to any positive effect. A smouldering match (wick) was carried separately, and after a measured charge and crude, spherical bullet had been rammed into the barrel with a closure of wadding or even turf, the match was applied to the small hole atop the barrel which exposed the charge. There followed a loud crump, a billow of smoke, and if the firer was lucky, the ball followed a more or less wobbly trajectory towards the target.

Rate of fire was not, as you might imagine, particularly high in the early days. But what bright commanders realised was that it was cheap to make, and took virtually no training to use. Overnight, the skill-at-arms of the glorious mounted knight was trumped by the peasant with a gun. Even the excellent longbow needed years of practice and a strong arm to use properly, and crossbows were expensive, and required winches to draw back the bowstring. With the handgun, which evolved to become known as the matchlock and then flintlock musket, a local militia could hold their ground against the best in a matter of minutes.

As the period progressed, the leaders of Europe quickly adopted the new formations of pike and shot in various proportions, with a few exceptions. The Spaniards, for example, maintained feared units of sword-and-buckler men until well into the seventeenth century, and the Swiss concentrated on huge pike formations, extraordinarily disciplined troops who could out-march and outfight almost everyone they met on the roughest of terrain. But by the time of the Thirty Years War and the English Civil Wars in the seventeenth century, both sides of a battle looked much the same, with a ratio of about one pikeman to every two musketeers in infantry regiments.

Faced with impregnable infantry formations, cavalry dallied with

Colonial expansion during the Renaissance: the Siege of Tenochtitlan, 1521, where the Spanish *conquistadores* Pedro do Alvorado and Gonzalo de Sandoval overcame a stubborn Aztec defence. This stunning 28mm game was created by Troop of Shewe and demonstrated by the Escape Committee at Salute 2007. As you can see, the era presents a wealth of options for the wargamer!

Parliamentarian horse and foot advance towards Montrose's Scots in a 28mm English Civil War game played using the free *Very Civile Actions* rules that can be downloaded from The Perfect Captain's website at *http://perfectcaptain.50megs.com/vcactions.html.* The mastery of mixed formations of matchlock muskets and pikes is one of the main challenges of the mid-seventeenth century.

a tactic known as the *caracole,* where rank after rank of pistol-armed cavaliers discharged their weapons at point blank range and then trotted to the rear to reload. Faced with any opponent more inclined to come to grips they were of course, to use the modern parlance, toast.

Gradually, realising that their expensive armour was not entirely bullet proof[1], cavalry began to trade metal for speed. Instead of the lumbering charge of the massive destrier warhorse of the medieval period, they evolved to be armed with perhaps a helmet and breast-and-back of steel, atop a sturdy buff leather coat with boots and gauntlets and the charge was now delivered at the steady canter, if not the full-on gallop. A good, straight broadsword with basket hilt and a brace of pistols completed the accoutrements and, most revolutionary of all, common men could be found in the ranks, with the aristocrats forming the officer class.

Another arm was quietly developing as the years progressed: artillery. At first, as dangerous to the user as the target, and inconceivably heavy and immobile, it was confined to siege operations for battering down walls. But by the time of the English Civil War, there were a number of serviceable calibres that could be used in battle and some lighter types that could even be moved during the action. Gustavus Adolphus of Sweden even experimented with lightweight 'leather' guns. But another aspect of these developments was the emergence of a new, educated and intelligent class of gunners who understood the science and skill required to use these new weapons.

The scene was set for a more democratic game of death.

---

1 *Armour of this period was, in fact, often guaranteed as 'pistol proof' and many museums house examples of breastplates with the tell-tale dent where this had been tested. Against the heavier musket ball, however, they offered less protection.*

The Tricorne Era

There followed a period of just over a century, known as the Age of Enlightenment, which produced not only some of the greatest advances in human understanding of the universe and the laws that govern it, but also what might be seen as truly the first 'world war' and a bevy of commanders who are still regarded as amongst the greatest commanders in history. Two of these stand head and shoulders above the rest: the Duke of Marlborough and Frederick the Great.

In terms of weapons and organisation, three things happened of great significance.

Firstly, a simple, cheap device was invented that homogenised infantry formations and made them even more formidable and tactically flexible than they had been before: the socket bayonet. This was one of those developments that seems so obvious now, but which was revolutionary in its effect. It meant that every infantryman could now be both musketeer and pikeman, sufficiently mobile to march wherever the general wanted and deliver massed volley firepower, whilst having the ability to successfully withstand menacing cavalry by the simple expedient of slotting a converted dagger onto the end of the musket. A previous incarnation, the plug bayonet, had literally been a knife shoved into the open-ended barrel, with the obvious detrimental effects on the soldier's ability to shoot.

This simple application of genius suddenly freed the commander in the field from the need to provide 'castles' of pike for the muskets to shelter beneath, and the battlefield became a much more fluid environment. Disciplined infantry could keep pace with walking cavalry, advances and retreats and counterattacks and reinforcement became less entangled affairs, and the business of training soldiers for war became more streamlined. But more than this, the infantry, with its disciplined volleys of musketry, delivered often at point-blank range, became the 'queen of the battlefield' and there were recorded instances of steady infantry stopping charging cavalry dead in their tracks, quite literally, using firepower alone and even declining to fix bayonets.

How were the cavalry to respond to this? All but a very few units that retained breast- and sometimes back-plates (known now as cuirassiers) dispensed with armour altogether. Now, they relied instead on the charge with cold steel to close the distance across the deadly 'killing ground' of a couple of hundred yards as quickly as possible, hoping to either terrify the infantry with their approach or literally smash through them should they manage to make contact. In reality, the cavalry often formed up on the wings of the battle opposite their enemy counterparts, and spent the day whirling and duelling with them in charge after charge while the infantry decided the day in the centre. Good commanders learned to husband their mounted arm carefully, waiting to unleash them on an already unsteady enemy, turning a withdrawal into a headlong rout.

In parallel with this, another form of soldier emerged – or perhaps,

The Battle of Neerwinden, 1693, a game set during the early horse and musket era, when a portion of many infantry units still carried pikes or were armed with 'plug' bayonets. This 28mm battle was staged by veteran wargamer and experienced demonstration game organiser Barry Hilton to showcase his *Beneath the Lily Banners* ruleset but, as is often the case, such a game attracts many onlookers who admire the expert brushmanship on the figures and the stunning miniature architecture. In this instance the terrain building talents of Adrian Howe are much in evidence. As you will see, the newcomer should not be intimidated by such a display of scenic prowess, but rather inspired to try new ideas and techniques.

Mollwitz 1741, presented in 'classic' style using massed 30mm Spencer Smiths (the very figures used in Charles Grant's *The War Game* in 1971). Whilst the aesthetics are much simpler and more 'toy soldier' in approach, they do have the benefit of throwing the linear tactics of eighteenth century warfare into stark relief, with battalions manoeuvring in stately fashion.

again in line with classical precedent, re-emerged: light cavalry and light infantry. Used primarily for scouting and harassing the enemy on the march, excelling in ambuscades and reconnaissance, they were often found wearing the gaudiest and most flamboyant uniforms. Hussars and Grenzers were found amongst the wilder fringes of the Austro-Hungarian empire, and began to be copied by other nations. Chasseurs, Jäger, Freikorps, Jäger zu Pferd, Uhlans, Light Dragoons – all of them found homes in the increasingly fashion-conscious nations of Europe.

The artillery quietly kept pace with everything else. The number of calibres of gun were reduced to more manageable proportions; metallurgy improved the casting of gun barrels and iron shot; the weight of gun carriages was reduced, and thus the number of horses needed to haul them; and the training of gunners became more professional. Guns were organised into batteries of four, six, eight or ten pieces of the same calibre that could be limbered up and moved, if necessary, during the battle, and initial experiments were made with horse artillery that could, in theory, keep up with advancing cavalry. A well-placed battery could now dominate an area of the battlefield like never before, and with deadly new munitions such as howitzer shell (a hollow ball filled with gunpowder lobbed from a short-barrelled gun at high trajectory, which would explode when its fuse burned down) and canister (in effect, a giant shotgun cartridge, actually a tin can filled with musket balls that disintegrated upon leaving the cannon barrel, scything down anything in its path), both infantry and cavalry feared its attentions. In some armies, units of infantry were accompanied by small-calibre 'battalion guns' that added extra punch to their firepower.

For the wargamer, there is a certain purity about 18th century warfare

Perry 28mm British and Hessian infantry close with American militia and Continentals at the Battle of Long Island, 1776. This was one of the largest American War of Independence wargames I have ever witnessed, organised by 'Eclaireur', the author of the popular *British Grenadier* rules, based on Dave Brown's *General de Brigade*. One aspect of the AWI is that infantry predominate, with cavalry and heavy artillery being relatively scarce.

Tarleton's cavalry crashes into and routs American militia in another AWI (also known as the American Revolution) game, this time Cowpens at the home of master sculptor John Ray, whose collection is entirely his own creation. Some of the miniatures are even unique one-offs in Milliput. These 30mm masterpieces are reminiscent of the hobby's early sculptors such as Edward Suren.

A magnificent 6mm rendition of Poltava, 1709, the key battle fought between the Swedes and Russians during the Great Northern War, seen at The Other Partizan in Newark. An unusual subject for a demonstration game, the Humberside Wargames Society did a tremendous job of creating a game that looked just like a contemporary battle painting. The look and feel was achieved using Baccus Miniatures and a painted board and backdrop. The photo below shows a close up of Swedish cavalry thundering towards the Russians — you can see these charming, tiny miniatures are surprisingly detailed.

An immense 28mm rendition of the Battle of Blenheim, 1704, involving over 4,000 beautifully painted miniatures and excellent terrain measuring 24 feet by 6! The inset photo shows the intense fighting around the key village of Blenheim, with much cotton wool in evidence providing the pyrotechnics! All these miniatures were lovingly painted by Matt Slade and Martin Holmes over a five year period, an example of the extreme dedication that wargamers, passionate about a particular period, often display.

that is reminiscent of the classical ancient period: the intriguing challenge of paper/scissors/stone, where the sides are well-matched with similar infantry, cavalry and artillery, and so the skill of the commander and his eye for the ground and ability to seize opportunities counts for a great deal. The main battle lines are dominated by highly disciplined infantry and cavalry, but with irregulars and light troops on the fringes and on the march, there are plenty of opportunities for achieving surprise.

There is one other fascinating aspect of this period, and indeed of the late Renaissance, which we should mention here: sieges. The attack and defence of towns and cities became a major part of warfare and the source of a new kind of arms race, one fought between gunpowder and metal on the one hand, and stone and turf on the other. The great engineer of the age was Vauban, who was responsible for some of the most remarkable feats of military engineering ever undertaken. His work still stands, surrounding many towns in France and Belgium, and is instantly recognisable because of the multi-pointed star-shaped outlines of his defences. Viewed from ground level, the walls are actually deceptively low and hard to see – proof, in itself, of his genius.

This came about because upright castle walls became terribly vulnerable to cannon that were able to collapse defences that had stood for centuries in a matter of hours. Vauban realised that to give the defenders a chance, he had to make city walls immensely thick at the base, angled to deflect incoming rounds harmlessly over the defenders' heads and surrounded by all manner of ditches and ramparts and bastions to make any head-on attack suicidal.

To overcome such an impregnable position, an attacking army now had to invest a huge amount of time and effort cutting the place off from the outside world, before embarking on a lengthy process of digging complex, zig-zagging trenches towards the walls and emplacing their own artillery in the hope of eventually breaching a small section of wall that could then be assaulted. This became such a precise art that a defending garrison commander could time his surrender to the very hour when an assault might be expected, and capitulate with honour intact. But woe betide the town governor who chose to resist beyond this point.

Vauban, it should be noted, was a shrewd cookie, and sold his services to both sides, earning fortunes for designing a town's defences, and then again for acting as a, ahem, 'consultant' for the attackers.

The Napoleonic era

Napoleon Bonaparte, by virtue of a coup d'état, made himself First Consul of France on 9th November 1799 and thus, effectively, dictator. It is at this moment that historians agree the shift from the "Revolutionary Wars" to the "Napoleonic Wars", since the original ideals of the Revolution had now been distilled into the personal ambitions of Napoleon Bonaparte. By 1800, the French star was clearly in the ascendant and in most cases, the battlefield tactics that had been born out of necessity when dealing with untold numbers of raw recruits, and that had been forged in the heat of battle, were proving their worth. Fast moving columns of infantry, flanked by excellent cavalry and artillery that was increasing in both mobility and potency, and organised into self-contained divisions and army corps, were proving too much for the old regimes, hidebound to 'linear' warfare and long supply lines, to deal with. However, by around 1809, France's opponents were beginning to learn some hard lessons that they would put to good effect in the later battles, especially after 1812, when Napoleon's army was a shadow of its former self, with most of his hard-fighting veterans dead or wounded, littering the battlefields of Russia, eastern and central Europe and Spain.

If you're the kind of person who enjoys the panoply of war, the Napoleonic period is undoubtedly likely to grab your attention. Uniforms

The effect many Napoleonic players dream of: a vast wargames table, with wonderful terrain and a carpet of miniatures! This 15mm Waterloo game involved thousands of finely painted figures on a huge table. Here you can see the French cavalry sweeping up to attack the Allied lines (left) to the south of La Haye Sainte farmhouse, with massed artillery in support.

Don't be intimidated by the museum-quality terrain pictured elsewhere: here is a large Napoleonic game played in veteran gamer John Preece's garage on plain green baize cloth over books and newspapers. The battle, based on Fontenoy 1745, was hard-fought by a French army (left) commanded by Yours Truly, faced by John's abundant and stubborn Prussians, using the *Charge!* rules. Happily, I managed to avenge a previous defeat!

28mm French Chevaux Légers Lanciers. These powerful light cavalry were formed by re-arming regiments of dragoons after Napoleon encountered Polish lancers. A versatile favourite amongst tabletop French generals!

A party of 95th Rifles (led by a famous fictional character) disembark from a ship crewed by Spanish guerrillas in a Peninsular War scenario laid on by Durham's Chosen Men at the Partizan show in Newark. The miniatures are all 40mm size, much favoured by gamers who specialise in skirmishes and smaller encounters. A great deal of hard work went into the scenery, including the dockside and ship, as well as the exquisitely painted miniatures.

At the other end of the wargaming scale, a Baccus 6mm British army awaits the French onslaught in a game presented at The Other Partizan by Neil Shuck of the *Meeples & Miniatures* podcast. The troops are based for use with the *Polemos* ruleset, also produced by Baccus.

28mm Prussian Landwehr defending the church at Plancenoit, 18th June 1815. Part of a stunning display at – yes, again! – The Other Partizan 2007, laid on by Stephen Maughan of Waterloo Wargames.

Another impressive 6mm game: Wagram, 1809, with the Austrians (left and centre) being assaulted by French columns arriving from the right. The game was created by Steve Jones of the Newark Irregulars and shows how fairly simple terrain with some clever brushwork can be very effective at this scale. The buildings are from a range produced by Timecast. Small scale figures work very well for large 'massed' battles such as this.

reached their spectacular apogee, topped off with shakos and busbies with tall plumes; jackets and pelisses were adorned with yards of cord and lace and dozens of glittering buttons; men were laden with shiny belts and buckles and finished off with tight breeches and boots for the cavalry. Truly, this era was a military fashion parade.

And now imagine a table groaning under hundreds, perhaps even thousands of such miniatures, representing Austerlitz or Borodino or Salamanca or Waterloo – some of the most famous and spectacular battles in history took place as Napoleon sought to dominate the whole of Europe and beyond. I have been privileged to witness some Napoleonic games where it has been a joy to simply stand and stare, let alone play. Many wargamers who love this period spend their entire lives doing nothing but amassing larger and larger collections of beautifully-painted miniatures, but this isn't a requirement, because it's perfectly possible to play much smaller skirmish or small unit games set in this period. Remember the television series *Sharpe*, based on the (much better) books by Bernard Cornwell? Well, there's even a ruleset based on those stories of the escapades of a British officer in Spain and Portugal.

It's for this reason that the Napoleonic Wars have a magical appeal – the games look glorious, whether large or small, and set in the desolate wintry wastelands of Russia or the sweltering heat of the Spanish plains. The balance between the three arms of infantry, cavalry and artillery is nearly perfect, with none completely dominating the other, and tactical success demands a keen eye for ground and tremendous timing.

Can you break the British squares at Waterloo or reproduce Kellerman's charge at Marengo? Can you command an army corps at Leipzig, the vast Battle of Nations, or disrupt French supply lines in Spain with your handful of green-jacketed 95th Rifles and *guerrilla* allies? I can't think of a single wargamer I've ever met who has never played and enjoyed the challenge of at least one Napoleonic game, and I doubt you'll be any different!

19th century 'European' warfare

This comparatively short era is taken to include all the European wars after the Battle of Waterloo in 1815 up to the Franco-Prussian War of 1870-71. It therefore covers the Crimean War and the various conflicts that arose as a result of Italian and German unification, including the Franco-Austrian War of 1859, the Prusso-Danish War of 1864 and the Austro-Prussian War of 1866. I have put the word "European" inside inverted commas because there is also a fascinating series of conflicts to be explored that took place in Central and South America, known as the Wars of Liberation, that both looked and felt strikingly European in nature, even though they took place on the far side of the world.

Though these conflicts had far-reaching outcomes for world history – Prussia's ascendancy in central Europe would lead to the First and Second World Wars – they are, curiously, 'niche' periods in wargaming terms.

It looks European, but it isn't – the Battle of Maipo (Maipú) 1818, fought by South American rebels and Spanish royalists, during the Chilean War of Independence. This game, staged at Salute 2008, used converted 1/72 plastic figures. American gamer John Fletcher has subsequently launched a range of 'large' 15mm miniatures that can be found at *http://www. grenadier productions.com/*

Colourful 28mm Mexican troops from the Mexican-American War of 1846-1848. It can be seen how little uniform fashions had changed in Central and South America since the Napoleonic Wars.

Perhaps the reason is that, other than the Crimean War, which has a reputation of being a British folly, none of these wars involved English-speaking nations (though the British were, of course, heavily involved in colonial expansion, which we shall come to shortly). Regrettably, xenophobia plays a part in history and, consequently, wargaming!

Nevertheless, I would heartily recommend them as conflicts not only worthy of study, but also an endless source of tremendous wargaming challenges. They were often bloody affairs, with troops wearing uniforms sometimes even more spectacular than their Napoleonic forbears, deployed in mass formations, but now advancing into the teeth of a leaden gale, as rifled and breech-loading firearms of much greater accuracy were increasingly deployed.

Despite mounting casualties, the officer class still believed in *la gloire* and the chivalry of earlier times, leaving lessons to be learned. Who amongst us has not heard of the infamous charge of the Light Brigade at the Battle of Balaklava? Fewer people are aware of the much more successful charge of the Heavy Brigade at the very same battle, and fewer still of the remarkable feats of courage performed by our European neighbours in the other conflicts listed above, such as Von Bredow's "Death Ride" at Mars-La-Tour in 1870.

As a final note, the 19th century in Europe is an era that can often benefit from the use of smaller scale miniatures, such as 10mm or even 6mm, to represent the huge formations that manoeuvred across vast battlefields and whose weapons reached farther than ever before.

Part of Gravelotte-St-Privat 1870, a major battle during the Franco-Prussian War, played at the home of retired Major-General John Drewienkiewicz using a host of 10mm miniatures from the splendid collection of Andrew Brentnall. Using Keith Warren's *To the Last Gaiter Button* rules, the game was played over two days by eleven players and three umpires! The pencil gives a useful scale reference; the 'sandwich' dial discs have a 'V' cut out on the underside to reveal numerals and are used to track casualties.

British and Allied troops begin the long slog up the slopes above the River Alma during the Crimean War of 1854-56. This was another impressive game staged by Crawley Wargames Club, this time using 6mm Irregular Miniatures on a marvellous sculpted terrain. Once again, micro scale figures can portray the 'grand sweep' of a large battle in a relatively small space.

Beautiful 28mm Perry Miniatures Carlist War figures, depicting the little-known conflicts of 1833 to 1876 that bedevilled the Spanish during the nineteenth century. Michael Perry can be credited with bringing these colourful troops to the attention of British wargamers. This game was seen at Partizan, of course. You've just got to love all those berets!

A splendid *Little Wars* style game staged at Salute by the Continental Wars Society. The figures are modern, sculpted by Aly Morrison under the guise of Shiny Toy Soldiers and marketed by Spencer Smith Miniatures. The conflict depicted here is the Prusso-Danish War of 1864 and was played in true Wellsian toy soldier style on a rug, as it should be!

Union cavalry advance to the front, supported by artillery. These are 40mm miniatures, an unusual scale for the American Civil War, but beautifully presented at The Other Partizan 2005. The snake rail fences in the foreground are a real trademark of battles on the American continent.

More cavalry, this time 15mm, and lots of them! A recreation of Brandy Station, the largest cavalry encounter of the ACW, played at the home of John Drewienkiewicz (known to his friends as DZ). The photo shows just a tiny section of the battlefield, the Confederate left flank commanded by the author, who was praying for reinforcements!

The Battle of Shiloh, a 6mm demonstration game played at the now, sadly, defunct 'Whiff of Grapeshot' show at the Firepower museum in Woolwich. With thousands of miniatures on the table, including some ingeniously-modelled paddle steamers on the river and hundreds of trees, it made an impressive display.

The American Civil War

One of those conflicts that has been a mainstay of the wargaming hobby since its early years, in many ways the American Civil War of 1861-65 was more modern than the contemporary European wars. The lethality and range of weapons increased enormously, evolving from Napoleonic muzzle-loaders to breech-loading rifles, carbines and artillery that swept away any advancing enemy. The uniforms worn were normally a lot less gaudy than those worn by European armies, but troops were initially still deployed in dense, Napoleonic formations until huge body-counts prompted the use of many more skirmishers in advancing clouds. Cavalry behaved much more like mounted infantry, armed with carbines and pistols, with a few sabre-armed cavalry versus cavalry clashes like Brandy Station as exceptions.

But the notable developments were really to do with the increasing industrialisation, particularly of the North. Railways and the telegraph permitted a huge, continent-wide theatre of operations, where orders could be transmitted and large numbers of men and material could be moved at previously unimaginable speed.

Naval ironclads, armies hunkered down in trenches and merciless siege warfare chillingly presaged the events of WWI. Like some of the larger battles in Europe, encounters such as Gettysburg were measured in days, rather than hours, as not just regiments and brigades, but entire divisions and army corps were fed into the line. As a result, this is another conflict that can benefit enormously from the use of smaller-scale miniatures if you want to really feel like a General Grant or Lee or J.E.B. Stuart.

The ACW, as it is commonly known, is often recommended for beginners because of the comparative ease of bringing simply-painted troops to the table, and the dash and vigour of the resulting battles. But like all challenging games, the clash of Union and Confederate forces is easy to play, but difficult to master, which is as it should be.

A key moment of the Battle of Gettysburg, 1863: Pickett's charge, as the Confederates launch a desperate attempt to crack open the Union line which nearly succeeded, but was swept away by withering fire from the Northern defenders. 15mm miniatures, in a game using Dave Brown's *Guns at Gettysburg* rules, seen at the Cavalier show in Tonbridge in 2007.

Colonial warfare

When we refer to 'colonial' wargaming, we generally mean empire building, especially by Britain and France, in Africa, India and the Far East. It is not a 'period' as such, because it incorporates conflicts as early as the eighteenth century in India and as late as the 20th century inter-war period in the North-West Frontier and Middle East. Generally, however, we think of such conflicts as the Anglo-Zulu Wars, the Mahdist wars in the Sudan, the Boer Wars, the Boxer Rebellion and France's involvement in Sub-Saharan Africa including the exploits of the famed Foreign Legion, who crop up in surprising places – perhaps their greatest exploit was the famous last stand in Camerone, Mexico, in 1863.

European technological superiority defeated mass bravery in all but a few cases, but small European forces could and did find themselves over-stretched or punished when they became over-confident. Of course, the Boer War saw the British trounced by an enemy armed with precisely the same weapons, but with much greater aptitude for using them in a superior way.

Lessons learned from conflicts such as the Boer War led to the mass introduction of camouflage for the very first time and saw the beginnings of that strange, very modern phenomenon – the empty battlefield, where troops are trained to lie down and take cover and the range and accuracy of their weapons means that men can open fire and cause casualties at much greater distances. In fact, there was little difference between the men who returned from South Africa in 1902 and those who marched off to war in 1914.

Colonial wargaming is ideal in many ways, because it ranges in scale from small skirmishes on the one hand to pitched battles on the other. It is also possible to complete a project in fairly short order: for example, I have a British force for the Zulu Wars consisting of a single battalion of infantry, with a few cavalry and a couple of guns, and these do battle with around 80 Zulu warriors who can be 'reincarnated' as required when I

28mm Perry British colonial troops from the Mahdist Wars 1881-1885 with (inset) their terrifying enemies charging pell-mell towards them.

A magnificent 28mm Sudan game with fortified town created by Paul Darnell, a highly talented terrain maker whose work dominated the show scene for some years in the late 'noughties. The colonial period is ideal for imaginative model making and exotic table layouts, including river craft such as those shown here for typical 'gunboat diplomacy'.

A column of Newline 20mm 24th Foot advances across the author's wargames table. The Anglo-Zulu War of 1879, which in reality only lasted some six months, holds an endless fascination for wargamers because it typifies the redcoats versus natives genre and looks spectacular on the tabletop. It offers a relatively inexpensive way into the hobby, too.

At The Other Partizan in 2010, the South East Scotland Wargames Group staged this very colourful Indian Mutiny 1857-58 game. Games set in the sub-continent present a tremendous array of opportunities for the wargamer, ranging from European-style encounters between regular troops to skirmishes between irregular warbands.

A creeping barrage approaches the British trenches as German assault troops move in for the kill. This magnificent 28mm dioramic game was staged by Great War Miniatures and features the skills of Dave Andrews and Aly Morrison. The convincing explosions, by the way, are made using barbeque skewers and mock clump foliage, sprayed black.

There's one aspect of WWI gaming that everybody seems to love: aerial combat, either as part of a game which includes land-based forces, or as a stand-alone game using rules such as *Wings of Glory* (previously *Wings of War*). Here, a Fokker D.VII flies over Dave Andrews' stunning trench system terrain.

The beasts that broke the deadlock. Early tanks accompany infantry in the Battle of Amiens 1918, as demonstrated by Rich Clarke of TooFatLardies at Partizan 2009, using their *Through the Mud and the Blood* rules. The miniatures are 28mm size on yet more excellent trench sytem terrain, built this time by Sidney Roundwood.

want the effect of the British being assailed by several waves of attackers. A similar system would work for many colonial conflicts.

Colonial games are ideally suited to imaginative scenarios, such as the arrival of a force to relieve a beleaguered outlying fort, or a party on a gunboat sailing up a dangerous stretch of river, or a punitive expedition advancing to deal with troublesome tribes. Who could not be inspired by old movies like *Zulu, The Four Feathers* or *Beau Geste*?

Most importantly, colonial gaming can often provide a great deal of fun and a valuable reminder that all empires are eventually doomed!

World War One

For a long time, very few people gamed WWI. It's easy to understand why – the stories of the horrors of the trenches have been handed down for generations, reinforced by grisly TV documentaries and movies like *Oh, What a Lovely War* and *All Quiet on the Western Front*. Little interest was shown in reproducing the ghastly wasteland of the Western Front, though many more showed an interest in the swirling dogfights that took place thousands of feet above the heads of the Poor Bloody Infantry.

The facts are that the initial open style of warfare quickly bogged down on the Western Front, but the Eastern Front remained relatively fluid, and events in the Alps, the Middle East and East Africa had a very different complexion if for no other reason than the particular challenges offered by the terrain and climate in these places.

But our overwhelming impression is of senseless, industrialised warfare, involving colossal forces scythed down by deadly machine guns and long-range artillery.

However, a number of wargamers took a closer look at the history and uncovered a rich vein of tactical challenges for the wargamer, including the increased use of specialised troops, tactics and weapons developed especially to overcome the impasse. These included hand grenades, flamethrowers, trench mortars and, eventually, tanks, though the full potential of armoured fighting vehicles was not realised during the war. Many of us are already familiar with the terrifying developments in artillery, including the huge howitzers and field guns capable of throwing high explosive, shrapnel and, worst of all, gas munitions many miles into enemy lines. Even here, however, there were innovations, such as the quick barrage just before an offensive and the 'creeping' barrage that advanced just in front of the troops tasked to take territory, rather than the long bombardments, sometimes lasting days, that had preceded earlier battles.

As a result, a surprising number of rulesets have appeared in recent years, accompanied by a number of attractive ranges of miniatures. Perhaps curiously, these are mostly 28mm figures, aimed at reproducing small-scale trench raids and the like, rather than the vast offensives that are more suited to campaign play on maps.

Land operations of the First World War are unlikely to ever challenge the attractions of, say, the Napoleonic era or WWII, but they are certainly

Save the Czar! A typical 'Back of Beyond' scenario, featuring forces common from around 1917 (the Russian Revolution) through to the early 1930s, with the Great Powers getting involved in each other's business in the most unlikely places. In such games, be prepared to expect the unexpected and indulge in adventure! This 28mm game was staged at the SELWG annual show, held at Crystal Palace.

worthy of consideration, and air wargaming with miniature biplanes and triplanes is extremely popular.

In addition, there are other interesting conflicts between the World Wars such as the Russian Revolution, the upheaval in Germany's Weimar Republic and the Spanish Civil War which can form the basis of somewhat quirky projects for the wargamer looking for something a little different.

World War Two

Anything I say here is dwarfed by the immensity of both the conflict itself and the resources available to the wargamer. Perhaps because it's the war that many of the doyens of the hobby (and, indeed, many of our own relatives) actually fought in, WWII has featured ever since the emergence of the modern hobby in the 1950s. It is also a period that has a huge following in the closely associated hobby of military modelling and I, like many others of my generation, grew up making hundreds of AFV models such as those produced in 1/76 by Airfix and the larger, 1/35 scale ones by Tamiya. As a result it is, you might say, in the blood of the hobby.

WWII also appeals to the innate geekiness of little boys, with the plethora of weapons and vehicles and their various capabilities. It also has the attraction of featuring combatants from almost every nation on earth with, of course, the emphasis on the major powers of Britain and the Commonwealth, the USA, Russia, France, Italy and Japan.

WWII represented total war, fought on land, sea and in the air. The ultimate outcome was, of course, the world-changing atomic bomb. The conflict also saw the first intercontinental ballistic missiles – Hitler's V1s and V2s that terrified the citizens of southern England. But other innovations also came thick and fast, such as radio, radar, night bombing,

An astonishing 6mm rendition of Operation Deadstick, also known as the D-Day attack on Pegasus Bridge, created by Maidstone Wargames Society. Research included Google Earth and aerial reconnaissance photos to create a precise scale reproduction. The facsimiles of the bridge and buildings made use of 3-D printing!

A 15mm game staged by Loughton Strike Force, "Kharkov 1943: Assault on Dzerzinhinsky Square", with plentiful Russian armour accompanied by infantry and artillery, assaulting the devastated city. 15mm is extremely popular with WWII gamers, not least because of the efforts of Battlefront with *Flames of War*.

A huge 1/35 scale Sword Beach on D-Day game seen at Salute, the biggest show in the UK's wargame event calendar. If you decide to launch yourself into the larger scales such as this, be aware of the additional costs and storage problems involved! For these reasons, such (literally) large-scale ventures are usually undertaken by clubs, as seen here.

A magnificent micro-scale recreation of Pearl Harbor 1941 by the South London Warlords and seen at the now sadly defunct Redoubt show. Here, a combination of ships, aircraft on wires (with markers for torpedo tracks) and stunning miniature architecture make for an eye-catching game. The scale here is 1/3000.

Like WWI, an aspect of WWII gaming that is a perennial favourite is air combat, especially set during the Battle of Britain, with Spitfires and Hurricanes duelling with Me109s, Fw-190s, Dorniers and Heinkels. Several innovative rulesets serve this market, such as *Check Your Six*, *Wings of Glory* and *Bag the Hun!*

Afrika Korps armour returns fire on the author's simple wargames table during a game of *Blitzkrieg Commander* (*BKC*). These diminutive 1/285 GHQ miniatures (here mounted on MDF bases) are exceptionally detailed for their size and can allow the gamer to have a much more realistic impression of weapon ranges relative to the size of the models.

German troops with a StuGIII in support lie in wait for Canadian infantry at Caillouet, 1944, as presented by the Shepway Wargames Club at Bovington. This 20mm scene shows some of the superb scenic modelling skills that one often encounters at shows – indeed the terrain is frequently as important to the players as the game itself.

sub-machine guns, shaped charge ammunition, paratroopers and other airborne troops, large-scale amphibious landings and Blitzkrieg with armoured and mechanised forces. Over-arching all this, politics – fascism, communism, obedience to the Emperor and democracy – emerged as motivating factors for war rather than historic, dynastic or religious claims.

The appeal of gaming the Second World War is, of course, that it is fast-moving and exciting. It is perfectly possible to play a game involving no more than a few squads of men or handful of tanks one day, perhaps using large-scale miniatures, and a huge scenario involving entire brigades across a front of many scale miles the next using 1/285 or even smaller models. Most gamers concentrate on a particular phase of the war to begin with, such as the Western Desert, the Normandy landings, Hitler's invasion of Russia or the struggle against Japan in the Pacific, but you'll find them readily branching out to collect other nationalities or phases of the conflict. Some prefer the quirky, oddball vehicles and weapons of the early war, whilst still more revel in commanding the *über*-weaponry of the late war, such as the famous German Panther, Tiger and King Tiger tanks. Good rulesets make this possible, whilst still achieving a balanced game.

Like Napoleonics, I know few gamers who haven't done at least some WWII gaming, and with the upsurge in popularity of this period (largely driven by Battlefront's *Flames of War* system), you'll have no trouble finding opponents.

The modern era

This brings the historical hobby right up-to-date. It's now quite common to see games at wargames shows depicting, for example, British infantry with their Warrior armoured vehicles slowly advancing through a mud-brick village in Afghanistan, a UN battlegroup holding off hordes of Chinese attackers in Korea or US Air Cavalry sweeping over the jungles of Vietnam. You can also find non- or semi-military games such as civilian rioters facing down a force of police and paramilitaries, and there is great interest in the actions of elite units like the SAS or US Navy Seals.

Some gamers feel uncomfortable playing games showing the actions of men and women who are either still alive or recently killed or wounded, or indeed depicting what is now known as 'the war on terror' at all, but we need to keep this in perspective: this is still a game, no real people are killed and in fact it can be highly instructive to be faced with the kind of decisions that our soldiers have to make on the front line every day. Moreover, I've seen online discussions with veterans of current and past conflicts and, to a man, they seem interested in such games and pleased that we should try to understand the dangers they face. And of course, we should not be hypocritical – many of the historical forces our hobby represents hardly behaved like angels and many computer games show warfare in much more grisly and troubling detail than miniature wargaming ever will.

Even more so than WWII, I can't possibly give a complete overview of the post-1945 era, but suffice it to say that whatever conflict interests you, it's probable that you will find the appropriate miniatures, vehicles and aircraft in one scale or another somewhere. Google is your friend!

Fantasy gaming

You might think that the fantasy genre began with JRR Tolkien, *The Hobbit* and *The Lord of the Rings*, but of course it really began much earlier – thousands of years earlier! Writers like Tolkien and the legions that have followed him in creating epic tales of Good versus Evil rely on something deeply ingrained in our very being as humans – myth and legend. The academic Joseph Campbell wrote a book called *The Hero's Journey*, in which he describes the common elements of storytelling worldwide and throughout history, and it is these common threads that fantasy writers use to create powerful stories of mankind facing extraordinary danger, usually reliant upon the heroic presence of key individuals to achieve victory or to complete a quest.

Tolkien's great works appeared in print in the mid 1950s, and the 'hippy' movement of the 1960s seized upon the books, inspired by the search for treasure in a dragon's lair or the dungeons of an evil king, or the quest to find a particular totemic item – a ring, for example – that holds special powers that can be conferred upon the bearer. Of course, the item itself usually proves as dangerous to the wielder as to his enemies, draining their life force should they risk making use of the artifact.

There has always been the option, therefore, to play fantasy games on a very small scale, with just a handful of figures or even, in the case of *Dungeons & Dragons*, simply in the minds of the players, with everything firmly in the realm of the imagination, from the armour and weapons of the adventurers to the demonic beasts they encounter. On the other hand – much to the satisfaction of commercial figure manufacturers – there

What we all used to think of as a 'moderns' game: a NATO Chieftain tank takes a bead on Warsaw Pact armour, somewhere in Germany, after the Cold War turns 'hot'. This large and visually appealing 28mm game staged at Salute in 2008 was unusual in that Third World War games are often played with micro-armour.

An Afghan local looks on as British soldiers reconnoitre a village in Helmand province as a convoy rolls through. An all-too familiar sight on our TV screens and one which many wargamers are uncomfortable recreating. Seen at Broadside 2012, staged by Rainham Wargames Club using Osprey's *Force on Force* modern rules.

A Chinook helicopter disgorges elite British troops in this game set in Sierra Leone's recent civil war and staged by Deal Wargames Society. The gamer wishing to recreate modern conflicts needs plenty of non-European scenery and a healthy collection of helicopter models.

Many people's idea of fantasy gaming, especially in 'heroic' 28mm size, is a result of the dominance of Games Workshop's *Warhammer Fantasy Battles* system and indeed, many a youngster has come to the hobby via this route because both the rules and the miniatures are available in High Streets across the world. The photo shows an impressive force of Dark Elves painted by the very talented Roger Smith of Hassocks in Sussex.

This spectacular *Demonworld* fantasy siege at Colours 2008 featured thousands of 15mm miniatures on a striking terrain including what can only be described as flying bits of rock! This is certainly beyond the means of the average individual wargamer, but makes for an inspiring club project. Staged by the Wednesday Night Wargamers.

Characters from *The Lord of the Rings* turn at bay to confront pursuing Dark Riders. These miniatures in the author's collection are from Games Workshop, but Tolkien's work has long been an inspiration for other rules writers and manufacturers.

is a raging thirst amongst players to stage epic battles in which hundreds of miniatures clash, representing both humans and a diverse selection of other races, many of which owe nothing at all to Tolkien's imagination.

Therefore, alongside miniatures representing vaguely medieval humans, you will find not only the elves, dwarves, orcs and goblins mentioned in *The Lord of the Rings*, but also ratmen, vampires, undead zombies and skeletons, creatures from the depths of Chaos, reptiles, giant insects, beastmen and many more. And of course, there are miniatures available for the myths and legends of ancient times, including centaurs, minotaurs, hydras, wyverns, griffons and so on.

But I'd be refusing to acknowledge the elephant in the room if I failed to mention that fantasy gaming, like sci-fi gaming, is dominated by Games Workshop, whose *Warhammer* rules and miniatures have taken hold across the globe. Views about this differ, and some question whether it is healthy for the hobby to be under the sway of a single company, but the fact is that you can travel to almost any country in the world and be sure to be able to find an opponent if you collect *Warhammer Fantasy Battle* miniatures.

Most fantasy battles are fought using 'heroic' scale (i.e. large) 28mm miniatures, because aficionados tend to enjoy painting their figures to an extremely high standard, often treating each one as an individual, rather than simply one of a mass. And it is certainly true that these miniatures, whether sourced from Games Workshop or elsewhere, are usually beautifully sculpted and reward having such attention lavished upon them. (Quite apart from anything else, they are often rather expensive compared to historical miniatures, though you can save money by buying plastic miniatures in bulk, such as Games Workshop's 'battalion boxes'.) You will find a wide range of blogs and websites online where highly skilled painters freely demonstrate their art.

A game of GW's now sadly out-of-production *Advanced Heroquest* in full swing at the author's home. As with *Dungeons & Dragons*, small parties of player characters and their henchmen venture into the subterranean lairs of various nasty creatures including, here, a species of ratmen known as Skaven, hoping to win fame and fortune. A great after-dinner game even for 'civilians'!

But you don't have to be an exhibition-quality painter to enjoy fantasy gaming any more than in any of the historical periods mentioned, and there are further options in smaller scales, such as Games Workshop's *Warmaster* and *The Battle of Five Armies* (which you can find listed on their website under Specialist Games) and a host of other ranges going down to the 6mm beauties produced by, amongst others, Baccus.

Nor indeed, do you have to stick to what is commercially available: there is nothing to stop you creating your own world entirely, inhabited by people, creatures and demons of your own devising. Who knows, you may become the master of a creation that others end up following and buying into – just make the triumph of Good far from a foregone conclusion, and you'll have years of exciting gaming ahead of you.

Sci-Fi gaming

Science fiction is the most recent wargaming genre to emerge, and comes entirely from literary and cinematic sources, coupled with the endless possibilities offered by the very real science going on in laboratories across the world right now.

The first stories we can recognise as science fiction were written by H G Wells (*The Time Machine* was published in 1895 and *The War of the Worlds* in 1898) and Jules Verne (*Twenty Thousand Leagues Under the Sea* was published in1870, *A Journey to the Center of the Earth* in 1864 and *Around the World in Eighty Days* in 1873). Since then, countless short stories and novels have been published which, together with the vast output from Hollywood, have fired the imagination of generations.

Like fantasy gaming, sci-fi gaming can take several forms, ranging from the small and intimate to the grand and epic. A popular format is akin to *Dungeons & Dragons*, or perhaps a pirates game in a historical context, and involves a small number of adventurers – often characterised as somewhat shady traders – discovering an apparently abandoned space ship drifting in space. They board the ship with the intention of salvaging, plundering or repairing it, only to discover that they aren't as alone as they thought they were...

Assuming they survive the encounter with whatever unpleasant manifestation turns up, such games then allow the survivors to gain experience and trade items, just as in fantasy's *D&D*. Indeed, Rick Priestley's original game *Rogue Trader*, which later morphed into the mega-popular *Warhammer 40,000*, posited just such a scenario.

At the other extreme, there are rulesets proposing titanic struggles between entire races, spread across vast galaxies and involving armies of millions. Like fantasy battles, numerous races are involved, both human and alien, and games can be fought in the endless deep of space or on the surface – or, indeed, interior – of strange worlds quite unlike our own. Think of *Star Trek, Star Wars, Dune, Starship Troopers, Aliens, Predator, Babylon 5, Battlestar Galactica* – these can form the basis of countless games, and miniatures are available for all of these and more besides.

Who would have thought tie-dyed cloth would be back in fashion? Here, however, it serves well as an effective Martian landscape for "Earth Attacks", a 1/72 Victorian Sci-Fi game staged by the Staines Wargamers at Cavalier in Tonbridge. This has very much an H G Wells *War of the Worlds* feel to it with 'steampunk' and colonial attributes.

"I lost my heart to a Starship Trooper..." Well, never mind, because the game based on the *Starship Troopers* movies, featuring vast numbers of giant bugs, crops up regularly on the circuit, as demonstrated here at SELWG by the North London Wargames Group, whose participation games are deservedly popular and highly entertaining.

Some impressive models for *Warmachine*, a popular game from Privateer Press. These models, beautifully painted by Adam Smith, represent the Protectorate of Menoth: like all fantasy and sci-fi games, prepare to get used to the flavoursome names as well as the game!

In this vein, the *Warhammer 40K* rulebook tells us, "There is no time for peace. No respite. No forgiveness. There is only WAR." In other words, if you're looking for subtlety, look elsewhere! But supported by their worldwide chain of shops and a vast range of miniatures, Games Workshop are clearly appealing to a younger audience and the fact is that many a teenage lad takes their first steps into the hobby by way of a team of Space Marines battling against a horde of Orks or Tyranids.

But of course, science fiction can take other forms, such as post-apocalyptic scenarios (*Mad Max*, *I am Legend*, or even *Shaun of the Dead*), alien invasion of Earth (*Independence Day*, *War of the Worlds*)

Sci-Fi games can be an opportunity for the gamer's imagination and sense of humour to really let rip. Here, seen at a GW Games Day, *Warhammer 40K* Orks launch their landing craft from 'H(uge) M(assive) S(hip) Da Bismork' – you can judge the scale of things because those Orks on deck are around 32mm tall! The landing craft were also decorated with amusing graffiti.

Just because they're slow doesn't mean they aren't deadly... Zombie games are a perennial favourite, coming somewhere between sci-fi and pulp as a genre, and of course linking to interests in the undead, such as vampires, and boosted by countless movies and TV series. Here, zombies create chaos in a town centre, an *Occult Wars* participation game at The Other Partizan 2006 using 40mm Monolith figures.

or situations where machines have become self-aware and rebel against their human overlords – think of *Blade Runner*, *The Matrix* and *I, Robot*. Even the popular TV series *Doctor Who* has a cult following of gamers, as does the story of reptilian takeover in *V*. And of course, the superhero and comic book genre is alive and well, inspired by *Superman*, *Spiderman*, *Batman*, the *X-Men*, *Captain America* and the rest of Marvel Comics' output. The fact of the matter is that if a sci-fi movie or television series has been made, it's highly likely that someone, somewhere is gaming it, either with miniatures or as a role-playing game. This is often made easier because of the merchandising that comes alongside any such enterprise these days, with a host of 'official' toys and models.

A popular offshoot of science fiction is 'steampunk', in which it is imagined that certain aspects of Victorian technology had advanced beyond what was really achieved at the time. Much of this is inspired by H G Wells and Jules Verne, and has resulted in some visually stunning creations. Imagine, therefore, combinations of Leonardo da Vinci and the industrial revolution, such as steam-powered armoured fighting vehicles, with armour of brass rather than steel and incorporating some high-quality teak panelling. Airships abound, and if a chap loses an arm, not to worry, it can be replaced with a fancy clockwork thing of brass, copper and wrought iron in a jiffy, perhaps with a magnifying monocle to match. Think of movies like *Wild, Wild West*, *The City of Lost Children*, *The League of Extraordinary Gentlemen*, *The Golden Compass* and the new *Sherlock Holmes* offerings as examples.

Like fantasy, however, you should not feel constrained by the output of others. Why not create your own dystopian vision of the future, people it with towering cities and glittering technology of your own devising, and have it fought over by warring factions of sentient duck people and meerkats? (Don't laugh, I've seen the figures...) Like all wargaming, as long as the result is challenging and fun, then you will have achieved your aim.

Conclusion

This has been the briefest scamper through the various historical periods and other genres available to the wargamer, and I am bound to have offended some by omission or misrepresentation, for which I can only apologise in advance. However, I hope that you will have gained a reasonable impression of the vast range of options available to you as you embark on this wonderful hobby, and that the photographs provide you with some inspiration to pursue your own passions. The chapters that follow are intended to help you achieve that.

Warhammer 40K with a twist: the Spanish-style setting makes this still one of the most intriguing sci-fi games I have seen at a show, in this case Cavalier in 2008, staged by Crawley Wargames Club and titled "Purge the Xenos". The fact is, of course, that you can set your sci-fi games wherever you like – you might imagine that you have to seek out an other-wordly setting, but there's nothing whatsoever to prevent you locating your futuristic games right here on planet Earth in some post-apocalyptic future or when visited by aliens/zombies/vampires... Take your pick!

4

SOMETHING TO FIGHT FOR

Terrain and Scenery

I t would be wrong to say that you can't fight wargames on just a plain, billiard table like surface with no features whatsoever, but the attraction pretty soon palls, so wargamers, like model railway enthusiasts, have become adept at creating terrain for their model armies to fight over and scenery to place on top that affects the ways in which those forces can be seen, move and fight.

Just what do we mean by these terms, which have cropped up several times already, and how to we go about representing them?

The word terrain derives from the Latin *terra*, meaning "earth" and *terrenum*, meaning "ground". In other words, when wargamers talk about terrain, we mean the surface across which our model troops move and fight, and the other objects placed upon it. Hills, trees, rivers, woods, buildings, walls and so on are properly known as *scenery*, since they help us to 'set the scene'. Let's take a look at how we represent them, the role they play in our wargames, how we can either find them ready-made from commercial outlets or make our own.

The playing surface

We commonly refer to the playing surface as simply 'the tabletop' because, for many wargamers, that's precisely what it is. Whilst, as a young boy, the lounge carpet was frequently the venue for my games with toy soldiers, the experience of careless feet, knees or domestic animals crushing and scattering entire battalions led to me shifting to the dining room table as soon as I could persuade the adults in the house that the fate of my armies was much more important than whatever they were doing. I occasionally

This is how many of us started: a plain dining room table, unpainted plastic figures and a few scattered pieces of crude scenery. The games were just as exciting – perhaps even more so – as the gaps were filled in by childhood imagination based on the books we had read and the films we had seen.

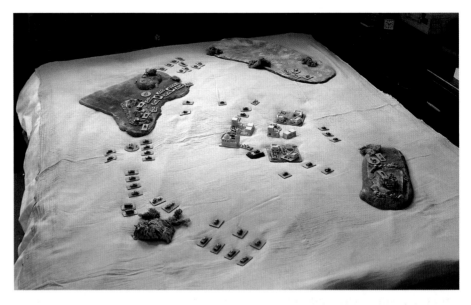

Tears before bedtime? It's perfectly possible to play games on your bed, which can be covered with appropriately-coloured sheets or blankets, but of course you will need to pack up before you tuck in! This sort of surface really demands that you use multiple basing for your troops and area basing for your scenery, such as woods, or they will topple and roll down undulations.

ventured to play games on my bed, covered with a green sheet, but whilst fine for WW2 tank games, my little Airfix men struggled to stand up on the undulating peaks and troughs, let alone the pillow hills, in those days before I realised that multiple basing for troops was the answer.

And so, like many before and since, family meals alternated with pitched battles between hordes of Romans and Ancient Britons, War of Independence Continentals and British Grenadiers, Waterloo British and French, and American Civil War Union and Confederates. From time to time, I saved up my pocket money and paid a visit to the local DIY store and purchased large sheets of chipboard, plywood or hardboard to create ever larger surfaces on which to play. Since we lived in a fairly small house, storage was always a problem, so several of my gaming boards ended up hinged in the middle or cut in half, so that they could be tucked discreetly behind cabinets or even the family upright piano.

In the early years, I didn't even bother with painting the boards, happily shoving plastic men around atop a plain, brown wilderness, but a concurrent interest in model railways led me to gradually invest in some flock grass here, some lichen bushes there, a handful of trees and so on. I think I must have been about eleven or twelve when suddenly, my lust for better-looking terrain sprang to life, and I could often be found elbow-deep in balsa wood, glue, paint and plaster, creating all manner of scenic items.

However, let's stick with the playing surface for the minute, because it potentially represents one of your biggest investments, and also the one you're going to have to live with the longest.

As has been discussed earlier, the size of tabletop you require is closely linked to the size of battles you wish to fight and the size of miniatures you wish to collect. Naturally, as with most wargamers, you're going to end up with figures from all sorts of historical – and perhaps even fantasy and science fiction – periods, representing different armies, and probably at different scales. But, for the moment, let's assume that I've done my job reasonably well and, by the time you've finished this book, you're thinking to yourself, "Hmm, this Hyde chappie has tickled my fancy, so d'you know what? I'm going to give this wargaming malarkey a go."

The next chapter, called "Assembling your Forces", deals directly with the choices you will face when starting a collection, but let's just say, for the minute, that you want to open your account using the vast array of 1/72 scale plastic soldiers that can be found in almost any toy or hobby shop, before committing to more expensive options from specialist producers. Once painted and based, these little fellows look tremendous, and I know many wargamers who have never felt the need to 'graduate' to anything else.

Now, these miniatures tend to come in boxes of around 40-50 infantry or a dozen cavalry for just a few pounds, so you won't have any trouble building up forces quite quickly should you so choose. Given that my recommendation is for most games to be played with around a dozen units per side, with perhaps 36 infantry figures or 12 cavalry per unit, then it's clear that a couple of dozen boxes will enable you to assemble the forces of both sides – great news for the budget-conscious, since at the time of writing, this would come to less than £150 for over 700 infantry and nearly 100 cavalry, with some artillery too.

Now, if we look at our typical unit of infantry, using our standard base sizes (see "Basing troops on page 358), each will require six bases of six figures, mounted in two ranks. This gives us a frontage of around 270mm, or about 10½ inches, when deployed in line. A cavalry unit of two squadrons of six, deployed side by side, would be four bases of 60mm, thus 240mm or around 9½ inches.

So, if you were to deploy your dozen units – say, eight of infantry, three of cavalry and a battery of artillery – in line, as a single line of battle, with

My well-worn custom-made wargames table, measuring 8 feet by 6, in my attic studio. I had to wait over 35 years to have a playing surface like this – and now, for most of the time, it's covered with all sorts of other 'stuff' associated with the working life of a wargames magazine editor, including samples from wargames companies set up for photoshoots, paperwork and my painting tray!

appropriate small intervals between the units of around an inch (25mm), then you would require a total frontage of 3,235mm (3.23m) or over ten feet! Panic not, because a number of factors would tend to prevent this.

First of all, there are likely to be obstacles in the way of achieving this drillmaster's paradise. All those features mentioned earlier, the hills, woods and whatnot, rather get in the way and make it unnecessary and undesirable to lay all your troops out in one long, thin line. Secondly, it's not even desirable: such a line is very weak and easy to break through, so the sensible general would keep a substantial second line, or reserve, to reinforce and replace the first. In fact, a little reading of military history shows that formal orders of battle and deployments were drawn up for just this purpose, with units being given specific places in the first or second lines of battle. And finally, a good general would always keep a powerful reserve 'to hand' to throw into the attack or defence at a critical point if required, to cover a retreat or to exploit an enemy rout.

And so, in very rough terms, it is unlikely that your army will require more than four to five feet of frontage when deployed, meaning that a table some six feet, or 1.8m wide, will normally suffice.

Now, what about depth? There are two factors at play here. The first is the range of weapons in our games, since it would lead to an almighty bloodbath if, once deployed, our miniature men found themselves immediately within short range of the enemy's muskets and cannon. On the other hand, whilst it's ideal if our troops have some leeway for manoeuvre, it would be very tedious indeed if they had to spend move after move just shuffling into long range before being able to open fire.

This is where the rules writer has to do some juggling to find the right balance of ground scale to time scale, so that the moves are long enough to bring opponents into contact in a reasonable time, whilst ensuring that players have sufficient space to achieve meaningful tactical movement

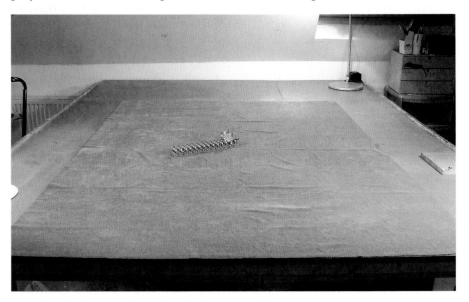

The cloth – a Games Workshop 'battle mat', to be precise – measures 6 feet by 4, a typical size for a wargame, though looking small here on my own table. The figures are a battalion of 30mm miniatures for size comparison. A cloth this size will be suitable for up to a dozen or so units a side maximum when used with 28-30mm miniatures for horse and musket games.

A game played recently on the full 8' x 6' surface covered by two battle mats. Here you can see that both armies are deployed at sensible intervals, with reserves in support and plenty of space to manouevre. The miniatures on the left are from the collection of Essex wargamer Iain Burt and those on the right are my own. The setting for 'The Battle of Coinville' is entirely imaginary.

even when under fire. The reality is that in scale, even smoothbore cannon would be able to shoot beyond the distant table edge if they chose, but in fact most fire was held until the shooting could be 'effective', which was a much shorter distance of, usually, less than a thousand yards.

So, if we glance at my own rules, the average, medium cannon have a long range of 1440mm, but a medium range of just 720mm, or just over 28 inches. Given that most games begin with the opposing troops deployed some six to ten inches onto the table, this means that a surface some four feet across is just about sufficient for most games to begin with some space to manoeuvre outside of close cannon range. Of course, there are many scenario options that will have enemies coming onto the table much further away than that, especially if the short table edges are used, and on the other hand, it can be fun to have the armies arrayed slightly closer, so that they really have to get stuck in without dithering!

So, it's pretty safe to assume that you can't go far wrong with a tabletop measuring around six feet by four (1.8m x 1.2m) for starters, and indeed there are huge numbers of gamers who never progress beyond this. I am lucky to have a permanent table measuring six feet by eight (1.8m x 2.4m), with hinged extensions to take up to twelve feet by six (3.6m x 1.8m) for really large games, but I have to confess that I haven't used the biggest size for years.

Of course, if you decide to use smaller miniatures, such as 15mm, 10mm or even 6mm, then such a table will do very nicely for some very grand battles indeed, leaving you plenty of room for manoeuvre beyond even extreme cannon shot if required. I am myself raising considerable armies for the Peninsular War using 6mm miniatures, and hope to be able to recreate some of the largest historical encounters here in my attic studio.

There is another consideration when it comes to deciding upon your table depth – your physical ability to reach troops in the middle, a factor made all the more acute if you are a person of a certain girth, such as myself! (Okay, okay, I'm working on it...) The fact is that six feet is already a bit of a struggle, and more than that becomes a real challenge. The late Charles Grant and his son, my friend Charles Stewart Grant, used to play on a surface atop an old table tennis table, which measured nine feet by seven. Melees in the centre of that monster must have been accompanied by a certain amount of sweating and cursing!

A degree of latitude can be achieved depending on the height of the surface above the floor, and here it comes down to what is the most ergonomically comfortable for yourself. Needless to say, in a game which requires long periods spent with your back bent over a playing surface, take your time in making your decisions before investing in a custom-built structure in order to avoid back problems.

From table to battlefield

How can we make a plain table look less like a table? Well, if you're stuck with the actual, unmodified dining room or kitchen variety to start with, then you can begin by acquiring a simple, green cloth (or a sandy coloured one, if your theatre of operations is a desert, or plain white if the setting is snow-covered). To represent an area of flat land, simply use it as you would a tablecloth, and cover the table. I'd advise using a few blobs of Blu-Tack around the edges of the table to stop it sliding off at an inopportune moment, but that's basically it.

A surprisingly effective grassland look can be achieved by using towelling. Shop around for a plain coloured bath towel which has a relatively short 'pile' to it, so that your little men don't get tangled up. If you can't find the precise shade of green you're looking for, don't panic – just buy a plain white one and then get a couple of pots of Dylon fabric dye (one yellow, one blue), mix them together until you get the colour you

A variety of ground coverings on top of a Games Workshop 'battle mat', ranging from a coloured sheet, through painted hardboard, model railway matting and carpet tile, to cheap lengths of cloth bought and dyed. There's also a piece of the wargamer's favourite 'wheat field' – teddy bear fur! The blue cloth is of course for naval games.

need (in fact a tiny touch of red might help to create a warmer colour) and then pop the whole lot in a bucket of hot water or in the washing machine according to the Dylon instructions. Your life partner may not fancy the resulting grass green colour, but you'll love it! (By the way, don't keep your precious battlefield in the airing cupboard along with household towels...)

It should come as no surprise that several companies now offer ready-made cloths to give a slightly more realistic appearance to your bare ground. These vary in price and quality, and come in different forms.

Firstly, there are those which are made from thick brown paper, to which various colours of sand and flock have been adhered using glue. Two drawbacks to this are that the glue tends to lose its adhesion over time, and the surface abrades, leaving you with a bald patch on your surface and a mess on your floor. Secondly, the paper backing can tear, which is very annoying!

Next, there is the type of base cloth sold by Games Workshop, which they call a 'battlemat', which is similar to the first type, but uses a soft cloth backing instead of paper. The mock-grass surface also seems to be superior, since it has been adhered using an electrostatic charge as well as some form of superior adhesive. The benefit of these is that they can be easily folded up and put away until next needed, yet seem to lose the creases once used again. I have a couple of these, which means I can cover my entire 8' x 6' table if required.

Recently, a number of gaming mats have come onto the market that use a rubberised material on top of a flexible base cloth, Some of these come pre-coloured, others are available plain so that you can paint them yourself. They are available in a variety of colours and textures, and at least a couple of companies have sprung up producing entirely customized designs (see Baueda, for example, or The Terrain Guy). The common denominator is high quality – and a high price.

Finally, there are a number of commercially-available cloths made from felt of various thicknesses, either plain or decorated with splodges of colour to break up the monotony of a single colour. (And there is nothing, of course, to prevent you doing this yourself.) Some are even screen-printed with a bird's eye view of fields, rivers, streams, hedges, rocks, scrub and so on to enhance the impression of realism. And for gamers who are either adapting a boardgame, or who prefer to have movement and ranges regulated by a fixed grid, a number of manufacturers give you the option of having these same cloths with a grid of hexagons superimposed.

Almost all these cloths are available via the internet, as well as in specialist wargaming shops and at wargaming shows. Ranging from perhaps £15 to £30 at the time of writing, they represent a relatively inexpensive way of disguising the domestic origins of your playing surface. Of course, if you have a good local fabric store, you may turn up a bargain for a home-made attempt at a fraction of this price. The customized mats mentioned above are, of course, much more expensive.

Some say that one of the visual disadvantages of the base cloth is that

The impression of rolling countryside that can be achieved by simply placing books under a standard Games Workshop battle mat. The edges are secured to the surface beneath using Blu-Tack. The Foundry Miniatures sheep, shepherd, dog and roaming bear are all from the author's collection and have seen action many times!

it is dead flat and therefore does not resemble the natural contours of the landscape, with rolling hills and valleys and streams and rivers and so forth. Well, a simple approach is to place items *underneath* your cloth to create the necessary undulations. A simple starting point is to use piles of books – I would recommend heavier hardbacks, because they shift less easily – or magazines, piled one on top of another in decreasing sizes, to create shelved 'contours' able to accommodate your miniature troops.

The first thing to note is that this really doesn't work with the paper-backed cloths. Secondly, even with the cloth surfaces, the slopes of hills can shift and slide in the most alarming fashion and troops, even when on multiple bases, can show their disapproval by slipping, sliding and even rolling downhill in the most annoying fashion. And it's not just the troops – other scenic items placed on top, whilst looking fine initially, can find themselves subject to earthquake-like forces if the gamer accidentally tugs the cloth or, worse still, attempts to leave the table with a corner caught in his clothing.

No, these days, what most wargamers do is use the cloth flat, to cover the playing surface, and then put all scenic items on top. This makes it easier to fix the basecloth securely, using pins, or Blu-Tack, or even have it glued permanently to the baseboard. It's quick, convenient and, with the right scenic additions, can look very good indeed.

I'm somewhat old-fashioned, because I have actually painted the surface of my wargames table a mid-green, with some mottled patches of darker and lighter greens. This is because, as you will see in many of the photographs in this book, some of the games I play are what might be described as 'old school' or 'classic' in visual style, bearing some resemblance to the type of games played by the early doyens of the hobby between about 1955 and 1975. For this reason, the bases of my eighteenth century troops are also painted a simple, plain green. We shall come to

An example of the common approach nowadays – using a basecloth with scenic items placed on top. This is actually a rather crowded table for a large battle – this type of close terrain with hills and woods is best suited to skirmishes, larger actions with predominantly light troops, or for games set in later periods such as WWII.

some further explanation of this later, but the advantage to me is that I don't *have* to use a base cloth at all: I can simply place scenic items on the tabletop, lay out my armies and start playing.

However, as a man with very catholic tastes, I dabble in all sorts of wargaming, so I also have a couple of GW battlemats, a desert mat and have also owned terrain squares, which we shall look at shortly.

Adding relief

One of the biggest challenges for the wargamer using a flat tabletop is representing those terrain features that dip below the general lie of the land, such as streams, rivers, ditches, trenches, ponds, lakes and even some roads, particularly old-fashioned tracks that have been worn into the landscape by the passing of countless wheels, hooves and feet. The answer is to create a surface higher than the tabletop itself, which can then be carved into or moulded to create depressions.

One of the ways this used to be done – and very occasionally, still is – is based on the simple idea of a children's sandpit. If you're anything like me, you probably spent countless hours as a child, either in the school sandpit or on a beach somewhere, tracing shapes with your finger or a plastic spade, digging holes, filling them up with water, or making futile attempts to redirect the incoming tide around a sandcastle moat until the edifice crumbled. As mentioned in the introduction, this led to the back garden and extensive trench and bunker systems carved into my father's carefully-weeded flowerbeds, to be occupied by soon-to-die Airfix figures and Tamiya tanks!

A sand table is, essentially, a grown-up version of the sandpit. A reinforced framework with raised sides is made, into which is poured several hundredweight of fine sand to a depth of several inches. This can be coloured with paints to represent the natural landscape, and of course, most importantly, if kept damp it can be moulded into precise shapes denoting hills, valley, gorges, cliffs, beaches and so on. Miniature houses can be placed upon it, trees can be stuck into it, until a quite remarkable three-dimensional map has been built. For many years, military academies such as Sandhurst relied upon just such recreations to train young officers in the finer points of strategy and tactics, and anyone fond of old wartime movies will have seen sand tables used time and again to brief bomber command pilots, officers leading commando raids and so on.

But before you get your wallet out and head for the nearest DIY store to buy up their stock of bagged sand, here are a couple of things to consider.

First of all, sand – especially wet sand – is heavy. Very heavy. There are true stories of wargamers forgetting to reinforce the floor of upstairs gaming rooms and living to regret it.

Secondly, the creation of such silicone wargames terrain is both time consuming and messy. Anyone who has spent time at a beach knows that somehow, the darn stuff gets everywhere, and is the devil's own job to get rid of.

Thirdly, several gamers who have experience of sand tables report that, like the Bermuda Triangle, they have the disturbing ability to mysteriously swallow entire platoons without trace, only for them to reappear at some future date like an archaeological find in *The Mummy Returns*.

No, on second thoughts, let's confine sand tables to the annals of history where they belong.

An alternative approach is to create the kind of scenic layout beloved by railway modellers. In the old days, I remember setting to with crumpled and torn newspaper and gallons of wallpaper paste to create epic, and very messy, layouts. I gradually learned that it's best to create a wooden 'former' underneath, so that the high points have sufficient support and the surface is of a more even depth, which aids drying. On top of this, in

Back in the day... Veteran wargamer Donald Featherstone crouches over his beloved sand table, an almost mythical construction that was capable of swallowing entire armies. Writing this in 2012, I can report that I don't know of a single wargamer who still owns a sand table. Perhaps they don't build houses strong enough any more. Photo used with Don's permission.

Wargames scenery being constructed from carved polystyrene glued onto thin MDF board at The Wargame Holidays centre in Crete. The board helps to prevent the polystyrene from warping and also makes the scenery more durable and solid. Photo courtesy of Jon and Diane Sutherland, who are also regular contributors to *Battlegames* (now *Miniature Wargames*).

those early attempts, I would paste plain white wall lining paper, which provided the surface to be painted and flocked. The more skilled (i.e. grown ups) were already using Plaster of Paris as a top coat, and since then it has been possible to buy plaster-impregnated bandages of various kinds which set rock hard, just as a plaster cast on a broken leg does.

The most common material used for such layouts nowadays is polystyrene foam. All of us will know the basic material so beloved of the packaging industry, which comes formed into all sorts of bizarre shapes and sizes to accommodate TVs, washing machines, dishwashers, microwaves and all the electrical goods churned out in the industrial age.

In fact, that sort of plain, white polystyrene is troublesome stuff, being tricky to carve cleanly, crumbling at the slightest provocation and it's tricky to paint too. Nowadays, modellers use a somewhat denser compound, the kind used for insulation boards and specialist modelling. Coloured pale blue or pink, this is much easier to carve to shape and doesn't crumble, meaning a huge saving in hoover time!

A major advantage of using foam to create the contours is the reduction in weight compared to the old methods, as well as an increase in durability. The 'hollow' nature of the old method using a frame and papier maché meant that it was easy to damage, whereas terrain made with high density foam is really quite strong. This makes it much easier for gamers to make and transport surprisingly elaborate layouts with comparative ease.

When planned and executed properly, these techniques can produce a highly detailed surface that the wargamer/modeller can then decorate accordingly. A first step is to give the whole piece an undercoat of domestic, water-based emulsion paint (known as latex paint in the US). Personally, I would recommend the addition of a good dollop of PVA adhesive (that's white woodworking glue, for those unfamiliar with the term, usually available in large tubs as well as tubes). Some people use the paint as-is, others mix in some fine building sand to give texture, and yet others use commercial exterior wall paint, which already contains texturing.

It's best to start with an overall dark colour, such as a very dark brown, and once that has dried, go over this with a 'wet dry brush' of a mid brown to create a realistic earth effect. (The technique of dry-brushing will be explained later.) Some gamers then apply patches of watered-down PVA adhesive and sprinkle scatter material and grass-effect flock as appropriate; others, looking for a simpler life, simply continue the painting process with a coat of mid-green followed by a lighter or yellow drybrush to simulate grass. Of course, you can go to whatever extent you like in creating your earth and grass effects.

One of the most dramatic effects to be achieved is that of water, either still or moving, using either resin or other liquids capable of emulating good old H_2O. Resin (used in the creation of fibre glass) is pretty nasty stuff, needs to be handled with care, requires the surface to be proofed against it and can take some considerable time to cure. The more recent substitutes, such as those sold by Woodland Scenics, are much more benign, and can be used to create waterfall effects as well as standing water and watercourses without the fire hazard or the house stinking for a week afterwards.

And in case you're wondering, the answer to that question that just popped into your head is that you paint the bed of the stream or lake first, before applying the water effect. Just as in real life, it's the earth, not the water, which is coloured, unless it's full of particulates like dissolved calciferous rock or mud.

The final effects that can be achieved with such dioramic layouts can be utterly stunning, as you can see in the photographs accompanying this section. Truly, this is model-making of the highest order, easily achieving (and, in my experience passing) what might be described as 'museum

Beautifully rendered water effects on a WWII E-Boat pen layout seen at the Battlegroup South Bovington show, which is held annually in the Tank Museum.

quality'. Around the world, there are certain individuals and clubs with a reputation for staging 'demonstration' games at shows who are well known for their depictions of battlefields from ancient to modern and beyond, and some of the masters of this art have achieved little miracles of terrainscaping.

So, why don't all wargamers do things this way?

Well, first of all, it's extremely time consuming. Secondly, it can be expensive – it's one thing putting something like this together for a special occasion, but what happens to it afterwards? After all, there are only so many times you will want to manoeuvre your troops over exactly the same terrain and the fact is that, shockingly, many of these elaborate layouts are simply discarded after the show for which they were built. (A canny few manage to sell their efforts to collectors who, it must be said, require a huge amount of storage space!) Thirdly... Well, we've already touched on that. Just like a model railway layout, once such a diorama is built, that's that, whereas the vast majority of wargamers want fresh challenges with each game they play – and that means a change of scenery. I might be fighting with the 8th Army in the Western Desert one day, and then a pirate skirmish in the Caribbean the next, and then a large nineteenth century battle in an Alpine pass the next, so obviously, I need a change of scene.

Tempting tessellations

The compromise is to use terrain that can be broken down into interchangeable sections. Most commonly, such terrain is divided into squares or hexagons that are isomorphic or modular, which is to say that they are designed so as to be able to fit together in a variety of ways whilst maintaining a seamless appearance. As an example, if a terrain square has a road or river leaving one edge, then a neighbouring square through which

Alistair Birch advances the Russians in a game of *Shako* being played on typical TSS square tiled terrain. Many wargamers prefer to use these than a mat, and they do have the advantage of rivers and trenches being 'sunk' into the surface. The only disadvantages are storage and their somewhat fragile nature, as the white polystyrene from which they are constructed can be easily damaged.

Kallistra's 'Hexon' terrain system uses a clever scheme of interlocking boards held together by simple plastic clips underneath, whilst additional terrain items are placed on top. They manufacture hill slopes that have been cunningly designed to allow many permutations, but you can also buy simple hills and escarpments ready-made. Individual hexes are 10cm wide from flat side to flat side.

that road or river is also to pass must have its road or river meeting the other at exactly the same point. For convenience, this is usually designed to occur halfway up each edge. This means that the watercourse or track can meander about as much as it likes within a square, as long as it returns to that midpoint when it reaches the far edge.

Given these limitations, terrain squares are extremely popular, and in fact can be given further permutations with the addition of half-size or double-sized units forming a rectangular shape within the overall tessellation of squares.

Only a limited number of regular polygons can form tessellations of this kind. Triangles are not really practical, so the next shape that wargamers have seized upon is the hexagon. Long popular amongst boardgamers for wargames, the hexagon is frequently used both for battle and campaign gaming, since it allows for regulated movement, unit facing and weapon ranges in a slightly more natural way than squares. It was only a matter of time, therefore, before miniatures wargamers decided to experiment with tabletop wargames, adapting 'traditional' rules to use hexes, or attempting larger-scale renditions of the kind of games usually played with cardboard counters. Nowadays, some rules are written to be able to use either hexagons or traditional 'freestyle' tape measure movement and ranging without a grid.

Obviously, whilst it is perfectly possible for the amateur to construct interlocking square terrain boards, hexagons, whilst not impossible, are more of a challenge, but both are now available commercially. Various companies make polystyrene squares (see the Appendix), either with the hills attached to the baseboard or separate, and Games Workshop make a small range of vacuum-formed plastic squares that come with a built-in locking mechanism to hold them together. Hexagonal terrain is available from GHQ in the USA and Kallistra (under the name Hexon) in the UK.

Larger polystyrene hexes being used for a recreation of the Battle of Long Island during the American War of Independence. The miniatures are 28mm size, so you can tell that these hexes measure about 10" across. With plenty of other scenery placed on top, they make for a convincing landscape, and unless dislodged, the hexes blend together quite well.

For a most part, this type of square terrain is around 50mm (2") deep, allowing features to be sunk around 25mm into the boards whilst retaining enough strength to prevent breakage along the line of the feature. Interestingly, the hexagonal terrain often comes much thinner. The Hexon terrain from Kallistra starts at about 10mm depth, and is made from a harder plastic compound with a flock material applied to the surface. Extension parts are available to create hills, which rise to a greater height above the general surface. Similarly, GHQ have a terrain creation system called Terrain Maker® which starts at just ¼" (6mm) deep, through a range of thicknesses up to 1½" (38mm). Here, the wargamer is left to add all the surface detail themselves, using techniques described in detail on the GHQ website.

Of course, there is nothing to stop you making your own terrain squares. You could use 50mm insulation board, as has been described above, cut into squares and then carved using craft knives and a hot wire cutter. If you've never seen one, this is essentially a horseshoe-shaped device, with a very thin wire inserted between the prongs. The whole thing is connected to a small battery, and when the trigger is pressed, this heats up the wire so that it cuts, to use a cliché, like a hot knife through butter. It takes a bit of practice, and you need to avoid breathing in the fumes, but once mastered, you can produce highly naturalistic curves.

A good way of combining multiple materials is to use thin – perhaps 5mm or quarter inch – MDF or plywood as a base, onto which you then glue the polystyrene. This adds strength and rigidity, as well as a little weight. This can help prevent the squares shifting around too much during games. If you plan to have a river, then you simply cut the shape out of the polystyrene completely, ensuring that the edges are sloped to resemble your riverbank, and then stick the two pieces aligned with the outer edges of the board base, leaving the wood exposed as the riverbed.

A diagrammatic representation of just some of the permutations of terrain square needed to cover most eventualities, ranging from the completely plain to the complex. I have only shown squares in classic 'temperate zone' green – what if you need desert sand, scrub or arctic wastes? This is why the cost of terrain squares is often borne by clubs, who may also have the storage space for an extensive collection (and the insurance for the not inconsiderable fire hazard...). Note how all roads and rivers exit the centre of the squares' edges. For coastal regions, you will also need some plain blue tiles. Incidentally, you may have noticed that the terrain tile captioned "River with road bridge" has no bridge! This is because you will need to place a bridge of your own on top of the tile where the road meets the river – it isn't moulded into the square. The same thing goes for most other terrain features, of course, including hills, which are generally laid on top of the tabletop surface as stand-alone items, though they can be incorporated as shown here.

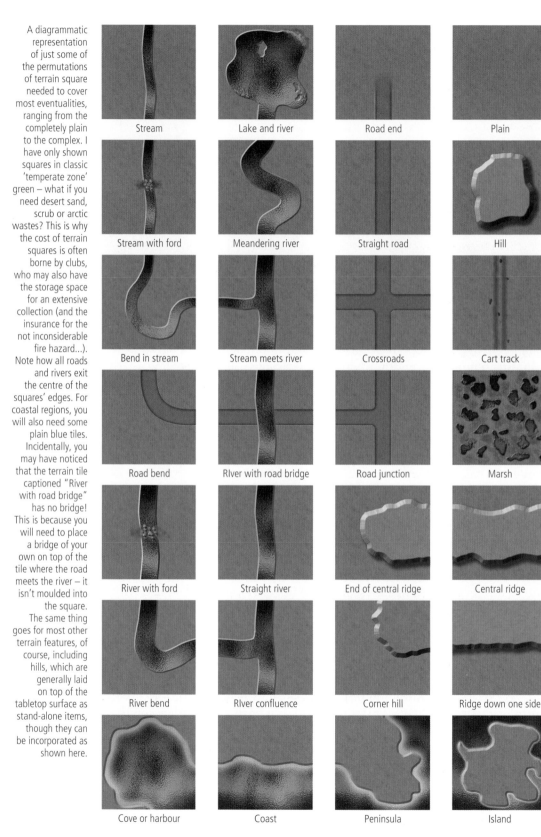

Stream   Lake and river   Road end   Plain

Stream with ford   Meandering river   Straight road   Hill

Bend in stream   Stream meets river   Crossroads   Cart track

Road bend   RIver with road bridge   Road junction   Marsh

River with ford   Straight river   End of central ridge   Central ridge

River bend   RIver confluence   Corner hill   Ridge down one side

Cove or harbour   Coast   Peninsula   Island

A cheaper option is to use carpet tiles. These are easy to find in flooring and DIY stores, and usually come in squares of around 50cm (20") with a coloured top layer made of various kinds of synthetic wool-like material, mounted on a black, rubber-like base. In the past, I have made my own terrain squares from green carpet tiles, and created 'below the surface' rivers and roads in them by actually scraping away the top material to make indentations, which I then painted blue or brown and finally varnished. Hard work and messy, but surprisingly effective.

And a final option for the highly budget-conscious is to just use flat MDF squares with rivers and roads painted on. If you have a modicum of artistic talent, they can be made to look quite good and, given a couple of coats of matt varnish, can be extremely durable and easy to pack away.

When it comes to choosing a size for your boards, you should pay heed to your playing area, and divide it accordingly. The most common size is 24" x 24", which means that a typical 6' x 4' table will require a minimum of six squares. However, it might not suit your storage arrangements to have such large squares, so an alternative might be 12" squares (24 will be needed as a starting point) or an intermediate size, although this would lead to them either falling short of, or overhanging, the edge of the table. You can, of course, make 'filler' rectangles to cope with this, but ultimately, it creates a lot of work for not much gain.

Another factor to consider is the size of miniatures you intend to play with. If you're a fan of the micro-scales, then 12" squares might give you plenty of room within each square for your rivers to meander and your roads to fork and turn. On the other hand, if you're using 20mm+ size troops, you'll probably find that a bit cramped, and prefer the greater space of a two-foot square. Fans of 15mm could go either way.

Of course, it doesn't take a mathematical genius to work out that whilst half a dozen plain 24" squares is fine for starters, the number of additional squares you will need starts adding up, whether you're buying them commercially or making them yourself. You will need at least enough river squares for such a feature to stretch right across the table from end to end – that would be three – and similarly for roads. Then, of course, we have an obvious need for squares containing a road meeting a river at 90° where the banks are high enough to demand a bridge, and another where it is shallow and fordable. And, of course, some sections of river will be straight, but others need to meander more realistically, and then you will need at least a couple where the river bends and exits via an adjacent edge rather than opposite... Start thinking about roads, with crossroads, junctions and forks, and whether the route is a main, metalled one or just a cart track, and the combinations really start to mount up. Fancy some coastal terrain? Don't get me started.

Hexagons are a bit more tricky, of course, because the rows of hexagons 'wiggle' up and down by half a hex with each row, and the sides are pointy! I know that's not a terribly scientific description, but you get the idea. In fact, Kallistra sell their Hexon terrain in sections of six hexagons arranged as two rows of three. The hexagons themselves are 100mm (4") across, and a box of 21 of these boards covers an area 3' x 4', and two boxes will cover a 6' x 4' table. The GHQ version comes as individual hexes, into which you carve rivers and roads and wadis (dry river beds in the desert) as required, but interestingly, Hexon equivalents come either flat or rugged, but never indented, though of course there's nothing to stop you experimenting.

In any case, it's clear that as long as you have sufficient storage space and a reasonable budget, commercially-available terrain squares or hexes can be a very attractive choice and certainly, if you are able to share the cost with other club members, it can be a good way forward. Making your own will also demand a certain amount of patience and modelling skill of your own, a learning curve that can only be overcome with trial and error, though a great deal of good advice also exists online and in various wargame magazines such as my own *Battlegames*.

Rivers and roads

Perhaps inevitably, the way forward for many, if not most, wargamers is to combine a reasonably attractive cloth covering for your table with scenic items placed on top, and in fact this is how I play the vast majority of my own wargames. But whichever course you choose, the challenge then comes to enhance the basic terrain layout with the rest of those items necessary to set the scene for our wargames.

Let's deal with those items that are potentially the trickiest first: rivers and roads.

Of course, it's entirely possible, if you've gone for the classic green-painted board such as I have, to simply draw these features onto your table using chalk, pastels or something similar, so that they can be erased afterwards. Indeed, when I was a boy, this is precisely what I did, and there must be bits of hardboard rotting in a tip somewhere bearing the

Simple roads made by slicing 60mm wide strips from a standard carpet tile and then applying a little judicious emulsion paint. You can see how the green helps to blend the straight edges into the tabletop and of course, you could embellish this further with lichen and static grass.

Various 2-D scenic items created using card and water-based paints. These cheap and cheerful items can be created in no time at all and are great for practicing your impressionistic terrain painting skills. I've got some pieces, such as the wide, raging river, that I've had for years and they still do sterling service. The 28mm Foundry English Civil War cuirassier painted by Jez Griffin gives an idea of scale.

ghostly shadows of games long forgotten. I would not advise trying this on a Games Workshop or other commercial cloth, however, as I think you'll find the marks trickier to erase!

Another very simple option is to use strips of appropriately-coloured cloth. Cut them to a standard width, including as many meanders and turns as you like, and simply lay them on the tabletop where required. Depending on the choice of material, they can look just fine, and of course some cloths, such as corduroy, can make surprisingly effective ploughed fields, for instance. The main problem with cloth is fixing it in position and preventing the edges from curling up – some double-sided sticky tape can help here.

Next up the ladder in terms of sophistication is to make completely flat watercourses and roads, using something as simple as cereal packet card. If you've got any skill with watercolours, acrylics or even household emulsion paints (those little test pots can be very useful here), it's possible to create a very artistic renditions of rivers, streams, gullies and roads. This is cheap and easy to do, and of course if you find you need more, you can quickly produce them yourself. A little sand or scenic flock along the edges – job done. A tip: it's a good idea to wet the pieces of cardboard on both sides and then let them dry flat before using water-based paints on them. This helps prevent warping. You can also finish off with a protective coat of modelling spray varnish or diluted PVA.

Having mentioned carpet tiles a little earlier, they can of course be cut into strips, rather than used whole, to emulate roads and rivers. Once again, take care to cut them to a standard width – say, 60mm for roads or 100mm for rivers – so that they will match up end-to-end. Bulges and meanders along their length don't matter, and in fact are desirable; it's the ends that need to match up.

If we want to achieve something a little more realistic, but haven't got the benefit of a surface such as polystyrene into which sunken features such as this have been moulded or carved, then we have to cheat by laying something onto our playing surface which has been built up around the edges to give the impression of it sitting lower than the surrounding terrain.

This can be achieved with the plain card method above, but adding a little household filler along the edges, but the flexibility and absorption of the card means that the banks are likely to become brittle. A better solution is to use either thicker brown carton card (also known as 'corrugated' card), hardboard or very thin MDF, which can be bought as thin as two or three millimetres (⅛").

Here's a step-by-step lesson of how to do this, which first appeared in Battlegames magazine issue 10 (still available as a PDF download from my blog at *http://henrys-wargaming.co.uk*). Of course, adapt these suggestions according to your own skills and requirements.

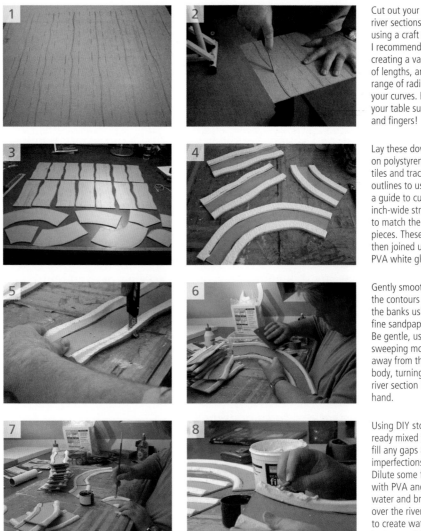

Using thin MDF, hardboard or plywood, draw parallel lines with inner dashes indicating the watercourse. Make the outer lines naturally undulating.

Cut out your river sections using a craft saw. I recommend creating a variety of lengths, and a range of radii for your curves. Protect your table surface and fingers!

The first batch cut out. It is important, for the time being, to ensure that the marks showing the watercourse width are clearly visible and match end-to-end.

Lay these down on polystyrene tiles and trace the outlines to use as a guide to cut out inch-wide strips to match the base pieces. These are then joined using PVA white glue.

Once the glue has dried, shape the riverbanks using a long blade. Always cut AWAY from exposed fingers! Ensure that the ends match all the other sections.

Gently smooth the contours of the banks using fine sandpaper. Be gentle, using a sweeping motion away from the body, turning the river section in your hand.

Using diluted PVA (about 1 part PVA to 3 parts water), give everything a thorough coat. Turn all the sections over and coat the back as well – this helps to prevent warping.

Using DIY store ready mixed filler, fill any gaps and imperfections. Dilute some filler with PVA and water and brush over the riverbed to create water texture and ripples.

For rubble, use cat litter, grit, small stones or scenic 'talus' (a posh word for grit) in various grades. Apply blobs of PVA to the riverbed on inner curves, and scatter freely.

For a natural look, start with the biggest rocks and boulders, adding finer grades of material, and finally a scattering of fine sand. Leave to dry thoroughly before brushing off excess.

Now undercoat everything with a wet mix of mid-grey, using artists' acrylic, or a mixture of household emulsion paint. This helps to kill the bright white of the filler.

Useful colours for this project: Oxide of Chromium Green; Monestial Green; Hookers Green; Raw Sienna; Burnt Sienna; Raw Umber; Burnt Umber and Payne's Grey.

Apply a wet coat of Raw Umber, painting up the inside of the banks and amongst the rocks, followed by a wet coat of Burnt Umber, using a smaller brush, along the centre.

Paint Raw Sienna up the banks and, where you want a ford, over the top too. Then apply thinned coats of Hookers Green and Monestial Green to represent deep water.

Apply a dilute wash of Payne's Grey around the rocks. Mix Raw Umber with the original Mid Grey and a touch of white, and apply to the rocks using a wettish dry-brush technique.

For fast-flowing water around rocks, semi-dry-brush pale grey, then white, to create foam and streaks on the surface. Ensure all turbulence runs *downstream*.

Apply as many coats of varnish to the watercourse as you can stand doing, leaving each to dry for the recommended time. The more coats, the more convincing the effect.

Once the varnish has dried, give the banks a basic coat of Oxide of Chromium. Don't forget to leave patches of Raw Sienna and Raw Umber showing where appropriate.

To demonstrate the simplest finish, I used ordinary scenic flock. Start with a thinned PVA glue over the banks, and sprinkle the flock liberally, tapping off the excess once dry.

The finished river sections. At this point, if you're keen, you could add extra scenic items, such as bushes, reeds, small trees and other vegetation.

Naturally, a similar technique can be used to make roads and tracks. You might wish to make the banks lower, or leave them off entirely, and apply filler along the length of the road, which you can then score with a stick or old paintbrush end to simulate cart tracks. With a bit of dexterity, you can carve the end of a matchstick or old paintbrush handle to simulate hoofprints in the mud.

Depending on your theatre of operations, you might undercoat your road sections with a dark brown, and then drybrush successively lighter tones of brown on top. It's perfectly possible to simulate cobblestones or flagstones, again using some kind of card or wooden former pressed into the surface, or scoring the impressions into the surface using a sharp implement or fine-tipped pen. Some brave souls even cut the shapes out using very thin card and apply them one by one!

To finish off your roads, just like the rivers, apply some scatter material and flock to represent small stones and grassy patches. You might even want to dig a few divots into the surface and treat them with water effects to simulate puddles, or create some snow and ice patches for winter wars.

Another thing I have seen which creates a very effective road surface is sandpaper, which comes in several grades to suit the size of your miniatures, extra fine for 6mm men up to coarse for 28mm troops. For modern, asphalt road surfaces, consider the dark grey 'wet and dry' paper. Either type can be stuck to the road shapes you have made, and then coloured by drybrushing or washing to add to the effect.

Of course, whatever you think of making at home, there's probably already a commercial version available, and this is certainly the case with rivers and roads. A recent arrival on the market are rubberised strips which can be painted up very easily, and then laid over your terrain, however undulating the surface. On the DIY front, one of the contributors to my magazine, Kerry Thomas, wrote an article about using pond lining rubber to create roads, which looked very effective indeed.

A number of manufacturers sell river sections created from vac-formed plastic or moulded resin, either unpainted or ready-painted. If you're in a hurry to get gaming and don't mind spending some money, these are of course an extremely attractive option. Be careful with your purchases, however, as some types of resin are far from indestructible if dropped.

A recent option for rivers is to use opaque plastic glass, the kind which has a 'rippled' effect for providing privacy in bathroom windows. This can be found in some DIY stores or specialist glazing or plastics suppliers. An alternative is 'frosted' effect self-adhesive film, which can be applied to plain, transparent plastic. The idea here is that you cut it to shape, paint the *underside* of the plastic and, hey presto, instant river! Of course, you can then disguise the edges by adding banks and other scenic effects in the same way as described above.

After a while, you'll soon develop that 'wargamer's eye' and you'll never walk around a DIY store or look at a piece of packaging in the same way again!

Fantasy scenery seen at Games Workshop's Games Day, created by the GW team and displaying plenty of fantastic imagination. The orc warships look suitably ramshackle in comparison with the monumental dwarven architecture.

Finally, let's not close our minds and imagine that all wargamers require scenery that looks like it has stepped out of the pages of *National Geographic*. Fantasy and science fiction gamers, for example, can give free rein to their imagination and adapt these techniques for more exotic landscapes. Creating a river flowing with molten lava or unspeakably revolting goo, for example, is largely a matter of exaggerating the texture of the watercourse itself and giving it an exotic paint job. Instead of subtle browns, blues and greens, it's time to splosh on vibrant reds and oranges and yellows, bursting from beneath a surface coat of black and greys for a volcanic outpouring, or slime greens and pus yellows for a putrid pit of poison. Let rip!

Ponds, lakes and marshes

Only a modicum of intelligence is required to figure out the fact that areas of standing water, such as ponds and lakes, can be created in precisely the same manner as rivers, except that instead of strips laid end-to-end, you will need to cut out a more or less irregular shape from your card, hardboard or MDF and build up the banks around it slightly before treating the central area and colouring it as above.

Something to think about before you launch into such a project is whether the water is still or moving, how deep it is and whether the banks are marshy or dry.

Still, but deep lakes are often found in mountainous areas, right up to Alpine 'col' lakes, high up in the peaks. Sometimes these are fed by waterfalls, which can make for a spectacular modelling project. The likelihood is, however, that you won't often play wargames set amongst such scenery unless you become interested in Napoleon crossing the Alps or the extraordinary, high-altitude battles fought between the Austrians and Italians in WWI.

Other still lakes (as well as man-made reservoirs) are found in rolling or flat countryside closer to sea level, and are usually shallower, with gently sloping banks. A variation on this is the large pond, which can often be found in boggy ground, even at high elevations such as the Scottish Highlands. Because of the peaty nature of the earth there, the banks are often nothing at all, and the transition from dry ground to wet catches out many a walker.

Then, of course, there are the large, tidal lakes such as Scottish lochs, where the banks may even take on the appearance of a beach at low tide and these substantial bodies of water, sometimes many miles across, can be extremely deep.

Besides these, there are any number of man-made ponds, ranging from the tiny back garden home for a few goldfish, up to abandoned quarries and reservoirs of various kinds. Near where I live in the South Downs of England, we also have 'dewponds', dug by herdsmen over centuries to collect rainwater and night dew for their flocks and herds.

Now, unless you have a particular scenario in mind that requires a huge swathe of your tabletop to be occupied with water features, then the fact is that a couple of pieces will probably stand you in good stead for the rest of your wargaming life. Therefore, I'd recommend perhaps three such items: a small one, representative of the typical village pond (you could even add a few ducks) or abbey pond, where the monks kept stocks of fresh fish; a small lake, such as might be found almost anywhere, sufficiently large to pose a serious obstacle so most troops will prefer to go round, unless they have boats; and an area of boggy, marshy ground which, whilst not necessarily deep, will again serve as difficult or impassable ground in many scenarios. In terms of size, assuming you are using 20-28mm miniatures, the pond could be perhaps 6" (150mm) square or thereabouts; I would make the lake more substantial, perhaps 18" (450mm) across

Caught in the badlands! A selection of home-made ponds and marshes of various sizes made by the author. These are all based on thin MDF and landscaped using the techniques described here. A visit to wargames shows and a keen eye when reading wargaming and model railway books provides plenty of inspiration – not to mention getting out and about to see the real thing!

or even a little larger if you have the table space; and the boggy ground maybe around 12" (300mm) in diameter. It would enhance your tabletop to perhaps make a few smaller pieces of marsh as well, to indicate an area with firm ground running between more dangerous footing, which can make for exciting games, especially Dark Age ones.

When colouring your watery scenes, remember the rule that the deeper the water, the darker the colour. To indicate gently shelving banks, start with quite a pale sandy colour (adapt this to the intended location – in the Alps, for example, the rock is pale limestone, but in other places it might be granite or sandstone or whatever the local rock is) and gradually apply darker shades until the central area is very dark indeed if more than a few feet deep. For the boggy areas, the water is often very peaty, and so a distinct brown colour should be evident. With a bit of practice, it's quite easy to blend one colour to the next using a small 1" (25mm) household decorating brush. As for the paint itself, you can use artists' acrylics or household emulsion. Be aware that these water-based paints can dry quite quickly, so you might want to invest in a tube of drying retardant from a decent art shop.

Particularly with boggy areas, you will want to add some reeds around the edge. You can use old paintbrush bristles for this, or unwound sisal string, or the kind of nylon hairs you find in washing-up brushes. The banks of all these pieces will be enlivened by the addition of a few small rocks and bits of gravel or coarse sand and perhaps a few small bushes, made from moss or model railway lichen. The only limit is your time and imagination.

If the lake has moving water, you might want to indicate a few small waves approaching the sides. These should be made using ready-mixed household filler applied with a brush and a stippling technique *before* painting the watery area. Once dry, apply the water effects and then lightly drybrush the wave crests with pure white. Don't overdo it!

As a final touch, on boggy areas and ponds in particular, sprinkle a small amount of scenic flock onto the last layer of varnish as it's drying to simulate duckweed and algae. Be careful to hold the flock in your fingers quite close to the surface as you do this, or it will spread too widely.

Trees

Just as with rivers and roads, there are a wide range of options available to the wargamer ranging from the expensive and commercial to the cheap, cheerful and home-made. One of the great bonuses for the wargamer is that the model railway community already has a huge industry churning out realistic trees and bushes by the million – no kidding! Wargames shops may be few and far between these days, but model railways are still available in high streets up and down the country and are a treasure trove for greenery of all kinds. You can even buy specific species of tree, and in several different sizes. In this day and age, of course, a few minutes spent Googling will reveal the most tremendous online catalogues of arboreal loveliness, ranging from the simple and inexpensive to the remarkably variety-specific and costly, and some of these are listed in the Appendices.

For the most part, as a wargamer, you'll probably content yourself with trees that look either evergreen (good for mountainous and tundra games) or deciduous (the standard type of tree seen in most European and American settings). Of course, if your wargaming tastes are more exotic, then you'll probably want tropical palms and, who knows, perhaps African Baobab trees.

If you've got the modelling bug and want to have a crack at making your own, a good place to start is your own garden or the local park and undertake a massive twig hunt. This is, it has to be said, most viable for larger miniatures of 20mm and upwards, since finding pieces appropriate for the micro-scales is more difficult and, in fact, not really required, as trees can be rendered more symbolically at those scales using just a trunk, rather than needing branches too.

Anyway, what you're looking for are twigs around 5-10mm thick at the 'trunk', with more slender branches coming off them. If you're standing under a tree looking for these, move yourself over to the shrubbery, where you're likely to have better luck. I seem to recall that various types of thorn hedge and privet bushes produce the most useful specimens, though of course you'll need to remove those nasty thorns!

An alternative to twigs is wire. That may sound odd, but what I mean is thin garden wire, which tends to come in bundles. To form the trunk and branches, first bend the lengths in half to form a bundle of loops, and grasp the open ends in one hand. Now, with the other hand, create three, five or seven (an odd number always looks best) little groups of loops at the other end, and twist them together. These are the 'branches'. Once accomplished, grasp the 'trunk' just below the branches and twist all the open ends together as tight as you can to form the trunk, leaving an inch

Commercial trees from Woodland Scenics (left) and Last Valley (right). The tree on the left is made from a plastic trunk and clump foliage; that on the right from natural twigs and rubberised horsehair.

or so at the open end. Now do as you did for the branches to form the roots, using the untwisted lengths at the open end.

With a bit more tweaking, you can quickly form quite an attractive skeletal tree. If you're really clever and have spread them sufficiently, you'll be able to balance the tree on your tabletop by its roots alone.

The next stage can be achieved in one of two ways. You can wrap the wires using masking tape before painting, or you can give the whole thing a good coat of ready-made filler and leave to dry. Once that's done, undercoat using a very dark brown, green or black, and then use drybrushing techniques to create a natural colour which, by the way, is much more often a greenish grey of some kind, rather than a child's colouring book brown.

If you've gone the twig route, the colour might already be spot on, but a coat of PVA or matt varnish wouldn't hurt to help preserve what is, after all, a perishable material. Twigs will also require some additional footing. This can be achieved by inserting some lengths of wire part-way into the branch to form roots as above, or you could use a circle of MDF and insert a thin screw from the underside up into the trunk. I wouldn't trust glue on its own, even hot glue or epoxy, but used in addition to the screw and wire, they can help disguise the join. You can also build up some filler around the base of the tree to blend it into the groundwork, as will also be done with the wire trees.

So far, so good. What about foliage? There are a huge number of commercially-available flocks and scatter materials available, and those made by Woodland Scenics, Realistic Modelling Services and others are ideal, particularly what is known as 'clump foliage'. You could use coloured sawdust or pet bedding (the finer hamster bedding is best) or even dried herbs, though I would advise you to only use an old, stale pot which has lost its fragrance lest your wargames room be forever perfumed!

Small commercial deciduous and conifer trees based by the author. The tendency is to use tiny trees like these for 6 or 10mm gaming, and larger ones for 20 or 28mm games, with 15mm games being decorated with something in between; but of course, in real life, trees come in many different sizes and so should they in our games.

Making a tree using garden wire. Stage 1 is to create a bundle of wire roughly 12" long, fold them in half and then, holding the looped ends, twist the central third or so of the length to form the trunk. The loose ends will create the roots.

Cut the looped end and twist the strands at either end to create roots and branches. I then stuck this onto a base made of thick card for ease of handling before applying a coat of thick-ish PVA adhesive and allowing everything to dry.

Now apply a coat of household filler, Milliput or – as I did – air-drying clay such as Das Pronto to completely cover the wire armature. This is messy and takes some patience! Once this has dried (it takes a few hours), give everything a dark undercoat.

Now finish painting the trunk and branches – bear in mind that real trees aren't just brown; greys and greens feature too. Then, using a clump of painted horsehair or other suitable material, add flock or foliage texture using plenty of PVA glue and voilà!

The first step is to take your wiry or twiggy trees and add some kind of bulk to the top, since it's extremely unlikely that you have been able to render every single branch and twig in your miniature version of the real thing. Nor would it be practical, since it would be impossibly delicate!

There are three materials that are easy to get hold of that will do the job. The first is rubberised horsehair, available from upholstery suppliers (or even your granny's old sofa). Tear off a piece, tease it out a little to loosen it, then glue onto the branches, making sure that they pass through it to hold it firmly. You can use water-based, spray or household adhesive for this, such as UHU or Bostik.

The next option does NOT take kindly to water-based paints: wire wool. Available from DIY stores and ironmongers, wire wool can be bought in several grades and in this instance, the medium or coarse grades are fine. Again, tease it into a rough ball shape, and stick to the branches.

And finally, you can use clumps of moss or model railway lichen, which can be adhered in the same way as horsehair.

Once dry, it is important to undercoat the foliage base, again using a dark green, brown or even black. For the wire wool, you must NOT use water-based paint for this or it will RUST! Use a car spray paint instead, which is oil-based, and make sure you do so in a well-ventilated area.

Finally, apply your foliage of choice after applying a spray adhesive to the bulk material underneath. Shake off the excess into a collection tray and *voilà*, you have a lovely tree.

When I was a little boy, I used to use pine cones sprayed green, but you never see that these days. Perhaps I'm getting old! Conifer trees can also be made using the 'bottle brush' technique by unravelling string and laying strands of increasing length between two pieces of wire. You then hold the ends of the wire with a pair of pliers and start twisting. This is, I warn you, fiddly and likely to lead to sudden expletives.

A simpler method is to use foam – the kind found in kitchen scrubbing pads or for cushions is ideal. Cut this to a rough conical shape, tease out a few irregular bits to create a slightly more natural shape, then stick a piece of dowelling or a piece of wire (with roots as described above) up the middle for a trunk. Undercoat the whole lot, and then when dry, apply scatter material as for the deciduous trees, but using a darker green.

By now, you may already have decided that making your own is just too much trouble and have left me to ramble on while you popped off to your local model shop and returned with an armful of oaks and elms, pines and spruces. Be that as it may, we're still not quite finished, because there's the small matter of making your trees stand up and arranging them in a fashion that is wargame-friendly.

My advice is to have some trees which are singles, and others that are mounted together on bases to form copses and woods.

The singles are easy. Home-made ones can be attached to bases as already described. I'd make the base somewhat irregular in shape, rather than exactly square or circular. Commercial trees often have a plastic trunk and roots, and these can be stuck down using a hot glue gun, or epoxy or household glue. Once the attachment is firm enough, usually after 24 hours, you can apply some filler to blend the join and then apply scenic effects to match your preferred style, ranging from a very simple coat of paint and perhaps a scattering of flock to match your tabletop, or with simulated fallen branches, perhaps a puddle or two, some wild flowers... It's up to you.

Wargamers normally create woods and copses by mounting several trees onto a scenic base. This can be as large or small as you like, but I wouldn't make it bigger than around 12" (300mm) square, if for no other reason than ease of storage. If you need an extensively wooded area in a game, then it's better to combine several such pieces, together with your supply of single trees.

Unlike model railway enthusiasts, who are seeking to create a miniature facsimile of the original, wargamers have to bear in mind the practicality of placing troops on their battlefield. This means that a decent gap needs to be left between your trees to allow you to manoeuvre troops between them. What we tend to say, therefore, is that the outline of the wooded base denotes the full extent of the wood, and the model trees placed therein are representative of what would, in reality, be perhaps an almost impenetrably bosky region. So, rather than feeling the need to cram your square foot of real estate with a rather expensive assemblage of foliage, it will do just fine to randomly attach half a dozen or so (again, odd numbers actually look best), add a bit of scenic artistry between and around them, and that's that. I have seen some marvellous work by wargamers and I'm sure the photographs accompanying this section will give you a good idea of what can be achieved.

A simple arrangement of trees on a base made from thick packing card, which is then decorated. The outline of the base indicates the extent of the wooded area and troops moving across it have their movement reduced.

Coniferous woods made by mounting trees on old CDs. It is important to coat the discs with a thick coat of PVA which acts as a primer for all the painting and scenic effects. Here, various types of scatter material, static grass and 'tufts' have been used to create the illusion of woodland. Note that each base contains several trees of varying heights, essential if you want to avoid the 'plantation' look.

You can also create woods for wargames by simply placing individual trees together. If you have trouble moving your troops through the wood, you can simply move the trees to one side. However, beware of the 'Burnham Wood' effect where entire forests can seem to creep across the wargames table!

Another quirky but popular method of creating smaller copses is to use old CDs as bases. It's no bad thing to use your wargames as a clever way of recycling the sort of stuff that would normally go in the bin, and CDs and DVDs are a landfill nightmare, so why not give it a go? You can see some I created myself here, and I hope that you'll agree that with the right degree of landscaping, they are pretty effective, and even the distinct circular shape isn't too troublesome. Of course, even that could be disguised somewhat by 'nibbling' the edge with pliers.

Of course, the base of your wood doesn't have to be flat, and can be built up using the techniques for creating free-standing hills we will be looking at shortly. This can be very effective for fantasy or Dark Age games to create the impression of ancient barrows and burial mounds as can be found right across the British Isles, for example.

Another neat trick I first saw in the Games Workshop, *How to Make Wargames Terrain* (which, incidentally, I recommend to you thoroughly and unreservedly) is to create a wood in two parts: an outer periphery, together with a central area which can actually be lifted out to accommodate troops! This marvellous idea is called a 'doughnut' wood, and is something I've been wanting to try for some time. This notion of being able to remove bits so that models can fit inside is something we shall see again later.

Bushes and hedges

Hedges are, of course, more or less a neat line of bushes that have grown together, so the materials used for both are more or less the same, and your first port of call really has to be the lichen beloved of model railway modellers.

Lichen is amazing stuff. *Wikipedia* tells us, "Lichens are composite organisms consisting of a symbiotic association of a fungus (the mycobiont) with a photosynthetic partner (the photobiont or phycobiont), usually either a green alga (commonly Trebouxia) or cyanobacterium (commonly Nostoc)". Gosh! And there was me thinking it was just miniature shrubbery. Leaving the science aside for one moment, the fact is that lichen is ubiquitous for the wargamer. It comes in all sorts of colours and shades, so you can pick precisely the right tone for Normandy bocage or Wild West tumbleweed. Available in packs both large and small, you can create an entire enclosed field system or just add a few tiny bits to the bases of your miniatures to achieve a highly realistic ground effect, along with sand, gravel and scenic flock, as you will see later.

For individual bushes and shrubs, there's really no simpler way than to take a thumb-sized lump of lichen and drop it onto the tabletop. If you're more tidy-minded than that, then of course you can fix some to a base that you have already landscaped, either as single pieces or covering enough area to indicate a larger area of shrubs and bushes.

Lichen also takes paint well, and drybrushing can be particularly effective. Medium-sized pieces of green lichen can be given a touch of

yellow to indicate gorse; if you pluck small pieces of a dark green or brown lichen, dot it around your landscaping in clumps and drybrush with purple or pink to indicate heather. If your setting is more modern, such as a townscape, neat little rows of lichen can be dotted with reds, whites, oranges and yellows to indicate bedding plants.

Lichen can also make good hedges, especially if fixed to a base of card or thin MDF. Treat the base first, including chamfering the edges to help it blend into the battlefield, to make it match your ground colour, then stick pieces of lichen along its length. Use varying sizes for wilder, countryside hedges, or similar sizes for a tended town hedge. You could even do a bit of miniature topiary!

A good idea I picked up from wargamer Adam Williams is to create 'bocage' type hedges by attaching lichen – and the occasional tree – to half-round wooden beading. This creates a nice raised bank effect and also provides a good anchoring point for the trunks of miniature trees by drilling into it. I recommend making such hedgerows in lengths of around 6" (150mm), both for ease of storage and flexibility of layout.

Extra realism can be achieved with either bushes or hedges by applying the 'clumped foliage' scatter material we have seen previously. A dip in dilute PVA adhesive, or a quick spray, followed by a dunk in a tub of the stuff works well, then just tap off any excess once dry.

It has to be said that lichen is pretty cheap stuff, but for the really budget-conscious, a trip into your own garden pays dividends. Whilst wild lichen normally grows in extreme locations, such as on mountain rocks and in arctic tundra, you may strike lucky, but you're more likely to find moss. The warning here is that moss is famously water-absorbent, and so will need to be thoroughly dried before use, after which you can apply paint effects as required. You can also buy moss in garden centres –

The hedgerow at the top is again based on a cheap pan scourer, but this time with flock applied using PVA adhesive to create a summery, leafy look. In addition, a couple of sprigs of Woodland Scenics 'Fine Leaf Foliage' have been inserted – real hedges often have trees and shrubs growing in them. The bottom 'bocage' hedge was made using half-inch half-round beading painted brown, with clumps of lichen stuck to it before flocking.

it's used for lining hanging baskets and the like.

A final tip comes with a story, which I suspect to be apocryphal, but who knows?

Kitchen pan scouring pads. Interestingly, they almost always tend to be green, and the story goes that when Woolworths (or whoever it may have been) came up with the idea, they had to decide what colour to make them, and some bright spark in the design department happened to be a wargamer and instantly suggested green, because he already saw their potential for wargames scenery!

These pads are usually roughly ¼"-½" (5-10mm) thick, and can be easily cut with sharp scissors or a Stanley knife. What could be simpler, then, than to cut strips off the pad to the height you require, and pop them on the wargames table? Since they are very light, they are prone to falling over, so fixing to a base is a good idea. Again, I would recommend perhaps a lick of paint and perhaps a sprinkling of scatter material to make them look more natural, but they are a simple and highly effective scenic item for wargamers on a budget.

As you would expect by now, hedges can be found in all shapes and sizes, courtesy of the wargames scenery and model railway industries. Available either in long pieces, or already cut to a standard length, they tend to be reasonably priced and again are an investment that I myself have made, being long on ambition but short on time.

Just a final suggestion here is to add some bushes to your woodland bases. Most woods and forests have some kind of undergrowth, particularly where there are open glades or where trees have fallen, or around the periphery where more light gets in, and whilst we don't want to overly impede our miniature men, a few clumps here and there can result in a highly pleasing appearance.

Walls and fences

As soon as you approach human habitation, you find people trying either to keep things in, or keep them out. The shepherd wants to keep his flock safe inside the pen, and keep the nasty wolves away. Or the problem may be neighbours; just as it is with suburban gardens, so is it also writ large with landowners jealously guarding the boundaries of their estates. And at the extreme, we have examples such as Hadrian's Wall and the Great Wall of China.

A less obtrusive form of obstacle is the fence, ranging from a few strands of wire strung between uprights to the mighty rail fences so beloved in America, which formed fearsome barriers to progress in the War of Independence and the Civil War.

There are a number of simple ways to make walls either quickly, cheaply, or both.

Method 1 is to cut lengths of strip timber (usually pine) to the right length, sand the faces and corners slightly (this helps your paint to adhere as well as taking off the obvious machined corners) and paint an appropriate colour. A coat of thinned PVA may help paint adhesion, especially if there are any knots in the wood. Depending on the scale of miniatures you are using, simply choose the timber size accordingly. A quick look at a local builders' merchant website shows widths of stripwood as narrow as 21mm (around ¾") by 9mm (about ⁵/₁₆"). It tends to come in lengths of around 2.4m (nearly eight feet), so a single piece will give you enough for sixteen lengths of 150mm (6"), though I would recommend that you make some shorter lengths as well to allow for field entrances, gates and so on. For stability, mount the pieces on bases of card or thin MDF if you wish.

To make your wooden walls more realistic, you can add scored or drawn lines to imitate brickwork (paint the wall in an appropriate dark

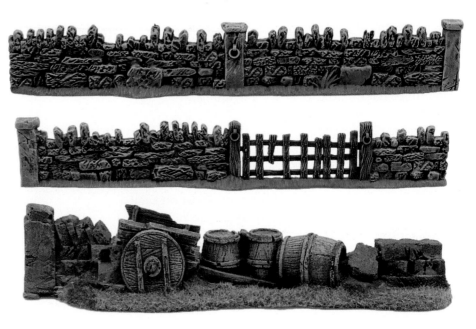

Walls. These are all produced by CItadel/Games Workshop, the top two being later versions which are now produced in unpainted grey plastic. They are quite fun to paint, simply using a black undercoat followed by successively lighter greys and green for the base. The bottom wall with added impedimenta came pre-painted. Both types are pieces from sets containing additional sections.

red or shade of brown first), or stonework (paint the wall a shade of grey or, for Cotswold limestone, buff). All such walls will benefit from a few splodges of green to represent mosses and lichens, or the addition of some small patches of PVA glue with some scatter material applied.

In hotter, southern European climates, walls are often constructed like the buildings, with brick or stonework beneath a coat of limewash or plaster. This is most easily simulated with pre-mixed household filler, or paint with some fine sand mixed in, brushed over the wood. Before it dries, scrape off a few areas at the corners or along the bottom to simulate the plaster having worn away or fallen off. When the filler has dried, give it a coat of very pale grey or buff, then drybrush the raised areas white, before then painting and patterning the scraped-back areas to simulate the underlying brick- or stonework.

Method 2 makes use of air-dried clay of the kind you find in hobby shops and art suppliers. In my youth, it went under the brand name of Das Pronto, which is still available, but there are other brands available too.

The first variation is to make lengths of wall to the size you need them, scoring or patterning the surface as required before allowing them to dry. One of the great benefits of this material is, of course, that you can make curved wall sections as well as straight ones, and also do some more decorative work to simulate field entrances, gateposts, fancy walling techniques and so on. Ensure that they are placed on a completely flat surface when left to dry. Once dry, I'd recommend a coat of thinned PVA before painting.

The second variation – for the truly obsessed – is to make hundreds of tiny little bricks and then become a miniature bricklayer. Oh yes, truly, I have seen it done. Do I recommend it? Not really!

Method 3 takes you to your local aquarium centre or builders' merchant

The top wall has been in the author's possession since the very early 1970s. Such vac-formed Bellona relics are now highly collectible. The centre wall uses the 'glued grit' method described here, and the third is made from a simple piece of stripwood, mounted on a base and coated with sand and PVA before painting.

in search of grit or gravel, which you can buy in large bags (and in aquarium shops, you can even choose the colour). You need a grade which is an average of perhaps 3-6mm in diameter (around ¼"). An alternative is cat litter – I'd recommend the silicone crystal version because the clay type may disintegrate if wet adhesive is applied.

You will need to ensure that the surface you work on is either plastic or well sealed in some other way, because what you now do is literally build your wall sections from the bottom up, using plenty of PVA adhesive or household glue, such as UHU or Bostik. For this reason, I'd recommend basing your walls on either card or thin wood. You'll need to be very patient with this method, because you'll only be able to lay a couple of courses each session, so a production line method is best. With luck, by the time you've finished laying the first stones on strip number 24, the glue on strip number 1 will be set!

Even though, when finished, these walls will be 'stone' coloured, they will still benefit from a coat of paint to remove the natural shine of the gravel. You can either undercoat, paint and then drybrush, or paint them an overall stone colour followed by a thin wash to bring out the relief.

Method 4 makes use of that old wargaming staple: polystyrene or, if you can get it, the specialist pink or blue modelling foam that we have mentioned before. Easily cut to the length, height and thickness required, you can use it in combination with the methods described above to create highly realistic walls. You can also sculpt it with a sharp scalpel to indicate stonework, cracks, rubble or masonry. With care, it can even be bent into curves. The trick here is to score the inner face with 'V'-shaped cuts from top to bottom – removing material this way allows the foam to curve more easily without compression bulges. Once set to shape, a good coat of PVA and filler disguises everything.

I have seen methods 1 and 3 combined quite effectively. Take your pieces of thin stripwood, coat the sides with PVA adhesive and then coat them with a layer of gravel. Once dry, a thinned coat of filler, followed by your preferred painting method, can produce an excellent result.

A final tip: many walls in town settings or around grand houses have 'capstones' or tiles along the top. These can be recreated with pieces of thin card or plastic (a use for old credit or reward cards!) stuck along the top before texture is applied to the sides. In hotter climates, the classic, curved terracotta tiles can be simulated using corrugated cardboard, or box card with the top layer peeled off.

As with all these scenic hints and tips, the commercial alternative always exists. You will find walls aplenty in specialist wargames shops, at wargames shows, in model railway stores and even in your local High Street Games Workshop, as well as on eBay and countless other online stores. Walls commonly come cast in resin or plaster of some kind; the resin types benefit from a wash in lukewarm water with some washing up liquid to remove mould release agent.

Fences are next on the list of consideration, and of course represent a

Both these fencing lengths come from the same Games Workshop set as the walls seen previously. The top one is interesting because it reminds us that fences have to conform to whatever pre-existing vegetation there might be, such as a tree. The lower fence includes a section of wattling, a very traditional method. Again, simple dry-brushing techniques have been used to paint these.

potentially more daunting prospect for the cack-handed. For this reason, I'd recommend making the commercial variety your first port of call, but here are some ideas for those doughty souls willing to give it a go.

You need to start all fencing with a base of the appropriate length. For classic two- or three-bar fencing, you will need either $^1/_{16}$" balsa wood or the ice lolly sticks you can buy in packs – or raid your local Costa or Starbucks for stirrers! In addition, you'll want some ¼" square softwood or balsa for the uprights. You could try using card for the bars, but you'll definitely need wooden uprights.

Now, you need to decide how far apart your uprights will be (use one of your miniatures alongside the fence length to judge what looks right – the answer will probably be three or four inches (75-100mm) for 28mm miniatures), and mark on your base where they will sit. Then you need to cut your uprights to length, lie them down alongside your base, and mark on them where the crossbars will go. Your crossbars will want to be no more than about 5mm wide (the stirrers or lollipop sticks come around this size) and the simplest method is to cut them to the length of your base, so that their ends will protrude slightly beyond the outside uprights. If you're really clever, you can do the maths and work out the post distances to create a 'seamless' look to a long length of fence.

Once you've done this, apply adhesive (white PVA wood glue is best) and create your fencing lying flat on your work surface. I would recommend pinning the bars in place until the glue dries, before then removing the pins and giving the whole lot a quick coat of thinned PVA to seal it before painting.

After this is done, place the fence upright in position on the base and glue in position. You should use household glue or even a hot glue gun for this to create a strong bond. One option is to use foam board (sometimes called 'sandwich' board) for your bases, which is about 3-5mm thick. You can cut into this with a scalpel to create hollows to take the uprights, so that they are fixed more securely. I would also recommend chamfering the edges to disguise them, and applying a coat of thinned household filler and some scatter material to disguise the joins.

For the advanced modeller, some barred fences have the horizontal bars passing through the uprights, rather than just nailed to them. Achieving this is tricky, but possible, by cutting vertical slots into the uprights with a scalpel. Work with care, so that you don't split the upright, then cut the parallel bars to length and insert and glue the ends into the uprights.

You only have to walk around your local area to see many other types of fencing, such as plain, upright planks (which have a horizontal batten across the back of them, top and bottom); slightly overlapping clapboard (which also need horizontal reinforcement); panel fencing (a modern type, not really used before the 20th century); and, if you live in the country, wattle fencing (long, thin branches or 'withies', laced in and out between uprights). All these can be achieved with the materials discussed already, such as card, balsa wood, coffee stirrers and so on. For the withy fencing, you could use wire, or the bristles from an old broom, or even the thin bamboo found in Chinese place mats.

If you live in the USA, you will be used to another type of fence, the split-log 'snake' rail fence which was such a characteristic obstacle for troops both during the War of Independence and, nearly a century later, the American Civil War. Its zig-zag line across the landscape is such an iconic sight, but many have tried and failed to make an effective miniature representation of it.

The best attempt I have ever seen is by Paul Davies, who writes for *Wargames Illustrated* magazine. His method, which makes use of cocktail sticks or wooden barbeque skewers, depending on the scale you are

Paul Davies' very effective snake rail fencing, as described in the text, with 15mm British Light Dragoons rushing off to quell the rebellion. Photo courtesy of Paul Davies.

More snake rail fencing in abundance on the wargames table of retired Major General John Drewienkiewicz, this time forming part of the backdrop to a huge 15mm Brandy Station game using a modified version of *Fire & Fury*. Note also the lovingly modelled *demolished* fence sections – apparently the real things can be shoved over by horses quite easily.

working to, can be found beautifully illustrated in a PDF download from the magazine's website – see *tinyurl.com/6kskyt9*.

The method is not for the faint-hearted or impatient, but as long as you follow the instructions carfeully, the result is simply wonderful.

I have to close this section with another web address, this time for Renedra Ltd, who make a splendid selection of fences for 28mm wargamers, including snake (they call it 'worm') fencing, picket fences and more besides: see *renedra.co.uk/webstore.html*.

Hills

Let's leave the small stuff of scenery for one moment to tackle the big stuff, the major lumps and bumps in the ground that provide height, cover and impede movement – hills.

As we have seen, in the old days, we used to make undulating terrain using *papier maché*, plaster bandage and other equally messy and arcane methods, but thinking and techniques have changed over the years, so let's apply a little thought here.

Let's look at this more closely, and how we can actually make our contoured hills.

It is perfectly possible to create individual, shaped hills consisting of more than one contour, apply scenic effects and then place them on the tabletop to represent high ground. However, to maximise flexibility, and increase the number of battlefield permutations for our games, we tend to make individual, separate contours which can then be stacked one upon another, from large to small, to create an infinite number of variations. This allows us to vary not only the height, but also the steepness of slope, by moving the edge of one contour closer to or further away from the edge of its partner beneath.

Unless a slope is so steep as to be only passable to specially-trained mountain troops, there should always be sufficient space between the contours for at least a base of infantry to stand.

There are any number of materials you can use, and over the years, I've tried most of them. Various thicknesses of sheet wood are easily obtainable from builders' merchants, including cheap off-cuts from larger sheets which can often be picked up for a few pence. I know some gamers who find old pieces in skips (known as dumpsters to our American readers) where houses are being demolished or renovated, which are totally free.

For ease of use, I would recommend MDF and chipboard, both of which cut easily with an electric jigsaw (wear a mask when cutting MDF, which releases tiny particles). Both these take paint well, and are heavy enough to 'sit' well on the table.

As an alternative, the various types of either expanded polystyrene or high density foam work well too, though the expanded polystyrene tends to crumble and deposit a fine layer of bits everywhere, which annoyingly also carry a static charge, so they stick to everything!

Cut out a variety of irregular shapes, ranging from two or three quite large base pieces, perhaps 24" (60cm) across, to much smaller ones of perhaps only 4" (100mm). Make some round, some long and thin, some curved, and so on. The idea, as mentioned above, is to permit as many permutations as possible.

Now you can choose to either leave these shapes cliff-sided, which may look strange but will allow you to use the contours you have created *either way up*, thus effectively doubling your output; or you can chamfer the edge to create a slope of around 45°, which looks more naturalistic, but of course then means that you can't use the piece upside-down.

If you decide to add the slope, you need to use appropriate tools. For polystyrene or the foam, you can use a sharp hobby knife or hot wire cutter, before smoothing with some fine sandpaper. For the MDF or chipboard, it's a tougher proposition, but is possible with careful use of the electric jigsaw, a variety of wood files and some sandpaper. Take your time.

Now you have your contour shapes, the first option is to proceed straight to painting. As always, I'd recommend sealing the surface with a coat of thinned PVA, before then undercoating with a dark colour (black or dark brown) and a top coat of mid green. As previously, by all means go to town adding some groundwork effects, either with textured paint, or with patches of adhesive and scatter material to create a grass effect. Of course, if desert warfare is your thing, you could add fine sand to some appropriately sand-coloured paint and then apply. With the polystyrene and foam, you can also add some indentations with your thumb or fingertips to look like shell holes, small ponds, or even small streams or wadis which can then be treated as previously described. On the whole, though, unless you have plentry of storage space where these items can

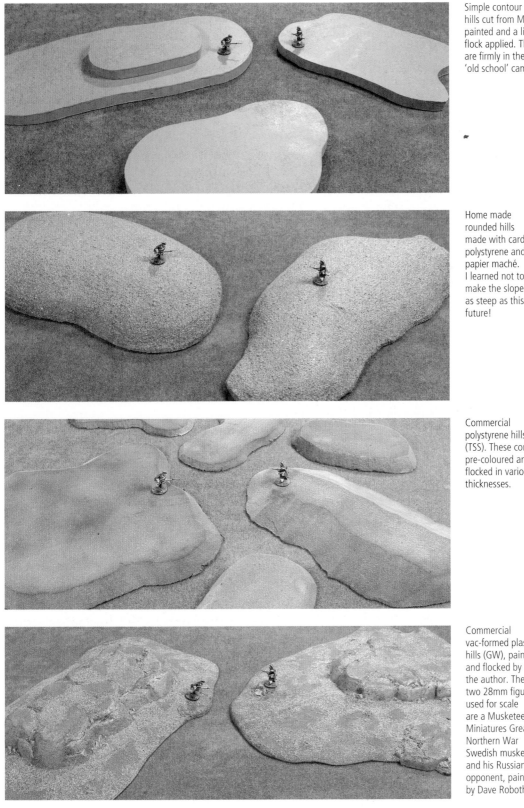

Simple contour hills cut from MDF, painted and a little flock applied. These are firmly in the 'old school' camp.

Home made rounded hills made with card, polystyrene and papier maché. I learned not to make the slopes as steep as this in future!

Commercial polystyrene hills (TSS). These come pre-coloured and flocked in various thicknesses.

Commercial vac-formed plastic hills (GW), painted and flocked by the author. The two 28mm figures used for scale are a Musketeer Miniatures Great Northern War Swedish musketeer and his Russian opponent, painted by Dave Robotham.

be kept without bashing against one another, I would keep things simple.

Bear in mind that the objective is to get your hills to match your groundwork as closely as possible, or they will look somewhat odd perched on top of terrain which doesn't resemble them in the slightest!

Obviously, once this is all dry, you can turn the slab-sided version of contour over and decorate the other side as well.

Another highly effective technique for the shaped contours I was shown by veteran wargamer Phil Olley is to cover the finished shape with pieces cut out from the gaming mats we discussed at the start of this chapter. It's easier to do with the cloth-backed type, as sold by Games Workshop, as this will stretch to the shape you are covering and permit you to poke it into any recesses, which is not quite so easy with paper-backed gaming mats, but not impossible – try soaking the paper in a thickish dilution of PVA, or even heavy-duty wallpaper paste first, so that it becomes pliable.

Phil goes back over the applied cloth and cuts some pieces away, applying highly realistic ground, rock, boulder and water effects to achieve a stunning result.

In my experience, you can never have too many hills. Once you've got plenty for the centre of the table, consider making some that have a straight side, suitable for putting right at the edge of the table, or even two straight edges for a corner. Games Workshop do, in fact, make a vac-formed plastic hill which comes in two halves, and therefore with two straight edges, so you can have a pair of half-hills entering from the side of your table, or clip them together to form a long ridge. Very useful. And then there are cliff edges leading down to a beach or scree-strewn slope below, giant columns of rock as seen in Arizona, and so on... The list is truly endless.

And don't forget that this technique of creating hills from layers is also the key to making spectacular man-made structures like pyramids and zigurrats. There should be no boundaries to the imagination.

The foam and polystyrene offer the most options for unusual hill and mountain projects, because they can be cut, sanded, shaved, plucked and even melted into the most amazing shapes and lifelike structures. Over the years, one also has accidental discoveries, such as the lunar-landscape effects of using oil-based paints or solvent-based adhesives on polystyrene. A very useful tool is a heated screwdriver, soldering iron or pyrogravure, but take extreme care with these flammable materials!

It goes without saying – but I'll say it anyway – that you can buy ready-made hills. I've already mentioned Games Workshop, but another popular supplier is Total System Scenic who make a wide range of hills in all sorts of shapes and sizes to accompany their isomorphic terrain square system. Kallistra also make hills to go with their Hexon hexagonal terrain system, including rocky crags. A quick hunt on eBay and other online stores will turn up a host of independent scenery makers who sell slopes of all heights and inclines, from the inexpensive to the pricey.

Bridges

There are so many other items with which you can adorn your wargames table, but for the purposes of this book, I'm only going to cover two more: bridges and houses. Let's talk first about river crossings.

As seen earlier, when making river sections, you can add material to the river bed to create the appearance of a ford or shallow water where people and animals can step or wade across in relative safety, but obviously the desired way of crossing a watercourse is via a bridge. Over the course of human history, there have been countless methods of making bridges, right up to the modern suspension and cantilevered structures beloved of award-winning architects, but I'm going to cover just a couple of historical examples of the kind you might expect to encounter pretty much anywhere in the civilised world and which, therefore, armies would need to deal with in the course of an action.

The first is a simple wooden, plank bridge of the kind known to ancient writers, and crossed by countless hoplites, legionaries, knights, men-at-arms, musketeers, pikemen and their ilk since time immemorial.

You need a strip of card – make it the same width as a base of infantry, or wider if you're going to allow cavalry to pass over it too – and it needs to be at least three times the width of your river or stream sections, so roughly 12" (30cm) wide for one of our rivers. Now, score it from side to side at around the 4" (10cm) and 8" (20cm) marks, and bend it slightly.

Now what you need are some rough planks cut from either balsa wood or thin card, which you glue perpendicular to the first piece of card, all along its length, but making sure that your bends aren't covered, so I find it useful to start with two pieces either side of the two bends.

Finally, you need to create the four uprights that will actually support the bridge above the river bed by way of crosspieces running beneath the bridge between them which give support. You can use balsa or ¼" square

A wooden plank bridge created using the techniques described above. The miniatures are 28mm Russian Heavy Weapons from The Plastic Soldier Company.

stripwood for this. If you're really keen, you can use twine or thick cotton to add the rope lashings, or bits of whittled matchstick as dowel pegs driven in to join the supports to the crosspieces.

Seal with PVA and then Robert is, as they say, your mother's brother.

By adding more central sections, you can create a bridge to cross a wider river; leave off one end section, and you have a jetty on a lake or out to sea.

A stone bridge may appear to be a trickier undertaking, but in fact it doesn't have to be. In essence, we're talking about two sides plus a road surface. To keep it simple, take your time drawing one side of the bridge onto thick card or 5mm foamboard, and cut it out with a sharp scalpel. You can then trace around this to create the shape for the other side or even, if you have some skill, tack it down with a bit of Blu-Tak or double-sided tape and simply cut around it.

One of the critical measurements is the width of the arch. If you want your bridge to be a stand-alone piece, the arch must be wide and high enough to pass over the banks of your river sections. An alternative is to make the bridge *part of* one of your lengths of waterway. You do this by creating a river section which is a cross shape, of which two arms will be the river and the other two, road. These parts should extend out from the riverbank far enough to accommodate the full length of the bridge, plus a little extra.

Having defined your arch shape, you need to sketch the arc of the road surface above this on the inner surfaces of your bridge, making sure they match on both sides.

For the road surface itself, use either reasonably thick card or, again, 5mm foamboard, and score parallel lines at intervals of 5-10mm across its length, to permit bending, and then attach to the arc described on the inside of the bridge sides. Two tips here: use an adhesive which dries

Valeri Ulanen (old 30mm Spencer Smith plastics converted from hussars for the author's fictitious campaigns) cross a stone bridge made by the author using foamboard and card. Is that the famous Baron von Münchhausen on his half-horse looking on? (It is – this stunningly rendered Eureka Miniature was painted and based by New Zealand gamer Kerry Thomas.)

A more elaborate commercial bridge, cast in resin and then painted by the author. This bridge is produced by Hovels. The smaller bridge behind is of unknown manufacture. The game in progress here was a huge 'imagi-nations' game played at East Ayton in 2011, and shows troops of Andy McMaster's 'Savage Swans' in the foreground and Iain Burt's Gateway Alliance behind.

quickly, but not instantly, as you may need to reposition slightly as you go; and you can use long, dressmaker's pins inserted from the outside to keep the road in place while it dries. Another tip is to make the road surface longer than the bridge itself so that it can be blended into the baseboard at either end, or trimmed back as required. You can always trim off excess – you can't add insufficient length back in.

Once dry, the road surface and sides can all be textured and painted as before, and if you have made it as part of a river section, of course the whole thing can be convincingly blended together as one.

You can attempt bridging projects as elaborate as you like. I have come back from many holidays in Italy, for example, brimful of ideas for monumental, multi-arch miniature bridges, but the fact is, not only would they rarely see action, but where on earth would I keep them? Besides, there is again the fact that several manufacturers, such as Hovels, make lovely bridges in resin that take paint nicely and will serve very well.

Buildings

Our last stop in this scenic extravaganza brings us to human habitation, be it the humble hovel or the lord's manor house, the village church or the city cathedral, the haybarn or the back garden privy. They are important because, in game after game, they form the very objective for which you are fighting, be it a tiny hamlet or a fortified town.

There are two approaches to miniature architecture: the representative and the functional. On the one hand, we want our little houses to look like real ones, but they also have a function in our games, in that at some point, they are likely to be occupied by our miniature soldiery and will be attacked and defended. Nor are their aesthetics unimportant, since many gamers find that they are able to express some aspect of their personality through the way their buildings look, and they are a powerful way of communicating a sense of place in a wargame. It would not do, for example, to have an edifice resembling the Taj Mahal in the middle of a Waterloo refight; nor would an ancient Greek temple sit well in a game set during the Falklands War. On the other hand, such odd juxtapositions might look terrific in a fantasy or sci-fi scenario.

Step one, then, in your journey into miniature architecture, is inextricably linked with the decisions you will be making about choosing a period for your wargames armies. Clearly, if you are drawn to Dark Age or Medieval warfare, that will very much dictate the style of architecture you will need to represent on the table, and you'd better get practising with wattle and daub and timber structures! However, British medieval architecture, whilst obviously having many similarities, is not the same as Swiss or Italian medieval architecture. A postcard sent from Chipping Norton in the Cotswolds, for example, shows a scene strikingly different from Zurich or Florence, though the buildings may date from precisely the same year. One of the skills wargamers develop is decorating their tabletop with items that can create a real sense of place with just a few items, whilst much of the rest of the scenery can be pretty generic.

The rules in this book focus primarily on the horse and musket era of central Europe, from around 1685 to 1815, which covers what we have come to know as the Baroque and Georgian periods.

The Baroque was awash with intellectual and artistic cleverness, which basically means lots of twiddly bits, such as floral decoration, *putti*[1] and those magnificent trophies of arms found carved above grand entrances, town gates and even painted on interior walls using *trompe l'oueil*[2] techniques. The clothing of the period was very flouncy, with wide hats, huge wigs, lots of lace, big cuffs and coat tails. The word 'decadent' comes to mind.

The Georgian period, however, was a reaction against this, a return to intellectual and architectural purity, inspired by the ancient Greeks. Architecture became simpler and more solid, based on the triangle and the column extolled by the Venetian Andrea Palladio two centuries earlier. Entire elegant terraces of such houses survive in places like Brighton & Hove, Bath, Edinburgh and London, as well as in cities like Boston on the Eastern seaboard of America. In terms of fashion, coat tails gradually became shorter, wigs and hats got smaller (and lost a corner, as the tricorne was replaced by the bicorne); but by the time of the Napoleonic period, the gaudiness began to increase again, particularly with the influence of the Hussar, which added lace aplenty to military jackets.

These changes were not universal, however, and many places in central Europe went about their business as they had always done, building in the

---

1   *Putti are those little plump cherubs that adorn countless stately homes in England built during the time of Queen Anne and the Duke of Marlborough, both in paintings and sculptures.*

2   *"Fools the eye", a method of painting a flat surface to create a three-dimensional effect, extremely popular in stately homes of the Baroque period such as Blenheim Palace.*

Very simple and neat houses seen in a classic *Little Wars* game staged by the Continental Wars Society at Salute using 42mm Shiny Toy Soldiers designed by Aly Morrison. The walls have been covered with brick-pattern paper, the roofs with tile paper. The patterned rug is optional!

A five-bastion fortress behind its *glacis* (the grassy slope shielding the foot of the walls and concealing a wide ditch). This Starfort Models example is manned by 15mm Essex Miniatures; the houses inside are from Hovels and the backdrop was created on the author's Mac and printed onto paper.

Dusk falls over a little Flemish town in May 1940 as the brave Belgians muster to face the onrushing Germans. This beautiful 15mm game, complete with working street lights, was created by members of the Crawley Wargames Club and seen 'on tour' around the shows in 2012. It must surely rank as one of the most delightful – indeed, magical – demonstration game scenes ever created.

same, traditional ways that had been handed down from father to son for many generations. And whilst stone and brick were the favoured building materials in Europe, the Americas, with their vast forests, emulated European architecture with wood frames and clapboard. In hotter places, such as the Indian subcontinent, most of Africa and the Middle East, mud brick was still the traditional medium, together with various forms of wickerwork.

I can't possibly cover every theatre and period here. My advice is simply to read as much as you possibly can, use online resources and take lots of photos if you take a holiday anywhere that the military history interests you. For example, I'm interested in the Peninsular War, so every snap taken in Spain or Portugal is a potential piece of reference material.

To keep things simple, let's assume, for the moment, that you'll be trying the rules in this book, and therefore require some buildings that have the right look for north/central Europe at any time between about 1740 and 1765, covering the Wars of the Austrian Succession and the Seven Years War.

The fighting took place across a broad swathe of the Continent, stretching from what is now Holland and Belgium, northern France, across Germany, Poland, and down into Austria and what is now the Czech and Slovak Republics. There was even fighting in Italy, quite apart from what happened in the Americas, India and beyond. This gives you plenty of scope to try out your skills in due course!

If you're not fussed about having buildings that aspire to realism, then it's perfectly possible to simply cut blocks from a piece of timber, then cut again at an angle to form the roof lines before giving them a coat of paint and drawing on details such as doors and windows. You can add chimneys and balconies using pieces of balsa wood or scrap card. For games with micro-scale miniatures such as 6mm or even 3mm, many gamers find this

A hamlet of really simple block buildings made from pine strip, with thin card roofs, balsa chimneys and all detail simply painted or drawn on. These examples are suitable for 6mm or 10mm gaming. Top tip: give everything a coat of diluted PVA white glue before painting because it seals in any wood resin.

approach perfectly adequate. However, most gamers eventually aspire to achieve something more than the purely representational, so let's look at how we achieve this.

Our basic building materials for miniature buildings start with card. As a boy, I began with cereal packet and other packaging card, though this can be prone to warping quite badly, because one side is sealed with printing inks and even varnishes, and the other (grey or white) side is highly absorbent. It is therefore advisable to wet the card first and then dry it whilst either stretching it using masking tape around the edges, or under pressure, such as a pile of books. It can then be worked on with less risk of warping.

A good artists' suppliers or stationers should stock a bewildering array of card of various kinds. Mounting board is a good choice, since it is a couple of millimetres thick and less likely to distort. You can buy this in either white or black, and sometimes in a range of browns too. A couple of big sheets (they usually come in A1 size (841mm x 594mm, that's a little over 33" x 23") will be more than enough to get started.

Another board material that is extremely popular these days is foamboard. It comes around 5mm thick (good suppliers have a range of thicknesses) and consists of a 'sandwich' of polystyrene between two sheets of card. The great thing here is that it is light, strong and does not warp, but can be glued using the same household or PVA wood glues applicable to normal card.

Of course, I used to make all my buidlings from balsa wood, and occasionally still do. Much loved by the model aircraft and boat communities, it is widely available in hobby shops as well as from specialist suppliers. See the Resources section at the end of the book for contacts. Rather than balsa, some people use thin MDF or other wood types. These of course produce a more solid and durable structure, but at the cost of

These balsa wood buildings created by the late Charles Grant hold something of an iconic status for wargamers as they featured in the 1971 classic *The War Game*. They received a public outing at Partizan in 2007 when the battle of Mollwitz, featured in the book, was refought. Note how the buildings are actually built to a smaller scale than the figures, but actually look fine.

These lovely buildings were made by Phil Olley for the May 2006 recreation of the Battle of Sittangbad from the classic book *Charge!* at Partizan. Created primarily from lightweight foam card, they are masterpieces of wargame 'stage setting', having the appearance of being very solid. Foam card is very easy to work with but can dent easily.

weight, and they are not as easy to cut with standard craft knives as the card-based products or balsa.

These materials can all be used on their own to create an attractive house, but I would add a couple more things to the list of necessaries before starting. Some Sellotape is jolly handy for taping joints together whilst you wait for glue to dry, or for holding things in position. As well as the very sticky, standard type, I also find the low-tack version extremely useful, as it can be peeled off without removing the surface with it.

Secondly, because you may be mixing materials, such as card and balsa wood, or applying exterior details like beams, you might want to keep a few good dressmaking pins handy to secure things in place where tape would be more difficult or could potentially get stuck down itself.

Another tip here is that for buildings in particular, a 'bits box' can be extremely useful, especially for things that could be used as embellishments to your houses. Some lengths of dowel could make decent chimneypots; some clear plastic might work well for window glass; some bits of thin chain could be just the thing for a drawbridge, and so on. Some people's bits boxes grow out of control, and in the case of Jon Sutherland, even led to his wife Diane writing a regular column in my magazine showing what can be done with all the odd stuff he squirrels away!

Before we get started actually making a simple building or two, let me state the obvious again by saying that not only can you find a phenomenal variety of architectural bits'n'bobs for sale (some of which I heartily recommend, such as plastic roof tiles, brickwork and other textures), but you can also buy entire buildings for any period of history and any theatre of operations, for any scale, either painted or unpainted. There are also companies producing 'card terrain', which essentially means that they are PDF files you can download and print out onto card at home before cutting out and assembling them. Again, a look at the Resources section of the book will reveal more.

But, as with everything else so far, let's assume you're going to give it a go, and the first thing you need is a plan of your house so that you know what size things need to be.

For the time being, you'll only need three tools: a sharp knife (I find surgeons' scalpels best, available from good hobby shops, but any good, sharp craft knife will do); a steel ruler; and the adhesive of your choice.

Because of the size limitations of this book, you can find full-size versions of these plans online at the *Wargaming Compendium* website: *www.thewargamingcompendium.com*. These are in PDF format, so you can download them and print them out at home.

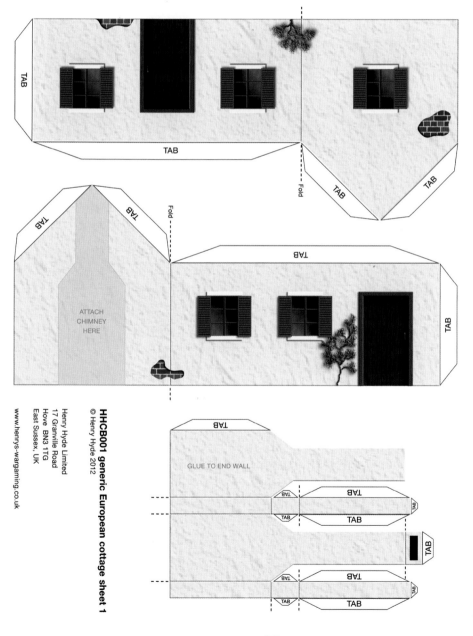

HHCB001 generic European cottage sheet 1
© Henry Hyde 2012

Henry Hyde Limited
17 Granville Road
Hove BN3 1TG
East Sussex, UK
www.henrys-wargaming.co.uk

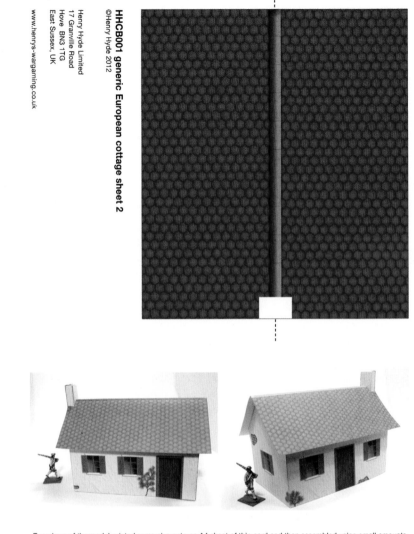

HHCB001 generic European cottage sheet 2
©Henry Hyde 2012

Henry Hyde Limited
17 Granville Road
Hove BN3 1TG
East Sussex, UK
www.henrys-wargaming.co.uk

Two views of the model printed same size onto an A4 sheet of thin card and then assembled using small amounts of household glue. You may wish to add corner strengtheners inside to increase durability. A Spencer Smith 30mm miniature has been placed alongside to give an indication of scale. By scaling the sheets during the printing process, the building can be made to suit any size of miniature. Permission granted to print the building as many times as desired. Resale forbidden.

The first one is a simple, generic cottage, with four walls, a roof and a chimney, which you can print out onto paper and stick down onto the material of your choice. Some inkjet and laser printers will actually accept thin card, but this is unlikely to be thick enough to prevent warping, though by all means give it a try.

Just as an aside, many wargamers have noticed that wargame buildings actually look better if they are made slightly smaller than the scale of miniatures you are using. For example, if we equate 28mm miniatures with a scale of around 1/60, then you will find that they look perfectly happy beside buildings created to 1/72 scale, even though they clearly won't fit through the doors. This is most often the case when you are fighting large battles – the smaller the action, the more closely the scales of building and miniature should match. One benefit of this is that you can reduce the size of your buildings, which reduces the storage problem. It also makes it easier to gain access to your troops, since a 'true scale' building at $1/60$ can be quite a tall object, especially if multi-storey and decorated with tall chimneys! However, as with all aspects of this hobby, do whatever you feel looks right.

Cut out around the edges carefully using a craft knife, making sure you leave the tabs for gluing intact. Where the shape is to be bent, score along the line using the back of a knife – you don't want to accidentally cut right through – and then use the edge of a ruler to work against as you gently bend into shape. The tabs will require the most extreme bending, to make sure that they will lie flush against the inside of the part to which they must be stuck.

Always do a 'dry run' test first. I'll say that again: ALWAYS do a 'dry run' first! Only when you're entirely happy that you've understood what goes where should you proceed to applying the glue. The dry run also shows you where the helping hand of a little Sellotape or a pin will be necessary.

I have a couple of useful tips for those moments when you are assembling a building and require nice, square corners where the walls meet at right angles.

The first is Lego. Marvellous stuff, and many of us have some lying around, either from our childhoods or pilfered from our offspring. You need a baseboard and enough bricks to make two or three courses. Then, quite simply, you make your Lego walls the right length and width to fit *inside* the building you are making, so that it acts as a former and ensures that the walls dry square to one another. If it's not quite the right size, a few shims of card slid between your card building and the Lego will do the trick. Of course, you don't need Lego – a small, sturdy box, for example, could be used to the same effect. The most important thing is that your former is solid.

Something else I would advise is to add hidden corner strengtheners. A simple approach is to use 5-10mm (¼"-½") square wooden trim, simply cut to length and stuck inside the corners. Alternatively, take a sheet of card or thin sheet wood that you know to be absolutely square, mark the right angle and cut the corners off. These can then be stuck inside the corners of your building, making sure the hypotenuse (that's the long side) is the one that's innermost, or you'll get some very wonky walls! If you want to be really belt and braces, you could add these both top and bottom of each corner.

When it comes to adding the roof to the top, make sure the tabs are folded in sufficiently along the top of the walls and particularly the gable ends, where they must be at 90° to the wall, then apply the adhesive and, with the ridgeline already pre-scored and folded, pop the roof on top. This is a classic case where some tape or pins applied from the inside can really help. If you are using a more robust material then you could even use elastic bands to keep things in place until dry.

And so, *voila!* You now have a little whitewashed cottage that can be used for games set pretty much anywhere in Europe from around 1650 onwards. By all means feel free to take out your paints and brushes and get more artistic, especially if you make several and don't want them to look identical. I would also recommend that you disguise any exposed card – the edges of the roof, for example, would benefit from a touch of terracotta, or even a simple mid brown. You can also cut out the door and then stick some tape down one edge to make a hinge, before re-applying it in place, so that you can actually open the door or have it standing ajar.

Another simple variation is to change the roof from terracotta to slate grey, or even to thatch. The colour is easy enough to change, either by applying a series of black washes, or by turning the roof piece over and applying your own styling. Simply draw the tile shapes you want using a ruler (or freehand, if you're feeling brave) and use watercolour or acrylic paint with a broad brush to apply the colour. As long as you've pressed hard when drawing the tiles (a sharp pencil or biro is useful here) then the pattern will show through.

If you want to get really fancy, you can try making the tiles out of paper or very thin card and stick them to the roof before colouring. This adds a very effective texture which can be painted and then drybrushed with a lighter colour to add even more relief. Whichever method you choose, be sure to check, either by popping outside to look at your own tiled roof if you have one, or checking some photographic reference, to ensure that you get the pattern right. It's one of those things that immediately looks odd if done wrong!

If your taste is for southern Europe, corrugated card is a very useful

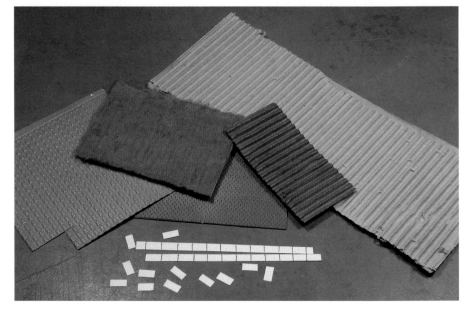

Materials for roofing. As well as a couple of commercial plastic types for slates and tiles, and teddy bear fur soaked in PVA for thatch, useful things you can find around the home include thin card (cut into individual slates, or leave as strips but with the tiles drawn or scored on them) and corrugated cardboard – damping the surface makes it easy to remove the outer covering, producing perfect 'Spanish' tiles.

material for making Mediterranean tiles and of course, as I have already said, some of the companies supplying the hobby produce excellent versions in plastic.

Thatched roofs might seem quite a challenge, but again these can be rendered simply with paintbrush, paint and pens. A more textured variation can be achieved using household filler. Apply a thin layer and then, before it hardens, comb it with an old toothbrush to produce the right texture. Once it's dry, it can be painted and drybrushed very effectively. A final version makes use of fake fur, which can be found in fabric shops. Cut a piece to the right size, with a slight overhang along the edges, then soak it in barely diluted PVA glue and stick onto your roof, Again, before it dries, comb it with an old toothbrush to finish the look.

Before we move on, we need to consider the practical application of our buildings. Do we want to be able to actually place troops inside, or shall we remove any garrison from the table and note its presence on a piece of paper or some other way? And secondly, how do we wish to represent any damage inflicted on the building, including it potentially being reduced to rubble or smouldering ruins?

Let's look at the first question. For the most part, when you're making your own buildings, they are hollow, so it is a simple matter to lift up the building, place the appropriate number of infantry inside (no horses or guns, they ruin the carpets) and pop the building back on top of them. As long as this doesn't happen very often, this is fine, or buildings can start to creep across the table in the most mysterious fashion, and your opponent might start complaining that your garrison has strangely moved from medium to long range from his artillery.

Many commercial buildings, however, are cast in solid resin, so with these it is necessary to work out the 'footprint' of the building and adjudicate how many miniatures it may contain. Then, when troops wish to occupy the building, the appropriate number are removed from the table and placed to one side, with a note being made. Alternatively, you can draw a floor plan for the building and place it on a side table. Then, when troops move in, they can be placed on the floor plan in such a way as to indicate their position.

BUILT UP AREAS

Another approach is to have Built Up Areas (BUAs) that are capable of being occupied by a set maximum number of troops – this is the approach I take, because it eliminates a lot of potential arguments about precisely how many men can be crammed into each miniature building. That number is, in reality, often far fewer than you might think, because our model buildings represent, in scale, a much larger footprint than the single building they portray. The area covered in fact denotes not just several buildings, but alleyways and streets between them, gardens, outhouses and other obstacles. Troops in close order would not be able to maintain their formation once inside; the ranks would thin, men would have to

A Built Up Area. This one is for 6mm or 1/300 miniatures. For European settings, large farms are popular, especially those based on the look and feel of the famous La Haye Sainte and Hougoumont at Waterloo.

spread out, some would be in upper storeys or basements, hiding behind rose bushes in the garden or crouching in the vegetable patch, and so on. And so the 'footprint' of the occupiers would spread out and disperse to fill the periphery of the area we define as our conurbation.

This approach also helps you to make your layout more attractive, since you can define a Built Up Area as, say, 200mm (8") square, and fill it with as many buildings, hedges, trees, bushes and so on as you like. We then arbitrarily decide that such an area can be occupied by no more than four bases of infantry of any kind. Although, on the face of it, this means that more close order miniatures can occupy the area than, say, skirmishers, the nature of the terrain means that the differences are ironed out in our rules to compensate. Close order troops will be forced to spread out, whilst skirmishers may well find themselves in closer proximity to their fellows and in any case, troops trained to skirmish were perfectly capable of operating in closer order under such circumstances.

Clusters of such Built Up Areas can be placed together to form our villages, towns and cities. You can also, if you wish, create a larger baseboard with several Built Up Areas on it, including roads and so on, as long as you are clear what should be defined as the BUAs. Similarly, you may well end up with model buildings in your collection that don't fit neatly into our defined BUA measurements. No matter: simply make an arbitrary decision about how many bases it can contain, and that's that.

Under my rules (see Chapter 7), infantry and their small battalion guns are the only troops allowed actually inside the buildings and who may therefore benefit from cover. Cavalry (unless dismounted) and guns are allowed to move between BUAs on roads or tracks, but may not benefit from the cover afforded by, nor directly assault, a BUA.

DAMAGE TO BUILDINGS

Back in the early days of gaming, in 1971, a lovely man called Charles Grant wrote a book called *The War Game* that bewitched me, and one of my favourite recollections even now is a pair of black and white photographs captioned thus: "The shell of a house is removed, leaving its ruins" and then "Infantry defending a ruined building. It accommodates seven men, the same number as it would do in an undamaged state."

For years afterwards, all my balsa wood houses were made in two parts: the outer shell, as described above, which can of course be made from any of the materials discussed; and then an inner shell of ruins, as seen in the photograph below, which is my homage, if you like, to the late Mr Grant.

Since our rules do indeed permit buildings to be reduced by shot and shell, I see no reason for not considering a continuation of this tradition which is, I think, not only charming, but also rather practical. For a start, there's no fudging which Built Up Areas have been demolished and secondly, the inner ruins act as a terrific former for your outer building shell, to keep it square at the corners and add general rigidity.

The trick, of course, is to ensure that your ruined walls actually fit inside the outer walls. So, for example, if your house walls are 150mm long by 75mm wide, and you are using 5mm foam board, then your ruins must not be bigger than 140mm x 65mm. Try it and see! In fact, I'd knock a millimetre or so more off this – you want the fit to be snug, but not so airtight that you'll have trouble removing the outer shell. Furthermore, you may want to apply paint or filler or other effects to the inner ruins to make them look the part, and that takes up space too. Inside the perimeter, you can do what you like – some rubble, a couple of scorched and fallen beams, some scattered roof tiles – but don't go overboard because you will probably want to place troops inside. A great deal can be achieved with some textured filler and a good paint job.

Building with outer shell removed revealing the ruins inside. This is very easy to do – just remember to make the ruined walls slightly shorter than the actual building! The ruins should be large enough to accommodate the base size of your troops.

Since the outer shell now needs to fit over the ruined walls, if you plan to add corner reinforcement to your buildings, then you either need to leave a gap at the corners of the ruins, or place the reinforcement further up inside the shell. As a guideline, I would recommend that ruined walls are no taller than about an inch (25mm).

With the potential effects of artillery in mind, it will be apparent that whilst solid cannon shot (contrary to Hollywood portrayal) do not explode, and therefore do not present much of a fire risk *per se* (though there are famous examples of where they were heated in braziers to become red hot before firing, especially against ships, as at the siege of Toulon), howitzer shells, on the other hand, certainly do. Filled with gunpowder, their explosion could not only cause fires in itself, but also the shards of metal casing it sprayed about were extremely hot. Even if a building did not catch fire immediately, pieces could lodge themselves in dry timber or fabric and smoulder for some considerable time, waiting for the right breath of fresh air. Bear in mind also that, in the pre-modern era, as well as wooden furniture, most households had animals, and many had thatched roofs, so straw and hay lay about in abundance, the ideal kindling material.

Our rules, therefore, cover the potential for a conflagration, but how should we represent it on the tabletop? Clearly, we don't want to actually set our miniature edifices aflame!

Returning again to Charles Grant, he proposed an ingenious device made up of two sheets of thin card, shaped and painted to resemble flames. Each had a slot cut into the lower part, and when fixed together at right angles, they could sit atop a model house quite comfortably.

Nowadays, however, things have moved on and wargamers have come up with some truly ingenious ways of indicating smoke, flame and explosions. Cotton wool figures in a number of options, since it can be

Inferno! A building has caught fire, as shown by the simple flames made from card and painted with acrylics – an overt homage to *The War Game!*.

A more elaborate way of depicting smoke and flames using wire wool, with additional paint and kapok added. This marvellous vignette was made by Phil Olley for his Cossack Rebellion game at Partizan.

dyed with thinned paint and then teased out to indicate smoke, though it has to be said that the colouring process rather takes the fluffiness out of it. Kapok, the sort of padding used to stuff teddy bears and the like, is a better option. Another alternative is wire wool, which again can be teased into interesting formations and painted. A word of warning: as mentioned when discussing the manufacture of home-made trees, DO NOT use water-based paint on the bare wire, or your wire wool will rust overnight and crumble away to dust. (Can you tell by now that I'm speaking from bitter, personal experience?)

Some people actually glue the base of the wire to a heavy object hidden inside, to aid stability. You might use an old spray can top, for example, or even a large steel nut from a hardware store. Fix the wire wool to the weight using epoxy.

By creating a conical shape, you can paint the lower, pointy end with vibrant reds, oranges and yellows to simulate flames. Once the wire is undercoated, you can happily use acrylics, though I would recommend keeping them thick. The application of some clump foliage scatter material to the wire wool, either using spray adhesive or right after the first undercoat of spray paint, can give a startling realism to the smoke effect.

I have seen some great effects used by well-known display gamers such as Barry Hilton, Phil Olley, Aly Morrison and Dave Andrews, and some of the photos here show just what can be achieved with a little thought and practice.

Storage

Regardless of the scale you decide to game in, you will quickly build up a collection of hills, rivers, bridges, houses, trees and all the other stuff that wargamers inevitably accumulate. If you can't stand the thought of this, then you either need a very understanding friend who will look after everything for you, or a club where everything is owned jointly and kept on club premises, or take up boardgaming.

Clearly, in practical terms, you need to plan ahead and make sure that you have plenty of shelving, cupboard or box space to accommodate your new acquisitiions. You can be sure that there will be three or four threads to your collecting woes, as books, magazines, model soldiers and scenery compete for your ever-shrinking real estate. Oh, and paints and brushes too, so make that five. Your potential passion for antique militaria is just gilding the lily, so stop it.

As you will see with model soldiers in the next section, your aim is to keep your acquisitions safe, clean, dry and in reasonably good order. I have become a great fan of the tough, clear plastic boxes sold by The Really Useful Box Company, available direct at www.reallyusefulproducts. co.uk but also through all good business stationers and many other outlets. Readers in the USA and mainland Europe and Scandinavia will be pleased to know that you can also get hold of these excellent items by simply tagging the name of your own country on the end of that URL, so /usa/, /germany/, /sweden/ and so on.

These boxes come in a wide variety of sizes, with the variety of footprint and depth meaning that it would take a very odd object indeed not to fit into one size or another. Highly recommended.

Cardboard boxes of various kinds are fine as temporary storage, but the trouble is that they can be affected by damp and can also get crushed in the most alarming fashion as box piles upon box over time, and eventually the unfortunate items at the bottom fall victim to gravity.

A slightly better option are box files, as sold by business stationers. These usually come in a standard size to fit A4 or foolscap paper. Some come with a hinged, spring-loaded clip inside to keep papers in place, but you don't want that, just a plain interior and a lid top, with or without a clip fastening. They are deep enough to house almost any terrain for 15mm or below; for 20mm and up, you might get single-storey buildings, bushes, hedges and small trees inside them, but larger trees and taller buildings will be problematic, though they can of course be stored in other ways.

Another source for storage solutions is a large furnishing store, such as Ikea. A trip to your local branch will reveal all kinds of little boxes, drawers, baskets and even entire cabinets of drawers suitable for both hiding your hobby and keeping things safe, and generally speaking, the prices are reasonable.

The one thing likely to defy storage attempts are your hills, since they come in all shapes and sizes. The best solution here is to simply stack them carefully, but don't make the stacks too high. If you have gone for the slab-sided contour look, they can of course be stored on their edge, in the same way that polystyrene terrain squares can.

Enough for now – I cannot possibly give you an exhaustive list of potential solutions, but at least I have made you aware that *you will need* a solution!

5

ASSEMBLING YOUR FORCES

Meet the Troops

And so, the scene is set, the table is laid, and your battlefield awaits the tramp of tiny feet upon its surface. Babbling brooks sparkle amid miniature glades, and windmills turn and grind microscopic corn to feed a myriad of tiny mouths. But where are they? What of these small soldiers and their equine companions? Show me their shining brass cannon and the fluttering flags beneath which they tramp to war. Let us cast our gaze, then, over the pieces with which we play our games, what choices to make, where to find them, how to assemble and paint them and organise them into regiments, and much, much more besides.

Size and cost of miniatures

We discussed the topics of size and scale earlier and now, most specifically, you're going to have to decide what size of miniature you're going to start collecting and for which period. As we saw when looking at miniature buildings, whilst many items used in your wargames can be termed 'generic' as far as scenery is concerned – a hill is always a hill, a tree is always a tree – your choice now is inextricably linked with the period you wish to recreate. But in addition, the question of aesthetics raises its head, together with finance (a heady brew), coupled then with a realistic appraisal of your own skill as a painter and, how dull, that question of storage again.

Now, you don't have to take this advice, but I'm going to give it anyway. If you've never played any wargames before, and you're not sure how your interests might develop in the future, and you don't want to spend a lot of cash finding out, then start as many – perhaps even most – wargamers have, pretty much since the modern hobby began in the late 1950s, with plastic figures.

The brand name "Airfix" is inextricably linked with the birth of the hobby, almost as though one begat the other when the first 1/72 scale figures in boxes began to line the shelves of toy shops at the eye level of eager young boys (and many, it has to be said, who were not so young at all). Nowadays, however, as you will see in the Resources chapter, there are a great many other companies that have joined the fray, and confusingly, several of them make each other's products under license! But before long, the names Italeri, Esci, Revell, Zvezda, HäT, Imex, Waterloo 1815 (yes, an odd choice of company name, I'll agree) and others will become familiar, as they are readily available in many toy and model shops, as well as online. Even Amazon stocks model soldiers these days!

Another great benefit of starting with plastic (technically, what wargamers call 'soft' plastic, which is extruded polythene) is that there is a marvellous website, run by enthusiasts, called Plastic Soldier Review at *www.plasticsoldierreview.com*. Given that, as you will see, wargaming is an extraordinarily diverse hobby, it is incredibly useful to have a website where every single release of 1/72 plastic soldiers is reviewed and photographed. The dedication of the site owners, who are completely independent, is to be applauded.

For your first foray, as far as this work is concerned, I'm going to recommend that you start with a handful of boxes of Napoleonics, some British, some French, which we shall gradually add to as you learn the rules and develop your skills. As I write this, a typical box of figures costs less than £10. For the purposes of this demonstration, I ordered some figures from Amazon.co.uk. The Italeri British Napoleonic Infantry 1815 were £9.24 for a box of 48 figures, which works out at 19.25p per figure. The Italeri British Light Cavalry (which, technically, are Light Dragoons), actually cost slightly less, at £8.29 per box, which includes 17 men and their horses, making them just under 49p per complete figure. By shopping around, particularly if you're prepared to take your chances on buying up someone else's old collection on eBay, you might of course be able to reduce the cost even further.

Now, the fact is that with 'soft' plastic figures, particularly the infantry, there are almost always a few poses included in the box that are pretty useless as far as wargamers are concerned, though this situation is gradually improving as manufacturers come to realise that when we buy figures, we tend to buy a *lot* of them, and therefore our requirements ought to be at least acknowledged! However, even if we were to discard up to a quarter of the figures in each box (and normally it is far fewer than that), our plastic infantryman would weigh in at no more than about 25p per figure.

Now, let's take a quick look at one of my favourite manufacturers of metal miniatures producing to the same scale, or thereabouts: Newline Designs (*newlinedesigns.co.uk/*). Sean Pereira sculpts lovely little Napoleonic men at 20mm size, which technically is around $1/87$ scale, but owing to the phenomenon known as 'scale creep', in reality they are fairly compatible with most 1/72 scale plastics.

An interesting case study in comparative sculpting: Newline Napoleonic 20mm infantry miniatures next to their 1/72 plastic brethren from Italeri, British on the left, French on the right.

Just a very small selection of the hard plastic miniatures currrently available for different periods, scales and types of wargaming.

The Newline figures come in packs of four infantry for £1.90 or three cavalry for £3.30, which equates to 47.5p per infantryman or £1.10 per cavalryman. By purchasing entire unit packs, for example the British Foot Advancing (24 infantry for £9.50), the cost for a foot figure comes down to around 39.5p each; a cavalry unit, such as British Light Dragoons, containing 10 figures for £9.50 again, brings the cost of their horsemen down to 95p each. You can even buy their Bargain Packs: 100 infantry or 36 cavalry for £32.50, reducing the cost still further to 32.5p per infantryman or just over 90p per cavalryman.

Why the price differential? Well, the most obvious reason is that white metal (somewhat akin to pewter)[1] is an expensive commodity whose constituent elements are subject to fluctuations in price on the world markets, particularly in recent years. The second reason is that many producers of metal miniatures are small companies – indeed, frequently one-man-bands – who cannot possibly hope to compete with the scale of output of the plastics manufacturers who, in turn, need to be able to make large investments up-front for the tooling and production costs of their mass-produced figures.

Interestingly, the last few years have seen a sudden explosion in the number of 'hard' plastic miniatures becoming available, spawned in a couple of cases (Perry Miniatures and Gripping Beast) by companies

---

1   *Many people describe metal wargames figures as 'lead', but in fact this has not been the case for a long time, and the major constituent element is tin, which can be mixed in varying proportions with antimony, lead, cadmium, bismuth, and zinc.*

previously known for their high quality metal figures. Currently, most offerings are in 28mm size (Perry, Warlord, Victrix, Wargames Factory), but The Plastic Soldier Company began producing 28mm, 1/72 *and* 15mm right from the start. You'll read more about these offerings later.

There are other things besides price that influence wargamers. The first is that, with most metal figures, you can choose precisely which pose you would like your infantry to be in. Since, apart from skirmish wargames, the 'look' most wargamers are after is the mass effect of cohesive units advancing to battle, we find little use for miniatures in odd poses, waving at one another, reloading, or apparently dancing some sort of jig. There is a party game called "Airfix charades" occasionally played by veteran gamers, in which they attempt to adopt some of the more curious poses found in early boxes of Airfix figures, whilst onlookers try to guess which box they are from. "Aha!" cries one, "that's the running figure waving its hand in the air from the Confederate Infantry set!" Or, "British Napoleonic infantryman stabbing the ground!" and so on.

As you will see from the photos in this book, there is something magnificently menacing about large battalions of infantry, all in identical 'march attack' or 'advancing' poses, tramping inexorably towards the enemy. With metal miniatures, you can achieve this from the word "go". Some wargamers also like their cavalry to be similarly dour, trotting with shouldered swords, though many prefer the charge *à l'outrance* pose, with sword or lance outstretched, thundering towards the foe on galloping charger.

Some wargamers, however, prefer a little variation, particularly in their cavalry, and it is possible both to buy a variation of poses or, indeed, do one's own conversions.

To achieve a similar uniformity with plastic figures is simply a numbers game: if you buy enough boxes, you will amass sufficient models to create

Just some of the variety of soft plastic figures available to create, in this instance, a British Napoleonic army at low cost. Even larger ranges are available for the French, with Austrians, Prussians and Russians available in some numbers too. The smaller nations lag a little further behind, but manufacturers like HäT produce a few. If you go for metal figures, the range is both wider and more specific.

entire battalions in similar poses. As a boy, I can remember walking into a local toy shop and emerging with perhaps ten or a dozen identical boxes of Airfix figures, to create battalions all firing, marching and so on. With plastic cavalry, I really wouldn't worry so much, as the plastics manufacturers tend to give them all fairly active poses on vigorous horses, so they can be used pretty much straight out of the box.

Another reason some wargamers prefer metal is 'heft', simply what the miniatures feel like in the hand and in use on the table. This probably has its roots in equating weight with value – after all, we pay more for a pound of cheese than we do for eight ounces – and it is certainly true that if you choose metal miniatures over plastic, your wallet will feel much lighter but your table will be groaning. However, given that the quality of the vast majority of plastic figures these days is at least the equal of, if not superior to, most metal miniatures, the argument is really nonsense. The fact is that many of the plastics manufacturers are in a position to afford the most skilled sculptors in the business, and their appreciation of anatomy and proper proportions is usually apparent. Of course, beauty is in the eye of the beholder, and taste is such a highly personal thing, so you will end up making your own choices, which is just as it should be, and if the physical weight of the figures in your collection is important to you, then so be it!.

Let's look briefly at some other figure sizes, to give you an indication of comparative cost.

It would be unfair to say that any scale is more popular than another, since the statistics are pretty much impossible to come by, so let's look in turn at 25/28mm, 15/18mm, 10mm and 6mm. The first two categories are divided by a slash because of what is known as 'scale creep'. For whatever reason, 25mm and 15mm have both succumbed to sculptors gradually making their miniatures more 'heroic', shall we say, in stature, so that entire ranges have seen a strange increase in height. Games Workshop sculptor Aly Morrison was recently quoted in a magazine article. Game designer Rick Priestley challenged him about the proportions of a recent sculpt:

"'He's a big chap isn't he?' I suggest with all the tact I can muster.

'Oh no! He's exactly the right size for a 28mm figure', replied Aly shamelessly. 'He's exactly 31mm tall!'"[2]

Let's pluck a well-known 28mm manufacturer from the list of possibles – and there are many, as you will see – and take a quick look at Perry Miniatures (*www.perry-miniatures.com*). I have chosen them because they produce both metal and hard plastic to the same scale.

Their "BH6 British/KGL[3] Infantry centre companies advancing, shouldered arms, covered shako" set contains six miniatures, noted as

---

2   *Wargames Soldiers and Strategy magazine issue 55, p.14. Knowing Aly myself, I have also heard him make similar comments confirming the drive to 'heroic' proportions.*

3   *King's German Legion, the Hanoverians who fought alongside the British during the Napoleonic Wars.*

28mm miniatures look grand, but weigh in as the most expensive. Here, French troops negotiate a town during the 1812 Battle of Maloyaroslavets, staged by the Bedford Gladiators at Colours 2012. The miniatures and scenery are typical of 'wargames standard', designed to be practical and look good at normal viewing distance.

being in their price code A band, which makes the set £6.50, or £1.08 per figure. They are considered by many gamers to be some of the finest miniatures in the business, but you can certainly see how a leap in figure size also leads to a leap in price!

Now to the cavalry. Sticking again to our direct comparison, their pack code BH37, "British Light Dragoons charging" gives you three cavalry figures at price code B, which is £8.00, or £2.67 per figure.

Their plastic offerings are certainly more attractive to the budget-conscious, as long as you are prepared to plunge into the task of snipping, filing and gluing before you take out your paintbrushes. Code BH1, plastic British Line Infantry box set (36 Line Infantry, 4 Riflemen) comes in at just £18 for the 40 figures – that's a mere 45p per figure. They don't yet have British Light Dragoons in plastic, but for comparison, their box FN140, French Napoleonic Hussars 1792-1815, costs £18 again for 14 mounted figures, or roughly £1.29 each. The cost benefits of hard plastic are plain to see, and the quality of the finished miniatures is identical to their metal brethren.

Now let's look at 15mm metals, and here I'm going to go to an old, well-established company which, though it has changed hands a couple of times over the years, is still going strong and has been a mainstay of the hobby since the late 1960s: Miniature Figurines, known to most as Minifigs (*www.miniaturefigurines.co.uk*).

They have an extensive range of Napoleonic Miniatures, and continuing our comparison, their code 6NB, "Centre [company] March Attack Belgic" [shako][4] comes as a pack of eight figures for £2.55, or just under 32p per

---

4 *The nature of British infantry headgear changed in 1812, during the Peninsular war, from a plain, conical 'stovepipe' shako to the 'Belgic' type, which had a lower crown but also a standing front panel which stood taller.*

Armies of 15mm miniatures are, for many, the best compromise in terms of look and cost, though the much sought-after AB Miniatures shown in this photo are hardly cheap. Here, exquisitely painted elite French carabiniers crash into Russian cavalry, as the Loughton Strike Force depicted the French assault on the Grand Redoubt at Borodino, 1812.

figure. 2NBC "Light Dragoon (shako)"[5] gives you four miniatures for that same price tag of £2.55, in other words just under 64p per figure.

Let's downscale, and take a look at Pendraken (*www.pendraken.co.uk*) who produce a nice range of metal 10mm Peninsular War miniatures, amongst others. They sell figures as entire battalions or regiments and so, for example, we find a "British Line Infantry Battalion" code PB1, containing 30 figures, on sale for £3.50. Now you really are getting bang for your buck, as this comes out at under 12p per infantryman. For the same price, PB4 "Light Dragoons" gives you 15 cavalry at just over 23p a figure.

Now, let's make the pips squeak and go over to Baccus 6mm (*www. baccus6mm.com*), owned by one of the biggest personalities in wargaming, Peter Berry, who offers his weeny warriors in handy packs.

NBR14 "Line Infantry – Belgic Shako" gives you no less than 96 figures, mounted in strips of four (at this scale, handling individual figures is, to say the least, challenging) for £5.50. NBR18 "Light Dragoons – Shako" provides 45 figures for £6.60. Our final comparison, then, comes out with infantry at under 6p each and cavalry at under 15p each.

Finally, there would be howls of derision in the online halls of the wargaming community if I failed to mention a clutch of other scales that can claim a place in this gallery.

At the micro-scale end of the range, where we found 6mm, I should properly declare that this equates to 1/300, which has been around for a long time, especially for WWII and modern era games, where these tiny miniatures are well suited to the much greater weapon ranges and speeds of armoured fighting vehicles (AFVs) and motorised transport. A very close relative is 1/285, a scale which American company GHQ has

---

5 *As opposed to the colpack adopted later, as several British light dragoon regiments were converted to hussars.*

pretty much claimed as its own with it's range of astonishingly detailed micro-armour.

In recent years, enterprising individuals have pushed the 'micro' aspect of micro-gaming even further, and it is now possible to find so-called 'pico' ranges created in 3mm and even 2mm sizes for the ultimate bird's eye view. Such microscopic marvels are available for horse and musket era troops, as well as post-1939 conflicts and those from Polish company Oddzial Osmy simply have to be seen to be believed. At 2mm size, Irregular Miniatures will supply you with an entire army for just £12.50! This makes talking about the cost of individual figures at this scale something of a nonsense.

Of course, just as the cost of such miniatures is consequently much smaller, they permit truly epic battles on a standard 6' x 4' table and your average game could be played on a single 2' square terrain tile!

At the other end of the scale, quite literally, are two sizes that, until recently, were best appreciated by collectors of miniatures for display, rather than gaming. In the early days of toy soldiers, 40mm and 54mm sizes (equivalent to approximately 1/45 and 1/32 respectively) were common, and many a simple and brightly-coloured miniature of these dimensions tramped across the living room carpet. Nowadays, of course, originals of this type change hands for substantial sums in auction rooms and online.

54mm in particular gradually became the standard size for highly detailed kits, both in metal and polystyrene, for military history enthusiasts to assemble and paint for display in dioramas and vignettes. In my teens, I was an avid modeller of Napoleonic kits from Airfix and Historex – I could never afford their metal equivalents from Greenwood & Ball, Hinchliffe and others.

The main attraction of these larger figures for most people was the

Micro-gaming in 6mm. These are mostly Adler figures being used to recreate the Battle of Borodino, 1812. There were more than 8,000 miniatures on the board! The French are attacking from the left towards the Russian redoubts at top centre. This is the kind of grand scenario for which 6mm miniatures are perfect. The game was organised by the Old Guard Wargames Group.

accuracy of both the anatomical proportions and the uniforms, together with the stunning results that could be achieved with a good paint job. Nothing could have been further from my mind than playing with them.

But for others, a small number at first, their impulses were different and they saw no impediment to gaming at this scale, happy to spend as long assembling and painting a single figure as others might in colouring an entire battalion. And of course, the price tag associated with such miniatures is consequently higher, though some manufacturers like Airfix produced boxes of 1/32 scale solid plastic Napoleonic figures that were a fillip to gamers, but are no longer available other than by chance finds on eBay. Just recently, British manufacturer Victrix has created a range of 1/32 scale Napoleonic hard plastic kit models, sold in boxes of 16 infantry for around £22. We hope this range develops further, because one of the major problems is that most manufacturers over the years have treated this scale as either the territory for highly-detailed collectors' figures (such as the exquisite Historex) or as toys for youngsters. Most infuriatingly, ranges are incomplete, although Austrian manufacturer HäT (*www.hat.com*) are making an interesting range that so far covers the continental European powers, but hasn't yet reached the British. A box of 18 infantry comes in at around £9.00, so 50p per figure; they have not yet made any cavalry, however, so you would have to look at perhaps Italeri, who produce some Napoleonic cavalry at this scale, with 16 figures per box for around £13.50, or about 85p per figure.

Clearly, the sheer size of such miniatures means that the average wargamer will only have sufficient space to deploy forces for a skirmish, rather than a pitched battle, with the possible exception of those able to play outside in a large garden in clement weather (and whose house pets can be trusted not to run off with an important leader at a critical moment!). Nevertheless, for very small-scale actions, the benefit of 54mm

At the other end of the scale, here is a selection of 54mm Victrix plastic figures, these depicting a battle in the Peninsular War, with British troops in the foreground and on the right. The effect is completely different to the 6mm battle shown opposite – individual miniatures are very much paramount, and come under much greater scrutiny from onlookers.

40mm Mexican troops assault American positions during a game set in the Mexican -American War of 1846-48, staged by Penarth & Distric Wargames Society. 40mm occupies an interesting place in the range of sizes, being large enough for super-detailed sculpting and painting, but just small enough to still be manageable for substantial games.

is that a great deal of individual detail and character can be portrayed which is just not possible at smaller scales. However, on the downside, the scenery required for such games is, of course, of an entirely different order, presenting an enormous challenge in terms of size, storage and expense.

Just in passing, let me mention 1/35, a scale commonly used in the production of model AFV kits by giants in the field such as Tamiya. Some gamers do indeed use this scale, but it is usually confined to WWII skirmishes, although I have seen it used for some huge and impressive demonstration games staged at major wargaming shows.

The case of 40mm is an interesting one. Long dormant in wargaming terms, it has seen a steady revival over the last five years or so, with several new ranges coming to market, especially for horse and musket era gaming. Their intermediate size makes them attractive to collectors and keen painters, but they are still pleasing as wargaming pieces since their 'footprint' is not that much greater than some 28mm miniatures.

40mm miniatures are, however, comparatively expensive, and at the time of writing, there are none available in plastic. For the purposes of our comparison, I have found price information for the Sash & Saber (the company is American) range as stocked by Old Glory UK (*www. oldgloryuk.com*) whose miniatures are currently designed for the Peninsular War, rather than Waterloo. They come as 'Starter Packs' (code 40NAP002 "British Infantry, Centre Companies, Stovepipe Shako, March Attack") of 20 miniatures for £35.00; and 'Command Packs' (40NAP201 "British Infantry Command") of five for £10.00, a total of £45.00 for 25 miniatures, or an average of £1.80 each for our typical battalion. Their light dragoons wear the characteristic Tarleton helmet of the Peninsular War. The starter pack is 40NAP016 British Light Dragoon Troopers, Tarleton Helmet (7 mounted miniatures in kit form) for £35.00; and the Command Pack is 40NAP211, British Light Dragoon Command, which

The author's own 30mm Spencer Smith miniatures in action recently, defending the walled building in an imaginary battle against more Spencer Smiths owned by visiting wargamer Iain Burt. These figures are cheap, easy to paint and have a certain 'je ne sais quoi' for enthusiasts of the 'old school' approach.

includes three miniatures for £18.00. With ten figures for £53.00, you're therefore looking at an average of £5.30 per cavalry figure.

Finally, I simply have to mention a size much loved by the doyens of the hobby back in the 1950s and 1960s: 30mm, which equates to around 1/60. Incredibly, those very figures, such as those sculpted by Edward Suren, Holger Erikkson and Barry Minot, are still available from Tradition of London and Spencer Smith Miniatures. I happen to be a great fan of their slender and well-proportioned elegance that lends a certain style to wargames, and their prices are comparable to 28mm miniatures. Spencer Smith's own ranges, now cast in white metal but based on a range originally cast in plastic, are a real option for beginners because they are not overloaded with detail, are simple to paint and, in fact, perhaps the cheapest figures for their size to be found anywhere. You will see lots of them in action later in this book, as your author has a sizeable collection of them!

If you order Napoleonic 30mm Willie figures from Spencer Smith (*www.spencersmithminiatures.co.uk*), then British Line Infantry cost £1.40 per miniature and our light dragoons will set you back £2.65 each. This makes them more expensive than the 28mm option, but the fact is that gamers tend to collect 30mm because of the style of the miniatures and their whiff of a bygone era. Nor are 30mm miniatures always expensive – Spencer Smith's own eighteenth century miniatures come in at just 45p per foot figure and £1.30 for cavalry, though it must be stressed that these venerable sculpts are devoid of the level of detail expected by most of today's wargamers.

A close cousin of 30mm is 1/56, which has come into vogue mainly because of a single range of beautiful eighteenth century miniatures created by a private venture called Minden Miniatures owned by wargamer Frank Hammond. The status of this enterprise is something of a curiosity, perhaps best described as 'semi-professional', but the quality of the product is beyond question.

Recently, American wargamer Jim Purky has established a similar enterprise known as Fife & Drum, also selling high quality 1/56 miniatures for the American War of Independence. Details of these, and all known current manufacturers, can be found in the Resources chapter.

If we assume, for a moment, that our average infantry battalion for our games will be 24 figures or so, and a cavalry regiment will be two squadrons of six, so twelve in total, then an approximate comparative cost per unit is as follows. Of course, all these prices are given as at the time of writing in March 2012, and are subject to fluctuation, and of course some manufacturers' goods are less expensive than others, but these are reasonable averages.

Size/Scale	Cost per infantry battalion	Cost per cavalry regiment
40mm metal	£43.20	£63.60
30mm metal	£33.60	£31.80
28mm metal	£25.92	£32.04
28mm plastic	£10.80	£15.48
20mm metal	£9.50	£11.40
15mm metal	£7.68	£7.68
1/72 soft plastic	£4.62	£5.88
10mm metal	£2.88	£2.76
6mm metal	£1.44	£1.80
3mm metal	£0.60	£0.78
2mm metal	£0.10	£0.30

How miniatures are made

Before we plunge into the techniques used to paint and base our figures, I thought it might be instructive to say something about how they are actually made.

The manufacturing processes used to create our miniatures are undergoing something of a technological revolution, as we shall see, and so are the methods for actually sculpting them, as the power of computers increases exponentially year on year, enabling skilled operators to sculpt in three dimensions using nothing more than the power of pixels and their own skill with the hardware and software. Nevertheless, the cost of deploying such technology is still huge, and therefore well beyond the means of the one-man-band, though I am sure that in the years to come, that will most assuredly change.

Let's begin, then, with the basics.

In order to sculpt a figure, the first thing you need, before you pick up any materials, is some reference. This might come in the form of a very patient friend who is willing to pose while you snarl and curse your way through your first few efforts. An alternative is to use photographic reference and an artists' mannequin, which can be posed in almost whichever position you like. One problem with photographic reference is that it usually shows only one viewpoint; ideally, you need front, back and both sides. Of course, after a while, you might be able to work without any reference at all, and I have been privileged to see a number of highly skilled miniatures sculptors at work who seem to be able to conjure tiny little human beings out of thin air and blurred fingers. Such expertise does not come, I must assure you, without a huge amount of practice!

Of course, in this digital age, there are also pieces of software that can help. One that springs to mind is *Poser* from Smith Micro. Frequently used for 3D animation, the full version is not cheap, but you may be able to download a demo or old version which will be fine for our purposes.

One of the great skills of the miniaturist is being able to capture not only the correct human proportions (and as you familiarise yourself with the different ranges available in the hobby, you will see that some sculptors are more successful at this than others), but also the way that cloth falls and folds, together with the effects of movement and carrying weight. For example, a musket weighs several pounds, a backpack often considerably more, and this affects the way a soldier carries himself.

Even more challenging are horses, a beast that is far easier to portray incorrectly than correctly, and you will find that this can influence your choices of cavalry quite considerably.

Anyway, assuming you have assembled the correct reference material, you will find that the Plasticene loved by sculptors of the past has long since been replaced, since it simply cannot withstand the rigours of modern production methods which involve high pressures and heat in the mould-making process. Nowadays, there are two favoured materials, both of which are essentially based on two-part epoxy: Green Stuff and Milliput. Green stuff gets its name because the two parts are blue and yellow, and once mixed... Milliput is much more reminiscent of old-fashioned clay or putty, and comes in two forms, a standard buff-coloured mix or the finer white one, which is the form preferred by miniaturists.

Milliput modelling clay and Green Stuff both have their respective adherents. As mentioned, Milliput is more like the type of clay you may even have used at school or college when making wonky ashtrays or fruit bowls. It can be heavily wetted to make it more pliable and behaves just as you might expect. Green Stuff is more 'plasticky', and is particularly excellent for rolling very thin to make capes and flags and clothing. It also acquires a much smoother surface finish than Milliput, which carries a slight, chalky texture. When fully dry, both become rock hard, are extremely strong and can be carved or sanded.

Both brands are stocked by good hobby and gaming shops and Games Workshop sells its own brand of Green Stuff.

If you're new to the concept of sculpting, however, you may be forgiven for not realising that in order to prevent a sagging figure, your starting point

Created in under 30 seconds – I know, because I witnessed it! Michael Perry's wire armature for a 28mm Napoleonic infantryman, Although it's just a bit of twisted wire, it already has life.

lies not, in fact, with clay of any sort, but with wire, in the form of an armature. In essence, an armature is a 'stick man', onto which the clay is then applied and built up to achieve the final, fully rounded appearance. I have seen an armature made in front of my eyes with an old paperclip and a pair of pliers by Alan Perry who, along with his brother Michael, is one of the modern masters of this art form. On the other hand, you can even purchase pre-formed armatures from, amongst others, Ebob Miniatures (*www.ebobminiatures.com*).

Sculptors seem to make use of an astounding number of corks. I don't wish to imply anything about their drinking habits, but a ready supply of these (the real thing, of course, not those nasty modern plastic imposters) would appear to be a prerequisite for the aspiring creator of wargames miniatures. Quite what they will do when screw tops have completely taken over, I have no idea.

Anyway, with the armature firmly embedded in its cork, which acts as both handle and support, the sculptor gets to work, building up the basic shape before then applying a top layer onto which the final details are applied. As a rank novice, this process takes me hours; on the other hand, veteran sculptors tell of having to make several every day when in the employ of some of the industry's hard taskmasters (who shall, of course, remain nameless).

If you want to become proficient at ancient warfare, colonials or fantasy figurines, then you had better undertake an intensive study of anatomy, because lots of bare flesh is on show. On the other hand, if you stick with the popular horse and musket period, it's all the minutiae of uniform and headgear differences which are most apparent, together with the characteristic firearms of the period.

Either way, once you have created your first few

Greens in various stages of production, created by Michael Perry for their 28mm medievals range. You can clearly see how the miniature is built up in stages, gradually adding (in this case) more Green Stuff over the wire armature. Michael clearly likes to get the legs right first!

figures and had them cast, you start to build up a 'library' of bits that can be applied to figure sculpts. Your first effort may well consist entirely of Green Stuff or Milliput, but when you look at the publicity web pages of experienced sculptors, you can see that their 'Coming Soon' page usually shows miniature work in progress consisting both of Green Stuff and previously cast parts. This makes sense: if you are sculpting a range of British Napoleonic Infantry, for example, you want to make sure that their muskets, water canteens, cartridge pouches and so on are the same, since these would be standard issue, whilst you concentrate on showing differences of facial expression and physical build. See, for example, "Metals workbench" and "Plastics workbench" on the Perry website at *http://www.perry-miniatures.com/*.

Perhaps completely uniquely at this stage, highly regarded collector and wargamer John Ray, who sculpts all his own figures, sometimes makes the green his final product, and has it painted to an exquisite standard, ensuring that this is a total one-off that can never be recreated. The result is beautiful and, of course, priceless, the envy of a host of aficionados who follow his output with great interest, myself included.

Once the raw 'green' is completed, this is normally used to make a 'master' figure, which is in fact a single casting of the green that the sculptor must ensure carries the final level of detail and precision required for the final product. It is from this master figure that the final production mould is made, and casting can begin. You may be interested to know that the green is often made slightly larger than the final figure, since some shrinkage can occur during the casting of the master figure.

Now, in the beginning, moulds were pretty tricky to make and dangerous to use. I can remember reading in one of Donald Featherstone's early books the methods used to make a mould from Plaster of Paris, starting with blocks of Plasticene. You had to set your master figure halfway into a Plasticene block, making holes for the pouring chute and also divots as 'locators'. Then, surrounding this block, you created sides from wood, which you clamped together on your table, before pouring in a layer of plaster, which had to set completely before you continued. Oh, and I hope you remembered to coat the exposed part of your figure and the Plasticene with Vaseline so that you could then prise the plaster off the Plasticene.

Naturally, this ruined the original Plasticene mould half, but hopefully left your figure intact. Now, turning the whole lot over, you could re-set the wooden sides and pour in a second lot of plaster to complete the mould.

Eventually (perhaps 48 hours after you started), you would have two mould halves and you could set your master figure to one side, assuming it survived the ordeal. Now began the process of carefully cleaning up the mould, and cutting channels that would allow air to escape as the metal was poured in the top.

Hopefully, by now, the plaster mould was completely dry – if not, it could explode when the hot metal was poured in! Clamping the thing together between two pieces of wood and with your hand protected by

A 40mm Prince August figure emerging from its home-cast mould. Photo courtesy of Phil Olley. The pouring and vent holes can be clearly seen. Great care must be taken when clamping the halves together and pouring.

fireproof gloves (adding asbestos into the toxic mix, why not?), with your windows open to let the fumes escape and your wife's favourite milk pan sacrificed to the cause, you added the magical silvery metal to the pan and watched it melt, puddling like mercury until it reached just the right colour. Then you poured, tapping the mould on the workbench to make sure it reached every nook and crevice... And waited.

After a couple of minutes, with luck, the mould would be cool enough to open again and there, in all its glory, was your miniature, surrounded by a spray of run-offs and flash, which would now need to be trimmed and filed and carved to achieve a facsimile of the original master.

If you were lucky, the mould had survived and you might be able to cast ten, twenty, fifty more. Occasionally, you might reach the heady heights of a hundred, but by then, the plaster mould would be showing the scars of its many encounters with hot metal, and you'd probably have to throw it away and start again.

Fortunately, sometime in the 1960s, some bright spark thought to put silicone rubber to good use in the model making industry. Silicone rubber is extremely durable, takes detail well, and can withstand high temperatures, all good characteristics for wargames miniatures.

The first moulds were still 'drop' moulds of the type originally created in Plaster of Paris, enabling the casting only of one, two or very few miniatures at a time. The metal travels down through the mould using gravity alone, which of course means that it may have trouble reaching particularly fine or finicky bits of the casting. Thus, it frequently happened that miniatures would turn up missing bayonets, swords or even the extremities of their anatomy. A good caster, of course, would spot these defects and pop the offending miniatures back into the melting pot, but on a busy day, they often got through unnoticed.

Interestingly, you can still buy moulds of this type for home casting via Prince August (*www.princeaugust.ie*). This Irish company still manufactures moulds, and all the necessary accoutrements, for a wide range of miniatures in several scales, and they can even be found on sale in some toy shops. Many of the figures are what might be described as 'demi-ronde', which is to say that if looked at from the edge, they appear flattish. This is one way of them avoiding the undercuts that can prove so troublesome when trying to release a casting from a mould, and is ideal for the amateur homecaster.

The popularity of such figures persists amongst some wargamers, especially those who are fond of the old-fashioned, slightly 'toy soldier' look that some describe as 'old school' and others as 'classic'. One such is Phil Olley, who has kindly provided us with the photo opposite of a miniature emerging, like a butterfly from its chrysalis, fresh from the mould, so that you can see the two mould halves.

The next development came about as a result of casters wanting to ensure that the molten metal could reach every nook and cranny of the mould, and thus the centrifugal casting process was born.

A centrifuge is, to all intents and purposes, like an old fashioned upright spin dryer or, perhaps more accurately, a record player. The two mould halves are made using circles of silicone rubber, about an inch thick and 12" (30cm) across. The pouring hole is cut to receive the molten metal in the centre, with feeder channels running out to the figures, which can now be cast in multiples, making mass-production possible. The cutting of the mould and all the pouring and venting channels is a considerably skilled job, and many sculptors also learn how to do this, as it helps them to comprehend the limitations imposed by the technology. One aspect

The results of a fresh spin of a centrifugal mould, here in the hands of its creator Roger Jenkins of Gripping Beast. A surprisingly small amount of metal is required to create a dozen figures or so; any excess is then trimmed off and thrown back into the melting pot. The central column shows where the molten alloy is poured in. The depressions around the edge are the 'female' locating holes that fit over the 'male' lugs in the other half.

that is important to understand is that this process is quite 'flat', so figures in particularly expressive poses may have to be cast in more than one part to achieve the final desired look once assembled.

As before, the two mould halves are carefully located together, normally using ball bearings set into the rubber, so that the fit is snug and no slippage can occur. Occasionally, one finds a figure that clearly shows signs (usually a distinct ridge) that the two mould halves have not been properly located before casting begins. Flash can also occur where metal has escaped along the join of the mould halves if they are not mounted tightly enough. The mould is set to spin at several hundred RPM, so that as the hot metal enters, it is flung out to the farthest recesses of the mould.

Depending on the size and type of miniature, a single spin might produce anything from a handful up to several dozen castings with a single ladle of metal. They can be released from the mould just seconds later, since the silicone rubber copes so well with heat and the metal itself cools quickly. Any defective castings are just popped back into the pot and another spin is made.

I have seen this process many times at different companies, and I still think it's like alchemy! That moment when the mould is opened to reveal its glittering contents is simply magical.

The vast majority of metal wargames figure manufacturers use this method. The set-up costs are not prohibitive, and both melting pots and centrifuges can be bought at different sizes. Many hundreds, even thousands of miniatures can be made in a single day in this way.

The final process to be described is that of injection moulding plastic figures. The process is essentially the same, whether it is for 'soft' plastic polythene or 'hard' plastic polystyrene figures, many of which are also hollow, rather than solid, and come in multiple parts like a typical plastic model aircraft or tank kit.

I'll start with the production process first, which essentially consists of molten plastic (which often starts life in pellet form before melting) being injected between two mould halves that are firmly clamped together. Here, it is the pressure of that injection process, rather than centrifugal force, which drives the liquid into every corner of the mould. The mould itself is normally made from stainless steel, rather than silicone rubber, since a metal mould has the weight and stability to withstand the extreme pressures involved, can be etched to take a great deal of surface detail, and is also an excellent conductor of heat which aids the rapid cooling process.

The nature of injection moulding means that the various components included in the mould are joined together by a 'sprue' which comes out of the mould attached to the parts. This ensures that no components are lost and eases the packing process. In fact, as someone who has been designing packaging for a hard plastic figure manufacturer (The Plastic Soldier Company), I can tell you that the boxes are designed to be just large enough to fit the requisite number of sprues – the sprue determines the box size, not the other way round. The wargamer himself

One of Renedra's high pressure injection moulds with the Perry Miniatures cavalry sprue it produces. The brass fittings are where the molten plastic enters and leaves the mould. These parts are made to fine tolerances from high-quality materials and give an idea why setting up a plastic miniatures line is so expensive. Photo courtesy of Renedra.

then removes the individual figures and other components from the sprue using clippers, a chore to which we have become accustomed in exchange for the comparative bargain price of plastic figures.

Both metal and plastic figures often arrive coated in a mould release agent. Nowadays, it's highly unlikely to be Vaseline, but my advice is always that a brief wash can work wonders for paint adhesion later.

The interesting thing that has come about with the advent of plastic figures is the notion of the 'three-up' figure. This is a 'green' or master figure produced at three times the size of the final figure – in other words, a sculptor working on a miniature that will eventually be 28mm tall makes a 'three-up which is actually 84mm tall. This enables them to work at a much greater level of detail than would otherwise be possible. These three-ups are then reduced using a 3D pantograph system, which essentially involves computer scanning the original, reducing it digitally and then outputting the data directly to a computer which creates the mould.

In recent years, however, an alternative has evolved which requires no actual physical sculpt at all: CAD 3D. Computer Aided Design in three dimensions has now reached such an advanced level that some systems link hardware input devices to software so that the designer can *feel* as though he is actually sculpting clay. The tool, which can move and rotate in all directions, emulates the sculptor's hand scraping, pushing, pulling, squeezing and cutting at the raw material, in a similar fashion to the astonishing machines used by surgeons to practice procedures without the need for a live patient or cadaver. A simpler form of the software can be used for what are known as 'straight line' projects, such as vehicles and tanks, which can be translated almost directly from engineering diagrams. Many of us already have this type of software on our PCs or Macs for designing home interiors or gardens.

Once the digital sculpt is completed, it can then be output directly to the mould-making process as described above.

One advantage of these digital sculpting techniques is, of course that it is very clean in comparison. Secondly, the digital sculptor can zoom in to an almost infinite degree in order to achieve a high level of detail. Detractors, however, point out that whilst the software is powerful, the quality of the product is only as good as the person inputting the data, and can we really expect a computer operator to achieve the beautiful results of someone who works with 'real' materials and tools?

Well, the proof will be in the pudding for that one, and my suspicion again is that as a new generation grows up that is more familiar with the computer mouse than the feel of clay under their nails, we can only expect future results to be astounding. Whether they will be able to incorporate as much 'character' into their digital sculpture will be the test of whether what they are doing is really art, or just industrial science.

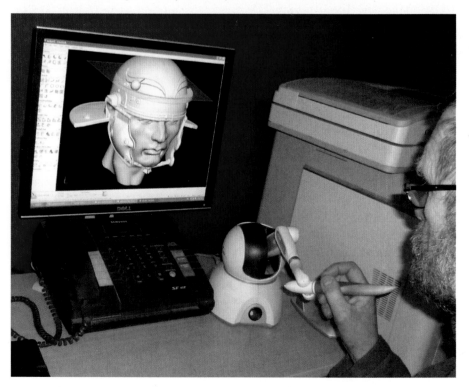

The process of digital sculpting has come a long way in recent years to the point where it can now be performed on a home- or office-based PC. The key tool is the haptic device that you can see the sculptor holding in his right hand, the equivalent of a mouse in standard PC programs. It is programmed to give feedback to the user, so they can literall 'feel' the medium they are working with as if they were sculpting real clay. Photo kindly supplied by the very talented Bob Naismith.

From Box to Battle

So, now I'm going to assume that you've taken the plunge and made that fateful decision to part with a few pounds to recruit your very first unit. I'm assuming that, sensibly, you want to keep the costs down initially until you're convinced that this is the hobby for you.

Your first investment, of course, may well have been in this book, rather than the figures or, if you're lucky, perhaps some kind soul has given you this volume as a present – if so, please thank them for me, both for supporting a struggling author and, we hope, for setting you on a lifelong path to happiness! Either way, let's look at what you need to get started.

Miniatures

In the 'Meet the Troops' section earlier, we examined the alternatives on offer in some detail and of course, it is entirely your choice as to which size of miniature and period of history you prefer, whether metal or plastic. However, for the moment, I'm going to make the bold assumption that initially, you'll want to try out the rules in this book, which recreate the 'horse and musket' period.

There is no simpler way to start than to pop along to your nearest toy or hobby shop, or perhaps visit a model stockist online to purchase a couple of boxes of 1/72 'soft' plastic figures. For the purposes of this demonstration, I initially bought four boxes from Amazon, all from Italian manufacturer Italeri: code 6095 British Infantry 1815; code 6094 British Light Cavalry 1815 (these are actually Light Dragoons, unlike the box 6040 they label as 'Light Dragoons' but which are actually hussars!); code 6002 French Infantry Napoleonic Wars 1805-1815 (wearing shakos, as opposed to Revolutionary Wars bicornes); and 6008 French Hussars (labelled Napoleonic Wars 1806/7 but, for our purposes, perfectly acceptable).

You could, of course, persuade a friend to recruit and command one side – either British or French – and thus halve your expense, but for the time being I'll assume that you might not have the luxury of an opponent yet, or perhaps are the parent of a prospective one whose purchasing power is synonymous with your own!

Now, what have we got for our money (less than £40 + postage at the time of writing)? For the British, we have three sprues of infantry, containing 48 figures, and three and a half sprues of cavalry, totalling 17 cavalry. The French have two sprues of infantry, but with 50 figures in total, and two sprues of cavalry, again with 17 cavalrymen in all. Please note that manufacturers are at liberty to change the content of their boxes, so what you see here may not match precisely what you buy – and indeed, you may have chosen to purchase something entirely different! However, my reason for buying these particular sets is that they will permit the creation of two balanced forces where neither side has a particular advantage. They will also enable you to get used to the basic aspects of the rules first, and then you can add other troop types in due course.

My initial purchases to create two modest forces of British and French using Italeri 1/72 soft plastic figures.

Preparation and tools

So, you've got your boxes of figures in front of you: What do you need?

First of all, you'll need some clear space to work on. This may seem obvious, but as you'll learn with this hobby, as soon as you start collecting figures, you build up quite a collection of other 'stuff' that goes with them.

I'm lucky enough to have a converted attic studio which serves me well as a writer, designer and, of course, wargamer, but after a decade of use, believe me, even my '*Loftwaffe*', as it is affectionately known, has accumulated far too much clutter and empty space is at a premium! Therefore your first task must be to allocate an area of at least two feet wide by perhaps two feet deep (or as far as your arms can reach, in fact) as a working area. The central part will need to be kept clear for whatever you are working on at the time, with the periphery used for your paints, brushes, water pots, tools, kitchen paper (for drying brushes or mopping up spills) and so on.

Games Workshop make a very useful 'paint station', which is effectively a plastic tray, but with recesses moulded for your paint pots, holes to stand brushes in and so on. At more than £20 as I write, there are certainly cheaper home-made options but, if you're in a hurry or don't have the wherewithal to undertake customised tray-making, it could be the best choice for you to get started. One aspect I do like of the GW product is that they have shaped the edges so that it will sit on your knees if you feel like watching TV at the same time.

The other critical aspect is light. You can never have too much light, but I have seen so many people who don't even make the best use of what they have. First of all, don't try to work with your back to the light – you're casting a shadow over whatever you're working on! Far better to sit either facing the light, or with the window to one side, preferably the side of your active arm (in other words, the right if you're right-handed). In addition,

A well-organised work station with everything the miniature painter needs close to hand, including reference material and notebook. Well, that's how I *start* each session... Wargamers are always interested to see how others arrange their workspace, and I've seen some gamers with wonderfully elaborate racks for their paints, for example, but as a beginner, you just need the basics.

invest in at least one good 'anglepoise' desk lamp with a daylight bulb. During the day, you can have this shining from overhead to eliminate shadows. If you plan to work through those long winter evenings, I'd recommend having at least two desk lamps, shining from opposite sides, as well as the general overhead light in your room. Be aware that 'tungsten' bulbs, as well as many of the new 'low energy' bulbs, can cast a coloured light, either yellowish or pinkish in tone, which will affect your perception of colour. Therefore, I recommend you hunt down 'daylight' bulbs wherever you can and stockpile them!

Step 1 of our preparation is to carefully clip or cut the figures (and their bases, in the case of the cavalry) from their sprues. Don't try using ordinary household scissors – you'll mangle the plastic and probably ruin the scissors too. I recommend either a sharp hobby knife (the segmented kind where you can snap off the tip once blunt are good), a surgeon's scalpel (the vee-shaped type with a flat edge, not the curved ones) or a pair of hobby clippers. Scalpels are available from all good art and hobby suppliers as are clippers – again, Games Workshop sell their own brand if you happen to be in the High Street.

Also at this stage, you can look for imperfections, which tend to come in three forms: flash (where plastic or metal under pressure has oozed out between the mould halves, creating a flat 'halo' around certain parts; mould lines (where imperfectly-aligned mould halves lead to a slight 'step' effect at the join); and 'tags', which are thin pieces where the material has followed escaping air along pre-determined 'vents' cut into the mould.

Tags are usually very easy to snip off with clippers. They are rare on plastic models, because the method of casting on sprues tends to prevent this, but quite common on metal miniatures, especially on the 'pointy' bits like the ends of weapons or slender equipment. Often, they will come away with just a slight twist between the fingers.

Using clippers to remove figures from their sprues. Hold the figure firmly and keep the flat side of the prongs towards the part you are extracting in order to ensure a clean cut with no protrusion left afterwards. Clippers like these work fine for both soft and hard plastic miniatures.

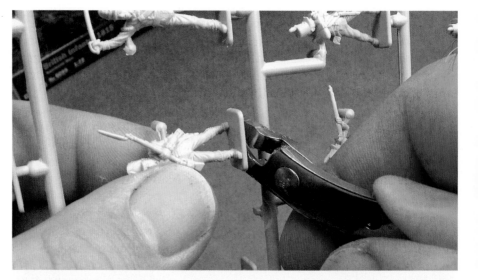

Removing flash and mould lines is much easier on metal and hard plastic figures than with soft plastic. Here, I'm filing a hard plastic Perry Miniatures ACW cavalryman using an oval-section file. With purely gaming-quality models, I'm not fussy enough to resort to fine grades of wet and dry paper.

Gently washing your miniatures in lukewarm water with a little detergent is important to remove any residues and prepare the surface for painting, whether they are metal or plastic. Here, a considerable number of Zvezda ancient Greeks are being given a bath before a thorough rinse. Don't be tempted to use the dishwasher!

Flash is somewhat harder to deal with and you'll need a different technique with plastic figures compared to metal ones. Starting with the easiest, flash on metal miniatures sometimes comes away with a light brush of the fingers, but more stubborn flash will require careful filing with round or elliptical modellers' files, sometimes known as 'mouse tail' or 'rat tail' files because of their size and profile. A good set of such files can be obtained from any good DIY or hobby store, or even an old-fashioned ironmonger, if you have one. Hard plastic miniatures can be scraped with a scalpel, keeping the blade almost perpendicular to the surface, followed by a quick file. Always file gently across the mould line at a slight angle. Expert modellers finish off with an extremely fine grade of 'wet and dry' abrasive paper. Whether metal or plastic, remove any dust or filings with a soft brush before proceeding.

For soft plastic figures, flash is much rarer nowadays, but if it does occur, it's a pain, because polythene does not like being filed. The only way forward is to use a very sharp scalpel, held at a shallow angle to the surface, and shave the flash away. Needless to say, a very steady hand is required.

Mould lines are treated in the same way as flash, but may require more material to be cut away to eliminate the fault. If the mould lines are very prominent, you are quite within your rights to return the figures and ask for replacements or your money back as they are unfit for purpose. I am always amazed at how tolerant wargamers are of poor manufacture: the problem is that, if people won't complain, the manufacturers may well be unaware of the problem and matters won't improve. As long as the approach is made courteously, most suppliers will happily replace or refund any faulty castings, especially since metal figures can simply be melted down again to make new miniatures and a good company will want to protect its reputation by keeping its customers happy. As a consumer, you have rights!

The next step may surprise you: we're going to wash the figures. All miniatures, whether metal or plastic, arrive with a residue of mould release agent, which needs to be removed in order to help our paints to adhere properly. The simplest way to do this is to fill a washing-up bowl or plastic bucket with some lukewarm water to which a few drops of washing-up liquid have been added. Pop the figures in and swish them around for a couple of minutes, then drain (I use a colander) and rinse them well to remove the detergent.

For metal figures, you can now just leave them to dry thoroughly on an old tea-towel or some kitchen paper. By all means put them near a radiator in cold weather, but not *too* near – we don't want warped weapons!

For plastic figures, however, I recommend a further stage: a bath in dilute vinegar. Vinegar?! Yes, that's right – re-fill your bucket or bowl with cold water and add a couple of capfuls of **spirit** vinegar (that's the clear stuff, not dark brown malt vinegar, which can leave your miniatures smelling for months) and toss your plastic figures in to soak for at least a couple of hours. I've not experimented with fancy wine or berry-flavoured vinegars, which are rather more expensive!

I tend to leave my figures to soak overnight, and then rinse and dry them the following morning, ready for the next stage.

What the vinegar solution does is microscopically etch the smooth surface of the figures, providing a better 'key' for the stages that follow. It's a process that has been arrived at over many years of experimentation by thousands of gamers who, in the early days, used to see their lovingly-applied paint literally flaking off before their eyes. By following this process and using acrylic paints as demonstrated below, your handiwork should last you for many years to come.

Next, you need some PVA adhesive, the commonly-available white glue that is used in various forms by everyone from schoolteachers in class to woodworkers making fine furniture. It's water-soluble and dries completely transparent, with a semi- to gloss finish. You'll need an old jam jar and an old brush (a small household decorating brush or a cheap nylon-bristled art brush is fine), together with a plastic tray or surface of some kind. Sounds mysterious? Right, let's get started.

Put a good blob of the glue into your empty jam jar. For a typical box of figures, I'd reckon on a heaped teaspoonful, though I tend to use a mass-production method, so I start with around a heaped tablespoonful. Don't forget, you can always keep any left over for future use as long as you have the lid for your jar and, to make sure you keep the air out, a bit of 'cling film'. Now, dilute the adhesive until you have something like a 25:75 glue:water mix which is the consistency of creamy milk. Make sure the glue is completely dissolved – you don't want any unexpected lumps, so keep stirring until it's thoroughly mixed.

Now, take your old brush, load it with the mixture and splosh it liberally over each figure, one at a time, making sure it gets into all the nooks and

Here are our ancient Greeks again, being given an undercoat of dilute PVA adhesive. You can see that I'm applying the mixture quite liberally. I then leave the figures for a few minutes before going back and soaking up 'pools' of excess PVA using a small brush or a piece of twisted kitchen tissue. Note the use of coffee stirrers to mount the figures in handy rows.

crannies. Try not to overload the figures: if you've overdone it, just take a little kitchen roll and use a corner to soak up any excess. Now pop the figure down on your plastic tray, pick up the next one, and on you go. (You should, by now, have guessed why I recommend putting the completed figures on a plastic tray – don't make the mistake I did of letting them dry onto wood or newspaper, which can lead to many expletives.)

As you're doing this, you can hold the figure's base with tweezers or simply with your fingers, an option that has the added benefit of peeling satisfying layers of dried glue from your digits afterwards.

If you have any multi-part miniatures, such as the cavalry, cannon or wagons, it's advisable to glue them together first before applying the PVA so that the joints are sealed. Because of the soft nature of the plastic (which is actually a form of polythene), not all adhesives bond it terribly well, but nowadays there are special types of superglue specifically for plastics of this kind – your local DIY store and a host of online hobby outlets will be able to make recommendations. If in doubt, universal adhesives like Bostik or UHU are fine.

If you want a really 'belt and braces' approach, you can pin soft plastic parts together very easily using, you guessed it, ordinary dressmakers' pins and a pair of pliers or wire clippers. Insert the sharp end of the pin into the top of the horse in the middle of the saddle, and then snip it off leaving just a few millimetres showing. [Safety note: mind your eyes during this process – it's best to hold on to the end of the pin as you snip it to prevent it pinging skywards with potentially dangerous consequences.] Once this is done, apply adhesive and impale the rider on top of the pin, pushing down until he is nicely seated on the horse. Leave the adhesive to dry thoroughly before coating the figure with PVA.

Once the PVA is dry, it seals the surface, preventing the plastic itself from oxidising (an annoying process which can lead to certain plastics

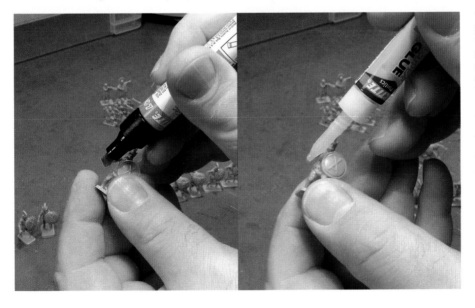

The two-step process required to use the type of superglue created specifically to stick soft plastic. On the left, the primer is applied with a special type of marker pen, then the actual adhesive is applied after allowing the primer to activate for a few seconds. It really does seem to make a difference to the strength of the bond compared to standard superglue. The figure's hand will hold a spear.

drying out and becoming brittle) and also provides an excellent priming for the painting stages that follow.

From this point on, the process is identical for both plastic and metal figures. Some people debate whether the recent 'hard' plastic miniatures require the PVA stage – in my opinion, it can do no harm, and certainly provides a useful filler for any small gaps left during assembly.

Preparing to paint

Nowadays, probably 90%+ of gamers and collectors use acrylic paint on their miniatures. In the old days (and I'm old enough to remember the late 1960s and early 1970s), there were only two options: enamel paints, which came in tinlets and glass jars; and artists' oil paints, which came in tubes. Both were oil-based, smelly and difficult to use with finesse, and the process of cleaning your brushes alone could have you faint from toxic fumes. Nevertheless, when mastered, they could produce beautiful results and some miniatures painters still use them to this day (particularly oil paints for horses).

Such techniques are for another book: what I intend to do here is help you get a reasonably good-looking army on the table in a reasonably short space of time, using all the tricks available to the modern wargamer, of which there are many, and you will have to decide what suits you best. The good thing is that these techniques will work on the humblest plastic figure as well as on the most expensive metal miniature. Some of them work better on larger miniatures, and others on tiny ones such as the 6mm castings mentioned earlier, but initially, we're going to get some paint onto those 1/72 figures you just invested in, then get them neatly based so we can play a little game.

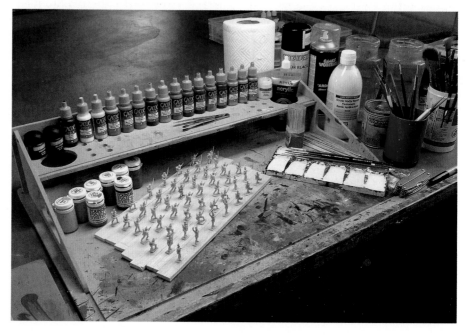

To get started with painting, you need a couple of dozen paints (fewer if you're happy to mix) and some varnish. I've also included a can of durable spray varnish – I'm very much a 'belt and braces' man! There is also a small collection of brushes here, ranging from a very fine 00 up to size 4 or so to quickly cover large areas and an old, soft brush for 'drybrushing'. With these, two pots of water and some kitchen towel.

PAINTS

You won't need many to start with. We'll start with black, white, mid-grey, bright red, a bright yellow, 'flesh' (which is obtainable is several shades), dark blue, light or sky blue, mid-green, dark green, dark brown, chestnut brown, a somewhat paler 'leather' brown or tan, and three metallic colours – gold, silver and 'gunmetal', which is a dull steel shade that, if you prefer, can be made by mixing silver and black. All these colours are available in small pots. Finally, we'll need some varnish to protect our paintwork. You can, in fact, use a coat of the same dilute PVA solution we used to prime the plastic miniatures, but most gamers tend to use either a matt or semi-matt spray varnish, or a brush-on artists' varnish such as Windsor & Newton's 'Galeria' acrylic medium matt varnish. If you want your miniatures to be super-tough, then you can apply a coat of polyurethane gloss varnish first, followed by a matt varnish to improve the visual effect.

Wargamers will happily debate the merits and demerits of different ranges of paints for hours, but in the end, it comes down to personal preference. Some people like the 'feel' of certain paints on the brush, others are more concerned about 'coverage' – in other words, will a single coat be sufficient, or is the paint more transparent, requiring further coats to build up to the final colour required? Some paints mix better with others in the same or different ranges, whilst others still can stand being diluted to a greater or lesser degree.

Many of these factors are affected by one of your very first choices: the colour of undercoat. Some people prefer to work from light to dark, beginning with a white or very pale undercoat and gradually adding thin washes of colour which collect in the folds and recesses, leaving the ridges pale. Others start with a black or very dark undercoat, doing the very opposite, building up the highlights, leaving the dark colours in the recesses. And then another school prefer to begin with a mid-tone, such as a grey, and use that as the basis to both create highlights with paler colours and shadows with darker ones. Finally, a recent innovation has been to actually undercoat the figure with the colour which predominates the most in its final uniform or costume, in the hope that this will save time: so, for example, we could undercoat our British infantry in red or our French infantry in dark blue, simply adding the remaining colours.

A final trick that has come to the aid of the speed-painter in recent years is 'dip', which is basically varnish to which pigment has been added. The idea is that you paint your miniatures with no shading or highlighting at all and then, once dry, dunk the miniature into the varnish, shake off the excess and then leave to dry. Hey presto! The result is a shaded, highlighted and varnished miniature in double-quick time. (In fact most wargamers refine this process slightly to create more subtle effects, but the basic process is as simple as I've described.)

What we're going to do is look at a number of alternatives, but first of all, let's choose some paint.

Once again, I have to mention Games Workshop as one of the places where you will most readily find acrylic paints suitable for wargames miniatures. If your interest has veered towards the historical, you are going to get some puzzled looks when the pleasant, if sometimes over-zealous, members of staff ask you what army you intend to paint and rather than answering "Chaos Marines" or "Clan Pestilens Skaven", you say "Waterloo campaign British and French". (For extra kudos you could point out to them that sometime *White Dwarf* editor Mark Latham had a set of Napoleonic rules published by Warhammer Historical called *Waterloo* featuring thousands of models sculpted by GW designer Alan Perry. Don't be surprised if you only get a blank look in return.)

Games Workshop paints, branded as 'Citadel' and just overhauled at the very moment that I was finishing writing this book, now come in six varieties: so-called 'Base' paints, of which there are currently 34 at the time of writing, have a somewhat thick consistency and are designed to cover in a single coat; standard 'Layer' colours, of which there are now 70, are the 'standard' range with many potential uses; 12 'Shade' colours, which are effectively washes, useful for producing shadows; a brand new range of 15 'Dry' colours, specifically formulated for drybrushing; four 'Glaze' colours that are like an ink wash; six 'Texture' colours for decorating bases; and finally four 'Technical' products, which include an acrylic medium, a gloss varnish, a primer and the new liquid 'Green Stuff'.

Now, if you're prepared to shop around, you can find identical colours much cheaper, or even bigger ranges. My first stop would be a brand called Coat D'Armes, distributed by Black Hat Miniatures (*www.blackhat.co.uk/ coat_darms/paintcolours.php*) and sold by a number of wargames traders often seen at wargame shows. Coat D'Armes paints are very similar to the original Citadel colour range in every respect. They also produce three washes and a textured paint for bases called 'Brushscape'.

Another popular range is manufactured by Foundry (*wargamesfoundry. com/paint_and_brushes/*). The Foundry range, again similar in character to the Citadel range, has one unique selling point: they are available in sets of three, consisting of the basic colour, highlight and shade for each tone. Thus, for example, Bright Red (15B) is accompanied by a brownish Bright Red Shade (15A) and orangy Bright Red Light (15C) – ideal for the beginner who may lack confidence mixing their own colours, or handy for the more experienced painter who simply can't be bothered!

A Spanish company called Vallejo (*www.acrylicosvallejo.com/gb/*) produces a huge variety of colours that are very different in character from those mentioned so far. There are two ranges: 'Game Color', which contains highly pigmented colours most suitable for fantasy gaming, though it has to be said that they work equally well for those historical periods where brightly-coloured uniforms and costumes were the order of the day; and Model Color, a vast array of some 220 tones suitable for the most rigorously authentic models. Two offshoots of this are the Panzer Aces range specifically formulated, as the name suggests, to reproduce the colours of WWII armoured fighting vehicles and their crews, and Model Air, featuring extremely finely-ground pigments suitable for use in an airbrush. Vallejo also have a range of brush-on powdered pigments for 'weathering' vehicles and figures.

Generally speaking, Vallejo colours are much thinner in consistency and more transparent than the other ranges mentioned above. This makes them suitable for the painter who prefers to build up colour and tone using a series of semi-transparent washes and glazes rather than a more impressionistic, 'impasto' style using thicker paint with more pigment.

You are unlikely to find Vallejo in high street stores, but they are often stocked by the better hobby shops and wargames stores and are commonly available at historical wargames shows.

Two more brands you may come across in toy and hobby shops are Humbrol and Tamiya. Humbrol, now owned by Hornby along with Airfix, were synonymous with wargaming for decades with their extensive range of enamel paints, but these are now also available as acrylics, similar in character to the Citadel/Coat D'Armes/Foundry ranges above. Their emphasis has shifted more towards the model railway and model aircraft enthusiast, rather than the military uniform aficionado. See *www.humbrol. com/paints/all-paints/*. Tamiya, well-known Japanese manufacturers of highly detailed large scale AFV models, have a modest range of acrylics stocked by those outlets where you find their kits: see *www.tamiya.com/ english/products/list/acrylic_1.htm*.

There are other brands of paint out there that I have failed to mention, such as Testor's Model Master brand, simply because I have no experience with them, but I think that I have provided enough for you to make a reasonably informed choice, bar one option: artists' acrylics, such as those produced by Rowney and Windsor & Newton. If you have any skill at all with paint on canvas, you may well be aghast at the thought of collecting

Hobby paints from a few manufacturers, including Citadel, Vallejo and Foundry (others are available); and some artists acrylic and oil colours from Rowney, Liquitex, Reeves and Winsor & Newton. Watercolour, poster and gouache paints are not really suitable for miniatures as their formulas are not plastic-based and so do not 'grip' plastic or metal surfaces by forming a skin.

dozens, nay, perhaps even hundreds of pre-mixed shades and tones when you know perfectly well that, with a little experience and confidence, you can mix any colour you like from just a handful of primary colours. Well, if that is indeed the case, good luck, and I can only admire your confidence. The problem for most wargamers, however, is that they want the colours on their palette to be reproducible, lest the tenth battalion of British infantry they paint looks alarmingly discordant with the first they completed. For sure, a certain amount of variation is desirable, but for those lacking skill and confidence with colour mixing, the pre-mixed colour ranges on offer have many advantages.

Where I am entirely in accord with the colourist, however, is when it comes to horses. Real artists acrylics, like oil colours, can achieve a natural effect and slight sheen that leaves paints from pre-mixed pots looking dead by comparison. Perhaps it's a trick of the eye, or even the figment of my imagination, but we'll take a quick look at the use of artists' colours for horses later on, and they can also be used for the first stage that we are about to embark upon shortly – undercoating.

BRUSHES

Having chosen our paints, we have to apply them with something, and your choice of brushes is critical.

In the days of oil-based paints, which effectively kept our implements bathed in a balmy moisturiser, brushes might last for years. The textbooks of the time encouraged us to invest in the finest sable brushes and we would happily spend a whole week's pocket money on a single brush, knowing that it would still be giving us good service in two, three, even five years' time.

Acrylics, however, are merciless on brushes. Many people I know report recurrent problems of brushes losing their points alarmingly quickly and

A selection of brushes of different types and prices ranging from dirt cheap to rather expensive, including sable, synthetic, hogshair and nylon, and in different shapes both round and flat. Some are used only for figures, some for terrain. Don't be fooled into thinking that smaller brush = finer point, because often a larger brush will hold its point better and for longer.

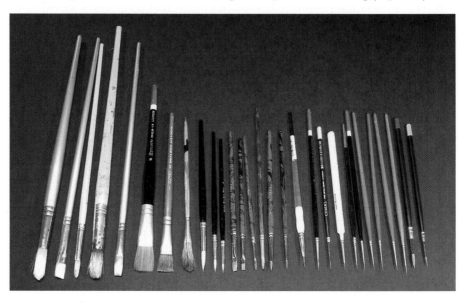

developing the dreaded 'hook' point. The onset of this condition can be delayed by punctilious care, but the fate seems inevitable.

For this reason, wargamers tend to have a fearsome array of brushes for different purposes, ranging from broad, flat brushes for light dry-brushing, through a wide range of 'round' brushes for general work, down to tiny tiddlers for the finest detail. As you'll see in the photographs included in this book, it's not beyond the ability of some painters to add the pupils to tiny eyes and the buckles to miniature shoes.

For the purposes of this demonstration, however, you will need only four brushes.

First, a general purpose flat brush, about 1/4" to 3/8" (6-10mm) wide. This can be used for applying broad washes of colour, dry-brushing and also for painting scenic items such as houses.

The second is a largish round brush, about size 6 to 8. This is a good, general-purpose brush which, if the point is maintained, can be used for anything from undercoating figures to applying broad areas of colour to coats, jackets, trousers and so on. It's an excellent size for painting horses and equipment like wagons or cannon. Both this and the flat brush can happily be synthetic.

Your third brush needs to be finer, perhaps a size 2 or 3 'designer' round brush, which has long bristles that come to an excellent point. This versatile instrument will be the one you use the most, so experiment with nylon, synthetic and natural sable. Ignore hogs' bristle – those are for oil painting on canvas. You want the hairs to be soft, supple and springy, so that they retain the point whilst being flexible. Such a brush can cope with everything but the very finest detail.

The final brush will be for the most delicate work, and different painters swear by their own preferences. I would go for a good sable brush, size 1 or possibly 0. It is possible to buy really tiny brushes, such as 00 or even 000, but in my own experience, they tend to deteriorate more quickly and are of very limited application – perhaps for the pupils of eyes or small buttons. In any case, let me restate the case that it is the point that counts, not the overall size of the brush, and in my experience a 1 or 0 holds its point far better and is more useful for other jobs such as applying fine highlights, braid and so on.

You can find brushes in any good art shop or online. Games Workshop sells its own brushes, as do several of the other companies we mentioned earlier who also manufacture paint, but after four decades of practice, I've come to the conclusion that these brushes are overpriced and frankly not of the best quality. Steer towards those companies used to dealing with artists, illustrators and graphic designers such as Windsor & Newton. Another brush maker I thoroughly recommend is Rosemary & Co, a small company making a superb and diverse range of brushes – see *https:// www.rosemaryandco.com/*.

In due course, you might want to add a fifth brush to your collection – that'll be one of the first three mentioned above once it gets old and scruffy, and no longer suitable for painting figures! Many a brush can serve out its retirement still doing useful work when basing your figures, or for undercoating or varnishing, or for painting or weathering your scenery. What you don't want, however, is to hang onto a brush once it starts shedding bristles – there's nothing more annoying than standing back to admire your own handiwork, only to spot an errant hair embedded in the paintwork! However, even in death, a brush can live on, with the trimmed hairs appearing as tall grass or reeds or sheaves of hay on a scenic base. The handle can then be used as a convenient stirrer or modelling tool.

A couple of tips about brush care.

- NEVER scrub your brushes point-first onto the bottom of the jar to clean them. This is the fastest way to murder a good brush! Always use a gentle swishing action in the water to clean the bristles. If you do have any stubborn paint that has accumulated near the ferrule (that's the metal tube that holds the bristles together in a bunch), then gently press the top of the bristles against the side of the jar and roll the brush back and forth. (This is why I use a jar rather than an opaque container so that I can see what's happening.) Another option is to draw the brush gently across a smooth surface, such as a clean palette, applying slight pressure to the top of the bristles near the ferrule as you spin the brush slowly between your fingers. You can also use your fingers to gently squeeze the bristles in order to release any dried-on paint, before rinsing again.

- To keep a good point on your brush, dry it by drawing it gently across kitchen paper, then use your tongue and lips to bring it to a point before storing. Don't be squeamish – acrylic paint is non-toxic. If you want a really fancy option, there is such a thing as 'brush soap' which can be bought at art and hobby stores but, to my mind, this is an unnecessary expense except for the very finest sable. Good old spit works every time!

- Store your brushes point upwards, not lying on their side. This protects the point, ensures even drying and enables you to instantly recognise the brush and its condition.

FINAL CONSIDERATIONS BEFORE PAINTING

Right, let's assume that you've now got yourself a small collection of tools, paints and brushes and you're sitting at your well-lit desk space ready to start. Just a couple more things to get ready.

You're going to need water. Use two pots or empty (well-washed) jam jars or coffee jars, fill them three-quarters full with clean water and place them side by side to your front right (for a right-handed person) within comfortable reach, but not so close that you might knock them over. You use one jar to clean the brush, the other for clean water to add to the paint to dilute it. Some expert painters go to the length of using distilled water to eliminate contaminants such as lead or calcium, but to be honest, ordinary tap water is perfectly okay for 99.9% of jobs.

Where you have water, you need something to dry it up, so I keep a roll of kitchen paper or tissue on the table, with one or two sheets torn off ready for action. You will also need this when preparing to use dry-brushing techniques, for which you wipe almost all the paint off the brush before lightly flicking the hairs across the object, leaving a tiny amount of paint on any raised detail such as buttons, braid, folds of cloth and so on, as you will see. I also wrap a piece of kitchen paper or a rag around a paint pot when I shake it – better safe than sorry!

I would also recommend a palette of some kind. You can buy cheap, plastic paint palettes at any art or hobby store, but an old, plain white plate or saucer will do, as would a piece of plain glass or a white bathroom tile. Any of these can be picked up for just a few pence or found around the house. You want the palette to be white so that your perception of the colour being mixed is not affected by any background colour. For this reason, you might also want to place a piece of plain white paper underneath the glass if that is your choice.

If you want to keep paint from tubes wet between sessions, then you can create a 'wet' palette. Lay a sheet of absorbent kitchen paper inside a plastic container – old take-away meal containers are good for this – and add enough water to make it thoroughly damp, but not overflowing. Now cover this with greaseproof or baking paper, and squeeze your paint onto this surface. Cover the container using the original lid or clingfilm, and the paint will stay fresh for days. You can top up the water with a few drops whenever you like.

Another useful thing to have around are cocktail sticks or matchsticks or ice lolly sticks that can be used for stirring paint, or transferring paint from pot to palette. You could also use an old paintbrush for this, as well as for adding drops of water to the paint. Some people use a small eye-dropper for the same purpose, or a small 'squeezy' bottle. In fact, Vallejo

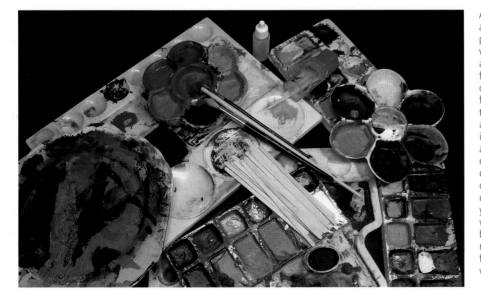

A variety of the author's well-used palettes and a variety of bits and pieces useful for stirring and dispensing paint from pots. One of the great things about acrylic paint is that it dries to a plastic skin, so once it's dry, you can happily mix different colours on top as wet as you like and they won't be affected by any pigment residue (unlike, for example, watercolours).

paints come in small, squeezable bottles custom-designed to enable you to add paint one drop at a time. It's a good idea to use a cocktail stick or old brush for mixing paint on your palette, saving your best brushes for actually painting.

I'm extremely lucky to have good eyesight, but if you're not so fortunate, you might want to consider some kind of magnifying device. These are available either as free-standing units, leaving your hands free, or as 'goggles' that can be worn on your head, over your spectacles if you need them. Some even incorporate a small light, rather like a miner's lamp. Another option is the 'anglepoise' magnifier, which often incorporates a ring light around the outside. Whichever option you choose, the main thing is that you must be comfortable using it, or you will be too distracted to paint the fine detail you bought it for in the first place!

If you are going to use spray paint for undercoating – there are advantages and disadvantages we shall discuss shortly – then you must ensure that you have a well-ventilated area in which to do this. If you work indoors, the danger is that you can inhale all kinds of unpleasant and potentially dangerous fumes, as well as particles of the paint itself. I have no idea what undercoat may do to the inside of one's lungs, but I can't imagine that the results are beneficial in any way, so at the very least, a face mask is a good idea.

In an ideal world, you would have a 'spray booth', a facility much loved by graphic designers in days gone by when they had to use Spray Mount adhesive to secure columns of type onto art boards during the page design process. A spray booth works in precisely the same way as the extractor hood above a modern cooker, sucking nasty things away from you and, via a pipe, expelling them through a filter and then to the outside. The genuine article is, however, extremely expensive – nearly £1,000 for an A2-sized booth – but you may be able to pick one up second-hand or rig something up with an old vacuum cleaner or, indeed, kitchen extractor hood. The cheapest alternative of all is to do your spraying outside or in a well-ventilated shed.

Naturally, you'll want to have any reference material to hand, such as your books covering period uniforms or other material to inspire you, such as drawings, photographs or magazine cuttings. I sometimes find that one of those stands used by cooks to keep recipe books open can help, or an old music stand.

And finally, for your own comfort, you may wish to have some kind of beverage to hand and perhaps some soothing music or even a chatty podcast, such as *The View from the Veranda* (*www.viewfromtheveranda. co.uk/*), where you can hear your author ranting with host Neil Shuck about various aspects of the hobby...

Oh, a quick tip: put your beverage on the opposite side of your work area to your water pots. I've lost count of the times that a perfectly good cuppa *and* the paint job have been ruined by dunking my brush in the wrong liquid!

Painting

"At last!" I hear you cry. Yes, we've taken a while to get to this stage, but by now, I hope you're fully prepared. Let's get started.

UNDERCOATING

For the purposes of this first demonstration, during which I intend to teach you how to get a smart army onto the table reasonably quickly, we're going to begin with a black undercoat and build up the colour from there. This also has the advantage of eliminating the need to create shadows and prevents unsightly gaps in the paintwork – nothing screams at you on the wargames table quite like a bit of white undercoat that has been left uncovered. Black is also kinder to reds, a prominent part of the British uniforms, as white does have the tendency to turn them pink. On the other hand, we must understand that black can 'kill' some other colours, such as yellows, that have lower opacity, so we shall have to compensate accordingly. With experience, you'll choose your undercoat colour according to the final look of the figure required, the skin tone and uniform colours desired, the techniques you'll be using and so on.

We'll begin with the British infantry which you will, by now, have washed, cleaned up and primed with your diluted PVA mixture. Naturally, ensure that you've washed your hands thoroughly before embarking on this next stage – grease is the enemy of water-based paint! On a hot day, use kitchen paper or a clean cotton rag to keep your hands clean and dry.

To ensure that the figures are both kept clean and are easier to handle, attach them to a strip of wood or card, spaced an inch or two apart. This will enable you to use production-line methods and speed up the process considerably. You can use a little Blu-Tak under each base, or a little blob of household glue – just make sure that the figures are attached firmly but *temporarily*, not permanently! An alternative is to mount them individually

Method 1: spray undercoating your miniatures. Several thin coats are better than one, thick, soggy coat. TOP TIP: wear surgical or rubber gloves for this job or be prepared, like the author in a hurry who forgot, to spend some time with a scrubbing brush and soap! Of course, the 'Rolls Royce' option is to have a spray booth with extractor fan, with the figures mounted on a plinth or rotating surface inside.

on plastic milk carton tops. I've even seen some painters mount figures on all four sides of a stick, which they then hold vertically and spray from all directions, producing what might be mistaken for a medieval weapon! If such a technique suits you, then go for it.

That done – and I tend to work on a battalion of infantry or a regiment of cavalry at a time – choose your weapon. If you decide to use a spray, such as matt black car paint or hobby paint, then ensure that the can has been shaken vigorously for at least a minute or so (you'll be able to hear the ball bearing doing its work inside the can). Now spray your strips of figures from about nine or ten inches (25cm) away, moving smoothly from side to side several times. Then, turn the figures around 180 degrees and repeat, before turning them 90 degrees so that you get all their sides, and again 180 degrees to spray from the opposite side. I usually do a final spray from directly above before inverting the can and doing a short spray to clear the nozzle. This whole process will probably have taken only a couple of minutes.

Once this first coat is dry to the touch (after about five minutes), I then lay the figures on their side and do another session, coating the undersides of the arms, legs and equipment, turn them over and repeat. Once done, stand the figures up again and leave them to dry for at least an hour.

As you will discover with practice, no matter how hard you try, spray paint has the infuriating habit of failing to reach every nook and cranny unless you hold it so close to the figure that the result is an unsightly, blobby finish, with over-applied paint sagging as it dries. Much better to apply several thin coats than one heavy one so that important detail on the figure is not obscured.

The second option, which is somewhat more controllable and less potentially hazardous to health or furnishings, is to undercoat the figures by hand.

Method 2: undercoating by brush. This is much more controllable, but make sure that the brush you use doesn't shed hairs, which can frustrate your final paint job.

Create a diluted (about 50:50 or 40:60 with water) mixture of black and, using your largest brush or even small house painting brush, apply liberally to your figures and set them aside to dry. Make sure that you get paint into all the nooks and crannies. Again, don't apply the paint too thickly, or you will obscure important detail. One coat may well be enough – we shall be applying further colours over this basecoat after all – but sometimes soft plastic miniatures are moulded in surprisingly garish colours, so you may wish to obscure this as much as possible.

Acrylic paints dry extremely quickly, usually within an hour or two at most, and often far, far quicker. The warmer the room, the quicker the water content evaporates, leaving the pigment bonded to the surface. Acrylic is, in fact, a type of plastic, so what you are actually doing is applying a microscopically thin pigmented 'skin' over the figure. Once acrylic paint is dry, the pigment is 'set', unlike with, say, traditional watercolours, which can be blended with other colours applied later, or 'lifted out' with clean water and an absorbent tool such as a dry brush, cotton wool or a sponge.

The process would be identical were you using a white or any other colour undercoat. You may, in fact, prefer to use white for the French infantry since a large portion of their uniform is, in fact, white, as you will see from the artwork on the box they came in.

PRODUCTION LINE PAINTING

Once the undercoat has dried thoroughly (which may be within an hour or so, but I would always recommend leaving it for longer, possibly overnight), you can start applying the basic colours.

It's a matter of personal choice, but I always begin by painting what I can see of the little men themselves – and for this period, that means the face and hands. I also feel that this brings them to life straight away and they 'call' to me to get on and finish them! Many wargamers feel differently and prefer to paint the flesh last, and I'm sure you'll develop your own preference.

Apply a few drops of pale flesh coloured paint (such as Citadel Kislev Flesh) to your palette and dilute it by adding the same amount of water or slightly less. Make sure that this is well mixed, producing a smooth, creamy consistency. In the case of Vallejo paints, which are much thinner, you will need much less water.

Taking your large round brush, gently pick up enough paint to about half-fill the bristles. DON'T flood the brush right up to the ferrule. With your other hand, pick up your first strip of figures, take a deep breath, and off we go.

Proceed along the strip of figures painting the faces first. Don't push the brush, always pull. Just cover the facial area from just below the brim of the hat down to slightly under the chin and round the sides slightly to where the ears and side of the neck are. Don't attempt to paint the front of the neck, which would be in shadow anyway, and leave a fine line of black above the collar if you can, but don't fret if your hand isn't steady enough

Diluting the flesh paint on the palette. You're aiming to create the consistency of creamy milk.

Picking up paint on your brush. Hold the brush at an angle and don't 'stab' the palette, but rather draw it through the paint. Don't flood the brush with pigment: you want to be able to control the flow as you paint.

Painting the faces a basic flesh colour. If you're feeling adventurous, once the first colour has dried, you can add a little white and highlight cheeks, noses and chins.

After the faces, do the hands, which again can be highlighted with a little paler flesh colour if you have the patience.

just yet. We can always correct it later, and practice makes perfect.

Once you've done all the faces, do all the hands, again leaving some black near the cuffs.

The big brush is fine, as long as it has a good point. We are not bothering about fine facial features here but, as you'll see, the final effect will be surprisingly effective and absolutely fine for our purposes. Throughout this process, don't worry at all if you splash paint over other parts – we'll be going over with other colours and have plenty of time to smarten everything up. If you accidentally make a big blob, just use the corner of a bit of kitchen roll or tissue to soak it up, then move on.

For now, that's the flesh done and we'll proceed to the next stage.

Sticking with the British infantry for the moment, here's your first bit of 'uniforminfo', as it used to be called in *Military Modelling* magazine many years ago. The Italeri figures in the box are listed as suitable for 1815, which is the year of the Battle of Waterloo (June 18th). However, there are actually two types of uniform included in the box. You'll have to look carefully, but all the figures on the bottom half of the sprues standing firing or squatting and firing (and yes, I'm as baffled as you as to why that pose wasn't simply a kneeling figure instead!), together with those reaching into their cartridge pouch and the other pair advancing with their musket held at waist height, are wearing what is known as a 'stovepipe' shako, which was worn from 1800 onwards. The shako worn by the remaining figures on the upper half of the sprues, with the 'false' front which stands higher than the crown, is called a 'Belgic' shako, and was introduced in 1812. Some units, such as Light Infantry regiments, however, continued to wear the stovepipe shako until the end of the war.

Now, it is certainly true that the Battle

of Waterloo and the 100 Days campaign which preceded it is, as we have seen, a fascinating period of history, but I am going to suggest that we paint our units in a manner suitable for the Peninsular War which preceded it in Spain, Portugal and southern France up to Napoleon's first defeat in 1814. The other figures we have obtained in our initial purchase are all suitable for this period, and this choice will give us far more scope in how we deploy our troops in wargames. Waterloo, Quatre Bras and Ligny were huge battles, whereas many actions fought in the Peninsula are well within the grasp of the average wargamer to recreate in their entirety, or close to it, should you choose to do so. Moreover, should you wish to expand your collection to include Austrians, Russians, Prussians and others, the vast majority of the battles they fought against Napoleon also took place before 1815.

Back to our painting and, in practical terms, this simply means that we're going to paint our British in white trousers, rather than grey ones. Although, technically speaking, grey was the standard issue after 1811, the troops in the Peninsula had terrible supply problems until the end of the war and white was still common right up to 1814, as well as all manner of 'make do and mend' and 'homespun' alternatives.

To give you an indication of how varied appearances in reality were, here's a veteran sergeant describing the situation when some previously 'missing' men turned up at the end of the war:

"The captain of my company, who had been like myself through the whole campaign excepting when actually in hospital, pretended not to know them when he saw them, and asked them, "Where on earth do you come from? You certainly don't belong to my company,

The difference between a stovepipe (left) and Belgic shako (right).

Painting the trouser fronts white...

...and then the backs. The undercoat will show through slightly because the diluted white paint has low opacity, but this is fine. Leave the boots black.

Adding a second coat of white to the upper surfaces, leaving the appearance of shadow where there is only one coat.

Tackling the crossbelts. Take reasonable care, but don't fret too much if you wobble.

Adding straps to the backpacks. Sadly, military units of this period really liked white leather and straps!

Adding the remaining white straps to the rolled greatcoat and elsewhere.

The next bits of white to tackle are the turnbacks on the jacket tails, where visible.

by your appearance." He then called me to say if I knew them. I remarked, "They seem to have been in luck's way about their clothes, at any rate;" and so they did, for whilst ours were as ragged as sheep and as black as rooks, theirs were as red and new as if they had never been on, and their shoes were to match, whilst ours were completely worn out by our continual marches, the captain's being quite as bad as any private's."[6]

This, of course, applied to all armies once they had been on campaign for a while, rather than simply parading on manoeuvres or at royal palaces. So, as your painting grows in confidence, you might wish to make future units somewhat more ragged in appearance, but to begin with, let's stick to the basics.

Using long, easy strokes (always pulling the brush towards you – pushing the brush can damage the bristles), paint the trousers, starting at the waistline where you can see the edge of the jacket, and moving down towards the feet, but leave the boots black. I suggest painting all the fronts first, then reverse the stick in your hand and paint the backs. You're just looking for nice, even coverage. Once you've completed one strip, pick up the next and do all *their* trousers, and so on.

This is pure production-line: by doing the same item over and over, you become much quicker after a while, and there's no unnecessary stopping and starting.

By the time you've finished the last one, it's possible that the paint on the first one will already be dry. Again, this will depend

---

6 "The Autobiography of Sergeant William Lawrence, A Hero of the Peninsular and Waterloo Campaigns", p.192-3 (Chapter XX), Project Gutenberg, www.gutenberg.org/files/29263/29263-h/29263-h.htm#page192

on the temperature of the room, humidity and so on. Either way, the paint should dry within a few minutes.

Now, white is one of those colours which has a low opacity (in other words, it tends not to cover very well), so the effect so far may look distinctly greyish. So now, I want you to repeat the process, but this time only painting the upper surfaces which would catch the light. So now, concentrate on the thighs, tops of the knees, shins, tops of the calf muscles and so on.

Done that? Good. Now, clean your big brush, and pick up the smaller one, probably a number 2 or so with a really good point.

Those British have really distinctive white crossbelts, holding up the bayonet and cartridge pouch respectively, so we're going to do those next.

Again, load the brush with white paint – a little less than last time – and move along the ranks. You should soon get into a nice "one, two, one, two" rhythm as you use the point of your brush to cover first the strap coming over the right shoulder, then the left, and so on. These British jackets are quite a challenge, so you're getting to practise some fiddly stuff right away, but nice, steady breathing and a degree of patience wins through. Some people prefer to actually hold the figures upside down for this, so your strokes go from the waist to the shoulder. Try it and see. Either way, remember that you don't want to force your brush point right into the corners which will be bathed in shadow anyway.

Having done the fronts, turn the figures round again and we'll do the back packs. You might want to switch to your smallest brush for this, cleaning the size 2 before you move on.

I'll be honest, knapsacks can be a pain, but once more, the production-line process really helps. Examine the figures first, and you'll see that the crossbelts and

"Is there no end to the white?" I hear you cry? Nearly there – these are the musket straps.

Our drummers need something to drum, so we add some white drum skins. If you're feeling adventurous, you could tweak the colour to make a slightly darker patch where the drum sticks have worn the skin.

Adding the yellow facing colour to the 9th Foot, beginning with their collars...

...and completing them with their cuffs and other minor details, such as epaulettes. If you splash onto the jacket area, don't worry, it will all be covered by the red later.

This shot shows 9th Foot figures with their facing colours complete. Refer to illustrations and other reference material – such as images found online – for more precise details if you like.

Now we tackle the blue facings of the 2nd Foot. Please, don't get hung up on this stage: we're creating an impression, 'painting the unit, not the man' as a wise man once told me.

If you get a bit of a splash onto the white trousers or belts, just dab it with a tissue, let it dry, and then touch up later.

At last, some spanking British scarlet. Leave a small gap of undercoat around the edges to indicate shadow and help define the area if you can. If not, don't worry, we'll be doing some quick shading later. Don't rush this stage.

haversack strap pass under the epaulettes on the shoulder and between the backpack and the figure's back. This requires just two blips of white paint per figure, and I suggest you do those first.

Now, these fellows have a rolled greatcoat and canteen on top, with a strap left and right over the blanket roll and another in the middle. One, two, three should be your rhythm as you just pull the brush point towards you. Then you have the two straps running down the backpack, swish, swish, done.

There's a bit more white to do. Turning the figures round and looking at them from the front, you can see that the haversack straps pass over the shoulder and under the arms, so *where you can see them*, paint them. I used italics there because it is a common disease amongst wargamers and modellers to paint even the stuff that can't be seen at normal viewing distance (usually 2-3 feet – 60-90cm – or even more). Unless you intend to enter painting competitions or take macro photos of your units for publication in a magazine, don't do it: that way lies madness.

Almost there. On some of the figures, there's the haversack located on the hip, underneath the water flask. A quick dab and you're done.

Now, I know that British infantry have white buttonhole tape on the front of their jackets, but we're going to leave that for the moment.

The final bit of white I'd like you to paint now is the strap on the underside of each musket, which is well illustrated on the box front art. A quick swish between the figures' hands, and then again to add a bit just beyond that (but stopping well short of the muzzle) and you're done. Oh, you might want to just finish with a blob of white on the top and bottom of each drummer boy's drum.

Any other white you can see we shall

either ignore or add as a detail using a different technique later.

Now, just as indicated on the box, we are going to represent two different regiments with these figures, one with blue facings, the other with yellow. (Facings originated as contrasting coloured lining to coats which were revealed by being buttoned back in the days when coat tails, double-breasted lapels and cuffs were more voluminous.)

The facing colour is visible on the collar, cuffs and epaulettes. In the case of officers, their lapels were lined with facing colour but, on campaign, they were usually worn buttoned across with only two rows of buttons showing on the front of the red jacket or with just a small triangle of colour showing on the upper chest where one corner had been buttoned back, as is just about visible on the officer figure waving his sword.

So, the unit in stovepipe shakos is going to have yellow facings – let's call them the 9th (East Norfolk) Regiment of Foot, and the others sporting Belgic shakos are going to have blue facings: the 2nd (Queen's) Regiment of Foot. Both were present at the Battle of Salamanca in 1812. In terms of uniform, the one major difference between them was that the drummer of the 9th Foot wore old-fashioned 'reversed' colours, which is to say that his jacket was yellow with red trim, as opposed to the style in the 2nd Foot, where the drummer wore a red jacket faced blue. Both had additional lace adornment on their sleeves, which we'll come to later.

So, what I'm going to suggest is that we paint the facing colours before the jackets. Start with the yellow ones. Why? Well, partly because it's much safer to have yellow paint on your brush before the blue, in case you haven't cleaned your brush properly!

Off you go then, although with the yellow paint, use less water to dilute it because you need more pigment to cover with yellow

Once all the red has been done, add a little yellow to the mix. The proportion should be roughly 1 part yellow to 5 parts red

Using this orange/red, highlight the upper surfaces of the arms, chest and so on where the light would be falling on them, leaving the darker red in the shadows.

Use black to touch up any areas that you feel need more definition, such as backpacks, cartridge boxes, the officers' scabbards, headgear, boots and so on. Take reasonable care at this stage.

The greatcoats receive our attention next. In the field, the greatcoat was often lost or discarded, if it didn't wear out, and would be replaced with locally-made blankets or coats, so feel free to add variations.

The water canteens – where present – should be a mid-blue for the British. Again, on campaign, these items often went missing and were replaced with all sorts of improvised containers.

The good old 'Brown Bess' musket gets our attention now, with a coat of mid- to dark brown.

If you're feeling up to it, there's an annoying leather canteen strap to deal with. Small brush, steady hand, breath held...

Preparing to drybrush. Yes, pick up barely diluted paint on your brush and then gently wipe it off onto a tissue or kitchen paper. Sounds daft, but...

than you do with some other colours. Use your finest brush for the collars and again, you'll probably want to do them in two stages, front and back. Then the epaulettes on the shoulders of those figures where any are still visible under those straps we painted. Then the cuffs, just a band around the bottom of the sleeve less than a millimetre wide. Finally, the drummer boy's jacket, though not much more than the sleeves are visible what with the drum, pack, knapsack and all those straps.

All done? Good, put those aside, clean your brush thoroughly and now do the blue facings for the 2nd Foot. Remember to treat the drummer the same as the rank and file here.

As you're painting the facing colours, do your best to avoid splashing the white trousers and belts. Load your brush with somewhat less paint than previously and taking care not to flick the bristles. If you do splash, don't panic: use tissue to soak up the spill and then quickly use another brush to apply some clear water to the affected area, then dab again with the tissue. This should remove most, if not all, the pigment and you can paint over it again later.

Okay, time for some British scarlet! Reds are another part of the spectrum that sometimes have opacity problems, so as with the yellow, don't over-dilute.

Go through exactly the same procedure as before, painting those bits that are still visible of the jackets after all that other stuff has gone on. For the most part, we're talking about the sleeves, a bit of the front and perhaps some of the sides. The back of the jacket, apart from on the officer and sergeant, is pretty much completely covered by the backpacks. Once again, if you can – and practice makes perfect – leave a fine line of black showing at the join.

Once you've done the first coat, I'm going to introduce you to the first attempt at paint mixing to create a highlight.

If you add white to red, you get pink, which is *not* the highlight colour for red (though it can be used sparingly to 'fade' it). What you actually need is a dull orange, so on your palette, where you should still have a little of the red left over, add a couple of drops of yellow. Not too much – we're not talking fluorescent here – but just enough to 'turn' the colour into a distinctly tawny shade. Add a little extra water if needed.

Now, just as you did with the second run on the trousers, apply this colour to the upper surfaces that might catch the light, meaning the upper arms and, depending on the position of the figure, possibly the front or rear of the forearm. Some of the 'flank company' figures have a device on the shoulder known as a 'wing', which should also receive a small dab in the centre.

By now, your miniatures are really coming alive. Not far to go.

Next stop, if you haven't done so already, get rid of your dirty water and refill the jar. You might want another cuppa by now too.

If your knapsack straps went a bit squiffy, now's the time to straighten them by simply applying a fairly dense coat of black over any errant white bits. Just a smooth, vertical stroke between the straps, followed by one either side, will do. You can also touch up the black boots and shakos if you need to. At this point, you will have already achieved quite a smart figure.

Greatcoats next, and these are a mid-grey. Again, simply paint stripes between and outside the white straps and a bit on the ends.

Water canteens are a dull mid-blue, which can be achieved by simply adding a touch of grey to sky blue.

The muskets – no surprise here – are chestnut brown. Just paint the upper surface and sides, leaving the white strap showing underneath. We'll leave the barrels and bayonets, along with other metal objects, until last.

Here we see the result as the bristles 'dust' the raised detail of the jacket lace. British lace distinctions were fiendishly complex in reality, and had buttons fastening the single-breasted jacket; hence our desire to be impressionistic only for now.

You can also drybrush the white cords that hang across the front of the Belgic skakos. Make sure you brush only *across* the detail.

Painting the plumes. Again, it's fine to keep things simple, but it shouldn't be too challenging to give your light bobs green plumes, for example. After this stage, I did a bit of tidying up and applied little white stripes of lace to the cuffs.

The first of the metallic colours to apply is gunmetal for musket barrels and as a base coat for bayonets and swords. You can mix your own colour simply enough using black and silver. Musket barrels were often 'browned', making them very dark.

The pointy bits – bayonets and swords – are simply rendered in silver, though again, you can be more subtle if you wish and add an intermediate iron or steel colour.

Right, I'm going to classify this bit as 'optional' because it is fiddly: a quick touch of leather brown for the strap which passes over the chest, from top left to bottom right as we look at it, and around the water canteen. If the very thought makes you faint, don't bother.

Now, we're going to use another technique called drybrushing. Use your size 2 for this, not the tiddler. Have a piece of kitchen roll ready on your work surface.

Gold serves perfectly well for the polished brass fittings of sword hilts and the badges on the front of hats. In reality, the musket had some brass fittings but at this scale, they would be invisible.

Create a fairly thick mix of white paint on your palette, dip your brush into it, then wipe almost all of it off. Yes, that's right, effectively paint onto the kitchen roll to absorb the majority of the paint. I tend to use my left thumbnail to test the result, which should be just the faintest trace of paint coming from the brush. Now quickly brush across the surface of the figures in the areas where the box art shows there should be white button lace, across those shoulder 'wings' for flank company figures, and across the front of the Belgic shakos that have hanging cords (the stovepipe shakos don't). All you're trying to do is *hint* at these details, not slavishly paint the moulding. This, my friend, is impressionism.

The officers have a crimson waist sash that can be added after mixing a little blue with red to make crimson.

Take care of your brush during this process and try not to let the paint completely dry on the bristles. "Dry-brushing' is not an entirely literal description, as it's actually semi-dry. You might prefer to use a cheap brush for this instead, though the ability to place the paint accurately is still important.

It's possible you may overpaint somewhat but, as before, don't panic, you can always go over and touch up any mistakes.

Time to deal with the drummer boys of the two units. The simplest one is that of the 2nd Foot shown here. The sleeve lace is tricky – just do white chevrons if that's all you can manage. Paint the drum in the unit's facing colour.

Next, I'd do the plumes. On the Belgic shakos, they are on the left side, but in the middle on the stovepipe shakos. These plumes were coloured white for grenadier companies, white over red for the centre or 'battalion' companies and green for light companies. Since British battalions had ten companies, this means that just a couple of each of our two units here should have either the white or green plumes, and the rest white over red although, to be honest, painting all of them white over red will do no harm for our purposes. If you do want to denote the light company, which can be used for skirmishing, then my suggestion would be to use a couple of the figures standing firing in the Belgic shakos and a pair of the squatting firing from the stovepipe shako group. The green, by the way, should be a mid-tone, grassy green such as Citadel's 'Warboss Green'.

On the last lap, now. We leave the metallic colours until last because they actually contain tiny metallic flakes which, if you're not careful, float around in the brush cleaning water and can end up embedded in your other colours.

First, gunmetal. A quick swipe along the top of every musket does the trick and, where present, coat the bayonets too. I also use gunmetal to undercoat the officers' swords.

Next, silver. Bayonets and swords get a coat of this, as do the mess tins on the knapsacks and the officers' scabbards. If you're feeling really adventurous, you could put the tiniest blob on the firing mechanisms of the muskets.

Gold (actually brass, but at this scale...) is used for the regimental badges on the shako fronts and a dab to indicate the hilt of the officers' swords.

Final touches: mix a little dark blue with some red to create a crimson suitable for the sash around the officers' waists. Add some white chevrons to the 2nd Foot's drummer boy's sleeves, and red ones to the 9th Foot's drummer boy. Their drums should be the facing colour of the unit, then drybrush white cords over the top, and finish by painting the drumsticks pale brown. And lastly, paint a bit of hair around the back of each man's head using a variety of browns and dark greys.

The fancier of the two is that of the 9th Foot, who wears 'reversed' colours, with a yellow jacket and red facings.

Now you can mix up a series of browns and whizz along adding hair to the back of the men's heads. A few pork chop sideburns might be in order too.

Paint the bases green, then it's time to stand back and look at the overall impression of your unit, and make any final corrections if they are needed. For example, I realised I had forgotten to paint the mess tins! Set them aside to dry thoroughly.

The final painting stage is to add a simple dark brown colour wash with a big, soft brush, which picks out all the details on the miniature without you having to labour for hours. A similar effect can be achieved using 'dip' as explained elsewhere.

Now what we're going to do is finish up with another technique that will help the detail to 'pop' – a wash.

Take dark brown or black and put a few drops into either a saucer or some other small, dished receptacle. Some wargamers use old paint pots for this purpose. Now add water until you get a *very* thin mix, perhaps 1:10 or even 1:20. Using your large brush, apply this wash to the figures and leave to dry. The pigment will settle in the recesses, shading the facial features and other detail.

Advanced techniques can add further detail and shading/highlight effects, but for gaming purposes, a quick shade of this kind is fine.

An alternative to paint that has become available in recent years is the 'wash' (now known as 'Shade') formula from Citadel, a very fine pigment suspended in an acrylic solution that has remarkable qualities that are best experienced, rather than described. Three colours in particular are favourites of mine: Gryphonne Sepia (now known as Seraphim Sepia), Devlan Mud (Agrax Earthshade) and Badab Black (Nuln Oil). And I have already described the 'dip' process which would obviate the need for shading at this stage. Other painters use artists' inks, but my advice is always to try new materials and techniques on a single figure first, rather than potentially sacrificing an entire regiment to unsatisfactory results.

There you are – you're done.

Well, almost. We've got to varnish and base these figures yet, but that can happen tomorrow. In the meantime, give yourself a pat on the back and take a break.

Finished and ready for varnishing (top) and then with the varnish applied (below). I used a spray varnish (Citadel's Purity Seal) followed by a brush-on matt varnish (Vallejo). The figures have been removed from their temporary homes on the painting sticks – this may leave some unpainted areas around the edges of the bases where they have been 'masked' by excess glue, but don't worry, as they can easily be touched up if you want to use the miniatures 'as-is' or will be concealed by the basing which comes next.

Varnishing

Welcome back. Your figures should now be completely dry and ready to take another coat which both protects them and brings out the lustrous colours. You might also want to take this opportunity to check over the figures for any splashes or things you missed.

Just as with undercoating, one of the simplest alternatives is to use spray varnish. It's available from DIY stores, hobby shops, Games Workshop and online.

Just as with undercoating, take your strips of figures and spray them as before, but you will only want one or two light coats, and you don't need to worry so much about the undersides: the varnish is to enhance the appearance of the figures and protect them from handling.

Some people – and I'm one of them – use a hard-wearing gloss varnish first, and then finish off with a coat of matt varnish. Others use a matt varnish, and then go over with a brush-on gloss varnish to highlight metallic and shiny leather parts. Others just use a single coat of semi-matt or silk finish varnish and leave it at that. And a few don't even bother to varnish them at all. However, particularly for soft plastic figures, I certainly wouldn't recommend leaving them unvarnished.

If you prefer to use brush-on varnish, follow the instructions on the container. Pay particular attention to whether your brushes need to be cleaned in water or a solvent, such as white spirit. I would recommend that you stick to acrylic-based, water-soluble types if possible. I would also advise keeping a brush purely for varnishing, so that it contains no traces of any coloured pigments.

So now you have some very pretty, painted figures, and you just need to base them.

Basing

This is where I shall refer the gentle reader to "Basing troops on page 358 where I indicate the suggested base sizes for your troops. In the case of close order line infantry of the kind most commonly found during the Napoleonic Wars, I advise 20mm x 20mm per figure, or 60mm frontage for a base containing two ranks of three. Given that these Italeri miniatures are quite small and slender, you may prefer to reduce these distances by a quarter to give a more authentic, closely-packed appearance, in which case your bases should be 15mm square per man, or 45mm x 30mm per six figures. If you choose to do this, then all other distances in the rules should technically be reduced by one quarter as well, which is already incorporated if you use the 'Base Width' references I have provided. If you go for larger, 25 or 28mm miniatures, then I'd stick to the 20mm frontage per man. If you head upscale to 40mm figures, then increase the infantry bases to 25mm square.

There are a number of materials you can use for basing figures. When I was a boy, I was happy with old breakfast cereal packets, and if you want a really cheap option, it's perfectly viable. The problem with cereal and other food packaging card is that it's generally too thin and can warp easily as soon as you try to paint it or apply scenic effects.

Pubs used to be a rich source of beer mats, but you never see them any more, so our next option is to visit an artists' suppliers and obtain some 'mounting card' of the kind used to frame pictures. This is a couple of millimetres thick, cuts easily with a sturdy craft or Stanley knife and can take a certain amount of paint without warping. Moreover, it's usually available in a variety of colours, including a useful dark green or earth brown. A typical brand is Daler Rowney Studland Standard Mountboard which comes in large, A1 sized sheets. Some suppliers only sell it in a pack of ten sheets, which would last you most of a wargaming lifetime, but any good art shop should be able to sell them singly.

If you decide to make your own bases, you'll need a good steel ruler as well as a sharp knife, and a hard pencil (2H or harder) for marking out the bases before cutting out. I'd also recommend a 'set square', one of those large triangular devices that help you to draw right angles.

Even better materials that are readily available nowadays are very thin plywood and MDF. You can buy sheets of thin (3mm) MDF from your local DIY store as well as specialist shops, but thin (1-2mm) plywood is best purchased from specialist suppliers, such as 4D Modelshop in London (*www.modelshop.co.uk/*). Ply is as easy to cut as card – but for both thick card or plywood, always use several gentle strokes rather than attempting to cut right through with a single stroke, which can either lead to the blade getting stuck or snapping or, even worse, 'skipping' after getting stuck, which is a quick way to lose a finger.

MDF is a tougher proposition and, to be honest, I'd recommend buying pre-cut bases if this is your material of choice. Companies like Warbases (*www.warbases.co.uk/*) offer a wide range of sizes straight from stock and, as I know, will happily cut to any size you require. And they are *cheap*!

Various basing options, including the packaging of the miniatures themselves, mounting board, the card backing from pads of paper, thin plywood, commercially-made thin MDF and plastic bases and even magnetic sheet with steel paper (very useful if you like to transport your figures inside a steel toolbox). You can use beer mats as well, though these are harder to find nowadays.

If you prefer plywood, Litko, based in the USA, produce a wide range of pre-cut sizes and again will make anything you like to your own specifications. (*www.litko.net/*). Litko's bases are laser-cut and arrive with a wonderful smell.

Another material that used to be in plentiful supply in the old days was linoleum tiles, but you almost never see them these days and, if you do, they come pre-glued with a peel-off backing, which is not at all what we want. If you happen to find an old pile hidden away somewhere, grab them! They were easy to score and then snapped cleanly, making them ideal for our purposes, and took paint well.

Some gamers mount their figures on thin steel bases and then line their carry-cases with magnetic paper (or base the figures on magnetic card and keep them in steel toolboxes). There can be no objection to this, if you are likely to want to transport your armies on a regular basis. The main enemy here, of course, is rust, so you will need to ensure that the bases are thoroughly primed, painted and varnished to prevent moisture getting in. For the appropriate materials, try Magnetic Displays in the UK (*www. magneticdisplays.co.uk/*) or Litko again in the USA.

Now, when it comes to basing, the next choice you need to make is this: will you group all your miniatures into sixes for infantry and threes for cavalry (with some of the exceptions noted in the "Basing Troops" section of the rules), which will require you to keep a note of individual casualties either on a notepad or using some kind of indicator behind the unit, such as a small die; or would you prefer to remove individual casualties as they are inflicted, which will make your units look a little more ragged under fire, but eliminates bookkeeping? The other consideration is that with the former method, your typical unit of perhaps 18-24 miniatures will require only three or four hand movements per turn to move, whereas if you use the method I am about to describe, it trebles the time taken to shift your

Time to choose: individual bases, that can be mounted on movement trays or multiple bases, with the whole unit in, say, sixes for line infantry, which will require you to keep tally of casualties; or a combination of numbers mounted together as shown by the 15mm miniatures here, as a compromise to speed up movement but also allowing casualty removal.

A beautiful little 28mm scene of a roadside preacher by Barry Hilton showing just what can be achieved with a dioramic approach, treating groups of figures as little vignettes. This was spotted at The other Partizan in September 2007.

regiments. For the kind of small games you are likely to be playing initially, it really makes little difference, a matter of seconds per unit. When you decide to embark upon really big battles, however, all those extra seconds mount up – but on the other hand, they are offset by the reduction in administration to keep track of casualties.

Personally, I have ummed and aahed about this for years, but have finally come to the conclusion that I prefer to take the casualties off as they are caused, and also don't like to see units trailing counting devices behind them as if they were 'Just Married'. I fully accept, however, that this is purely a matter of personal choice, and some wargamers go to great lengths to have the best of both worlds, using 'casualty' figures placed behind the unit or cleverly camouflaged dials with numbers on, for example, and the photographs in this book show some of these ideas in use.

If you do follow my method, you can always use a card tray, cut to the size of the full six-figure base (or three figures for cavalry), with or without a lip to prevent them sliding off, placed underneath the permanently-mounted figures to speed up moving them on the table.

One final consideration is for the aesthetics of the game. It is much easier to create attractive scenic effects on a large base than a small one. I have seen some really stunning work over the years, where an individual base of figures, or a group of bases arranged in a particular way, create a mini-diorama all of their own. Some gamers will even omit one or two figures from a base, just to create more room for 'scenicking', as my American friend Bill Protz calls it, or convert miniatures so that some are falling wounded or a horse is rearing. The possibilites are endless for the gamer who is also a dedicated modeller and painter, and because it is the base that counts, rather than individual miniatures, the rules are unaffected.

Whatever decision you've made, now's the time to prise the miniatures you have painted carefully off the strip of card or wood that has been their home for a while now. Be gentle: use a penknife or dinner knife to slide under the base and lever the figure away. If you encounter resistance, move to attack from a different angle, but eventually, they should pop right off. By all means line them up neatly to admire your handiwork. Of course, keep the strips they were mounted on for future use.

Now take your bases, either cut to size yourself or purchased and, using a strong adhesive (I tend to use UHU or Bostik all-purpose glue), stick your figures neatly in place. Given the variety of poses we have in a typical box of soft plastic figures, there are a number of alternatives. Place kneeling or squatting figures in front of standing ones, or group figures with similar poses onto the same base. Another alternative is to have purchased several boxes of figures and wait until they are all painted before basing them. Before painting, you can collect all the standing firing ones together, or all the figures 'at the ready' and so on, and paint them up as units, so that your regiments are instantly recognisable by their pose, as well as their facing colours.

The fact is, however, that as with almost everything in this hobby, it's all down to personal taste: if you don't mind your units having a higgledy-piggledy appearance, that's absolutely fine. Some wargamers go to great lengths to have units where, for example, almost all the figures are firing, but just a few are reloading, or one or two falling wounded, or some heads are turned to face in a different direction and so on, to create a more 'lifelike' appearance.

Either way, make sure that you have placed the figures in two, fairly neat ranks (regular European-style troops should have a neater appearance than irregulars such as Grenzers or militia), and that the figures are not placed too close to the edge, so that the bases can all be lined up both

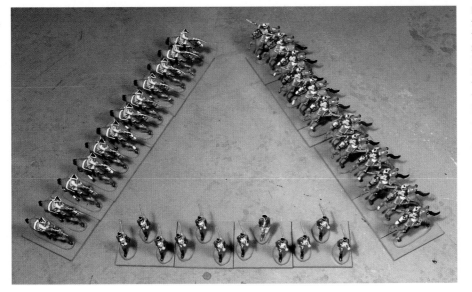

I base regular troops, such as the heavy cavalry shown on the left, in a very, well, neat and regular fashion! Irregular troops, such as the hussars on the right and the skirmishers in the centre are given more leeway.

side-by-side and front to back easily, without one man's musket poking another's in the back. This is called 'ranking up', so that our miniatures can form neat, coherent blocks to indicate that the unit is in line, column or, in the case of infantry, square. When we come to apply scenic effects, we shall also take care not to let anything dribble over the edges for the same reason.

For the time being, however, I'd advise sticking to basics and getting your first unit ready for action.

Once your figures are glued to their bases, I would again advise leaving the adhesive to harden for 6-12 hours before adding any scenic effects.

EMBELLISHING YOUR BASES

Now, it is perfectly acceptable, at this point, to simply take out your pot of mid-green, pick up your number 8 brush (or even your flat brush) and give the bases of your figures and the bases you have mounted them on a single coat. Don't add too much water – you want to get the job done in one go. Take care, of course, not to splash the green onto your lovingly painted miniatures, and take your time. Remember, by the way, to paint around the *edge* of the bases – I have seen so many otherwise perfectly respectable units of minatures ruined by a stark white or pale brown line underscoring the unit. Yuck!

However, basing is an art form in itself, as I indicated above, so I'm going to show you a simple method of making your bases more attractive.

What you need is some fine sand – silver sand, the kind used in children's sand pits is best, and is available at DIY stores in large quantities or from hobby suppliers in much more sensible amounts. You can use ordinary builders' sand, and may even be able to pick up a handful for free at a nearby building site, but do ask permission first! Builders' sand is much more coarse and liable to contain gravel. It is also dirty, so although this may sound bizarre, I recommend washing it first using a fine seive or muslin and then dry it on a baking tray in a warm oven.

Okay, once you have your sand, the next thing you want is your PVA adhesive again and an old plate, saucer or other dished container. You'll also want a really old brush that you don't mind ruining, or something that you can use as a small spatula, such as an ice lolly stick.

In your receptacle, make a gooey mix of sand, glue and a blob of dark brown paint. You're looking for something that looks a bit like the chocolate cake mix your mother used to make, rich and granular. Now, using whichever implement you choose, apply this to the bases, making sure you get between the figures' feet and disguising the edge of their bases as far as possible. Don't apply it too thickly, or it will just run off the edge as it reaches its own level.

An alternative method is to coat the bases with PVA first and then dip them into a tub of the fine sand, tapping off the excess once dry and then following up with a coat of dark brown. Or you could also use textured exterior wall paint instead of the sand, which can be found in a range of colours at DIY stores. I'd recommend a dark, chocolatey brown, but any dark to mid brown will do.

Once this first coat is dry, apply a coat of drybrushed mid-brown or earth colour.

Finally, we can apply some kind of grass effect. The first option is to simply paint patches of green on the bases, leaving some of the earth colour showing, then mix in some yellow and apply a drybrushed highlight. The second option is to apply 'flock'.

We came across flock, also known as scatter material, earlier in the book when discussing making terrain. It comes in many different colours and shades, but is essentially what model railway enthusiasts use to depict grass. At its simplest, you can use sawdust or hamster bedding, stained green using fabric dye such as Dylon and left to dry. There are many more sophisticated varieties available nowadays, available from model shops, Games Workshop or online from companies like Woodland Scenics, which are made from synthetic materials. A single bag or tub will last you a long time, so a few pounds represents good value for money. You can also buy various grades of coarse sand and gravel known as talus or scree, useful for representing small boulders, but of course you may also be able to source such material from the wild (which also describes some gardens I have seen...)

The best way to use flock is in small patches. Apply some PVA to an area on your base and, using some tweezers, apply a clump of the flock, press it in, leave it to dry, then tap off the excess. If you're feeling particularly creative, you can use any of the techniques outlined before for making scenery, such as water effects for puddles or streams, trimmed brush bristles for tall grass or reeds and so on. I tend to add a small rock here and there with a dab of glue. Once dried, these can be painted and drybrushed to tie them in visually to the rest of the base.

You can also add tufts of taller grass, either home-made or manufactured. Companies like Silflor and Ziterdes make pre-formed tufts which you can stick to your bases before adding scatter material or flock. Alternatively, you can make your own from the bristles of old brushes or even, for larger scale miniatures, nylon broom or scrubbing brush bristles. The commercial variants come pre-coloured, whilst you will need to paint home-made tufts.

The very last job is optional and will be invisible. Turn the base over and, on the underside, make a note of the name of the unit. You can write on a label first, if you prefer, and then stick that on the underside. And while you're at it, why not add the date you completed them? Then, in years to come, you can look back fondly at your early work and see how much progress you've made.

See the photos overleaf to see these techniques in action.

Congratulations. You have just completed your first units, which are now ready for action and for displaying proudly on your shelves. They are bound to be the veterans of your army in your heart!

The first stage is to apply a mixture of fine sand, mixed with PVA adhesive, bown paint and just enough water to make it flow. Take your time, using an old, small brush and cocktail stick, making sure you completely cover the miniatures' bases, then leave to dry thoroughly.

Drybrushing with a pale earth colour over the textured layer. I used quite a 'wet' drybrush technique to cover most of the dark brown. You can, of course, research the predominant soil colour in your theatre of operations or for a specific battle – perhaps the soil should be sandy, or full of clay, or reddish in tone.

The final stage: scenic grass. Here I have used self-adhesive tufts (bottom right), followed by patches of diluted PVA onto which I am applying standard static grass. Again, you could use different colours to represent a particular theatre of war or time of year, though most wargamers opt for generic basing as shown here. Once dry, invert the bases and tap to remove any excess.

NEW PAINTING CHALLENGES

So, you now have a couple of British infantry battalions under your belt, let's think about how to approach the French.

Again, you have the box art to guide you, which makes it clear that the two main colours you're going to need here are white and dark blue. Also notice how the French legwear is different – they wore breeches reaching to the knee, but the lower half of the leg was covered by black gaiters. These had brass buttons up the side, but for wargaming purposes I really wouldn't bother with attempting to paint those at this scale. Similarly, there are buttons down the outside of the folded back lapels on the front of the jacket – again, only worth attempting if you are capable of microscopic accuracy. If you are painting 28mm figures or larger, these buttons are often sculpted with exaggerated height and can be attempted.

I would recommend that you start with a black undercoat again. This time, pay particular attention when painting the white crossbelts that pass over the front of the coat, which is also white, to leave a faint line of black between the two. Take your time and remember the production-line methods you have already used on the British.

For highlighting the blue jacket, I would add a little mid-grey and white to the basic colour, rather than just white, which can result in an artificially pale colour.

What you will notice is that there is actually a slight discrepancy between the artwork on the box, which shows men wearing coats with tails down to the back of the knees, and the figures inside the box who are actually wearing jackets with much shorter tails, the so-called 'Bardin' regulation style of 1812. However, I wouldn't worry about this – it just means a bit less blue and red to paint round the back!

As before, I'd advise leaving the metallic parts until last, and this time you'll have the chinscales to paint which some figures have around the chin as you would expect, but others have turned up on the sides of their shakos.

The contents of one box of Italeri British now painted and based – two battalions arranged in line with their light companies deployed to skirmish. Most wargamers would probably purchase several boxes at once, gathering together duplicate figures so that each unit is formed by miniatures in similar or identical positions, rather than the mixed look we have here.

French infantry battalions in 1812 consisted of six companies – four 'centre' companies of fusiliers, one of grenadiers and one of voltigeurs (skirmishers). Grenadiers had a red collar, red stripes on their shakos, red epaulettes and a red plume; voltigeurs had yellow collars, green and/or yellow epaulettes, yellow stripes on their shakos and a yellow or yellow-over-green plume. The fusilier companies had red collars and epaulettes, but different coloured pom-poms (a sort of small plume which is what all the figures from the Italeri set are wearing): the first company had dark green pom-poms, the second sky blue, the third an orange-pink and the fourth violet. Colonels had white plumes, majors red-topped white and a *chef de bataillon* had red. More junior officers and non-commissioned officers wore white pom-poms, with those in voltigeur companies wearing yellow and grenadiers red.

Welcome to the minutiae of Napoleonic uniforms! The fact is, however, that a welter of regulations were issued which often never reached, or were blatantly ignored by, the colonels of regiments in the field, a practice which has kept Napoleonic enthusiasts arguing to this day.

You may not have got around to buying any reference books yet, but an extraordinary amount of material is available online: see, for example, *www.napoleon-series.org/military/organization/France/Infantry/ Line/c_Reeselineinfantry.html* for line infantry reference and then *www. napoleon-series.org/military/organization/France/Cavalry/Hussars/c_ Reesehussars.html* for the French hussars we'll be tackling in a moment.

When you finish painting your French infantry, I'd advise using dark brown as the wash over the men's faces, but use black for the rest of the figure, which works better with the French blue compared to the dark brown over the British scarlet uniforms. Then varnish and base as before.

Excellent: by now, you should have two battalions each of British and French line infantry, already a collection capable of providing an entertaining game.

White features heavily on the French, so make use of the techniques described earlier to highlight areas that would catch the light. The French, especially grenadiers and veterans, were noted for their love of moustaches, so you might like to add some facial hair! This battalion comprises figures in the same pose taken from several boxes.

Perry 28mm *hard* plastic ACW cavalry figures on the production line. Here, the riders are painted separately from their horses. Pale colour horses – except, I would argue, greys, such as the dapple grey shown here – are best given a coat of white first with the colour built up using washes. The troopers' horses are being painted as bays, mostly a mid-brown with black points.

However, let's add some cavalry.

I mentioned that it is a good idea to assemble soft plastic cavalry prior to applying the coat of PVA, so if you have not already done so, go ahead and complete that process now. With the rider pinned to the horse's back and the horse firmly glued to the base, you should have a perfectly stable object for painting once temporarily attached to your painting stick. Another option for cavalry, if you want to give them more individual attention, is to attach them to screw-on milk carton tops that are about 30mm in diameter. By holding the plastic top, you keep greasy fingers off the figure and can rotate it to reach difficult parts really easily.

It doesn't matter whether you tackle the French hussars or the British light dragoons first. Undercoat the entire miniature just as previously, and then paint the rider, saddle, saddle cloth (technically called a *shabraque*), the reins and bridle. Cavalry presents new challenges as you come to grips with the intricacies of saddlery, lots of buckles, fur busbies and metal helmets, especially for heavy cavalry (including French dragoons).

PAINTING HORSES

Now, for the horse itself, it's worth spending a little time understanding horse colours. Most people these days, unless you're very lucky or a fan of horse racing or other equestrian sports, hardly ever get to see a real horse in the flesh. The important point for us is that horses have a variety of colours and markings that are related to the particular breed, and whilst infinite variations are possible, there is a logical system at work, particularly in regard to military horses.

Most army horses in use since the 17th century are of the 'warmblood' type, sometimes known as hunters. There are also some lighter Arabian types, the breed favoured by the racing fraternity, and heavy cavalry have often been mounted on types of heavier 'cold blood' horse, many derived from the medieval destrier.

Just as the army likes its men to have a regular, regimented appearance, the same goes for the horses. The vast majority of cavalry were mounted on 'bay' animals, describing a colour which is, basically, brown or tan, but can vary from a dark bay to a light bay. Another common colour was chestnut, a reddish brown.

True black horses are extremely rare: they are usually very dark brown. Dark horses were (and still are – see the current Life Guards and Blues & Royals on parade) often the preserve of heavy cavalry, whereas pale horses, such as duns and light bays, were frequently used by light cavalry.

Truly albino white horses are also uncommon: more often, the onlooker is really describing a very pale grey, and greys can vary enormously in tone from near-white through to almost black. The most common variety of grey is the 'dapple' grey. The famous, and very beautiful, Andalucian and Lippizaner mounts used for military dressage are greys.

White and very pale grey horses were most commonly ridden by those who needed to stand out on the battlefield, such as senior officers, trumpeters and standard bearers, but there were, of course, a number of units who famously rode grey horses, such as the Royal North British Dragoons, more commonly known as the Scots Greys.

I have included a chart of the more common horse colours here, but I would also recommend typing "horse colours" into Google and you will be presented with a wealth of helpful websites.

One of the most important aspects of horse colouring to understand is that of 'point' colouring and markings. As you will see, many types of horse have dark or even black legs, tails and manes, some have dark legs, but lighter tails and manes, and others are more or less a single colour overall. But most horses that are not white or pure black have some kind of white marking at the extremities of the legs or on their heads.

A stocking is a white marking that extends up to or just above the knee; a sock extends from midway down the cannon (that's the straight bit that looks like a human shinbone) to the hoof; a pastern is a white marking extending just from the fetlock to the hoof; and a coronet is a small white marking just around the top of the hoof.

On the head, you can have a white snip just on the nose, a star on the forehead, a broad blaze or thinner stripe down the front of the face, and a horse with a head that is completely white at the front is called "bald".

The secret, therefore, to having a very naturalistic looking cavalry unit is to simply paint all the bodies the same colour (chestnut with black manes, tails and lower legs, for example) and then give each horse slightly different white markings. I start with the first horse having no marks on the lower legs, the second with one stocking, the next with two, the third also with two but on diagonally opposite legs, the next with three, and so on. Few horses have white marks on all four legs, by the way, most have two or three, although a 'horsy' friend of mine tells me that modern owners who use their horse for jumping prefer no white leg markings because it can, apparently, be a sign of weakness in that leg.

Horse Colour and Markings Chart

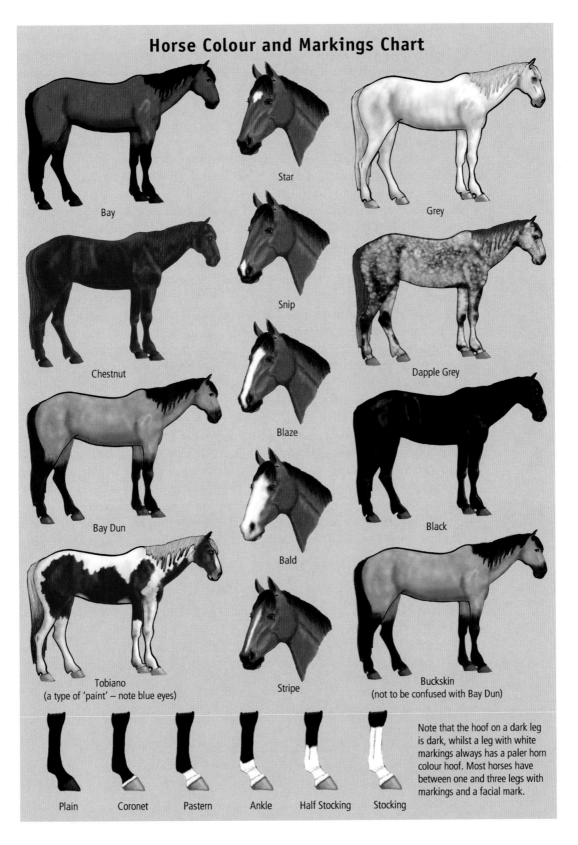

Bay

Star

Grey

Chestnut

Snip

Dapple Grey

Bay Dun

Blaze

Black

Tobiano
(a type of 'paint' – note blue eyes)

Bald

Stripe

Buckskin
(not to be confused with Bay Dun)

Plain   Coronet   Pastern   Ankle   Half Stocking   Stocking

Note that the hoof on a dark leg is dark, whilst a leg with white markings always has a paler horn colour hoof. Most horses have between one and three legs with markings and a facial mark.

Another important consideration is hoof colour. Horses' hooves are basically the equivalent of our toenails and are, essentially, horn, so choose natural horn colours such as beige, tan or grey. The simple rule is this: if the leg colour is pale or has white markings, then the hoof should also be pale; if the leg is dark or black, then the hoof will also be dark.

If your horse is going to be very dark in colour, then undercoat it black or very dark brown. I've even seen black horses undercoated with dark blue – it's surprisingly effective. If, in the other hand, the animal is a lighter colour, anything from a chestnut up, then undercoat it white and build up the horse base colour in thinner washes. This allows the undercoat to show through slightly on the raised areas, creating a natural sheen. Tie everything together visually at the end of the process with a very thin wash of dark brown which will settle in the recesses and create more definition.

This is why more experienced painters often use artists' oil colours, or acrylics with some 'retardant' added, which extends the drying time considerably. By applying a fairly generous coat of this type of colour, you can then take something absorbent like a small piece of sponge and gently wipe the paint off the raised surfaces such as the horse's rump, flanks and the side of the neck. The artists' paint dries with a very naturalistic sheen and can even leave the original brush marks showing in a way that resembles hair.

Dapple grey horses present a real challenge, but the results can be spectacular. Start with a black undercoat, and then do a basecoat of mid-grey extending down to the upper legs. Now, with your mid-range brush, apply clusters of white dots on the upper surfaces and flanks of the beast. The legs should be left darker, and can then have white markings the same as any other colour of horse. Having good reference material to hand here is really important.

A final tip is that very pale coloured horses often have a slight pinkish tinge around the nose and mouth. I suggest taking just a drop of flesh

A large cavalry battle between French and Austrian forces, fought entirely with soft plastic figures from the collection of Andy Crofton. Soft plastic figures make an encounter like this relatively inexpensive, a matter of pence per figure rather than pounds, and they look great! The rules in use were *Shako*.

coloured paint, make a very thin wash, and apply just a drop to the nose.

Your cavalry, now that they are proudly mounted on beautiful horses, can then be based in exactly the same way as the infantry. Note that the British light dragoons and French hussars are both examples of regular, close order light cavalry, although little more than half a century earlier, hussars were considered very much 'irregular' and rather wild.

In due course, you'll want to add other cavalry types to your collection – cuirassiers, dragoons, carabiniers, chasseurs à cheval, lancers and others – but for the time being, the figures you have represent around two large or three smaller squadrons per side, which is quite enough to start with.

ARTILLERY

I would suggest trying a handful of games with the infantry and cavalry first. Don't forget that one company of each battalion is trained to operate as skirmishers, and the French had superior numbers in this regard for quite some time. However, the companies trained to skirmish were also perfectly capable of taking their place in the line alongside their fusilier and grenadier colleagues – see Chapter 8 "Learn by Playing" on page 395.

Anyway, before long, you're going to want to add some firepower to your forces, and so once again, I'd recommend that you consider starting with the inexpensive option of some more plastic figures. For both the British and the French, Italeri have made the interesting decision to produce the somewhat more exotic horse artillery for the British and French first, rather than the more prosaic foot artillery. However, the French come with a limber included with the crews and two guns, whereas the British do not! For this reason, you might want to track down Airfix Set 01746 Waterloo British Artillery (again, these are Royal Horse Artillery wearing their distinctive fore-and-aft 'Tarleton' helmets, so are suitable for the Peninsular War as well).

This is a classic example of where some of the large manufacturers, often primarily classifying their wares as 'toys', have not considered how infuriating it can be for the wargamer and collector to not be able to find matching sets and this is, of course, why many wargamers frequently move across to metal figures. I am hoping that before long, the Plastic Soldier Company, who are planning to release sensibly-composed Napoleonic sets, may get round to solving the problem as far as our artillery are concerned, but for the moment we must either make do with what is available – or go metal.

Using metal miniatures for your artillery is not such a bad idea. For a start, you don't need much – just a single gun model, representing a battery per side should keep you going for some time. (The allocation was roughly one gun per battalion, so a battery of six guns would serve up to six battalions of infantry, plus cavalry supports.) As a rule of thumb, I'd add a battery of guns for each eight to ten units under your command, perhaps a little more for games set in the later Napoleonic era – refer back to "Troublesome Artillery on page 26.

1/72 Plastic British Foot Artillery from Revell (left) and its metal equivalent in 20mm from Newline on the right. As you can see, though nominally roughly the same scale, there is quite a size disparity, as well as the Revell figures being somewhat more slender, not to say 'willowy'! You pays yer money...

Checking the Newline Designs website (*newlinedesigns.co.uk/*), their 20mm ranges are compatible with the popular ranges of soft plastic figures, though they will appear a little chunkier. A 9-pounder gun model, together with limber, horse team, riders and crew, comes to a little over £10 plus postage. I would suggest that represents excellent value for money, so for around £20, you could order foot artillery for both the British and French (the French should have a classic 8-pounder gun, but Newline currently only make a 6- or 12-pounder, so take your pick). Note that the British guns have a single trail, whilst the French 'Gribeauval' carriage has a split trail.

Cleaning up metal castings has already been described – you'll mostly need your small files, and to be honest, the Newline miniatures are pretty clean. You might want to use a bigger file for underneath the bases to ensure that they are flat enough to allow the figure to stand up.

Give the castings a wash, but you can skip any vinegar or PVA treatments and go straight to undercoat. Everything after that is the same. So, the gunner figures, riders and draught horses should pose no problems whatsover. There are a few more straps and traces to do, and if you have the right reference to hand, you can really go to town adding extra bits and pieces with thin wire or cotton. Just a note, then, about gun barrels and woodwork.

Guns of this period were cast in bronze which, when polished, looks like brass. Some armies – such as the Austrians – painted the barrels black to protect them from the elements, which was also common at sea. For bronze barrels, paint them gold and then simply give them a wash of dark brown.

Gun carriages were painted according to tradition: see the table opposite:

Austria	Yellow with black fittings
Baden	Dark grey
Bavaria	Light grey
Britain	Blue/grey
Brunswick	Olive green
Denmark	Red with yellow fittings
France	Dark olive green
Hesse Darmstadt	Medium blue
Naples	Light blue
Prussia	Light or medium blue
Russia	Very dark green
Saxony	Dark grey with yellow fittings
Sweden	Blue/green
Württemberg	Natural wood with yellow fittings

It must be pointed out that the precise shade of many of these colours is still subject to often heated debate, so don't worry too much. The Foundry paint range contains a useful set of Napoleonic artillery colours covering several of the nations listed above.

Other metal fittings on the carriage would have been iron, including the wheel rims, and therefore painted black to prevent rust unless otherwise specified.

For your artillery base, you may wish to mount your limber permanently, but put your gunner figures on individual bases so that they can be removed if casualties are suffered. In addition, keep the gun itself as a stand-alone piece, so that it can be hitched to the limber when moving or placed on the separate battery base when deployed. You may wish to cut your artillery bases with sides angled at 45° to indicate the field of fire achievable without needing to turn the battery.

Hard plastic miniatures

There is now a wide and ever-expanding range of hard plastic 28mm historical miniatures on the market from manufacturers such as Perry Miniatures, Victrix, Warlord, Gripping Beast and Wargames Factory that have joined the already vast selection of fantasy and science fiction figures sold by Games Workshop and others. The common factor is that they all need a certain amount of assembly before painting, so I thought I'd give you a quick step-by-step lesson on how to cope with this additional work.

This process will require you to obtain some additional materials and tools: polystyrene cement, the same kind as you would use to assemble any other plastic kit; a couple of sculpting tools for working with filler – these can be obtained in cheap sets from artists' suppliers or even on eBay; and the filler itself, either Green Stuff or Milliput, as can be seen in the photos overleaf.

When tackling hard plastic miniatures, a useful armoury of items includes clippers, rat-tail files, tweezers, two-part epoxy filler, superglue and polystyrene adhesive, a hand drill, a scalpel with fresh blades and fine-grade wet and dry paper.

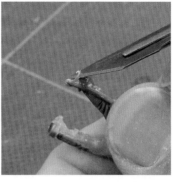

If you find flash that needs to be cut away, take your time and make sure your fingers and thumbs are well out of the way!

Polystyrene adhesive needs to be applied with precision to prevent it flooding the joint and spilling onto the visible surface, so you can use a 'needle' applicator like this...

Sometimes you will encounter small objects that are best applied using tweezers. You can even 'stab' small parts with a dressmaker's pin if they are particularly resistant to being picked up! Any tiny hole will be filled during painting.

... or a brush applicator like this. You only need to apply adhesive to one of the surfaces to be joined. After joining, press the two halves together firmly for 30 seconds or so.

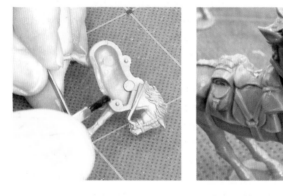

Inevitably, some parts will not fit perfectly and the gap at the join will need filling. You can buy liquid 'green stuff' filler for very small gaps.

Cleaning off mould lines by scraping with the edge of a sharp scalpel. Don't lean the blade in the direction of scraping or it will dig in and cut, damaging the figure.

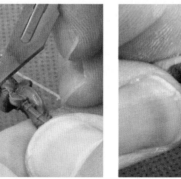

For larger gaps such as the horse's neck above, use two-part epoxy filler, either Milliput or 'green stuff', so-called because the two constituent ingredients are yellow and blue, producing a green substance when mixed. It can be rolled very thin.

FLAGS

One of the great attractions of many eras of history is the heraldry of national and unit pride expressed by the carrying of flags and banners. The technical term for a regimental flag is 'colour' for infantry and 'guidon' for cavalry. You may have watched the modern-day ceremony of Trooping the Colour that takes place in London on Her Majesty the Queen's official birthday every year. Here, you can see the individual regiments of the Guards Brigade, including the Foot Guards and Horse Guards, marching past the Queen so that she may honour the regiment and all that have served it in the past, as witnessed by the many battle honours embroidered on the colour.

The exception is artillery: whilst for infantry and cavalry, their colours or guidon are their rallying-point in battle, for artillerymen, their guns serve the same purpose and many gunners have died rather than allow their pieces to fall into enemy hands. Hence the King's Troop Royal Horse Artillery, who also parade on the Queen's birthday, carry no flag, but they and their guns take precedence over all other units on parade.

Now, the figures we have been painting up to now are somewhat bereft in the flag department. The French infantry do indeed have a couple of flags, but they are pretty scrawny, and for some reason, the sculptors didn't see fit to give the Italeri British infantry any flags at all, whereas in reality, every British battalion carried two flags – the regimental colour, displaying the unit's battle honours on a background matching the unit's facing colours, and the King's colour, which was essentially a Union Jack with the unit's number in the centre. Together, they are called a 'stand' of colours. The French carried but one large colour per battalion (80cm – 31½" – square, considerably smaller than the British colours which were six feet – 180cm – square), but in fact for them, it was the pole – or, more correctly, the golden imperial eagle perched atop it – that was more important than the coloured cloth, which carried slogans about liberty, egality and fraternity and the regimental and battalion details.[7]

Cavalry units would also carry a guidon but, because of the nature of their work, it was often left with the baggage behind the lines for safe keeping and the trumpeter became the focus of attention. This was also true for specialist light infantry units, such as the famous 95th Rifles, who frequently operated in a dispersed formation, and were called together by the blowing of a horn or bugle (and the hunting horn was frequently used as a badge by light infantry units).

Now, whilst there are some beautiful flags available commercially, it's fairly easy to make your own flags for infantry units using nothing more complicated than a computer printer and a piece of thin wire. You can even download free flags from the Web. As always, it's important to start

---

7 *The design of French flags changed during the Napoleonic Wars. Up to 1804 the design included multiple diamond shapes, but in 1804 was changed to a distinctive central white lozenge shape with blue and red corners. This then changed to the more familiar 'tricolour' format after 1812.*

with good reference material if you're making your own, but let me give you a head start by giving you my renditions of the Regimental Colour and King's Colour (the one that looks like a Union Jack) for the 9th Foot here:

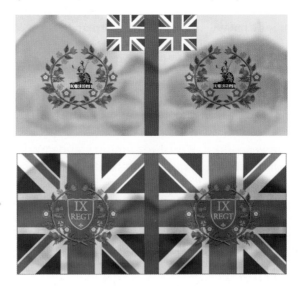

And for a typical French infantry regiment of early 1812 in the Peninsula here (the 34th Ligne, which saw extensive action in Spain).

You are welcome to photocopy these, but they are also available for download from the website at *www.thewargamingcompendium.com* as PDF files, so that you will be able to enlarge or reduce them if required to match whichever scale of miniatures you prefer.

There is also another marvellous online resource that has been around for many years offering free flag downloads as mentioned in the text above: see *www.warflag.com/flags/select.shtml*.

Once you have downloaded the flags, print them out onto a sheet of good quality paper, perhaps even 'photo quality' but not, of course, glossy. Then, once the ink is thoroughly dry, cut them out and apply adhesive to the rear (use household glue such as UHU or Bostik or undiluted white, PVA adhesive) and glue them around a piece of thin wire. Thin wire comes in many forms – you can buy it at garden centres or from hobby suppliers. Brass wire is preferable, because it won't corrode. Once the glue has dried, you can undercoat and paint the flagpole. Each nation

Flags rendered in different ways: simple printouts on paper (top left); commercially printed (Adolfo Ramos, top right); painted on tin foil (bottom left); and finally, painted on linen (Barry Hilton, bottom right). In all cases, whether printed or not, you should eliminate any white edges that might be showing, using a touch of paint or even marker pens. The linen version needs to be soaked in PVA to create a suitable surface to take paint. If you're printing flags yourself, consider using wide self-adhesive address labels, eliminating the need for messy glue when wrapping them round your flagpoles.

had its own conventions: the French painted theirs blue; the Austrians had red, black, yellow and white stripes spiralling along the length of the staff rather like a barber's pole; the Prussians painted theirs white; Italian, British and Saxon infantry had plain, varnished wood; Polish, Nassau and Württemburg infantry flagpoles were black; Hungarian infantry used light blue and white bands; Würzburg had red and white bands; but other nations seem to have either painted or not painted the poles at the whim of the colonel.

If you are feeling particularly creative, then you can of course paint the flags rather than simply print them, and many wargamers see it as a matter of pride that they have painted their own flags onto either fine linen (though in fact, real regimental colours are made of silk) or tin foil. Of the two, the fabric is the most challenging and I wouldn't undertake it lightly. Tin foil (in fact ordinary aluminium foil as used for roasting your chicken), on the other hand, is easy to work with, and can be folded, rolled and crinkled into all manner of realistic poses.

Let me make it clear where I stand on this. I would love to have the time to paint my own flags, but I don't. What I do instead is design flags for my own fictitious countries, which I then print out, and when it comes to historical flags, there are a number of people who produce beautiful renditions of the originals and sell them at very reasonable prices, so they get my business! But as you'll see from the photographs in this book, hand-painted flags can look spectacular.

Note that many wargamers create flags that are much larger in scale than the originals would have been, in order to increase the visual spectacle of unit heraldry on the tabletop.

FURTHER ADVICE

I have barely scratched the surface of the endless possible approaches to painting and basing miniatures, but I hope that this has been enough to demonstrate the basic principles and get your creative juices flowing. I have quite deliberately concentrated on 'production line' techniques to get your figures onto the gaming table quickly, but if you prefer to lavish more individual attention on them, be my guest. Many gamers like to paint officers, drummers, colour bearers and so on as one-offs, since they tend to receive the most scrutiny at the table.

All the magazines mentioned in this book carry articles about painting and basing. And nowadays, of course, there are an ever-growing number of websites and blogs with a huge amount of useful hints and tips from painters of all standards and styles.

The key is this: don't be afraid to experiment and don't allow snobbery to dictate where you get your advice. You might not enjoy fantasy gaming or science fiction, for example, but these genres have seen some of the most extraordinary breakthroughs in miniature painting techniques. Try something on a spare figure – if it doesn't work, you can always paint over the mistake and try something else. For many wargamers, painting and collecting is at least as important a part of the hobby as actually playing the games, and you will find it an endlessly fascinating and challenging aspect of wargaming.

6

FROM SMALL TO LARGE

Wargames for All Occasions

Y ou can play a wargame with as few as two miniatures, or you can play with tens of thousands and they can be equally enjoyable, though it is likely that the former will require less time and dedication than the latter! This section of the book will show you that there are a host of options between those two extremes and that you can easily find something to suit your temperament, interests and, indeed, your wallet.

Just two miniatures: the duel

Probably the very first fights on the planet were between pairs of micro-organisms swimming in the primordial soup, and there remains something very primal about a one-on-one encounter. In ancient times, there was gladiatorial combat; in medieval times, the tournament and the joust; and from the Renaissance through to the late 19th century, the duel, a form continued in air-to-air combat above the trenches in WWI and over the English Channel in WWII. In modern times, the duel is perpetuated in sporting forms such as boxing, martial arts, even tennis or golf, though to my mind, there needs to be a personal, physical risk at stake.

The duel was killed off by technology as much as anything else. A prime component of such an encounter was being able to look one's opponent in the eye, to know that he is at, or barely beyond, the reach of one's arm in an arena where the outcome is to kill or be killed. The duel was subject to rules to which all participants had to adhere: it needed to be 'fair'. Thus duellists agreed to certain terms and were represented by 'seconds' who were not emotionally involved in the dispute. It became customary for weapons to be identical, or nearly so, in order that one side could not claim that the other had an unfair advantage. Duelling swords and pistols were customarily made in matching pairs for this reason. Even as late as in the vapour-trail ridden skies of the Battle of Britain in 1940, where Spitfires and Me109s twisted and rolled in the blue heavens, the pilots respected one another as putting their lives at risk with little or no protection in machines that frequently crashed of their own accord, let alone with the additional provocation of tracer bullets.

Such niceties have been thrown out of the window in modern warfare: the objective is to kill one's opponent at the greatest distance possible – including 'over the horizon' if necessary.

However, in wargaming terms, recreating a duel is very simple to do, and can be achieved in a number of ways. Technically speaking, you don't even need the miniatures, though they are certainly part of the fun and the visual appeal.

For the purposes of this demonstration, we're going to simulate the thrill of the arena in ancient Rome and its provinces, and I am very fortunate in that my own magazine, *Battlegames*, carried a set of rules for gladiatorial combat called *Habet, hoc habet!* written by Arthur Harman, which he has graciously permitted me to reproduce here with some modifications.

The idea of a duelling game is to produce a fast and furious few minutes of fun. It is not a cerebral exercise, nor can it ever truly reproduce what it's like to be inside a hot and heavy suit of armour with someone trying to knock your head off, or in the centre of a gladiatorial arena with a crowd of thousands baying for your blood. However, you might work up a sweat and, if you want to be the next Russell Crowe, this could well be your thing!

So, what will you need?

First of all, a couple of gladiators. The scale really doesn't matter in the least. It may well be that, if you have children of your own, their toyboxes may already contain some gladiators that will be perfectly suitable. At the time of writing, several companies make gladiators. Some of my favourites come from Miniature Figurines, one of the oldest wargames figure manufacturers, who also make a suitable selection of wild animals threatening to take chunks out of the combatants. Other good ranges in 28mm scale are available from Crusader Miniatures (*www.crusaderminiatures.com*) and Foundry Miniatures (*wargamesfoundry.com*) to name but two, and two companies have produced 'soft' plastic sets of gladiators: Italeri and Pegasus (see *www. plasticsoldierreview.com* for reviews).

I have produced a set of cards and half the 'arena' playing area (you can simply photocopy it twice and stick the two halves together), but you can also download these items from the *Wargaming Compendium* website as PDF files to print out at *www.thewargamingcompendium.com*.

A *secutor*, one of the 'heavy' types of gladiator similar to a *murmillo* or a *Samnite*. Illustration by Ann Prescott.

Although this game has been designed primarily to portray a bout between a *murmillo* and a *retiarius*, there is no reason why the basic system could not be adapted to reflect the differences between the various types of gladiators, as suggested later.

For readers unfamiliar with the Roman arena, here is a brief description of the principal varieties of gladiator.

THE SAMNITE

The first gladiators in 264BC wore armour based upon that of Rome's Samnite enemies, defeated by her Capuan allies in 308BC. Samnites wore a vizored helmet (*galea*) with a huge crest and plumes, leather bands (*manicae*) on their exposed right arms, leather or metal greaves (*ocreae*) on their left legs, and carried a stabbing sword (*gladius*) and large, rectangular shield (*scutum*).

THE THRACIAN

An innovation of Sulla, though portrayed in third century BC reliefs in Etruria, Thracians wore helmets, bands of leather (*fasciae*) round their thighs, two greaves, and the gladiators' usual protection for the right arm. They carried a curved sword or scimitar (*sica*) and a small square or curved shield (*parma*).

THE MURMILLO

During the Empire, *myrmillones* were the usual opponents of Thracians or *retiarii* (see below). Armoured and equipped similarly to a Samnite, the murmillo derived his name from the sea-fish (*mormylos*) crest of his helmet.

THE RETIARIUS

This gladiator wore no helmet and carried no shield. His only defensive armour was a leather or metal shoulder-piece (*galerus*) worn on the left shoulder, and arm and leg bands. His weapons were a trident (*tridens*) or harpoon (*fascina*), a dagger and a net (*rete*), attached to his left wrist by a leash so that he could draw it back if he failed to throw it over his opponent.

A typical *Thracian* gladiator. Illustration by Ann Prescott.

THE ARENA

The playing area, or arena, is simply a circle of stout cardboard, divided into squares sufficiently large to contain the base of one figure, but no larger (see overleaf). One inch or two centimetre squares will be suitable for 25mm models. In the interests of a fast and furious game the arena should have a diameter of no more than twelve squares. If you consider your beautifully painted figures deserve a more atmospheric arena than a mere cardboard circle, you can construct surrounding walls and entrance gates to provide a realistic background, and draw the movement grid on artistically 'blood'-stained sandpaper.

Finally, each player must have his own complete set of the Playing Cards as shown on the next few pages.

EXPLANATION OF THE PLAYING CARDS

The Playing Cards fall into three groups:
- Action Cards, indicating the gladiator's movements and other actions.
- Defence Cards, showing how the gladiator will react to an attack.
- Hit Cards, which are used to resolve the outcome of an attack or a blow.

The arena for our gladiator game, which you can photcopy at whatever size is required to fit your miniatures. You can also download this image as a PDF file from the book's website.

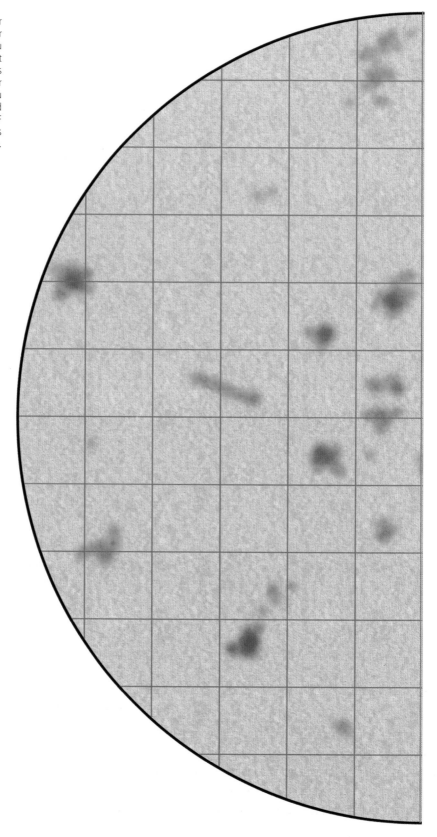

To create some period atmosphere – and because this game was designed originally to enliven Latin lessons for preparatory schoolboys – the captions are written in Latin. I have also followed the Latin style of using capital 'V' where modern English would use a 'U'. Translations are given in brackets and may be added to the cards if desired, but my experience is that players soon become familiar with the Latin expressions.

ACTION CARDS

- **PROCEDO** (I advance): gladiator may move **one** square in any direction, including diagonally (like the king in chess).
- **OPPVGNO** (I attack): gladiator may move **two** squares in a straight line, including diagonally, **provided** that moving two squares will bring him into a square **adjacent** to his opponent. Retiarius may also use this card to move two squares in a straight line and **stab** at his opponent across one square (but not diagonally) between them, provided he has his trident. Should this prove impossible, then treat this card as PROCEDO (see above).

The following Action Cards **may be played by retiarii only** and should be discarded from the packs of players using other types of gladiator.

- **RETE IACIO** ("I throw the net"): retiarius may throw his net, provided that it has been recovered since being thrown previously (see below), at his opponent if no more than two squares (but not diagonally) separate them.
- **RETE RECIPIO** ("I recover the net"): retiarius retrieves his net and coils it ready to throw again. He may not throw the net until this card has been played, but may both recover and throw again in the same turn.
- **TRIDENTEM IACIO** ("I throw the trident"): retiarius throws his trident at his opponent, provided that no more than four squares separate them. To retrieve his trident, the retiarius must move into the square where it is deemed to have landed (directly in front of the opponent if blocked by SCVTVM; immediately behind his opponent's original position if avoided by VITO) and not be involved in combat whilst in that square.

DEFENCE CARDS

- **VITO** ("I avoid/dodge"): gladiator sidesteps any attack or the retiarius' net. The player moves his figure one square in any direction of his choice, including diagonally, provided that the figure ends the turn out of contact with the attacker (i.e. not in an adjacent square), or to one side of the line of flight of a spear/trident. The other Defence Card may be played only by *murmillones* or other gladiators carrying shields.
- **SCVTVM TOLLO** ("I raise the shield"): murmillo blocks any blow or deflects a thrown spear/trident, but does not automatically avoid the net (he will be deemed to have avoided the net only if he can guess the retiarius' choice of Hit Card – see below).

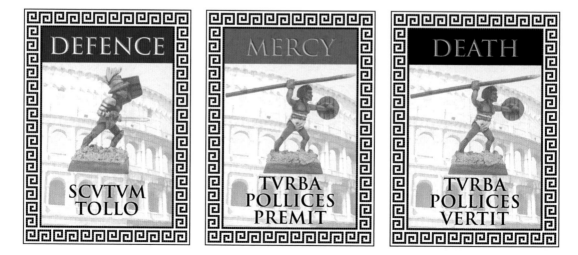

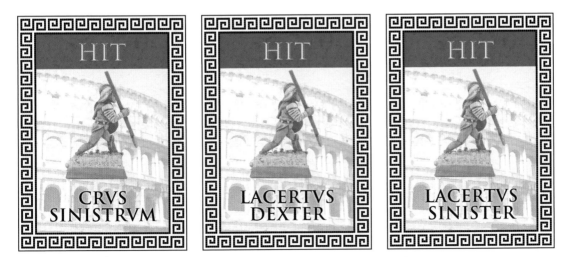

You can use the blank given at the end of the series of cards here to create additional actions or hit locations should you wish. Note that extra, optional cards have been provided for more specific hit locations as described in the text under "Ideas for additional rules/ variations".

NB Any Action or Defence Cards which are played, but cannot fulfil their intended purpose – RETE IACIO, for example, when the retiarius has previously thrown, but not yet recovered, his net – count as PROCEDO.

THE PLAYERS' DECKS OF CARDS

MURMILLONES	CARD	RETIARII
21	PROCEDO	21
3	OPPUVGNO	5
3	VITO	6
3	SCVTVM TOLLO	0
0	RETE IACIO	3
0	RETE RECIPIO	3
0	TRIDENTEM IACIO	2

These combinations of cards have been found to give a satisfactory game, but for a quicker, bloodier combat, reduce the number of defence cards held by both gladiators.

HIT CARDS

These indicate the area of the body at which the attacker is aiming/which the defender is protecting.

- **CAPVT** (head): a blow to the head kills a retiarius, who has no helmet, but only wounds *murmillones* and other gladiators with helmets.
- **CORPVS** (body): wounds any gladiator.
- **MEMBRA** (limbs): wounds any gladiator.

Successful hits are recorded by giving the victim tokens – coloured counters or smaller copies of the appropriate Hit Cards – which result in the number of cards a player may hold in subsequent turns being reduced by one, as shown below:

MURMILLONES	HIT CARDS	RETIARII
Two hits = 1 card	CAPVT	One hit kills
One hit = 1 card	CORPVS	One hit = 1 card
Three hits = 1 card	MEMBRA	Two hits = 1 card

NB When a gladiator has suffered two hits to the body, he is badly wounded and must plead for mercy.

Murmillones have helmets, and so can take several blows to the head; retiarii do not, so a blow to the head will be fatal. Neither gladiator wears body armour, so a wound in that area will be severe. Both gladiators wear guards on their right arm; *murmillones'* left arms are also protected by the shield, and their lower legs by greaves.

(For a simpler introduction to the game for younger children, have any hit, other than CAPVT on the retiarius, cause the loss of 1 card – though this does perhaps make it too hard to disable the latter.)

When a player has only one card left (which he must play as a Defence Card) or the combination of cards in his hand permits no movement (VITO and SCVTVM, for example) he must appeal to the crowd for mercy by drawing either:

- **TVRBA POLLICES PREMIT** (The crowd signals thumbs down): mercy! Gladiator lives to fight another day...or:
- **TVRBA POLLICES VERTIT** (The crowd signals thumbs up): death! The winner cuts the loser's throat.

(This follows the interpretation put forward by Michael Grant that the thumbs up or down gestures actually had the opposite meanings to those popularly attributed to them today.)

SEQUENCE OF PLAY

1. Decide which player will be the retiarius and which the murmillo by dicing or tossing a coin.
2. The retiarius discards all SCVTVM cards from his pack; the murmillo discards all cards marked RETE IACIO, RETE RECIPIO and TRIDENTEM IACIO.
3. Both players put their Hit Cards – CAPVT, CORPVS and MEMBRA – to one side for use when necessary, together with TVRBA POLLICES PREMIT and TVRBA POLLICES VERTIT.
4. Players shuffle the cards remaining in their packs thoroughly and place the packs face down in front of them.
5. The opposing figures are placed on opposite sides of the arena, directly in front of the respective players.
6. The retiarius draws **five** cards; the murmillo **four** cards.
7. Both players secretly select a Defence Card (see above) from their hands and place them face down beside their packs. A player who does not have a Defence Card in his hand must play another Action Card to bluff his opponent.
8. Each turn, the retiarius plays his cards first and moves his figure,

resolving any attacks or blows before the murmillo plays his cards. The retiarius always plays three Action Cards; the murmillo two cards (always subject to the number of cards left in his hand as a result of wounds inflicted in previous turns). A player may choose to discard an Action Card, rather than move his gladiator in accordance with it, by playing it face down with his other Actions for that turn.

9. Should the net or trident/spear be thrown, or the moving figure start his turn in or enter a square adjacent to his opponent **at any point during his turn**, an attack must be resolved immediately, as described below. Once the attack has been resolved, any remaining Action Cards for that gladiator may be played. Note that a gladiator may only attack once in his turn.

10. When both players have played their Action Cards for that turn, resolved any attacks, combats and wounds, they then return all cards, including Defence Cards, which have been played, to the bottoms of their respective packs, and draw new cards to make up their hands for the next turn, subject to any wounds received. Defence Cards which have not been played count as part of the players' hands for the next turn: they may be played again or saved for future use, as the players prefer. Alternatively, the players may agree before the game that unplayed Defence Cards must be returned to the pack at the end of a turn.

11. Repeat stages 7-10 above until one gladiator is killed or unable to move. In the latter case, the player must draw a card to determine the verdict of the crowd as described above. The victor may take on a fresh opponent, recovering half the cards lost for wounds in the previous bout (rounded down to the nearest whole number, subject always to a minimum loss of one card), or both players may draw fresh gladiators for a new contest.

A *retiarius* confronts a *murmillo* in a typical gladiatorial encounter. Illustration by Ann Prescott.

RESOLVING ATTACKS/COMBATS

An attack/combat takes place whenever: the gladiator whose turn it is to move plays RETE IACIO or TRIDENTEM IACIO; starts his turn in or enters a square adjacent to his opponent; or is unable to move out of a square adjacent to his opponent (such as a murmillo trapped in a net).

When an attack is made, the potential victim must reveal his Defence Card. If he has anticipated correctly, the attack fails and no further resolution is necessary; if he has not played a suitable Defence Card, the attack will be decided by the Hit Cards.

The Defender chooses one of his Hit Cards and places it face down before him. The Attacker then plays one of his Hit Cards face up, whereupon the Defender's card is revealed. If the two cards are identical, the blow is blocked and the Defender escapes unscathed; if not, he is wounded, or sometimes, in the case of a retiarius, killed if the Attacker played CAPVT (see above).

Tokens representing hits are given to the victim and, if necessary, the number of cards in his hand is reduced by one for the rest of the game, as described above.

A murmillo who is trapped in the net by failing to play VITO against RETE IACIO will be deemed to have escaped from it if he survives comparison of Hit Cards unwounded. If he does not, he remains in the net for the following turn only – in other words, the retiarius takes his next turn immediately, after which play then proceeds according to the usual sequence described above.

IDEAS FOR ADDITIONAL RULES/VARIATIONS

Add extra Hit Cards, such as **BRACCHIVM DEXTRVM/SINISTRVM** (right/left forearm), **LACERTVS DEXTER/SINISTER** (right/left upper arm), **CRVS DEXTRVM/SINISTRVM** (right/left leg), **PECTVS** (chest) and **ABDOMEN** (belly), allocating different degrees of severity to each. Increasing the number of cards held in the players' hands would be necessary to prevent fights coming to too rapid a conclusion! Greater atmosphere and more tension due to the increased likelihood that blows will not be blocked will result.

Shield-carrying gladiators would, of course, be automatically protected against BRACCHIVM SINISTRVM or LACERTVS SINISTER – unless wounds inflicted on their right arms forced them to drop the shield and fight left-handed with the sword. Wounds to one or both legs could prevent the playing of OPPVGNO, or even VITO.

The exact combination of cards in a player's pack might be adjusted to reflect differences in the armour and weaponry of various types of gladiator: thus a Thracian, armed with a curved, slashing sword and carrying a round shield, might be given fewer SCVTVM cards than a Samnite, whose larger, rectangular shield may have afforded slightly more protection, but more PROCEDO and OPPVGNO cards as he was somewhat more mobile.

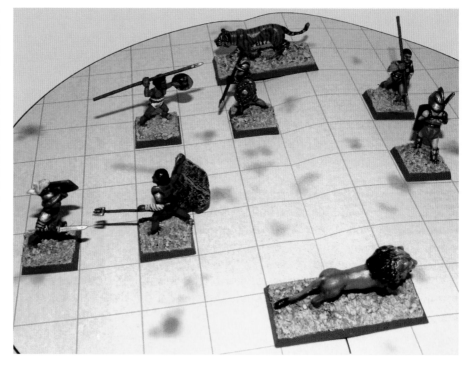

A frantic gladiator game in progress. The miniatures are all Miniature Figurines painted by the author, including the lion and tiger adding extra spice to the game! The arena is simply the original *Battlegames* centrefold design created when Arthur's article was first published.

Individual gladiators might be given combinations of Action and Defence Cards to reflect their ability or personality. RVFVS SCROFVLVS, for example, a dogged, but unimaginative heavyweight slogger of a murmillo, might be given extra SCVTVM cards, but fewer VITO and OPPVGNO cards, and be capable of suffering more wounds to the head or chest (by reducing the number of cards lost from his hand thereby) than his agile opponent, the retiarius QVINTVS VELOX, who has no SCVTVM cards, and, being unarmoured, can be killed by a thrust to PECTVS or ABDOMEN.

I am grateful to Arthur for allowing me to include such an excellent (and educational!) game in the *Compendium*. He has asked me to add:

"I set out to develop rules for gladiatorial combat in order to enliven Classical Studies and Latin lessons, determined to produce a game with simple, easily memorized rules which pupils could play with a minimum of supervision in real time.

"I abandoned the traditional wargame structure of scale moves, combat resolution by dice and the consequent need to refer to rules or charts during play, in favour of an adaptation of Andy Gittins' system for his 'David and Goliath' game, which I had seen demonstrated at the Conference of Wargamers.

"My thanks to Miss Jeanne Battye, Headmistress of North Bridge House Junior School, for her support of the initial development of the game; to Miss Kate Mitchell, Head of Juniors, and Mrs Jacqui Thompson, both of Wimbledon High School, for allowing further playtesting by Year 4, and to my

Latin/Classical Studies pupils (too many to mention by name) for their enthusiastic playtesting of the game during the last fifteen years."

Now, if ancient Rome isn't your thing, you might prefer the idea of being d'Artagnan of the Three Musketeers, and that's certainly a viable option: Redoubt Enterprises, for one, do a very nice range to suit (*www.redoubtenterprises.com*). Another alternative and a particular favourite of mine is the world of medieval foot tournaments, where men in armour fought for the honour of their lady – and often substantial prize money.

If you think you might be interested in playing larger medieval games at some point, then there are two good options. In 1/72 scale, companies like Italeri and Zvezda produce some very nice figures, and in 15mm and 28mm scale, there is a wide range on offer. A trip to your local Games Workshop will present you with a selection of Bretonnian and Empire figures that are suitable – you only need a couple, and individual figures are sold in blister packs. Meanwhile, Games Workshop designer Michael Perry has created a lovely range of 28mm medieval figures for Perry Miniatures, in both metal and plastic. Or how about a fun alternative for this, which will save you time and effort?

Use children's toys.

Amongst the most attractive are the beautiful Schleich figures from their 'Knights and Fighting Heroes' range. Illustrated here, in the red corner, we have their Foot Soldier with Sword and, in the blue corner, the Foot Soldier with War Hammer. For a fiver each, they stand 90mm (3½") tall and come ready-painted to quite a high standard. All you need to do is play with them!

Schleich knights in combat, part of a wide range of such figures. Great for introducing kids to the hobby, these beauties are collectible in their own right.

Several miniatures: the skirmish

It is, of course, perfectly possible to play games with several combatants a side: indeed, in ancient Rome, they often staged combats between numbers of gladiators and even, as you will know if you have watched Ridley Scott's movie *Gladiator*, mock battles. But skirmishes are such a common feature of warfare that I want to take this opportunity to introduce you to them on our journey into the possibilities offered by wargaming.

Skirmishes are, in fact, perhaps the most common form of encounter in warfare throughout history. It implies a meeting of small forces, perhaps as few as half a dozen a side, such as small patrols. On the other hand, they may be the prelude to something much bigger, such as when the 'point men' of advance guards jostle for position while they wait for the main body of their army to arrive. It could begin with a mere scout, who is then supported by the rest of his patrol, who then call up the rest of their squadron or company. This, in turn, may escalate as the rest of the battalion or regiment arrives, perhaps supported by other troops, artillery and so on.

Such an engagement may fizzle out as one side decides that it is outnumbered or low on ammunition or too far from home; on the other hand, a full-blown battle might ensue within hours of the first meeting.

A skirmish is also an apt way to describe those engagements that are on the fringes of military history, such as innumerable fights in the Wild West of America, any number of colonial engagements and 'policing' operations, and the efforts to deal with piracy on the high seas and the myriad islands of the Caribbean and elsewhere. It's also true to say that the vast majority of action seen by soldiers since the First World War have been skirmishes of one kind or another, where an individual squad or platoon slogs along as part of a much larger campaign that they cannot possibly grasp as a whole. Indeed, as we see on our television screens

A typical skirmish game, this one Gripping Beast's *Saga* set in the Dark Ages. Skirmish games are certainly not 'poor cousins' in the wargaming world – some wargamers play nothing else, preferring to assemble a wide range of forces for small actions than spend their hobby time amassing divisions, corps and armies for Armageddon-like encounters!

almost every day, this is the nature of the war in Afghanistan, where close-knit units of soldiers are subjected to surprise encounters with equally small units of Taliban in skirmishes that may last a few minutes or several hours. For most soldiers, their experience of war is, in fact, a never-ending sequence of skirmishes.

And of course, skirmish games are highly suited to non-historical encounters in fantasy, science fiction or other genres such as 'pulp' gaming, a term that covers recreating scenes from lurid 1950s novels, movies and comic books: *King Kong* or *The Land that Time Forgot*, anyone? Games Workshop's highly successful Warhammer 40K is, essentially, a skirmish game and whilst a number of large battles are described, many of the encounters in *The Lord of the Rings* are running skirmishes, fending off various types of evil creatures such as orcs, goblins or Black Riders.

Skirmishes also incorporate many types of small-group adventure game, often conducted as role-playing games where each participant takes the role of one of the miniatures on the board. *Dungeons and Dragons* is the classic example, but there have been many more, such as *Heroquest* and, for science fiction fans, *Rogue Trader*.

Many wargamers cut their teeth on skirmish wargaming. After all, it's easy to get started: you don't need many miniatures, nor do you need a large table area or substantial amounts of scenery. The key point is that the miniatures on the table are representative of nothing more than themselves – which is to say, a scale of 1:1.

Now, you might wish to try skirmish wargaming with whatever miniatures you are going to be collecting for your main wargaming interest, be that horse and musket, ancients, Renaissance, WWII or whatever you are most drawn to. For the purposes of demonstrating this type of gaming, however, I'm going to take you on a journey way out West, to the frontier towns of the 1870s and 1880s, where the tumbleweed blows.

A Wild West game in progress. The marshal and his posse are confronting the baddies near the lumber yard at top left. This simple layout measures a mere four feet square and the buildings are all PDF downloads from Eric Hotz's Whitewash City range printed onto paper then mounted onto old breakfast cereal packets, including the railway tracks. The base boards are 5mm MDF.

What are we going to need? As ever, a playing area, and for this, I would recommend something between three and four feet (1-1.25m) square. More space is nice, but really not necessary for the kind of 'quick and dirty' game I have in mind.

A good reason for choosing a Wild West setting is that the scenery can be as cheap and simple as you like, particularly given that there is some superb paper scenery available. What do I mean by 'paper' scenery? Quite simply, it is scenery produced as PDFs to download and print out onto paper or card – or, of course, you can design your own. Our gladiatorial arena was a very simple example, but a number of designers have created extraordinarily detailed artwork for entire Wild West towns, including hotels, saloons, outhouses, workshops, warehouses – even railway lines.

The bad guys: a gang of Mexican bandidos from the author's collection, painted by the extremely talented Jez Griffin of Shakespeare Studios. These cut-throat varmints are clearly out to cause trouble! The 32mm miniatures are from Black Scorpion, who have an excellent range of Wild West and Pirate figures. Crates and barrels from Frontline Miniatures.

We're the law in this town! The sherrif, his deputies and some of his posse making ready to hunt down the lawbreakers and bring them in – dead or alive! More wonderful Black Scorpion miniatures, these painted by the author. Whitewash City card buildings.

Once I had discovered Eric Hotz's 'Whitewash City' (see *www.erichotz. com/whitewash.html*), I never looked back. One of the other advantages of the Whitewash City buildings is that they come with detailed floor plans showing doors, windows, stairwells and so on. Items of furniture are marked too, but several companies produce excellent items in resin or white metal that can enliven a scene considerably.

You don't even need to buy any miniatures, if you don't want to, because it's perfectly possible to buy PDF people! Such 'paper flats', just like the scenery, can be printed out and mounted upright on a simple card base. Some paper flats depict the front and rear views of the figure, others show the sides. Such 2-D pieces are not to everyone's taste, but they are certainly by far the cheapest and quickest way to get playing. If you decide that you like the setting a lot, then you can of course graduate to 3-D models in the scale of your choice. Try Wargame Vault *www.wargamevault.com* and you can download a vast range of free paper figures from Matt Fritz's *Junior General* website at *www.juniorgeneral.org*.

If, like me, you feel the urge to play Wild West with more characterful miniatures that can take their place in your collection, then there are a host of manufacturers who produce suitable figures. Perhaps the most extensive ranges are made by Artizan Designs (*www.artizandesigns.com*), Black Scorpion (*www.blackscorpionminiatures.com*), Dixon Miniatures (*www.dixon-minis.com*), Knuckleduster (*www.knuckleduster.com*), Old Glory (*www.oldgloryminiatures.com* then look for 25mm Figures > West Wind > Cowboy Wars) and Wargames Foundry (*wargamesfoundry.com*).

Okay, so let's assume you have assembled a gang of bad guys and a posse of lawmen. To be strictly correct, we should, of course, duplicate each figure on horseback as well as on foot, but for the demonstration game, we'll assume that the horses have either been tied up at the edge of town or perhaps they're being fed at the livery stables.

The last things you need are a tape measure (the steel, retractable kind used for DIY is perfect, and most wargamers have a couple of these in their 'ready to go' box) and some dice. Nothing fancy here, just the standard six-sided type (d6). Two will do, but more is good. And finally, a pack of ordinary playing cards, including the jokers. Make sure they are well shuffled.

Now, set up a scenario – a good, old-fashioned bank robbery will do, or a posse catching up with the bad guys at their hideout – with a nice selection of typical buildings for the period, including the bank and, somewhere, the Sheriff's office. As well as the two opposing teams of characters (I would recommend perhaps four per side to start with), you can also have innocent townsfolk wandering about, referred to as Non-Player Characters (NPCs), and we'll deal with them later. It's also a good idea to have other stuff literally lying around: some crates and barrels, local produce, lumber, perhaps a horse trough and so on. You'll get some ideas from the photographs.

It might prove an incentive for the bank robbers if you actually make

A definite case of lurking... The bandido lookout keeps a sharp eye open for the sheriff's men.

the prize more tempting. A £1 coin or a dollar bill is fine – don't overdo it or real shots might be exchanged!

The objective, therefore, is for the bandits to make it to the bank, rob it and make good their escape. The lawmen, meanwhile, will have to prevent the getaway.

So, here are the rules.

WILD WEST SHOOTOUTS

Each turn, the players cut the deck. Highest card wins and moves first. The cards are replaced in the deck, and the deck is shuffled. The player can move or fight with all, some or none of his characters as he sees fit, according to the circumstances. If a player draws the Joker, he can carry out a bonus action with **one** of his characters (e.g. walk 4", turn 180° *and* fire his pistol, or mount his horse *and* canter 12").

Each character should have a clearly defined 'front' arc, indicating his (or her, if Calamity Jane, Belle Starr or other female character) 90-degree field of vision. Either side of this are two 90-degree 'flank' arcs and finally a 90-degree 'rear' arc.

A character that has taken two hits is considered dead or unconscious; a 'Hard Man', such as a gang leader, Sheriff or US Marshal can take three; townspeople or innocent bystanders only one. Horses take one wound only. A record can be kept on a sheet of paper, or some kind of counter placed beside the character when it is wounded. Only one Hard Man per side is permitted in normal games and is designated the leader.

Killed characters, horses or NPCs are laid down, rather than removed, and count as low obstacles (hard cover for any prone figure).

Permitted actions each move

Characters on foot may
Walk 4" and turn up to 180°
Run 8" and turn up to 90°
Walk 2" carrying a heavy object
Crawl 1" facing any direction
Stand up, kneel or lie down losing ½ move
Cross an obstacle such as a wall, fence or hedge up to chest height
Climb/descend one storey using the stairs
Climb 2" up any other obstacle (e.g. crates, woodpile) or mount/dismount a wagon
Scale up to one storey of the outside of a building with hand-holds
Jump or vault a gap up to 2" wide or obstacle less than ½" high
Mount a horse or wagon
Jump onto a horse or wagon from above
Shoot a Winchester or other magazine-loading rifle once (aimed)
Shoot a Winchester or other magazine-loading rifle twice (quickfire)
Reload three rounds in a Winchester or other magazine-loading rifle or late period pistol
Reload one round in an early 'cap and ball' pistol (e.g. 'Navy' or 'Army' Colt or Le Mat)
Shoot a muzzle-loading musket or rifle or carbine once
Half reload a muzzle loading musket or rifle or carbine
Shoot a double-barrelled shotgun twice (a single barrel each time, incl. at different targets)
Shoot both barrels of a double-barrelled shotgun simultaneously once
Reload a double-barrelled shotgun
Shoot a pistol once (aimed)
Shoot a pistol twice (quickfire)
'Fan' a pistol (unaimed)
Throw a knife or other object
Throw a lasso (rope)
Engage in brawling (hand to hand)
Open a door and step through
Close a door and move away
Open a window
Pick up a heavy object
Light a fuse and throw dynamite
Pick up and throw a small object

Characters on a horse may
Move up to half distance and dismount
Walk 6"
Trot 12"
Gallop 24"
Turn up to 180° if walking or trotting
Turn up to 90° if galloping
Jump an obstacle such as a wall, fence or hedge up to chest height
Jump a gap up to 4" wide
Jump off his horse
Shoot a Winchester or other magazine-loading rifle once
Reload three rounds in a Winchester or other magazine-loading rifle or revolver
Reload one round in an early 'cap and ball' pistol (e.g. 'Navy' or 'Army' Colt or Le Mat)
Shoot a muzzle-loading musket or rifle or carbine once
Half reload a muzzle loading carbine (takes two turns)
Shoot a double-barrelled shotgun twice (a single barrel each time, incl. at different targets)
Shoot both barrels of a double-barrelled shotgun once
Reload a double-barrelled shotgun
Shoot a pistol once (aimed)
Throw a knife or other object
Throw a lasso (rope)
Use the horse as an aid to climb an obstacle
Load or unload saddlebags onto or from a horse
Engage in swordplay (hand to hand)

The sheriff and his posse moving past the saloon and miners' tent hotel, with a sneaky bandido sniper visible top right.. Buildings from the Whitewash City range, barrels, crates and water trough from Frontline Wargaming, miniatures from Black Scorpion.

Characters on a wagon may
Move up to half distance and dismount
Walk 6"
Trot 12"
Gallop 24"
Turn up to 180° if walking
Turn up to 90° if trotting
Turn up to 45° if galloping
Jump off the wagon
The following apply to passengers only, not the driver (who needs both hands)
Shoot a Winchester or other magazine-loading rifle once
Reload three rounds in a Winchester or other magazine-loading rifle or revolver
Reload one round in an early 'cap and ball' pistol (e.g. 'Navy' or 'Army' Colt or Le Mat)
Shoot a muzzle-loading musket or rifle or carbine once
Half reload a muzzle loading carbine (takes two turns)
Shoot a double-barrelled shotgun twice (a single barrel each time, incl. at different targets)
Shoot both barrels of a double-barrelled shotgun once
Reload a double-barrelled shotgun
Shoot a pistol once (aimed)
Shoot a pistol twice (quickfire)
Throw a knife or other object
Throw a lasso (rope)
Use the wagon as an aid to climb an obstacle
Load or unload one large or two small objects
Engage in brawling (hand to hand)

MOVEMENT PENALTIES AND RISKS

- Players should agree on any steep slopes, broken or swampy ground, rivers or streams deeper than 12" (on foot) or 24" (on horseback or wagon) or ravines, all of which reduce speed by half whilst passing through them.
- A character on foot may *walk* backwards at half speed.
- A wagon carrying more than two thirds of a full load moves at half speed. A full load is composed of up to six objects, which might be the driver and five passengers, or the driver plus five large crates or barrels or ten small ones. You should decide what constitutes a large or small object for each scenario.
- If a character attempts to climb a structure or jump or vault an

obstacle or jump onto or off a horse or wagon, he must roll a d6 to see if he falls. A 4, 5 or 6 means he has made the climb or jump successfully and may be placed on the far side of the obstacle, ready to move again next turn. A roll of 2 or 3, however, means that he has fallen, but escaped injury, so may not do anything else until next turn. If jumping a gap or stream, the character is placed midway across. A roll of 1 means that not only has he failed, but he also takes an automatic Hit and must attempt to Save against possible wounding, requiring a 4, 5 or 6 to do so.

- If a character attempting to climb has the benefit of his horse or a wagon, then add 2 to his climbing die roll. *This applies to the first storey or equivalent only.*
- If the character has fallen from a height, then add 1 to the Save requirement for each storey from which he has fallen (i.e. a character falling from the first floor needs a 5 or 6, and from the second floor he needs a 6. From the third floor or above, the wound is automatic. Fortunately, there weren't too many tall buildings in Wild West towns!)
- You may wish to allow characters to climb trees in some circumstances. Treat them as buildings for climbing and falling.
- All obstacles must either be climbed, jumped, vaulted or moved around, including casualties. It is not permitted to simply ride or drive over them.
- Drawing or holstering a revolver or pistol can be done at no cost.
- The minimum gap required for a character to pass between other characters, or another character and an obstacle, is 1" on foot, 2" on horseback, 3" on a wagon.

WEAPONS

A Winchester 1873 held fifteen rounds. A typical revolver, whether the later type firing cartridges or the earlier 'cap and ball' type, held six rounds[1], hence 'six-shooter'. A derringer or 'Saturday night special' held two. There were still many old-fashioned single-shot, muzzle-loading weapons in circulation, such as cavalry carbines and even old muskets and rifled muskets from the Civil War, as well as comparatively rare hunting weapons, 'buffalo guns' and the like.

As well as the classic 'six shooter' pistol, some gunfighters carried a heavier pistol such as the Colt Dragoon, the Colt .45, the .45 Schofield, and the Remington, which were more accurate and had a slightly longer range, but could not be 'fanned' like the six-shooter.

Another interesting weapon was the Le Mat pistol, a nine-shot revolver which also had a second barrel housing a small shotgun cartridge, with about half the range of a normal shotgun. If a character is armed with one

---

1 *I am reliably informed, however, that many cowboys and gunslingers often left the chamber under the hammer empty to prevent accidental discharge if the hammer caught on clothing.*

of these rarities, then once per game he may flip the switch and use this scattergun as if it were a single barrelled shotgun, but halving all the range bands.

A cowboy would also normally carry an all-purpose knife of some kind, and hunters would have skinning knives, perhaps even the famous 'Bowie' knife. In a pinch in a bar fight, however, any nearby object such as a bottle or poker would do!

Other favourites of the movies are Dynamite and TNT which were used for mining and came rolled into paper-covered tubes to which a fuse was attached. A later development was Nitro Glycerine, a highly unstable compound which came in liquid form, stored in jars. A good bank robber might also avail themselves of a strong acid of some kind to burn through complicated locks.

Some weapons may be improvised from whatever is to hand, such as a lumberjack's axe, a miner's spade, a blacksmith's hammer or a piece of wood. You should decide what is available for each scenario.

Make my day... The sheriff confronts Quick Draw McGraw outside the saloon on Main Street. He's tagging along with the bandidos in the hope of making a fistful of dollars and securing his lethal reputation.

SHOOTING

A character may shoot at any time, but suffers penalties to accuracy if moving as shown below. He may shoot at anything within his field of vision, including at a target outside his front arc, but suffers a penalty to accuracy.

Weapon	Range		
	Close 5+ to Hit	Medium 7+ to Hit	Long 9+ to Hit
Derringer	0"-2"	n/a	n/a
Six-shooter	0"-4"	4"-8"	8"-12"
Heavy pistol or Le Mat	0"-5"	5"-10"	10"-15"
Smoothbore Musket	0"-5"	5"-10"	10"-15"
Muzzle loading carbine	0"-6"	6"-12"	12"-18"
Rifled Musket	0"-8"	8"-16"	16"-24"
Winchester	0"-10"	10"-20"	20"-30"
Single Shot Rifle	0"-12"	12"-24"	24"-36"
Shotgun	0"-5"	5"-9"	9"-12"
Thrown weapon	0"-3"	3"-6"	6"-9"
Lasso	0"-2"	n/a	n/a

The table shows the total required on two dice for each range, with the following modifiers *for each shot fired* (i.e. if 'fanning' all six shots from a six-shooter, each shot is worked out with a -4 modifier):

Shooting Modifiers			
Target walked in its turn	-1	Firer is walking or turning	-2
Target ran or trotted in its turn	-2	Firer is running or trotting	-4
Target cantered in its turn	-3	Firer is cantering	-6
Target galloped in its turn	-4	Firer is galloping	-8
Target is lying down/crawling	-2	Firer is wounded	-4
Target is behind soft cover	-2	Firer resting long weapon on wall etc	+2
Target is behind hard cover	-4	Firer is prone or kneeling	+2
Looking up at target	-2	Looking down at target	+2
Target is prone	-4	Target is kneeling (not shotguns)	-1
'Fanning' a six-shooter	-4	Quickfiring Winchester or pistol	-2
Firer is green	-4	Firer is sharpshooter or gunslinger	+4

This may look like a lot of modifiers, but you'll soon get used to them and before long will know them by heart.

- Soft cover offers concealment, but won't stop a bullet, so includes bushes, fences, boxes, barrels, wagons and so on.
- Hard cover offers both concealment and stops the passage of bullets, so walls, rocks and stouter constructions come into this category. I tend to count buildings as hard cover *unless the target figure is standing at a window* to fire out. Horse troughs, heavy lumber, tree trunks, railway lines and some other objects (indoors as well as outside) should also be agreed upon as 'hard' cover.
- A simple record should be kept of the rounds fired. By far the easiest way to do this is to use matchsticks, tiddleywinks or some other form of counters, which are moved from one pile to another as they are used up. Alternatively, make a note on a scrap of paper and cross off rounds as they are used.
- A limit should be set on the number of extra rounds carried so that the game does not descend into an endless gunfight! If we assume that all characters start with their weapons loaded, then it would seem appropriate that a maximum of 15 extra rounds per man are carried on bandoliers, belts or in pockets or pouches, the equivalent of one complete reload for a Winchester. This can be increased or reduced for specific scenarios.
- Dynamite should only be available in small quantities, lest the game descend into Armageddon. It counts as a thrown weapon, so consult the table Weapon/Range table above, take into account any modifiers and roll to hit the target.
- If the dynamite misses, we must find out where it has landed. Roll a single d6: a roll of 1 or 2 means it has fallen 2" short of the target; 3 equals 2" to the left of the target; 4 means 2" to the right; and 5 or 6 means it has overshot the target by 2".
- Whether the dynamite hits or misses, we now roll another die. This determines how long the fuse burns for before the dynamite explodes. A 1 or 2 mean it explodes immediately; a 3 or 4 means it explodes at the end of the opponent's next turn; a 5 or 6 means it explodes at the end of *your* next turn. Obviously, in the latter cases, it means that the dynamite can potentially be picked up and thrown back (but see Guts below).
- Dynamite has a 2" blast radius, any character or NPC within that distance when it exploded is considered 'hit'. If the explosion occurs inside a building, the effect is greater and the blast radius is 3".
- Any figure suffering a Hit must now attempt to Save by rolling a 6 if hit at close range for the weapon firing, 5 or 6 if hit at medium range and 4, 5 or 6 if hit at long range. If a Save is not rolled, the figure suffers a wound. It is therefore possible that a figure may be killed outright in a single move if hit multiple times. Dynamite always counts as being at close range.
- A lasso never inflicts a Hit, but must be on target to be effective – see overleaf.

- If a character is 'hit' by a lasso, then he is pinned and may not move or defend himself. A sensible option at this point might be to surrender!
- If a character on foot is lassoed by a character on horseback, he may be dragged behind the horse and suffers an automatic Hit every turn. A saving throw of 4, 5 or 6 is required to prevent a Wound and of course the Guts rule does not apply because the character can't run away.

BRAWLING

When opposing figures actually come into contact, a brawl takes place. This is done very simply by opposed die rolls, with modifiers as below:

Brawling Modifiers	
Character ran into contact	+1
Character is higher than defender	+1
Character is 'Hard Man'	+1
Character is behind cover (first round only)	+1
Character on horseback fighting opponent on foot	+1
Character on horseback using sword against opponent without one	+2
Character is outnumbered	-1
Character is wounded	-3

Brawls are simultaneous, so both players roll their dice at the same time. The highest modified roll wins the fight, the loser is hit and is pushed back 1". If the scores are equal, the fight is drawn and continues next round.

In order to prevent a Wound, the loser must roll a 4, 5 or 6 on another die. If the attacker used a knife, club, rifle, musket, carbine or Winchester, then this is increased to a 5 or 6 to prevent a Wound, and if the character

An effective way to end an argument: give 'em both barrels! Shotgun Joe adds real punch to the sheriff's posse, but he can be vulnerable while reloading and range is limited.

is on the receiving end of an axe, sword, sledgehammer or miners' spade blow, a 6 is required.

If a character is outnumbered, all attacks must be received at a -1 disadvantage. If a situation involving several miniatures is unclear, break it down into as many 1:1 fights as possible and then the remaining brawl should become clear.

Brawling on horseback is called swordplay, and is only permitted between characters armed with swords. Though rare, it should be included for military characters who take pride in using *l'arme blanche*!

GUTS

Clearly, taking a hit is a shocking business, and a sensible human being would run for cover, but on the mean streets of Deadwood, a man's gotta do what a man's gotta do, and that takes guts.

Our rule is simple: if a character takes a Hit, regardless of whether he is wounded or not, he must test for Guts. The only modifiers are for a Hard Man, who may add 1 to the die roll, but if the character is actually wounded, he must deduct 2.

Roll a d6 – a score of 4, 5 or 6 is required to pass and continue. If he fails, he must run (or gallop, if on horseback) directly away from the threat towards the nearest cover during his next turn (or as many turns as required to reach it) and remain there for a further turn. If the retreat takes him off the board, then his part in these events is over.

If the character has also been wounded, then he will remain in cover for the rest of the game unless reached by a Hard Man, Doc or Friendly Lady on his side who can patch him up (this takes three turns) and get him back in the fight.

NON PLAYER CHARACTERS (NPCs)

Another fun aspect of Wild West – or indeed any skirmish – gaming is the addition of more or less innocent bystanders who are not controlled by either player as such, but can put a spanner in the works of either side.

Every Western town has its typical characters, such as barmen, undertakers, the mayor, the local newspaper owner, any number of cowboys and farm hands, the local priest, shopkeepers, doctor, the town drunk, the bank manager and his clerks, the hotel and saloon owners, local landowners and ranchers and, of course, ladies of the night. If there is a railroad nearby, then there will also be the station with the station master and, probably, the telegraph operator, warehouse owners and so on. A mining town has miners and, very often, Irish and Chinese labourers, who would probably also be running the local laundry; and of course, every good Western town needs a travelling salesman selling quack remedies.

This is without stretching our scenario to include the Plains Wars and other conflicts with the Native Americans, in which case you could add the Indians themselves and the US Cavalry, or, even earlier, the Alamo, Davy Crockett and so on.

The point is that you can add townspeople to your heart's content, each housed in an appropriate building, doing their best to go about their own lives whilst the goodies and the baddies are shooting it out on Main Street. Each of these NPCs is controlled in the following way.

For every player turn, roll a d6. The total score is the number of NPCs on the move that turn. NPCs always move at walking speed. The player whose turn it is decides *which* NPCs will move, but their opponent decides *where* they will move. When the turn passes to the other side, roles are reversed. It is perfectly acceptable for a NPC to move multiple times, or for different NPCs to be selected.

NPCs will never willingly move into the line of fire of an exchange of gunfire that is already taking place and, if they find themselves in such a position, must be moved away at the earliest opportunity.

Good guys (lawmen etc) must never shoot at an enemy character that is within 1" of a NPC. The baddies have no such restriction and may even deliberately use a NPC as a 'human shield' by moving into base-to-base contact with the NPC and hiding behind it, though they cannot shoot whilst doing so.

POTENTIAL REFINEMENTS

Of course, there are all manner of extra details you could add to a set of rules like this. They are far from perfect, and you should feel free to adjust them according to how you 'feel' about the period and the setting.

For one thing, there were a host of different weapons, of which I have chosen just a small selection to be representative of the Wild West. If you wish to add more, or adjust the ranges or effects of what I have listed here, then by all means do so.

Similarly, you could go into more detail about the location of wounds. If a wound is caused, you could roll a pair of d6, with these suggested results:

2	Head shot, killed outright
3	Left shoulder, cannot use long firearm
4	Left arm, cannot hold pistol
5	Left leg, cannot walk or run
6, 7, 8	Body, immobilised
9	Right leg, cannot walk or run
10	Right arm, cannot hold pistol
11	Right shoulder, cannot use long firearm
12	Heart shot, killed outright

Finally, there are all manner of special characters you might like to introduce. The Hard Man is just one and, in the Shooting rules, I have introduced the Sharpshooter who is more accurate with long weapons like the Winchester or carbine, and the Gunslinger, whose weapon of choice is

Some of the author's Black Scorpion cowboys and lawmen. One of the great things about Wild West miniatures is that most of them can be used as either goodies or baddies, appearing as a law-abiding citizen in one game and then as a rootin' tootin' gun-slingin' bank robber the next. There are few periods in which your miniatures have such versatility.

the heavy pistol or revolver and is capable of firing both his revolvers in a turn (though not fanning them). You might want a Brawler who specialises at, well, brawling, or the Trick Rider who can master a horse, enabling it to jump higher and further or turn faster. How about a Dynamite Expert who can cut fuses more precisely and throw it more accurately, or an Inspiring Leader who can add a point or two to a character's Guts test? Over to you...

RECRUITING YOUR GANG

Something that you will find is common in wargames rules are points systems. The idea is that each troop or character type is worth a certain number of points, to which various weapons or types of armour or morale ratings can be added, and these are also given a points value. The idea is to permit the fielding of completely different forces if necessary, but which still have the same or similar fighting values.

So, for example, in our Wild West game, we might say that each side has 50 points to begin with – let's call them "Dollars" to make things a bit more atmospheric. To hire a standard cowhand or bandido (with just one Wound) costs $5; a deputy or experienced gunman (two Wounds) costs $10; and a sheriff or gang leader (three Wounds) costs $20. It costs an extra $5 for any special skill, such as Sharpshooter, Gunslinger and so on.

Now for the extras. A horse? $5. A wagon with a team of two horses? $15. Standard revolvers come at $2 each, whilst a heavy pistol is $5 and a Le Mat $8. A derringer or a knife costs just $1, as does a muzzle-loading smoothbore musket, whereas a shotgun is $7. A Winchester costs $10, as does a single-shot rifle, whilst a muzzle-loading carbine or rifled musket costs only $3. A lasso rope is only $1, whereas a stick of Dynamite is going to cost you $5. A decent sword for a cavalry type would be $4. A complete restock of ammunition would cost $1.

These are, of course, just suggestions, but you can see how you'll have to make choices right from the start.

Like many adventure games, it's great fun to have the result of one game affect the next, in a species of campaign (about which I shall be saying a great deal more shortly). Your games should include some kind of reward for both sides: a simple approach is to say that the bad guys are aiming to get away with a stash of cash from a specified location, whilst the good guys are attempting to prevent this and earn a reward in the process. For example, let's say that a gang is trying to rob the bank which contains $100, then the reward on their heads should be $25 each, dead or alive. Any money earned can then go towards purchasing new kit for the next game, or recruiting new team members to replace those killed last time. You could also pay a doctor to treat the wounds suffered in the previous game, assuming the character wasn't killed outright, at a rate of, say, $10 per wound.

You might also like to introduce 'intermission' games, such as the gang visiting a local saloon where they might win – or lose – money on games of Poker or Roulette or Black Jack, thus affecting their ability to purchase recruits and equipment next game.

And finally, you could introduce awards such as the gaining of skills for particular feats. For example, a character that manages two or more kills at long range with a rifle or other long arm could be upgraded to Sharpshooter for free at the end of the game, whilst a character that wins two or more Brawls could be classified – naturally enough – as a Brawler. The only limit is your imagination.

And if that all sounds too much like hard work, there are some excellent rules available to purchase that include pretty much everything you can think of and more besides.

The end is nigh: the last of the gang are holding out in the goods yard, doing their best to make an end that will be sung about.

Reaching the next level: battles

As you start collecting miniatures for your chosen historical period, there comes a point where you are moving beyond the forces that would be appropriate for a skirmish – say, at most, a few dozen miniatures per side, representing a couple of companies or squadrons – but are not quite at the stage where you feel that you can field sufficient men for a real battle. This is an awkward sort of fight to classify, and historians often refer to such situations with words like "engagement", "encounter" or even the lovely "affray". To be classed as a full-blown "battle", there needs to be something more at stake, a specific objective or piece of ground, whereas the type of tussle we are referring to seems a more transient, though not necessarily less hard-fought, affair.

A classic scenario for a fight of this type is the raid, where one side decides to send in a force sufficient to do the job, hopefully with the element of surprise, and then get out again. We are very used to such things in a modern context, from the birth of the Royal Marine Commandos and other 'Special Forces' such as the SAS onwards, but they also took place frequently in earlier times. The Royal Navy, for example, was famous for ferrying forces of Royal Marines hither and thither to land on enemy shores, create havoc, and then either depart or take possession of their new conquest, such as a fort or remote island. On the other hand, the horse and musket era abounds with cavalry raiding parties, aiming to either find their own forage or prevent the enemy from gathering theirs, or to cut lines of communication.

Sometimes, these raids took on a life of their own and could be rather larger. One good example is the Austrian Lieutenant General Hadik's Raid on Berlin in 1757[2] and a little later, Confederate General JEB Stuart was famous for his large raids during the American Civil War.

Many of the battles fought during the American War of Independence and the Seven Years War in America were, by European standards, very small indeed and could easily fall into this category. Indeed, one of the blessings of these conflicts for the wargamer who wants to get into action quickly is that with just a few units, it is possible to recreate some of the most important actions of the wars in America. The War of 1812 also saw many smaller actions, as did many of the wars of independence in Central and South America during the 19th century.

Such mid-range affrays are also the stock-in-trade of medieval games and its offshoot, fantasy wargaming. In medieval times, a lord would have his retinue, consisting of units of archers, men-at-arms, billmen, spearmen and so on, numbering anything from a few hundred up to thousands, depending on his rank. A senior lord such as an earl or a duke would also number mounted knights and men-at-arms amongst his followers.

The English Civil War is another classic period where many of the battles were quite small, confined to opposing forces in a particular

2   See Charles S Grant's "Wargaming in History Volume 4" pp 155-159, Ken Trotman 2011

locality. Although almost contemporary with the cataclysmic events of the Thirty Years War in Europe, the battles and sieges were very small in comparison and therefore, from a wargamer's point of view, much more achievable.

It is easy to see why such a model works well for fantasy gaming too, where the player can add to his army unit by unit, increasing both the overall strength of his force and the possible options available to him for any given scenario.

Now, I'm not going to provide a separate ruleset for this type of action, because it is not so very different from the slightly larger battles for which the full ruleset I have included in Chapter 7 is designed. My suggestion is simply this: base your troops precisely as you would for the main rules, but double all the quoted ranges and unit sizes.

The effect of this is to make your battalions into half-battalions or large companies. By keeping movement rates the same, we are effectively halving the time scale of each turn. As a result, we also need to halve the number of casualties inflicted, so simply work out the results of shooting as in the main rules, and then halve the result.

Melees are slightly different, because in reality, they were often decided very quickly anyway, so my advice would be to keep hand-to-hand results precisely as they are, but if you prefer to prolong the outcome of such fighting, then by all means halve melee casualties as well.

But at some point, you will realise that your collection has reached a point where you no longer want to worry about the fate of individual platoons and companies of men, and you feel ready to tackle the main prize: the full-blown battle, where you are commanding full regiments, brigades and even divisions of troops.

MILITARY ORGANISATION

Perhaps this is also a good point to pause and think about just what we mean by some of the terminology of military organisation that you will encounter with increasing frequency. let's start at the beginning.

An individual man or woman in the land forces can go by different names. 'Soldier' is the generic term, but each part of the army and marines have their own, special terms to describe them:

- Private in the infantry or marines (who also use the word 'Marine')
- Trooper in the cavalry (which may include helicopter forces or tanks)
- Gunner in the artillery

Obviously, different countries have their own, specific system of ranks and titles, but the British system ascends from the private soldier through lance corporal, corporal (or bombadier in the artillery), sergeant, staff or colour sergeant, company (or squadron in the cavalry) sergeant major and regimental sergeant major, who is the senior non commissioned officer (NCO) in a regiment. Just to confuse matters, Guards regiments call a corporal 'lance sergeant' and the Household Cavalry equivalent is 'lance-corporal of horse'.

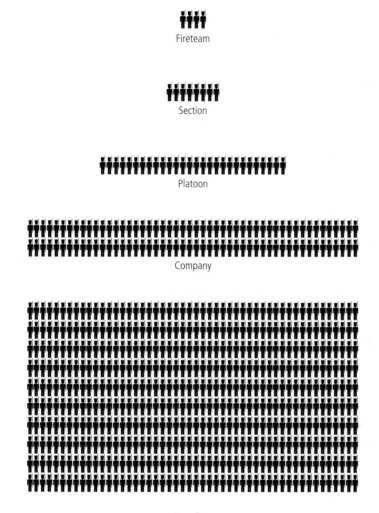

Fireteam

Section

Platoon

Company

Battalion

Diagram illustrating organisation from section to battalion level. During the horse and musket period, the platoon was used as the basic element for the control of musketry, but was not a permanent administrative unit. Also, modern British battalions as shown here are about half the size of their paper strength in earlier times, and now have five companies instead of ten.

The Commissioned ranks (i.e. the officers) begin with second lieutenant (also known as an ensign in the Guards or cornet in the cavalry), then climb through lieutenant, captain, major, lieutenant colonel, colonel, brigadier, major general, lieutenant general, general and end at the giddy heights of field marshal.

Let's look at what these people are trained to command in today's army.

- **Fire team**: approximately four men commanded by a lance corporal
- **Section**: two fire teams comprising 8-10 men commanded by a corporal. This also happens to be the number of men who can fit into the standard Warrior armoured vehicle.
- **Platoon** (infantry) or troop (cavalry or artillery): three sections, totalling some 30 men, commanded by a captain, lieutenant or second lieutenant. During the horse and musket era, platoons were not permanent units, but rather an expedient sub-division of a battalion

used to co-ordinate 'firings' so that a third of the battalion fired whilst another third loaded and the final third stood ready.

- **Company** (infantry) or **squadron** (cavalry) or **battery** (artillery): three platoons amounting to about 100 men, commanded by a major. Historically, a company was actually recruited, paid for and owned by a captain, who effectively 'leased' his company to the colonel. This is why we call a business a 'company'.

- **Battalion** (originally infantry): nowadays, five companies commanded by a lieutenant colonel, amounting to between 550 and 750 men including staff and support. The battalion has historically been the primary element of tactical manoeuvre for the infantry, whereas it has been the battery for artillery and the squadron for cavalry. Nowadays, however, a typical infantry battalion may be spread over a huge area of operations.

- **Regiment**: nominally commanded by a full colonel but in practice, commanded by a lieutenant colonel. In modern times, the battalion and regiment have become virtually synonymous since most regiments consist of only one battalion. However, for the cavalry, whose regiments often consist of more than one squadron, and the artillery, where a regiment might have several batteries, the regiment still has an administrative function. In previous eras, even as late as WWII, a typical infantry regiment might have several battalions.

- **Brigade**: commanded by a brigadier, a brigade is a unit of manoeuvre consisting of several battalions or regiments, perhaps up to 5,000 strong depending on the attached support and auxiliary units. The Brigade of Guards is an example of a permanent arrangement, as is 16th Air Assault Brigade. Historically, brigades were convenient groupings of troops of a particular type – infantry, cavalry or artillery – capable of independent action or supporting other brigades of the same or different types, such as a cavalry brigade supporting infantry.

- **Division**: a major-general has at his disposal two or three brigades with a total manpower of 10,000 or more. A division has historically been a grouping of mutually-supporting troops, such as infantry with cavalry (or nowadays armoured) support and artillery, logistics and so on. Such a force is capable of looking after itself for an extended period. A comparatively modern idea which started with Napoleon, who was the first to use divisions to outmanoeuvre his enemies who were still wedded to eighteenth century ideas of an army being divided into 'wings'. Interestingly, a 'battlegroup' is a much smaller modern 'division' often seen in recent conflicts in Afghanistan and Iraq, for example, that may only be the size of a battalion or regiment, but has infantry, armour, engineers and so on.

- **Corps**: a group of divisions, rarely seen outside a major war. Not to be confused with the expression meaning a particular branch of armed services, such as 'the United States Marine Corps'.

- Above this level, major wars may see the birth of Armies and even

Army Groups, such as those involved on the Eastern Front during WWII.

Really big battles

It is my sincere hope that the rules I have provided in Chapter 7 will serve you for some considerable time as you grow your collection of horse and musket era armies and play games that range from perhaps a brigade or two per side (that's roughly six to ten units) up to quite large games of even a couple of divisions or, in Napoleonic terms, a small corps consisting of perhaps 12-20 units. Beyond this will depend on your ability and enthusiasm to recruit fresh troops to the cause and, of course, the space you have available. Most wargamers are happy to achieve this kind of level and play countless games in which they take the role of a divisional commander or perhaps one of Napoleon's Marshals, or a subordinate of Frederick the Great or one of Maria Theresa's generals. Moreover, there is much to be said for a happy wargaming life at this level.

For some wargamers, however, this simply isn't enough, and the desire arises to play the part of Napoleon or Frederick, Gustavus Adolphus or Tilly, Louis XIV or Marlborough, commanding entire armies on the broad plains of Europe, sending many tens of thousands of miniature men to their fates.

There are several ways to approach this.

THE LITERAL APPROACH

You can – and some people do – continue collecting gargantuan armies at your chosen size of, say, 28mm miniatures until the floors are groaning under the weight. Couple this, if you are able, with an enormous space to accommodate a huge table, and you might just be in business. In fact, I use that word advisedly, because there are, in fact, businesses set up to help wargamers achieve this very dream by proxy – wargames holiday centres.

The Wargames Holiday Centre near Scarborough circa 1986 with Salamanca in full swing. This shows the main, centre table measuring 24 feet by 6 feet and you can just see another behind the players on the left. The British attacked from the left and the French counterattacked (successfully) from the right and far end of the table.

An immense refight of Waterloo organised by *General de Brigade* author Dave Brown. Quite apart from the magnificent layout and hordes of beautifully-painted 15mm miniatures, the most striking aspect is the number of players involved. Large games such as this produce plenty of excitement and tension – just like the real thing, though fortunately, no real blows were exchanged!

In my youth, I was fortunate to be able to attend a long weekend gaming the Battle of Salamanca, 1812, at the original Wargames Holiday Centre in Scarborough, owned by the late Peter Gilder, who has been mentioned earlier as the creator of Hinchliffe figures from the late 1960s through to the early 1980s. Peter created a set of rules called *In the Grand Manner*, which reflected his preference for very large games played with large (36+ figures) battalions of his own 25-28mm miniatures. The space available was enormous – a custom-built outhouse with a table some 24 feet long, divided into three sections measuring six feet, six feet and three feet wide respectively, with gaps to allow one to reach troops in the middle of what was, in effect, a 24' x 15' monster. It was a dream come true to be able to play with the thousands of beautifully-painted miniatures that lived in cabinets around the walls. It was even more gratifying to play the French commander Marmont and reverse history!

There is still a UK-based Wargames Holiday Centre, now based in Kingsclere, Berkshire (see *www.wargameshc.co.uk*) where you can play large, historical games, and another in Newark, Nottinghamshire called The Bunker (*www.thebunkergames.com*) which specialises in smaller movie-inspired 'pulp' games such as *Indiana Jones*, *633 Squadron*, *The Magnificent Seven* and *War of the Worlds*. What fun!

But if you feel like sipping cocktails by the pool while recovering from the exertions of commanding the Union at Gettysburg or an armoured division in Normandy, then the new Wargame Holidays in Crete may be just the place for you (*www.wargameholidays.com*).

Of course, if you collect smaller miniatures, such as 15mm, 10mm or 6mm, then space is not as much of a problem, but if you use the same set of rules for huge battles as for smaller ones, it's going to take you an awfully long time to get through a game. This can be partly overcome by having more players; indeed, the kind of games organised by the Wargames

Holiday Centre and by wargames clubs frequently field between three and ten players per side, each commanding a division or so with an overall commander co-ordinating their efforts (or, at least, attempting to).

One benefit of the multi-player game is that it can recreate actual battlefield command problems quite accurately. Assuming that such a large gathering has at least one umpire in place, then all manner of mayhem can result when orders go astray, reinforcements fail to arrive or enemy appear unexpectedly on one's flank. The other interesting thing is how quickly it can happen that the divisional commanders guard 'their' sector rather jealously, failing to offer help to their neighbours but demanding reinforcements for their obviously more important task. On the other hand, a team that cooperates well can sometimes overcome seemingly insurmountable odds.

However, such games place a huge onus on the organisers to choose the teams well and sacrifice their own gaming enjoyment to the greater good of the occasion. As I know from personal experience, it can mean a great deal of preparation and hard work to keep things ticking over smoothly, especially when the gaming action gets tense and nerves begin to fray!

BATHTUBBING

So, if lots of troops on extensive terrain doesn't excite you or is way beyond your means, what else can we do? Well, the second method is called 'bathtubbing', an odd expression I agree, but let's get to grips with the concept.

When you were a child perhaps you, like me, played with toy ships in the bath. I can remember that my father had bought me a set of small, plastic ships representing a number of the famous vessels from the Second World War, some German, some British, with evocative names such as *Tirpitz*, *Bismark*, HMS *Hood*, HMS *Devonshire* and so on. In my eyes, these six or eight toys became entire fleets battling on the high seas and my knees, poking out of the water, became islands around which they fought, with an occasional massive waterfall descending from the heavens when I turned on the taps to top up the hot water!

'Bathtubbing', then, is the practice of scaling down a battle to suit the arena we can actually fit into our house: in this case, not the bath, but our wargames table, be it six feet by four or whatever we can manage.

The late Charles Grant – whose name has cropped up several times already – was a master of this, and famously wrote a number of articles in magazines like *Military Modelling* and *Battle* where he recreated anything from the ancient Battle of Marathon to Fontenoy or Mollwitz. His son, Charles S Grant, has continued this tradition in his *Wargaming in History* books for Ken Trotman, using units from his own fictitious armies to represent their historical counterparts.

What this means, in essence, is that rather than having to assemble the vast number of figures required to recreate a battle like Waterloo at our standard figure:man ratio of, say, 1:20, we declare that each of our miniature battalions represents something larger instead, such as a brigade. Even a giant battle such as Waterloo then becomes potentially manageable. Roughly 73,000 British and Allied troops, joined later in the battle by nearly 50,000 Prussians, faced some 77,500 French. At a figure:man ratio of 1:20, this would require 3,650 British and Allied miniatures, 2,500 Prussians and 3,875 French. It's possible, and indeed I've seen it done, but it's a lifetime's work for a single collector!

By bathtubbing, however, we can take a different approach. Let's say that, like me, you have access to a table some 8 feet by 6 feet and let's make the assumption that you are using the cheap option of 1/72 scale soft plastic miniatures mounted, in accordance with my *Shot, Steel and Stone* rules included in this book, on bases with a 45mm frontage.

Waterloo has three key landmarks: the Château of Hougoumont on the French left, and the farm of La Haye Sainte in the centre, and the villages of Papelotte, La Haie and Frischermont on the right. If we assume that each of these is represented by our Built Up Areas – La Haye Sainte could be just one, but Hougoumont should be at least two and the cluster of villages on the eastern flank perhaps three – then this leaves us a mere three feet or so between each of these famous landmarks in our miniaturised mock-up.

For his part, we know that Wellington drew up his army in roughly three lines on the ridge of Mont St Jean. Some troops were placed near Braine L' Alleud off to his far right, but this is 'off table' as far as we are concerned.

Now, if we take the British table edge to represent Wellington's ridge, we can see that we have eight feet maximum to contain our troops. We

The Battle of Mollwitz, 1741, a classic piece of 'bathtubbing' undertaken by the late Charles Grant for his classic 1971 book *The War Game*. This recreation of *his* recreation was undertaken by 'The War Gamers' at Partizan in 2007. Son of Charles Grant, Charles Stewart Grant, is standing, centre, talking to Laurence Baldwin, one of the show's organisers. The miniatures are all original Spencer Smith plastics.

shall want to garrison Hougoumont with some light troops, perhaps as much as a large battalion of four stands (I am assuming that we are using the 'standard' configuration of the rules here – if you prefer the 'old school' look with bigger units, then the number of units can be halved). In fact, during the course of 18th June 1815, Wellington sent as many as 12,000 men in this direction as they fought hard to repel the 14,000 or more Napoleon used to attempt to take the place. La Haye Sainte needs to be occupied too by a small battalion, perhaps a couple of bases of light infantry.

Behind them on the ridge, the rest of the Allied army is arrayed. If our average sized British battalion uses, say, four bases of six figures, then its total frontage is 180mm or just over 7". With a small gap between each unit of perhaps an inch (25mm), then the fact is that our front line of units on the ridge can number no more than around twelve. For wargaming purposes, to allow sufficient room for manouevre, we would also probably wish to reduce Wellington's three lines of troops to just two. As a result, we are looking at perhaps just a couple of dozen British and Allied units at the most, including those posted in the buildings.

Now, in terms of proportions, we know that Wellington had some 54,000 infantry, 13,500 cavalry and 5,000 artillerymen serving 150 guns, or proportions of 10.8 : 2.7 : 1. So, if we assume a total of 24 units in our British /Allied army, then some 18 of them should be infantry, four should be cavalry and three artillery. This very neatly equates to 18 infantry battalions, four cavalry regiments and two artillery batteries of eight guns each – let's say 408 infantry figures, 48 cavalry and 16 gunners.

For the French, Napoleon commanded roughly 53,500 infantry, 15,500 cavalry, and 6,500 artillery with 250 guns, proportions of 8.2 : 2.5 : 1. Given that they outnumbered the British slightly, we can allow them an extra unit, giving a total of 25, of which 17 should be infantry battalions, five cavalry regiments and and three artillery batteries of eight guns. This is represented by 408 infantry figures (the same as the British), 60 cavalry and 24 gunners.

Make no mistake, even a game such as this will prove a formidable undertaking for an inexperienced wargamer, and you may wish to make your first attempt using just half these numbers, but it is certainly attainable by the enthusiast within perhaps a couple of years of diligent collecting, and of course even sooner if you use smaller scale figures.

And let's not forget, if you're impatient or wish to economise, you can halve the number of figures mounted on each base or even simply play with cardboard warriors.

The point is that it has been found on numerous occasions that such a scaled-down portrayal of the original, if carefully thought through, can still produce results remarkably similar to the original battle upon which it is based. As long as the proportions of troop types are correct – and this must include the morale gradings of A (élite), B (steady) or C (suspect) – then the magic seems to work pretty much every time.

CHANGE THE SCALE

For many wargamers, however, this kind of 'fiddling' is unacceptable, because it leaves the wargamer trying to be Napoleon or Frederick whilst also dealing with the minutiae of command at the level of a colonel. Surely, they point out, the Emperor Napoleon or King Frederick would not be concerned with whether a particular colonel orders his battalion to form square at a particular moment, nor even, perhaps, whether they choose to open fire or charge with the bayonet.

In fact, the argument goes, the Commander-in-Chief has only one question on his lips: did they win, or did they lose?

Now, it has to be said that the vast majority of wargamers seem perfectly happy to experience command at both the level of the general and that of the colonel, and my own *Shot, Steel and Stone* rules contained in this book have been written with that in mind. We seem to enjoy ordering massed miniature soldiery to their dice-borne deaths, but at the same time like to get up close and personal with the action when it happens, willing each die to turn up a 6 and praying for each battalion to hang on in that melee just one turn longer. In fact, I have gone quite some way to abstracting certain aspects of play to speed things up, but it is, of course, possible to go one step further.

This is where self-contained boardgames have the advantage in some respects. Many have been produced over the years that are focused entirely on just one battle, be it Waterloo, Gettysburg, Marathon or Malplaquet. Rules have been devised that reflect the potential outcomes of just that one day, and the troops are cardboard counters on a cardboard terrain of tesselated hexagons, marked with combat and movement abilities, divorcing the players from the attachment that naturally arises when they themselves have laboured for hours with paints and brushes to make those little men appear 'just so'.

As someone who has played this kind of game, I can say that the best of them are very good indeed and boardgaming can become an engrossing hobby in itself. But here, we are concerned with the aesthetic attraction of playing games with miniature soldiers, so what can we learn from boardgames that can help us to achieve our goal of commanding huge armies, from the general's perspective, in a game that lasts perhaps an afternoon or evening rather than days?

Well, the clue is in the abstraction. We have to make it crystal clear what level of command we are interested in, and here, it is that of the Commander-in-Chief. We want to be able to make those dramatic, sweeping decisions that we read about in the history books, where the general sends in the cavalry, smashes through the enemy line and then orders in the reserve to complete the rout. We don't want to be bogged down with "Enemy at 100 paces, fire!", "Form square!" or "Fix bayonets!" Exciting though these things can be, they belong at a much lower level of command.

In the process of doing this, we have to allow our miniatures to become cyphers, representing the appropriate types of units, but without worrying

An ACW game seen at the (sadly defunct) 'Whiff of Grapeshot' show in London. Here, the value of 6mm miniatures for recreating corps- and army-level actions is clear, with the sprawl of large forces across the landscape realistically portrayed on a table just 8 feet by 6. The Confederates (top) are putting up quite a fight as the Union attempt to feed in reserves.

overmuch about their individual formations or even strengths. If we say that a single base of infantry now represents a battalion, then the four bases we have painted to represent a single battalion up till now become a brigade of four battalions; a single gun model can now represent an entire battery, and so on.

It is here that the smaller scales such as 6mm really start to come into their own. Their diminutive stature means that they can be used in far greater numbers and a big battle really does start to look like those contemporary battle paintings we all admire. There are, of course, some wargamers who develop the skill of painting angels on pinheads, but for the most part, they take the advice of Peter Berry, owner of Baccus Miniatures, who says "paint the unit, not the man". And there is, of course, an extensive range of scenic items available for small-scale gaming – see the Resources section.

It is at this point that I cease to be prescriptive. How you create your units for the Grand Tactical game is entirely up to you. A strip of five Baccus 6mm infantry figures has a frontage of 20mm (for aesthetic reasons, I prefer to mount them two-deep, so ten to a base, which I make 15mm deep), which would also accommodate three cavalry figures or one gun and crew. That's fine, but you might want your units to have a more beefy look, so by all means say that a unit consists of two or more bases – it really doesn't matter, other than in terms of what feels and looks right to you. Obviously, the more stands per unit, the more miniatures and space you will need.

Now we need to think about terrain. We shall continue to make use of the Built Up Area concept for settlements, but we now obviously need to think about geography. What was previously a mere stream now assumes the proportions of a major river; a copse of trees becomes a large wood; and a minor contour is now a mighty ridge. Well, that's absolutely fine, because we are no longer worried about an occasional hedgerow or shallow ditch, nor even of an individual building, because now we are shifting to a much higher level, where such details are meaningless. As the general, we shall be telling brigadier X or major-general Y to take their brigade or division and attack position Z, and leaving it entirely up to them how they decide to overcome such obstacles.

As for you, dear reader, this is where you need to put in some work, researching the Orders of Battle for the armies involved in the historical encounter you wish to recreate. Pay particular attention to the chain of command, so you can see that, for example, at the Battle of Waterloo, Napoleon's Armée du Nord consisted of the Imperial Guard plus I Corps, II Corps, VI Corps, III Reserve Cavalry Corps and IV Reserve Cavalry Corps. Each of these corps, commanded by a Marshal of France, was sub-divided into divisions. Taking I Corps (commanded by Comte d'Erlon) as an example, his total of 19,800 men were made up from the 1st Division under Quiot, the 2nd Division under Donzelot, the 3rd Division under Marcognet, the 4th Division under Durutte, the 1st Cavalry Division under Jacquinot and completed by 46 guns under the command of Desales.

Let's drill down further. Quiot's 1st Division, numbering 4,183 men on 18th June 1815, comprised two brigades, the 1st Brigade under Colonel Charlet and the 2nd Brigade under the delightfully named Baron Bourgeois. It also had six 6-pdr guns and two 5.5" howitzers attached, plus artillery train troops and some pioneers.

Charlet's 1st Brigade had seven battalions of infantry: four battalions of the 13th Légère and three battalions of the 17th Ligne.[3]

For our purposes, this is as far as we need to go as the infantry battalion or cavalry squadron or battery of artillery are the building blocks from which our game is assembled.

You will find some suggestions for adapting the *Shot, Steel and Stone* horse and musket era rules included in this book on the website at *http://thewargamingcompendium.com*.

Campaigns

There comes a time in most wargamers' lives when stand-alone games played within the confines of a single tabletop are just not enough. For them, the challenge needs to move from the tactical to the strategic, and the only way to achieve this is through a campaign.

Now, it is of course possible to recreate the huge sweep of, say, the D-Day invasion of Normandy in 1944 and the 'race to the Rhine' that followed, or Frederick the Great's campaigns in Silesia or, much earlier, Alexander the Great's or Julius Caesar's conquests. However, as with all things wargaming, my suggestion is to start small in order to avoid disappointment and to get used to the idea of the outcome of one game having consequences for the next.

---

3   See, inter alia, *The Waterloo Companion* by Mark Adkin, Aurum Press, 2001 p.57

LINKED GAMES

It just so happens that I love campaigns and have a real passion for certain types of more involved campaign games involving fictitious nations that we shall look at later. But let's begin with the very simplest kind, a series of linked games.

A real general knows that every battle has at least three possible outcomes: a victory, in which his forces drive the enemy from the field and occupy the ground held by the enemy and, perhaps, beyond; a stalemate, in which both sides exhaust themselves in their efforts to outdo the other, arrive at a tense stand-off or depart in opposite directions to recover; or a defeat in which, calamity of calamities, the general must do his best to keep control of his troops and extricate them from a dangerous situation whilst fending off a pursuing enemy.

Now, what this means in practice is that the commander must always keep a reserve, either to exploit an opportunity to achieve the victory or, conversely, to plug an inconvenient hole should some of his own troops decide that they've had enough. In most wargames, the players tend to want to just see as much action as possible for all their units, paying scant regard to the concerns of a real general.

By means of a campaign, however, it can become immediately apparent that conserving one's forces is a sensible idea. This isn't to say that you shouldn't hurl your best troops at the enemy if you're sure the right moment has arrived, but it should make you think twice about having a 'death or glory' attitude in your games!

A simple method is this. Play a first game on a table set up as you desire. Whoever wins this first game then designs a layout that would make sense as if it were a continuation of the first table, but one table width to the rear of the losing player's position in game 1, as in the diagram below, where you can see that terrain features continue from one to the other.

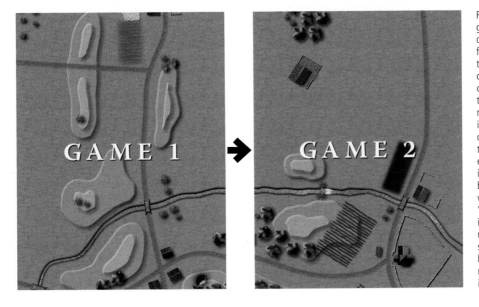

Red force win game 1, and so designs the table for game 2. Here, the river must clearly continue onto the next table, as must the road. The logical interpretation of the stand of trees in the south eastern corner is that it might become a larger wood, and so on. You might wish to introduce certain restrictions to the system so that both sides have a reasonable chance in the next battle.

Keep a note of the casualties suffered by both sides during the first game. For game 2, use the same forces as in the first game, but the victor is permitted to regain 50% of the casualties suffered in game 1, whilst the loser may only recover 25%. You might also like to spice things up by allowing the possibility of reinforcements: both sides roll a d6 – the victor can add one new unit on a roll of 5 or 6, whilst the loser requires a 6.

Such a campaign could continue until either a specific objective is achieved, or a set number of tables have been covered (say, a maximum of three in any direction) or one side falls below 50% of its starting strength.

A variation on this is where the two sides have been compiled from lists of troops using points systems, so that instead of 'raw' casualty numbers, the calculations could be made using points. Under such a system, for example, an infantry base might be worth 10 points, whilst a light cavalry base is 15 points, a heavy cavalry base 20 points and a gun 50 points. Therefore, if the victor suffered 100 points of damage in game 1, he can choose 50 points of replacements for game 2, and he may decide whether that should be, say, five infantry bases, or two light cavalry bases and two infantry, or just one gun, and so on. Obviously, he can't replace any figures that weren't casualties in the first place – that can only be done via the reinforcements die roll.

Making maps

Linked games can be great fun, and are especially suited to club competitions, in which a number of players can participate using this simple format. However, the true aficionado of strategy recognises instantly that there is something missing: a map.

If you are recreating a historical campaign then the best advice is to read as much as you can and most military history books contain excellent maps that can form the basis of your campaign. In fact, in recent years some wonderful titles have appeared that consist of almost nothing but highly detailed maps and blow-by-blow accounts of the manoeuvres and battles fought over the ground they depict. These maps can be photocopied and gridded with squares or hexagons, and you can then make use of the rules outlined later in this chapter.

However, many wargamers enjoy designing their own, completely fictitious, maps, even if the games they intend to play are set in a particular historical era. This may seem odd, but wargamers are inventive folk!

A simple starting point for such campaigns is to use the linked games mentioned above as the basis for a map, filling in the surrounding areas by extending the roads, rivers, hills and so on. This is a very quick way to create a large area that can then be campaigned over again at some point in the future.

Another starting point for a wargame campaign map can be, of course, a real map. What you need to have done first, however, is decide what level of forces will be confronting one another: is this a local campaign, typical of the sort of thing that happened in, say, the English Civil War,

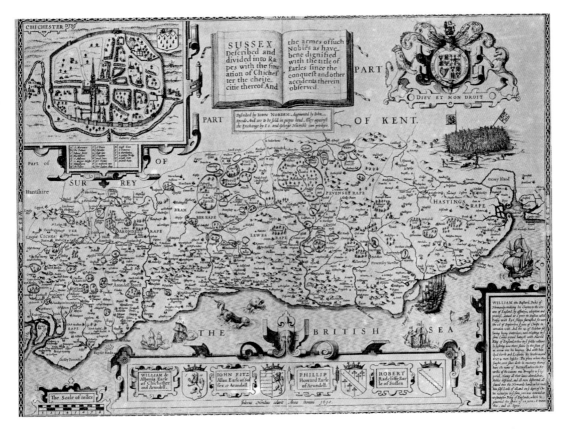

A map of Sussex by John Speede and engraved by Hondius in 1610. We can be fairly certain that it shows a county largely unchanged for centuries and would form a marvellous basis for a campaign. Note that the English Channel is labelled "The British Sea". The inset map shows the city of Chichester and the fleet of ships indicates the landing place of William the Conqueror and the Normans at Pevensey Bay in 1066. From the Sussex County Record Society collection, call number PM118.

or perhaps neighbouring baronies facing off in medieval times; or are we at the level of, for example, a division or corps or 'wing' of troops manoeuvring during the horse and musket period, aiming to capture a significant city or concentrate against a divided foe; or, at the top end, perhaps you are aiming to recreate the Normandy landings on D-Day or the entirety of Napoleon's invasion of Russia in 1812?

Let's look at the first level, a local campaign during the medieval or Renaissance period, though of course it could be of whatever era you like. It's possible that you have two rivals, the King's man Sir Percy Wossname, and his dastardly Parliamentarian rival, Thomas Thingummy, also a landed magnate but a follower of Oliver Cromwell. Each side probably has no more than a few hundred, or at most a couple of thousand, troops at their disposal, probably some infantry, some cavalry and a couple of small artillery pieces. It's likely that they are fighting for control of a market town and its surrounding countryside, and the two rivals may well live in fortified manor houses. The area in dispute is likely to be just a part of a single county, certainly less than fifty miles by fifty, which equates to a day's ride.

This is an ideal piece of ground to learn the art of campaigning, and your first port of call should be a good Ordnance Survey map, or perhaps a highly detailed road atlas. If you can get it, naturally, a period map is even better for atmosphere. Select a suitable area – you could cut a 'window' out of a piece of cardboard to the same scale as the map and then move it around until whatever is contained within the area looks just right. If you want to disguise your area of operations, then change the scale, so that one mile equals two or vice-versa.

The next stage is to create a copy of the map, but (unless your campaign is set in the post-1945 era) remove all signs of human development that have been built since your chosen period. In most cases, this will mean eliminating all motorways, railway lines, tunnels, pylons and suburban sprawl. Many 'A' roads in fact follow ancient routes, as do 'B' roads and ungraded country lanes. On British Ordnance Survey maps, ancient monuments, castles and country houses are conveniently marked, and you may well find perfect candidates to house your rivals.

Another popular approach is to take the outline of a real country or continent – Australia, for example – and turn it on its head, so that north becomes south. It's surprising how unrecognisable an otherwise familiar outline can become: we are so used to seeing the globe from a Euro-centric standpoint or, even more specifically, an Anglo-centric one, simply because the cartographers who designed the maps upon which modern geography is based were British and champions of the Greenwich Meridian!

Our inverted Australia can now be switched to any scale we choose, either remaining the vast continent it actually is or, by telescoping it down, perhaps shrinking to a mere desert island over which bands of pirates and natives can fight. The interior, instead of being largely empty, could become home to rolling downland and woods alive with the chirruping

It's Australia, mate, but not as we know it... A huge change of scale and some imaginative names, and your campaign is underway. Such an adventure could be a purely 'historical' pirate game, or perhaps involving fantasy elements in a very *Pirates of the Caribbean* fashion. Another trick is to take a country or county that is landlocked in reality, but plop it in the middle of an ocean to make it an island or even a mighty continent, with vast armies fighting across 'Liechtensteinia' or 'Surreyvia'.

Dread Point · Old Scraggin's Mine · The Murk · Skeleton Bay · Hopeless Sands · Treasure X · Lighthouse Hill · Hell's Mouth · Isle of Doom · Screaming Cliffs · Shipwreck Strait · Captain's Head · Cutthroat Cove · Hangman's Point of birds; on the other hand, perhaps it might inspire you to create an inhospitable Mordor-like landscape for a fantasy campaign. The choice is yours.

The requirement is the same: to populate your map with enough towns, cities and villages, rivers and roads, hills and valleys, forests and woods to make it seem real and give space for your troops to manoeuvre. Don't expect things to move along nicely if you cover your continent with jungle and swamp! On the other hand, you do want to break up a completely barren landscape with at least some mountains and valleys that might prove challenging to even the most futuristic of assaults, forcing commanders to think about lines of advance and possible concealment of enemy forces. And of course, a planet can be more than skin-deep, with tunnels and caves and even underground or underwater cities.

CREATING YOUR OWN WORLD

My personal preference is for entirely fictitous countries fighting entirely fictitious campaigns over entirely fictitious maps. I'll say more about what are nowadays called 'imagi-nations' in a little while, but let me first explain how I go about this kind of world creation, which has a long and honourable tradition.

My favourite period is the horse and musket era, specifically the eighteenth century. Inspired by the historical reality of a myriad tiny states, principalities, duchies, bishoprics and electorates, I long ago decided to follow the lead of the late Charles Grant and his own creations of Die Vereinigte Freie Städte and the Grand Duchy of Lorraine, as outlined in his 1971 book *The War Game*. My own warring nations are Prunkland and Faltenland, though there are others now inhabiting their world, such as Granprix, Grenouisse, Gelderstaad (enough with the Gs already!), Schwitz, Borscht, Byzarbia, Schmeissberg-Donau and others.

I first created my maps for these places based on some ideas outlined by the late Tony Bath in his seminal book *Setting Up a Wargames Campaign*, published in 1986. I later described the process in great detail in the first twelve issues of my magazine, *Battlegames*, but I shall summarise the process here as I don't assume you to have read that august publication!

All you need, to begin with, is some paper, a pen or pencil, and some dice. Nothing fancy: A4 or US letter-sized paper to begin with, though you may later wish to transfer the results of these jottings onto something larger and of higher quality in due course. The dice are just the standard d6 variety, though you are perfectly at liberty to use some of the fancier polyhedra to add variety should you wish.

As above, your first task is to decide precisely what area of operations you want. For my purposes, I'm creating a continent, country by country, though these nations are not, for the most part, terribly big. Divide the area on your paper into large squares. In my case, each of the squares represents approximately 25 x 25 miles (625 square miles). You might call these 'geographical units', because what we now do is determine the overall character of each of these substantial tracts of land using our d6 friends.

Roll one die for each square. A score of 1-4 means the area is basically flat; a 5 or 6, means you've got hills or mountains. Just make a quick note in each square as you progress, then pick up the dice and roll again.

For each square you denoted as flat, a score of 1-3 means that it is open ground, be it prairie, desert, savannah or ordinary grassland. A roll of 4 or 5 means the square contains light woods; a 6, on the other hand, means densely wooded, forest or, where appropriate, jungle.

Now for the hill squares. A 1, 2 or 3 means bare hills; 4 or 5 creates wooded hills; and a 6 means that square is mountainous, with or without forest depending on your personal preference to suit the world you have in mind.

My original notes on graph paper for the creation of more detailed terrain of Grenouisse and Granprix, with their neighbours Gelderstaad and Faltenland to west and east respectively and Schwitz to the north east. Here you can see the outcomes of the first dice rolls. Already, a landscape was being created in my mind's eye. The dotted lines indicate approximate national boundaries and coastlines.

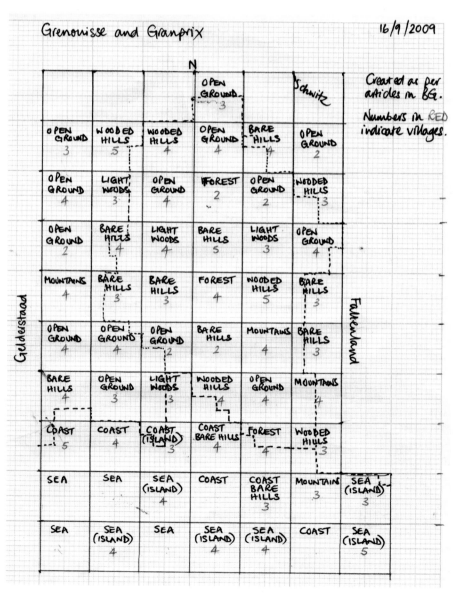

Voilà, you are now staring at a sheet of paper that contains a new world just bursting to be seen, admired and pillaged.

SQUARES OR HEXAGONS?

Now, the next stage is both a matter of personal preference, experience and human resources – creating a gridded map that uses either squares or hexagons.

That sounds fearsomely complex, but really, it isn't. Let me start with the last point first.

Every 'normal' map you look at is gridded in squares. Ordnance Survey maps, road maps, even atlases all use the standard square in order to make use of coordinates. The Biebersfurt (capital of Prunkland) A-Z will tell you that Verlorenstraße is on page 27, grid reference G6. We flick to page 27 and follow the letters across the top, A, B, C... er, G, and then run our finger down, 1, 2, 3... 6. Aha! Indeed, there's Verlorenstraße, just off Nirgendwostraße.

In standard mathematical parlance we are, of course, talking about x and y coordinates, the standard method of desciding a point in two-dimensional space. And, for the most part, jolly useful they are too.

The problem when it comes to wargames, however, is that squares require a surprising amount of more detailed administration. Think of it like this. On a chess board, which is gridded in squares, the bishop or queen, which can move diagonally, can reach a square that is adjacent to their current position, but on the diagonal, in half the time it would take, say, the rook, which can only move forwards or sideways. The consequences for a wargames campaign could be absurd, with a player who moved his army diagonally running artificial rings around an opponent who moved horizontally or vertically.

This is where those human resources potentially come in, because ideally, you need an umpire who can keep track of the exact position of troops moving realistically across the map, whilst keeping the results secret. Thus, Player 1 could inform the umpire that he intends to move his cavalry patrol off the road to the farm at X, whilst Player 2 might be anticipating him to move along the road to the bridge at Y, so he tells the umpire that he wishes to set up an ambush in the woods nearby. The umpire keeps a 'master map' showing the precise positions of each unit of both sides, but sends back only sketchy reports to the two players, revealing only what could actually be seen by the forward elements or scouts on either side. This is, of course, just like *Kriegsspiel*.

The problem for most wargamers is that, first of all, they don't have access to an umpire and secondly, they themselves don't have time for the minute level of bookkeeping this requires.

In my experience, switching to hexagons solves these problems and, even if you do have the luxury of an umpire, it will help to reduce paperwork all round.

This is because hexagons allow for a somewhat more natural movement, having six faces instead of four, and encourage a slightly more abstracted method of play. We simply decree that, for the most part, movement is adjudicated to simply be from hex centre to hex centre, requiring one 'Movement Point' to do so. We'll look at this in more detail shortly.

DETAILING YOUR MAP

Back to the map. We're going to take the regional variations you have created on the schematic and transfer them to the map proper. I use paper gridded with hexagons – you can buy this commercially or just download a sheet to print out from the *Wargaming Compendium* website at *www.thewargamingcompendium.com*. Each of the squares we created translates into an area five hexes by five, with each hex representing an area some five miles across, a unit of measurement I have found extremely convenient for determining map moves. Initially, I just work lightly in pencil so that I can change or erase things easily, and simply giving general indications of high ground, woods and so on.

At this stage, I add rivers 'by eye' – that is to say, I look at the geology that has been brought into being and picture what would happen if I poured a giant bucket of water over it. Where would it flow? Logically, rivers start as mere springs, brooks and streams in high ground and flow downhill, either gradually in flat areas or more precipitously in the mountains, where you might like to mark a few waterfalls.

You can roll one or two dice to decide how many major rivers there should be: I settled on around half a dozen in a country like Faltenland, which is also divided from its neighbour, Prunkland, by the mighty *Sturmwasser*. By all means take away a die if your country is intended to be desert, or add one for a rainforest zone. Once you have your major rivers, add tributaries, again using simple logic and your artistic eye to determine where they should run. Don't forget that your main rivers should swell slightly in width each time they are joined by a tributary.

Rivers normally head towards the closest ocean or large lake, but a glance at any atlas will show that isn't always the case, because slightly higher ground may intervene, leading them on meandering courses to reach their final destinations.

All this beautiful scenery is crying out to be admired by an indigenous population. Once again, roll a die for each of the squares you created: a score of 6 means there's a major settlement somewhere in that area. I modify the die roll to make things more logical – add 1 if there is a major river in that square, and add 2 if that river forms the border between two countries (creating plenty of frontier towns). On the other hand, deduct 1 from the die roll if the square is hilly and deduct 2 if it is mountainous. You might also choose to do the same if your definition of an empty square is 'desert', and again if the square is dense forest or jungle. Of course, these are suggestions, and I'm sure that you can think of plenty of major cities high in the mountains or on wide open plains with nary a soul to be seen.

Now you can add some villages. they appear by the simple expedient of

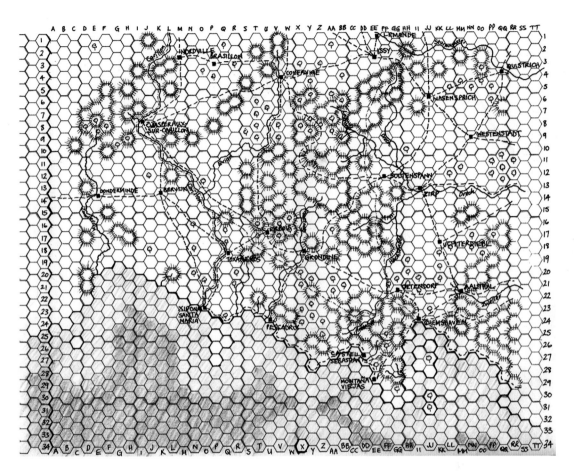

rolling two average dice (2, 3, 3, 4, 4, 5). If you don't have an average die, simply count 1 as an extra 3 and 6 as an extra 4. Again, you can adjust the score as you see fit, perhaps adding a die on a broad flood plain or near the coast, and subtracting one in mountains, forests and so on. As ever, it's your world, so you decide.

You need to create a road network too. Start by creating more or less straight routes between your major towns and cities, obviously diverting somewhat if there are large hills, wide rivers or dense forests in the way. Even in the twenty first century, such major feats of engineering are often shunned by fund-starved governments. Then, look at the network you have created and think about where minor routes might branch off to reach smaller towns and villages. Until we look at detailing individual hexes, that will do. As an alternative, canals were quite common in the horse and musket era, particularly for bringing food and other natural resources to the city from the countryside or mining areas.

The final touch at this stage is to name the places on your map. It's perfectly okay to 'steal' the names of real places, or you can get inventive. You might be happy to settle with Roundtop Hill, Blue River and Green Wood, or you might, like me, prefer to show off a bit, adding a little humour or a smattering of foreign languages, or both. You've got to live with the

The development of Granprix and Grenouisse. The red outlines equate to the earlier squares that have now been translated into hex arrangements. Initial pencil detailing has now been worked over using a Rotring pen and ink, and place names have been generated from my imagination and a selection of dictionaries, including French (for Grenouisse) and Catalan and Spanish (for Granprix). Rivers and main roads have now also been plotted.

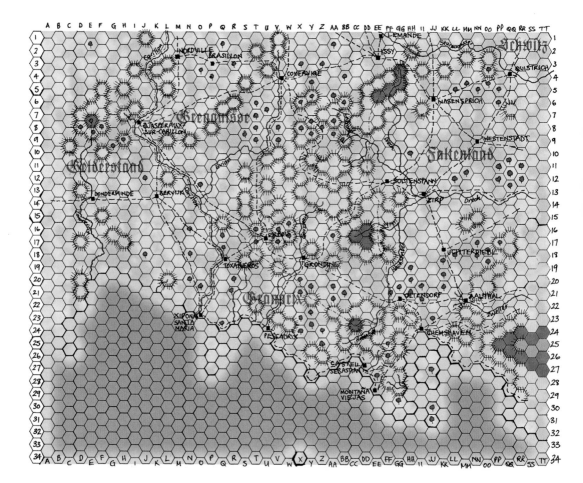

The final map, coloured using a combination of hand tints scanned in and Photoshop. By leaving the original hand drawing and lettering, the effect of an entirely non-digital map is retained. This map was actually used for a multi-player campaign in 2010-11 and resulted in a series of exciting and memorable wargames that featured in *Battlegames* issues 26-28.

place, so it's your call. In my fictitious nations, I've used German, French, Dutch, Spanish, Catalan, Italian, Russian and Czech so far, and a new country I'm creating is testing my ability to make things up in Arabic. Of course, I can't speak all those languages, but a supply of good dictionaries and, nowadays, online translation services means that the linguistic world is your oyster. And of course, if you learned Latin or Greek at school, your passage throught the ancient world is assured.

Now, let me make it clear that it's perfectly fine to stop right here. Beyond this point lies the stuff of advanced campaigning or, as it is also known, madness. It is a path I know only too well!

From this point on, I start looking at the individual hexes, rather than the 5 x 5 'squares', and I now consider the different types of terrain in economic terms. I work out the overall economic traits of each hex, and each of these is given an appropriate productivity in terms of the local currency per annum, which will be important later when I start calculating national income and the resources available to raise and maintain armies and navies.

And finally, of course, there are the inhabitants of this marvellous place. I create the population, ranging from perhaps just 100 people per mountain hex or fewer, through cultivated hexes teeming with village life which might support around 2,000 people, up to the capital city that might be home to 100,000 or more. As ever, you should adjust numbers to suit your historical (or fantasy or science fiction) timeframe.

DETAILING THE HEXES

The map you now have is perfect for the vast majority of your campaigning needs: see the rules at the end of this chapter. In fact, it's only if and when your forces encounter the enemy that there's a chance you might need more detail, and my advice is to wait until that happens before doing any more work.

The fact is that, unless you have a sudden and irrepressible urge to test your sanity, you will only ever detail a fraction of the map you have created. This is because, true to life, you will find the same bits of ground contested again and again, whilst huge swathes remain empty, unloved and unvisited. On the other hand, key towns, crossroads, bridges, mountain passes, fortresses and harbours will change hands time and time again. Why? Because they are strategically important, whereas the rest of the glorious countryside you have dreamt up off the beaten track will remain just that – off the beaten track, until such time as you embark on the Tourism Wars of 2150.

Let's imagine that your detachment has encountered an enemy brigade in hex D21 and neither you nor your opponent backs down. It's at this point that you need to take a closer look at the specific terrain in that hex.

I keep a supply of hexagons measuring 20cm from corner to opposite corner printed on tracing paper. The actual size is unimportant, but I have found this a convenient size to fit onto a sheet of A4 (210mm x 297mm), with sufficient space around the hex for making notes and a key to the symbols I use. The hex is further gridded into 25mm squares which of course overlap the edges slightly. These can prove useful if one ever needs to create an adjacent hex.

First of all I sketch the general details obtained from the previous stage in pencil, using some artistic licence to add key elements. Trial and error is the best possible practice for this kind of thing, and of course referring to real maps to gain inspiration is a given. Once I'm happy with the overall balance, I ink them in with a Rotring pen (though any draughtsman's pen or thin fibre tip will do).

For the next stage, adding hills and woods, I make use of a pair of percentage dice. Technically decahedra (d10) or dodecahedra (d20), they are marked 0 to 9 (twice on the d20). Normally, the wargamer (or roleplayer, for that is the milieu in which they are most frequently found) uses a pair of differently-coloured percentage dice, with one representing tens, the other units – a roll of 00 is deemed to mean 100.

The system is simple: for each of the 25mm squares (either whole or partial), roll the dice. For each hex distance the hex you are detailing is from the relevant terrain type on the big map, deduct 10% from the

A finished hex – in this case, the city of Castell Sebastian located in hex DD27. You can really – pardon the pun – go to town on the detailing. With its south-facing slopes, I decided that wine would probably be made in the area, so vineyards appear as well as normal woods. Other, smaller villages, hamlets and farms are also scattered about, and the town itself is obviously a masterpiece of seventeenth century military engineering around an old town centre.

chance of it occurring in the square you are detailing. That sounds much more complicated than it actually is to do. For example, if you are working on an area three hexes distant from the nearest 'hill' hex, there's a 70% chance of hills occurring in any of your squares. If woods occur five hexes away, the chance is 50%.

Don't be afraid to adapt these results to create something that looks right. If you're getting too many small hills dotted around like molehills, move some and clump them together to form a larger undulation, or take some of them to mean an additional contour. If all your woods are dispersed around the perimeter like a halo, drag some of them inside or, as an alternative, deem some of them to be orchards or vineyards.

Beyond that, everything is a matter of taste, including the addition of minor roads and tracks, beaches and cliffs along the coastline and little hamlets and farms dotted around. Finally, you can add more detail to your towns and fortresses, right down to individual streets and buildings if you wish. The more work you put in, the greater the long-term satisfaction of having created a completely unique place from your own imagination.

And that, of course, is why wargamers have coined the now popular term 'imagi-nation'.

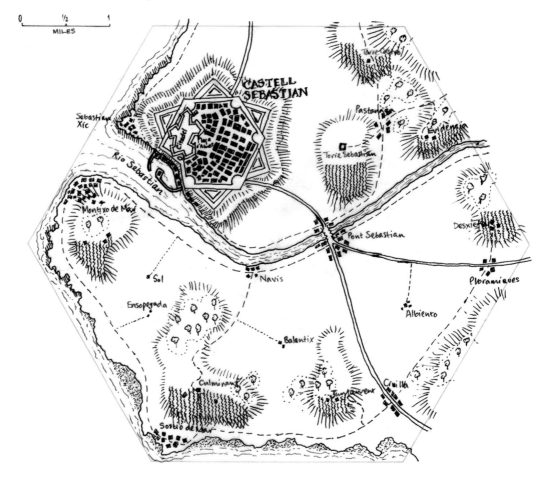

Uniforms and Standards, 1745, Das Königliche Heer von Prunkland

The national colours are white and red, and continue to predominate in the uniforms of His Majestys armed forces. Some detail changes have been made.

The Infantry
Musketeers

(left)
Regt. No I , von Eintopf (Red facings)
A musketeer of the first company, first battalion.

(right)
Regt. No. II. von Renscher (Orange facings)
A sergeant of the second company, first battalion.

Note the various edging styles on the hats, the shapes of lapels and the grouping of buttons on them

ADDING FLAVOUR

There are some who can use a created country as a venue for historical forces to do battle, but as you might guess, my feeling is "Why stop there?" And thus the forces of Prunkland, Faltenland and all the others were born, sons of the soil of my own madness!

Creating your own armies has several advantages. You have complete control and if, on a whim, you decide that bright pink is the most fetching colour for your grenadiers, so be it. A canary yellow for your hussars? Right away, sir. At a stroke, those timid and nitpicking souls who lean over your shoulder and whine "I think you'll find..." are banished. Nor should the onlooker scoff overmuch, because a glance at any tome detailing the uniforms of armies down the ages shows just how gaudy the art of military tailoring has been throughout history. Would you have invented the costume of the landsknechts or, indeed, hussars? Indeed, I think it safe to say that few of the creations I have seen from wargamers' minds have been as remotely preposterous as the 'real thing' has often been.

In fact, those of us who tread this path are pretty respectful towards our forces' historical counterparts, if for no other reason than to maintain the correct period flavour. Military fashion in the mid-eighteenth century, for example, was very different from that in the late nineteenth, so having regiments of musketeers in long-tailed coats but sporting the *Pickelhaube* on their heads would just not seem right, just as having Greek hoplites wearing the Roman *lorica segmentata* would look out of place.

That being said, there is huge satisfaction to be had designing the uniforms for fictitious troops, and of course your choices can be influenced by your own ability to paint the figures. Plain red coats and black trousers? Why not? On the other hand, if you're a practised brushman, then you can add all the lace and feathers and flounce you fancy. Go for it!

ADDING PERSONALITY

The other way of adding character is to create a background for your units and their commanders which can have a direct bearing on their performance in combat. A unit raised in a mountainous region might well

A page from the author's campaign diaries, proudly proclaiming "Uniforms and Standards, 1745, Das Königliche Heer von Prunkland" (the Royal Army of Prunkland). The uniforms of Von Eintopf Musketeers and Von Renscher Musketeers are shown. I had plans to create entire volumes of such meticulously recorded sartorial splendour but alas, real life has so far prevented me from achieving this ambition. One day...

make good candidates for a regiment of light infantry, perfectly at home on the slopes of hills or the dark recesses of a dense forest. A different future awaits men from the plains where they are at home on the backs of galloping horses, the natural breeding ground for cavalrymen. The towns and villages you have created can lend their names to your units or, as was often the practice in earlier times, they can be named after their commander.

I've always taken pains to ensure that every single unit in the armies I create has a named colonel, and sometimes a lieutenant colonel or major too, who can lead their regiment to glory or defeat on my tabletop battlefields. The First Regiment of Musketeers they may be, but they take the field proudly as Regiment von Eintopf; those cuirassiers are von Brettlingen and that battery is commanded by von Rikoschtezki. These are the names that stir the soul of every Prunklander, and many more besides. Each of them is recorded in my campaign diary, their exploits set down in pen and ink (much more satisfying than the blank tapping of a keyboard) so that, in my dotage, I can sit in my rocking chair and be transported back to that glorious charge, that furious firefight, that magnificent last stand.

But, more than this, these commanders have been brought to life by using a technique well known to the role-player. Each of them has been given a series of characteristics like so:

Name	Int	Init	Cour	Char	Str	H
Von Eintopf	77	73	24	97	24	88
Von Negretto	97	14	31	88	69	96
Von Brettlingen	29	41	01	32	35	77
Von Czapka	14	14	44	84	08	72

Running along the top, we have Intelligence, Initiative, Courage, Charisma, Strength and Health. Each characteristic has been generated by rolling a pair of percentage dice, the score shown becoming that character's factor for each item.

The results are the personalities of each commander. So, Von Eintopf is a pretty bright chap with lots of good ideas, and it's a good job that he has the enormous charisma to persuade his subordinates to carry them out for him because he's, shall we say, a little lacking in the courage department, perhaps because he's evidently a bit of a weedy chap, though unlikely to drop dead for anything less than a cannonball.

Von Negretto, on the other hand, is blessed with a towering intellect but an utter incapacity to make his mind up. Lucky for him he manages to disguise his dithering with charm.

Von Brettlingen and von Czapka are both cavalrymen, the former commanding a regiment of cuirassiers, the latter commanding hussars. Perhaps it's a requirement of the job to be a bit dim when you're asked to charge headlong at the enemy all day, though von Brettlingen will clearly be following his men, not leading them. In fact, there's not much to commend this fellow at all, whilst von Czapka is probably adored by his men, despite his feeble frame and lack of, well, anything else to commend him at all!

Such characteristics can be used in your games to add piquancy. Say, for example, that you, as commander in chief, wish to send a change of orders to one of your units. You might give a bonus to units whose commanders are highly intelligent or, more simply, roll against their intelligence to see if they understand the order. The gifted von Negretto is likely to have no problems at all, whereas von Czapka, on the other hand...

If your commanders are foolish enough to get themselves involved in a melee, then it is possible that they might be wounded or even killed. Should this happen, roll against their strength to see if they suffer a wound – here again, von Negretto is likely to fare better than von Czapka – and then, if they are wounded, roll against their Health to see if they survive.

The point is that, having created these characteristics, you can use them in innumerable situations where you might wish to adjudicate the ability of a particular unit commander to respond to a situation, either on his own account or, in the case of a senior commander, in terms of how he might be able to influence other troops nearby, for better or for worse. Clearly, his personal Courage and Charisma could have a great effect on those around him in a crisis.

The bottom line in all this is: make stuff up! The more use you make of what you have created, the more interesting and unique it will become.

The whole point of a campaign is to lead to cracking good games and a sense of camaraderie amongst the players. I can think of no better examples than the games played at East Ayton in 2011 and 2012 by the motley crew who frequent the WD3 online forum, who came together under the author's umpireship to play out the climax of 'The Grenouissian Intermezzo' in 2011 and 'B-Day in Byzarbia' in 2012. This shot shows the climactic Battle of Pescadrix in 2011, with no less than 13 imagi-nations represented!

Campaign rules

I have used these rules for several campaigns now, and they have been whittled down to what I know will work. By all means fiddle with them to make them more complex if you desire, or simplify them if you can.

1　Each campaign move represents one week of real time.

2　Each hex represents an area approximately five miles across. For campaign movement purposes, a hex's terrain is simplified to a single terrain type. Since the individual hex's map is only drawn up in detail once contact has been made, the cartographer should make the specified terrain type predominate when drawing the more detailed version. Even an apparently empty or remote hex is likely to have small tracks, a few farms or cottages, minor watercourses, small woods and so on.

3　Every unit acting independently, including scouts, ADCs and generals if moving alone, should be given a coordinate and its movement tracked separately.

4　Every force acting independently should be given a designated commander, and his characteristics noted. These are his Intelligence, Initiative, Courage, Charisma, Strength and Health, each expressed as a percentage (simply roll a pair of percentage dice) as described earlier.

5　At the end of each campaign week, opponents should declare their coordinates. No indication of the forces present in a hex should be given unless contact is made. These initial declarations simulate rumour, sightings by members of the local population, reports from spies and so on.

6　Movement is considered to be from hex centre to hex centre.

7　Movement is considered to be simultaneous, and a record must be made of the route taken by troops in case contact takes place part-way through a week. Should it become apparent that troops have had a 'near miss' and crossed each other's paths during the week, then their movement should be tracked back to the point where they made, or nearly made, contact, and a fair decision taken about whether they would have seen each other and perhaps engaged. This will be determined by the terrain in the hex and the time of day.

8　Troops may move less than the specified distances, but will be adjudged to have been stationary for that proportion of the move less than the maximum distance permitted. All movement is deemed to start at the beginning of the week, so any time spent stationary will be after the appropriate time spent moving has expired. For example, a unit of hussars that moves only three hexes cross country at normal rates will be deemed to have finished moving halfway through the week and to have remained stationary thereafter.

MOVEMENT POINTS (MP)		
Troop type	**Normal**	**Forced**
Close order infantry	2	3
Grenzer / Jäger	3	5
Heavy cavalry	4	6
Light/irregular cavalry	6	9
Field artillery (4-12pdr)	2	3
Wagons / siege guns	2	n/a
Generals/ADCs/couriers	20	n/a
Scouts	Add 50% according to type	

MOVEMENT POINTS – BOATS (MP)	
Situation	**Speed**
Downriver	6
Upriver	4
On lakes	5
On canals	5
Ships at sea following wind	12
Ships at sea against wind	6

MOVEMENT FACTORS (MF)	
Terrain type	**Movement Factor**
Cross country	1
On roads	½
On hills	2
In woods	2
To pass through a defile	+1
On roads on hills	1

The above factors are cumulative. Defiles are defined as bridges, towns and gaps of one hex or less between obstacles.

9   No movement is allowed on the upper two contours (shown as purple and white respectively on my maps) as these are considered to be the highest slopes where normal movement for bodies of troops is impossible. Players may elect to allow irregular infantry or Jäger to move in small detachments on such terrain with appropriate penalties.

EXAMPLES

An infantry battalion spends all week marching at normal pace along a road. It has 2 Movement Points (MP), divided by the Movement Factor (MF) of ½ for moving on roads, so it can move 4 hexes along the road that week.

A Grenzer battalion is force-marching. It wants to move half the week along a road, and then turn off and start moving cross-country. Its force-march gives it a total of 5MP. It expends half of them along the road, costing 2½ MP to move 5 hexes; and then they can move another 2½ hexes cross-country. (To simplify, one could move 2 hexes cross-country, and allow the other 1/2 hex to be carried over to the next week's move.)

A heavy cavalry squadron moving at normal speed on a road passes through a small town in the second hex that week, and then begins to ascend a hill on the far side. To move the first two hexes under normal circumstances costs just 1MP, but the town acts as a defile and costs another 1MP. They therefore have 2MP remaining to use climbing the road on the hill, allowing them to progress 2 hexes further.

A light cavalry patrol is force-marching cross-country. Two hexes away are some woods beside a river: they have been ordered to cross a bridge over the river and travel another two hexes off-road in hilly country to form a screen to protect the bridge. The patrol's force-march allows it 9MP. It expends 1 in the first open hex cross-country, and then 2 in the woods hex, plus 1 for crossing the bridge. This leaves 5MP. To move the two further hexes off-road in the hills expends a total of 4 Movement Points, leaving 1 in hand, so they are adjudged to have reached their destination

10 Forced marches are permitted once every five map move weeks. A record should be kept of the unit's moves in order to verify its ability to force march. The forced march need not be the last of the five moves, and a unit does not have to force march.

11 Forced marches may be 'carried forward', such as 10 normal moves followed by two forced marches. However, no more than three consecutive forced marches are possible, and no unit may force march in a week after it has fought two actions or more.

12 Each side has six boat models representing river barges (or such other quantity as agreed upon by the players beforehand: it should not be possible for more than a brigade to be transported by boat at any one time). A boat model may carry half an infantry battalion (maximum four bases in our 'old school' variant tactical rules, so halve this for the standard version with fewer miniatures per battalion) or cavalry squadron (again, no more than four bases) or a battery of artillery of up to eight guns (four bases)and their crews. Artillery limbers and caissons must be transported separately. You may of course adjust this rule to suit your own campaign circumstances.

13 Players may decide that a number of small, local craft are also available. The quantity may either be agreed beforehand, or decided randomly on arrival in a town or city beside a watercourse. In any case, the number of extra craft available should be limited to an additional 50% capacity, with the possible exception of capital cities and major sea ports.

14 Each boat in use must be given a map coordinate. They may be captured or destroyed, and no replacements may be built during the current campaign season.

15 Boats may be dismantled and taken overland by wagons, and therefore will move as wagons, but *on roads only*. In order for this type of move to be carried out, wagons must be detached from infantry or cavalry regiments who must offload the supplies normally carried in them. To do so requires 1MP deducted from the wagon's move. The regiments concerned must designate a town or village as their magazine and supply centre, and must remain within two hexes of it until their wagons return to them. (You may decide to raise a special pontonnier unit instead.)

16 To load boats onto wagons requires one wagon model per boat model and takes one week to carry out. To place boats back in the water after overland transportation requires half a week, including making ready for sailing. No troops may embark or disembark during the loading or unloading process.

17 To judge whether the riverbank terrain is suitable for the loading or unloading of barges, throw a d6: 1-3, unsuitable; 4-6 suitable. Loading and unloading is permitted anywhere along the length of a canal as long as the prevailing terrain is not marshy or wooded.

18 To ferry troops across a river using barges previously assembled for the task requires half a move. Each boat may only ferry its usual capacity in a normal move, which includes embarkation and disembarkation, but it may return to the opposite bank again ready to embark further troops at the beginning of the next move.

19 Crossing rivers other than by bridge or boat is not permitted for artillery or wagons. Infantry and cavalry may attempt as follows:

    February-April   No fording allowed due to melt water

    May-October   Throw a d6: 1-3 no luck; 4-6 takes 1 move

20 If the crossing attempt is unsuccessful, inform opponent of terrain conditions when he is within one move distance of the river crossing point attempted and perhaps indicate this on your master map. (This may be done by an umpire if one is available.)

21 To embark infantry on boats requires half a move, others need a whole move. To disembark infantry requires a quarter of a move, others need half a move.

22 Boats on rivers may not climb hills! This is only possible on canals with locks. Where present, locks on canals do not appreciably delay movement, which has been averaged over a week and includes brief pauses anyway.

23 No troops may cross canals other than by bridges or boats.

24 When opposing forces meet in a hex, their strengths should be declared by the players as follows:

1 figure	SCOUT
2-50 figures	DETACHMENT
51-150 figures	BRIGADE
151-300 figures	WING
301-500 figures	ARMY
501-1000 figures	GRAND ARMY
1000+ figures	SUPREME COMMAND

Troops inside towns should be declared thus:

1-50 figures	SMALL GARRISON
51-300 figures	MEDIUM GARRISON
301-500 figures	LARGE GARRISON
501+ figures	GRAND GARRISON

slightly before the end of the week.

An 8pdr artillery battery is ordered to pass through a forest three hexes wide to a town the other side. The general who ordered this should be shot. It would be quicker to call in your pioneers to build a road!

These numbers are based on a figure:man ratio of approximately 1:20, so adjust to suit your own wargame rules as required.

25 Once contact has been made, and strengths declared as above, then further intelligence may be gathered. Each side rolls one d6: 1 = no further intelligence gathered; 2 = more accurate estimate of enemy numbers obtained, + or – 10%; 3 or 4 = as for 2, but also approximate proportions of infantry, cavalry and artillery; 5 = as for 3 and 4, but also with more detailed indication of troop types (grenadiers, heavy and light cavalry etc); 6 = complete information about the enemy force.

26 The die roll should be modified according to the intelligence and initiative of the local commander, reflecting the likelihood that he has sent out patrols and scouts to reconnoitre the enemy. Commanders with intelligence below 30% should deduct 1 from their die roll; commanders with intelligence above 70% should add 1. The same applies to initiative, and the scores are cumulative. Thus a small force with a commander of high intelligence and initiative can find out a great deal about a much larger force, whereas an army with a dullard at the helm might stumble around learning very little about the enemy it encounters.

27 Once strengths have been declared and further intelligence gathered, players may decide to fight or retire. If both sides accept the challenge, then draw up a more detailed map of the contact hex and the side which gathered the most intelligence may decide on the battlefield to be fought over. If one side declines, then it must retire to the hex it previously occupied on its route and their opponents may occupy the disputed hex. Both sides can elect to retire if they wish, or simply stand their ground without fighting. Should this happen, both sides will gain full knowledge of each other's forces in the hex.

28 Troops in hexes adjacent to a contact may arrive to reinforce. Full details of the flanking force, its commander and the order of march of the units concerned should be written down and sealed in an envelope (or given to the umpire if you have one). Throw four d6. The score indicates the time at which the force might arrive on a 24-hour clock (with, obviously, 04.00 hrs being the earliest). On the appropriate battlefield move, take the initiative factor of the flanking force commander and throw two percentage dice, one for tens, the other showing units 0-9. If the throw is lower than, or equal to, his initiative factor, the force arrives on time. If not, it is delayed by one move for every 5% over the required throw, fractions rounded up.

29 The order of precedence for command in the field, if the commander-in-chief or designated field commander is not present, is as follows:

i. Royalty
ii. Guard
iii. Other élites, e.g. grenadiers
iv. Cavalry, unless above – élite cavalry outrank élite infantry
v. Infantry, unless above
vi. Artillery (never rank as élite for chain of command)
vii. Engineers
viii. Commanders of irregular units
ix. Other e.g. medical staff

30 The place of precedence in battle is the right of the first line, followed by the left, then the right of the second line, and so on. It is in battle alone that artillery takes absolute precedence over all other arms and may be placed where the commander desires.

31 Fortress towns should be classified thus to indicate their maximum capacity:

i. 3rd class fortress   250 figures
ii. 2nd class fortress   500 figures
iii. 1st class fortress   1,000 figures

These are based on a figure:man ratio of approximately 1:20, so adjust to suit your own wargame rules as required.

32 Players holding towns at the conclusion of the campaign season benefit from the tithes and taxes appertaining to those places. The capital of a country is worth 10,000 thalers; other cities are worth 2,000 thalers each. Large towns are worth 1,000 thalers, small towns just 500. Your map should have a key indicating the size, and therefore value, of each of your major settlements. Villages are of negligible value, and so ignored to simplify the rules, but you may decide to give value to a certain number of them to represent special trades carried out in them or resources nearby.

33 A town or city taken after a practicable breach has been made, or after a siege lasting more than four weeks, has its value halved owing to the necessary expenditure on repair. Sieges will be dealt with separately.

34 Each regiment of cavalry, battalion of infantry or battery of artillery requires a wagon model which represents its supply train. If a unit's wagon is lost, destroyed, or captured by the enemy, that unit will suffer -1 on all its combat and morale die rolls in battle until it is found, recaptured, or replaced by a new wagon. Replacement wagons must be sent from the point on the map baseline where the unit originally entered the theatre of campaign. A unit may march to intercept its replacement wagon.

Another example from the 'Grenouissian Intermezzo' campaign.

General E Pickled of the Gateway Alliance has sent a cavalry squadron to reconnoitre the capital city, Pescadrix, in hex U23. When they get there, they encounter a 'Large Garrison' as well as several outlying patrols of 'Detachment' strength. The city is in fact stuffed with troops belonging both to Granprix and one of its mercenary allies, Aytonia. Their response to the appearance of the enemy Detachment is to drive them off with cavalry patrols, and the Gateway troops accede to this, retiring to hex T23 where they establish themselves in the small fishing village of Pont de la Ciutat al Mar. Since the Gateway's troops retired, no further intelligence is gathered.

PIONEERS

In his excellent *Wargaming in History Volume 5*, Charles Grant lists some of the tasks for which engineers and pioneers should be used. They include trenches and other battlefield earthworks such as redoubts, abatis and *chevaux de frises*, and the building and demolition of bridges. Some tasks can only be performed by the specialists themselves, whilst they can supervise others, directing the work of ordinary line infantry.

The capture of enemy colours can become quite a propaganda coup in the course of a campaign, with much bragging and needling following such an event. Some gamers have even been known to build miniature monuments to humiliate their opponent still further!

35 A unit which captures a wagon from the enemy benefits from +1 on all its combat and morale die rolls if it takes part in any engagement within one week of the capture.

36 Wagons may be carried on boats as per artillery.

37 Engineers and pioneers should gain bonuses in sieges, construction, demolition and route clearance. Your tactical rules should reflect this.

38 Veterans are troops that have taken part in five or more actions in which they have both inflicted and received casualties. However, an otherwise veteran unit which consists of 50% or more new replacements who have not fulfilled this criterion is no longer veteran. A choice must therefore be made between keeping units up to strength or gaining the bonus. It will be noted that most units will survive with their recovered wounded rejoining the unit later, and these recovered casualties *do* count towards the status of veterans. Veterans are distinguished by their increased fighting and morale factors which are usually covered in the tactical rules. Note that it is also possible for élite troops to become veterans.

39 Casualties suffered in battle are subdivided as follows:
    i.   20% are dead, severely wounded or otherwise unable to fight
    ii.   20% recover next day (light flesh wounds or knocked out)
    iii.   20% recover after one week (concussion, other light wounds)
    iv.   20% recover after 2 weeks (more serious wounds)
    v.   20% recover after 4 weeks (severe but recoverable wounds)

40 Wounded are automatically captured if their unit routs. Otherwise, they are helped by comrades to the nearest garrison town to receive treatment, requiring two helpers per casualty. Recovery may not begin until the casualty has reached hospital.

41 A losing commander may surrender his casualties after battle even if no rout occurs, as indeed may a commander whose position is so perilous that he wishes to spare further suffering – an agreement being made between opponents prior to engaging, if desired.

42 Prisoners require one guard for every ten captives.

43 Regiments taken prisoner must surrender their regimental colours and standards, unless allowed by their captors to keep them. The capture of enemy colours should provide a battlefield morale boost for the troops concerned for one campaign week following the event. Naturally, the unit that has lost its colours should receive a morale penalty for a longer period, perhaps one month.

44 The minimum force that must occupy a town for it to count as a gain for one side or the other at the end of the campaign season is a company of infantry or squadron of cavalry.

45 No more than 10% of a side's total force may occupy a single town at the start of the campaign season.

46 Points may be awarded for battles and sieges: 10 points for a win, 5 points for a draw, 0 for a loss. Deduct 1 point for every 5% losses incurred.

Whether you're using squares or hexagons, there is a map-movement technique you can use instead of an umpire if you and your opponent are able to meet on a regular basis. I recall this first being described by Don Featherstone in *War Game Campaigns*, and it involves a large collection of match boxes (though any small box with a drawer will do).

Quite simply, each box is allocated to an individual grid square or hexagon, and they are glued together to form a miniature chest of drawers, with the *x* coordinates running left to right and the *y* coordinates from top to bottom marked on both ends of the drawers. Each player has his own, large-scale copy of the map, and a collection of counters, each representing a unit or brigade in his army.

Moves are made alternately, and when Player 1 is moving, Player 2 turns his back. Having calculated his positions at the end of the campaign day or week (whatever time period is deemed best), Player 1 puts the counters corresponding to his units in the appropriate drawers. Then Player 2 takes his turn and, of course, if he opens a drawer and discovers an enemy piece inside, then he announces contact has been made and the decision is made whether to proceed to a set-down on the tabletop or, such as in the case of a mere scout uncovering a much larger force, one side may elect to retreat.

CAMPAIGN DIARIES

One of the real joys of a campaign is being able to look back in later years and re-live the experience. Nowadays, of course, many people prefer to record their wargames online in the form of a blog – something I shall be looking at in Chapter 10 – but there is, I find, something particularly wonderful about stumbling upon a good campaign diary.

I have kept written records of my games for as long as I can remember (I still find bits of paper with scribbled notes and sketch maps dating back to the 1970s), but it was when my friend Guy Hancock joined me in bringing my Wars of the Faltenian Succession to life, beginning in 1986, that I really began to take this pleasant administration seriously. I bought a perfect-bound A4 notebook, with narrow ruling, from a stationers and it became the home for all my campaign thoughts.

The move for each campaign week occupied four pages, as you will see in the photos overleaf: one double-page spread held the names of all my units and their dispositions, giving the hex reference and any notes I thought important about their condition, where they were heading and so on. The following spread was then filled with jottings about the campaign week, including any encounters with the enemy, my strategic concerns, what I thought the enemy was up to and, most importantly, the list of enemy declarations. This was followed by the results of any encounters, casualties incurred, and any adjustments should a unit end up in a different hex to the one intended as a result of the week's events. Your diary is also a great place to indulge in a little, how shall we put it... Propaganda!

In addition to the diary proper, I also kept a lever-arch file, filled with correspondence between the players (much of it rather less diplomatic than you might imagine) and a series of sheets of tracing paper, in which I coloured in the hexes according to that week's declarations. This proved very useful in making sense of what Guy was up to strategically – a function which, more than 25 years on, might be achieved using software on your PC or Mac or even an 'App' on a mobile device.

Have fun campaigning – it's the best kind of wargaming there is.

Spreads from the author's campaign diary for 7th-14th March 1744 (1991 in reality) during the 'Martinstaad Crisis' phase of his ongoing 'Wars of the Faltenian Succession' campaigns. The lower spread gives map coordinates and notes, revealing the forces of Prunkland closing the vice on the capital Martinstadt; and then the upper spread makes the author's jubilation at his success pretty clear! Note also the diagram of a somewhat complex encounter in hex V33, where in true eighteenth century fashion, unpleasantness was avoided.

320

7

SHOT, STEEL & STONE

Horse & Musket Era Rules
for European Warfare 1685-1845

I t seemed to me that a book about wargaming that didn't include a full set of rules would leave the reader frustrated and disappointed, so it would hardly be fair of me to create such a monster myself! Surely, I reasoned, a newcomer to the hobby, having listened to all the theory and learned so much about the hobby in the preceding pages, would want some way of putting all those ideas into practice. Here, therefore, is my contribution to that ever-growing library of wargames rules that I dearly hope I have inspired you sufficiently to wish to explore for yourself.

The troops at your disposal

INFANTRY

Infantry are men trained to march and fight on foot. In the eighteenth and nineteenth centuries, private soldiers were normally drawn from the lower classes of society, such as unskilled labourers or peasants, but occasionally they were men with a trade or education. A substantial number were petty criminals who had been offered the alternative of serving in the army, rather than serving a prison sentence. Particularly in the German states, the rank and file sometimes included members of the aristocracy serving as cadets. Officers were usually of noble blood, but also counted a few long-service veterans promoted from the ranks amongst their number.

The usual armament of the period was the smoothbore musket, which

Portuguese infantryman c.1704. © Bob Marrion

was muzzle-loading and largely inaccurate: hence the need for mass volleys. Infantry firepower had increased substantially, thanks to the greater reliability and rate of fire of the flintlock compared to the matchlock. To this would be attached a socket bayonet when charging home or repelling cavalry. Specialist units of 'light' infantry were issued with rifles, also muzzle-loading, and much more accurate, though slower to load.

Infantry in some units carried a 'hanger', or short sword, in addition to their bayonets. This proved most useful for chopping firewood or carving chickens over the campfire!

During sieges (rarely on the battlefield), certain élite troops were issued with grenades – crude devices of hollow iron filled with gunpowder, and fitted with a burning fuse. These were often as dangerous to the user as to the enemy, but were useful for attacking entrenchments and fortifications. Since it was necessary to stand up in very close proximity to the enemy when throwing the device, 'grenadiers' tended to require above average bravery.

The 'poor bloody infantry' have always needed stamina to carry their weapons and equipment. The Age of Reason was no exception. In addition to a uniform consisting of shirt, waistcoat, coat, hat, knee breeches, woollen stockings, gaiters and shoes, the infantry private was burdened with crossbelts bearing cartridge pouch, bayonet, knapsack and haversack, which contained additional clothing and rations, cooking and cleaning implements and any personal possessions. And after all that, he picked up his musket!

An officer was much better off, with a uniform made from better quality materials, wagons to carry his baggage, a fine sword and occasionally a weapon such as a spontoon or halberd. Noncommissioned officers often had such a polearm, for keeping the men in line. The ensign, a young second-lieutenant, would normally have the job of carrying the battalion's colours, as is still the case in the British army. In some armies, this job was given to a veteran NCO.

The infantry may be further subdivided as follows:

American militiaman 1775.
© Bob Marrion

- **Militia** were generally poor quality, part time troops who had often been chosen by ballot to defend a town or region. By its very nature, militia was highly variable in quality, usually consisting of young or very old men and others disinclined to the military life, often infirm and understandably averse to risking their lives. George Washington said that relying on militia was like "... resting on a broken staff". The occasions when militia gave a good account of themselves were rare enough to be of note, such as the battle of Bunker Hill. Poorly equipped and poorly led, it was only when defending hearth and home that they sometimes matched regular troops.

- **Musketeers**, and **fusiliers** (the latter originally guarded trains of artillery and gunpowder armed with a 'fusil', an early flintlock which posed far less danger to the ammunition wagons than the burning match fuses of matchlocks), formed the backbone of the armies of our period. They were the unsung heroes of all battles, trained to wield musket and bayonet in the service of their country. Whether volunteers or conscripts, the army was their life, for better or for worse. Assuming they survived combat, these men frequently became veterans of ten, twenty or even thirty years in the service. Generally reliable and highly disciplined in combat, they became inured to hardships to a degree which we would find shocking. Loyalty, however, was variable, and desertion was a persistent problem for almost all armies. In some armies, fusiliers had a semi-élite status, and were issued with headgear similar to grenadiers.

France: Musketeer, Regiment Anhalt 1762.
© Bob Marrion

- **Grenadiers** were usually selected from amongst the biggest and toughest men, often veterans of several campaigns. Whilst in some armies forming companies that were nominally part of the line battalions, in action they were frequently grouped together into élite battalions, either to add power to an attack or to plug a gap. The discipline and training of grenadiers, together with their veteran status, set these men apart from other troops of the line. They were expected to set an example, and this was reflected by better pay and more privileges. The most distinctive mark of a grenadier was his hat. This was either the 'mitre' type, often with a front plate of metal, embossed and engraved with elaborate designs, or the 'bearskin' type of fur, usually with a cloth top or hanging bag. Prussian and Austrian grenadiers are examples of these two styles. The hat derived from the original function of grenadiers – throwing grenades, which was tricky when wearing the tricorne hat of the musketeers. The size of some grenadier caps, however, shows that its symbolic importance was far greater than its practicality. A regiment of grenadiers in battle array was a most imposing sight.

Britain: Grenadier Royal Scots 1684.
© Bob Marrion

- **Guards**, the ultimate élite units, were practically indistinguishable from grenadiers in terms of their uniforms, apart from the use of 'royal' colours for their facings. For example, British guardsmen wore dark blue facings – and still do. Perhaps the most famous guardsmen were those of Napoleon's élite Imperial Guard, known as the *grognards* (grumblers) who were

France: Grenadier of the Imperial Guard 1815.
© Bob Marrion

cosseted by Napoleon and only used *in extremis* to crush the last enemy resistance. Famously, at the end of the Battle of Waterloo, their defensive squares refused to surrender and were slaughtered. The important factor is prestige. Guards regiments attracted the aristocracy to their ranks, and even the rank and file were frequently of noble blood or highly experienced veterans. Their pay was far better than that of troops of the line, which made them an expensive commodity. Small wonder, then, that they were rarely exposed to the dangers of the battlefield, and were commonly envied by their countrymen. But their loyalty to the person of the monarch was fierce, and the title of many of these units, such as *Gardes du Corps*, was a literal description of their function to guard the head of state. Curiously, the Austrians never raised any guard units for the battlefield at all.

• *Grenzer* were irregular troops, originally raised in the wilder fringes of the Austro-Hungarian empire as a form of militia. (Their name originates from the German word for border, *Grenze*.) However, the native warrior character of these men was soon recognised, and

Austria: Grenzer Regiment Oguliner 1762.
© Bob Marrion

they served in vast numbers with varying degrees of distinction throughout our period. Less disciplined than troops of the line, they felt ill at ease with the formal, linear battlefield tactics of the day. Given the opportunity for ambushes, raids and reconnaissance, however, they rated very highly and pulled off some spectacular successes against the Prussians. A parallel can be drawn with the British use of Highlanders, whose appearance struck fear into many opponents. They were also feared by the civilian population of the territories through which they marched and their conduct, when let off the leash of authority, could hardly be described as exemplary. *Grenzer* were fiercely loyal to their overlords, and were not prone to the desertion suffered by many of their fellows in regiments of the line.

- **Chasseurs** or *Tirailleurs* to the French, *Jäger* to the Germans and, in due course, Light Infantry and Rifles to the British, were the regular army's answer to the *Grenzer* for skirmishing. Originally drawn from hunters, gamekeepers and foresters, but later supplemented by any man who showed a talent for marksmanship and initiative, the main attributes of a *Jäger* were his marksmanship with a rifle and his ability to make the best use of difficult terrain and cover. This also meant that they were encouraged to use that most uncommon of commodities in an eighteenth century army: individual initiative. Their job made light infantry almost as élite as grenadiers, though they were sometimes ridiculed as using cowardly tactics by the more stubborn defenders of the old order. Such jibes were most often occasioned by fear, however, which usually exaggerated the actual effectiveness of the rifle. *Jäger* traditionally used the hunting-horn as their badge, and tended to be clad in the closest thing you will find to camouflage in the eighteenth century, typically uniforms of green, grey or brown.

Britain: 60th Kings Royal Rifle Corps 1799.
© Bob Marrion

- **Freikorps** ('free battalions'), a type of unit commonly found in the Prussian service, were, in effect, private armies serving the king under the command of their proprietor colonels. Their reputations ranged from very good to utterly diabolical, some being extremely well-led, others being little better than bands of brigands and cutthroats in uniform. Some units amongst their number, such as that of von Kleist, performed creditably but, referring to their common uniform and conduct, Frederick described them as "Triple blue, and three times damned to the devil!"

Prussia: Musketeer, Frei Battalion Le Noble 1756.
© Bob Marrion

Britain: Trooper,
Life Guards 1712.
© Bob Marrion

CAVALRY

Cavalry are men trained to march and fight on horseback. This includes dragoons, who had by now become disinclined to dismount and fight on foot in the manner of their predecessors, even though many armies persisted in training them to do so. Cavalry were usually recruited from agricultural labourers who had some experience of dealing with horses, and their officers were almost invariably landed gentry, schooled in the saddle from early childhood. In this sense, history really is another country, since even the most experienced horsemen of modern times will leap into their cars, or take a bus or train for everyday transport. In the eighteenth century, horses *were* the transport, and a cavalryman had a very strong bond with his mount that is hard to imagine nowadays.

Cavalry were usually armed with a sword of some kind – typically a sabre or broadsword – which was used to thrust or cut. A great deal of training was devoted to their proper use, and most cavalry attained a high level of skill. Lances were issued to some eighteenth century units, such as the Prussian Bosniaks, but compared to later times they appear to have been relatively ineffective when used by battlefield units. In the Napoleonic period, however, the lance came into its own as a devastating battlefield weapon in the French and other armies.

Our cavalrymen were often heavily armed in addition to their swords. A pair of pistols (occasionally more) and a carbine or short musket were common additions. However, the average cavalryman was no musketeer, and firearms were normally used only when on patrol, skirmishing, outpost duty or duelling. Against infantry, cold steel reigned supreme, though the pistols might serve as a backup at very close quarters.

In addition to weapons, the poor horses were beasts of burden indeed. A cavalryman was bedecked with all the impedimenta we mentioned for the infantry, plus his sword or lance, tall boots for the heavy cavalry, a breastplate (and sometimes backplate) for the cuirassiers, an iron 'secret' head protector inside the hat, bridle, saddle, pistol holsters, shabraque or saddle cloth, forage bag, stirrups, blanket roll and other bits and pieces appropriate to the horseman's art. It is, then, small wonder that the horseflesh selected was nothing like the modern racehorse! Indeed, you might be forgiven for thinking, were you to travel back in time, that the heavy cavalry was mounted on cart horses. It must be appreciated that the horses were bred for the job – heavy hunters of the Percheron and Hanoverian type were best, with smaller breeds (but hardy nonetheless) for the lighter cavalry.

We should pause to consider what we mean by light, medium and heavy cavalry. As we have just seen, the terms refer in the most literal sense to the size of the men and horses and the load they were burdened with. However, it also alludes to their battlefield use. Heavy cavalry (such as cuirassiers) was a strike force, intended to punch a hole in the enemy's line. Light cavalry (hussars being a prime example) was opportunist, harrying, ambushing and raiding the enemy, though also capable of taking its place in the traditional battle line. Medium cavalry – the dragoons – could fulfil either role, but as our period progressed it became almost indistinguishable in appearance and function from its heavier brethren. Prestige accrued to the heavyweights, whilst the light cavalry had a more fashionable and exciting image. Cavalry may be further subdivided as follows:

1st Corps of Shropshire Yeomanry Cavalry 1795.
© Bob Marrion

- **Militia** cavalry, often called 'Yeomanry' in Britain, could be said to be the worst of all possible worlds! Either they were infirm men and boys mounted on old and flea-bitten nags; or they were country gents on expensive horses, more attracted by pomp and glory than by the dangerous methods of earning these accolades. If a man had invested a personal fortune in his mount, then the disinclination to expose the beast to shot and shell must have been enormous. Moreover, a yeoman's horse would not have received the rigorous training of a true military mount, which involved controlled and careful exposure to terrifying noises, sights and smells. Thus the horse would not have been conditioned to resist its instinctive wish to head home at the first sign of trouble, bearing its grateful rider with it. Militia cavalry, then, could hardly be counted upon to strike terror into the enemy.

Britain: 9th Dragoons 1751. © Bob Marrion

• **Dragoons**, the mainstay of the cavalry, were originally mounted infantrymen armed with a firearm known as a 'dragon' and were often found wearing a uniform identical in cut to the infantry. In some armies they persisted in wearing gaiters and shoes instead of boots, in recognition of their possible role on foot. Dragoons were highly versatile, capable of charging home with the heavy cavalry, yet able to fulfil outpost, reconnaissance and patrol duties alongside the light cavalry. Dragoons often had their own élite companies of horse grenadiers, with distinguishing headgear – some were even trained to throw grenades on horseback! There are certainly records of their dismounted use, and they were still frequently armed with a firearm somewhere between a full musket and a carbine in length; but the fact is that their 'medium' cavalry status made them extremely useful both on the battlefield and on campaign, able to fulfil many functions. In short, the dragoons were to the cavalry what musketeers were to the infantry: ubiquitous and generally reliable. History proved, however, that dragoons would soon return to their dismounted role, as the huge increase in firepower and weapon ranges seen in the later nineteenth century rendered the traditional use of cavalry as a shock arm impossible. European armies tried to hold onto their glorious past for longer than the Americans, who by the time of the Civil War had realised that the best use of cavalry was as a highly mobile mounted infantry to 'get there the fustest with the mostest'.

Britain: 1st (Royal) Dragoons 1815. © Bob Marrion

• **Cuirassiers**, known in German as *Kürassiere*, were the élite cavalry of the time, taking their name from their heavy breast (and sometimes back) plate. (*Cuir* is the French word for leather, the

328

France: Cuirassiers
du Roi 1704.
© Bob Marrion

material from which early body armour was made.) Their outfit was completed by thick, heavy leather boots and gauntlets, and either a substantial helmet or an iron skull cap or 'secret' concealed beneath more commonplace headgear like the tricorne hat. The 'lobster' type of cuirassier in three-quarter armour and closed helmet had really disappeared by the early eighteenth century. By no means capable of galloping any great distance, their charges were usually delivered at a stately trot or canter, with unit cohesion being the prime tactic. We should be careful not to be blinded by visions of a solid wall of men and horses bodily crashing into the enemy and trampling and sabring them down, although this did happen occasionally. During our period, the famous Spanish tactician Santa Cruz demonstrated to his men how cavalry could be kept at bay with nothing more than a stick, and well-trained infantry could and did hold their ground. Nevertheless, the threat of the steamroller onrush of determined heavy cavalry could only be countered by a steady nerve, and most shaky troops would turn tail and flee at the very prospect. Certainly the heavy cuirasses provided a high degree of protection against musketry and badly aimed bayonet or sword thrusts, and this feeling of invulnerability greatly improved the morale of the men. There are many instances of cuirassiers turning the tide of a battle with a well-timed attack on a shaky enemy line. Note that the British had another form of heavy cavalry known as 'horse' who did not wear breastplates but were identical to cuirassiers in other respects.

Britain: 10th
Hussars 1815.
© Bob Marrion

- **Hussars**, cousins to their countrymen on foot the *Grenzer*, made a great impression during the Age of Reason, and their fashions persisted in popularity well into the nineteenth century. They were born to the saddle,

Britain: 8th Light Dragoons 1790. © Bob Marrion

superb swordsmen, excellent shots with a pistol and renowned for their drinking and wenching exploits. When they first appeared from the plains of Hungary, they were disdained for their unmilitary and highly irregular conduct but soon won respect, and almost every country in Europe eventually raised units of hussars. Brave to the point of madness on occasion, a hussar would ride straight at anything – when the circumstances were of his choosing! Like the *Grenzer*, ambushes, raids and reconnaissance were home to the hussar, and the linear battlefield was a strange place for him. However, Frederick the Great trained his hussars to take their place in the line of battle with notable success; but the more 'regular' he made them, the less effective they became at their traditional duties. True to form, the British were very tardy in raising hussar units, preferring 'light dragoons' who performed the same duties but, being regulars, were easier to control. In the end, many of these regiments were converted to hussars, as the true, irregular character of the hussar was lost and their extravagant dress was adopted merely as a statement of military fashion.

France: 7th (Vistula) Lancers in Spain, 1811. © Bob Marrion

- **Lancers** (known in German as ***Ulanen*** and in French as ***lanciers***) were notably scarce in western Europe during the Age of Reason and failed to make any real impression. Frederick the Great, having converted some hussars to lancers, was so utterly dismayed by their performance in action that he changed them back again! During the reign of Napoleon Bonaparte, however, the French Empire recruited large numbers of lancers, having been impressed by the redoubtable Polish cavalry they encountered in 1807, and eventually added two regiments of these formidable light cavalry types to the Guard. If well-used, lancers could move at light cavalry speed but strike with the impact of heavy cavalry, making them extremely useful. They were also the ultimate weapon in pursuit, capable of doing great execution on scattered troops because of their longer reach.

France: Elite Company of the 13th Chasseurs à Cheval in Spain, 1811.
© Bob Marrion

- *Chasseurs à cheval*, or *Jäger zu Pferde* in German, were originally, as their name implies, mounted light infantry. Few in number during the eighteenth century, they nevertheless grew in popularity until in the Napoleonic period, they figured in many armies, having abandoned their role on foot for one akin to hussars or light dragoons. The French raised large numbers of these useful cavalry, including the Chasseurs à Cheval de la Garde Imperiale, Napoleon's favourite regiment, whose undress uniform he wore daily. Like their infantry cousins the *Jäger*, they usually wore a green uniform, and in some armies were armed with a rifled instead of a smoothbore carbine.

- **Guard cavalry** were the élite of the élite. So much prestige was attached to such units that arguments could persist for years between aristocratic families who felt slighted by a promotion or appointment given to a rival. The finest horses, the strongest men, the best equipment, the gaudiest uniforms – all these led to a groaning expense list for any exchequer called upon to provide funds for such a unit. Guard units could be cuirassiers, dragoons, hussars or any other type, but were distinguished by their close association with the sovereign and their precedence over all other units in the

Britain: Royal Horse Guards 1760.
© Bob Marrion

army. Nonetheless, the points raised concerning guard infantry can also be made here, that a guard unit might see less action than a unit of the line, and all the vast expense could count for nought. However, a guards regiment of cavalry serving in the presence of its monarch would have a tremendous sense of its own honour and prestige that it would have been inclined to preserve above all else. Their distinction was as much moral as physical and, as Napoleon summed up, "The moral is to the physical as three is to one."

- **Cossacks**, often armed with a long lance, were ten-a-penny in Russia. Much like the hussars in temperament and duties, many Cossacks behaved worse than bandits, were tribal in outlook and even less inclined to see a true battlefield than the hussars. Often controlled by local warlords, they were, however, murderously effective at their best, cutting supply lines and raiding deep behind enemy lines. In 1812, they were to gain notoriety, combining with the weather to annihilate Napoleon's Grande Armée. In the Age of Reason, however, these most unreasonable of fellows remained firmly on the fringe.

ARTILLERY

The artillery are men trained to fight using ordnance such as guns or howitzers, and who generally marched and fought on foot. Frederick the Great , followed by the Austrians, experimented with horse artillery, mounting the gunners on the limbers – by the end of the Napoleonic Wars, each gunner also had his own horse and was armed with a sabre, though the Austrians persisted with an oddly modified ammunition caisson on which the gunners rode called a *Würstwagen*, literally translated as 'sausage cart'. Other gunners rode on a padded seat fitted to the gun carriage itself – what an adventure that must have been!

A display at the Firepower Royal Artillery museum in Woolwich, London, showing a British Napoleonic 9-pdr cannon being fired. Note that, in reality, both gunners would need to stand well clear of the piece to avoid serious injury!

The artillery was generally considered to be beneath the dignity of the aristocracy, who were suspicious of its mix of science and alchemy. It was thus the educated middle classes who excelled in this arm, which was the reason it became one of the more professional arms.

Britain: Royal Artillery 1756. © Bob Marrion

Considering the fact that the industrial revolution still lay some years ahead, the artillery became remarkably powerful. It can be roughly subdivided into three categories – infantry support or 'battalion' guns; field pieces, including howitzers; and siege artillery. These divisions are connected with the weight of shot fired, and therefore the size of the equipment itself and the supply 'tail' it required.

The weapons were actually quite simple. A barrel was cast from bronze or iron, a fairly hit-or-miss affair which required tremendous craftsmanship to produce high quality results. The idea of casting the barrels solid, then drilling out the bore, was technologically advanced for its time and caught on only gradually. Previously, every gun was cast from an individual mould which was destroyed as part of the process. Small wonder that consistency was not a strong point of eighteenth century foundries.

The idea of rifling a gun did not catch on until the later nineteenth century – the Jäger had unique armament in this respect. Similarly, breech-loading, although tried in earlier times, had to wait until another century before it became widespread because of the difficulty of sealing the mechanism successfully. The result was a smoothbore weapon, mounted on a sturdy carriage, with no recoil mechanism apart from any incline on which the battery was sited. Refinements were largely confined to metallurgy and the design of the carriage, which gradually led to a decrease in overall weight of the piece.

Prussia: Gunner c.1700. Note the ornate 'portfire' which held the glowing match used to ignite the powder in the vent. © Bob Marrion

A roundshot was basically a sphere of iron, propelled by the explosion of a measured charge of powder. It then proceeded in a more or less erratic fashion (due partly to the 'windage' or gap between ball and barrel, and partly due to the uneven casting of the ball itself) until it hit the ground – the 'first graze'. What happened then depended on the nature of the ground, the amount of powder used to propel it, and the elevation of the piece which fired it. If the ball had followed a flattish trajectory and

A 5.5" howitzer on display at the Firepower Royal Artillery museum. The barrel mounted in front is 6" calibre.

the ground was firm, it continued by a series of bounces or ricochets until it lost momentum and rolled along the ground to a halt. It must be stressed that the ball was capable of killing or maiming anything in its path from the moment it left the barrel until it came to a complete standstill. Many a foolish soldier lost his foot when trying to stop a seemingly harmless ball as it rolled along. The power of the ball in its early flight was capable of murderous destruction, knocking down whole ranks of men and horses in the most dreadful fashion.

Contrary to Hollywood portrayal, cannonballs did not explode! Howitzers, however, did fire crude exploding projectiles in the form of shells. These were hollow iron spheres, filled with gunpowder, which was ignited by a fuse. The fuse itself was lit by the propellant charge in the

A rear view of the same howitzer showing the gunners' tools strapped to the trail and clearly showing the ammunition coffers either side of the barrel.

barrel, having been trimmed to explode the shell on or above the target.

France: Artillery Train Conductors, Egypt 1801. These men were tasked with driving the teams of horses attached to limbers and ammunition wagons.
© Bob Marrion

Like their larger brethren, the siege mortars, howitzers had short, stubby barrels and fired at a high trajectory. Unlike guns, whose calibre was expressed as the weight of shot they fired, howitzers were normally known by the width of their bore, such as 5.5". Curiously, some countries used the equivalent weight of stone shot as their calibre.

The effects of shellfire were as much moral as physical. In wet ground, howitzer shells could bury themselves harmlessly and the erratic fuse could lead the shell to burst far too early in its flight, making it as dangerous to the user as the target. Nevertheless, a shell landing in the middle of closely packed ranks could have a devastating effect and cavalry horses in particular could be terrified, even if left unwounded. Most buildings in our period were timber framed and howitzer shells were ideal for setting them on fire, thus denying their use to the enemy. Howitzers also had another use – taking shots at enemy troops in 'dead' ground, behind hills and so on. In these times, this was of course a highly speculative sort of shooting in the absence of trained forward observers equipped with radios. A lucky shot, however, could have a startling effect on troops who had assumed they were safe!

Both types of gun could fire caseshot or canister. This was, in essence, a tin can, containing balls as small as musket balls, though sometimes larger, and occasionally scraps of iron, nails and so on. On leaving the barrel of the gun, the container disintegrated, producing a lethal hail of pieces which spread out as it progressed. In short, canister was like a giant shotgun cartridge. Its range was naturally limited, but artillerymen were able to produce the most appalling carnage at close quarters against the densely packed infantry and cavalry formations of the day. Due to their wider bore, howitzers produced a greater spread, but field gun canister could carry slightly further.

The bigger calibres of gun and mortar tended to be used in sieges, for the destruction of fortifications. Much effort went into designing fortresses to resist their power, particularly in France and the Low Countries. Their sheer size and weight made them virtually immobile and cannon calibres of more than 12-18lb rarely appeared on the battlefield.

SPECIALISTS

It is worthwhile mentioning some of the more esoteric combatants who, at the beginning of the horse and musket period, were often civilians contracted for the duration of the war or even just a particular siege or campaign. Only gradually did these services come under the auspices of

Britain: Officer, Royal Engineers, Egypt 1801. © Bob Marrion

France: Miner, Egypt 1800. © Bob Marrion

Spain: Pioneer, Infantry Regiment Zamora 1809/10. © Bob Marrion

France: Surgeon, 16th Légère, Spain 1808/9. © Bob Marrion

France: Drummer, Guides à Pied de Bonaparte, Egypt 1801. © Bob Marrion

the armies themselves – indeed, the artillery was still under a different government department in some countries, such as Britain. Needless to say, this led to difficulties and somewhat erratic standards.

- **Engineers** were highly qualified individuals who designed fortresses, fortifications and earthworks for the defence of strategically important places. Vauban was probably the most famous example of a military engineer. These people also held the secrets of attacking the places they had designed! Their work was therefore the stuff of sieges. The city of Lille is a splendid example of the engineer's art.

- **Sappers and miners**, who were often volunteers from the line regiments, were the men who dug the 'saps', 'lines' or 'parallels' (types of entrenchments), of the attacking force during a siege, or burrowed underneath the walls of an enemy fortress to lay explosive charges intended to demolish the fortifications. Their work was extremely dangerous, and the men usually received a bounty for their bravery. In most armies, they were organised separately.

- **Pioneers** were primarily big, strong men with carpentry and building skills, the predecessors of the modern combat engineer. They were often attached to regiments a few at a time, and were used to clear and repair the march routes, construct palisades or other wooden defences and so on. Originally regarded as artisans and labourers of little value, pioneers gradually won respect as tough and brave men and many are remembered for their heroic deeds in battle.

- **Surgeons** ranged from the genuinely dedicated scholar of medicine to the barber's shop quack. Wounds received in horse and musket period battles, compounded by the shock of amputation without anaesthetics – other than liquor – and post-operative infection resulting from unsterilised surgical instruments and the lack of antibiotics, frequently resulted in death. One may speculate that the fear of wounds contributed a great deal to rates of desertion. Some countries had more compassion than others, organising stretcher bearers and hospitals, but it was not until later in Napoleonic times that medicine was given a higher level of prestige as a result of the work of Baron Larrey.

- **Musicians** in the form of bands of drums, brass and woodwind instruments, featured in all armies of the time, particularly once the 'cadenced' march in step was introduced. The drum or bugle was used to relay orders to the troops above the din of battle, and every army had tales of courageous men who continued to play whilst in grave danger. Less well publicised is the equally common vanishing of those types at the first shot! As noncombatants, musicians traditionally served as stretcher bearers and medical assistants.

- **Farriers** were a type of vet-cum-blacksmith attached to the cavalry. As well as their primary job of keeping the horses properly shod, they were also issued with axes to dispatch wounded or suffering horses and then cut off a hoof as proof to their country's exchequer that the horse had died.
- **Pontoniers** were specialists trained and equipped to create and then dismantle bridges for the army. Their name derives from the word 'pontoon', a type of flat-bottomed boat. Anything from just a few to dozens of these would be anchored in place across a river, and decking laid between them across which the troops could march. Access to a good pontoon train could give a general excellent strategic possibilities.

Organisation and tactics

INFANTRY

The basic infantry unit was the battalion, consisting of some 500-1000 men. A regiment could consist of more than one battalion, but the first battalion was usually the senior, with second or third battalions often remaining at the regimental depot for recruitment and training purposes.

The battalion was further subdivided into companies, usually of about 50-100 men. In most armies, one company in each battalion was composed of grenadiers, though as we have seen, these were frequently detached and joined with other grenadier companies to form élite units. In some cases, there was also a company of light infantry or *Jäger*, sometimes even armed with rifles, though curiously, Napoleon forbade his troops from using this more accurate weapon.

When using its muskets, a battalion was normally divided into 'firings' or platoons. These did not always perform as strict subdivisions of companies, but the idea was for the firings to shoot in a strict sequence, so that there was always a reserve of loaded muskets. Some armies simply fired by ranks. In the stress, noise and smoke of battle, however, sooner or later this complex process usually degenerated into men firing at will (known in German as *Heckenfeuer* or *Rottenfeuer*), with or without commands.

A battalion usually marched in column, but deployed into line to fight. Columns, though a matter of academic debate (particularly in France), appear not to have been used very often for attacks. The principal reasons seem to have been the untidiness of it, the inability of the officers to control the 'herd' instinct of men bunched together in a dense column, and the fact that such closely packed men presented an ideal target for artillery. It is reasonable to speculate that the column was itself the formalisation of the tendency of frightened men to bunch together.

A line was normally three ranks deep, sometimes four, and *in extremis* might form up in only two ranks. Three ranks seems to have been the compromise between protecting against cavalry and bringing as many muskets as possible to bear. Fans of the British army might like to note that the famous two-deep line was developed quite late in the period, as a result of its experiences in the American War of Independence.

The square, as a defensive formation against cavalry, was little used early in the period, but became more common during the Napoleonic Wars. This was partly due to the greater discipline and firepower of the eighteenth century soldier, who seemed not to require the reassurance which the square provided. Nevertheless, once an army began to retreat, leaving gaps in the line, or when a body of troops on the march found itself ambushed by hordes of hussars or Cossacks, then the square was certainly a sensible option for self-defence.

Infantry usually advanced slowly, with frequent stops to check alignment – the trickier the terrain, the more stops they made. A stately 60-75 paces per minute was the norm, with muskets shouldered to prevent nervous men from firing too soon.

Firefights usually began at a range of under 200 metres, a distance that would make the serried ranks sitting ducks with modern weaponry, but which was considered long range in the smoothbore era. In fact, it was only when troops were within 100 metres or less that musketry became really effective and some volleys were delivered virtually toe to toe.

Most fights were decided by musketry alone, the side suffering heavier casualties tending to conclude that enough was enough and heading to

A close-range musketry duel between Brunswick and French troops of the Napoleonic era in 1815. 28mm Perry Miniatures in action at the Partizan show. The little LED light 'flames' in the kapok smoke are a lovely touch.

Crunch! A classic infantry melee ensues as massed French columns crash into a battalion of Nassauers in line. This is going to be messy! Ideally, the attacking columns would have been harassed by skirmishers as they approached and then sent packing by a determined volley, followed by a charge – but things look bad for the unfortunate men of the German duchy here.

the rear. The point at which this happened was influenced by other factors too, such as leadership, the support and encouragement of other units, the terrain – even how tired the men were.

Attacks with the bayonet rarely caused many casualties, but often had a striking morale effect, particularly once steady volleys had sapped the resolve of the defenders. The usual outcome was that the defenders made off in great haste rather than hang around to be skewered.

Hand to hand fighting, or melee as it is known, was far more likely to occur in confined spaces such as houses or fortifications, or in chance encounters in woods or fog. Some authors point to the lack of recorded bayonet wounds as evidence that melees almost never occurred – but a trained soldier would often parry with the bayonet, then smash the butt of his musket into the enemy's chin (or other soft parts), rendering him just as *hors de combat* as if he had been stabbed. In a tight corner, an unconscious opponent is as good as a dead one! There are recorded instances, however, of the ferocity of Hungarians and Croats in particular, who regularly carried – and used – a vicious sabre.

Against cavalry, infantry would hope to bring down sufficient horses and riders with musketry to literally form a barrier to their progress, slowing them down so that more volleys could be delivered to discourage them altogether. Even if the horsemen did manage to come to close quarters, all was not necessarily lost for cool-headed infantry who presented a continuous hedge of bayonets – horses do not like sharp and shiny objects thrust at their noses, and they shy away. Disordered or shaky troops, however, could expect to be burst through and sabred by determined cavalry, and routing troops could expect little mercy.

The lighter troops, such as *Grenzer* and *Jäger*, performed rather different duties. *Grenzer* were capable of marching and fighting like troops of the line, but were rather less disciplined and nowhere near as controllable.

Perhaps the most famous light infantry of all, thanks to the novels of Bernard Cornwell: the 95th Rifles in action in broken ground in Spain, lying in ambush for the hapless French. The beautiful miniatures are the creation of Bill Gaskin, terrain by Paul Darnell.

Happiest in broken terrain and tricky country, they were masters of *la petite guerre*, launching raids and ambushes. Provided that they did not meet determined opposition from regular troops, they did rather well, and were justifiably feared.

Jäger, on the other hand, fought in open formations and extended order, acting on individual initiative, using trees, bushes, rocks, walls, fences and minor undulations in the ground as cover. They excelled at picking off officers and NCOs, producing a morale effect on their opponents far in excess of the number of casualties they inflicted. The downside of their tactics, however, made them extremely vulnerable when attacked by formed bodies, especially cavalry, and they would ordinarily avoid approaching too close lest they were caught. Their weapons allowed them to keep their distance, however – rifles were capable of reasonably accurate fire at 300 metres or more, but were slower to load owing to the difficulty of ramming a 'patched'[1] ball down the rifled barrel. For this reason, *Jäger* often worked in pairs, covering each other in turn. Many nations were worried by the *Jäger*'s use of individual initiative in an age when rigid discipline was prized, and there were never very many of them until the Napoleonic era, when their numbers grew exponentially. In Britain, the ground-breaking Light Division fought in the Peninsula and there surely cannot be anyone with even a passing interest in military history who has not heard of The Rifles, the famous 95th Regiment and 5th Battalion, 60th Regiments of Foot made famous by the exploits of Richard Sharpe in Bernard Cornwell's novels.

---

1   *The bullet was wrapped in a patch of greased, thin cloth, leather or pigskin to help it grip the rifling when the weapon was fired, thus improving accuracy. See http://www.95thrifles.com/Old-Website/Articles/Patch/*

THE SQUARE

At this point, I really must say something about the famous 'square' formation which is such a characteristic of the Napoleonic period in particular, though it also features in various forms in many eras both before and after. A square was normally created by a unit of infantry threatened by cavalry. In essence, a battalion would halt, and then 'fold back' the companies on either side of its centre company to form two sides and a rear, all facing outwards. This was obviously quicker to perform if the battalion was in column, rather than stretched out in a long line.

In order to make itself a true bastion of defence, the sides of the square needed to be at least three, preferably four ranks deep. The front rank would kneel, the butts of their muskets on the ground beside their right knees for solidity, with their fixed bayonets pointing up at roughly 45 degrees. The second rank would stand, muskets with fixed bayonets thrust forward 'at the ready'. This would then leave the rear one or two ranks able to fire through the intervals. This compact formation would, therefore, present a formidable hedge of bayonets towards the enemy cavalry which, as we have seen, were not likely to wish to impale themselves on this fearsome abatis[2] of steel.

The important thing about a square is that it has no flanks. Unlike a line, or even a column, it makes no difference from which angle the enemy approaches – wherever they come from, they are greeted by the certainty of sharp, steel points if they come too close, and the additional possibility of being shot.

This latter fact is not quite so straightforward. Let's imagine our average enemy dragoon, say, mounted on his large horse of sixteen to seventeen hands height, together with all his equipment as described above. We are probably talking about a total weight close to a ton.

What your average infantryman does not want is that lot dropping on his head, especially if it arrives at a steady trot or canter, ranging from perhaps ten to twenty miles per hour. (As we have seen, the nature of the beast itself, the desire to maintain cohesion and the likelihood of churned-up ground makes it unlikely that many charges were delivered at a full, rolling gallop.) It doesn't take much arithmetic to work out that the potential force at the point of impact would be colossal, and in fact the few instances of a formed square being successfully broken and destroyed by cavalry were mostly caused by just this: a dead or dying horse and its rider careering into the side of a square, crushing the defenders beneath it or injuring them with its flailing legs, allowing the rest of the cavalry to pour through the gap and set about the infantry. (The battle of Garcia Hernandez in Spain, 1812, is just one such instance.)

Therefore, it became a matter of nice judgement not only when to give the order to form square so that it was fully closed by the time the cavalry

---

2 An abatis was a formidable obstacle formed of the branches or trunks of trees laid in a row, with their sharpened tops pointing towards the enemy.

arrived, but also when to actually shoot at the attacking cavalry. The Battle of Waterloo in 1815 is a famous example of where the French cavalry swirled around the British squares, their tight squadron formations broken and unable to penetrate the defenders, and themselves being picked off by the infantry as they passed. Ideally, therefore, the infantry would wish to hold their fire until they were certain that shooting would not endanger their own formation. In addition, given that it would take even the best-trained infantry twenty to thirty seconds to reload their muskets, they would have to be certain that they had a reserve of loaded muskets at all times, lest the enemy cavalry took advantage of the face of a square suddenly being entirely denuded of its firepower.

A square could, of course, be formed by more than one unit, and indeed there are many instances of two or more battalions, even an entire brigade, combining to form a much larger square formation. This happened at Waterloo, where the entire ridgeline commanded by Wellington was covered by infantry squares in a mutually-supporting chequerboard formation, making a true death trap for the repeated mass cavalry charges delivered by Marshal Ney.

Looking at earlier times in the horse and musket era, we are more hard-pressed to find instances of battalion squares being formed to repel cavalry in major battles, but they were most certainly used in difficult country when threatened by those vagabonds of war, the hussars or *Grenzer*, or when the infantry as a whole felt vulnerable. During the Marlburian period, there were indeed examples of huge squares being formed, as described by David Chandler:

> "At Fleurus in 1690, for example, the Dutch foot formed a vast square of 16 battalions after the flight of their cavalry, and proceeded to execute a model withdrawal to Charleroi which Luxembourg was in no way able to prevent. A second outstanding example was in July 1705, when 10 Bavarian battalions under the Comte de Caraman formed up into one square at Elixhem – again after the rout of their supporting horsemen – and successfully held off Marlborough's cavalry attacks and outdistanced his foot and guns until they found safety under the guns of Louvain. 'Which plainly shews,' comments General Kane, 'that if a body of Foot have but Resolution to keep their Order, there is no Body of Horse dare venture within their Fire.'"[3]

Now, here's Christopher Duffy, the premier historian of the Seven Years War, describing the Austrian use of squares just a few decades later:

> "Squares were formed by one, two, three or four battalions at once. The procedures at the time of the Seven Years War were so slow and difficult as to be virtually inapplicable in a full-scale

---

3 David Chandler, p.122-3, "The Art of Warfare in the Age of Marlborough", Spellmount, Staplehurst, Kent, 1997

Infantry in squares arranged in a mutually-supporting chequerboard formation near La Haye Sainte on the field of Waterloo await the onslaught of massed French cavalry. 28mm figures from a game staged by Loughton Strike Force at Salute.

battle, and were attempted only *in extremis* when an isolated unit was in danger of being overwhelmed by cavalry during a retreat or in open country. Even then, wrote Cogniazzo, any trust which the troops might repose in this formation was likely to be misplaced, for unless they knew what it was like to be hit by a cavalry charge, they had no conception of how terrifying the experience could be. An intelligent commander would instead manoeuvre in column and take advantage of any useful features of the ground to cover his flanks, front and rear. More commonly, the infantry faced the horsemen in lines up to six ranks deep, with the rearward ranks reversed if necessary if the cavalry came at them from behind."[4]

And now, let's hear what he has to say about the Prussians of Frederick the Great in respect of the infantry square, for which the most meticulous regulations certainly existed:

"Despite its impressive appearance, the square remained a formation 'which was beloved by the King but scorned by the generals'. Unless a battalion happened to be caught on its own in open ground, it was infinitely simpler to deal with swarming cavalry by causing the rearward rank to turn about and open fire. If the worst came to the worst, and the infantry were swamped by the cavalry, the best hope of survival was to lie flat on the ground, hoping to stay out of reach of the sword blades, and get up again after the cavalry had passed on to other business. The *Battaillon-Garde* was overrun twice in

---

4   Christopher Duffy, p.407, "Instrument of War: Volume 1 of The Austrian Army in the Seven Years War". The Emperor's Press, Rosemont, Illinois, 2000.

this way at Kolin in 1757, yet was able to retire from the field
in a semblance of order."[5]

Mind you, you wouldn't want to try that against Napoleonic lancers or Cossacks!

So why, at the end of the eighteenth century, did forming square suddenly become the fashion again? One of the answers lies in the French Revolution, the *levée en masse* which recruited tens of thousands of raw recruits to the colours, and the response of France's enemies which was, in due course, to mimic this conscription – with the exception of Britain.

As we have seen, well-trained, highly disciplined and steady infantry could still potentially see off attacking cavalry with cool nerves and musketry, but such skills were at a premium. The sheer terror induced by the rumbling approach of cavalry should not be underestimated – watching the Household Cavalry on parade is something I would recommend to any wargamer – and half-trained conscripts, if they are not to run away, need to be corralled. The formations of column and square are ideal for this, because they give the occupants a tremendous sense of security. With their fellows on either side, and the sense that their backs are covered, with the officers and NCOs posted in the centre of the formation close behind them, it is clear to the nervous soldiers that the safest plan for them is to simply stay put.

Even amongst the comparatively highly disciplined British, whilst the two-deep line was an excellent choice for musketry, allowing every weapon to be brought to bear for volley fire, officers knew that for facing cavalry, the square was the only sensible option. The danger of not doing so was brought home with ferocity during the battle of Albuera in 1811, when three infantry regiments of Colborne's brigade were virtually annihilated by French cavalry during a thunderstorm which rendered their muskets unable to fire. A fourth regiment, the 31st Foot, was in fact saved as a result of forming square in time.

It should not be imagined that a square was entirely invulnerable. Apart from the possibility already mentioned of a stricken horse ploughing into the men, it can easily be guessed that such a rigid formation was hardly able to jog around the battlefield. Whilst it is not true to say that squares were completely immobile – there are plenty of examples in history of them shifting position, even covering considerable distances – this would obviously have to be done at a very modest pace indeed in order to maintain the square's cohesion. Usually, the rear of the square would about-face, and the men in the sides would make a quarter turn, before heading off. Naturally, if cavalry approached once more, an emergency stop would have to be made and the men faced outward again, a procedure hardly conducive to winning a race.

Moreover, if the enemy cavalry were supported by infantry or, even

---

5   *Christopher Duffy, p.122, The Army of Frederick the Great, The Emperor's Press, Chicago, Illinois, 1996.*

worse, artillery, then the square was in real trouble. The proximity of the cavalry would force the unit to remain in square, only able to bring one quarter of its muskets to bear compared to any enemy infantry facing them of equivalent strength; and enemy artillery would be able to position itself just outside effective musket range (which, after all, was not much more than 100 metres) and flay the square with a barrage of canister, shot and shell. Such a bombardment would quickly reduce a square to a bloody ruin, as happened to units of Napoleon's Imperial Guard in the closing stages of the battle of Waterloo.

CAVALRY

The basic cavalry unit was the squadron, a regiment consisting of as many as ten squadrons, but more usually four to six. A squadron normally had 120-160 troopers, armed and mounted according to their type. Battle reports tended to speak of the total number of squadrons present, rather than regiments, because squadrons were capable of independent action. In battle, groups of squadrons or regiments formed cavalry brigades.

In previous eras, cavalry had been trained to use mounted firepower and in some armies this theory persisted into the Age of Reason. The manoeuvre, known generally as *caracole*, involved ranks of troops trotting up to the enemy, firing their pistols or carbines, then retiring to reload. Whilst infantry consisted of unwieldy formations of pikes and matchlocks, this was feasible. Even when the bayonet – simply a dagger jammed into the musket barrel – was first introduced, the cavalry was able to persist with the caracole because the infantry couldn't fire! The socket bayonet, however, changed the situation drastically. Cavalry attempting to use firepower found themselves out-ranged and out-shot and they disintegrated under a hail of lead.

Consequently, the charge with cold steel was rekindled after a long

You can imagine the thunder of hooves as massed French cuirassiers advance up the hill. These are 28mm Perry Miniatures, seen during a game at Partizan in May 2009. For the author, heavy cavalry are one of the major attractions of the horse and musket period and using them correctly is one of wargaming's greatest challenges. Marvellous!

absence, and the Prussians in particular turned the heavy cavalry into a formidable shock arm. Faced by Austrians who had more natural ability, the Prussians drilled their cavalry in a rigorously disciplined fashion, to the point that even their hussars could confidently charge on the battlefield. As has been seen, the morale effect of a charge was often greater than the physical impact, since in order to retain alignment and cohesion, the horses were rarely allowed to gallop during the attack, though this was the ultimate aim of Frederick's reforms.

Against opposing cavalry, this remained true, horses not being naturally inclined to use their heads and chests as battering rams. Usually, a passage would be forced through the intervals between the troopers, an exchange of sword thrusts or slashes taking place as they did so. This made cavalry adopt lines two or three ranks deep, with some considerable interval between them, so that second and successive ranks and squadrons acted as a reserve to reinforce an overwhelmed front rank or exploit success.

The heavy broadsword was considered the appropriate weapon for heavy cavalry, riding boot to boot. It was used to thrust at their opponent, the edges often being quite blunt. To prove the point, cavalry wounds from swords were most often found on the right forearm. Light cavalry, particularly hussars, used the curved sabre. This was a slashing and cutting weapon, and consequently they tended to use more open formations which allowed room to wield these weapons. Lances were the preserve of light cavalry types and we have seen that they proved generally unpopular in the eighteenth century. The Lanciers de Saxe appear to have been one of the few units to gain any distinction with this arm – and every lancer in this unit was accompanied by two dragoons! During the Napoleonic wars and after, however, the use of the lance increased enormously, and to devastating effect.

Cavalry were rarely used against fresh, unwavering infantry. A cavalry

Light cavalry reconnaissance. These are 28mm Ural Cossacks, very much from the wilder fringes of Eastern Europe, but used extensively by Russia during the Napoleonic Wars in particular to harry units on the march and cut supply lines. Swarms of Cossacks plagued the French as they retreated from Moscow in 1812, adding to Napoleon's misery. Eureka miniatures painted by Kerry Thomas.

Cavalry in a dismounted role. These dragoons are from Andy McMaster's imagi-nation of Altefritzenburg, part of his 'Legion of the Savage Swans'. Historically, dragoons and light cavalry were often called upon to operate on foot in the reconnaissance role or when they lost their horses, as happened to many French dragoons in the Peninsular War. Napoleon raised entire regiments of foot dragoons.

commander needed the talent of *coup d'oeuil*, the ability to judge the terrain, the state of the enemy and timing, so that a sudden attack could be launched which caught the enemy in the flank or off-balance. When done well, this could lead to the complete collapse of the enemy's line; when poorly judged, a bloody repulse could result.

Cavalry were kept busy off the battlefield by being the eyes and ears of the army. Cavalrymen had to range far and wide to find suitable fodder for their mounts, and this was institutionalised in the light cavalry by using this activity for reconnaissance, ambuscades and intelligence gathering, whilst attempting to prevent the enemy from carrying on the same business. One might think that this gave the cavalryman a golden opportunity to desert, with a horse making his getaway all the easier. It seems, however, that the cavalry were not as prone to desertion as the infantry; whether the superior pay and prestige brought greater loyalty, we can only speculate.

Cavalry also protected the flanks of an army on the march, and had to be ready to wheel into line to drive off attackers. If surprised in this way, we find that the dragoons may have occasionally dismounted to hold a strong point until help arrived. It was also when on picket duty, reconnoitring or out foraging that cavalry used their firearms, both to defend themselves, alert their comrades to danger or shoot a hare for the pot.

ARTILLERY

Field guns and howitzers were normally organised into batteries. Originally, a 'battery' was the earthwork emplacement where siege guns were sited to 'batter down' the enemy's walls; the term then came to be used for a fire unit of four to twelve guns (depending on national artillery organisation) when deployed for battle.

It would be as well to explain the organisational jargon for artillery here since, given what I explained in "Military organisation" on page 286, some confusion might arise. In British service, horse artillery fire-units were 'troops' by analogy with the cavalry they sometimes accompanied; foot artillery fire-units were referred to as 'brigades' when meaning the men, guns, horses and attendant vehicles, but as 'companies' of artillerymen. A two-gun section of a fire-unit of either kind was a 'division'. During the eighteenth century, there was rarely any higher regimental structure for the artillery and we have already seen that many people did not perceive the guns to be part of the 'proper' army.

The guns were extremely heavy and difficult to move. This meant that a commander had to site his guns very carefully at the outset of a battle or siege, since they could not easily be switched to counter unexpected threats. The positions chosen were preferably on a low eminence or ridge, so that they could use their ammunition to best effect.

Batteries tended to be placed along the line to give converging fire to support an attack or provide defensive fire across a broad front; it was in the Napoleonic era that the concept developed of the 'grand battery' consisting of perhaps dozens of pieces. Many battalions of infantry were also provided with little 2–3 pounders, which they dragged along with them, to give added effect to their musketry. Their effectiveness is debatable but they would certainly have had a morale effect.

In theory, artillery could open fire at ranges of a mile or more. However, the main problem was observing the fall of shot or shell, in order to make corrections. Against a moving target, this was clearly absurd. Similarly, it was considered dishonourable to aim at individuals such as generals. The artillery confined its showing off, therefore, to shooting at the enemy's own artillery in an attempt to either destroy it or force it to move position.

By far the most common tactic was to bombard the dense troop concentrations of the enemy's foot and horse. Whilst the theoretical

Napoleon's first love, the artillery – though this battery is ranged against the French! This impressive Prussian artillery was seen in a game staged by the League of Gentleman Wargamers at The Other Partizan in Newark, September 2008. A wonderful array of cannon and gunners, and even the equipment needed to refit guns in the field, is supported by squadrons of Landwehr lancers.

Ah, now Bonaparte is happy! A quite superb 28mm rendition of French Napoleonic artillery by Barry Hilton, based in accordance with his *Republic to Empire* rules which are more realistic than most rulesets in portraying the area that should be occupied by a battery in action. Here, it's absolutely clear that supporting units could not possibly just casually stroll through a deployed battery. *Magnifique*!

maximum range of even a smoothbore cannon might be as much as a couple of kilometres in ideal conditions, fire commenced at well under 1500m in the majority of cases. The first few rounds would be ranging shots, so by the time really effective fire began, the range to an advancing enemy would probably be 800m or less. The cannonade would continue until the enemy was under 400m distant, when the gunners would ordinarily switch to canister, unless the foe was ensconced in some strong point or building.

Howitzer shells would not be fired at less than about 100m range, as the barrel could not be elevated sufficiently. Much closer, and the shells would in any case be dangerous to the gunners firing them.

Another serious limitation faced by artillery was smoke. The battlefields of the eighteenth century were smothered by billowing clouds of the stuff, the result of black powder propellants for both cannon and muskets. Like a dense fog, this meant that you could often not see the man beside you, let alone an enemy unit 2,000 metres away. This also reduced rates of fire, since there is no point shooting at a target you can't see. Moreover, recognition of friend and foe became a nice business, and one can find several instances of fire being held for heart-pounding minutes as a unit approached in order to discover its true identity, and just as many cases of tragic misidentification when units blazed away at units they didn't recognize – losses to 'friendly fire' or 'blue on blue', in modern parlance.

The artillery was horse-drawn by teams of four to ten horses – even more for the heavy siege pieces. A transition was gradually made from having the horses in tandem to having them in abreast, which obviously reduced the road space occupied by the guns and utilised the strength of the horses more effectively.

Ammunition for resupply on the battlefield was carried in caissons.

These were special wagons, usually containing a combination of shot or shell and canister, together with pre-measured, bagged charges of powder. The caisson also often had a spare wheel for the cannon carriage. Larger wagons would be employed for the transport of ammunition on the march.

The limber was the means of attaching the harness of the horses to the gun itself for transporting the weapon around the battlefield and on the march. The limber might often have a box containing sufficient ammunition to commence an engagement, and often in early horse artillery, the gunners sat precariously on the limbers.

Horse artillery was an attempt to give mobile fire support to units of cavalry, and Frederick the Great was a great experimenter in this respect. Do not, however, confuse the capabilities of eighteenth century horse artillery with its much more numerous, fast and powerful Napoleonic equivalent.

Grand tactics and strategy

Small wonder that the majority of commanders preferred to avoid pitched battle in the Age of Reason. The troops were expensive to recruit, train and maintain; the general's sovereign would be clamouring for 'safe' successes; disease and desertion would be nibbling away at the strength of his army; allies would be causing politically strenuous situations; and given equal numbers, the outcome of a battle might as well be decided by the toss of a coin. Sieges were so much more scientific, it seemed, so that once a place was surrounded it was possible to calculate fairly accurately, barring disasters, when it would fall.

Just as Marlborough stood this concept on its head at the beginning of the eighteenth century, so Frederick the Great was to do during the mid eighteenth century and Napoleon at the turn of the nineteenth. During the War of the Austrian Succession and the Seven Years War, the Prussians had a superbly disciplined army, but it was inferior in numbers to its enemies. Frederick could not afford the luxury of detaching armies to besiege heavily fortified towns in a leisurely campaign, yet still have sufficient troops in hand to ward off a relieving force. Nor could he afford campaigns of gentle manoeuvre with no result, since the ring of enemies he faced threatened the very existence of Prussia. Similarly, Napoleon felt himself surrounded by enemies, and had to adopt an aggressive campaigning style to eliminate his opponents in quick succession. Of course, this would eventually land him in trouble by making more enemies...

Decisive encounters on the battlefield thus allowed the Prussians, and then later the French, to use their prowess, and Frederick and Napoleon to use their particular tactical genius to the greatest effect. Their repeated ability to trounce their enemies was remarkable, but they did not always have things their own way. Their opponents learned to counter many of their tactics, so that by the end of their supremacy, neither Prussia nor France had achieved as much as their battle honours might seem to indicate.

In broad terms, the dispositions of an army in battle array depended on a number of factors:

- The terrain to be fought over
- The number, type and quality and of troops at hand
- The numbers and dispositions of the enemy
- The amount of time available for preparation
- The character of the commander
- The system of precedence and honour

Whilst most of these factors seem straightforward, the last might need some comment. In the seventeenth and eighteenth centuries, the regiments in an army were graded in terms of seniority, or precedence. Thus a guard cavalry unit would obviously take precedence over a militia infantry battalion. However, the system often had roots in the actual date a unit was raised – the 'older' the regiment, the more seniority attached to it. This was complicated by whether the unit was granted royal favours, and the position in the nobility occupied by the colonel of the regiment, who might also be a general commanding a brigade of regiments! We can imagine the arguments that resulted as commanders jostled for their proper place in the line of battle, and the potential disasters resulting from trampled egos.

An army usually formed up in two or three lines of units, the rearmost acting as reserve. The most prestigious placing was at the right of the first line, then the left, then the right of the second line and so on. This produced a rather hidebound and inflexible disposition which only an above average commander could overcome.

Frederick the Great usually broke this static, linear mould by concentrating his attack on the flank of his enemy, overthrowing it and then rolling up the rest of the opponents' line. The 'oblique order' was a general description of this type of attack, and was useful for an army fighting against greater odds.

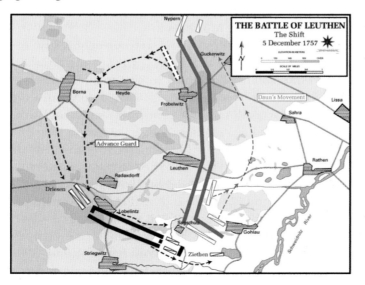

Frederick the Great's finest moment: his outflanking of the Austrian army at Leuthen in 1756 using what has become known as the 'oblique order'. *Map: Wikimedia Commons, created by the United States Military Academy's Department of History. Cartographers Mr. Edward J. Krasnoborski and Mr. Frank Martini.*

The Emperor Napoleon benefited from the French Revolution having completely overthrown the system of aristocratic privilege. Units were grouped together into self-contained divisions and corps, able to act independently both on the march and in battle. This system proved strategically devastating in the early campaigns against more hide-bound opponents of the old regime, with the curious exception of the British in the Peninsular War. Ironically, however, the Marshals of the Empire appointed by Napoleon himself created their own system of rivalries and jealousies which were to provide the undoing of Napoleon's own plans on several occasions! Moreover, France's enemies learned quickly, and by the end of the Napoleonic Wars the Prussians in particular had created their own army organisation out of the ashes of defeat which eventually enabled them to play a key part not only in Napoleon's defeat at Waterloo, but also to eventually dominate the third quarter of the nineteenth century.

There is insufficient space here to describe all the campaigns and battles of this period. I strongly suggest that if the mere taste I have given in this introductory section has interested you, then put the Bibliography to good use at your nearest library or online. The majority of wargamers gradually accumulate their own libraries of reference works on their favourite period and any newcomer who joins a wargames club or an online forum will find veterans of a generous nature from whom they may borrow or glean information.

Tactical tips

The essence of battlefield tactics is not so different from chess, in that what you are seeking to achieve is an overwhelming superiority of force at what the Germans call the *Schwerpunkt*, the point of greatest effort. In chess, this means bringing your most powerful pieces to bear on the opponent's king, until it has nowhere to go, which is known as 'checkmate'. Notice that just as in war, some chess pieces can act at 'long range', like the queen, bishop or rook; and others need to get close in to be effective, like the pawns and knights, even your own king.

In a wargame, this translates as finding your enemy's weak spot, and channelling everything you do to achieve a breakthrough right there. This will require an understanding of how long it takes for each troop type to reach that place on the battlefield, and what they can do once they get there, which is something you learn from experience and practice, practice, practice. Obviously, artillery can strike from a long distance, but is even more powerful if it can get in close; cavalry can charge from some way off, but have to achieve their victories at close quarters with sword or lance; whereas infantry are slower, but have the benefit of musketry to blast away from a modest range; and light infantry can snipe and wear down the enemy at the critical point from a safe distance.

Really, it's not so different from that childhood game of paper-scissors-stone. Artillery can cause carnage, but heaven forfend if the cavalry manage to get amongst them; cavalry are tremendously dangerous if they

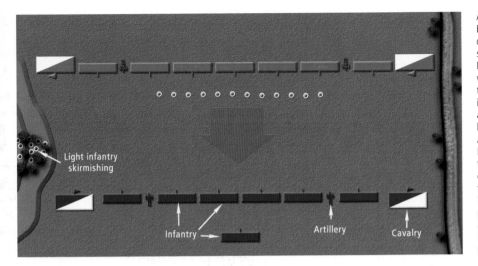

A solid defence by Blue, making use of difficult terrain to secure either flank. Note the small, but vital reserve and the skirmishing infantry taking advantage of both height and cover. An unimaginative Red enemy would find it difficult and costly to break through a defence like this, needing perhaps as much as a 50% superiority in numbers to be sure of victory.

Light infantry skirmishing

Infantry

Artillery

Cavalry

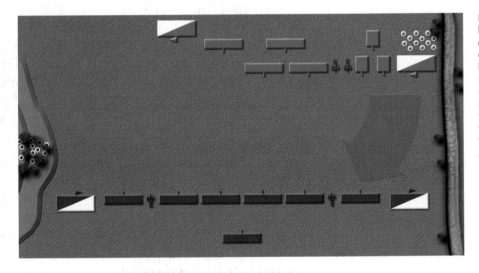

Here, Red focuses his strength on one part of the enemy's line, hoping to crush it before Blue can respond. Artillery is massed to destroy the 'schwerpunkt' where the blow will be delivered. A variant of the 'oblique order', this relies on speed and determination. Note infantry deployed in column for moving quickly with cavalry and skirmisher support.

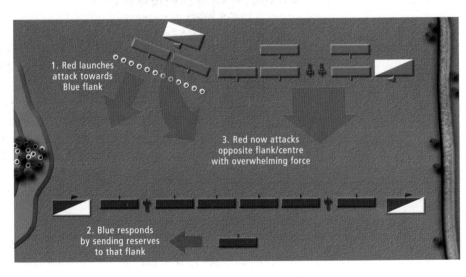

1. Red launches attack towards Blue flank

3. Red now attacks opposite flank/centre with overwhelming force

2. Blue responds by sending reserves to that flank

Red uses a diversionary attack to draw in the enemy's reserves before delivering the fatal blow elsewhere. This requires very fine judgement and timing, but can be devastating if successful. Note how Red's right flank cavalry appears to be supporting one attack, but can then switch rapidly to protect the flank of the main thrust.

can close fast enough, perhaps from an unexpected direction, to catch infantry or artillery off-guard; and infantry can blast away to great effect, but are slow and vulnerable to the range of artillery or the speed and power of cavalry if taken unawares.

Of course, one of the skills of generalship is not letting your opponent realise that you have spotted their weakness until the last possible moment. This may mean making feints or diversionary attacks at other places on the battlefield, whilst husbanding your troops in preparation for the big punch. For example, you might send your light cavalry to cause a real nuisance on one flank, whilst planning to attack on the other. With luck, this attack will grab your opponent's attention, leading him to feed reinforcements into that sector until bang! – in goes your main attack, just when he has run out of responses.

Your tactics in a battle will be decided by a number of factors. The simplest type of battlefield formation is to have your infantry in the centre, with cavalry on the flanks. Place your artillery in a position affording the optimum field of fire: moving it after battle commences is both slow and a waste of good time in which it could be inflicting casualties. You may have a contingent of horse artillery providing more mobile firepower to soften up enemy units which your cavalry will attack.

Another thing to try is to use 'dead ground' to switch troops from one flank to another. This is a gambit often overlooked because of the 'helicopter view' of most wargames. Assume, therefore, that you agree with your opponent that you will allow 'hidden' movement by way of sketch maps of the battlefield, or some other agreed mechanism. Units could therefore appear initially on one flank, and then slink away via map movement to appear at a critical moment on the opposite flank, just as happened in several real-life battles. (This ploy is made much easier if you have a willing umpire for your game, who can monitor all such activity with impartiality.)

Always pay attention to the terrain in your games. You can, of course, just play on a boring, green cloth with no features whatsoever, but you'll soon grow tired of that. Strive to portray more realistic terrain, and your games will become hugely more challenging and enjoyable. A river with a bridge creates enormous problems for a general if there's an enemy waiting on the other side. Logically, if there's a bridge, there will probably be a settlement of some kind, ranging from a small hamlet to an entire city. And if you're in a river valley, there will probably be low-lying, marshy ground that impedes movement. And perhaps a copse of trees or two... You get the picture.

Now, think about your army. If you've got to take that bridge, placing your artillery will be critical. You want to keep the enemy away from the crossing, but without endangering your own men, so shooting straight up the road to the bridge not only lacks imagination, but you'll be cursing after a couple of moves when your own men block your field of fire. Your cavalry will love the open spaces and flat ground on either side of the river, and of course they can move fast, but they'll be in real trouble if you lead them into the marshes or they get tangled up fighting in woods or city streets. For that you need your infantry, who are great at both taking and holding ground and, more specifically, your light infantry types will be right at home where the going is tricky and they can make up for lack of numbers by using trees, walls, hedges and bushes as cover.

On the other hand, if you're the one defending, you'll probably have fewer troops (at least, I hope so, or the attacker will have next to no chance and besides, wargames with identical sides are really, really dull – this is where wargames really differ from chess), so it's extremely important to spot your own weaknesses and plug them. Try to put yourself in your opponent's shoes. If you were them, what would you be trying to do? Where does the terrain favour the defence or the attack? At what point is he going to be most vulnerable? Certainly, the moment they step onto that bridge is going to be critical – can you place your artillery and infantry to make it a deathtrap? Are there any other points on the river that are fordable where he could potentially outflank you? Can you shelter your troops from the inevitable incoming bombardment? And critically, how much of your force can you set aside as a reserve, out of harm's way until absolutely needed? I have seen a handful of infantry or a squadron of cavalry completely change the fortunes of a game when thrown in just as the enemy tide has crested the defences, to then be thrown back pell-mell in utter rout.

For your own sake, apart from any stipulation in the rules, you should make a sketch map of your dispositions and write down the objectives of your army at the beginning of the game, which will only allow a certain degree of latitude to your individual battalions and squadrons. Objectives for your army may be as simple or as complex as you like – but remember that the more complicated the plan, the more can go wrong. The best tactics tend to be simple, but a shrewd commander will take into account the possibility of victory or defeat, and have contingency plans to match.

Don't be afraid to experiment if the terrain or the troops under your command demand an unconventional approach. But if you stray too far from the historical possibilities, the rules will penalize you. For example, opening fire with muskets at extreme range is unlikely to cause many casualties. Two hundred years on, we have a great deal of hindsight, and the temptation is to use troops in a fashion more reminiscent of later periods. Don't do it! If you want to indulge in some fantasy and pit a Napoleonic army against a Frederican one, then go ahead – but don't try to fool yourself into believing that it looks like the eighteenth century.

And finally, forgive me for repeating this, but always keep a reserve! *I'll say that again*: **always keep a reserve**! Having a reserve will allow you to turn a win into an outright victory, or prevent a defeat from becoming an undignified rout. Depending on the battle, a reserve might be a single company of infantry or squadron of cavalry or a whole division. Its size is often immaterial – it is its morale effect which counts.

A huge 15mm game based on the battle of Aspern-Essling 1809, staged by Loughton Strike Force at SELWG 2012. The French are advancing from the left to meet the Austrians arriving from the right. Here you can see some of the items commonly used by wargamers who play Dave Brown's *General de Brigade* rules, such as devices for recording casualties and the current state of units.

The simple pleasures of a game of *Shot, Steel and Stone* played at home. This 'old school' look is still loved by many, but is entirely a matter of my personal choice – you can use whatever figures you like, in whatever scale, painted and based to the standard that pleases you. A game using my rules, but played with, say, Pendraken 10mm Napoleonics, or Fife & Drum 28mm American War of Independence miniatures, or even Baccus 6mm Marlburian figures, would look very different. Wargaming is a very personal hobby and only you can decide on 'the look' you wish to achieve. Over to you...

SHOT, STEEL AND STONE

The Rules

The scope of the rules

- These rules are suitable for actions set in Europe, North America and South America in the period 1685-1845 or thereabouts. Future works will deal with periods to either side of this rather broad era.

- Options are given for representational figure scales averaging 1:30 and an 'old school' option of around 1:15. However, the base or 'element' is the important part of this game, not the number of miniatures placed upon it, which the player is at liberty to change to suit their own taste and, indeed, wallet. As a result, there is no need to re-base any armies you already have.

- The ground scale is not precise, but may be taken to equate about 1.5mm to 1 metre, or 1:667 for the standard game, and half this for the 'old school' variant, so 3mm to 1 metre or 1:333.

- Base Widths (hereinafter BW) will be used as units of measurement.

- For the standard game, each complete turn may be taken to approximate 20-30 minutes of actual 'battle' time. A game representing an entire day may therefore be fought in perhaps 12-24 turns, depending on the forces engaged. I recommend the use of scenarios and proper objectives in conjunction with acceptable losses to determine actual game length. Small games can be played in between two and four hours.

- References are made to d5, also known as average dice or dAv, marked 2, 3, 3, 4, 4, 5 (simply re-roll any 1s or 6s on a normal six-sided die); d3 (1, 1, 2, 2, 3, 3, so count 1 and 2 as 1; 3 and 4 as 2; and 5 and 6 as 3); and finally d2, which means 1, 2 or 3 count as 1; and 4, 5 or 6 count as 2. Standard d6 always means 1, 2, 3, 4, 5 and 6.

- A free Quick Reference Sheet may be downloaded from the website accompanying this book at *www.thewargamingcompendium.com*, where you will also find additional material for and commentary on the rules.

- It is deemed that every point on the battlefield can be seen from every other point unless terrain or scenery is interposed or, with the agreement of both players, weather conditions apply as part of a campaign or specifically designed scenario.

- If a situation arises that is not specifically covered by the rules, flip a coin, roll a dice or just make something up and accept the outcome like gentlemen!

Armour classes and dressing

For most of the horse and musket era games you will play, the vast majority of the troops you will use are unarmoured, with the exception of cuirassiers.

Unarmoured	Troops wearing no armour at all, with the possible exception of some kind of helmet or protective headgear, whether infantry or cavalry. They may even be naked or semi-naked, but in any case not wearing anything offering greater protection than ordinary cotton or woollen fabric on their bodies, however extravagantly embellished (e.g. hussars). The majority of troop types from this period of history wear no armour and operate in open, loose or close order.
Heavy	Troops wearing more metal protection such as cuirass, tall boots made of stiff leather, thick leather gauntlets and epaulettes to protect the shoulders. They always wear a helmet. Cavalry horses might not be armoured at all. These troops operate in close order.
Extra Heavy	Mounted troops from very early in the period who still wore more armour than the 'Heavy category described above, such as tassets to cover the thighs and armour for the upper arm. However, their horses are unlikely to be armoured. These troops operate in close order.

Morale Classes

Class	Description
A	Élite: regular guards, grenadiers, irregular fanatics and personal bodyguards, veteran regulars and other distinguished troops; and picked or hardened irregulars
B	Steady: trained regulars with combat experience, experienced warrior irregulars
C	Suspect: poorly trained regulars, militia, inexperienced or timid irregulars, pressed levy and otherwise unwilling or timid troops

Basing troops

Artillery should be mounted facing the short edge, all others facing the long edge.

The standard base size for 20-30mm figures is 60mm x 40mm. (I actually base my own Spencer Smith infantry on 45mm x 40mm because I prefer a more closely-packed look with these slender miniatures, and this applies to many of the earlier 'old school' manufacturers and 25mm miniatures. However, **note that our Base Width measurement remains at 60mm.*** *See note overleaf.*) And remember, I have already said that *you do not have to re-base your troops if you prefer not to do so.*

For 15mm troops, I recommend reducing the standard base width by a third to 40mm x 30mm or thereabouts. For 10mm or smaller scales, I recommend bases of 40mm x 20mm, but mount more miniatures per base.

Alternatively, you could reduce base size to 30mm x 20mm or smaller in order to increase the number of units on the table. As long as the system you use is consistent, it really doesn't matter and the individual wargamer can choose whatever suits his own collection best.

- Close order infantry should be based six miniatures per base.

- Loose order infantry should be based five miniatures per base.

- Open order infantry should be based four miniatures per base.

- Skirmishing infantry should be based three miniatures per base.

- Close or loose order cavalry should be based three miniatures per base.

- Skirmishing cavalry should be based two miniatures per base.

- Artillery can optionally not be based permanently, but arranged as one gun and its crew on a temporary base when deployed, with limbers and so on based separately. Battalion guns, where present, require a crew of two per gun; light artillery three; medium artillery four; heavy artillery five; and howitzers three per gun. These crews also indicate the normal number of dice to be thrown when shooting.

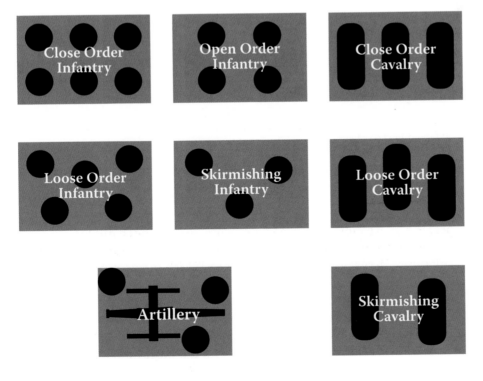

Infantry capable of skirmishing or operating on close/loose order can, if you prefer, be duplicated on different bases OR mounted as close/loose order and then moved apart with a gap of one base width between them when skirmishing. They could also, for example, be mounted as two separate bases of a single rank of three each, and then moved into a long, thin line when skirmishing. It's really up to you!

Close Order regular infantry and cavalry should be mounted as neatly as possible in straight lines. Irregular, Loose Order infantry and cavalry and skirmishers should be placed more randomly. Open Order is actually a formation adopted by highly trained troops, and so whilst there is more space between models, they should still be placed in an orderly fashion.

The horse and musket era saw some really huge battles, so the use of smaller scale miniatures is recommended to those who would prefer to act as a true general. Some suggestions are given in the Resources section.

Note from "Basing troops" on page 358
*The astute reader will recognise that placing infantry on smaller bases than cavalry will result in the infantry having more bases able to fight in melee – one extra, in fact, per 180mm of frontage. Given the historical ability of eighteenth-century infantry to repel cavalry, I am comfortable with this decision and playtesting has shown that heavy cavalry, well handled, are still perfectly capable of overcoming this numerical disparity. As an option, if your eighteenth century infantry are mounted on 60mm x 40mm bases, you may wish to give them a bonus of +1 against cavalry in melee.

Unit size

Size	Bases	Notes
Extra Small (XS)	1 (2)	The equivalent of perhaps a company or two of infantry or squadron of cavalry, roughly 150-200 men. A single gun or howitzer model.
Small (S)	2 (4)	An under-strength unit, or small battalion or regiment of 300-400 men. Two gun or howitzer models.
Normal (N)	3 (6)	The standard operating unit for infantry or cavalry, equating to something like a battalion or regiment at campaign strength of around 500 to 600 men. Three gun or howitzer models.
Large (L)	4 (8)	A powerful battalion or regiment or well turned-out warband or other irregular unit at full strength or thereabouts, numbering up to perhaps 800 men. Four gun or howitzer models.
Extra Large (XL)	5 (10)	An exceptionally large unit of up to 1,000 men. This is an extremely unusual size for a regular unit, but might be achieved by a 'gathering of the clans' or a pressed levy. Quantity should not, of course, be mistaken for quality. Five gun or howitzer models.

- The unit sizes in brackets reflect what in amongst wargamers have come to be called 'old school' preferences for visually appealing units consisting of an average of 36 miniatures or more. All weapon ranges and other distances in these rules have been adapted to suit this. It is perfectly feasible to halve these numbers in order to fit more, smaller units on the tabletop.

- Note that the 'old school' variant is much better for representing intermediate sizes of artillery battery, such as six or ten guns. For Reaction test purposes, such a battery counts as the next higher size.

- Units of infantry act as cohesive bodies. Detaching sub-units is not permissible before the Napoleonic period unless specified by the scenario. However, the standard unit for cavalry, consistently referred to in contemporary Orders of Battle, was the **squadron**, which would normally be represented by two to four bases. A full regiment of cavalry might consist of anything from two to eight squadrons.

- Note that until the late eighteenth century, many armies allocated small calibre (often 3-pdr) 'battalion' guns to their infantry in varying numbers. For simplicity, if using the 'old school' variant, these rules permit one battalion gun model per infantry battalion, crewed by two figures dressed in the same fashion as the parent infantry unit.

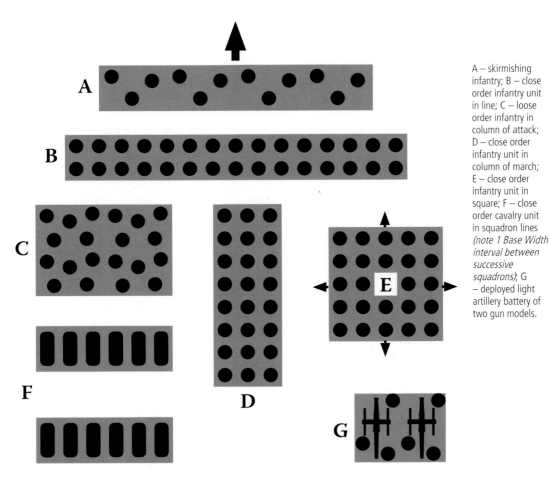

A – skirmishing infantry; B – close order infantry unit in line; C – loose order infantry in column of attack; D – close order infantry unit in column of march; E – close order infantry unit in square; F – close order cavalry unit in squadron lines *(note 1 Base Width interval between successive squadrons)*; G – deployed light artillery battery of two gun models.

Typical unit formations

- Standard formations during this period included the **line**, the **column of attack** and **column of march**. In addition, infantry were often trained to use the **square** as a defensive formation, a tactic that reached its apogee in the Napoleonic period and then in later colonial wars. Highly disciplined infantry in the eighteenth century would often turn the rear rank about as an alternative: see "Turning rear rank about" on page 381.

- Note that column of attack was rarely used before the Revolutionary Wars in Europe, and therefore should only be permitted in pre-1789 games with the consent of both players for specific scenarios.

  Skirmishing infantry and cavalry would adopt a constantly moving 'cloud' formation in which individual soldiers would move forward to shoot, then reload whilst their companion fired and they would make best use of whatever cover was available.

- NB **Column of march is not permitted to troops within 12BW of the enemy** unless specified by the scenario.

Skirmishers

One of our challenges is representing units, or portions of units, that are able to operate in both close order and open or extended order. Before the French Revolution, units of light troops or grenadiers were often composed of the light and grenadier companies from several different regiments, brought together to form a *corps d'élite* for a specific purpose. Alternatively, they were small units of *Freikorps*, *Jäger*, *Chasseurs*, *Tirailleurs* and so on, used to harass the enemy from difficult ground such as woods or steep hills. From the end of the eighteenth century, however, it became common for each regiment or battalion to have a company of grenadiers and one of light troops, nominally posted on each flank of the unit. The light company was trained to operate ahead of the battalion on the march and, in battle, to spread out in front of their follows to create what has become known as a 'skirmish screen'. Several nations went on to create entire battalions of troops capable of operating in either close or skirmish order, the *infanterie légère* and the light infantry (such as the famous 43rd and 52nd Regiments) and 5th Battalion, 60th and 95th Rifles.

The aim of a skirmish screen was twofold. Firstly, they would snipe at approaching enemy, hoping to kill or wound their officers and NCOs in particular in order to spread confusion and panic in the enemy's ranks. And secondly, they would be tasked with dealing with the enemy's own skirmishers, such as the famous *voltigeurs* that swarmed in front of French attack columns, in order to prevent disruption of their own parent unit.

In earlier wars, skirmishers tended to operate as independent companies or even smaller groups, tasked with denying terrain features or built up areas to the enemy, or holding other difficult ground, or infiltrating through such ground to threaten the enemy's flank. They were also used more extensively in *la petite guerre*, on raiding parties, ambuscades, reconnaissance and infiltration. The American War of Independence saw a great deal of this sort of action, but it should be remembered that the Austrian *Grenz* units had become famous on mainland Europe doing similar things on an even larger scale. Maria Theresa raised huge numbers of semi-regular units of both infantry and cavalry from the wilder fringes of the Austro-Hungarian empire, particularly the famed Croats and hussars. Such was the reputation of these troops that their clothing became a subject of fashion for the best part of two hundred years and their tactics were imitated from the forests of America and Canada through to the wastes of Russia.

Of course, the vastness of North America was also fertile ground for irregular troop types, such as the hunters and trappers who explored and colonised and traded in these huge arenas, and the Native Americans they encountered. Such irregulars saw service on both sides of the struggle, in which rival tribes were set against one another.

- For our purposes, the dispersed miniatures on a base of skirmishers already represent their typical formation, as does the somewhat ragged formation typical of irregular troops. In both cases, simply arrange the bases in a straight line, short edge to short edge.

- Portraying regular light infantry companies can be done simply by having one base per unit that is replaced by two bases of three infantry of just one rank, rather than the customary two ranks. When operating as a screen, the pair of half-depth bases (20mm for 28/30mm miniatures) are placed ahead of the parent unit at least 1BW apart. Any shooting directed at them is calculated as if shooting at troops in skirmish order. The pair of bases is treated as one for hits and all other reaction purposes. They may operate as skirmishers in

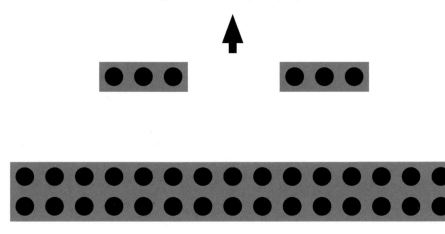

A Napoleonic-style infantry battalion of six bases, with one deployed as a single rank skirmish screen ahead of the main unit. Later in the war, entire battalions were capable of deploying in skirmish order, but in fact a reserve in close order was normally maintained.

all other respects, including movement, terrain effects, cover and so on, but must remain within 2BW of their parent unit at all times, unless specifically tasked separately by the local sub-commander or Commander-in-Chief.

- As far as the enemy is concerned, infantry fire must be directed against the skirmish screen rather than the unit they are shielding as long as the skirmish screen unit retains at least half its Strength Points. Thereafter, fire may be directed at the parent unit as if unscreened.

Strength Points

- Strength Points are allocated per base and then totalled for a unit. They are an indication of its ability to take punishment. Strength Points are normally shown visually by the number of miniatures mounted on each base, but a player wishing to use fewer – or smaller scale – figures may do so, making the necessary adjustments and perhaps recording hits on a tally sheet.

- **Once a unit has taken unsaved hits equal to half its initial Strength Points, it must retire from the battle** if it has not already been forced to do so by other factors explained in the rules. *This is known as a unit's Cohesion Limit.*

A scenario may specify, or players may agree, that specific units should be upgraded, downgraded or allocated additional or fewer Strength Points to more accurately reflect the historical performance of that formation under certain circumstances. During a campaign, units might also lose or gain Strength Points to reflect losses, reinforcements or subtle changes in morale.

Consult the rules for Shooting and Melee to find out how casualties are inflicted, the Disruption rules which show how units are disrupted, and the Reaction rules which describe the effects of casualties on the ability of a unit to carry on fighting.

Army size

For an average sized game on a table of 6' x 4', I recommend forces of around twelve units per side. This is not prescriptive, as it depends on the time available for the game, the armies being used, the terrain being fought over and so on. Difficult terrain will tend to slow progress, but armies with a preponderance of cavalry will move more quickly, than another consisting largely of infantry. In the Appendix to these rules on page 392 I have provided some simple, twelve-unit army lists as guidance. There are, of course, many more possibilities!

Deployment

- Opposing armies should be deployed 10-20 Base Widths apart (600-1200mm for 20-30mm figures, depending on whether you are playing the standard or 'old school' variant). This should of course be adjusted to take account of difficult terrain, the playing time available and so on, but this distance should allow some manoeuvring time before contact is made or firearms start to dominate the field. My preference is always for scenario- or campaign-driven deployment, but for casual games, here are a few suggestions.

- Players can use a file index card, blank postcard or the back of an old business card for each unit in their army, marking the unit's name and strength on the back. Alternatively, use standard playing cards and list what each card represents on a sheet of paper. An army consisting of more than one third cavalry may also have one blank 'dummy' card for every four units of any arm; other armies may deploy one blank per six real units. Both sides then deploy their cards within their designated deployment zones, face down, either simultaneously or alternately. When the last card has been laid, they are turned over to reveal the actual dispositions and are then replaced with the appropriate miniatures.

- Each side can draw a map of the tabletop, or the host or an umpire could provide this. Each side draws the position of their troops on their map as accurately as possible. When finished, the maps are revealed and the troops deployed as indicated. A mischievous umpire may, of course, exploit any ambiguity caused by the players' lack of cartographic skills!

- Each side can simply deploy their units one by one, alternating between the two players. Roll a die each to begin – highest may choose whether to deploy first or second. The side with the most cavalry may add 1 to its die roll, denoting the likelihood of superior reconnaissance.

- Erect a barrier or curtain along the centre of the table to mask deployment, which may then be carried out simultaneously. No peeking!

- For a really random option – assuming that you get on well with your regular opponent – both sides can lay out their armies according to their wishes, taking up their ideal positions for the terrain. Then roll 2d6 and your opponent may move this number of *your* units up to 2d6 inches in any direction, with the exception that no unit may be moved off the table or placed in impassable terrain. Repeat for the other side. I call this the 'sandstorm', and it isn't for the faint of heart!

Command structure

- An army is led by the **Commander-in-Chief** and must be divided into one or more commands, each of which should consist of between one and six units, usually of similar type, although they may be mixed. A Sub-Commander, who would usually be termed a 'Brigadier', leads each of these commands.

- In a small game with only up to six units, there is no *requirement* for Sub-Commanders and the C-in-C may take personal charge of the units under his command. You may, however, use additional sub-commanders if you wish and if their presence would be logical, such as for a cavalry brigade acting alongside infantry.

- Your command structure may always be adjusted to comply with a historical scenario.

- In large games, particularly in later periods, these commands may themselves be grouped together into divisions of up to six commands or brigades, led by a Senior Commander, who is still subordinate to the C-in-C. In modern parlance, these Senior Commanders would be major-generals or lieutenant-generals.

What is important is that you are represented by the C-in-C with, under normal circumstances, a number of Sub-Commanders leading various parts of your tabletop army. In large or multi-player games, there may be an additional tier of command between you and the various commands, which are themselves made up of groups of units.

- **The exceptions are light troops**, the skirmishing infantry and cavalry whose training or inherent nature means that they can be expected to move beyond normal command ranges and act on their own initiative; and artillery, whose gunners would be perfectly capable of determining whether the enemy was in range and the type of ammunition they should use. They may benefit from the proximity of a commander and friendly troops when hard pressed, but they are used to operating without guidance. Therefore:

- **Units of Horse Artillery, Skirmishers and Light Cavalry are not required to be commanded and can act on their own initiative**.

- Under normal circumstances, the player himself always counts the miniature general representing him on the tabletop as a Superior Commander, and any Sub-Commanders as Competent. Depending on the specific scenario, or if a historical battle is being represented, then the command abilities of both the overall Commander and any Sub-Commanders should be adjusted appropriately.

Command radius

- The C-in-C can command *any* unit within 10BW (Superior, A), 8BW (Competent, B) or 6BW (Cautious, C) of his base. Sub-Commanders can command any unit of *his own* command within 5BW (Superior, A), 4BW (Competent, B) or 3BW (Cautious, C) of his base.

- Command radius is always measured to the closest point of the unit(s) commanded.

- Once it has carried out its current orders, any unit *outside* the command radius must halt and await further orders. However, any such unit engaged in melee may continue to fight and A and B class troops may attempt to countercharge if charged, and may charge any enemy unit within their normal move distance.

Leadership tests

At the beginning of each player's turn, roll two d6 against the leadership of the C-in-C and each Sub-Commander.

- **Superior (A)** commanders have a Leadership Factor of 9; **Competent (B)** 8; **Cautious (C)** 7. In order to pass the test, the player must roll less than or equal to this Leadership Factor. The dice used should be left next to the leader in question until all the units in his command have been moved.

- *Any* unit within 3BW of an enemy unit acts on its own initiative and does not require orders.

- **A Commander or Sub-Commander who fails his roll** must deduct 2BW from the movement of all cavalry units under his command this turn, or 1BW from all other units. For example, a Cautious commander (rated 7) rolls 9. Cavalry under his command must deduct 2BW this turn, and his infantry 1BW from their normal move. This deduction is *compulsory*.

- **A Commander or Sub-Commander who rolls a double 6 has blundered** and must roll another d6 and consult the list below:
  1. All this commander's units deduct 2BW from their movement this turn
  2. All this commander's mounted units deduct 3BW and other units 2BW from their movement this turn
  3. As for 2, and any formation changes take twice the normal time
  4. As for 3, and no charges or countercharges are permitted
  5. As for 4, and all units shooting suffer a -1 penalty on their die rolls
  6. As for 5, and all units mêléeing suffer a -1 penalty on their die rolls

- **A Commander or Sub-Commander who passes the test** may move as many of the units under his command as he likes any distance up to their movement limit as dictated by their circumstances.

- **A Commander or Sub-Commander who passes his test by a margin of 2 or more may** *add* 2BW to the movement of all cavalry units under his command this turn and 1BW to all other units. For example, a Superior commander (rated 9) rolls 7. Cavalry under his command may add 2BW, and his infantry 1BW to their normal move. This addition is *not* compulsory.

- **A Commander or Sub-Commander who rolls a double 1 is really on top form**. Roll another d6 immediately and consult from the list below:
  1. All this commander's units add 2BW to their movement this turn
  2. All this commander's cavalry add 3BW and infantry 2BW to their movement this turn
  3. As for 2, and any formation changes may be carried out without penalty
  4. As for 3, and no deductions need be made for difficult terrain
  5. As for 4, and all troops eligible to shoot add 1 to their die rolls
  6. As for 5, and all troops eligible to melee add 1 to their die rolls
  Leaders have no other effects on shooting, either positive or negative.

- For the purposes of Reaction Tests, Sub-Commanders may add their Leadership Bonus only to nearby troops *under their own command*, but *not* to any unit led by a different Sub-Commander. The General, however, may confer his bonus upon *any* units within his command radius and able to see him. (See Reaction Tests later.)

- **If a General or Sub-Commander attaches himself to a retreating or routing unit,** he is adjudicated to be putting all his efforts into inspiring or rallying that unit alone and his Leadership bonus will apply *to that unit only* until he separates from it again. (See Reaction Tests later.)

Players, by prior agreement, are free to adapt this rule to allow for greater or smaller extremes. The intention is to represent the ability of high-calibre commanders to inspire their troops to greater efforts or, conversely, the reluctance of troops to obey a dullard, as well as those subtleties, such as the ground, weather conditions, and 'fog of war'.

In my experience, rules that prevent a player from carrying out any actions *at all* during a move can quickly lead to frustration because dice, being what they are, often produce runs that defy averages and can leave a player sitting on his hands for long periods whilst everyone else seems to be having fun. This is, after all, supposed to be a game...

Risk to leaders

- A Commander or Sub-Commander may not be specifically targeted on his own, but a leader who is *attached* to a unit which suffers casualties from shooting or hand-to-hand combat *is* at risk of becoming a casualty or being captured. Test as follows:

LEADERS AT RISK FROM SHOOTING

- A Commander or Sub-Commander who is attached to or within 1BW of a unit that suffers *at least 1 hit per base* (in other words, the number of hits taken by the unit as a whole is equal to or greater than the number of bases in the unit) is at risk. The shooting player now rolls 1d6:
  - 1, 2 = **a near miss**! The leader in question needs a new hat, but is otherwise fine
  - 3, 4 = **unhorsed**! The leader's horse is killed, and he may not move or issue orders for one turn until he remounts.
  - 5 = **wounded**! The leader is wounded, but not gravely, and needs medical attention for d6 moves, during which time he may play no part in the battle and command must be assumed by the Commander (if it is not he who has been hit) or nearest Sub-Commander. If the hit is from roundshot, a roll of 5 counts as a 6.
  - 6 = **calamity**! The leader is gravely or mortally wounded and command must be assumed by the Commander (if it is not he who has been hit) or nearest Sub-Commander but with a delay of d3 moves. All friendly units within 5BW must take an immediate Reaction test, suffering a deduction of -1 if it is a Sub-Commander, -2 if it is the general himself who is hit.

LEADERS AT RISK IN MELEE

- A Commander or Sub-Commander who is attached to or within 1BW of a unit that loses a round of melee and suffers *at least 1 hit per base* is at risk. The winning player rolls 1d6:
  - 1, 2 = **look out sir**! The leader in question suffers a bruise, but is otherwise fine.
  - 3, 4 = **unhorsed**! The leader's horse is killed, and he may not move or issue orders for one turn until he remounts.
  - 5 = **captured**! The leader falls into the enemy's hands and is escorted back to their own general in triumph. Terms may be negotiated for his release. If the hit is received from infantry, a roll of 5 counts as a 6.
  - 6 = **calamity**! The leader is gravely or mortally wounded and command must be assumed by the Commander (if it is not he who has been hit) or nearest Sub-Commander but with a delay of d3 moves. All friendly units within 5BW must take an immediate Reaction test, suffering a deduction of -1 if it is a Sub-Commander, -2 if it is the general himself who is hit.

Move sequence

1. INITIATIVE

At the start of the game, each player rolls a d6. Highest scorer may elect to go first or second. If one side has a higher calibre C-in-C, then that player adds 1 to his die roll. In the event of drawn scores, re-roll. Players then take alternate moves. A scenario may dictate that one side or the other has the Initiative for the first move or you may choose to dice every move.

2. DECLARE ORDERS

The player whose turn it is must now declare his intentions for *all* his troops for this turn. Players should agree before the game whether measuring is allowed before giving orders, moving or shooting.

PERMITTED ORDERS	
Voluntary	**Compulsory**
Charge (specify target unit/s)	Retire
Countercharge (specify target unit/s)	Retreat
Advance (specify direction)	Rout
Support (specify unit to support)	Disperse
Hold (specify position or terrain feature)	Charge (target unit/s will be dictated)
Retire	
Follow (specify unit to follow)	
Pursue (specify target unit/s)	
Evade	
Change formation	
Shoot (specify target unit/s)	

- Unless specifically ordered to charge or melee, no unit may approach within 1BW of an enemy unit.

- A unit within 1BW of an enemy that intends to charge them at the start of the enemy's turn must pass a 'raw' Leadership test in order to evade the enemy successfully, i.e. equal to or less than 9 if A class, 8 if B class and 7 if C class . If it fails, it is caught and must fight Disrupted.

- As noted above, units of Horse Artillery, Skirmishers and Light Cavalry are not required to be commanded and can act on their own initiative. If they do so, they will neither benefit from any bonus accruing to a commander's good leadership roll, nor suffer any consequences from a bad one. However, the intentions of such units should still be declared during this phase.

- Any unit within 3BW of an enemy unit acts on its own initiative and does not require orders. However, the intentions of such units should still be declared during this phase.

3. TEST FOR LEADERSHIP FOR SUB-COMMANDERS AND THE C-IN-C

This will determine what proportion of their commands, if any, will be able to move this turn.

- Assuming he passes his Leadership test, the C-in-C may opt to take command of *any* units within his Command Radius, but **if the C-in-C tests first and fails**, representing a catastrophic breakdown in the chain of command, **then that player's turn ends immediately after the troops he commands have completed their actions – none of his sub-commanders are permitted any orders.** This does not apply if the C-in-C is the only commander on the field, such as in a small game with half a dozen units per side or fewer.

- If the C-in-C attempts to issue commands to any units that one of his sub-commanders has already unsuccessfully attempted to command, then he suffers a -1 penalty to do so.

4. CARRY OUT REACTION TESTS FOR ANY CHARGERS AND DEFENDERS

- Warband units within charge bonus distance of an enemy to their front and able to do so *must* always Charge or Countercharge without requiring a Reaction Test.

- C class troops and Artillery may *never* Countercharge.

- Skirmishers and light cavalry may instead elect to Evade.

5. MOVEMENT

- **Carry out compulsory moves: routs, retreats and pursuits.**
  - □ **Routing troops** suffer no delay for turning tail and move directly away from the victors their standard move distance for the terrain they are occupying +d3BW. **Retreating troops** do likewise, except the additional distance is d2BW. Subsequent moves should be directly towards their own table edge.
  - □ **Pursuers** are permitted to move their standard move +1BW for infantry, +2BW for heavy cavalry or +3BW for light cavalry.
  - □ **If routing troops cannot find a gap** to pass through of at least 1BW to the flank of interposing friendly units, then they will shove their way through friends, disrupting any except skirmishers in the process.
  - □ **If pursuers make contact** with such a routing unit, it is automatically destroyed and removed.
  - □ **Retreating units may fight back**, with appropriate penalties.

- □ **Pursuers always have the option of rallying** at the table edge unless they are classed as Warband or Impetuous, in which case they must pursue their quarry off the table for d6 moves before being permitted to return. (Think of the Scots Greys at Waterloo, for example.)

- • **Move chargers, counterchargers and evaders.**
  - □ **Counterchargers and evaders of class B or C** suffer a compulsory delay of 1BW deduction from their move, and so will be caught at a standstill if the chargers are within this distance at the start of their move.
  - □ **A class troops** suffer no delay – their exceptional training and/or experience has taught them to read the signs of what is about to happen much more quickly.
  - □ **The charge bonus portion of a charging unit's move** must be made in a straight line, perpendicular to its frontage, and may only be claimed if it will enable the unit to actually make contact with the enemy.
  - □ **Any direction or formation changes** must be carried out in the normal portion of its move.
  - □ **A unit that moves less than its charge bonus distance** cannot claim the benefits of charging in the subsequent melee, as it has not built up sufficient momentum.
  - □ **Evaders who do not shoot at their attackers** move their standard move distance for the terrain they are occupying +d3BW
  - □ **Evaders who opt to shoot** before evading move their standard move distance for the terrain they are occupying +d2BW.

- • **Infantry units charged by cavalry may attempt to form square[6] or turn their rear rank about.**
  - □ **Permissible to close order and loose order units only.**
  - □ **Infantry of class B or C suffer a compulsory delay of 1BW deduction from their move,** and so will always be caught with the square not fully formed and count as disrupted if the chargers are closer than this.
  - □ For all other circumstances, the infantry are assumed to form square successfully **unless they roll a double 6 on 2d6,** when they count as disrupted and the cavalry may attempt to break in.

- • **Carry out normal moves, march moves and formation changes.**

- • **Move the C-in-C and other sub-commanders if desired.**

---

6   *If appropriate for the specific period/theatre being represented.*

6. Shooting

• Calculate artillery fire.

• Calculate small arms fire.

• Any charging unit taking one or more hits *per base* must stop 1BW short of its target and suffers 2 Disruption Points.

7. Melees

• **Hits from melees are calculated in an order determined by the reach of weapons.**

• **Certain weapons, such as pistols, count at Point Blank range only just before impact** and so their effect should be worked out before any hand-to-hand fighting and the results taken into account for the melee, but no Reaction Test should be taken until the melee has been completed.

8. Reaction

• Carry out any Reaction Tests necessary, including attempts to rally routers or pursuers.

The sequence from 2-8 is then repeated for the other side, which completes a turn.

Move Sequence Summary

1 Initiative
Add 1 if commander superior.

2 Declare Orders
Compulsory moves first, then voluntary

3 Test for Leadership
Test for C-in-C and sub-commanders in any order

4 Reaction Tests – Chargers & Defenders
Includes units wishing to counter-charge. Light troops may evade.

5 Movement
Compulsory routs, retreats and pursuits; then chargers, counter-chargers, evaders and infantry forming square; normal moves; and finally commanders and sub-commanders.

6 Shooting
Artillery; small arms; check whether chargers must pull up.

7 Melees
Point-blank shooting first, then fighting by longest weapons first.

8 General Reaction Tests
Includes attempts to rally routers and pursuers.

Converting base widths to millimetres for 25-30mm miniatures

BW	mm	BW	mm	BW	mm	BW	mm	BW	mm
1	60	5	300	9	540	13	780	17	1020
2	120	6	360	10	600	14	840	18	1080
3	180	7	420	11	660	15	900	19	1140
4	240	8	480	12	720	16	960	20	1200

Basic move distances

All movement is measured from front base edge to front base edge.

Type	Distance	Type	Distance
Close Order Infantry	3BW	Close Order Heavy Cavalry	5BW
Loose Order Infantry	4BW	Close Order Light Cavalry	7BW
Skirmishing Infantry	5BW	Loose Order Light Cavalry	8BW
Battalion guns	3BW	Skirmishing Light Cavalry	10BW
Horse Artillery (early)	6BW	Foot artillery	3BW
Manhandled field guns	1BW	Napoleonic Horse Artillery	8BW
Leader on horseback	10BW	Courier	12BW
Wagons	3BW	Boats (canal speed)	4BW

Movement penalties and bonuses

Situation	Movement Effect
Infantry in column of attack	+1BW
Infantry charging or pursuing	+1BW
Cavalry charging or pursuing	+2BW
Infantry about-face 180 degrees †	-1 BW
Infantry changing from column of march into line	-1 BW
Infantry or artillery shooting and moving or vice versa*	-2BW
Crossing difficult terrain or fording river or stream**†	-2BW
Any troops on good roads	+1BW
Crossing rough terrain**†	-3BW
Infantry moving though Built Up Area †	-1BW
Cavalry or artillery moving through Built Up Area	-2BW
Troops passing through defile narrower than 1BW	-1BW
Infantry stepping back	-2BW
Infantry lying down or standing up	-1 BW
Complex manoeuvre***†	-3BW
To mount or dismount cavalry****	-2 BW
To limber or unlimber artillery	-2 BW
Troops in Extra heavy armour	-1 BW
Troops in column of march §	Double basic movement
Troops not in column of march, but more than 12BW from nearest enemy	Add 50% to basic movement
Boat moving upstream	-2 BW
Boat moving downstream	+2 BW

* Includes evaders. Matchlocks may not move and fire. Thrown weapons have no penalty.

** Not permitted to artillery other than using defined tracks or roads unless permitted by special scenario rules

*** Changing formation or changing face by 90 degrees, cavalry changing face by 90 or 180 degrees, increasing or decreasing frontage, passing a defile.

**** One base in three must remain mounted as horse holders.

† Not applicable to skirmishers

§ Only permitted to troops at least 12BW distant from nearest enemy troops

- Troops in column of march make any additions or deductions *before* doubling the remaining distance.

- Troops charging a unit that manages to evade successfully lose their charge bonus and make a normal move instead. Movement bonuses or penalties resulting from Leadership Tests are unaffected.

Note that formal, Vauban-style fortifications do not impede movement – they were specifically designed to speed up the transit of troops. However, any areas of domestic housing that have been allowed to flourish inside or outside will count as standard Built Up Areas.

Interpenetration

Interpenetration simply means the situation where one unit wishes to pass through the ranks of another friendly unit. In all cases, it is only possible where the moving unit will pass through the other completely by the end of its turn. Therefore, if a unit has insufficient movement, the interpenetration may not be attempted, but it may move next to the friendly unit in order to make the attempt next turn.

- Skirmishers on foot, unless charging, may pass through, or be passed through by, any other friendly unit without either unit being affected.

- Close order units may pass through other close order units, but both will suffer 1 point of disruption as a result.

- Loose order units may interpenetrate any troops without disruption.

- The unit being passed through may not move, fire, or conduct close combat until the manouevre is complete.

- Units in square or column of march may not be interpenetrated.

- Charging or evading units (other than skirmishers) may not attempt to interpenetrate. Charging skirmishers may only pass through other skirmishers.

Shooting

- **Players may carry out the shooting in any order they choose,** subject to all artillery fire being calculated first and its results being taken before any other ranged shooting.

- A unit must be able to trace a direct and clear line of fire **at least 1BW wide** to the target.

- **The permitted Firing Arc for infantry, artillery and mounted skirmishers is 45° to either side of a line drawn from back to front of either side edge of a base.**

- **Close and loose order *mounted* cavalry may only shoot straight ahead.**

- **In order to shoot outside these arcs, the unit must turn.**

The permitted arcs of fire for infantry artillery and mounted skirmishers. Close and loose order mounted cavalry firing pistols or carbines from the saddle may only shoot straight ahead.

- **Only the front rank of *bases* may fire** unless the rear ranks or the target are standing on ground at least one contour higher, in which case fire from the rear ranks is worked out separately.

- **Shooting at bases involved in melee, either completely or corner-to-corner, is forbidden,** but *completely non-engaged* bases of a unit in melee are a legitimate target.

Weapon ranges

Weapon	Short	Medium	Long
Thrown*	1BW	n/a	n/a
Pistol	1BW	n/a	n/a
Carbine	1BW	2BW	4BW
Bow	2BW	3BW	6BW
Matchlock	1BW	3BW	6BW
Musket	1BW	3BW	6BW
Rifle	2BW	6BW	9BW
Light artillery	3BW	6BW	12BW
Medium artillery	4BW	12BW	24BW
Heavy artillery	8BW	16BW	32BW
Howitzer	3BW	9BW	18BW

*One use only

Shooting procedure

In order to cause hits, the following numbers of dice are thrown *per base* shooting. Hits are caused on a score of 4, 5 or 6 after all modifiers have been applied (see below). Note that a roll of 1 is *always* a miss.

- Close order infantry — 3
- Loose or open order infantry — 2
- Skirmishing infantry — 1
- All infantry inside Built Up Areas — 2
- Cavalry firing pistols — 1
- Cavalry firing carbines when mounted — 1
- Battalion gun — 2
- Light artillery — 3
- Medium artillery — 4
- Heavy artillery — 5
- Howitzers — 3, unless target is in confined space, then 5

At close range, all artillery may roll one extra die to simulate the effects of canister.

If the cumulative modifiers on the table that follows bring the total required to score a Hit to more than 6, then the shooting player must first roll a 6 for each base firing, then roll another die as follows:

Score required	Additional die roll required after first 6
7	4, 5 or 6
8	5 or 6
9+	6

Therefore **a double 6 is *always* a hit, regardless of circumstances.**

Shooting modifiers

These modifiers are applied to the *score on each die* rolled, not the number of dice rolled.

Dense target*	+1	Target unit in soft cover	-1
Enfilading target	+1	Target unit in hard cover	-2
Firing unit is A class	+1	Target unit in fortifications	-3
Firing unit is C class	-1	For each Disruption cause	-1
Target unit is in skirmish order***	-2	Target unit wearing heavy armour**	-1
Target unit is in open order	-1	First volley for muskets or carbines †	+1
Target is at short range	+1	Shooting unit moved (unless thrown)	-1
Target is at long range	-1	Target is BUA or equivalent	+1

* *Limbered artillery, infantry square, head or flank of attack column, head of any column of march*

** *Not applicable to artillery*   *** *Includes deployed artillery*   † *Not applicable to skirmishers*

Saving throws against shooting hits

Immediately after hits on a unit have been calculated, the enemy then has the opportunity to save those hits, depending on the type of weapon causing them – the more powerful the weapon, the harder it will be to save. Throw the same number of dice as those that scored hits on the unit.

Weapon inflicting hits	Saving roll required
Pistol or bow or thrown	3-6
Carbine, musket, matchlock	4-6
Rifle or howitzer shell	5 or 6
Smoothbore cannon	6

- **A base is lost as soon as Hits suffered equal the Strength Points value of a base of that unit's type**, normally equal to the number of miniatures mounted on it. Hits can be recorded using a small die, chit, marker or tally sheet to keep track of accumulated Hits.

Shooting at a charge

- Assuming that it passes its reaction test, **a defending unit armed with missile weapons may attempt to shoot at an enemy charging it or any friendly unit within its permitted arc of fire** during the *enemy's* Movement Phase, *in addition to* any shooting it may have done during its own previous turn.

- **If the enemy attack falls short**, either because the distance has been misjudged or because of the effects of the enemy's Command Roll,

then no shooting will take place in the enemy's move, and the unit must wait until its own, standard Shooting Phase. (However, this does not apply to evaders who manage to shoot and then successfully evade.) The consequence of this additional shooting may, indeed, be to prevent the enemy from making contact.

- Roll a d6: **1 or 2 means shooting is calculated as if at Long range; 3 or 4 at Medium range; 5 or 6 at Short range**. A class troops add 1 to their die roll; C class deduct 1.

- **Any charging unit taking one or more unsaved hits per base** must stop 1BW short of its target, suffers 2 Disruption Points and must take an immediate Reaction Test.

Counter-battery fire

In reality, counter-battery fire was often frowned upon as being of little value, but there were certainly times when the suppression of the enemy's artillery could prove crucial. When targeting deployed artillery, it has already been noted that the **working crews count as a skirmish order target and therefore cause a deduction of -2 to any unit targeting them**.

- **For each gun crew figure killed, that gun then rolls one die fewer when shooting**, and there is a risk to the gun itself. Any 'natural' roll of a 6 (i.e. before modifiers) means that the targeted gun has been hit, and another d6 should be rolled to determine the effect:

- **If hit by roundshot**
  1 = glancing blow, no further effect; 2, 3 = wheel broken, gun out of action for d3 moves; 4, 5 = carriage damaged, gun out of action for d6 moves; 6 = barrel struck and dismounted, gun out of action.

- **If hit by shell**
  1 = gun hit by small splinters, no further effect; 2, 3, 4 = wheel broken, gun out of action for d3 moves; 5 = carriage damaged, gun out of action for d6 moves; 6 = shell detonates ready ammunition, any figures/units within a radius of 1BW test as if hit by another round of howitzer fire.

Shooting at Built Up Areas and risk of fire

- **Built Up Areas** (BUAs) should be divided into units 240mm square[7], represented perhaps by a single house model with garden.

---

7 *This is a suggestion: use a size to suit your own collection, but around 4 Base Widths square. For larger BUA units, adjust the number of troops permitted to garrison the area accordingly.*

Such models can be single or multi-storey, but in reality represent a mixture of single- and multi-storey buildings, be they simple dwellings, churches, warehouses and so on, surrounded by clear land, low and high walls and so forth.

- **Each BUA unit may be garrisoned by a maximum of eight infantry bases of any kind**. The varying number of miniatures per base are irrelevant, since the terrain imposes what might be termed 'garrison order' on all occupants.

- **No cavalry are permitted to garrison a BUA unless dismounted**, but may pass through on roads.

- **No artillery is permitted to enter a BUA, with the exception of battalion guns or guns being placed in previously prepared positions** in accordance with a scenario, or travelling on roads.

- If shot at, **troops in buildings count as being in hard cover, and NOT additionally as skirmish, open, loose or close order**.

- **Each BUA is allocated 100 Strength Points (wooden) or 150 Strength Points (brick) or 200 Strength Points (stone)**. Fortifications are of an entirely different order, but for game purposes should be allocated 500 Strength Points as a minimum, with up to 1,000 Strength Points for Vauban-style defences.

- **If targeted by roundshot**, the damage caused in Strength Points is the total poundage of *model guns* firing (e.g. two 12pdr models = 24 points) added to the score of 1d6 per gun model. At long range deduct 2 from the die roll; at medium range deduct 1; and at close range, make no deduction. The building is destroyed when the Strength Points of the BUA are reduced to 0. For example, three 6pdr models shooting at medium range roll 2, 4 and 5, so the damage caused is 3 x 6 + (2-1) + (4-1) + (5-1) = 18+1+3+4 = 26.

- **If shot at by howitzers**, the damage caused is equivalent to the calibre of shell rounded down (e.g. 6" = 6, 5.5" = 5) plus the score of 1d6 per gun model. However, *howitzer shells are not affected by range*.

- In addition, **howitzer shells may also set buildings on fire**. For each howitzer model firing (or two models in the 'old school' variant), roll 2d6. If shooting at wooden buildings, a score of 9+ means they have caught fire; brick buildings take on 11+; and stone edifices on nothing less than a double 6.

- Once aflame, **unless extinguished within the first two turns of**

igniting, the fire burns for the rest of the game, with a risk of spreading to adjacent BUA units within 2BW in the direction of the prevailing wind (spin a pointer). Roll a d6 each player turn: wooden buildings catch on a 4+, brick on a 5+ and stone on a 6.

- **Any troops inside a building that catches fire must evacuate it immediately**. If they are prevented from doing so for any reason, they are lost.

- **A fire must be extinguished within the first two turns of igniting** by infantry whose bases are touching the building with their long edges. They may not do anything else whilst firefighting. To extinguish a fire, each base making the attempt rolls a d6. During the first move, a 4, 5 or 6 is required to extinguish the fire; in the second move, a 6 is needed. If the BUA is still under howitzer fire from the enemy, then a modifier of -1 must be applied. If any of the bases making the attempt roll a 1, then the building has collapsed suddenly, so the base is lost.

- According to the scenario, **areas of crops, or wooded areas** during times of drought may also catch fire using the rules outlined above.

Turning rear rank about

Some highly disciplined infantry, particularly during the eighteenth century, were capable of facing an attack in the rear, even by cavalry, by turning about the men in the rear rank. **In order to perform such an action, the infantry unit concerned must be A or B class and in close order**. Once the order is given, the unit may use one of its three allocated dice per base to shoot in the opposite direction to the rest of the unit.

Lying down

In exceptional cases, an enlightened commander might allow his troops to lie down to reduce casualties from incoming fire, but of course the consequences of troops being caught prone by, say, charging cavalry could be terrible. Wellington was one of the first generals known to have allowed his troops to do this, but it became more frequent as the lethality of weapons increased.

- **Infantry may lie down, losing 1BW of movement to do so.**

- **If targeted while prone**, the infantry count as being in Hard Cover to all but howitzer shell fire, which counts Soft Cover only.

- **Any troops except trained Light Infantry attempting to fire** whilst prone will suffer a -2 penalty.

- **Any troops caught whilst prone by the enemy** will suffer a -3 penalty on their dice rolls in melee as chances of survival would be very slim indeed.

Close combat (melee)

- The player holding the Initiative may carry out the melees in any order he chooses.

- **Only the front rank of bases may melee.** All bases counted as fighting must be in edge-to-edge contact and the maximum odds permitted are 3:1.

Reach and first strike

- **Units in melee that outreach the opponents they face always strike first.**

- Thrown weapons and pistols outreach pikes, which outreach cavalry lances, which outreach muskets with bayonets *unless the infantry is in formed square*, when its muskets and fixed bayonets outreach all cavalry.

- Infantry in *formed* square *always* strike first against cavalry. This is also possible for certain highly drilled infantry units in line in the eighteenth century, such as the British infantry at Dettingen.

- **Melees fought by troops with equal length weapons are simultaneous.**

- **A unit assailed from the flank or rear** does *not* outreach those opponents, however it is armed, and must suffer being attacked by the enemy before any survivors can fight back.

Close combat procedure

In order to cause hits, the following numbers of dice are thrown *per base* fighting. Hits are caused on a score of 4, 5 or 6 after modifiers have been applied (see below). Note that cavalry roll different numbers of dice according to whether it is the 'impact' phase of combat, subsequent rounds of melee, or they are caught at the halt or being pursued.

- Close and loose order infantry charging, with momentum, or following up add one die per base.

- A roll of 1 is always a miss.

Close or loose order infantry	3				
Open order infantry	2				
Skirmishing infantry and crews	1				
Heavy cavalry charging	5	Melee 4	Halted[8]/pursued	3
Napoleonic lancers charging infantry	5	Melee 4	Halted/pursued	2
Napoleonic lancers charging cavalry	4	Melee 3	Halted/pursued	2
Other light cavalry or Cossacks charging	4	Melee 3	Halted/pursued	3

- If the cumulative modifiers on the table that follows bring the total required to score a Hit to more than 6, then the player must first roll a 6 for each base firing, then roll another die as follows:

Score required	Additional die roll required after first 6
7	4, 5 or 6
8	5 or 6
9+	6

Therefore **a double 6 is *always* a hit**, regardless of circumstances.

Close combat modifiers

Pikes	+1	Unit is trapped or surrounded*	-2
Cavalry attacking square or equivalent	-4	For each disruption cause	-1
Cavalry attacking highly drilled infantry**	-2	Infantry fighting any cavalry	-1
Cavalry fighting cuirassiers	-1	Following up a close combat victory	+1
Unit is A class	+1	Unit is C class	-1
Enemy is behind soft cover***	-1	Enemy is behind hard cover or in BUA	-2
Uphill of enemy	+1	Reinforcing a melee	+1

Does not apply to troops in BUAs or other strongpoints unless enemy has broken in. ** *Applies to eighteenth century European and Scandinavian infantry.* *** *Does not apply to troops in woods unless they spend two full turns doing nothing except 'plashing' and felling trees to create horizontal barriers – vertical trees in their natural state are neutral cover in melee. Once done, that section of wood is treated as linear soft cover such as a fence.*

Unless the attackers outreach the defenders or have surprised them, all hand-to-hand fighting is considered simultaneous, so the defenders may now fight back, ignoring any casualties caused by their opponents until the end of the phase. **If outreached or surprised**, however, **the**

---

8   *As a result of an adverse Reaction test result.*

defenders must take any casualties or disruption suffered into account before fighting back. **If the defenders outreach the attackers, the attackers must suffer casualties first.**

Saving throws against close combat hits

As with shooting, after hits have been calculated, the opponent then has the opportunity to save those hits, depending on the type of weapon causing the hits. **Armoured troops add 1 to their saving die roll.**

Weapon inflicting hits	Save required
Sword, club, musket, bayonet, other hand weapon	3-6
Sword or lance if cavalry charged or reinforced, pike in general melee	4-6

- **A base is lost as soon as Hits suffered equal the Strength Points value of a base of that unit's type.** Hits are recorded using a small die, chit, marker or tally sheet to keep track of accumulated Hits.

Results of close combat

- **The side suffering the most *unsaved* Hits is declared the loser.** If unsaved Hits suffered are equal, then the melee continues *in situ* during the next player turn.

- **The losers are pushed back 1BW, plus ½BW per 1 Hit difference compared to those inflicted on the enemy.** A class troops ignore the first two Hits difference; C class *add* two Hits (for the purposes of this calculation only – they don't actually suffer two extra Hits!).

- **Any unit forced back 3BW or more breaks immediately** instead and will Rout next phase.

- A unit that wins a round of melee counts as 'following up' if the melee continues to a next round.

- **The position of combatant units following melee** should always conform to the winners.

- **Units following up a victory** may remain in contact with the enemy as long as doing so does not exceed their permitted movement.

- **If a melee continues after the first round,** bases on both sides behind their front rank may advance to either or both sides of the foremost bases, up to the limit of their normal permissible move, to join in the fighting in subsequent turns *but do not count as charging.*

- **If the losers of a melee Rout as a result of the subsequent Reaction test**, then the victors have the option of pursuing or not, except that Impetuous regulars and any irregulars must take a Reaction test themselves if the player wishes to *prevent* them from pursuing.

- **Any unit may only fight three rounds of close combat before breaking off and retiring** at least 1BW to recover, unless they are occupying a BUA, in which case their desperation enables them to fight on for as long as necessary, suffering 1 Disruption Point for each subsequent round of melee fought without rest to reflect their fatigue.

- **Heavy cavalry** roll one die fewer after charging, pursuing or meleeing for more than one round to reflect fatigue and winded horses.

Breakthrough

- **If a charging cavalry, camelry or elephant unit inflicts twice as many Hits as it receives or more, then the defending unit is broken through and immediately split in the centre**, counting this as two Disruption points (total -2). The attackers may then continue to advance any remaining move distance they may have left over as a Momentum Advance, and if this brings them into contact with further enemy, then they may fight a further round of melee, still counting as charging, but also as Disrupted.

- **The unit breaking through may veer up to 45° either side of its original line of advance** in order to contact further enemy units. If no such units exist, they must move straight ahead or remain where they are and either continue to melee if the original enemy unit survives or reform and rest for one move.

Reinforcing a melee

- To represent fresh squadrons joining a swirling melee, **cavalry squadrons are permitted to reinforce friends in an existing cavalry versus cavalry melee** by moving into contact either with enemy OR friendly bases already involved in the melee. They may not count as charging, but the enemy will require a higher die roll to save against attacks from these fresher troops. **The maximum odds permitted are 3:1 and only the front rank of bases of the reinforcing unit may participate.**

Capture the colours!

- A unit which is broken through by cavalry, or which retreats or routs as a result of losing a melee, risks losing its colours to the victors. The winning side rolls 1d6 – a roll of 6 means that the standards have been captured. The unit that has performed this deed gains a +1 on all Reaction tests for the remainder of the game, whilst the unit that has lost its colours suffers a -1 penalty until it can recapture them.

Turning rear rank about

- As with shooting, in order to perform such an action, the infantry unit concerned must be A or B class and in close order. The unit must first pass a Reaction test and, if successful, may use one of its three allocated dice per base to melee with a unit attacking it from behind.

Fighting in Built Up Areas

- **Refer to the Shooting rules above for permitted maximum garrisons** for BUA units.

- **To be eligible to attack a BUA**, a base of attacking troops must be placed in contact with the BUA so that its *entire* length is in contact.

- It is assumed that **the maximum force permitted to garrison a BUA unit** is also an indication of the limit of doors, windows, alleyways, walls and loopholes that permit access into, or egress from, the BUA.

- **Troops attacking a BUA may not count as charging** under any circumstances as they are having to negotiate obstacles.

- **If any bases of troops garrisoning the BUA under attack are destroyed, the attackers may break in** with the same number of bases on a roll of 5 or 6 on a d6. Any base that breaks in may then fight on equal terms with the defenders, but if it loses the subsequent round of melee, it is ejected. The troops breaking in count towards the maximum number of bases permitted in a BUA. For example, if a standard BUA already contains eight bases of infantry, no more may enter until at least one is destroyed or flees.

- **Troops garrisoning a BUA count as 'Supported'** until such time as the enemy break in, at which point their true condition must be taken into account.

Disruption

Under certain circumstances, the cohesion of a unit is disrupted which reduces its ability to shoot or fight hand-to-hand, and which may even reduce its morale.

- **The following effects, each causing 1 point of Disruption unless otherwise specified, are cumulative,** applied immediately and take effect for as long as the cause persists.

- **Disruption may be cleared at a rate of 2 points per turn** by the unit halting and doing nothing but reforming.

Cause	Cause
Unit crossed or fought in difficult or rough terrain this turn	Unit successfully attacked in flank or rear or surprised this turn
Infantry or artillery successfully charged by cavalry this turn	Unit has taken 1+ hits per base this turn
Charging unit failed to make contact this turn	Friends contact but unable to interpenetrate this turn
Unit contacted whilst attempting to evade this turn	Unit making Momentum Advance or pursuit this turn
Unit lost melee by more than 1 hit per base this turn	Unit routed this turn – requires 2 moves at halt to clear
Unit has fought two or more rounds of melee	Unit has been broken through this turn: *2 disruption points**
Charging unit stopped by shooting this turn	Unit escalading fortress or strongpoint this turn

* This applies whether the unit breaking through is friend or foe.

When to test reaction

Any unit must test its reaction when:

- **it wishes to charge or when it is being charged**.

- it suffers **1 or more unsaved Hits per base from shooting** (including when shot at during a charge).

- it **loses a round of melee**.

- it wishes to **rally from rout or pursuit**.

- **Friends rout through the unit or friends in sight are destroyed or dispersed** within 4BW of it.

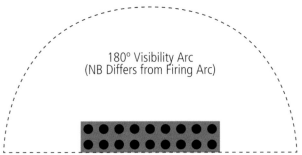

180° Visibility Arc
(NB Differs from Firing Arc)

- **Impulsive troops and Warband** must also test at the start of their next movement phase whenever enemy troops come within their charge range.

- Losing a base does not, in itself, require a Reaction test – only **casualties from shooting or losing a melee trigger the test.**

- **A unit which falls below 50% of its starting strength** must retire in good order, unless it takes further casualties and must therefore test again. The exception is troops within a BUA or fortification, who may continue to fight unless forced out by enemy action.

Reaction test procedure

- **Total the points applicable** in the Reaction test modifier table below, then **deduct 1 point for each Hit suffered during this turn only, and also deduct 1 point for each current Disruption Point.**

- **Add 3 points** if within command range, with no enemy troops interposing, of an **A class commander or sub-commander.**

- **Add 2 points** if within command range, with no enemy troops interposing, of a **B class commander or sub-commander.**

- **Add 1 point** if within command range, with no enemy troops interposing, of a **C class commander or sub-commander.**

- Then **roll 2d6 and add the score to the total.** A roll of double 6 *always means the unit has passed*; a roll of double 1 *always represents a failure, **regardless of other factors**. These represent the remote possibility of a rabble standing its ground or a crack unit turning tail.

- **In order to pass, the total score achieved must be equal to or more than the following:**

  - A class = 6
  - B class = 8
  - C class = 10

Example
A Normal-sized unit of B class musketeers loses a round of melee against a similar enemy unit, suffering three casualties to their two. It has 0 points for its size, it has been pushed back (-1) and has no cover (0). It is in close order (+2) and has friends in support (+2). Both its disruption and class are the same as the enemy (0) but it has suffered three unsaved Hits (-3). With a B-class sub-commander in range (+2) it must roll 6+ to continue.

Reaction test modifiers

Category	-2	-1	0	+1	+2
Size	XS	S	N	L	XL
Unit is	Routing	Retiring or pushed back	Static	Advancing or following up	Charging or pursuing
Cover	Closest enemy has hard cover	Closest enemy has soft cover	None	Hard	Fortified/ entrenched
Order*	Mob	Skirmishing	Open	Loose	Close
Security	Threatened	Isolated	Friends in sight	Friends close	Supported
Difference in disruption in mêlée	2+ causes inferior	1 cause inferior	Same	1 cause superior	2+ causes superior
Class in mêlée	Far Inferior	Inferior	Same	Superior	Far Superior

* Routing troops ignore these modifiers for order because they are disordered!

Reaction test definitions

SUPPORTED

Visible friends in good order, facing the same direction, within 3BW.

FRIENDS CLOSE

Visible friends in good order, facing within 45° of same direction, within 6BW. Engaged friends can only count as "Friends close", never as "Support" unless actually engaged in the same melee, against the same opponents as the testing unit. Artillery may support, or be supported by, any friendly unit within 3BW and facing the same direction.

FRIENDS IN SIGHT

Visible friends in good order, facing within 90° of same direction, within 9BW.

ISOLATED

No friends within 9BW, or closer friends not meeting criteria above.

THREATENED

Surprised by enemy unit, or enemy unit within their normal charge reach of testing unit's flank or rear.

DIFFERENCE IN DISRUPTION AND CLASS IN MELEE

These are determined by comparing with the enemy in contact.
- When attacking an infantry square or pikes, cavalry Cohesion is always classed as 'Far Inferior' and the infantry as 'Far superior'.

- A unit counts only its *current* size when testing, not its starting size.

Reaction test results

- A unit that passes its Reaction Test may continue as desired.

- If the unit fails to score the necessary total, consult the table below.

Unit is: Failed by:	Charging	Advancing	Halted/ Standing	Retiring	Retreating	Routing
1	Halt	Halt	Retire	Retreat	Rout	Rout
2	Halt	Retire	Retreat	Rout	Rout	Disperse
3	Retire	Retreat	Rout	Rout	Disperse	Disperse
4	Retreat	Retreat	Rout	Disperse	Disperse	Disperse
5+	Rout	Rout	Disperse	Disperse	Disperse	Disperse

- **Artillery crews that fail a Reaction Test with an outcome worse than Retire** abandon their guns, disperse and are removed. Crews with a Retire order may limber their guns and attempt to take them to safety if circumstances permit.

- **A regular, Impetuous unit that passes its test with an excess of more than 5 points** MUST charge the closest enemy unit at the first opportunity. The scenario should specify any units classified as Impetuous (such as the Scots Greys at Waterloo).

- **An irregular unit which passes its test with an excess of more than 3 points** MUST charge the closest enemy unit at the first opportunity.

- **All units with a bad outcome may test again in the following move.**

- **Routing units continue to suffer one additional unsaved Hit each complete turn after the first Rout move**, whether Pursued, shot at or not, representing the disintegration of the unit as it flees. This extra casualty must be taken at the start of the Reaction Test phase, before any calculations are made.

- **A general or sub-commander may attempt to rally routing troops by attaching himself to the unit**, but he must then remain with that unit for the rest of the battle and share its fate.

- **A Routing unit, which fails to rally when it reaches its Cohesion limit or the table edge**, disintegrates completely and is removed from play. **A Retreating unit** may continue to attempt to rally even after leaving the table, but will then require a full turn to reform and will then require the same number of turns to return as it took after leaving. **A Retiring unit** that has not reached its Cohesion limit may rally at the table edge, requiring a full move doing nothing else.

Reaction test results definitions

HALT

The unit has been stopped dead in its tracks, ceases to advance and must remain motionless during the movement phase of its own next turn, facing the enemy, neither advancing nor retreating.

RETIRE

At the start of the movement phase of its own next turn, the unit makes one half standard move for the terrain it is occupying away from the nearest visible enemy, facing the enemy. They will avoid impeding friends and move through gaps if at all possible. The move distance is NOT subject to Leadership variation.

RETREAT

The unit turns about 180° at the start of the movement phase of its own next turn, deducting ¼ move distance in the process, and makes one standard move for the terrain it is occupying +d2BW away from the nearest visible enemy. It will avoid impeding friends and move through gaps if at all possible. The move distance is NOT subject to Leadership variation.

ROUT

The unit immediately turns about 180° with *no* deduction from its move for doing so, regardless of which player's turn it is, and moves directly away from the nearest enemy its standard move distance for the terrain it is occupying +d3BW. It will continue to move at this speed during each of its own movement phases until or unless rallied to a better morale state, or the unit disperses or leaves the table. Subsequent moves should be directly towards its own table edge. If routing troops cannot find a gap to pass through of at least 1BW to the flank of interposing friendly units, then they will shove their way through friends, disrupting any except skirmishers in the process. The move distance is NOT subject to Leadership variation.

DISPERSE

The unit has been completely shattered and is removed from play.

Victory and defeat

Each scenario should state specific victory conditions, but in arbitrary terms, a side that has lost control of half its units, either killed or routing, has lost the game. It is possible, therefore, that both sides could lose! On the other hand, a scenario could dictate that the side which achieves its objective, may win despite any casualties suffered. In a campaign context, objectives and outcomes are more obvious and a prudent commander might wish to call it a day long before casualties force this upon him.

APPENDIX TO THE RULES

Typical 12-unit horse and musket wargame armies

SEVEN YEARS WAR AUSTRIAN

- 6 Normal B class Unarmoured Close Order Musketeer Regiments armed with muskets
- 1 Normal B class Unarmoured Loose Order Grenz Infantry Regiment armed with muskets
- 1 Normal A class Unarmoured Close Order Grenadier Regiment armed with muskets
- 1 Large B class Unarmoured Close Order Dragoon Regiment armed with swords and carbines
- 1 Large B class Heavy armoured Close Order Cuirassier Regiment armed with swords and carbines
- 1 Large B class Unarmoured Loose Order Hussar Regiment armed with swords, pistols and carbines
- 1 Normal (3 gun models) B class Medium Artillery Battery, gunners Unarmoured and armed with hand weapons and tools only

SEVEN YEARS WAR PRUSSIAN

- 6 Normal B class Unarmoured Close Order Musketeer Regiments armed with muskets
- 1 Normal B class Unarmoured Close Order Fusilier Regiment armed with muskets
- 1 Normal A class Unarmoured Close Order Grenadier Regiment armed with muskets
- 1 Large B class Unarmoured Close Order Dragoon Regiment armed with swords and carbines
- 1 Large B class Heavy armoured Close Order Cuirassier Regiment armed with swords and carbines
- 1 Large B class Unarmoured Loose Order Hussar Regiment armed with swords, pistols and carbines
- 1 Normal (3 gun models) B class Medium Artillery Battery, gunners Unarmoured and armed with hand weapons and tools only
- OR 1 Small (2 gun models) B class Light Horse Artillery Battery, gunners Unarmoured and armed with hand weapons and tools only

Seven Years War Prussian infantry advancing across Phil Olley's wargames table. 28mm Foundry figures painted by Phil himself and organised according to his own rules.

American Continental units painted by the very talented Steve Jones.

AMERICAN WAR OF INDEPENDENCE BRITISH

- 6 Small B class Unarmoured Loose Order Musketeer Regiments armed with muskets
- 1 Large A class Unarmoured Loose Order Grenadier Regiment armed with muskets
- 1 Large A class Unarmoured Loose Order/Skirmishing Light Infantry Regiment armed with muskets; the entire unit may act in either Loose Order or Skirmish
- 1 Large B class Unarmoured Loose Order/Skirmishing Highland Regiment armed with muskets; the entire unit may act in either Loose Order or Skirmish
- 1 Small A class Unarmoured Loose Order Light Dragoon Regiment armed with swords, pistols & carbines
- 1 Small (2 gun models) B class Medium Artillery Battery, gunners Unarmoured and armed with hand weapons and tools only
- 1 Large (4 gun models) B class Light Artillery Battery; gunners Unarmoured & armed with hand weapons/tools only – can be divided into two independent sub-units

AMERICAN WAR OF INDEPENDENCE AMERICAN

- 4 Normal B class Unarmoured Loose Order Musketeer Regiments armed with muskets
- 1 Normal A class Unarmoured Loose Order/Skirmishing Light Infantry Regiment armed with muskets; the entire unit may act in either Loose Order or Skirmish
- 1 Large B class Unarmoured Skirmishing Rifle Regiment armed with flintlock rifles; operating purely as Skirmishers – can be divided into up to 4 independent sub-units
- 3 Large C class Unarmoured Close Order Militia Regiments armed with muskets
- 1 Small B class Unarmoured Loose Order Light Dragoon Regiment armed with swords & pistols
- 2 Normal (3 gun models) A class Light Artillery Batteries; gunners Unarmoured & armed with hand weapons/tools only

AUTHOR'S NOTE

Huge thanks to AWI expert Brendan Morrissey who compiled these lists. He also provided supplements covering Loyalists and Germans for the British and French for the Americans that can be downloaded from the website. Brendan adds, "Historically, the British used elite formations – Guards, Grenadier/Light Battalions, Highlanders and a few excellent Line Regiments – to do almost all of the actual fighting... This contrasts with the American force, which will have few elites and some lousy troops, so the American player will almost always need to be the defender in any scenario."

Peninsular War British

- 6 Normal B class Unarmoured Close Order Musketeer Regiments armed with muskets. One base from each Regiment may be used as Skirmishers.
- 1 Normal B class Unarmoured Close/Skirmishing Light Infantry Regiment armed with muskets. The entire unit may act in either Skirmish or Close Order.
- 1 Extra Small A class Unarmoured Skirmishing Rifle Company armed with flintlock rifles. The Rifles normally operated purely as Skirmishers.
- 1 Small B class Unarmoured Close Order Dragoon Regiment armed with swords and carbines
- 2 Small B class Unarmoured Close Order Light Dragoon or Hussar Regiment armed with swords, pistols and carbines
- 1 Normal (3 gun models) B class Medium Artillery Battery, gunners Unarmoured and armed with hand weapons and tools only
- OR 1 Normal (2 gun models) A class Medium Horse Artillery Battery, gunners Unarmoured and armed with swords

Peninsular War French

- 6 Normal B class Unarmoured Close Order Musketeer Regiments armed with muskets. One base from each Regiment may be used as Skirmishers.
- 1 Normal B class Unarmoured Close/Skirmishing Légère (Light) Infantry Regiment armed with muskets. The entire unit may act in either Skirmish or Close Order.
- 2 Normal B class Unarmoured Close Order Dragoon Regiments armed with swords and carbines
- 2 Normal B class Unarmoured Close Order Chasseur or Hussar Regiment armed with swords, pistols and carbines
- 1 Normal (3 gun models) B class Medium Artillery Battery, gunners Unarmoured and armed with hand weapons and tools only
- OR 1 Normal (2 gun models) B class Medium Horse Artillery Battery, gunners Unarmoured and armed with swords

Another view of Barry Hilton's beautifully rendered Peninsular War battle, including a magnificent painted backdrop. Those British infantry are going to be hard to dislodge from their ridge-top position!

8

LEARN BY PLAYING

A Scenario to Hone Your Skills

The very best way to help you get to grips with the *Shot, Steel and Stone* rules for horse and musket warfare is to demonstrate them actually being used. To this end, I have devised a species of mini-campaign that takes place in Martinstaad, a small country that lies to the north of my favoured fictitious nation, Prunkland. Martinstaad was, until 1744, a neutral country, at which point my wargaming chum Guy Hancock (who commands the forces of Faltenland) and I, stymied in our attempts to invade each other's territory, decided to ignore the neutrality of our little neighbour and move to seize its land and considerable natural resources. Success would also result in achieving strategic superiority on the northern flank. What ensued was known as The Martinstaad Crisis 1744-45 and I am forced to overcome my natural modesty to report that the outcome was a complete success for Prunkland, with the capital of Martinstaad, somewhat confusingly called Martinstadt, falling to a majestic strategic plan devised by King Ludwig of Prunkland himself.[1]

The drubbing Faltenland received led to a peace that, in campaign terms, has now lasted more than two years – something of a record as far as the two bellicose neighbours are concerned, I can tell you. This has left Prunkland in a position to – how can I put this – pursue other interests abroad, including involving itself in affairs much further west, where it has been able to acquire new territories as a result of the recent (April 1747) war known as The Grenouissian Intermezzo, which featured as a three-part series in *Battlegames* magazine over the winter of 2011-12.

However, all has not been well in little Martinstaad since the cessation of hostilities between Prunkland and Faltenland because, understandably, the indigenous population are not entirely happy about being occupied, even by such smart, handsome and benificent fellows as my Prunklanders. As a result, trouble has erupted in the early summer of 1747, a popular uprising led by the exiled Elector Otto von Bonkelschwonk has wrestled control of the capital city from its Prunklandish occupiers, and the country's little army has reformed under the banner of freedom, vowing to throw out the southern invaders.

With the Prunklandish garrison of Martinstadt now held captive and the Governor of the fortress under house arrest, events have moved fast. King Ludwig of Prunkland has received the news, and has sent an emissary to make it clear to the rebels that they must lay down their arms and return to their homes, or worse will follow.

Let's take a quick look at a map showing central Martinstaad. This is a

---

1 *I seem to recall that the whole 'Martin' thing came about because a work colleague of Guy's was going to be involved in the campaign as a third party, but for reasons long forgotten, he had to withdraw, so he was commemorated by naming the country and capital city after him.*

scan from one of my old (circa 1992) copies, and you can still see some of the pencil marks from my workings at the time.

The capital, Martinstadt, can be seen at the top of the map, from which rebel forces have headed south, then turned south west after Rossdach, aiming to retake the key town of Überplink and the important road junction about 15 miles north east of the town. Prunkland lies to the south east of this map, beyond the city of Yaveltor on the Martinstaad side of the border, but also has a significant force much closer in the town of Vaastrich, which lies just to the west of this map.

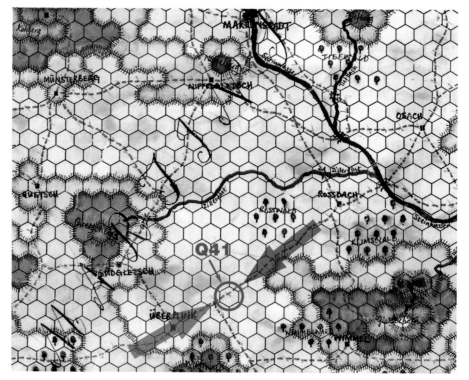

Our action begins at dawn on 29th May 1747 in hex Q41. (Alert readers will notice that this map was drawn using the hex paper turned 90° compared to the way I normally use it, for no other reason than that Martinstaad is a comparatively tall and narrow country, and so fitted the paper better that way. This means that the rows of hexes 'wobble' left to right rather than up and down, so the hex immediately to the left of Q41 is P41 and so on.)

A detachment of Prunklanders tasked with patrolling the Überplink-Rossdach road has been scouting the area north and south of the bridge across the Plattelbach. This is a small, single-span affair, built of local stone. Even though the stream is not very wide, the banks here are rather steep and, especially in the spring, the Plattelbach runs fast with meltwater from the nearby hills. King Ludwig's men have also been investigating the nearby villages of Trabensdorf and Elfershausen to the north and Jüngersbach to the south. The countryside hereabouts is green, rolling and very pleasant, supporting forestry, dairy, sheep and arable farming and as the dawn breaks, the crowing of cocks and the lowing of cattle can be heard through the mist that cloaks the valley.

In campaign terms, a contact is now made, whereupon Prunkland declares a Brigade (though as we shall see, the available forces don't exceed a Detachment by very much to begin with) and Martinstaad declares a

Wing. Both sides are happy to proceed to the more detailed hex as shown at the foot of the page.

Battle 1: advance guards clash at Knechtbrücke

In the vicinity of the bridge (known locally as the Knechtbrücke), the forces of Prunkland, commanded by one Brigadier von Protz, are as follows:

- A von Valeri Ulanen — 4 bases of light cavalry, B class
- B 1st company von Kleidemacher Jäger — 2 bases of light infantry, B class, armed with rifles
- C von Czapka Husaren — 4 bases of light cavalry B class
- D 1st battalion von Schmidt Musketiere — 6 bases of regular infantry, B class
- E 1st troop of von Fernschuß Artillerie — 1 base of light artillery, B class

Total: 17 bases of troops consisting of 24 cavalry, 36 line infantry, 6 light infantry and 1 gun. The letters refer to the map of the battlefield overleaf.

Approaching them from the east are the advance guard of Martinstaad's army, commanded by one Major General John McPreece, a somewhat mysterious figure, reputed to live in a remote castle on the wild coast of

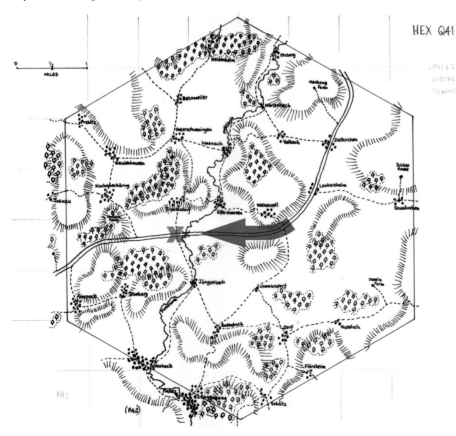

HEX Q41

My original, hand-drawn map of Q41, again with the pencil construction lines and notes visible. As you can see, this is an area of forested rolling hills and valleys, dotted with small hamlets, villages and farms through which the major road from Rossdach to Überplink passes. The forces of Martinstaad, strung out along the road as they decamp from their overnight stop around Dielkirchen and Lenkersheim, are debouching onto the plain and approaching Prunkland's Detachment of light cavalry and infantry, with a single gun, camped near the bridge.

Walesia and a wild goose if ever there was, now in the employ of the Elector of Martinstaad and keen to cement his reputation as a real up-and-at-'em firebrand. With him at the head of the column are the following:

- 1   Jesseldorf Light Dragoons   6 bases light cavalry, C class
- 2   Kaiserberg Chasseurs   6 bases light infantry, C class
- 3   Dolpermann Dragoons   4 bases heavy cavalry, B class
- 4   Osach Light Artillery   1 base light artillery, B class
- 5   Fendwiese Fusiliers   6 bases line infantry, B class

Total: 23 bases of troops consisting of 30 cavalry, 36 line infantry, 18 light infantry, 1 gun. The numerals refer to the map of the battle opposite.

For the purposes of our game, both commanders are rated as Competent, rather than Superior or Cautious. However, note that the composition of the forces is somewhat different in terms of numbers and morale ratings – campaigns, just like real wars, rarely see identical forces facing each other across the field and are all the better for it!

Now, this little action is eminently suitable for beginners, involving as it does a reasonable variety of the troop types typically encountered

A closer view of the area covered by the battle, showing the 6' x 4' table area used for battle 1 and a suggested area for a second, larger game, increasing from a comparatively small affray between advance guards who then receive reinforcements, up to a major clash upon which the success or failure of the Martinstaadian Revolution hangs. (It should be noted that Prunkland's historians refers to this period as the Martinstaad War of Independence since, as far as they are concerned, Martinstaad brought nothing revolutionary to the affair at all.)

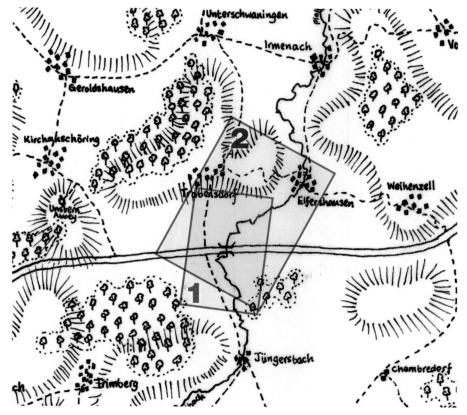

throughout the horse and musket period, although our action is very much an eighteenth century one (and A and B class infantry therefore have the option to 'turn about' to face attacks). Moreover, as we shall see, it forms the first of two actions (see the map opposite) that, as more troops are fed into the battle, increase the physical size of the encounter, the challenges for the player and the complexity of the tactical situation.

So let's crack on and take a look at the start positions for Battle 1.

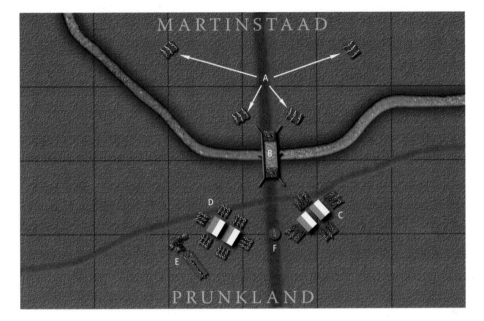

The bugles calling *reveille* have only just ceased their clamour and von Protz's men in camp are rousing themselves from their slumber, stumbling out of bed to stand-to for roll call. North of the road is von Schmidt's battalion of musketeers, arrayed around the camp as its companies form up. Nearby are the gunners of von Fernschuß artillery, checking equipment and tending to the limber horses as they settle between the wooden shafts. South of the main road, von Czapka's hussars are feeding and grooming their horses as the sun tries to break through the early morning mist that has settled in the valley near the stream.

On the far side of the stream are the light troops, doing what they do best, which is standing guard and patrolling in dispersed formation. The two platoons of von Kleidemacher Jäger are at either end of the bridge and beyond them, dispersed north and south of the main road, are von Valeri's lancers, the two squadrons arranged with one troop forward and one troop a few hundred yards nearer the bridge, facing somewhat north east and south east respectively. With the morning mist as it is, the lead troops are barely within sight of their fellows.

Brigadier von Protz himself (F) is on the road between the campsites, already planning his day with his aides, his intention being to hold the bridge with the *Ulanen*, musketeers and the gun, whilst sending von

Czapka and his hussars with the *Jäger* on a reconnaissance mission to the nearby villages.

Meanwhile, as you can see, having set off about an hour before dawn, Martinstaad's forces are heading west along the road and, as dawn breaks, they have reached the very edge of the table, with their order of march as follows:

1	Jesseldorf Light Dragoons	on the road
2	Kaiserberg Chasseurs	deployed half north and half south of the road
3	Dolpermann Dragoons	on the road, following the light dragoons
4	Osach Light Artillery	on the road, following the dragoons
5	Fendwiese Fusiliers	on the road, at the rear

Major General McPreece, never a man to be found far from trouble, is at the very head of the column with the light dragoons, peering through the mist ahead, his keen eyesight scanning the brightening horizon as the rising sun begins to burn away the early fog. Now he can hear the murmur of running water ahead, and what are those smudges that appear to be moving? Are they men, or just more grazing animals like the many they have passed in this region?

But now, McPreece sits bolt upright in his saddle, for the sound of a bugle call is unmistakable, whether muffled by mist or not.

"Quickly, men," he calls, "on your guard now. Make ready – the enemy are near!" His order is accompanied by the sound of hundreds of sabres raking from their scabbards and men checking the locks on their muskets.

In terms of the game, it is deemed that visibility in turn 1 will be just 24". As a result, as the forces of Martinstaad reach the eastern table edge, they are able to see – and be seen by – the platoon (for our purposes, a single base) of Kleidemacher Jäger at the eastern edge of the bridge, but not their companions at the western end. The four troops of von Valeri Ulanen are also visible, but Brigadier von Protz and his troops near the camp are, for the time being, still invisible.

The first thing that needs to be done is to roll a die for each side to see who has the initiative and, given that they are emerging from the early morning mist, justice is seen to be done – though only just – because Martinstaad rolls a 2 compared to Prunkland's puny 1 and, living up to his reputation as a firebrand, McPreece decides to go first and begins issuing orders.

TURN 1: MARTINSTAAD

Given that time is of the essence if he is to take and hold the initiative, Major General McPreece scans the situation quickly and orders the Jesseldorf Light Dragoons, a keen unit that has yet to see action, to charge straight ahead down the road in order to clear the light infantry he can see out of the way and seize the bridge. He is not worried by the two troops of enemy lancers to either side near the bridge – they are outnumbered by the light dragoons and, at the moment, appear to be facing the wrong way anyway! Similarly, the two troops of lancers closer to him, but further to the flanks, are isolated and can be dealt with by the Kaiserberg Chasseurs, another inexperienced unit who could do with a taste of success.

Note that neither the light dragoons nor the *chasseurs* (who are light infantry) *require* orders, since they can act on their own initiative, but it is considered good form to include them in the ordering process. They do both benefit from a good leadership roll if commanded, or suffer the results of a bad roll. In this instance, Major General McPreece is insistent that both the light cavalry and the light infantry are very definitely kept firmly under his control!

As for the rest of the column, they are to follow on as quickly as they can. Further orders will be issued as and when they reach the field of battle.

Having issued his orders (out loud, if you please, with no mumbling or shilly-shallying), McPreece must now discover whether the orders got through. Two dice tumble across the table – and come up 3 + 1 = 4, an excellent roll that means he can add 2BW to the movement of his cavalry and 1BW to the movement of all other troops, should he wish. Such a result might mean that his orders got through very quickly, or that the individual unit commanders receiving the orders are on good form today and so on; the specifics don't really matter, and can just be summed up by saying that luck is with Major General McPreece at this moment, though of course that might change...

Now, let's begin with the charge by Jesseldorf Light Dragoons, because that prompts a number of calculations – see "When to test reaction" on page 387. First of all, we need to discover whether the cavalry are up to the task in the first place, especially since they are inexperienced, C class troops; secondly, we need to find out what that platoon of von Kleidemacher Jäger intend to do, such as stay where they are and shoot at the onrushing cavalry, or shoot before attempting to evade, or just get out of the way altogether; and then we might need to discover how the light dragoons will themselves react to any casualties they receive. This may sound complicated but in fact, once you get the hang of it, the procedure becomes automatic and quite often, experienced players can just look at a situation, do a quick bit of mental arithmetic and decide whether it's worth rolling the dice or doing the full calculation at all: sometimes, it's just plain obvious what should happen.

However, for the time being, permit me to take you through the calculations in full, so that you get the idea.

Let's start with the Jesseldorf Light Dragoons. Consult the Reaction test modifier table on page 389.

They are a Normal sized unit, consisting of 6 bases	0
They are currently advancing (the charge has not yet begun)	0
They have no cover, but nor does the closest enemy	0
They are regular light cavalry in close order	0

They are supported +2

(The remaining factors, relating to melee, do not apply yet)

So far, we have a running total of +2, and being C class troops, they need to achieve a total of 10 to pass the test.

They have not yet suffered any hits, nor are they disrupted, so there are no further deductions to make.

On the positive side, the Commander-in-Chief is right next to them at this point in the turn, so we can add 2 points there, making our running total of +4.

Now, we pick up our pair of dice. With a total of 10 or more required, we can hear the drum roll as Major General McPreece attempts to score 6 or more. They roll to a halt and – it's a 4 and a 5, making 9. Added to the 4 points we already had in hand, this makes a total of 13 points, more than enough for the charge to proceed.

Now, the focus shifts to the little platoon (a single base in this instance) of von Kleidemacher Jäger on the bridge, who now hear the cavalry's bugler sound the charge, and see the advancing horsemen emerging from the mist with sabres glinting. There can be no mistake where they are headed, and the skirmishers must test to see whether they will obey orders or simply scatter. They are, at least, experienced campaigners and therefore B class, rather than the somewhat less reliable C class of the enemy cavalry, though not yet the veteran or elite troops who carry the envied classification of A class. Our *Jäger* therefore require a total of 8.

(If players agree, individual units can, of course, be nuanced for a campaign or specific scenario, perhaps introducing C+ or B+ at 9 and 7 points respectively, for example, or a truly awful C- requiring a total of 11 or more.)

Beginning with the table again, the single base, isolated from its fellows, is a mere Extra Small unit, so starts badly with -2. It is static, so nothing to add there and, as far as the enemy it is facing is concerned, it has no cover either, so another 0. It is in skirmish order – that's -1 – but it does have support, which adds +2. Like the cavalry, no melee has yet taken place, so no further factors from the table are relevant.

With a running total of -1, we need to reach a total of 8, leaving a shortfall so far of 9 points. The unit has suffered no hits or disruption, thank goodness, and it is within the command range of Brigadier von Protz, who adds 2 points, so it is left needing 7 or more from the dice roll – hardly a foregone conclusion.

There is hush in the room as two white dice skitter across the table. The first stops showing a 3 – oh dear! – and the second keeps rolling until... Aha! Its top face shows a 6! This makes 9, which, added to the +1 brought forward from our calculation, makes a total of 10, and the *Jäger* have passed the test.

A degree of teeth gnashing can be heard from the opposite side of the table, but now von Kleidemacher's men calmly decide to shoot at the approaching horsemen before evading back over the bridge to safety.

Now we refer to "Shooting at a charge" on page 378, where we can see that we need to determine the range at which the defending *Jäger* may shoot. A die is rolled (with no modifier, since the *Jäger* are B class) and the result is a 4, meaning that they open fire at medium range. (Medium range for a rifle is between 2BW and 6BW under normal circumstances, but the purpose of this test is simply to see how calmly the men will load and shoot under pressure – the *actual* range is irrelevant.)

Consulting "Shooting procedure" on page 377, we can see that the base of von Kleidemacher may roll just a single die. Looking at the "Shooting modifiers" that follow immediately afterwards, we can see that the target qualifies as a 'dense target', because it is an onrushing column of horsemen more than two bases deep, thus increasing the chances of hitting something and deserving a bonus of +1. On the other hand, the *Jäger* are having to remain calm whilst 'shooting and scooting', which may both affect their aim and reduce the time they have to load, aim and fire, so they suffer a -1 deduction, leaving them requiring the original 4, 5 or 6 to hit.

The single die rolls; the result is 5, so a very palpable hit.

Now, the light dragoons have a chance to save which, against a rifle hit, requires a 5 or 6 (the greater accuracy of the rifle means it is more likely to be on target and effective than a musket). This time, the die is black and suitably funereal, because the result is a 4 and a light dragoon falls from his saddle. (In fact, you can just remove a figure from the unit like I do, or use a small dice or marker next to the unit to record the casualty until the appropriate number of figures representing a full base of the appropriate troop type have become casualties. And, by the way, it really doesn't matter what colour die you use, I just tend to always use white for Prunkland and black for its enemies!)

First blood to Prunkland.

At this point, von Kleidemacher make good their opportunity to scarper and turn about, heading back over the bridge their normal move (5BW for skirmishing infantry), minus the compulsory deduction for B and C class troops of 1BW for the delay when reacting to a charge, minus 2BW for shooting and moving, but +1BW for being on a good road. This leaves the skirmishers with 3BW of movement, which takes them to a point exiting the far end of the bridge, partly on the road.

Note that we always measure front edge to front edge, so the *Jäger* base is turned about before measuring the movement available.

As far as the Jesseldorf Light Dragoons are concerned, even though they have suffered a casualty, it is just a single one, which is nowhere near sufficient to trigger a Reaction Test.

Now, this leaves the light dragoons in an interesting situation, because their starting point – the easternmost table edge – lies 67cm (that's just over 11BW) from the rear of the base of *Jäger* they are charging. With a normal move of 7BW, plus the charge bonus of 2BW and the bonus from Major General McPreece's leadership roll adding yet another 2BW, the light dragoons have a hefty 11BW of movement available to them; but out of reach is out of reach, and the lucky *Jäger* are able to make good their escape – *just*! As a result, the light horsemen lose their charge bonus and advance their normal move distance plus the leadership bonus instead – a total of 9BW, leaving them about a quarter of the way onto the bridge. (By the way, make sure your model bridges are wide enough to accommodate a standard Base Width or you will end up having to balance your miniatures in a most unsightly fashion.)

Major General McPreece, back on the baseline, takes comfort from the fact that his light dragoons have now effectively cut the line of retreat for the enemy's lancers, a situation from which they will be hard pressed to extricate themselves, and now turns to the Kaiserberg Chasseurs to do their duty.

The Martinstaadian skirmishers are ready and the company south of the road acts first, wheeling with the southernmost base as the pivot, the other two swinging round to bring their muskets to bear. Note that shooting and moving (or vice versa) incurs a deduction of 2BW, but with a basic move of 5BW, plus their Commander's leadership bonus of an extra Base Width, the *chasseurs* have plenty in hand and swing into position. Likewise, their comrades north of the road wheel to face the other troop of von Valeri Ulanen, whereupon the crackle of musketry begins. Both groups are just under 3BW from their targets, and therefore at medium range.

Starting with the chasseurs south of the road, one die per base is again permissible, and so three dice are rolled, the results being 3, 3 and 1. With a bonus of +1 for enfilading the target (that is to say, shooting from the flank and therefore liable to cause more casualties), things are looking up, but then come deductions of -1 for being C class troops and another -1 for shooting whilst moving, taking the scores down to 2, 2 and 0 respectively. Oh dear. A few bullets whizz close to the enemy lancers, but none hit home.

The company north of the road, however, have superior die rolls, with the dice coming up 1, 5 and 6. This is much better, and after deductions this equates to 0, 4 and 5 – two hits!

Now the lancers have a chance to save these hits, so von Protz picks up two dice and rolls: the outcome is 1 and 5, so one of the hits is saved (a 4, 5 or 6 saves against muskets), but the other is not and Prunkland suffers its first casualty. Honours even!

For such a small, isolated unit, even a single hit is significant, and because it amounts to one hit per base, a Reaction Test is necessary.

Von Valeri Ulanen are experienced, B class troops, so we know that a total of 8 or more must be achieved. Running through the table as before, a tiny unit suffers a -2 penalty; it is static, so that counts for nothing; neither it, nor the nearest enemy, have any cover, so again that amounts to another 0; the lancers are in loose order, so that's +1; and they have 'Friends close' (the nearest troop of lancers), so that's +1; and again we can ignore the factors relevant to melee only. Looking at other factors, the lancers have suffered a hit, so that's -1, and another -1 for Disruption as a result of suffering 1+ hits per base this move. Unfortunately, they are well outside Brigadier von Protz's command range. Before we roll the dice, then, von Valeri stand at -2 and they therefore require a roll of 10+ to pass the test.

Oh, dear. With a 1 and a 5 totalling 6, Prunkland's lancers are a long way from succeeding. Consulting the table on page 388, we can see that a failure by 4 for troops at the halt can lead to only one thing: a rout! This is going to be interesting.

In accordance with the rules, the lancers are turned about and before heading back towards the bridge, roll a die. A score of 3 results in 2BW being added to their normal move of 8BW, making 10BW in all. However, as they gallop towards the bridge, we can see that it is already blocked by the Martinstaadian light cavalry who have pulled up short after their intended charge, so the lancers have no choice but to turn aside and head north along the bank of the stream in an attempt to find an alternative crossing point. As a result, they end up some 3BW north of the bridge, desperately seeking succour!

All that remains for Martinstaad to do is move the heavy dragoons onto the table (allowing for the movement of their light dragoon cousins and an appropriate interval between units, the first two bases of Dolpermann Dragoons are placed on the road) and make a note of how far behind them the remaining units will be.

Unfortunately, Prunkland has not quite finished, because the routing lancers have passed within 3BW of their support troop located close to the bridge. Not surprisingly, seeing your comrades heading past you at full tilt in the wrong direction is likely to make one question one's own part in the proceedings, and so a Reaction Test must ensue.

So, here we go again. It's a tiny unit, so -2; static, 0; no cover either way, 0; loose order +1; and even worse, the unit is now threatened by the enemy cavalry to its flank, -2. Even though the unit is technically within the command radius of Brigadier von Protz, there are now enemy troops interposed between them who also cut any viable means of communication (the road) and no alternative route for communication has yet been found, such as a ford in the river. The upshot, then, is that we arrive at the end of the test with a defecit of -3, necessitating a roll of no less than 11 on two dice to reach our required total of 8 for B class troops.

A 2 and a 4 certainly won't do it, meaning a failure by 5. Consulting our Reaction Test Results table, we can see that this means that the unit doesn't even get the chance to run – it disperses instantly, and is removed from the table.

At which juncture, Brigadier von Protz can be heard stifling profanities, for even such a godly man as he cannot bear to see his precious lancers flee at the first shot! Fortunately, the remaining *ulanen* are unaffected because, thanks to the direction they are facing and the interposed Martinstaadian troops, they can't see what's going on.

The very last thing to do at the end of a player's turn is to move their commander(s) if they wish, and so Major General McPreece (6) trots forward to take station between the light dragoons and the heavy dragoons on the road, ensuring that as many of his men as possible remain within his command radius.

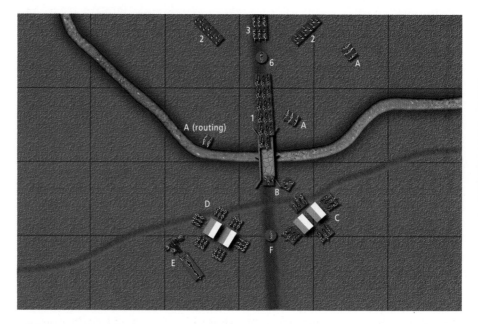

TURN 1: PRUNKLAND

"Revenge", Brigadier von Protz hisses through his moustache, "ist ein dish best served *eiskalt*. You vill pay for zis, McPreece!"

Before the brigadier even needs to issue any orders, there are some units that can act on their own initiative and one more that must respond to a compulsory order, so let's deal with the last first.

With one troop of von Valeri's *ulanen* completely dispersed, another, reduced from three figures to just two, is desperately searching for a way to cross the Plattelbach north of the bridge. I decided that there should be no potential crossing points within two feet either side of the bridge, so with a standard move of 8BW for loose order light cavalry, plus an additional 3BW for rolling no less than a 6 for their rout 'bonus' (hardly the right word under the circumstances, but it will do), the lancers gallop along the banks of the stream, scanning the water for signs of a fording place. In game terms, we can keep this process simple by saying that for each 12" (30cm) of unsurveyed bank scanned, a unit may roll a d6: a 1, 2 or 3 means that no crossing is possible; a 4, 5 or 6 means success. Seasonal variations are appropriate – add 1 to the die roll in high summer or during a drought, deduct 1 in winter or in early spring when the meltwaters are rushing down from the hills, or after torrential rain. Once a 12" section of river has been deemed fordable, this should be announced to the opponent too, or the result noted on a slip of paper if the enemy's troops are too far away to have been able to see the initial crossing, but revealed if they attempt to cross at the same spot. A section of stream or river will only be diced for once. You could, alternatively, cut a pack of playing cards, a red card meaning success, a black card meaning failure and so on.

As it happens, von Valeri's men are relieved to spot a shallow crossing point after travelling some 7BW to the north east, and turn to cross. The ford counts as difficult terrain, and so reduces their movement by 2BW, allowing them to cross the stream and emerge just beyond the far bank using the 2BW remaining.

Being light cavalry, the remaining two troops of lancers are also able to act on their own initiative. Given the sudden arrival of so many enemy, including the *chasseurs* who opened fire on 2nd Troop (though they did not cause any casualties), the most sensible option is for the survivors to join together and move away from the trouble for the time being to observe events. With 8BW of movement available (unaffected by any leadership roll to be made by von Protz, from whom they are currently cut off anyway), the troop nearest the bridge hurries to join their comrades to the south east and, once joined, they wheel about to face roughly northeast, keeping an eye both on the Martinstaadian light infantry and events on the road and beyond.

The next units to be able to act on initiative are von Kleidemacher Jäger and von Czapka Husaren. Let's start with the skirmishers. You will recall that the first platoon of *Jäger* managed to escape across the bridge by the skin of their teeth, outdistancing Martinstaad's Jesseldorf Light Dragoons after inflicting a casualty on them. Their comrades of the second platoon had simply positioned themselves beside the south west corner of the bridge, ready to defend themselves. Now, using their initiative, the first platoon sprints to the north west corner of the bridge across from their comrades, and the crackle of rifle fire begins (to which we shall return).

Meanwhile, von Czapka's hussars, rudely stirred from their breakfast, swing themselves into their saddles and, despite being slightly disordered, prepare to do what every self-respecting hussar has done down the ages – *charge!*

As we have seen, a unit wishing to charge must take a Reaction Test first, so let's run through this quickly:

With only 4 bases, von Czapka is a small unit	-1
At the point of testing, the unit is static	0
They have no cover, nor does the enemy	0
The unit is in loose order	+1
Owing to its dispersal, only 'Friends close' can be claimed	+1
The unit is disrupted (scattered around the camp)	-1
But Brigadier von Protz is nearby	+2

With no hits suffered so far, this makes a subtotal to carry forward of 2, so with a total of 8 required to pass, von Protz needs to roll 6 or more with two dice, and he obligingly rolls a 4 and a 6 totalling 10, so the hussars pass with flying colours and are gathered together into a column charging straight for the bridge. However, we don't move them into contact just yet because now, the Jesseldorf Light Dragoons must test to see whether they will stand to face the onslaught. Moreover, a formed unit in good order has the opportunity to countercharge, and Major General McPreece expresses his desire for his light cavalry to do just that.

Running through the test swiftly, we know they are a Normal sized unit, so 0; they are advancing, +1[2]; they have no cover relative to the enemy, 0; they are in close order, +2; they are certainly supported, +2; melee factors don't apply; they have one Disruption point (charging unit failed to make contact this turn); but Major General McPreece is right behind them, urging them on, +2. This gives them 6 points out of the 10 required for a C class unit to pass, so the dice roll needs to be 4+. Major General Johnny McPreece picks up the black dice, shakes them, kisses them, shakes them again, blows on them for luck and then rolls... a 3 and a 6, adding 9 to our subtotal, making a mighty total of 15. The inexperienced cavalry can be heard muttering, "Bring it on!"

With both sides hurtling towards a mighty crash on the bridge, all that remains is to simply determine precisely where it will happen. Don't forget that B and C class troops countercharging suffer a compulsory delay of 1BW before reacting. This is achieved by allowing von Czapka Husaren to advance 1BW first (just move the frontmost base, rather than the entire unit at this stage). Then we compare relative speeds. The hussars are loose order light cavalry, giving them a charge move of 10BW; their opponents are close order light cavalry, also charging, with a permissible move of 10BW on the road, so they are moving at the same speed. Therefore, we mark the point halfway between the two units and this is where the impact happens, so the units are moved forwards until they come into contact at this point, where they are left until the melee phase of the turn.

Bear in mind that all this action has happened before any orders have been formally issued: it is all possible as a result of light troops being able to act on their own initiative and, in the case of the *Jäger* near the bridge and von Valeri Ulanen on the plain beyond the stream, because some units began the turn within 3BW of the enemy, which also qualifies them for being able to act on their own initiative. Now, however, it is time for von Protz to get the rest of his men into action.

How disappointing, then, to see the Leadership Roll dice stutter to a halt showing 3 and 6, totalling 9: a failure by the smallest of margins, but a failure nonetheless. Such a result means that any cavalry or horse artillery under his command would deduct 2BW from their movement, and infantry and other artillery 1BW – not the end of the world, but alarming enough when enemy cavalry are heading in your direction!

In fact, Brigadier von Protz has only two units left to command, the remainder having acted on their own initiative. Von Schmidt Musketiere

---

2   *Note that they do not count as charging because during their turn, they were outdistanced by von Kleidemacher Jäger, so their potential charge was reduced to an advance instead.*

are able to begin shaking themselves out of their morning campsite parade, with four of the six platoons forming line facing the bridge, the remaining two hurrying as best they can to join them; and von Fernschuß's gun limbers up and sets off towards the northern end of the infantry line, hoping to find a suitable spot to unlimber and fire upon the enemy coming up the road. Having used their entire move allowance, the musketeers will not be able to fire, but nearer the bridge, von Kleidemacher Jäger are taking a bead on the enemy light dragoons on the bridge.

It is not possible to shoot at a base of enemy troops that is engaged in hand-to-hand combat, so the nearest stand of light dragoons is safe, but their comrades behind them on the tightly-packed bridge are fair game. The range to target for both bases of skirmishers is just over 1BW – short range for rifles and therefore +1. Shooting into the side of a column at an angle like this makes it a dense target, so +1, but this is countered by the fact that the enemy cavalry are at least partly shielded by the stone walls of the bridge, giving them hard cover and therefore -2 on the *Jägers'* die roll. So far, then, we have a running total of 0, so the skirmishers need to roll 4, 5 or 6 to hit but, in addition, the northernmost platoon moved, so they suffer another -1, meaning they need to roll 5 or 6 to hit.

Von Protz takes a deep breath, and the dice roll. For the northernmost platoon, a 5 – a hit; and for their comrades, a 6, a most definite hit! The Jesseldorf Light Dragoons therefore need to make two saving rolls, and with an outcome of 2 and 6, another trooper is removed. (It's fine to take shooting casualties from the rear of the column because, in reality, men would move forward to fill the gaps left in the forward ranks.) So far, the light dragoons still haven't taken sufficient casualties to trigger a Reaction Test for them.

With no more shooting to be done (note that under normal circumstances, artillery fires first and any casualties it causes are removed before musketry is calculated, but neither side has managed to get their guns into action so far), it's time to address the clash of sabres on the bridge. With one side charging and the other countercharging, there's little to choose between them, and with only one base per side able to make contact on the constricted roadway, this will be a close run thing. However, we must bear in mind that Von Czapka's men are seasoned campaigners and B class, whilst the men from Martinstaad are enthusiastic, but relatively untried C class, perhaps about to cross swords for the first time.

Let's refer to "Close combat procedure" on page 382 where we can see that both sides, classified as 'Other light cavalry or Cossacks charging', may roll four dice per base in the first round of melee when the impact takes place. The "Close combat modifiers" table that follows reminds us that, this still being Turn 1, the light dragoons are still suffering from disruption, so suffer -1 on their dice rolls; and being C class, they suffer another -1. However, I judged that they are slightly uphill of the hussars on the crest of the bridge, so should benefit with a +1 bonus for that, leaving them at -1 on their rolls overall. Von Czapka's hussars have no modifiers, so the combat rolls required will be 4, 5 or 6 for the hussars, but 5 or 6 for the light dragoons.

The Jesseldorf Light Dragoons roll first (it makes no difference, as melee is considered simultaneous unless one side is outreached or surprised): 1, 2, 2, 6 leads to just a single Hit on the hussars. Von Protz reaches for the white dice: 1, 3, 4, 6 – hardly shattering, but two Hits nonetheless. Time for the saving throws.

Saving against swords if cavalry charged or reinforced requires a throw of 4, 5 or 6 to save, and Prunkland promptly rolls a 5, so the single potential hussar casualty is saved. Martinstaad, however, is not quite so lucky: a 3 and a 5 mean that only one is saved, and so another casualty is removed.

Now, albeit by the slimmest of margins, Von Czapka Hussars have won the melee, and such an event has great significance for both the winners and losers because, first of all, the losers are pushed back 1BW, plus ½BW per 1 Hit difference, to which C class troops must *add* 2 points. Therefore, the Jesseldorf Light Dragoons are shoved back 1+½+ ½+ ½ = 2½BW, not quite enough to lead to their immediate rout, but close to it, as they are bundled back across the bridge.

What must follow is a Reaction test for the light dragoons. They have lost a base, but are still a Normal sized unit, 0; they have been pushed back, -1; they have no cover, 0; they are in close order, +2; they are still supported, +2. However, now the other factors come into operation, beginning with the fact that they are more disrupted than their opponents (1 cause, as opposed to 0), so -1; and they are one class inferior compared to the hussars (C class versus B), so another -1. In the entire turn (which includes Martinstaad's phase as well as Prunkland's), they have taken a hefty three hits, so -3; they have one Disruption Point, so -1; but Major General McPreece is still yelling at them from behind, so he counts +2. Adding this lot up, we arrive at a running total of -1. This means that, in order to reach their required total of 10, McPreece must roll nothing less than 11 or 12 on two dice.

Not only does he fail to do so, but in the most spectacular fashion imaginable. Snake eyes, double 1, and the fate of the light dragoons is sealed! Even if we treat the light cavalry as 'Halted' rather than 'Retiring', the Reaction test results table shows us that a failure by 5 points or more can only have one outcome: the unit disperses immediately, the men fleeing for their lives in all directions, not even routing as a semi-cohesive unit that might have a remote possibility of returning to the fray. No, they are obeying the law of devil take the hindmost, scattering to the four winds, and all Major General McPreece can do is gnash his teeth and remove the figures from the table.

Beyond the stream, Brigadier von Protz smiles a satisfied smile. "Zat," he murmurs, "vill teach zem. *Eiskalt!*"

Now, it must be noted that troops of any kind do not take well to the sight of their comrades being cut down and running away, so the rules state that if friends rout through the unit, or are destroyed or dispersed within 4BW (a distance of less than 150 metres in reality – close enough to hear the screaming and cries of distress and see enough to wonder if you'll be next), then a Reaction Test is necessary. Two of Martinstaad's units qualify: Dolpermann Dragoons and Kaiserberg Chasseurs.

We'll deal with the dragoons first. They are a steady, B class unit, so will require a total of 8 or more. At four bases, they are a small unit, -1; they are advancing, +1; cover is irrelevant, 0; they are close order heavy cavalry, +2; they have support (to either side and on the road behind, don't forget), +2; the melee options are irrelevant, and they have suffered neither hits nor disruption, so all 0; but the Commander-in-Chief is right there, so +2. With a running total of 6 already, they only need 2 points from the dice roll, which you might say they cannot possibly fail, since even 1+1 = 2, giving them the total they need; but *we always classify a roll of double 1 as a failure* (by 1 point for a Reaction Test), so roll they must.

McPreece breathes a sigh of relief as, incredibly, he rolls a 1 and a 2, giving him the bare minimum score of 3 required to pass!

The Kaiserberg Chasseurs, divided in two as they are, count each sub-unit as a small unit, -1; advancing +1; cover irrelevant, 0; skirmishing, -1; supported, +2. Ignoring the irrelevant stuff, they then add +2 for the general, leaving them with 7 or more needed to reach the required 10 points for C class troops. With rolls of 8 and 10 respectively, both groups pass and can continue.

Note that we do not test troops that have not yet entered the table, even if, theoretically, they may be approached by the fleeing light dragoons. We have enough calculations to deal with within the confines of our battlefield, let alone those that could be said to be necessary beyond it! Perhaps, if you have the services of a very patient and able umpire, upon whom you lavish gifts and favours, such a task might be undertaken, but I would advise against it.

So, now we have arrived at the very end of Turn 1, and we are left with just one final test: the isolated troop of von Valeri Ulanen that has routed across the stream must see if they might rally from their flight, or continue, or disperse completely. However, before we need to carry out any further calculations, another rule applies: any unit making more than one rout move suffers an automatic, extra hit for every additional rout move, representing the unit beginning to disintegrate. Our poor lancers made their first rout move in direct response to the shooting casualties, then another looking for a way to cross the stream, and therefore, at the start of this Reaction phase, must suffer another hit as described. This takes the tiny unit down to one figure, below half strength, and they must therefore retire whatever the outcome of any test – which, with the extra hit now suffered, can hardly be expected to be good. Nevertheless, as always, they have the chance to roll a double 6 which would allow them to retire with dignity, but they fail, rolling a mere 5, so they disperse for good.

This is the last calculation with which I shall burden you, because I think you'll have got the hang of things now, so for subsequent turns, I shall give you a simplified account. Besides, I want you to understand that in reality, you will pick up the move sequence and understand what needs to be done pretty swiftly, and you will also be equipped with the Quick Reference Sheets you can download from the website at *http://thewargamingcompendium.com* rather than needing to flip back and forth through this book.

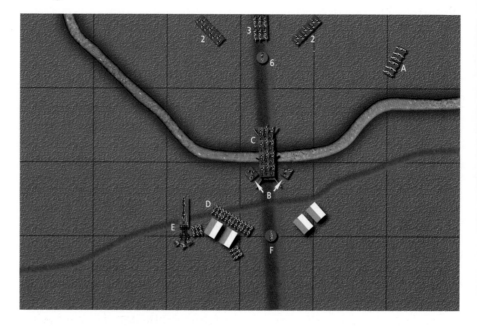

TURN 2: MARTINSTAAD

With his light dragoons following the principles of *sauve qui peut*, Major General McPreece is now confronted by Prunkland's hussars thundering across the bridge just a few hundred yards to his front so, with a long column of troops due to arrive shortly, he knows he has to stabilise the situation and sweep away the enemy light horsemen. At the same time, he needs to exploit the intelligence he gained when he saw the routing troop of enemy lancers manage to cross the stream about a quarter of a mile north of the bridge. With the enemy now rousing themselves in their camp, there is no time to lose.

Using their initiative, the southernmost group of Kaiserberg Chasseurs wheel slightly to face the remaining squadron of von Valeri Ulanen, now united as a single unit to the south. The *chasseurs* north of the road advance towards the stream, parallel with the road.

McPreece's orders are for Dolpermann Dragoons to divide into their two squadrons, the lead squadron to charge straight down the road at von Czapka Husaren, the second squadron to wheel right and head across country to the newly-discovered ford, where they will be able to cross and threaten the enemy on the far bank. The Osach Light Artillery, meanwhile, is to move to the right of the road where they will be able to unlimber in one or two moves to bombard the enemy's positions. Finally, the Fendwiese Fusiliers are to make haste towards the battlefield, where their firepower is desperately needed!

Now it is time for McPreece to test his leadership and he rolls 8, sufficient to simply pass the test, with no further effects. This is enough to send the dragoons into the fight, and the lead squadron spur their mounts towards the enemy, confident that their extra weight will see off the opposition.

Will the dragoons charge? A clean bill of health in the reaction test, including support and the general being close, means they only need a roll of 2+ to pass (though of course an actual double 1 would result in a failure, representing that slim chance that even a unit in a comparatively comfortable situation might just 'lose their bottle'), and they roll 9, so off they go.

As is standard practice, von Czapka's boys must also test to see if they will stand, and this they pass with flying colours, enabling them to countercharge. Taking into account the stipulated delay before they can sound the charge, they see the enemy dragoons begin to advance towards them with malice aforethought before their own trumpeter responds, but with their greater speed (light cavalry in loose order compared to heavy cavalry in close order), they are able to advance just over three Base Widths compared to just two for Dolpermann Dragoons, making the impact point on the road just over 10" from the eastern table edge. As a result, the area available for McPreece to deploy his men is shrinking.

The remaining movement is not terribly exciting, but the limber of the Osach Light Artillery manages to enter the table, though the gun itself is still hanging off the edge, and the head of the infantry unit in column of march behind them is still a couple of Base Widths shy of appearing.

With the movement completed, the shooting phase now arrives. With no artillery in place, we move quickly to musketry and, finding themselves within long range of Von Kleidemacher's platoon of *Jäger* on the north side of the bridge, the northernmost company of *chasseurs* takes a pot shot at long range, but misses. With a similar degree of marksmanship, the three bases of Kaiserberg Chasseurs south of the bridge open fire at von Valeri Ulanen, but, given modifiers for long range and having moved, they need 6s, and fail miserably.

Straight on to the melee between Martinstaad's dragoons and Prunkland's hussars, then. Both sides have just one base with which to fight, since they are in column on the road. Heavy cavalry charging fight with five dice per base; light cavalry charging fight with only four. The opponents are both B class and have no other modifiers to apply, so we are looking for simple rolls opf 4, 5 or 6 to hit and with neither side outreaching the other, rolls are simultaneous.

The tension is palpable as the hussars roll and cause two hits – and the dragoons do the same! McPreece looks on with gritted teeth: he'd hoped for more than that. Now saving rolls are made, and again the honours are even, with both von Czapka's men and Dolpermann Dragoons saving one each and suffering a single casualty. With honours even, no Reaction Tests are necessary and the melee must continue during Prunkland's turn. However, it is permissible for bases following the front rank to spread out to either side of the lead bases at a rate of one on each flank per turn, so more men will be able to fight.

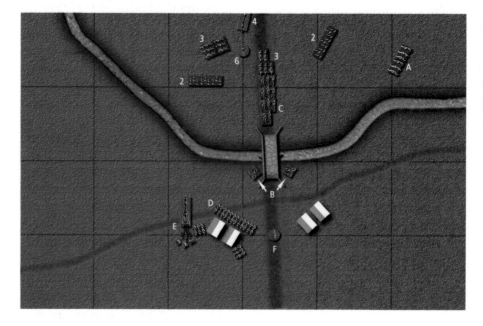

TURN 2: PRUNKLAND

A faint smile can be discerned crossing Von Protz's moustached face. His expensive *Jäger* have escaped, the brave hussars are putting up a stiff fight, stopping the enemy's heavy cavalry in their tracks, and his troops on the west bank of the Plattelbach have had time to organise themselves. In short, the initial panic is over, and now the tide will turn. His orders are for Von Schmidt Musketiere to continue forming up and advancing towards the stream, accompanied by the artillery to their left, and his light troops can carry on using their initiative.

Initiative first. The two platoons of von Kleidemacher Jäger join forces at the north west corner of the bridge, facing the enemy across the stream. Coming together like this makes them marginally less vulnerable, though they are still a Extra Small unit. The next act of initiative, however, has a rather more spectacular outcome: on the far side of the stream, the remaining squadron of von Valeri Ulanen sound the charge, and begin moving towards the enemy skirmishers to the south of the road.

Now, initiative or not, a Reaction Test is still required for the lancers to press home their attack, and everything is taken into account, including the fact that they are somewhat out on a limb. But, with a roll of 10 to round things off, there's no stopping them, and walk becomes trot becomes canter becomes gallop as they hurtle towards the foe, lance pennants streaming in the wind.

Now, what are the Kaiserberg Chasseurs to do? They are only C class chaps, and probably don't really want to be here, but test they must to see if they will stand or have the option of evading to safety. This is added to that and taken from the other, with the calculation finally ending with a requirement of at least 8 to pass the test. The dice settle at 2 and 5 – the test is failed by 1 slender point. Consulting the table of Reaction Test results, we see that this forces the unit to halt – it can neither advance nor retreat at will, it is rooted to the spot.

With doom descending upon them riding grey horses (Von Valeri Ulanen are famous for their dapple grey mounts), the men of Kaiserberg Chasseurs prepare to sell their lives dearly, raise their muskets to their shoulders, breathe deeply and hear their officers' soothing voices: "Wait, boys, steady, be sure to hit your mark."

Having rolled a 5 to see at what range they may open fire at the chargers, they are waiting, you see, until the lancers are nearly upon them and only now does a volley ring out. A whoop of delight as the dice fall 5, 5, 6, which will surely stop the Prunklandish horsemen in their tracks? But no, it is not to be, as the saves roll 2, 6, 6, only one saddle empties and the dreaded steel-tipped cavalry crash home.

In skirmish order and outreached by their enemies, there can only be one end for the *chasseurs* and, sure enough, an entire base of three figures is skewered, the unit is split asunder and broken through, and the whooping horsemen thunder on, suffering no casualties in return. But it doesn't end here, because with plenty of their original move allowance left, Von Valeri's men see the exposed flank of Dolpermann Dragoons, who have been fought to a standstill on the road by von Czapka Husaren, and urge their horses on to this new objective, taking the dragoons completely by surprise. Yet again, this time against sword-armed cavalry, they strike first and strike mercilessly, kebabbing no less than four of the enemy dragoons with no reply and again, rending the unit asunder.

Unsurprisingly, the single remaining figure of the first squadron of Dolpermann Dragoons considers his situation carefully and then vanishes, not wishing to hang around to become luncheon meat for the lancers. Cries of "Oi! Leave some for us!" can be heard from the ranks of von Czapka's hussars, who now find themselves unemployed and therefore use their own initiative to reform, forming line abreast astride the road.

Von Valeri's astonishing run of success could have had further consequences, because the surviving company of Kaiserberg Chasseurs are within 4BW of a friendly unit that has been destroyed or dispersed, as is the remaining squadron of Dolpermann Dragoons. However, because of the direction they are facing, these events are not visible to them (an Arc of Sight extends as a semicircle with its baseline along the front edge(s) of the unit's foremost bases, as shown in the rules). However, Martinstaad's light artillery, just entering the table, does have to test but fortunately, with the support of the general and a decent dice roll, they remain calm and continue.

Well, that was quite an initiative phase, and von Protz has not even rolled for his leadership yet, so he does so now, scoring an unspectacular 8. This is sufficient, however, for von Fernschuß Artillerie to make good headway towards the Plattelbach and the musketeers to now form up as a single line just beyond the camp.

Thus ends a move with which the brigadier can be very content.

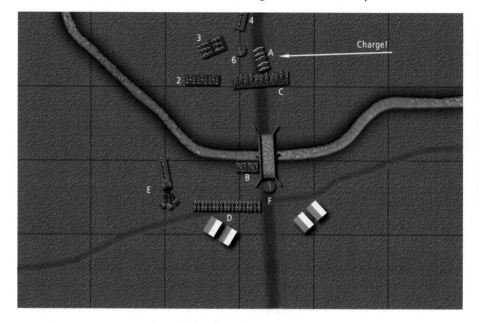

TURN 3: MARTINSTAAD

"Oh, dear. Oh, deary, deary me," mutters Major General McPreece. "Perhaps I should have a lie down, or a nice cup of tea, or perhaps one of those cakes with currants in and sugar on the top." It seems our firebrand has fizzled out.

One can understand his distraction, because he has just witnessed the destruction of half of his heavy cavalry almost literally at the tip of his nose and, given the option, I'm sure that any of us would wish to remove ourselves from such close proximity to the enemy. If those lancers had not been so preoccupied by the open flank of Dolpermann Dragoons, they might well have considered taking him prisoner, so he is lucky to still be in command. Clearly, however, the situation is not at all good, and thoughts of attack must now be given over to rescuing what he can from the situation and ensuring the safety of the remainder of the army approaching from behind.

The first thing we note is that because several units are within 3BW of the enemy, they are able to act on their own initiative without waiting for McPreece to finish his tea or make his mind up. The first bit of quick thinking comes from the Kaiserberg Chasseurs, who are bright enough to realise that they can turn to face the exposed flank of von Czapka Husaren and unleash a volley of well-aimed rounds down their serried (well, being irregulars, slightly ragged) ranks, so they execute a 90° wheel, though this is a much less formal manouevre for skirmishers than troops in close-order ranks.

Next comes the squadron of Dolpermann Dragoons, which has been heading north to the ford, but hearing the commotion, realises that its moment for glory has come. Turning about, the charge is sounded and a quick Reaction Test later, it is confirmed that they are ready for action, their target being the rampaging lancers of von Valeri Ulanen. At this point, therefore, the said light horsemen must also test, which they do, and pass almost casually. The opponents are very close, so close indeed that they are unable to claim the impact accruing to units that have achieved charge speed (for cavalry, they must have travelled at least 2BW). In fact, with the two units separated by only about 2½BW, von Valeri travels just 1½BW and Dolpermann only 1BW. This has important implications for the melee to follow.

Anyway, we must leave them where they are for the moment and turn our attention to the third unit capable of using its initiative because of the proximity of the enemy, and that is the Osach Light Artillery. Its options are limited in the extreme, barely on the table and hemmed in by other units, so it chooses to do the only sensible thing and unlimber at the table's edge next to the road, from whence it might be able to get in a shot. There was much sucking of teeth here, because its position at the edge of the table was moot, but in the proper spirit of wargaming, I decided to err on the side of generosity and the single gun was permitted to make ready.

Having done all that, it is time for Major General McPreece to gird his loins and take his Leadership Test – which he does, and fails by 1 point, rolling a 9. How tiresome for him, as his couriers evidently take a wrong turn and the infantry suffer a 1BW deduction. (Note that the dragoons, albeit not light troops, are able to act on their initiative and are therefore not subject to leadership penalties). As a result, only the first base of the column of Fendwiese Fusiliers makes it onto the table.

So, feeling generous, I allow the Osach Light Artillery to fire off its first roundshot in the direction of the southernmost troop of von Czapka Husaren but, evidently, the gunners are utterly discombobulated by all the excitement around them and despite having three dice at their disposal, none of them appear to work today.

Now come the Kaiserberg Chasseurs, with three dice to expend on the beckoning flank of the hussars. Fizzle, fizzle, phut. Rarely have I seen such a pathetic run of 1s and 2s. But there's more to come.

Glory be, here comes the thud. With von Valeri Ulanen able to outreach Dolpermann Dragoons, they get to fight first, although the coming together is at sub-charge speed, so the number of dice rolled is reduced to 'melee' levels. Although the lancers are 'carrying' a casualty, they still count as two bases, so they roll three dice per base, making six in all. Here we go – 6, 6, 5, 4, 4, 4. With no modifiers to apply, that means the Martinstaadian dragoons have to save three hits before they can respond.

Right then. 3, 3, 2.

McPreece buries his head in his hands.

Before they can strike a blow, the dragoons have been reduced to half strength and have been broken through, so whatever happens, they will be heading home next turn. All that remains to be discovered is the degree of alacrity with which they will perform this task.

There may, however, be compensation, because the surviving base does get its last chance to fight back and, in an act of defiance, one of their four dice scores a hit. "Hah! take that, you snivelling Prunklanders!" snarls McPreece.

Von Protz picks up a dice and tosses it casually across the table. 6. A save. I swear I can almost see a sneer.

Martinstaad's last cavalry has, therefore, been smashed, and just to add insult to injury, Prunkland's lancers have, as has been mentioned, broken through – again – and with most of their permitted countercharge move in hand, they can pretty much pick their targets at will. The *chasseurs*, yes, they look ripe, let's go and pick on them.

With a blood-lusting squadron of enemy *ulanen* bearing down on them, however, and after seeing their noble heavy cavalry routed, the Kaiserberg Chasseurs decide that they would be better off elsewhere and turn tail. However, their random die roll only adds 1BW to their movement and, as they reach the ford and begin struggling across, they are caught and annihilated by the jubilant lancers. The Plattelbach runs red this day.

Mercifully, despite the ghastly events in front of them, both the Osach artillerymen and the Fendwiese Fusiliers pass their requisite Reaction Tests and, for now, will continue to obey orders. But the Martinstaad turn ends, with the remaining heavy dragoons routing off the edge of the table and McPreece praying for reinforcements.

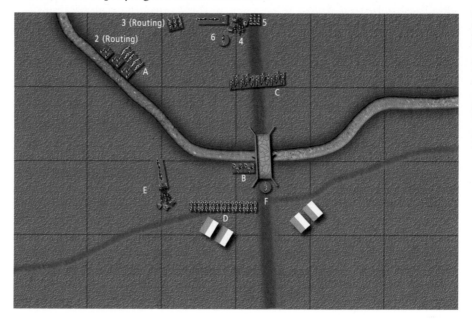

TURN 3: PRUNKLAND

There's little left for von Protz to do except tidy up and prepare for the enemy reinforcements that are bound to arrive wihin the next few hours. For now, he is satisfied to have done his duty and kept the bridge in Prunkland's hands. He knows that now is the time to call for help, and a courier is sent galloping westwards towards Überplink and the much larger force that he trusts, by now, is on its way. What is there left to do?

Again using their initiative, von Valeri Ulanen plunge into the stream at the ford, making their way back to the safety of the west bank where they can recover from their heroic exertions and, with luck, find some of their comrades from the other, less fortunate squadron in time for the next action. Von Czapka Husaren have a commanding position astride the road, and simply move back slightly closer to the bridge to stay at long range from the enemy gun and their infantry that are just arriving. Finally, von Kleidemacher Jäger feel confident enough to head back over the bridge to the east bank, from where they will be able to begin sniping at the enemy gun crew.

Von Protz's Leadership Roll is another competent 8, so von Schmidt Musketeers are able to move to their intended position on the west bank of the stream north of the bridge, and von Fernschuß Artillerie move into position on their left flank, though they do not have sufficient time to unlimber this turn.

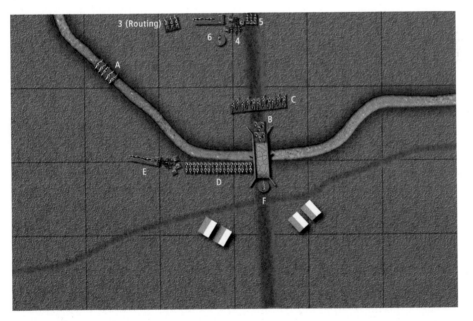

ENDGAME

Clearly, Martinstaad's advance guard has taken a drubbing, with only the artillery and line infantry left on the field, the remainder either dead, routing or dispersed – a comprehensive victory for Prunkland. And it is at this point that we must leave proceedings, perfectly prepared for a follow-up battle as reinforcements arrive for both sides, perhaps necessitating a move to a larger table to accommodate the extra forces involved and covering a wider area. It would be wonderful to regale you with the tales of the epic confrontation that followed – and perhaps, in another place, at another time, I shall, but we must leave it here for now.

My hope is that this exciting and action-packed little encounter at Knechtsbrücke will have served its purpose in whetting your appetite to get stuck in and play, demonstrating the rules and also showing you how some of the different troop types work. Admittedly, this was a battle dominated by light troops, particularly cavalry, and most pitched battles are much more affairs of line infantry, heavy cavalry and artillery, but I shall be posting other battle reports on both the website for this book at *http://thewargamingcompendium.com* and my own blog at *http://henrys-wargaming.co.uk*. You can also be sure that the forces of Prunkland and its enemies will march again in the pages of *Miniature Wargames* and elsewhere.

9

OTHER ASPECTS OF WARGAMING

Further Dimensions to Consider

J ust when you thought you'd got to grips with wargaming, it's time for me to introduce you to some of the other aspects of the hobby that, whilst they might not be of interest to everyone, must certainly be given an honourable mention in a work such as this, which purports to shed light on as wide a spectrum of wargaming as possible. These include naval wargaming, aerial wargaming and some of those other aspects, such as roleplay, 'pulp' gaming and solo wargaming that are almost hobbies in themselves. And finally, I want to give you some advice about those most modern aspects of the hobby, taking digital photographs of your games and miniatures and running a wargaming blog, which has nowadays taken over the role of a wargames journal.

Naval and pirate wargames

There are a substantial number of wargamers who, even if it is not their primary sphere of interest, have at least dabbled in naval wargaming at one time or another. Perhaps particularly for the English, our maritime history is studded with great names that echo down the ages, such as Sir Francis Drake and, of course, the redoubtable Nelson, whose age also inspired the marvellous *Hornblower* novels, subsequently recreated both on film and television, written by CS Forester.

As a young boy, I remember having a set of plastic toy ships to keep me entertained in the bath, and in later years spent some long winter evenings battling with the rigging on the Airfix range of ship kits. The Golden Sovereign, HMS Endeavour, HMS Victory and the Wasa all did their best to defy my patience, but eventually sat proudly atop the family's upright piano until they inevitably fell victim to careless dusting by my mother and, if I recall correctly, an ill-advised game of indoor football with my older sister. The result was a spectacular demonstration of fireships on our garden fishpond, accompanied by an air rifle cannonade, a fitting end to these proud vessels as they sank in flaming glory beneath the induced waves. Of course, I would not recommend that you follow my example, carried out as it was when I was fresh in years and green in judgement.

The problem always was, however, that in those days of the early to mid 1970s, whilst my armies of Airfix plastic soldiers were burgeoning along with my interest in land-based wargaming, I had no inkling of how to go about playing naval wargames. As far as I can recall, there was only one other lad in our school wargames club who had any interest in the genre, and he brought in a handful of WWI Dreadnoughts which really didn't 'float my boat', if you'll pardon the pun.

The other problem with naval wargaming was that everything about it appeared to be highly technical. The nuances of navigation, tides, wind and weather coupled with the somewhat baffling demands of gunnery at sea

Renaissance galleys clash in a recreation of the Battle of Lepanto 1471, seen at the Redoubt show in Eastbourne (now sadly dormant).

meant that one was often confronted with a welter of incomprehensible tables and data. Grey battleships on a grey sea – compared to the glorious sight of a horse and musket army on a terrained battlefield, it just seemed all too dull.

At that time, I had not discovered Donald Featherstone's title on the subject, let alone the Fletcher Pratt Naval Wargame, first created in 1928 and used to train naval officers during WWII[1]. Nor had I explored the small but exquisite ranges of miniatures designed specifically for this aspect of the hobby. But nowadays, things are different, thanks to a number of aspects that have brought naval gaming to the attention of a wider audience.

First of all, we need to thank Games Workshop for having created a fantasy naval game called *Man O'War*, which brought naval gaming to the attention of a huge number of gamers in the early 1990s. Although designed for fantasy, a number of its mechanisms and ideas were certainly applicable to historical 'age of sail' settings and were readily adapted by wargamers looking for a fun, rather than a highly technical, approach. Sadly, *Man O'War* and the models that accompanied it went out of production in 1995 and they are now only available, at considerable cost, on the second-hand market, though the rules and playsheets can still be downloaded at no cost from various fan sites.

In recent years, this was followed up by their cousins at Warhammer Historical (*www.warhammer-historical.com*), with Mark Latham's *Trafalgar* – he also happened to be the Editor of *White Dwarf*, GW's in-house magazine, at the time. This attractively-designed ruleset once again brought naval wargaming to the attention of the wider wargaming community and, whilst experts point out that some of its mechanisms are

---

1 See *"Fletcher Pratt's Naval Wargame"*, ed. John Curry, *History of Wargaming Project 2011*.

flawed, it has done a tremendous job of making even landlubbers such as myself take a second look at an aspect of the hobby I had neglected.

For more modern conflicts, *Victory at Sea* from Mongoose Publishing (*www.mongoosepublishing.com/miniatures/victory-at-sea.html*) is a popular system covering WWI and WWII. Again, a highly readable design and simple rules system lie at the heart of a game that has caught the imagination of a far wider audience than simply the typical naval gaming technophiles – even I've had a go!

There are, of course, dozens – perhaps hundreds – of other rulesets available, covering everything from the triremes of ancient Greece right through to the most modern, missile-equipped battleships and aircraft carriers. Well-known historian and wargamer Angus Konstam, in Charles Grant's *The Wargamers' Annual 2012*, mentions a handful of other sets that he and his pals at the South East Scotland Wargame Club, based in Edinburgh, have been happily using for some time, including *General Quarters* (for WWII games), *Fleet Action Imminent* (WWI), *Smoke on the Water* (American Civil War), *Perfidious Albion* (pre-dreadnought) and *Attack with Torpedoes* (coastal forces). To this list, for the age of sail, I would add *Grand Fleet Actions* and *Fire As She Bears*, both of which are available as PDF downloads from Wargame Vault (*www.wargamevault.com*). You can also find free rulesets on the appropriately-named Freewargamesrules (*www.freewargamesrules.co.uk*).

This form of gaming has been made much more attractive in recent years by the creation of some truly stunning small-scale models suitable for wargaming. Perhaps first among equals is the range created by Rod Langton (*www.rodlangton.com*) whose tiny 1/1200 and 1/300 vessels are, quite simply, miniature miracles, albeit priced accordingly. Close behind are the excellent models from GHQ's Micronauts range (*www.ghqmodels.com*), which include 1/1200 Napoleonic ships that match those from

The Nelson touch: a simple age of sail naval wargame in progress at Partizan.

Langton, and WWI, WWII and modern ships in 1/2400 scale. A name that has been around for a long time – the 1970s, in fact – is Navwar (*http://navwar.co.uk/nav/*) and now, a relative newcomer called Hallmark makes Napoleonic ships in 1/2400 scale and modern style battleships (1906 onwards) in an extraordinary 1/6000! Truly, a fleet in a cigar box.

Finally, it would not do to leave without saying something about one of the most popular forms of 'crossover' naval wargaming, which incorporates aspects of both naval and land wargaming – pirates. Who has not been captivated by the image of the lovable rogue, sailing the high seas, plundering treasure wherever he finds it, with a yo ho ho and a bottle of rum?

Whilst the tedious reality is that real-life pirates were hardly the cheery souls that literature and the movies would have us believe, and many of them came to very sticky ends indeed, it is certainly great fun to play pirate games pitching a cap'n and his scurvy crew against the wicked governor of a colonised island, the keen captain of a Royal Navy frigate and his sailors and marines, or indeed a competing pirate crew, as they follow a treasure map to find a chest stuffed with pieces of eight before the natives or the jungle send them to an early grave.

Rules for such games, whether home-grown or sold commercially, have been around for many years, but again it was Warhammer Historical who raised the stakes with their release of *Legends of the High Seas* a few years ago, based on the same successful mechanisms that had been tried and tested in their *Legends of the Old West*. This type of gaming focuses on the larger figure scales such as 28mm, and a number of manufacturers – my particular favourite is Black Scorpion, but Foundry, Eureka, Old Glory, Artizan, Redoubt, FreeBooTer and many others also have excellent ranges – cater for the gamer keen to raise hell on the high seas.

A pirate game in progress at the Wargame Holidays centre in Crete. Nowadays, there are a wide range of pirate, military and civilian figures from the 17th to early 19th century, together with ships cast in resin with wooden and metal accessories for the masts, davits and so on, that enable you to create convincing games of this type. Many wargamers go to great lengths to create their own ships and scenery. Photo © Jon Sutherland

Unless your crew is to remain landlocked, you will also need ships, and since 28mm represents something around 1/60 scale, you are confronted by the need for a fairly substantial model! A typical frigate of, say, 32 guns, measured in the region of 140 feet in length by 35 to 40 feet in the beam: scaled down, that's a model over two feet in length by 8" wide, and of course its mainmast will be roughly as tall as the ship is long. For this reason, most gamers confine themselves to smaller vessels, what in naval parlance would be called "4th rate" and below. These include some evocatively-named vessels, such as schooners, cutters, ship-sloops, corvettes, brigs, barques, luggers, chasse-marees, galleys, xebecs and so on, armed with anything from just half a dozen up to 24 guns or so.

Many wargamers make these themselves, although as you would expect, you can buy wargame ships for pirate games as kits. The point here is that what you want is the effect, rather than the detailed reality, of a period ship, because too much detail, especially rigging, simply gets in the way of your fingers and miniatures. As a guide, see Angus Konstam's helpful website at *www.edinburghwargames.com/Pirate%20Ships.htm*.

Pirate games are, in effect, a form of skirmish wargame, and the rules I have provided in this book for Wild West games can easily be adapted to suit the period from roughly 1620 through to the Napoleonic period – indeed, I plan to do so myself for a future work. The only additions needed are simple rules governing ship-to-ship combat, boarding parties, landings by rowing boat, swashbuckling combat aboard ship and adaptations of the weapons listed to include blunderbusses and those marvellous coconut hand grenades that were such a feature of *Swiss Family Robinson*. However, I have little doubt that your inspiration, these days, is more likely to be *Pirates of the Caribbean* and its sequels!

This cursory introduction is, of course, the mere tip of the proverbial iceberg, but I hope that these few pointers will inspire you to delve further if you feel you have 'the Nelson touch'. Perhaps the best starting point is to visit the site of David Manley (*www.btinternet.com/~david.manley/naval/naval.html*), one of the most respected naval wargamers alive, and use the links on his site for further exploration. For those of you who fancy being the next Blackbeard, then take a look at the Pirate Wargames Yahoo! Group at *http://games.groups.yahoo.com/group/PirateWargames/*.

Air wargames

My contact with air wargames followed pretty much the same trajectory as my dealings with naval wargames, except that as a boy, inspired by the adventures of Biggles and war movies like *The Battle of Britain*, *633 Squadron* and *The Dam Busters*, I made far more model aircraft than I did ships. As you may recall me mentioning in the introduction, my father had a particular love for and connection with aeroplanes which certainly filtered through to me, and I still find flying machines both fascinating and beautiful.

Playing with aircraft, other than in a somewhat childish *dakka dakka*

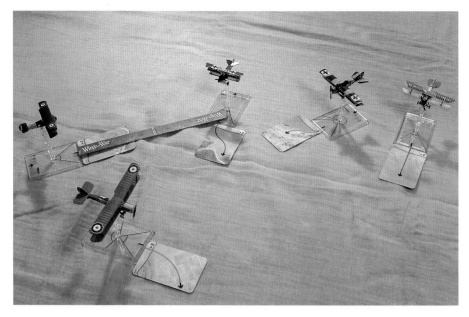

Wings of War (now known as *Wings of Glory*) game in progress. The Germans have 'jumped' a British reconnaissance patrol but the Sopwith Camel is able to open fire on the Dr. III while the Bristol tries to escape..

dakka neeeeooooowwwwww way[2], requires the introduction of something more than is needed for most wargames: the third dimension. Whilst naval games can be played on a completely flat board, and land wargames on an almost featureless one, save a few contours, air wargames really do need the gamer to 'think outside the box'. It is just a fact that gaining a height advantage plays a huge role in aerial combat, and depicting this satisfactorily in a game presents something of a challenge, especially if one is to avoid the same kinds of technical tedium that can bedevil naval gaming.

Of course, the other thing that air wargaming has had to contend with is the rise of the personal computer. In the early 1990s, I have to confess to being addicted to a number of flight simulation games which were, for the time, completely phenomenal experiences that put the player right in the cockpit. Nowadays, even the lay person is completely familiar with the concept of flight simulation for both civilian and military use. By comparison, the thought of shoving a model aeroplane around a board suspended by a bit of wire seemed pointless but, despite this, some innovative rules writers have managed to not only maintain the patient's pulse, but even give it something of a rebirth.

Whilst Donald Featherstone – inevitably – had already produced a book on the subject in 1966, I was not tempted to tackle air wargaming until the emergence, in 2004, of a game designed by Italian company Nexus. *Wings of War*, soon to be re-released by Ares Games as *Wings of Glory*, uses a beautifully elegant system that removes all of the technical aspects from

2 *Mind you, as a boy I was delighted with a couple of toys brought out by Dinky: a Hawker Hurricane that made machine gun noises, and a Ju-87 Stuka that actually dropped a bomb which, armed with a cap gun cap, made a satisfying bang on impact!*

the game and instead involves the player in making split-second tactical manoeuvre decisions in order to try to attack the opponent in his blind spot. It manages to do this by using a mixture of miniatures (though these are not strictly necessary), cards and boards on a tabletop, which can be terrained if the players wish. The movement cards are cleverly tailored to match the speed and manoeuvrability of each, individual aircraft type; so, for example, a Fokker DrIII triplane has a different range of options available to it compared with, say, a Sopwith Camel. Each turn, each player lays down a manoeuvre card of his choice simultaneously which, combined with models that can be raised or lowered using pegs in their stands to denote altitude, results in dogfights that are both great fun and surprisingly realistic.

Another clever factor is the shooting. If the enemy is in a player's field of fire and in range, he can be shot at, but die rolls are eliminated and cards indicating damage received are drawn instead. At close range, the player receiving fire must draw two cards, but at long range, only one. The results of these are kept secret unless the plane starts billowing smoke. Until a plane actually crashes, the opponent is kept guessing how much damage he has done, which leads to some intriguing situations. Is my opponent bluffing, or not? Has he made several consecutive left turns because his ailerons are damaged or because he wants me to *think* they are?

Given that the miniatures accompanying the game are themselves highly attractive and collectible, and that a novice can often put up a good fight or even beat a veteran player, it's small wonder that *Wings of War* quickly took hold and became something of a phenomenon. I know of many players who, like myself, would not call themselves air wargamers as such, but have happily invested in one or two of the boxed sets and a handful of extra aircraft for pick-up games at their local club or for a quick (and that is meant literally – it's possible to have a game in ten or fifteen

Hurricanes and Stukas mix it up over the English Channel in a Battle of Britain convoy protection game seen at the Whiff of Grapeshot show in Woolwich. The aircraft are 1/144 scale.

minutes) game at home with friends or even normally bewildered family.

Whilst *Wings of War* has enjoyed great success, partly because it fulfils the 'game in a box' principle, there are also many other rulesets that enjoy a high reputation amongst gamers, such as *Check Your Six!* and, from TooFatLardies, the cheekily-named *Algernon Pulls It Off* and *Bag the Hun*. Once again, to see what else is available I would refer you to the Freewargamesrules website mentioned above and to Wargame Vault, which has a wide range of card aircraft model kits to download – see *www.wargamevault.com/index.php?filters=40107_0_0_0*.

As far as other aircraft models are concerned, *Wings of War* uses 1/144 scale models and other manufacturers also produce metal, plastic and resin models at this scale, such as Area88, Bandai, Boford, Café Reo, Dragon, F-Toys, Furuta, Popy, Takara and Zvezda. There are, of course, many big-name plastic kit manufacturers such as Airfix, Revell and others, who make 1/72 kits of a vast range of aircraft from the dawn of flight onwards, but this size is not often used for air wargames nowadays because of the sheer space required to allow them to manoeuvre. They are, however, frequently used for WWII ground-attack aircraft in land-based games at 20mm or 1/72 scale and Stukas, Hurribombers, Typhoons and Ju-88s are common sights in WWII games. At the other end of the spectrum, it is possible to find models in the micro-scales of 1/300 (GHQ and Raiden models are actually 1/285), 1/600 and even a diminutive 1/1200 from C.A.P. Aero and 617 Sqn (see *www.magistermilitum.com/prodtype.asp?PT_ID=22&strPageHistory=cat*) that can be used, for example, alongside ship models for aircraft carrier operations. Rulesets like *Blitzkrieg Commander*, that are often played with micro-armour, take air support into account, aspects that can literally add another dimension to your gaming.

Once again, I have done little but point out the tip of the iceberg to you, but with luck, you will come to enjoy putting on your goggles and taking off into this fascinating aerial arena from time to time.

Roleplaying

We have already touched upon character creation for campaigns in the "Adding personality on page 309. The system I used was derived directly from perhaps the most famous roleplaying game of all: *Dungeons and Dragons®*. *D&D*, as it came to be known, designed by Gary Gygax and Dave Arneson and first published by TSR in 1974, gained huge popularity and retains its following today. So, just what was the attraction?

For a generation primed by the novels of JRR Tolkien and a blossoming list of other fantasy writers, *D&D* offered a means for gamers to enter that parallel world inhabited by elves, orcs, hobbits and humans, armed only with an expanding range of books and their imaginations. With one participant acting as the umpire or 'Dungeon Master' (DM), the rest of the group would spawn alternative personalities – what we might today call 'avatars' in an online context – with which they would explore the

Typical role-playing character models. These vintage figures include heroes, henchmen and some of their Skaven rat-being enemies who are highly suitable for subterranean encounters or urban skirmishes. You could adapt the skirmish rules used in this book or use *Warhammer Skirmish* or similar commercial rulesets. Vintage Citadel Miniatures and TSS buildings from the author's collection.

alternative universe laid out before them by the DM, guided by the hallowed tomes published by TSR.

That library quickly grew to more than a hundred books, which have subsequently been regularly revised and updated. The game, now published by Wizards of the Coast, is now in its 4th Edition, including the *Dungeon Master's Guide, Dungeon Master's Guide 2, Dungeon Master's Kit, Monster Manual, Monster Manual 2, Monster Manual 3, Monster Vault, Player's Handbook – Arcane, Divine, and Martial Heroes, Player's Handbook 2 – Arcane, Divine, and Primal Heroes, Player's Handbook 3 – Divine, Primal and Psionic Heroes...* The list goes on and on, incorporating scenario books and much more besides.

The key point about roleplaying in general, though, is that the player participates as an individual character. Everything that happens in the game is, in effect, happening to *you*: you have to imagine that you are actually right there, feeling weary from the weight of your armour as you try to fend off a horde of onrushing goblins, or struggling to remember your spells as you battle with an enemy wizard, or creeping around stealthily as you try to break into a guarded room to steal some treasure.

One of the other key aspects of *D&D* and its subsequent imitators is that it works best as an extended campaign, rather than as a one-off scenario. In this way, knowledge, experience and treasure can be accumulated so that your character gradually becomes more powerful and is able to tackle tougher challenges, a system directly mimicked by computer and online games such as *World of Warcraft*, where players spend countless hours working towards 'levelling up' – in other words, having their efforts rewarded by becoming a more powerful character, able to wield new weapons, cast new spells or perform other, more advanced feats.

Such systems are not, of course, confined to fantasy settings. Science fiction, 'pulp' (see below) and even historical storylines can benefit from just such an approach. Fans of popular fiction will readily recognise that a series of stories such as the *Sharpe* novels written by Bernard Cornwell, or the *Hornblower* stories by CS Forester, can readily be translated into just such a series of linked games in which the central characters accumulate knowledge, experience, skills, medals and promotions along the way.

One of the interesting aspects of roleplaying is that it can take several forms, either with, or without, miniatures or, indeed, even 'live', where the participants actually dress up as their characters and act out the fantasy, a form of gaming known as LARP (Live Action Role Play). This is a form which is really completely outside the remit of this work, indeed a world of its own in many respects, so let's concentrate on the first two.

I remember my own first experiences with *D&D* were confined completely to the imagination, without miniatures. The DM would hold a gathering at his house, with the lights dimmed, glasses filled and, no doubt, a somewhat herbal whiff in the air. With a low voice, he would announce, "You are entering a long, dark corridor. The walls are damp and slimy, the footing beneath you is somewhat slippery, and there's a foul smell carried on a faint breeze from somewhere ahead. You think you can hear distant screams and the grinding of machinery. What are you going to do?"

Well, this would be the prompt for some excited conversation amongst the players, sorting out the order of march, checking who had what (especially candles, lanterns, tarred torches, flint and rope, as I recall). The first, guttering torch would be lit, casting an eerie glow over the party and into the fathomless depths of the dungeon, and off you would go, checking for traps and doors and fearing an onrush of gribbly creatures at any moment. Dwarven or thief characters would be called forward to disarm traps or unlock doors; warriors would take the lead with their

The latest versions of the D&D Players' Handbooks (as at February 2013).

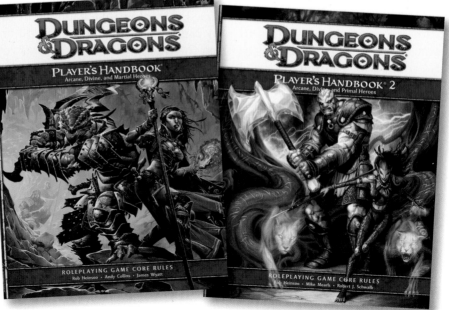

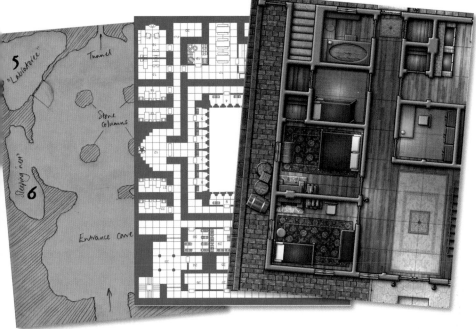

Dungeon maps range from the home-made, to popular 'blueprint' types, to beautiful full-colour renderings of caves, taverns, underground tombs and so on. (Examples here by the author, Oone's Blueprints and 0 HR: Art & Technology – the latter two available from *Wargame Vault* http://www. wargamevault. com).

armour, shields and strong arms; lithe elven characters with excellent bow skills would take post to guard against enemy approaching from afar; wizards would prepare their incantations to cast fireballs or turn enemy to stone; priestly warriors would mutter prayers to protect the party from evil creatures, and so on. One player would always be designated as the map-maker, to keep a record of where the team had been and what they had found. Woe betide them if they made a mistake!

What made it all even more interesting was that you could choose to play a Good, Evil or Neutral character, but this wouldn't be apparent to your companions until a crisis arose, so you could never trust your fellow adventurers completely.

The key, as ever, was having a great DM who not only had a mind of inestimable cunning, capable of setting the most dastardly traps for the players to escape from, but who was also a great story-teller, capable of evoking scenes of horror and desperation or, conversely, expressing a wicked sense of humour. He also needed a fine sense of judgement: obviously, he had the power to unleash the mightiest monsters and terrible horrors on the players, but such a game is always a team effort, and it can quickly unravel if players feel they have been hard done by and their sense of enjoyment can evaporate in an instant.

To assist him, the DM is armed with a formidable array of manuals, which he will have studied deeply, and an equally formidable array of dice, many of which are those glamorous polyhedra mentioned earlier, such as percentage dice. As a situation arises, the DM makes a mental calculation of the character's chances of succeeding in a particular enterprise, such as discovering a trap, climbing a rickety ladder or defeating an annoyed troll, and will determine the die roll required to pass the test. Ah, how the room hushes as the dice clatter across the table; ah, how the player shrieks as the troll's hammer descends to crush his skull. Let's hope someone has a healing potion with them!

With miniatures in play, of course, things are slightly different. Here, each player has his own figure, representing him as a hero in the game, and the DM lays out the dungeon section-by-section as the players explore. With a vast range of suitable scenery available these days, this can lead to some very attractive-looking games, and the range of both adventurer and monster miniatures on the market bears testament to the popularity of this type of roleplaying game (see "Wargame figure manufacturers" on page 475). One of my favourite games of this kind is *Advanced Heroquest*, originally available from Games Workshop but now, sadly, long out of production.

Certainly, as with fantasy gaming in general, sculptors in the roleplay genre display some remarkable creativity and many of the miniatures available are simply stunning, demanding a first-class paint job to match. There are many gamers who concentrate on this aspect to the exclusion of all else, and it is certainly an extremely rewarding pastime.

But there's a final type of roleplaying that has nothing to do with dungeons, dragons or even fictitious characters in historical settings – on the contrary, the aim is to discover something about real-life situations. Really, these events can be described as a form of *Kriegsspiel*, since the objective is to test the player's ability to cope with the pressures of real-life leadership.

For example, a group known as Wargame Developments (*www. wargamedevelopments.org*) has been involved with running such games for many years. The late Paddy Griffith was instrumental in organising games staged at the Imperial War Museum Duxford which sought to recreate strategic moments in history such as the 1940 Invasion of Southern England, the 1941 Invasion of Crete and the 1940 Invasion of Norway. In such games, umpires are almost as numerous as the players, in order to make the games as 'real time' as possible. Participants take the roles of the respective Commanders-in-Chief, with their complete staff, liaison officers and so on, and are confronted with the same decision-making crises as faced by their historical counterparts. Not for the faint-hearted! With a list of activities which rejoice in the names of 'Black Games', 'Command Vista Games', 'Lawn Games', 'Muggergames', and 'Underneath the Banyan Tree' amongst others, I thoroughly recommend a visit to their website where you can download their handbook for free.

I would also recommend a visit to *www.megagame-makers.org.uk/* to read about some of the extraordinary large-scale games that are organised regularly by enthusiasts.

Pulp gaming

Pulp games may, indeed, sometimes be operated as roleplaying games, and at other times as skirmishes, but the common denominator is that they are based on the stories contained in the 'pulp' novels and movies of

Pulp game in progress at Salute, in this instance a rendition of *Ice Station Zebra* which appears to involve a zombie crew shambling across the ice! Undead and zombie types feature regularly in pulp games recreating the atmosphere of 'schlock horror' movies. At least one major plastics manufacturer – Wargames Factory – produces a boxed set of 28mm zombies. You can never, or so I'm told, have too many zombies... The green lights on the submarine are also rather nicely rendered.

the late 1940s, '50s and early '60s. Many of these were science fiction or adventure novels, with hairy-chested heroes rescuing damsels in distress whilst, in the process, saving the world from giant insects/dinosaurs/aliens/vegetation/cannibals/Nazis/zombies/women [delete as appropriate].

Of course, this kind of schlock horror had a precedent from long before in the form of HG Wells (himself a wargamer, as we have seen) and his novels like *The Time Machine, The Island of Doctor Moreau, The Invisible Man* and *The War of the Worlds*. How pleasingly ironic, then, that his novels should be turned into wargames! Games set in a science fictionalised late Victorian world are sub-classified as 'Steampunk', a world with vessels made of gleaming copper and brass, fused with wood- and ironwork, powered by the boilers and pistons more commonly associated with the railway locomotive. Think also of Jules Verne with *Twenty Thousand Leagues Under the Sea, A Journey to the Centre of the Earth* and *Around the World in Eighty Days.*

Once again, some of the miniatures created for this type of gaming are quite extraordinary, and Steampunk has spawned a following and even an artistic movement all of its own.

So, if you fancy your chances at finding some rare archaeological treasures before saving the girl from the giant gorilla in the cave underneath the volcano, beating off a few T-Rexes and giant ants on the way to your steam-powered airship and then making a rendezvous with your brass and wooden submarine that will take you to your secret island paradise, then pulp gaming may be just the thing for you.

Solo wargaming

Yes, that's right: you don't need an opponent to play wargames. In fact, it's probably true to say that almost all wargamers have, at one time or another, played solo.

This is not to say that wargamers are just a bunch of 'Johnny Nomates'! It may well be, of course, that a wargamer might find himself moving somewhere distant from his previous regular opponents or to a town without a wargames club, but there are any number of perfectly good reasons to take up solo wargaming and some gamers actually *prefer* to game alone.

First of all, a solo game gives you the opportunity to try out a set of rules before testing yourself against an opponent who knows them better than you do. Much better, surely, to get to grips with the mechanics of a ruleset at your own pace, rather than in the competitive heat of a game against a live opponent? You can get used to the move distances, try out a few shooting phases and melees, run through a few morale checks and so on until you feel familiar enough with them not to need to refer to the rulebook every time. This will certainly gain the approval of your forthcoming opponents and ensure that you spend more time actually playing than checking the rules.

Even if you are familiar with a ruleset, you may have decided to raise a new army and want to check how it performs before committing it to a serious battle. For example, if you decide to use the *Shot, Steel and Stone* rules contained in this book, you might have initially raised, say, a Seven Years War Prussian army to face Austrians, but then you become interested in the western theatre and fancy trying British against French. What better way than to test your newly-painted redcoats in the comparative safety of a solo game or two, not unlike real-life contemporary commanders who send their troops on exercise?

At the same time, wishing to improve your tactical skills, a solo game is a great opportunity to try out different tactics to see what works and what doesn't. Line up the opposition in the same positions every time, but try different options with the other – cavalry on the flanks, cavalry in the centre, artillery concentrated, artillery spread along the line, a right hook, a left hook and so on. Such training will certainly bear fruit in your future games, and can also be extremely enjoyable.

Solo gaming is also an excellent tool for those wishing to write their own rules – believe me! In the three years or so it has taken me to complete this work, I have lost count of the number of solo scenarios I have tried out, ranging from a matter of a handful of troops on the corner of the table for ten minutes, up to more weighty encounters that have lingered on the table for days as I tested modifier x compared to modifier y for cuirassiers a versus dragoons b and so forth.

There are also certain types of game that are ideally suited to solo gaming. One of my private passions is siege wargaming, but this highly technical aspect of warfare is very much an acquired taste, I have to admit.

Charles S Grant is about to embark on some siege gaming of his own as I write this, and he has confessed that there will certainly be episodes that he will game alone, rather than with opponents. Indeed, back in the 1970s there was a marvellous series of articles in *Battle* by Ron Miles of Southampton following his marvellous Siege of Dendermonde, much of which was fought solo. As well as sieges, some have happily fought entire campaigns solo, especially if they are interested in the intricacies of supply, logistics and economics, aspects that are often sadly neglected.

As your knowledge of military history grows, you will certainly come across conflicts that you become passionately interested in, but which fail to even raise a flicker of interest in your wargaming chums, whether close or distant. The War of Jenkins Ear? The conquest of ancient Sumer? The Rif War? No worry, the fools can scoff as much as they like whilst you game contentedly, using whatever rules you like, in whatever scale you like, whenever it suits you.

Can't sleep? A new addition to the family keeping you awake? No worries: as you cradle the fruit of your loins, you can happily pace beside your wargames table, contemplating your next move.

Worried that your miniature armies aren't painted to competition-winning standard? Yes, many of us have felt the pressure to achieve 'pro' standards with the brush over the years, and almost all of us have realised that either our eyesight isn't up to it, our shaky hands won't comply or simply, quite frankly, that we can't be bothered. Really, life is too short to worry about such things and solo wargaming means that we never have to worry about a snide comment coming from across the table, no sound of teeth being sucked followed by "I think you'll find..."

But finally, there are those who simply find it preferable to game solo. Not for them the hurried setting up and taking down of a game to match

The lonely wargamer. The author playtesting his rules with a tricky scenario, taking plenty of time to enjoy the experience without the worry of an opponent who has to beat the motorway traffic home. Not everyone enjoys solo gaming, but it can be a richly rewarding experience, especially if games against 'live' opponents are few and far between or you are studying tactics.

their opponent's hurried schedule. So often nowadays, we're lucky if we can find someone who can spare more than a hastily-arranged afternoon or evening before work or family duties intervene. I know myself that as a young man, I thought nothing of spending an entire weekend playing a monumental game to a conclusion with friends; nowadays, managing to grab three or four hours seems like a victory in itself. We are all just so busy. But I am lucky and have a permanent wargames table so, on those occasions when it isn't covered with all the general clutter that tends to accrue in a wargame magazine editor's studio, I sometimes grab the opportunity to play through a scenario at a leisurely pace to its conclusion, or until one of my cats scatters units to the four winds!

But you don't have to listen to me: there's an excellent "Solo Wargaming" blog run by 'Jay' who lists his top ten reasons for solo wargaming at *http:// bit.ly/qOjB9u*. Take a look!

As you may have noted earlier, two authors in particular have contributed works on the subject of solo wargaming: Don Featherstone, whose 1973 work *Solo-Wargaming* remains unsurpassed; and Stuart Asquith, who wrote *The Military Modelling Guide to Solo Wargaming* in 1988 and *The Partizan Press Guide to Solo Wargaming* in 2006. Charles S Grant also wrote the extremely useful *Programmed Wargame Scenarios* for the Wargames Research Group in 1983. You can also subscribe to *Lone Warrior*, the journal of the Solo Wargamers Association – visit their blog site at *http://lonewarriorswa.com*. And finally, there's a Yahoo! group dedicated to solo wargaming at *http://games.groups.yahoo.com/group/ SoloWarGame*.

Having given you a general outline of the idea, let's look at some specific ways in which you can overcome what is bound to be your next question: how do you play against yourself? Surely, you can't have a balanced game

A range of solo wargaming books and magazines. Solo wargaming is still a relatively neglected field – the question is whether gamers have migrated from playing solo games with miniatures to shoot-'em-up games on their PCs which would be a shame, because there is a particular pleasure to be derived from the lone pursuit of wargaming perfection.

if you know precisely what your opponent is, err, I mean *you*, are going to do...?

Well, actually, you can. At its very simplest, it's entirely possible to play any of the games presented in this book solo 'as is', because they use alternate move systems – you just move from one side of the table to the other, and put as much effort as you can into doing your best for the side whose turn it currently is.

However, it's easy to add some spice to the mix right from the start.

DEPLOYMENT

Let's say that you want to play a game of *Shot, Steel and Stone* solo. Let's imagine that you have perhaps a dozen units a side, perhaps consisting of eight infantry battalions, three cavalry regiments and a battery of guns, which is fairly typical.

Instead of placing them along the baseline as you normally would, imagine that this is an encounter taking place on a misty morning and units may have gone astray in the fog. Divide each baseline into six sectors – easy if your table is six feet wide – and allocate each a number from 1 to 6. Now, simply roll a die for each unit: whatever the score, that is where it will arrive on the battlefield. Now roll another die for each unit: this time, the score indicates the turn on which it arrives.

Given the unpredictable nature of chance, it could happen that pairs of units appear all along the baseline on turn one, or everything might arrive in one massive traffic jam in one square on turn 6! However, the likelihood is that units will be fed in piecemeal over the first half dozen turns, and the job of the opposing generals is to cope with and make the best of this situation.

To add spice, you could 'favour' one side (let's call it Red), but give it the greater challenge by allowing the opposing side (Blue) to deploy as it wishes at the start of the game, with all units present, whilst Red is subjected to the random dice rolling just described. This creates a real race against time as Blue seeks to exploit the chaos in Red's line before all its reinforcements arrive.

FLANKING MANOEUVRES

It's even possible to achieve the flanking manoeuvres that are so difficult with a live opponent. Let's say that one or both sides are allowed to start with just eight of their twelve units on the table, deployed as they wish. The remaining four units are deemed to be a flanking force, tasked with arriving on one side flank or the other. The soloist can decide on the composition of these forces themselves, or have them randomly determined by rolling dice. In such an instance, then 1 or 2 means a cavalry unit, 3 means a light infantry unit, 4 a line infantry unit, 5 an elite grenadier or guard unit and 6 an artillery battery (or, in the case of ancients, another cavalry unit).

Having determined the composition of the force, the player rolls a die each turn to determine whether it arrives and, if so, where. On turn 1, the player would need to roll a 6 for the force to arrive; on turn 2, a 5 or 6 will see the force appear; on turn 3, a 4, 5 or 6 and so on until, obviously, the force will definitely arrive on turn 6.

Once the arrival is announced, its entry point must be determined. A roll of 1 means that things have gone badly astray, and the force turns up behind its own army – it took a wrong turn somewhere! A roll of 2 means it arrives two feet in from the enemy's baseline on the left flank; a 3 means two feet from the enemy's baseline on the right flank; a score of 4 has it arrive just one foot in from the enemy's baseline on the left; a 5 gives it an entry point one foot from the enemy's baseline on the right; and a 6, best of all, has it appear directly behind the enemy's centre, really putting the proverbial cat amongst the pigeons.

It would be sensible to assume that this force is accompanied by a suitably senior sub-commander, probably a brigadier, who can exercise control over the arriving force, lest they be stranded without further orders.

AMBUSH

One of the most entertaining types of scenario is that of a wagon train or column of troops attempting to reach safety in an outlying fort or camp in the midst of hostile territory. Whilst having a live opponent is fun, it's also one of the easiest to recreate in solo play.

It's best to play this kind of game along the length of the table. The specific period and setting is immaterial: it could be a Roman legion tramping through the ancient Teutoburger Wald, an army of Crusaders wearily advancing amongst the sand dunes of the Middle East, a Napoleonic French army warily scanning the surrounding hillsides in Spain, or a colonial British force marching to relieve a fort on the North West Frontier. All you need is a winding route and plenty of terrain from which an attacking force might suddenly debouch.

One of the other great aspects of this type of game is that the ambushing side doesn't need lots of figures – it's perfectly acceptable to have a 'clan' sized group of just a couple of dozen figures that might appear, fight furiously for a turn or two and then get killed or run off, only to appear again elsewhere.

The game begins with you commanding the wagon train, relief force or whatever it is, and you simply make the force move along the road or track towards its destination. It's important that the bulk of the force is tied to the road, either because it consists of heavy transport or its escorts who cannot easily move cross-country, though it is permissible to have a small proportion of the force capable of doing so. If you're feeling particularly cruel, you might decide that the force is also running low on ammunition, and restrict the number of turns on which it can shoot.

Each turn, as you approach your destination, roll a die for each potential hiding place (such as a wood, group of buildings or behind a hill) that comes within long shooting range of the marching force: a 5 or 6 means

The author playing a solo 'ambush' scenario. Small games such as this can be played within an hour or so or replayed several times to discover alternative outcomes. They are a particularly enjoyable aspect of campaigns; the participants might not be able to justify meeting up to play such minor actions, whereas the umpire can have great fun playing them solo and then reporting the outcome to the players.

that an ambushing force is present. Now roll another die: a 1-4 means that they are only inclined to shoot from a distance, whilst a 5 or 6 means they are made of sterner stuff and will attempt to attack the convoy and engage in hand-to-hand combat as long as they number ten figures or more. Now roll 4d6 to determine the strength of the force, ranging from a mere four souls up to as many as twenty-four warriors.

As a result, the convoy may be able to brush the opposition aside or could be faced with quite a battle on their hands before they can continue. In every case, the objective of the assailants is to destroy or capture as much of the convoy as possible.

You can use the standard morale rules from your regular ruleset to cover the attackers, or use a simpler '25%' rule, which is to say that they will tolerate losing up to a quarter of their number before scarpering back whence they came and disappearing.

The convoy must attempt to keep moving at all costs and you might like to set a time limit, such as twenty four moves, for the convoy to successfully reach its destination. This prevents Red from simply sitting back and waiting for the attacks to come to him and beating them off by circling the wagons – those supplies or reinforcements are needed desperately! You could also allow the garrison of the destination they are attempting to reach – it could be a fort or town – to sally forth with a small force in an attempt to assist the approaching force, but the proviso must be that the convoy is actually in sight from the town and within, say, two feet of the walls.

EVENT CARDS

Another simple way to enliven your games as a solo player is to make use of a pack of playing cards. Every card should equate to an appropriate instruction that must be followed, with Clubs and Spades referring to the Blue side and Hearts and Diamonds relevant only to Red. Shuffle the deck thoroughly and then, each move, a card is drawn and the appropriate action taken by the side to which the card refers. You can moderate the impact by deeming certain cards to be, in effect, 'blank' and on the other hand, the Jokers could apply to *whichever* side is currently taking its turn or, conversely, to *both* sides.

Let's look at an example pack:

- 2   Deduct 2BW from *all* moves this turn
- 3   Deduct 1BW from all infantry moves this turn
- 4   Deduct 2 BW from all cavalry moves this turn
- 5   1 randomly-determined unit cannot move *at all* this turn.
- 6   All this side's shooting suffers -1 penalty this turn
- 7   All this side's meleeing suffers -1 penalty this turn
- 8   All this side's meleeing benefits from +1 bonus this turn
- 9   All this side's shooting benefits from +1 bonus this turn
- 10   1 randomly-determined unit moves *double* this turn.
- Jack   Add 1BW to all infantry moves this turn
- Queen   Add 2BW to all cavalry moves this turn
- King   Add 2BW to *all* moves this turn
- Ace   An unexpected unit of reinforcements arrives. Decide where.
- Joker   A sudden downpour prevents *any* shooting this turn.

COURIER CARDS

Donald Featherstone famously introduced the idea of 'courier cards', back in the 1960s. This relied on the system prevalent at the time of writing orders for each unit under your command, instead of rolling dice for command and control, orders which could only be changed once a courier arrived from the general with fresh orders (or, of course, *in extremis* the general could make the journey himself).

The system is very simple: measure the distance between the miniature representing your Commander-in-Chief and the destination unit, or group of units such as a brigade, on the battlefield. A quick bit of mental arithmetic will give you the number of moves required for the ADC to reach that unit under normal circumstances (usually just two to four moves, depending on the terrain, given that couriers tend to move at cavalry charge speed in most rulesets). Now, for each turn that the courier is in transit, draw a card, with results that might be something like the following:

- 2   Courier killed by stray cannonball. Message lost.
- 3   Horse killed by stray cannonball. Courier continues on foot.
- 4   Courier goes astray, journey takes double expected time.
- 5   Horse goes lame, journey takes 50% extra time to arrive.
- 6   No effects
- 7   No effects

- 8 No effects
- 9 No effects
- 10 No effects
- Jack Courier makes good speed, add 10% to his moves.
- Queen Courier is lucky, journey takes 25% less time than expected.
- King Courier mounted on thoroughbred, moves 50% faster.
- Ace Courier is expert rider, journey takes half expected time.
- Joker Courier is captured by enemy who may act *immediately* on the intelligence.

SOLO CAMPAIGNING

To round up this brief introduction to the idea of solo gaming, it's worth considering the benefits of soloing an entire campaign. This may seem like a daunting and dreary prospect, but in fact, quite the opposite is true. To begin with, all those reasons for playing individual games solo are doubly true when it comes to campaigning. Here, you are free to pursue your passion for strategy at leisure and in your own, unique fashion.

One of my personal joys is keeping detailed campaign journals, an aspect which benefits enormously from not having deadlines. Without the pressing need to produce the next set of coordinates for your opponent and/or umpire, your rambling thought processes can go on for as long as you like. Fancy producing a side-story for one of your units? Go ahead. Perhaps just a single company of light infantry is making a foray into enemy territory to gather intelligence? Well, for you, this could become an exciting little sideshow that would be too time-consuming to be included in a competitive campaign, but a fascinating detour for a soloist. Feel it's time to update the uniform regulations for one of your warring nations? Go right ahead. Or how about some colonial expansion, taking some explorers and a unit or two of marines to some far-flung desert islands to

The author poring over his campaign maps and diaries. This is one of the most pleasurable aspects of wargaming as far as this writer is concerned, creating imagi-nations and seeing them develop as games are played, armies are manouevred and the countries and their peoples come to life. It's especially thrilling when other campaign participants add their own flavour and ideas.

see what they can find? Newsworthy stuff in a solo campaign!

Just as with tabletop battles, you can use dice- or card-driven systems to determine the actions of one side or the other, ranging from the deployment of forces along the frontier to what should happen each campaign move. As mentioned above, you might decide to confine your campaign to 'mini' campaign proportions, involving just a handful of units each side within a confined area, such as a raid across the frontier. On the other hand, with unlimited time, your ambitions can be far grander, encompassing wide-ranging manoeuvres with large forces, including sieges, casualty recovery, prison camps, economic and political background and so on. As a solo campaigner, indeed, these other aspects might be your primary field of interest, whereas the pressure for most conventional wargamers is to produce battles, almost to the exclusion of everything else.

One might try a system of cards, indeed, that determines the entire campaign, so that every campaign month, you draw a card and are faced by a fresh task, such as this:

- 2   One of your regiments is hit by dysentery. Determine casualties and prevent spread of disease.
- 3   The Chancellor warns of reduced revenues. Examine the taxation system and plan economic recovery.
- 4   Pirates/bandits are attacking coastal/hill towns. Prepare a force and deal with the problem.
- 5   Enemy prisoners have escaped from your prison camp. Prepare a force to track them down.
- 6   One of your fortresses is in a poor state of repair. Arrange for improvements.
- 7   You require more troops to garrison your border towns and fortresses. Raise new units of garrison troops or militia.
- 8   Your usual horse breeders have been hit by equine disease and replacement horses are reduced by half for three months.
- 9   Plan a raid on the enemy's capital city to capture their treasury and kidnap at least one dignitary for ransom.
- 10   Transport systems are inadequate. Plan and build a canal between two of your major towns.
- Jack   Your infantry's uniforms are looking tired. Re-design at least one major item of dress (hat, coat or trousers).
- Queen   Raise and equip a unit of engineers, pioneers, sappers or pontoniers.
- King   The weather becomes unusually hot for the next month meaning the army needs 25% extra to drink.
- Ace   The weather becomes unusually wet for the next month, reducing all movement by 25% and cannon fire by -1.
- Joker   There is civil uprising in one of your cities. Roll percentage dice to determine proportion of inhabitants involved, then deal with it causing as little bloodshed as possible.

Multi-player gaming

At the opposite end of the spectrum there are games with several or, indeed, many participants. Here, the challenge is to keep everyone interested and entertained for as much of the time as possible. There's nothing worse than to attend such an event, only to feel like the proverbial gooseberry for most of the day whilst everyone else seems to be having a good time. In these days of high petrol and transport costs, it's possible that people may have run to some considerable expense to participate, quite apart from any entrance fees or accommodation costs that may also have to be found.

The person organising such a gathering needs to have certain managerial skills, not only to ensure that the day runs smoothly, but also to make sure that each participant is matched to the appropriate level of command. If you're designing an event for your own club or group of players, then it's possible that you might know everyone reasonably well and therefore be aware that Bob is brilliant with cavalry, and therefore will be quite at home dealing with a cavalry division, whilst Jim has a spectacular record of losing his cavalry in turn 1 of every encounter, and therefore might best be given an infantry command! If you don't know your players this well, then as organiser, it has to be part of your job to find out by asking some pertinent questions on the entry form.

The same applies to the rules that will be used. Early in 2011, I had the privilege of helping to organise an event where the rules to be used were, in fact, those contained in this very book. As a result, everyone who took part was starting with a blank sheet, and had no preconceptions about how the rules should play, which troop types were likely to perform well and so on, other than from their own knowledge of military history. To my immense relief, the weekend went brilliantly and nary a murmur was raised about the rules, which went down well with veterans and beginners alike.

On the other hand, there are frequently large games organised around a particular ruleset – *General de Brigade* and *In the Grand Manner* are two that come instantly to mind in a Napoleonic setting – where at least a passing knowledge of the ruleset can make all the difference to one's enjoyment of the weekend. Fortunately, most wargamers are decent folk who will happily help to steer the newcomer through the mechanisms of an unfamiliar set of rules, but one shouldn't count on that.

Another peril of the multi-player game is that it's possible for a player to be given command of a sector that sees little, or indeed even no action during the day. Just what, such a player would ask himself, was the point of me turning up at all? Whilst wargames can be pleasing visual spectacles, and it is possible to share the excitement of those participants who are in the thick of the action, the mood can be somewhat different if the idle players are paying for the privilege. They have a perfectly reasonable expectation that parting with their hard-earned cash will lead to them at least shoving around some attractively-painted miniatures, even if their actions don't lead to them being the hero of the day. Therefore, the organiser needs to

Rich Clarke (centre) looks sanguine about our chances as corps commanders of the French Army defending Gravelotte St. Privat in 1870. Umpire John Drewienkiewicz, (blue shirt, left) in whose splendid 'bothy' the game was played, is explaining one of the finer points of the *To the Last Gaiter Button* rules to Dave Hathaway. For huge battles such as this, multi-player games are really the only sensible option. 10mm miniatures were used.

Multiplayer games don't have to be huge, complex affairs. Many small games are run at shows with several players participating, such as this one seen at The Other Partizan. Such mini-multiplayer games are useful for demonstrating new rulesets or providing entertainment for younger members of the crowd who may be in danger of getting bored whilst daddy does his soldier shopping! Evidently, that isn't the case here, however...

think ahead and perhaps allow a player who is in command of the reserve to also take charge of a few brigades somewhere more likely to see action. This may mean having one or two fewer participants overall, but lead to greater harmony during the day.

Multi-player games tend to be large affairs, played over tables much larger than a conventional two-player wargame. For example, the climax game played in the event I helped organise in 2011 covered an area no less than 24 feet by 6 feet (7.32m x 1.83m). What tends to happen – and this is an interesting insight in itself – is that the players in one sector become oblivious to what is happening in the other sectors. Concentrating on their own front of perhaps four to six feet (1.2m to 1.83m), they focus on the player opposite and enter their own little world. Depending on the pace of play, if you're not careful, the result can be that the left flank players are just about finishing move 6 whilst the right flank players are about to start move 8, which can be a nightmare for the umpire to unravel.

And that leads me onto another point: large, multi-player games really benefit from the services of an umpire – and, if possible, more than one. I know that over the course of the weekend I organised, the task of fielding questions from around a dozen players over two days, as well as resolving the small number of complicated questions that arose, together with the campaign back-story, was certainly challenging and enjoyable, but completely exhausting!

A good umpire certainly needs to be on top of his game throughout the event and it can help if he also has a mischievous sense of humour, being prepared to throw a 'curved ball' into proceedings to add a little spice. I have been fortunate enough to participate in a couple of games organised by retired Major General John Drewienkiewicz (known by his wargaming chums, at his own insistence, as DZ) at his lovely country home in Suffolk. These large games, the first an American Civil War battle (Brandy Station) and the second the Franco-Prussian War Battle of Gravelotte St Privat, ran not only with four or five players per side, but also with multiple umpires. DZ is particularly adept at prompting commanders to issue written orders and then, shall we say, 'forgetting' that he has scrunched them up in his pocket, only for them to reappear some considerable time later!

But, having indicated a number of potential pitfalls, the fact is that the highly-charged atmosphere of a large, multi-player game with thousands of miniature troops on the table can be truly wonderful, whether the game is historically-based or utterly fictitious. Playing the part of the French Marshal Marmont and reversing the historical outcome of Salamanca (1812) during a vast game at the original Wargames Holiday Centre is something I shall never forget; commanding a Confederate cavalry division at Brandy Station, throwing in charge after charge to keep the tide of Union troops at bay, was simply thrilling; and holding the flank at Gravelotte St Privat as the onrushing horde of Prussians carpeting the horizon swept towards the French positions was one of the most tense days I have ever had! And finally, seeing more than a dozen players who had played through a handful of campaign moves before arriving to command their entirely fictitious forces in battles fought over ground that had only existed inside my head up to that point, using my rules that had hardly been tested before battle commenced was, for me, the crowning glory: the true spirit of wargaming.

If you get the chance to participate in such a game, take it. You won't regret it.

B-Day in Byzarbia, the second of the immense East Ayton games umpired by the author, this time following on from the previous year's 'The Grenouissian Intermezzo'. Our protagonists were squabbling over the Granprixian protectorate of Byzarbia, a completely fictitious place with a distinctly North African flavour. The personalities of the players were shown not only by the armies they created entirely from their own imaginations, but also by their style of play.

ADVICE FOR THE DIGITAL AGE

10

Exploiting Technology for Your Hobby

Since the pioneers of the hobby wrote their captivating books in the third quarter of the twentieth century, technology has changed out of all recognition, from the simplest to the most complex aspects of what we do. But most of all, it is the power of computing that has affected the way we see our hobby – quite literally. Those early books and magazines were, after all, illustrated mostly with black and white photographs, taken with cameras that used film that had to be sent off to a laboratory, often via a branch of Boots the chemists in the High Street. If we wanted duplicate copies or enlargements, we had to pay for them and wait a week or two. Now, however, we can take untold numbers of photographs with a digital camera and, within minutes, select the ones we like and upload them to a blog or online album for all the world to see.

Here, then, is some advice for making the most of these revolutionary developments that have done so much to bring wargamers together around the world, giving us instantaneous access to the collections that others have created and the ability to discuss what we are doing, in real time, with fellow hobbyists across the globe.

Photography for wargamers

Being the Editor of a wargames magazine means that I am regularly sent articles with accompanying photographs that are, how can I put this – of variable quality? Whether or not you are taking photos that may be potentially published, or just for your own memories of a particularly exciting game or to record your latest beautifully painted unit, here are a few basic tips I can give you that should help improve your results.

- **Get yourself a decent digital camera**. I used to be a keen amateur photographer with what we would now have to term an 'old fashioned' film camera, but the fact is that nowadays, the advantages of digital cannot be ignored and the resolution available is now little short of astonishing. I can remember my first digital camera – won as a competition prize in 1996 – boasted 1 Megapixel. Wow! Then, about ten years ago, I bought a Fuji Finepix 6000 which had 6Mp resolution. It cost me the best part of £450, but transformed the results of my photography, and I still use this camera for most of my work, because the lens is superb – and that's the key. It's generally the case that those companies previously known for great optical equipment still produce the best lenses, and a good lens is the key to getting superior results. Finally, last year I realised that I wanted a small, portable option for taking with me on long walks or on holiday, and to my astonishment I found that the goalposts had moved again: for just over £50, I was able to buy a tiny Fujifilm Finepix AV which boasts an amazing

12 Megapixel resolution – twice the power for a fraction of the price! Okay, it doesn't boast as many bells and whistles as my older workhorse, but for photographing most wargames, it's terrific. So, no excuses, if your camera is more than a few years old, go shopping. The bargains available, particularly online, can be tremendous.

- **Don't use the camera's built-in flash**. The problem here is that, particularly at close range, the built-in flash simply blitzes the foreground and leaves the background in deep shadow. This is because objects that are too close simply bounce the flash straight back at the lens, causing a white-out. Far better to use natural daylight or, if that isn't available, extra lighting in the room, as you'll see later. If you have a larger camera with a mount for a separate flash, then try bouncing the flash off the ceiling.

- **Get yourself a tripod**. One of the most common errors is camera shake. If you want good results, it's really no good just waving the camera in the direction of the tabletop, pressing the shutter and hoping for the best, especially if you're working without flash which requires a longer exposure time. First of all, make sure that you buy a camera that is capable of being mounted on a tripod – the tell-tale sign is a threaded hole on the underside. Second, think about the kind of shots you're most likely to want to take. If you think that you're most likely to want to take close-ups using the camera's macro setting, then you won't need a full-blown, extending tripod. Instead, get yourself a mini tripod that will raise the camera just a few inches above the tabletop, or even a 'bean bag' camera support – a quick search even on Amazon or eBay reveals dozens and dozens of

The author's photography set-up, with a camera mounted on a sturdy tripod, a selection of additional lighting, a 'cube' for specific shots, and a selection of additional, smaller tripods for close-up work. There is also a smaller back-up camera – and the author's iPhone 4, with which this photo was taken! Of course, the other vital piece of kit not shown here is his iMac, loaded with Adobe Creative Suite.

variants, many of them costing less than £10. Of course, having a fully extendable tripod will give you many more options for taking shots of games, whether at home or at shows.

- **Get used to using a shutter cable release or timer**. The main cause of camera shake, after the simple acts of breathing or having a strong heartbeat (seriously), is actually pressing the shutter with your finger. This is especially prevalent now that most cameras don't even have proper viewfinders any more, just digital screens that you have to hold at arm's length in order to frame the picture correctly – a recipe for disaster if ever there was. I still really prefer a bulkier camera that I can hold firmly against my eye, rather like a sniper's rifle, which helps to eliminate shake. Even on a tripod, pressing the shutter manually can cause shake or a shift in position. The old-fashioned way is to use a cable release to press the shutter remotely – this will require a shutter button with a threaded hole in the top to take the cable. If not present, then you will need to use the camera's timed release function, which usually delays the picture being taken by anything up to 10 seconds, though less than half that is most useful for our purposes. Be aware that using this function can decrease battery life.

- **Use additional light sources**. When there isn't enough daylight, make use of two or three extra light sources. Be wary of standard, overhead incandescent light bulbs, or those new-fangled tubular fluorescent things that are now taking their place in the EU because of the controversial piece of legislation that became law in 2009, because they can create a 'colour cast' which can have your images turn out looking very odd indeed – the most common result is a yellow or

Left, a scene using just indoor daylight. The camera has done a pretty good job, but the long exposure required has bleached out much of the detail. On the right, just a single halogen anglepoise behind and above the camera has been added, and look how the detail suddenly 'pops' because of added contrast. No other adjustments have been made at all – the image would normally be brightened in Photoshop.

pinkish cast. The best option is to install 'daylight' bulbs, which have a faintly blueish tinge, but whites appear relatively true. Really good cameras have 'white point adjustment', which is to say that you can alter the camera's settings to compensate for any colour cast. This is usually done by taking a close-up photo of a piece of paper that you know to be 'true' white, which the camera then uses as a reference point to adjust subsequent images. When placing your light sources, have one on each side as well as above and, ideally, you would have one shining from above and behind the camera. The objective is to create a nice, even, natural light which eliminates excessive shadows, unless you are looking to create a special, dramatic effect. Obviously, if you have the wherewithal to invest in proper, photographic studio lights, then go ahead, but you really don't have to spend that much.

- **Multiply whatever light you have.** Even if you only have one or two extra lights, or simple daylight entering from one side, you can make use of reflective surfaces to bounce the light back into the scene. I often use a large sheet of plain, white card, but you can use a mirror or aluminium cooking foil or any other smooth, reflective surface. By the same token, it's a good idea not to wear brightly-coloured clothing when taking photos in strong light, as I have learned to my cost after discovering that my bright scarlet *Battlegames* T-shirt had affected some images I took at a show!

- **Learn how to use depth of field.** If you asked me what the most common fault was after camera shake and poor lighting, it would be this: images taken too close to the subject, where the depth of field is so narrow that the front rank figures are in focus, but not the rear rank (or sometimes not even the rear of the front rank!); or, taken from an angle, one end of a battalion in line is in focus, but not the far end.

Depth of field in action 1: using a very narrow aperture, in this case f 2.8, only a very small section of the centre of this line of troops is in sharp focus.

Depth of field in action 2: using a much wider f-stop – here, it's f.8 – much more of the line is sharply defined. Notice how changing the aperture also changes the light.

To get the full line completely in focus, however, it is necessary to move further away from the subject and shoot with a wide aperture. You can then crop the image as shown.

These outcomes are a result of the camera's aperture being too small, and thus focusing on just a very narrow part of the subject. What you need to do is open up the aperture, and thus get more in focus. Now, on a really good camera, you can set the functions so that the aperture takes priority, and then specify a wider aperture – say, f.8 or f.10 – as opposed to a narrow one – f.2.8 for example. On a cheaper compact camera, like my Fuji Finepix, the answer is *do not use the macro setting*, and move *away* from the subject. This tells the camera to open its aperture to take in a wider scene, though the focus will still be centred around whatever you have 'targeted'. To do this, aim at the primary subject of your image, press the shutter *halfway* down until it beeps, re-compose your shot if needs be, then press the shutter the rest of the way down. If you're using the timing device, do the same, but press the shutter all the way down *before* re-composing the shot, so that you adjust the scene before the timer releases and takes the shot. This isn't to say that the macro setting isn't useful – for focusing on individual miniatures and vignettes where you *want* the background to be more blurred, it's perfect – but in general, it's over-used.

- **Learn how to compose a pleasing image**. Time after time after time, I see images of the back of a line of advancing troops. How dull is that? This makes the subject recessive, which is to say that it is moving away from the viewer and thus diminishing in power and interest (unless knapsack buckles are your thing, of course), as well as presenting us with what is often the least attractive view of the miniatures. What you need to do is to get round the other side and take the photo showing them coming *towards* you, colours flying, their little spears or bayonets threatening, their little faces snarling in fury. The other trick is to create angles in your photos, which in turn implies movement and conflict. A simple, straight-ahead view with lots of horizontals is very, very dull, because it conveys stability and stasis. Just move slightly to one side, and take the same shot but looking along the line. Now, you have introduced perspective, which creates lots of nice diagonal lines rushing towards a vanishing point on the horizon. Drama! This also makes use of the depth of field mentioned above, and you can manipulate that to focus on the most important part of the scene. And finally, think about every image telling a little story, whether it be the calm before the storm, the glorious panoply of uniforms, a

Not bad, but a bit dull: not only are the Royal Marines showing us their backs in disgust, but they are also portrayed in a very undynamic, horizontal plane, which tends to appear static.

Same scene, same figures, different story. Notice how the diagonal lines suggest movement in the picture; we can imagine the redcoats advancing to tackle the scurvy knaves of Blackbeard's gang guarding their contraband. Black Scorpion miniatures painted by Jez Griffin and Ged Cronin. The house was made by the author's father in 1968.

dashing cavalry charge, the epic struggle of an infantry melee, the moment when the enemy turns tail and runs, or even a 'time stands still' moment such as the one I created for the cover of issue 9 of *Battlegames*, where one gunfighter has just outdrawn the other.

- **Use a false background**. If you are taking photos at a show or convention, then there's not much you can do about the background, although many people staging games are more than happy to clear away clutter such as dice, tape measures, coffee cups, drinks cans and so on. In your own home, however, you can be more creative. To eliminate unnatural background, you can simply use plain card, or a length of wallpaper lining paper unfurled and pinned or Blu-Tacked against a wall, or an old sheet pinned on the wall or draped over some cardboard cartons or a free-standing rack. If you're feeling more adventurous, you could even paint a background scene, much like a theatre set design, with rolling hills and sky, or an urban setting – whatever is most appropriate. You can also borrow from that stalwart of associated hobbies: model railways. It's quite common to see scenic backdrops on elaborate railway layouts, and these are even available commercially (see, for example, the Faller website at *www.faller.de*), should you not feel up to becoming the next Constable or Monet, or you could create your own as discussed on a number of model railway websites, such as *www.009.cd2.com/members/how_to/backdrops.htm* and in books like *Painting Backdrops for Your Model Railroad* by Mike Denneman.

• **Learn how to use software like Photoshop**®. In former times, you'd hand over your film to a processing lab and wait patiently for a week or two for your images to arrive. Sadly, many of them would come back as bitter disappointments, often with a judgemental label applied by the lab such as "Poor focus", "Camera shake" or "Too dark". The joy of digital photography is that we get instant feedback, switching the camera to view mode and immediately deleting the images that don't come up to scratch (or, at least, you should be – what's the point of keeping duff images?) Keen photographers in my father's day would, like him, fill the garden shed or basement with all kinds of dangerous chemicals, red and orange lights and huge enlargers that looked as though they had stepped straight out of an HG Wells novel; but nowadays, we have Adobe Photoshop® and similar image manipulation software. Because its use is fundamental to achieving great results, I'm going to say a bit more about it.

▫ **Understand the jargon**. The images from your camera will transfer to your PC or Mac in one of two formats: JPEG (sometimes spelled JPG), or Camera Raw. The latter is usually reserved for high-end cameras, and preserves the very finest and most subtle detail in an image for reproduction at much larger sizes or at much higher resolutions than you are ever likely to need. Other common file formats are TIFF/TIF and PSD (which is Photoshop's own format). Other graphics formats used on the web are PNG (pronounced 'ping') and GIF (with a hard 'g'), but they aren't suitable for your photos. A 'pixel' is simply a single bit of information about the image as represented on screen. The more pixels in an image, the higher its 'resolution'. The higher the resolution, the bigger the image both in terms of its actual dimensions, and its 'weight' in bytes. A 'Megabyte' is simply 1,000,000 bytes. And finally, you need to be aware that photography works in 'RGB' (red, green, blue) mode, which is used for manipulating light, whereas print works in 'CMYK' (cyan, magenta, yellow and black – the 'K' stands for keyline). 'Greyscale' is, of course, just black and white and shades of grey. As a result, you should expect to see some shift in colour values between what you see on screen and the final printed result, because the technology of manipulating light cannot ever completely match the potential results of applying tiny dots of pigment to paper. As an exercise, use a magnifying glass

A standard printed image of a 15mm vignette of a field forge (left) and a tiny portion of it enlarged to show the 'rosette' pattern of cyan, magenta, yellow and black dots from which it is actually formed.

to view the colour photographs in this book or any magazine up close: you'll see the 'rosettes' of tiny dots, with each of the four colour inks arranged in lines at specific angles. Compare that to zooming in on your on-screen image until you can see the square pixels arranged, mosaic-fashion, side by side. Both rely on the 'impressionist' effect so that they appear to merge and mix when you move away from the surface of the image.

- **Save your originals**. A JPEG is a format used to compress an image so that it is easier to store, or quicker to transmit via the internet. With the advent of huge hard drives and ultra-speed broadband, which the inventors could not have foreseen, these benefits are no longer quite so meaningful, but as the sheer size of images grows (most used to be 640 x 480 pixels, but are now frequently in excess of four times that size), JPEG technology is still useful. The important thing for you to remember is that JPEGs are *lossy*, which is to say that every time you save an image as a JPEG, part of the information it contains is lost by the compression process. (You can do an experiment by taking a sample image, and then repeatedly "Save As..." a standard-resolution JPEG several times. You'll be amazed at how quickly the detail becomes fuzzy. Most programs now allow you to specify how much compression – and therefore information loss – you will permit during the 'Save As...' process.) Therefore, *always keep your originals intact and stored separately* and work on a duplicate copy instead. The simplest way to do this is to open the original file, "Save As..." under a different name using the program's native format (such as .psd in Photoshop®, which keeps the duplicate intact) and then work on that version before saving as another JPEG. Be aware that a PSD file is much weightier, in terms of its Megabyte size, than a JPEG. In some software, such as Apple's iPhoto®, a copy is made automatically so that in an emergency, you can revert to the original.

□ **Crop, crop, crop!** Just as my mantra as an editor is to cut, cut, cut, the average photo contains all sorts of extraneous rubbish that has nothing to do with the subject of the image. Perhaps the most common phenomenon is that of wargamers' crotch – a beautifully-arrayed battlefield, teeming with delightful miniatures, with a background of the (mercifully) trousered nether regions of a row of players and onlookers. Not nice! Even without this, you'll find that your photos tell a more powerful story if you cut out empty background and, in effect, zoom in on the action. You might also find that the same photograph can provide more than one image, simply by cropping it differently – which will only be possible, of course, if you have saved the original intact as I advise above!

A standard image as it emerged from the camera (top). There's nothing fundamentally wrong with it, but just look at the difference in impact when it is cropped (below). The act of cropping makes us focus our attention on whatever you want the story of the image to be, and resonates much more with the viewer. Here, the titanic struggle between Regiment von Eintopf, desperately defending the farm, and the overwhelming numbers ranged against them is highlighted by cropping. In addition, subtle changes to the lighting and sharpness have been made in Photoshop to make the defenders behind the wall stand out more clearly. The presence of General E Pickled,urging his men over the walls, is also clearer, as are the proud colours of the Boleyn Regiment on the left.

□ **Making adjustments**. The three most common things I need to do to images I receive is to brighten them, remove colour casts and sharpen. Software like Photoshop® always has several ways of achieving the same results, some of which are simpler to learn than others. The beginners' route is to use the Image > Adjust > Brightness/Contrast control, and perhaps Image > Adjust > Photo Filter to eliminate any colour cast, followed by Filter > Sharpen to tighten things up after reducing to the size necessary for your purposes. (You should always apply the Sharpen filter *after* reducing the size of the image, and recent versions of Photoshop® also allow you to specify the resampling method when changing the image size – Bicubic Sharper is the one you need.) However, as a professional, my tools of choice are, first of all, Image > Adjust > Levels and/or Image > Adjust > Curves, which allow me to adjust and balance the brightness, contrast and relative colour values all in one go. As always with such things, practice makes perfect, but these tools permit much finer adjustments. Then, if any sharpening is necessary, I use Filter > Sharpen > Unsharp Mask which, whilst sounding like a contradiction in terms, again makes far greater control over the extent of the sharpening process possible.

If you can master the process I've outlined here, you're well on your way to achieving professional results. And of course, if in doubt, you should always refer to your camera's and the software's own manuals and its 'Help' facilities.

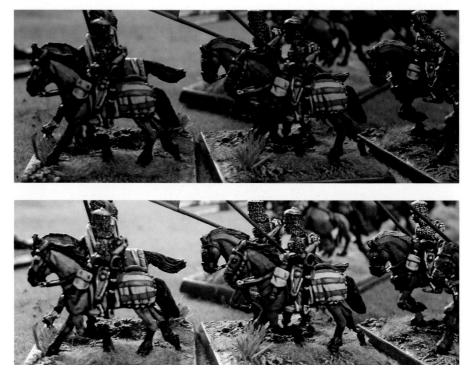

A typical shot taken at a wargames show on a dull day with poor lighting. I try to avoid using flash if I can, because it tends to 'blitz' the foreground and leave deep shadows behind.

The same shot after improvement in Photoshop, including adjusting the light levels, softening shadows and sharpening the image to help it 'pop'. These lovely Polish cavalry were seen in a Cossack Rebellion game staged by Phil Olley at Partizan.

Wargaming and the power of the internet

When I first started my *Battlegames* website back in 1998, there were but a handful of websites dealing with wargaming in the entire world. Now, the internet is awash with wargaming sites, the vast majority of them blogs maintained by individual wargamers. Why should this be?

Well, the first thing to say is that establishing and running a website has never been easier. I remember, with a kind of masochistic pride, that to create a website of any sort in those early days required the kind of study of arcane gobbledegook that would normally remain the preserve of a mathematician or, at a pinch, a practising wizard. HTML, JavaScript, Java, Perl, CSS and their ilk defied simple comprehension, buried as they always were within the pages of doorstop tomes whose weight was as eye-watering as their price. Companies like Macromedia made valiant attempts, with software such as Dreamweaver, to make the process easier, but they ended up being just as bloated and unwieldy as the processes they were intended to replace. For the lay person – and even for a web professional such as me – the creation of a website was a lonely and arduous process.

Until, that is, the concept of Content Management Systems (CMS) was born. Suddenly, you didn't need to labour offline to create content that then had to be uploaded – working directly via a standard web browser such as Internet Explorer, Firefox or Safari, it became possible to update your website quickly and simply without ever needing to understand the code behind the scenes. And with the arrival of WordPress and Google's Blogger, we were handed systems that were not only simple to use, but *free*.

Almost overnight, the World Wide Web was truly democratised and web designers such as myself started to lose their jobs. Why, goes the argument, should you call in a highly skilled and expensive designer when you could do it all yourself for nothing? Wikipedia tells us that as of February 2011, there were already more than 156 million public blogs in existence and the evidence seems to be that this number is increasing rapidly, alongside other social media accounts such as FaceBook, Twitter and media sharing sites such as Flickr and YouTube.

So, what do people use blogs for? In my own case, I use it as an adjunct to the 'official' *Battlegames* website to talk about the gaming and other projects that I'm involved in. Because I seem to have become increasingly busy, I don't update it as often as I would like, but there are many other wargamers who update theirs monthly, fortnightly, weekly – even daily. I can only admire their dedication! Most take the form of a kind of journal, in which the author (blogger) describes his latest games, the progress of his army painting, events he has attended and so on. A few are real gems, creating a kind of narrative, perhaps of an ongoing campaign or storyline. See, for example, American gamer Bill Protz's remarkable duo of blogs: Campaigns of General William Augustus Pettygree (*http://generalpettygree.blogspot.com*) and Campaigns in Germania (*http://campaignsingermania.blogspot.com*).

The blog has also been a boon to those of us who enjoy the fictitious wars of imagi-nations. Entire continents have been born online, jostling cheek-by-jowl with gamers whose interests are purely historical or fantasy or sci-fi. It takes only moments to upload photos, videos and other media to accompany enthusiastic text. You can count on it, for example, that even if you don't manage to make it in person to a particular wargames show, a handful of blogs will carry photos and commentary within twenty four hours – sometimes, even 'live' from the event itself, because of course, the advent of the iPhone, iPad and other 'smart' devices makes it possible to broadcast and upload wirelessly.

The other unique feature of blogging and other social media is immediate feedback. Make a blog post and, assuming that it has aroused the interest of passing traffic, you're likely to get a smattering of comments within hours. A really controversial or exciting post may get dozens, even hundreds of comments. To prevent scurrilous entries appearing, the blogging software allows you to monitor and censor feedback and block the dreaded 'spam' from undesirables trying to convince your readership that they should purchase dodgy pharmaceuticals and the like. It's possible also to block all comments, in fact – but part of the point of running a blog is to contribute to the wargaming community, if such a thing can be said to exist, and so hearing what others think about what you have posted is par for the course.

Generally speaking, I think it's fair to say that negative feedback on blogs is pretty rare. The vast majority of those who take the time to comment are encouraging and keen to praise the efforts of others. Online forums[1], on the other hand, can be much more dangerous minefields for the uninitiated, where keyboard heroes lurk to spit bile from the safety of their anonymous usernames, though they wouldn't dare say "boo" to a goose in the real world. However, you can also find the most incredibly helpful people, happy to answer the most obscure or naive questions with patience and wisdom – and answer them repeatedly, because it's just one of those internet things that newcomers tend never to read the archives, so the same questions come up again and again and again...

This also underlines one of the curious things about the internet. With 'conventional' media such as books, we read them from the beginning, through the middle to the end, gaining an understanding of the present condition by virtue of a guided tour through what went before. The World Wide Web is quite the opposite when you first encounter it: blogs, FaceBook, Twitter and news sites start with the present, the right here right now, and in order to comprehend how on earth we arrived here and what it all means, you need to 'drill down' into the previous posts, gradually unravelling things from the top down, much like an archaeologist scraping back layers of soil. Of course, while you take the time to do that, more and more layers are piling on top.

Of course, it's entirely up to you whether you run a wargames blog or not. The ether is littered with half-started, abandoned or simply orphaned projects. Something that occurred to me when I published the obituary for the late Paddy Griffith is that such efforts will no doubt outlive us all, our words floating around some inner space like digital ghosts until such time as a hard drive in a distant server is wiped clean by some disinterested geek and our data is lost forever.

But the final word about the World Wide Web and wargaming must go to those traders who, like me, might not be able to run a wargames business at all without it. Because of the internet, a website I started as a hobby project – nowadays, we would certainly call it a blog, though the term didn't exist in 1998 – was able to accumulate a following which led to me being able to launch a 'real' magazine in 2006. The irony, of course, is that when I sold my business in 2011, the fastest-growing sector of the business was digital subscribers who purchase electronic files online, bringing the whole thing full circle.

The explosion of online trade, both in terms of new purchases direct from manufacturers, traders and publishers via their online shops, and second-hand sales and purchases via online auction sites like eBay, has of course caused collateral damage. To find a high street retail store selling historical miniatures is now extremely rare: the little shops that used to be run by men of a certain age in cardigans have disappeared, crushed by extortionate rent and rates on the one hand and the sheer exuberance of online trading on the other. It has been proved repeatedly that for

---

1   *The correct term is "fora", I know, but as wargaming veteran Rick Priestley recently commented, does anyone actually use that word these days?*

specialist and niche goods such as those wargamers crave, we are far more likely to flourish our credit cards in the comfort of our own home than in the high street. Only key wargame shows offer a physical shopping venue nowadays and even here, we have seen the curious advent of a new habit: wargamers pre-ordering goods online to be collected at a wargames show. Does the retailer credit that sale to his website or to his attendance at the show? Has the purchaser actually saved money on postage by collecting it themselves at a time when public transport fares and the cost of fuel are, in the UK at least, going through the roof?

Whatever the precise accounting, the fact is that it has become possible for a one-man-band to advertise his wares worldwide at a tiny fraction of the cost of conventional advertising, and to respond almost instantly to customer enquiries – though this, of course, also has the flipside that one can never quite feel that you can close the office door behind you and leave work!

But the fact is that the internet is here to stay, and wargaming has unquestionably been one of the major beneficiaries, both for individual wargamers and the industry they support. The solo wargamer need never feel lonely again; the club need never worry about how to broadcast its events; and the small business knows full well that, given diligence and application, there are potential customers out there, all over the world, who can hear about and purchase its products and services. The hobby is now both local and global, twenty four hours a day, seven days a week, 365 days a year.

For wargaming, in one form or another, I'm convinced that the future's bright.

11

RESOURCES

Reference, Inspiration and Materials

Whether you decide to embark on your wargaming life and become a sculptor of your own miniatures, like John Ray, or prefer to simply assemble, paint and collect the current commercial offerings, or perhaps venture to undertake the occasional conversion rather than using a figure straight out of the box, the first thing you're going to need is reference material, sources of inspiration and the wherewithal to find the figures, terrain and other stuff you're going to need.

This applies whether the armies you intend to collect are historical, fantasy, science fiction or, indeed, that murky in-between place called 'faction', which is either imaginary events based on historical ones, rather like the *Sharpe* novels of Bernard Cornwell, or the 'imagi-nations' such as those I have created myself, that have been described earlier in this book.

The kind of reference material you will want as a wargamer comes in several forms: general historical background reference; specific reference about the war or battles you intend to fight; reference about the uniforms and clothing and equipment of the soldiers that fought in these wars; geographical reference, for setting up your tabletop battlefields; architectural reference, for making sure the buildings you put on your tabletop are in keeping with the place and the period; technical hobby reference, for advice about the painting and basing of your miniatures, and for sculpting or converting, or making terrain and scenery; reference about the manufacturers and suppliers of miniatures suitable for your chosen period; and last, but by no means least, a set of rules for playing your games.

Now, I hope that this book goes some way to satisfying some of those needs, but one of the most important items on the list is uniform and equipment reference, in which department we are blessed.

Books

When I first started wargaming back in the 1960s, I think there was one shelf in our local library that dealt with military history and only a handful of books about wargaming. It can still happen that you might stumble upon a particularly obscure conflict in a far distant part of the world about which little is known and even less has been written, but that is comparatively rare. Now, the opposite is true: for the most part, we have information overload.

For wargamers, our primary source material is still the written word and the work of an élite band, the military illustrators. Foremost amongst the publishers who have brought military history to life for at least two generations now are Osprey, whose *Men at Arms*, *Warrior*, *Vanguard* and *Campaign* series have been the mainstay of almost every wargamer.

These are slim volumes – some of them no more than 48 pages or so of quarto-sized paper – and they follow a familiar pattern of concise text, interspersed with photos of museum exhibits or, depending on the conflict or subject covered, contemporary photographs and occasional maps. The real joy for us, though, is that the centre eight pages are in full colour, with beautifully rendered uniform plates of troops from the time, or armoured fighting vehicles, fighter aircraft, ships or whatever else is appropriate. As someone who has done a bit of commercial illustration in my time, I can tell you that the skill and knowledge required to produce such exquisite work is no mean thing, and many of the Osprey artists have become world-famous for their achievements, such as Angus McBride, Peter Dennis, Brian Fosten, Gerry Embleton and others.

If you're anything like me, over time you will acquire a substantial library of these publications, as there seems to be no end to the list of useful works by Osprey. From ancient Egypt to the conflict in Afghanistan, you are pretty much guaranteed to find an Osprey book about it – and usually several. It has become part of wargaming and military modelling folklore that if you wait long enough, Osprey will almost certainly produce a title covering the most obscure reference material imaginable. A range which already includes *Fortress Monasteries of the Himalayas* and *Fairbairn-Sykes Commando Dagger* is clearly determined to leave no stone unturned in its desire to cover every conceivable subject of potential interest! Their website is at *www.ospreypublishing.com* and their books are stocked prominently in many high-street bookshops.

Whilst Osprey is perhaps the best known, it would be unfair not to mention other publishers producing noteworthy ranges. Casemate, an American company but now also with a strong presence in the UK and Europe, has made several shrewd acquisitions of smaller, specialist publishers, and they also distribute on behalf of other publishers. Perhaps their strongest suit is the huge range of WWII and modern military biographies they produce, but with nearly fifty companies under their wing at the time of writing, their remit is clearly much wider. My particular favourites are the books covering the late nineteenth century European wars from Helion, and the Napoleonic titles they have inherited from French publisher *Histoire et Collections*. Their output is enormous, and I would recommend that you visit their website at *www.casematepublishing. co.uk* to gain an impression of their complete portfolio.

And of course, I dare not forget to mention my own publishers, Pen & Sword, who have been a highly respected producer of military history books for many years, especially those titles that one might call more 'academic' studies of particular commanders or periods of military history. I feel they have a particular strength in ancient and Napoleonic history, but that's my own prejudice because, like Osprey and Casemate, they have a vast catalogue covering many subjects, including wargaming, of course! For fans of naval history, they have an exceptional range under the heading of Seaforth; I have an interest in the Age of Sail and some of their titles on this topic are truly outstanding. Their website is at *www. pen-and-sword.co.uk.*

Finally, I want to mention a very interesting niche publisher here in the UK that can be found at *www.wargaming.co* (that's correct – no .uk at the end). Let me quote their own remit:

> "The History of Wargaming Project aims to collate, preserve and make available key work from the history of wargaming. It includes wargaming books from Donald Featherstone, Charlie Wesencraft, Paddy Griffith, Phil Dunn, Phil Barker, Tony Bath, Fletcher Pratt, Terry Wise, Dunn Kempf and others. The project includes hobby gaming and professional wargames played by the American Army, the British Army, the Royal Navy and the RAF (scheduled to print in 2011). The project includes previously unpublished material. The lead editor is John Curry."

This is a laudable aim, and to this end, a whole swathe of books written by some of the early doyens of the hobby have been reprinted in softback format. The quality of reproduction has been variable, and they do not have the 'presence' of the original works, which were normally hardback, but the fact is that original first editions – as I know, since I own a fair few – have become astronomically expensive and as rare as hens' teeth. I can, therefore, only applaud John in his efforts to bring these seminal wargaming works to a wider audience for a fraction of the price.

One of the most exciting developments in the last year or so is that Osprey, Pen & Sword and Casemate have started releasing their publications as e-books, enabling you to read them on your PC or Mac, iPad or netbook, or even your mobile phone. Whilst I shall remain a fan of good, old-fashioned printed paper until the day I die (I am a bibliophile and books are, to me, a sensual experience as well as simply a repository of information), it's hard to argue with the fact that the potential exists to have your entire military reference collection with you wherever you go in this digital age.

As an aside, I just want to say a quick word about copyright theft. Downloading PDF files from 'torrent' sites or accepting them from an individual without payment to the publisher is *illegal.* It deprives the publisher, author, illustrator and designer of their rightful dues and it means they are less likely to commission new work or even survive in today's highly competitive marketplace.

There are also a number of publishers that have sprung up within the hobby who are also booksellers, so let's take a quick look at some of the better known ones.

Perhaps the best known is Caliver Books, whose sister company Partizan Press is well-known in the hobby for producing very smart books on a wide range of subjects, including military history, wargaming and re-enactment/living history. They have an especially respected portfolio on the English Civil War (owner/publisher Dave Ryan is a reenactor himself) and publish a huge range of wargames rules covering every period of history, as well as stocking pretty much every other set that has ever been published by anyone else! Retired Brigadier Charles S Grant, who wrote the foreword to this book, is writing a noteworthy series covering the campaigns of the Duke of Wellington which is being published by Partizan, as well as a number of wargaming titles. Dave Ryan can be found at wargames and living history events not only in the UK, but also occasionally on mainland Europe and even in The United States, on pretty much every single weekend of the year! See *www.caliverbooks.com*.

Ken Trotman Ltd, owned by the charming Richard and Roz Brown, are also booksellers, specialising in some of the rarer and more academic titles in military history, but they are also publishers of an increasing number of noteworthy titles, both in military history and wargaming. Charles S Grant figures again, having penned four out of the current five books in the breakthrough series *Wargaming in History* dealing with wargaming the eighteenth century, which I have had the privilege to design. The third title in the series, written by Major General John Drewienkiewicz, with Adam Poole, concentrates on the Battle of Gettysburg in the American Civil War and further titles are planned. Setting aside my involvement, I heartily recommend the books in this series because they are written by experienced officers who also have a passion for history and are both, I can tell you, some of the wiliest wargamers you'll ever encounter! This series also boasts some wonderful uniform plates by veteran illustrator Bob Marrion, who has a gift for conveying character, as well as accurate sartorial information, with his pictures.

Another significant small publisher based here in the UK has caught my attention in recent years. Helion, owned by Duncan Rogers, another wargamer, has published particularly noteworthy volumes on the European wars of the late nineteenth century, particularly the Austro-Prussian War of 1866 and the Franco-Prussian War of 1870-71. Their catalogue covers a much broader range of history, of course: take a look at *www.helion.co.uk* and, as mentioned above, their own range is also distributed by Casemate.

Another great resource for uniform and armour books is, of course, eBay (*www.ebay.co.uk* or *.com* or *.de* etc, depending on where you are), where you may pick up some amazing bargains or, on the other hand, manage to get your hands on the output of specialist publishers now, sadly, long out of business. One such is the Blandford Press who, in the 1960s and 1970s, produced a superb range of pocket-sized reference works called the Blandford Colour Series, including such gems as *Uniforms of Waterloo, Army Uniforms of World War 2, Uniforms of the Imperial Russian Army, Cavalry Uniforms, Uniforms of the Retreat from Moscow* and *Uniforms of the Seven Years War 1756-63*.

An alternative source for book lovers is AbeBooks (*www.abebooks. co.uk* or *.com*) which is a veritable treasure trove for second-hand books ranging from the commonplace to the rare, with appropriate price tags to match.

One cannot over-stress the importance of second-hand books as potential reference sources. Not so many years ago, many towns had second-hand bookshops aplenty, and university towns especially so. But my own home town, Brighton and Hove in Sussex, is a case in point: where we had at least a couple of dozen excellent outlets, there are now less than a handful, other than a few charity shops. All the second-hand book business has gone online.

If you are able to travel to at least one of the many wargames shows that are regular fixtures in the UK, the USA and elsewhere, then you will have better luck, since there are always booksellers in attendance, and you will not only be presented with a healthy choice of Osprey's mammoth output, but also usually at least one or two stallholders with a wide spectrum of second-hand books. Just here in the UK, Caliver Books, Ken Trotman and Paul Meekins (*www.paulmeekins.co.uk*) are regularly found at wargame shows; and in the USA, veteran bookseller On Military Matters (*onmilitarymatters.com*) takes his wares to the two largest shows in the US calendar, Historicon and Cold Wars, along with Aide de Camp Books (*www.adcbooks.com*).

It would be very blinkered of me indeed to be utterly Anglo-centric, though I must confess my lack of extensive knowledge of publishers beyond these shores. So, let me give you just a brief insight into military history reference publishing outside Great Britain.

In the US, a company called Uniformology (*www.uniformology.com*) has been scanning and restoring original military uniform plates for many years, and then making them available either in book form or on CD. An incredibly useful resource, they cover the works of great uniform illustrators such as Knötel. Richard Knötel was the most famous German military artist who painted from around 1890 until his death in 1914. His vast output of illustrations documented the uniforms of nearly every country in the world during and before his lifetime. If you find yourself drawn to the horse and musket period, these plates are a 'must have' and, especially on CD, they are tremendous value for money.

If the American Civil War becomes the focus of your interest, then you simply must be told about the superb work of Don Troiani, an illustrator of that conflict without compare. A number of books containing his work have been published by Stackpole Books – *www.stackpolebooks.com*.

At the expensive, but beautiful, end of the spectrum, the Military History Press (*www.militaryhistorypress.com*) produces some exquisite publications that would take pride of place on any collector's shelf, alongside some more affordable military history titles worthy of consideration.

For the French, we have already mentioned Histoire et Collections, now under the purview of Casemate, but they deserve a 'gold star' from wargamers for the fascinating range of martial material they have produced over many years, not least the wargaming magazine *Vae Victis*, which we shall come to later. See *www.histoireetcollections.com* and, if you are linguistically challenged, you will be relieved to find that the website

– and the books – have English versions! You will perhaps be unsurprised to learn that their uniform books mostly deal with Napoleon's armies, but they have a very nice range of military history.

For Italians, Edizioni Chillemi (*www.edizionichillemi.com*) produce a wonderful range of titles under the banner of *Storia Militare*, which are not unlike Osprey books in format, but which concentrate primarily on Italian subject-matter, which I actually find fascinating.

In Spain, a fledgling publishing company is emerging called Sátrapa Ediciones, which has only a handful of titles available at present, but is noteworthy for the stunning illustrations in its Osprey-like publications. Definitely worth keeping an eye on at *www.satrapaediciones.com*. Given the strength of the hobby there, however, I am surprised there are not more publishers producing reference works of Spain's proud, military past – perhaps I have just simply failed to find them.

Finding German language reference publishers has proved quite difficult. It seems that there are a fair number of translations available of the works by French artists Liliane and Fred Funcken and others, but many are now out of print and only available second-hand. A smattering of small publishers with military history lists do exist, such as Melchior Verlag (*www.melchior-verlag.de*) and Motorbuch Verlag (*www.motorbuch-verlag.de*), but I can only imagine that German historical wargamers rely heavily on English language sources. This does not seem to have changed since my days as a student there, where one sometimes stumbled upon small, university-based publishers who produced short runs of somewhat academic works on military subjects.

Magazines

You would think it very strange indeed for an author who is also the editor and publisher of a magazine not to mention this particular form of publishing at least briefly! And it is true that wargames magazines are a marvellous source of inspiration and information, which is why they exist in the first place.

Battlegames (*www.atlanticpublishers.com/magazines/battlegames/*), the magazine I gave birth to in 1996 and still design and edit for the new owners, is something of an oddity, because it focuses primarily on the playing of games and the exploration of facets of representing warfare on the tabletop, rather than treatises on military history *per se*. Whilst you may well find helpful articles about making wargames terrain, or painting wargames figures, or assembling an army as a project, you are less likely to find uniform details of a particular period or a description of a historical battle, simply because such information exists elsewhere in abundance, as you have seen, so why duplicate it?

The granddaddy of wargaming publications is *Miniature Wargames*, (*www.atlanticpublishers.com/magazines/miniature-wargames*) another independent monthly title until April 2011 when it was acquired by Atlantic Publishers. Whilst the nature of its content has varied considerably over the twenty-nine years it has been around, it seems to have settled into a mixture of strongly historical-based articles, looking at actual or potential wargame refights of real battles, and now a fairly large section featuring fantasy and science fiction gaming which is due to be transferred to a brand new, stand-alone publication *Dark Horizons*.

Perhaps the hobby's most 'glamorous' monthly title is *Wargames Illustrated*, (*www.wargamesillustrated.net*) which you can find in most large stationers on the high street. A bulky publication at well over a hundred pages, this magazine features lots of 'eye candy' – photographs of expertly painted miniatures on lovely terrain – together with frequent historical articles and illustrations, often based on work previously published in Osprey publications, in a high-gloss format. Previously independent, the magazine was bought out a few years ago by Battlefront, a New Zealand company famed for having created an extremely popular WWII game, *Flames of War*, which emulates the Games Workshop approach to sales and marketing and has certainly been responsible for bringing a great deal of 'new blood' into the historical side of the hobby.

Wargames, Soldiers and Strategy (*www.wssmagazine.com*) is actually a recently re-born version of a magazine previously owned by a Spanish hobby magazine consortium. Under the new ownership of the Dutch publisher Karawansaray and produced bimonthly, it has a very pleasing, clean design style, well-written articles, excellent photography and an interesting 'dossier' format, which has the content concentrated around a particular war or battle or period each issue, though there is plenty more to read as well. It is probably the most akin to *Battlegames* of all the other magazines.

The UK is not the only place where you can find glossy wargames magazines, and continental Europe boasts three of the best.

I have already mentioned *Vae Victis*, a superlative bimonthly publication from France produced by Histoire et Collections. As well as covering miniatures wargaming, *Vae Victis* is exceptionally strong on board wargames, and in fact contains a completely unique game and counters every issue. Other than a very short editorial "hello", the magazine is entirely in French, though their website has an English version – *vaevictis. histoireetcollections.com*.

From Italy comes an independent, quarterly publication *Dadi e Piombo* (*dadiepiombo.com*), again in full colour throughout. In many ways, I feel it is the Italian 'cousin' to *Battlegames*, with a very similar ethos, focusing on the gaming itself, with lots of 'how to' articles and a unique approach.

I have mentioned *Wargames, Soldiers and Strategy* already but I need to make clear that the Spanish language version that originally spawned it continues to exist: *Wargames Soldados y Estrategia* is available from *www. revistasprofesionales.com* but now has no connections whatsoever with the Karawansaray title edited by Guy Bowers.

Curiously, the USA does not, at the time of writing, have an equivalent printed magazine of its own. There have been a number of attempts in the past, such as *The Courier* (1968-2005) and *Historical Miniature Gamer Magazine* (which appears to have petered out in the last couple of years), but the most universally missed is *MWAN* (Mid West Wargamers' Association Newsletter), very much a unique one-man effort produced by Hal Thinglum, who sadly had to relinquish the reins owing to ill-health. Copies of these magazines do, however, turn up on eBay and at bring-and-buy stands at wargames shows.

All the periodicals mentioned so far focus primarily on historical wargaming, but of course the 'elephant in the room' that must be mentioned is *White Dwarf*, published monthly by Games Workshop and available in most high street stationers around the world. This 'magazine' is, in reality, a catalogue of Games Workshop products and a showcase for its own version of the fantasy and science fiction wargaming hobby, and you will not find products or services from any other company mentioned within its attractively-designed pages. That being said, the quality of the publication itself, and the toys on show within it, means that huge numbers of wargamers, whether or not they prefer this style of gaming, can derive inspiration from it. A good painting technique is universal, whether you are applying it to a World War I 'Tommy' or an orc!

There are other magazines too which, whilst not strictly focused on wargaming, can certainly provide a source of inspiration, reference or modelling and painting tips. *Military Modelling* (www.militarymodelling.com) has been around for a very long time indeed, and in fact spawned some of the classic articles on the hobby in the early days. The similarly-named *Model Military International* (www.modelmilitary.com), another monthly title, focuses much more on modern military hardware and Armoured Fighting Vehicles (AFVs). *Military in Scale* magazine (www.militaryinscale.com), on the other hand, also includes articles about building model aircraft. All these three are British titles.

In the US, *FineScale Modeler* (www.finescale.com) has a remit similar to the British titles, but also covers some civilian modelling projects, such as cars and trucks.

From Spain comes *Xtreme Modelling* (www.xtrememodelling.com), a bimonthly dealing with hyper-detailing post-1939 AFVs. They also have a range of books. The website is, it has to be said, somewhat confusing, but the quality of the models on display is top notch.

Bear in mind that you may find excellent tips not only in overtly military publications, but also in more peaceable pastimes – railway modelling is a good example. *Railway Modeller* (www.pecopublications.co.uk/railway-modeller.html), *Model Rail* (www.greatmagazines.co.uk/railways/model-rail-magazine.html), *British Railway Modelling* (www.model-railways-live.co.uk/Magazine/) and *Hornby Magazine* (www.hornby.magazine.co.uk) are just the tiny tip of a vast iceberg of monthlies serving a hobby which has some of the best terrain-making techniques to be found. Worth buying an occasional copy for the adverts alone – railway modellers have an astonishing assortment of flocks and trees and building materials.

Karawansaray also currently has two superb sister publications to *WSS* – *Ancient Warfare* (*www.ancient-warfare.com*) and *Medieval Warfare* (*www.medieval-warfare.com*) which, if those periods take your fancy, are an absolute must-have. Their content is very highly regarded in academic circles, as well as amongst enthusiasts, and the illustrations are wonderful.

From Spain comes another beautiful publication, *Desperta Ferro*, (*www.despertaferro-ediciones.com*) which deals with both ancient and medieval warfare. The text is all in Spanish, but it's worth struggling with a dictionary or online translator for the sublime illustrations alone!

The UK has the excellent *Military Times* magazine (*www.military-times.co.uk*) which presents a broad range of military history, uniform and armour reference, campaign and battle reports from ancient through to modern times. In addition, the BBC's *History* magazine regularly runs features on military subjects (*www.historyextra.com*).

Whilst it struggles to produce wargaming magazines, the United States certainly has an excellent range of military history magazines on offer. The eponymous *Military History* magazine (*www.historynet.com/magazines/military_history*) covers a huge range of topics of potential interest to the wargamer, and for wargamers, *Armchair General* is simply a must-have (*www.armchairgeneral.com*), presenting the reader with tactical and strategic challenges to solve. Publishers Weider History Group produce a number of other titles such as the highly-regarded *MHQ* (*Military History Quarterly*), *Civil War Times*, *World War II*, *Vietnam*, *America's Civil War* and, should you become interested in Wild West gaming, the appropriately-named *Wild West*.

It's probable that there are a host of other titles I've overlooked, and the magazine market changes constantly in any case, so it's possible that by the time you read this, some of those I've mentioned will have gone out of business, but others will have emerged. Nevertheless, I hope that this overview of what you might find on the shelves of your corner newsagents or high street stationers will have alerted you to keep your eyes open!

The silver screen

We should not neglect the potential inspiration and education that can be provided on-screen, either the small one in the corner of our lounge, or the large one at the local cinema.

Anyone with a television knows that, for example, the History Channel seems to have an absolutely bottomless pit of programmes about Hitler's rise to power and the excesses of the Third Reich though, to be fair, they have also produced some interesting programmes on ancient Greek and Roman warfare, the American Revolution, the American Civil War and others. My caveat is that some of these shows are extremely 'dumbed down' and display a level of xenophobia which beggars belief.

Programming on military subjects is extensive on other channels too: the BBC has regular documentaries, as well as series such as those by Dan and Peter Snow on *20th Century Battlefields* and *Battlefield Britain*;

and of course most of us are familiar with Channel 4's *Time Team* and the archaeological digs that frequently feature Roman, Anglo-Saxon, Medieval and later military finds.

The Discovery Channel has a popular program called *Mythbusters* that frequently puts arms and armour from different periods of history to the test. Whilst the presentation is sometimes rather silly, it nevertheless provides some fascinating insights.

In my opinion the best channel of them all is the USA's HBO, which has made some of the best television programmes on historical subjects ever created, with titles like *Band of Brothers*, *The Pacific*, *John Adams*, *Rome*, and *Generation Kill*.

And of course, over the years, many films have been made about military subjects, ranging from *Spartacus* to *Gladiator* and *The Longest Day* to *The Hurt Locker*. As long as the film itself has been well researched, it can help the wargamer gain a valuable impression of warfare at the time portrayed, though Hollywood movies must come with the caveat that they often sensationalise what is, in reality, a pretty dour business.

And if you're a fan of fantasy or science fiction, movies and TV programmes are often *primary* source material. *Aliens*, *Starship Troopers*, *Lord of the Rings*, *Dr Who*, *Star Trek*, *Star Wars*... Wargaming gives you a way of being Aragorn or Jean-Luc Picard without the need to travel to Los Angeles!

Military history societies and re-enactors

Perhaps unsurprisingly, when people with shared interests get together, they form clubs and societies where research can be shared and knowledge increased. A handful of these are available to the wargamer, some of which are exclusively focused on wargaming, whilst others combine this with re-enactment functions.

I shall list those of interest later, but the point is that it can be highly instructive to discuss detailed aspects of a particular period with fellow enthusiasts, whether face-to-face, online or via the pages of a society journal, and at least a brief acquaintance with re-enactment can, as I know myself, open a whole new world of understanding what it must have been like to be clothed, armed and accoutred as a fighting man in any period.

In fact, one of the grandees of the hobby, the late Brigadier Peter Young, distinguished soldier, historian and author of *Charge!*, founded the Sealed Knot in 1968, the well-known English Civil War re-enactment society which now boasts thousands of members.

As just mentioned, most such groups have some kind of newsletter or journal, and I simply must mention the granddaddy of them all, *Slingshot*, the journal of the Society of Ancients (*www.soa.org.uk*), a publication steeped in the history of wargaming since its earliest days, and debating chamber to many of the great names of wargaming for many years.

Other popular societies include the Pike and Shot Society (*www. pikeandshotsociety.org*) and its journal *Arquebusier*; the Napoleonic

Association (*www.napoleonicassociation.org*); the Victorian Military Society (*www.victorianmilitarysociety.org.uk*) who produce *Soldiers of the Queen*; the Society of Twentieth Century Wargamers (*www.sotcw.net*) whose newsletter is simply called *The Journal*; the American Civil War Society (*www.acws.co.uk*) whose newsletter can be downloaded as a PDF from their site; and let's not forget *Ragnarok*, the journal of The Society of Fantasy and Science Fiction Wargamers (*www.sfsfw.org*).

Clearly, this list is entirely Anglo-centric, and I can only apologise in advance to anyone whose worthy group has been omitted. You are always welcome, of course, to get in touch so that any future edition can be updated. I also know from my own experience that many large organisations actually consist of a myriad smaller, local groups, who may well have their own newsletters, purely for the consumption of their own members. There are also many re-enactment and living history groups whose output is only of peripheral interest to the wargamer.

The World Wide Web

As I have been writing this section, it struck me that one thing has changed beyond all recognition since anyone last sat down to write an all-encompassing book about wargaming in this way: the advent of the Internet. When Don Featherstone, already a veteran of the hobby, penned *Featherstone's Complete Wargaming*, published in 1988, the very first website was still three years away, and even then it was the preserve of high-tech academics at CERN in Switzerland.

How times change. I launched the first *Battlegames* website in June 1998, at a time when, as a graphic designer, most of my clients were still asking me "What's a website?" shortly followed by, "And why on earth would I ever want one?" At that time, there were literally a handful of websites dealing with wargaming of any kind, and I quickly found my site swamped with traffic from eager wargamers, fresh to the online world, hunting down everything there was then available about the hobby. With the birth of my own magazine still just a mere twinkle in my eye, I even advertised in *Miniature Wargames* to get more traffic, and none of the magazines at the time had a site of their own. Ah, innocent and heady days!

Now, it's hard to find a wargamer who doesn't have a blog, or a FaceBook account, or at least participate on one or more of the many online forums that litter cyberspace, ranging from the 'big daddy' The Miniatures Page (*theminiaturespage.com*), through mid-range and friendly places like WD3 (*wdlovesme.19.forumer.com*), to smaller niche sites, club sites and so on.

We're a particularly opinionated lot, so trying to follow a discussion on an online forum can be both confusing and, occasionally, intimidating. As with anything on the Internet, you often find that people are far braver when hidden behind the security of an anonymous username and a keyboard than they would ever dare to be face-to-face.

Be that as it may, you can find some astonishingly helpful folk online, some of whom turn out to be academics with expertise on a particular period of history, whilst others may be re-enactors or simply highly experienced gamers who can point you in the right direction to find what you need. And some of those blogs I mentioned earlier are truly inspiring, featuring images of beautifully painted collections, step-by-step records of how they have achieved the results they have and, of course, those all-important links to other sites that have inspired or helped them.

The short answer to the most powerful use of the Web is, of course, Google. Just enter your search terms, such as "wargaming", "Napoleonic uniforms", "fantasy scenery" or whatever it happens to be, and you're well on your way on an extraordinary journey of discovery. Pay particular attention to Google's powerful image search capability, since there are countless old engravings and colour plates online, along with huge numbers of photos taken at re-enactment and living history events depicting every conceivable period. A great deal of fantasy and science fiction art is also available online, and I hardly dare tempt you to type "Lord of the Rings" lest you be swamped!

Given the transient nature of the Web, there is little point me putting a list of wargaming blogs or other sites here. As we all know, links that work just fine one day may just bring up an "Error:404" message the next, and given that this is a book that, I sincerely hope, may still be read in years to come, I think it's far better just to direct you to my own site at *www. battlegames.co.uk* where you will find a host of links that I endeavour to keep up-to-date.

Your local library

Use it or lose it, as the saying goes, and never was this more true than when referring to the current state of local libraries. There was a time, for anyone over the age of thirty as I write this, when your local library was the *first* port of call when you sought reference material, whereas sadly, nowadays, it is all to often the last.

With libraries disappearing as a result of government and local government cut-backs, or simply because of under-use in these digital times, libraries are having to become imaginative to compete. But it is still possible to find treasure on their shelves and, of course, all countries have inter-library loan schemes so that they can obtain books and journals for you even if your local branch does not have a copy of their own. With some military history and wargaming books being rare, expensive or both, this is a tremendous resource which we neglect at our peril.

Besides, modern libraries are often nice places to visit, often with a coffee shop and comfortable chairs, and convenient desks where you can sit and make notes or augment your book reading with access to – you guessed it – the Internet! Many libraries also, like bookshops, arrange visits from notable authors or have talks given by academics, so keep your eyes open in your local newspaper for announcements.

I have a soft spot for libraries, I'll admit. From my early years, I was a regular visitor to those in Southend-on-Sea and Leigh-on-Sea in Essex and it was here, indeed, that I first discovered the seminal work that still influences me to this day: *The War Game* by Charles Grant. Together with a good school library, these places introduced me to a whole new world, opening my eyes to a wealth of military history and other literature without which I would be a different man today. For my GCSE A-levels, I ditched the notes from my English lessons and instead learned the art of literary criticism from books, resulting in an 'A' grade pass, defying my teacher's 'C' grade prediction. Reading really can change your life.

How sad the world will become if it loses real books and the libraries that house them. For me, the digital world is but a poor and cold imposter.

Museums

Obviously, there are far too many museums around the world to be listed here, but I took a straw poll amongst people who follow *Battlegames* on FaceBook and these are some of their favourties. In all cases I have given a website address where available, since websites tend to contain the most up-to-date information, opening times and prices as well as photographs of what to expect.

UK

Imperial War Museum London *http://london.iwm.org.uk*
Imperial War Museum North (Manchester) *http://north.iwm.org.uk*
Imperial War Museum Duxford (Cambridgeshire) *http://duxford.iwm.org.uk*
Bovington tank Museum *www.tankmuseum.org*
National Army Museum, London *www.nam.ac.uk*
Royal Armouries, Leeds *www.royalarmouries.org/visit-us/leeds*
Royal Armouries, Tower of London *www.royalarmouries.org/visit-us/tower-of-london*
Royal Armouries, Port Nelson, Portsmouth *www.royalarmouries.org/visit-us/fort-nelson*
The Combined Military Services Museum, Maldon, Essex *www.cmsm.co.uk*
The RAF Museums, London and Cosford *www.rafmuseum.org.uk*
The Muckleborough Military Collection, Norfolk *www.muckleburgh.co.uk*
The Tangmere Military Aviation Museum *www.tangmere-museum.org.uk*
Firepower Royal Artillery Museum, Woolwich, London *www.firepower.org.uk*

See also the very useful **Army Museums Ogilby Trust** website at *www. armymuseums.org.uk* which lists hundreds of regimental and other museums with links to their websites.

EUROPE

Hotel des Invalides, Paris, France *www.invalides.org*
Airbornemuseum Oosterbeek, Holland *www.airbornemuseum.com*
Oorlogsmuseum Overloon, Holland *www.oorlogsmuseum.nl*
Dutch Army Museum *www.armymuseum.nl*
HeeresGeschichtlicheMuseum, Vienna, Austria *www.hgm.or.at*
Stibbert Museum in Florence, Italy *www.museostibbert.it*
Musée de la Bataille de Rocroi *16 place d'Armes, 08230 Rocroi, France*
Royal Museum of Armed Forces and of Military History, Brussels, Belgium *www.klm-mra.be*
Palais des Beaux Arts, Lille, France (permanent exhibition of 1/600 models of Vauban's fortresses) *www.palaisdesbeauxarts.fr/spip.php?article63*
Zeppelin Museum Friedrichshafen, Germany *www.zeppelin-museum.de*
Bundeswehr Military History Museum, Dresden, Germany *www.militaerhistorisches-museum.bundeswehr.de*
Bayerisches Armeemuseum, Ingolstadt, Bavaria, Germany *www.bayerisches-armeemuseum.de/en/*
In Flanders Field Museum, Ypres, Belgium *www.inflandersfields.be*
Le Grand Bunker, Ouistreham, Normandy, France *www.musee-grand-bunker.com*
The National Swedish Museums of Military History, Stockholm and elsewhere in Sweden *http://www.sfhm.se/default____4443.aspx?epslanguage=EN*
The Doge's Palace and Armoury, Venice, Italy *www.venice-museum.com/doge.html*
National Army Museum, the Alcázar, Toledo, Spain *www.toledo-turismo.com/turismo/contenido/conociendo-la-ciudad/donde-mirar/museos/museo-ejercito.aspx*

REST OF THE WORLD

West Point, New York, USA *www.usma.edu/museum*
Royal Armouries, Louisville, Kentucky, USA *www.royalarmouries.org/visit-us/louisville-kentucky* which is housed at The Frazier History Museum *www.fraziermuseum.org*

Canadian War Museum, Ottowa, Ontario, Canada *www.warmuseum.ca*
Auckland War memorial Museum, Auckland, New Zealand *www.aucklandmuseum.com*
Royal Canadian Regiment Museum, London, Ontario, Canada *www.theroyalcanadianregiment.ca*
The Liberty Memorial and National WWI Museum, Kansas City, Missouri, USA *www.theworldwar.org*
National Air Force Museum of Canada, Astra, Ontario, Canada *www.airforcemuseum.ca*
Base Borden Military Museum, Ottawa, Ontario, Canada *www.borden.forces.gc.ca*
The Charleston Museum, Charleston, South Carolina, USA *www.charlestonmuseum.org*
Fort Sumter, Sullivan's Island, South Carolina, USA *www.nps.gov/fosu/index.htm*
The Naval Aviation Museum, Pensacola, Florida, USA *www.navalaviationmuseum.org*
Battleship USS Alabama, Mobile, Alabama, USA *www.ussalabama.com*
United States Army Aviation Museum, Fort Rucker, Alabama, USA *www.armyavnmuseum.org*
The National WWII Museum, New Orleans, Louisiana, USA *www.ddaymuseum.org*
Mississippi Armed Forces Museum, Camp Shelby, Mississippi, USA *www.armedforcesmuseum.us*
American Civil War Museum, Gettysburg, Pennsylvania, USA *www.gettysburgmuseum.com*
The Mariners' Museum, Newport News, Virginia, USA *www.marinersmuseum.org*
Jamestown Settlement & Yorktown Victory Centre, Williamsburg and Yorktown, Virginia, USA *www.historyisfun.org*
For links to various military museums in Australia, see *www.ozatwar.com/museums/militarymuseums.htm*
Rorke's Drift, KwaZulu-Natal, South Africa *www.places.co.za/html/rorkesdrift.html*
Isandlwana Battlefield, Route D897, Nqutu Rural, South Africa *www.historvius.com/isandlwana-battlefield-534*

Wargame figure manufacturers

This list is not, I fear, exhaustive, though it is reasonably comprehensive. Inevitably, by the time this book is published, some of those listed here may have sadly gone out of business or have been taken over by another company, whilst brand new enterprises will have happily sprung up to take their place.

Almost all do now, thankfully, have websites, which releases me from the monstrous task of listing their wares and prices, which quickly go out of date. Instead, I shall simply mention the sizes of miniature that they are best known for at the time of going to press and whether they produce historical (*H*), fantasy (*F*), sci-fi (*SF*) or role-playing (*RP*) miniatures.

Whilst there is a great deal of crossover between wargaming and the wider hobby of military modelling, I have not included companies here whose primary target is the modeller/collector, rather than wargamer.

Regrettably, whilst some wargames companies have excellent and very modern websites, a few still have sites that come straight out of the digital dark ages. You have been warned!

Those companies whose names have been highlighted with a star ★ are generally considered to be the better-known 'big players' of long standing, with extensive ranges, often in several scales. This is not to say that others listed here may not also be of excellent repute – it is simply that they advertise less, or I have little or no knowledge of them, and you should therefore check their websites and elsewhere for further information.

1st Corps 28mm metal *H* *www.1stcorps.co.uk*	**19th Century Miniatures (Old Glory 15s)** 15mm metal *H F* *http://oldglory15s.com*
AB (Anthony Barton) Figures ★ 1/76 and 15mm metal *H* *www.abfigures.co.uk* for WWII *See also Eureka Miniatures* *www.eurekamin.com.au and Fighting 15s* *www.fighting15sshop.co.uk for Napoleonic* *and other ranges.*	**Abandoned Mind Games** 28-32mm metal *RP* *http://abandonedmindgames.com*
Aberrant Games and Miniatures 20mm and 28mm metal *SF RP* *www.aberrantgames.com*	**Acies Edizioni** 15mm metal *H* *www.aciesedizioni.it*
Airfix ★ 1/72 and 1/32 plastic (often found in toy and model shops) *www.airfix.com*	**All the King's Men Toy Soldiers** 54mm metal toy-style miniatures *H* *www.allthekingsmentoysoldiers.com*
AMS Miniatures 15mm and 28mm metal *H F SF* *www.amsminiatures.co.uk*	**Armorum & Aquila Miniatures** 28mm metal *H* *www.aandaminiatures.co.uk*
A Call to Arms 1/72 and 1/32 plastics *H* *www.acalltoarms.co.uk*	**Accurate (Imex)** 1/72 plastics *H* *www.imex-model.com*
Adler 6mm metal *H* *http://home.clara.net/adlermin*	**Alternative Armies** 15mm and 28mm metal F *www.alternative-armies.com*
Andrea-Miniatures Collector-grade metal miniatures in many scales *H F* *www.andrea-miniatures.com*	**Armies in Plastic** 54mm plastic *H* *www.armiesinplastic.com*
Armourfast 1/72 plastic vehicles *H* *http://armourfast.com*	**Army Group North Miniatures** 1/56th WWII resin vehicles *www.agnminiatures.com*
Artizan Designs ★ 28mm metal *H RP* *www.artizandesigns.com*	**Art-Miniaturen** 1/72 metal *H* *www.schmaeling.de*

Askari Miniatures 28mm metal *H* www.askari-minis.com	**Assault Group** 28mm metal *H* www.theassaultgroup.co.uk
Aventine Miniatures 28mm metal *H* www.aventineminiatures.co.uk	**Baccus** ★ 6mm metal *H F* www.baccus6mm.com
Baker Company 28mm metal *H* http://bakercompany.co.uk	**Barony Miniatures** 28mm metal *H F* www.baronyminiatures.com
Barzso Playsets 54mm plastic *H* www.barzso.com	**Battlefield Miniatures** 20mm metal *H* www.battlefieldminiatures.co.uk
The Battleforge 28mm metal *F* www.thebattleforge.co.uk	**Battlefront** (Flames of War WWII) ★ 15mm metal *H* www.flamesofwar.com
Battlestandard Miniatures 28mm metal *H* www.battlestandardminiatures.com	**Baueda Wargames** 15mm, 28mm and 1/48 metal *H F* www.baueda.com
B&B Miniatures 20mm and 25mm metal *H* www.bandbminiatures.co.uk	**Bear's Den Miniatures** 15mm, 28mm and 40mm metal *H* www.bearsdenminiatures.com
Bederken Miniatures 28mm metal *F* www.bederken.com	**Bend Sinister** 10mm, 12mm, 15mm and 28mm metals *H* www.bendsinister.co.uk
Bicorne Miniatures ★ 25mm metal *H* www.bicorne.net	**Billy Bones Workshop** Paper armies http://billybonesworkshop.co.uk
Black Cat Bases 15mm and 28mm metals *H F SF RP* http://blackcatbases.com	**Black Hat Miniatures** ★ 15mm, 18mm, 25mm and 28mm metal *H F SF RP* www.blackhat.co.uk
Black Orc Games 28mm metal *F SF RP* http://100k.blackorc.com	**Black Scorpion** 32mm metal *H F RP* www.blackscorpionminiatures.com
Black Tree Designs 28mm metal *H F SF* www.blacktreedesign.com	**Blaze Away Miniatures** (including Cannon Fodder Miniatures) 15mm and 28mm metal *H* www.blazeaway.com.au
Bolt Action Miniatures (see Warlord)	**Boot Hill Miniatures** 28mm metal *H* http://boothillminiatures.co.uk
Brigade Models 28mm, 15mm and 6mm figures and vehicles *H F SF* www.brigademodels.co.uk	**Britannia Miniatures** 20mm, 25mm and 28mm metal figures and vehicles *H* www.britannia-miniatures.com
Caesar Miniatures 1/72 plastic *H* www.miniknight.com	**Calpe Miniatures** 28mm metal *H* www.calpeminiatures.co.uk
Campaign Game Miniatures 15mm metal *H* www.campaign-game-miniatures.com	**Castaway Arts** 28mm metal *H* www.castawayarts.com.au
Cavalcade Wargames 28mm metal *H F SF* http://cavalcadewargames.com	**Center Stage Miniatures** 28mm metal *F RP* www.centerstageminis.com

Conquest Games 28mm metal *H* *www.conquest-games.co.uk*	**Conquest Miniatures** 28mm metal *H* *www.conquestminiatures.com*
Copplestone Castings ★ 10mm, 15mm and 28mm metal figures and 1/55 vehicles *H F SF RP* *www.copplestonecastings.co.uk*	**Corvus Belli** *(including Infinity and* *WarCrow)* 15mm and 28mm metal *H F SF RP* *www.corvusbelli.com*
Critical Mass Games 15mm metal figures and vehicles *SF* *www.criticalmassgames.com*	**Crusader Miniatures** ★ 28mm metal *H* *www.crusaderminiatures.com*
Cold War Miniatures 28mm metal *H SF* *http://cold-war.co.uk*	**C-P Models** 20mm and 28mm metal *H SF RP* *www.cpmodelsminiatures.co.uk*
Crocodile Games 28mm metal *F* *www.crocodilegames.com*	**Cutting Edge Miniatures** 28mm metal *H* *http://cuttingedgeminiatures.com*
Dark Realm Miniatures 6mm metal *SF* *www.darkrealmminiatures.co.uk*	**Dark Sword Miniatures** 28-30mm metal *F RP* *www.darkswordminiatures.com*
Darwin Games 32mm metal *SF* *www.darwin-games.com.au*	**Dixon Miniatures** ★ 25-28mm metal *H* *www.dixonminiatures.co.uk*
Donnington Miniatures (aka Ancient & **Modern Army Supplies)** 15mm metal *H* *www.donnington-mins.co.uk*	**D&P Minis** 15mm and 28mm metal *H* *www.dadiepiombo.com/d&pm.html*
Drabant Miniatures 40mm metal *H* *www.drabant-miniatures.com*	**Dwarf Tales Miniatures** 28mm metal *F* *http://portal.dwarftales.com*
Eagle Figures 25mm metal *H* *www.eaglefigures.co.uk*	**East Riding Miniatures** *(also Platoon 20* *and Lamming Miniatures)* 15mm, 25mm and 28mm metal *H* *http://shop.eastridingminiatures.co.uk*
Ebob Miniatures 28mm metal *H F* *www.ebobminiatures.com*	**Elhiem Figures** 28mm metal *H SF* *www.elhiemfigures.com*
Elite 28mm metal *H* *www.eliteminiatures.co.uk*	**eM-4 Miniatures** 28mm metal and plastic *F SF* *www.em4miniatures.com*
Empress Miniatures 28mm metal *H* *www.empressminiatures.com*	**Essex Miniatures** ★ 15mm and 28mm metal *H* *www.essexminiatures.co.uk*
Eureka Miniatures ★ 18mm and 28mm *H* *www.eurekamin.com.au*	**Fantassin** *(see Warmodelling)*
Fenryll **28mm resin** *F SF* *www.fenryll.com*	**Fife & Drum Miniatures** 1/56 (30mm) metal *H* *http://fifedrumminis.blogspot.co.uk/*
Fighting 15s ★ 10mm, 15mm, 28mm and 40mm metal *H F* *SF RP* *www.fighting15sshop.co.uk*	**First Legion** 40mm and 54mm metal *H* *www.firstlegionltd.com*

Forge World ★ Large-scale resin models supporting the Games Workshop range *F SF* *www.forgeworld.co.uk*	**Foundry Miniatures** ★ 28mm metal *H* *www.wargamesfoundry.com*
FreeBooTer Miniatures 28-32mm metal *F SF RP* *www.freebooterminiatures.de*	**Front Rank Figurines** ★ 28mm metal *H* *www.frontrank.com*
Games Workshop ★ A vast range of metal, plastic and resin figures and equipment *F SF RP* *www.games-workshop.com*	**Gaming Models** 15mm resin *H* *www.gamodls.com*
Garrison Miniatures 25mm metal *H* *www.garrisonminiatures.com*	**GHQ** ★ *(sold by Magister Militum in UK)* 1/285, 1/1200, 1/2400 and 10mm metal *H* *www.ghqmodels.com*
Gorgon Studios 28mm metal *H F* *www.gorgon-studios.com*	**Gramodels** Resin vehicle kits in various scales *H* *www.gramodels.co.uk*
Great War Miniatures 28mm metal *H* *see www.northstarfigures.com*	**Green Eyed Minis** 15mm metal *F* *greeneyedminis.com*
Gripping Beast ★ 28mm metal *H* *http://www.grippingbeast.com*	**Grubby Tanks** 1/76 (20mm) resin vehicles *H* *www.grubbytanks.com*
HäT ★ 1/72 and 1/32 plastics *H* *www.hat.com*	**Hasslefree Miniatures** *(see also Mantic)* 28mm metal *F SF RP* *www.hasslefreeminiatures.co.uk*
Haus of Stuff 15mm, 20mm and 25mm metal *H* *http://wargame51.tripod.com/wargame.htm*	**Heresy Miniatures** 28mm metal *F SF RP* *www.heresyminiatures.com*
Heroes of the Dark Age 28mm metal *H F* *www.heroesofthedarkage.com*	**Heroics & Ros** 1/300 (6mm) metal *H* *www.heroicsandros.co.uk*
Hinchliffe 25mm metals *H* *www.hinchliffe.co.uk*	**Historical Miniatures.com** *(Stone* *Mountain Miniatures)* 15mm metal *H* *http://historicalminiatures.com*
Historical Products Company 20mm metal *H* *www.ebhpc.com*	**Historifigs** **10mm**, 20mm, 28mm and 40mm metal *H* *F SF* *www.historifigs.com*
The Hobby Den 20mm resin vehicles *H* *www.thehobbyden.com*	**The Honourable Lead Boiler Suit** **Company (HLBS)** 28mm, 40mm and 1/48 figures and vehicles, metal and resin *H RP* *http://www.hlbs.co.uk*
Imprint Models 1/50 scale vehicles *H* *www.imprintmodels.co.uk*	**Ironclad Miniatures** 25/28mm figures and vehicles in metal and resin *H SF* *www.ironcladminiatures.co.uk*
Irregular Miniatures ★ 2mm, 6mm, 10mm, 15mm, 20mm, 25mm, 42mm and 54mm metal *H* *www.irregularminiatures.co.uk*	**Italeri** ★ 1/72 and 1/32 plastics (often found in toy and model shops) *H* *www.italeri.com*

Kallistra 10mm metal Hordes and Heroes Medievals suited to *Warmaster H F* *www.kallistra.co.uk*	**Khurasan Miniatures** 15mm metal *H F SF* *http://khurasanminiatures.tripod.com*
Kingsford Miniatures 28mm metal *H* *www.kingsfordminiatures.org*	**Knuckleduster Miniatures** 28mm and 40mm metal *H* *www.knuckleduster.com*
Lancashire Games 15mm and 25mm metal *H* *www.lancashiregames.com*	**Langton Miniatures** 1/200, 1/300 and 1/1200 *H* *www.rodlangton.com*
Legio Heroica 15mm and 20mm metal *H* *www.legio-heroica.com*	**Lurkio** 15mm metal *H* *www.lurkio.co.uk*
Magister Militum ★ 1/285, 10mm, 15mm, 20mm, 25mm and 28mm metal *H* *www.magistermilitum.com*	**Man at War Games** 15mm metal *H* *www.manatwar.es*
Mantic Games ★ (*including Hasslefree Miniatures*) 28mm metal *F SF RP* *www.manticgames.com*	**Matador Models** 1/76 vehicles in resin and metal *H* *http://matadormodels.co.uk*
Matchlock Miniatures (*see Minifigs*)	**Mega Miniatures** 28mm metal *F SF RP* *www.megaminis.com*
Mercs 28mm metal *SF* *www.mercsminis.com*	**Minden Miniatures** 30mm metal *H* (*NB This is not a commercial business – see site*) *http://mindenminis.blogspot.com*
Miniature Design Studio 28mm metal *H* *www.miniaturedesignstudio.co.uk*	**Miniature Figurines (Minifigs)** ★ Vast range: 10mm, 12mm, 15mm, 20mm, 25mm and 28mm metal *H* *www.miniaturefigurines.co.uk*
Minimi Miniatures 20mm resin *H* *www.minimi.co.uk*	**Mirliton** 15mm, 20mm and 28mm metal *H F* *www.mirliton.it*
Mithril Miniatures 32mm metal *F* *www.mithril.ie*	**MMS Classic Models** 1/76 vehicles im metal *H* *www.mmsmodels.co.uk*
Moonfleet Miniatures 15mm and 28mm metal *H F SF RP* *moonfleetminiatures.com*	**Museum Miniatures** 15mm metal *H* *www.museumminiatures.co.uk*
Musket Miniatures 10mm, 15mm, 20mm and 25mm metal *H* *www.musketminiatures.com*	**Musketeer Miniatures** (*orders now handled by Gripping Beast*) 28mm metal *H* *www.musketeer-miniatures.com*
Mutineer Miniatures 28mm metal *H* *http://mutineerminiatures.com*	**Navwar** 15mm, 1/1200 and 1/3000 metal *H* *www.navwar.co.uk*
Newbold World 28mm metal *F* *www.newboldworld.com*	**Newline** ★ 1/72, 20mm and 28mm metals *H* *http://newlinedesigns.co.uk*

North Star ★ Distributor and retailer of many different manufacturers as well as own brand www.northstarfigures.com	**Odemars (Ykreol)** 1/72 plastic *H* www.ykreol.com
Oddzial Osmy 15mm and 1/600 metal *H* See Fighting 15s www.fighting15sshop.co.uk or http://picoarmor.com	**Offensive Miniatures** 28mm metal *H SF* www.offensiveminiatures.com
Old Crow 6mm, 15mm and 28mm resin *SF* www.oldcrowmodels.co.uk	**Old Glory** ★ 10mm, 15mm, 25mm and 40mm metal *H* www.oldgloryuk.com
One Monk Miniatures Paper armies for F and SF (print as big as you like) http://onemonk.com	**Otherworld Miniatures** 28mm resin or metal *F* www.otherworld.me.uk
Outland Games 20 and 25mm metal *H* www.outlandgames.net	**Outpost Wargame Services** 15mm and 28mm metal *H* www.outpostwargameservices.co.uk
Paper Tiger Armaments A remarkable range of PDF vehicles to print out and assemble www.papertigerarmaments.com	**Pardulon** 28mm resin figures and vehicles *SF* http://pardulon-models.com
Parkfield Miniatures 15mm and 25mm metal *H* www.parkfieldminiatures.freeservers.com	**Pendraken Miniatures** ★ 10mm and 28mm metal *H* www.pendraken.co.uk
Perry Miniatures ★ 28mm and 40mm metal, 28mm plastic *H* www.perry-miniatures.com	**Peter Pig** 15mm metal figures and vehicles *H* www.peterpig.co.uk
Pig Iron Productions 28mm metal *SF* www.pig-iron-productions.com	**Pithead 10mm Miniatures** 10mm figures and vehicles in metal *H* http://nowear.se/pitheadphp/www/page.php?paeid=5
The Plastic Soldier Company Ltd ★ 15mm, 1/72 and 28mm plastic *H* www.theplasticsoldiercompany.co.uk	**Prince August** ★ 25mm and 40mm home casting moulds *H* www.princeaugust.ie
Pulp Figures 28mm metal *RP* www.pulpfigures.com	**QRF Models** 15mm and 1/100 figures and vehicles in metal *H SF* http://quickreactionforce.co.uk
RAFM Miniatures & Games 15mm, 20mm and 28mm metal figures and vehicles *H F SF* www.rafm.com	**Ral Partha** 15mm and 28mm metal *F SF* www.ralparthaeurope.co.uk
Rapier Miniatures 6mm and 28mm metal *H F* www.rapierminiatures.co.uk	**Reaper Miniatures** 28mm metal *F SF RP* www.reapermini.com
Rebel Minis 15mm and 28mm metal *H SF* www.rebelminis.com	**Redoubt Enterprises** ★ 28mm metal *H* www.redoubtenterprises.com
Redstar Miniatures 1/48 metal and resin figures and vehicles *H* www.redstarminiatures.eu	**Reiver Castings** 6mm, 10mm, 20mm, 28mm figures and vehicles resin and metal *H SF* http://reivercasting.wordpress.com

Relic Miniatures 28mm metal *H* *http://relicminiatures.com*	**Renegade Miniatures** ★ 28mm metal *H F* *www.renegademiniatures.com*
Revell ★ 1/72 plastics (often found in toy and model shops) *H* *www.revell.de*	**R H Models** 20mm metal *H SF* *www.rhmodels.com*
Rif Raf Miniatures 28mm metal *H* *www.rifrafminiatures.co.uk*	**RSM95** 20mm and 25mm *H* *www.dpcltdcom.org/rsm95_007.htm*
Sash and Saber *(also see Old Glory)* 28mm and 40mm metal *H* *www.sashandsaber.com*	**Scarab Miniatures** 28mm and 1/48 scale metal *H SF* *http://scarabminiatures.com*
Scotia Grendel 1/300 and 25mm metal and resin *H F SF* *www.scotiagrendel.com*	**SHQ/Kennington Miniatures** 20mm and 25mm metal figures and vehicles *H F* *www.shqminiatures.co.uk*
Skytrex ★ 15mm, 1/200 and 1/300 figures and vehicles and 1/144 aircraft, metal *H* *www.skytrex.com*	**Sloppy Jalopy** 1/48, 1/56 and 28mm vehicles and figures in metal and resin *H* *www.sloppyjalopy.com*
Spencer Smith ★ *(incorporating Jacklex and Shiny Toy Soldiers)* 20mm, 30mm and 42mm metals *H* *www.spencersmithminiatures.co.uk*	**Splintered Light Minis** 15mm and 20mm metal H *F SF* *www.splinteredlightminis.com*
S&S Models 20mm and 28mm metal and resin vehicles *H* *www.sandsmodels.com*	**Stan Johansen Miniatures** 15mm and 28mm metal *H SF RP* *www.stanjohansenminiatures.com*
Steve Barber Models 10mm, 28mm and 42mm metal *H* *www.sbarber-models.clara.net*	**Stonewall Figures (Combat Miniatures)** 20mm metal *H* *www.stonewallfigures.co.uk*
Strelets 1/72 plastic *H* *www.strelets-r.com*	**TB Line Hobby Wargames** 10mm metal *H* *www.tridentebologna.it*
Thunderbolt Mountain 25mm, 30mm and 1/48 figures *H F* *www.thunderboltmountain.com*	**Tiger Miniatures** 28mm metal *H* *www.tigerminiatures.co.uk*
Tin Soldier UK 15mm and 28mm metal *H F* *http://tinsoldieruk.com*	**Tradition of London** ★ Classic ranges of 25mm and 30mm metal *H* *www.traditionoflondon.com*
Under Fire Miniatures 20mm metal *H* *www.underfireminiatures.com*	**Valiant Miniatures** 1/72 metal and plastic *H* *www.valiantminiatures.com*
Venexia Miniatures 15mm and 28mm metal *H* *www.venexiaminiatures.com*	**Vexillia Limited** 15mm metal *H* *www.vexillia.ltd.uk*
Victory Force 28mm metal *H F SF* *www.victoryforce.com*	**Victrix** ★ 28mm and 54mm plastic and metal *H* *www.victrixlimited.com*
Viking Forge 15mm and 25mm metal *H F* *http://vikingforge.datasquire.net*	**Walkerloo** PDF Napoleonic soldiers to print out and play *www.walkerloo.com*

Wargames Factory 28mm plastics *H F SF* *http://wargamesfactory.com*	**Wargames South** 10mm (1/144) metal figures and vehicles *H* *www.wargames-south.com*
Warlord Games ★ 28mm metal and plastic figures and vehicles *H* *www.warlordgames.com*	**Warmodelling** ★ 15mm metal *H* *www.warmodelling.com*
Warrior Miniatures 15mm and 25mm *H* *www.warriorminiatures.com*	**Waterloo 1815** 1/72 and 1/32 plastic *H* *www.hatitalywaterloo.it*
Waterloo to Mons 28mm metal *H* *www.waterlootomons.com*	**WD Models** 28mm metal and resin figures and vehicles *H* *www.wdmodels.com*
Wespe Models Resin models and kits in many scales *H* *www.wespemodels.ro*	**Wessex Games** 28mm and other scales in metal *H F SF RP* *www.blease.pwp.blueyonder.co.uk*
West Wind Productions 28mm metal *H SF* *www.westwindproductions.co.uk*	**Wyrd Miniatures** 28mm metal *F SF RP* *www.wyrd-games.net*
Zvezda ★ 1/72 plastic (often found in toy and model shops) *H* *www.zvezda.org.ru*	

Terrain and scenery manufacturers

Again, this list is far from the whole picture, especially since this sector is noted for one-man-band outfits to pop onto the radar for a time and then disappear, but the major players have been around for some time and are likely to remain happily serving the needs of wargamers for years to come.

Acheson Creations Resin scenic items *www.achesoncreations.com*	**Advanced Terrain** 28mm terrain items, including losts of ancient ruins *www.advancedterrain.com*
Amera Plastic Mouldings An interesting range of fortifications, tents and other useful items *www.amera.co.uk*	**A*M*S*I Miniature Landscaping** A variety of useful terrain and scenic materials *http://amsistuff.com*
Angel Barracks ★ Specialists in 6mm scenery *http://angelbarracks.co.uk*	**Architects of War** ★ A wide range of useful terrain items *www.architectsofwar.com*
Architectural Miniatures Custom-made (and beautiful) model buildings *www.architecturalminiatures.co.uk*	**Area 9** A relatively new company with a growing range of scenic items *www.areanine.net*
Armorcast A wide range of scenic and other items *www.armorcast.com*	**Battleboards** High quality terrain boards and accessories for wargames *www.battleboards.co.uk*

Battlefield Architect A variety of terrain items *www.battlefieldarchitect.com*	**Battlefield Terrain Concepts** A range of terrain and scenic items *http://battlefieldterrain.com*
The Battleforge Scenic accessories for F and SF *www.thebattleforge.co.uk*	**Baueda Wargames** ★ Some very interesting cenic accessories for 15mm, 28mm and 1/48 *www.baueda.com*
Billy Bones Workshop Paper scenic items (PDF format to print out at home) *http://billybonesworkshop.co.uk*	**Black Cat Bases** ★ A wide range of scenic items covering many periods – plus bases! *http://blackcatbases.com*
Brandlin Laser cut styrene building kits *http://brandlin.blogspot.com*	**Castle Kits** Scenic and building kits ideal for F and SF gaming and roleplaying *http://stores.castlekits.com*
CNC Workshop Miniature Scenery An intriguing range of slot-together scenery and terrain *www.miniaturescenery.com*	**The Colonial Steamboat Company** 15mm, 20mm and 28mm buildings and boats *www.colonialsteamboat.co.uk*
The Cthulhuminati Easier to see than to explain or pronounce! *www.cthulhuminati.com*	**Dwarven Forge** Dungeon building systems *www.dwarvenforge.com*
Ebob Miniatures A new range of buildings *www.ebobminiatures.com*	**Evil Mushroom Games** Scenic items especially suitable for SF *www.evilmushroomgames.com*
Fantascene ★ 28mm scenery *www.fantascene.net*	**Fieldworks** Buildings for 10mm and 15mm gaming, including lots of ruins *www.fieldworks.org.uk*
Forge World ★ Resin scenic items often suitable for more than just F and SF *www.forgeworld.co.uk*	**Fortress Models** Resin trench systems and gun emplacements *www.fortressmodels.co.uk*
Foundations of War Resin and plaster cast terrain products *www.foundationsofwar.co.uk*	**Frontline Wargaming** ★ 15mm, 20mm and 28mm wargame scenery and accessories *www.frontlinewargaming.co.uk*
Gale Force Nine ★ A wide range of battlefield scenery for fantasy and historical settings *www.gf9.com*	**Gamecraft Miniatures** Buildings in a variety of scales *www.gamecraftminiatures.com*
Games Workshop ★ Also produce a wide range of useful terrain and scenic items *www.games-workshop.com*	**GrandManner** ★ Exquisite 28mm scale resin model buildings and terrain *www.grandmanner.co.uk*
Hirst Arts Casting materials for creating your own buildings *www.hirstarts.com*	**Hotz Artworks** Paper (PDFs to print out at home) buildings and felt gaming mats *www.hotzartworks.com*
Hovels ★ A large range, especially of buildings, in several scales *www.hovelsltd.co.uk*	**Ironclad Miniatures** Bunkers, entrenchments and other scenic items in several scales *www.ironcladminiatures.co.uk*

J R Miniatures Buildings and terrain items in several scales *http://02a7218.netsolstores.com*	**JTT Microscale** Trees and other scenic materials *www.jttmicroscale.com*
Kallistra ★ Popular terrain providers, especially their 'Hexon' system *www.kallistra.co.uk*	**Kerr & King** Scenic and terrain items and scenic bases *www.kerrandking.co.uk*
K&M Trees ★ Trees, hedges and scatter material *www.kandmtrees.com*	**Knuckleduster Miniatures** Scenic items for their Wild West ranges *www.knuckleduster.com*
Kobblestone Miniatures Very attractive terrain and scenic items, especially buildings *www.kobblestone.ca*	**Lancer Miniatures** 20mm buildings, ruins and scenic items *http://lancerminiatures.com*
Langton Miniatures Buildings, earthworks and an exquisite range of age of sail ships *www.rodlangton.com*	**Linka** Re-usable moulds for creating model buildings *www.linkaworld.com*
Long Range Logistics Terrain and scenic items *www.longrangelogistics.com*	**Lurkio** Terrain for ancients gaming *www.lurkio.co.uk*
ManorHouse ★ Wonderful buildings, especially medieval/Mediterranean *http://manorhouseworkshopmindstalkers.wordpress.com*	**The Miniature Building Authority** A wide range of buildings and other scenic items *www.miniaturebuildingauthority.com*
Miniature Worldmaker A wide range of terrain and scenic items *www.miniatureworldmaker.com.au*	**Monolith Designs** A wide range of buildings and accessories in 15mm, 20mm and 28mm *www.monolithdesigns.co.uk*
Noch ★ Model railway scenics supplier with a vast range of useful items *www.noch.de/en/*	**NP Models** A pleasing range of model buildings and scenic items *www.npmodels.co.uk*
Old Crow 6mm, 15mm and 28mm resin scenery and buildings for SF *www.oldcrowmodels.co.uk*	**Oshiro Model Terrain** Pre- and custom-made items, especially oriental buildings *www.oshiromodelterrain.co.uk*
Paper Terrain A good range of PDF buildings and scenics to print out *www.paperterrain.com*	**Pardulon** Buildings and accessories for F and SF *http://pardulon-models.com*
Quantum Gothic A range of SF scenic items and accessories *www.quantumgothic.co.uk*	**Realistic Modelling Services** ★ A beautiful range of terrain and scenic items and services *www.realisticmodelling.com*
Renedra ★ Plastics casting company who also make useful scenic items and bases *http://renedra.co.uk*	**S&A Scenics** Scenery and terrain, including trees, suitable for many scales *www.scenics.co.uk*
Sabol Studios Custom terrain creation *www.sabolstudios.com*	**Scale Link** Model making accessories, especially fine etched brass items *www.scalelink.co.uk*

Scenic Express A vast range of scenic and terrain materials *www.sceneryexpress.com*	**Scheltrum Miniatures** Historical and fantasy scenery, buildings and boats *www.scheltrum.co.uk*
Silhouette MiniNatur A superb German range of model vegetation including Silflor tufts *www.mininatur.de*	**TableScape** Scenery for 25-30mm figures *www.tablescape.co.uk*
TB Line Hobby Wargames Hexagonal terrain and accessories for their ancients gaming system *www.tridentebologna.it*	**Terrain Warehouse** ★ A variety of terrain and scenic items *www.terrainwarehouse.co.uk*
TerranScapes A wide range of terrain and scenic items *http://terranscapes.com*	**Time Cast** ★ 6mm, 10mm and 15mm scenics, especially buildings *www.timecastmodels.co.uk*
Total Battle Miniatures ★ A lovely range of buildings and fortifications in several scales *www.totalbattleminiatures.com*	**Total System Scenic (TSS)** ★ Terrain and scenery, best known for their modular terrain boards *http://totalsystemscenic.com*
Urban Construct Terrain and modular 28mm scenery, buildings and fortifications *www.wargameterrain.co.uk*	**War Torn Worlds** Terrain items made from recycled tyre rubber *http://wartornworlds.com*
War Zone Gaming Terrain Sytems They do what it says on the tin! *www.war-zone.com*	**Woodland Scenics** ★ One of the premier suppliers of scenic and terrain items *http://woodlandscenics.woodlandscenics.com*
WorldWorks Games An extensive range of paper (PDF) terrain for F and SF *www.worldworksgames.com*	**Ziterdes** ★ An extensive range of terrain and landscaping materials *www.ziterdes.de*
Zuzzy Terrain and scenic items aimed mainly at the F and SF markets *www.zuzzy.com*	

Miscellanea

Paints, glue, brushes, decals, flags, modelling material and other bits and pieces that just refuse to fit into any other category – the other 'stuff' of wargaming. As ever, this list is liable to change at any time.

Acrylicos Vallejo ★ Manufacturer of a widely available range of superb acrylic paints *www.acrylicosvallejo.com/gb/index.html*	**Antenociti's Workhop** Truly a retailer with 'stuff' of all kinds! *www.antenocitisworkshop.com*
The Army Painter ★ Acrylic paint and 'dip' to achieve fast results when painting *en masse* *www.thearmypainter.com*	**Back 2 Base-ix Wargaming Products** An Australian firm providing a wide range of aids and accessories *www.back2base-ix.com*

Battle Flag Flags and decals *http://battleflags.blogspot.com*	**Battle Foam** Foam and bags to carry your armies *http://battlefoam.com*
Battlefront *(Flames of War WWII)* Paints, pigments and other accessories to accompany *Flames of War* *www.flamesofwar.com*	**Black Lion Decals** Decals for military vehicles *www.blackliondecals.nl*
Chapterhouse Studios **Custom** bits and pieces for *Warhammer* and *Warhammer 40K* *http://chapterhousestudios.com*	**Chessex** ★ Dice, dice and more dice, nothing but dice! *www.chessex.com*
Coat d'Armes ★ An excellent UK-based range of acrylic paints see *www.blackhat.co.uk*	**CorSec Engineering** A variety of intriguing gaming aids *www.corseceng.com*
Cotton Jim's Flags A very large range of – wait for it – flags *http://cottonjim.mybigcommerce.com*	**Crystal Caste** Dice *http://crystalcaste.com*
Daler-Rowney ★ Artists' paints, brushes and supplies *www.daler-rowney.com*	**The Dial Dude** ★ Clever dials for casualty and morale state visual recognition *www.the-d-d.net*
Dom's Decals A staggering range of tiny decals for vehicles and aircraft *www.domsdecals.com*	**Ebob Miniatures** ★ Sculpting tools, armatures, putty and more *www.ebobminiatures.com*
Fernando Enterprises ★ International miniature painting service *www.miniaturelovers.com*	**Figures in Comfort** ★ **Popular** foam trays and carry cases for your miniatures *www.figuresincomfort.net*
Flag Dude Flags for your wargame armies *http://flagdude.com*	**Gale Force Nine** ★ A wide range of useful accessories and playing aids *www.gf9.com*
Games Workshop ★ Inevitably, GW produce a host of 'stuff' in-house *www.games-workshop.com*	**GMB Designs** ★ Beautiful flags for your wargame units *www.gmbdesigns.com*
KR Multicase *(aka Kaiser Rushforth)* ★ A popular range of foam trays and carry cases *www.krmulticase.com*	**Liquitex** Artists' acrylic paint and supplies *www.liquitex.com*
Litko Game Accessories ★ A vast and popular range of useful bits and pieces to aid your gaming *www.litko.net*	**Little Big Men Studios** Transfers (decals) for wargame figures *www.littlebigmenstudios.com*
Magister Militum An assortment of paints, glues, dice etc *www.magistermilitum.com*	**Magnetic Displays/Coritani** ★ Magnetic and steel paper useful for basing and transporting figures *www.magneticdisplays.co.uk*
Plastruct ★ Vast range of polystyrene modelling parts – download their catalogue *www.plastruct.com*	**Rosemary & Co** ★ Superb artists' brushes *www.rosemaryandco.com*

Sabol Designs	Veni Vidi Vici
The Army Transport range of figure carrying cases www.saboldesigns.net	A wide range of transfers (decals) for wargames figures and vehicles www.3vwargames.co.uk
Warbases.co.uk Pre-cut MDF bases for your figures in any size you like www.warbases.co.uk	Winsor & Newton ★ Artists' paints, brushes and supplies www.winsornewton.com

Wargame shows, conventions and competitions

Every year, tens of thousands of wargamers flock to shows both large and small, all around the world. Of course, their specific dates tend to change each year and sadly, some lose the battle with finance and go out of business, whilst new shows are spawned to replace them. What follows is therefore not a definitive calendar, but it should give you an idea of what is likely to be happening where and, roughly, when, so that you can then make use of the ubiquitous Google, and announcements made in the regular magazines, to find your way to these gatherings.

Note that some of these events are, or include, wargame competitions for gamers who play specific rulesets (especially ancients) such as *DBA* (*De Bellis Antiquitatis*), *DBM* (*De Bellis Multitudinis*), *DBMM* (*De Bellis Magistrorum Militum*), *FoG* (*Field of Glory*), *WAB* (*Warhammer Ancient Battles*), *WFB* (*Warhammer Fantasy Battles*), *HoTT* (*Hordes of The Things*) and *FoW* (*Flames of War*).

Special thanks to Richard Tyndall (Tricks) of the Newark Irregulars upon whose hard work this is based.

The author (in the bright red T-shirt) chatting with *Wargames, Soldiers & Strategy* Editor-in-Chief Jasper Oorthuys, both of us dwarfed by the vast surroundings of the Excel Centre in London's Docklands, the venue of the annual Salute show. Hundreds of traders, thousands of customers through the door – a shopping mall for wargamers! There are also dozens of games laid on, both as demonstrations and participation events. It all makes for a very full day in April!

UK & EIRE

Event	Place	Usual month
Cold Steel	Evesham	
Barn HOTT	Bristol	
Milton Keynes 15mm DBMM	Milton Keynes	
Four Seasons Winter WAB	Stockport	
Albanich	Dumfries	
Scottish League 1st Round	Dumfries	January
Godendag	Usk	
Warpcon	Cork, Eire	
Crusade	Penarth	
Welsh Open DBA	Penarth	
Munster Open DBM	Cork, Eire	
PAW	Plymouth	
Vapnartak	York	
Northern DBM Doubles 1st Round	York	
Call to Arms	Newbury	
Hammerhead	Newark	
WAB GT	Manchester	February
Burton Ancients Doubles	Burton on Trent	
Corrivalry	Daventry	
Scottish League 2nd Round	Perth	
Cavalier	Tunbridge Wells	
South Cheshire Militaire	Crewe	
Innovation in Wargaming	Brentwood	
Leprecon	Dublin, Eire	
Bristol Brawl	Bristol	
Mersey Meltdown WFB	Liverpool	
Overlord	Abingdon	
Itzacon	Galway, Eire	
PAWS 15mm DBA Competition	Portsmouth	
HoTT Avalon	Glastonbury	
Armati by the Sea	Bournemouth	
Schiltron FoG/Armati/FoW	Glasgow	March
West Midlands Military Show	Wolverhampton	
Skirmish	Sidcup	
HoTT Cymru	Penarth	
Spring Skirmish	Yeovil	
Westbury Wars	Westbury	
Mansfield Spring Open WAB	Mansfield	
London Toy Soldier Show	London	
Whoops! Apocalypse WFB	Erdington	
Finn Mac Cool Cup	Dublin, Eire	
Northern DBM Doubles 2nd Round	Manchester	

Event	Place	Usual month
Scottish League 3rd Round	Whitburn	April
Society of Ancients Battleday	Bletchley	
WAB Spring Open	Mansfield	
Student Nationals	Sheffield	
Open War	Mansfield	
WPS Club Challenge	Nottingham	
Venta Silurum DBM	Caerwent	
Weymouth Battle Day AK47	Weymouth	
DBA Northern Cup	Sheffield	
BHGS Challenge	Ascot	
War Cry 15mm Pairs	Clevedon	
Salute	Docklands, London	
Four Seasons Spring WAB	Stockport	
Shieldwall SW Doubles 2nd Round	Slimbridge	
Fisticuffs	Weymouth	
Carronade	Falkirk	May
Legionary	Exeter	
Plastic Warrior Show	Richmond	
Rollcall	Oxford	
Battlegroup North	Elvington	
Lincombe Barn Table Top Sale	Bristol	
Midlands DBA Open	Alvechurch	
Beer and Pretzels	Burton on Trent	
Fear Naught FoW Campaign	Bovington	
PBI Day	Bournemouth	
Future War Commander	Slimbridge	
WAB Historical Weekend	Mansfield	
Celtic Championship	Belfast	
Triples	Sheffield	
Overlord Military Show	Horndean	
Partizan	Newark	

Event	Place	Usual month
Games Expo	Birmingham	June
Wappinshaw	Glasgow	
PAWS 15mm DBA Competition	Portsmouth	
Durham WG Group Open Day	Durham	
Broadside	Sittingbourne	
Saltire	Evesham	
Four Seasons Summer WAB	Stockport	
Weymouth Battle Day	Weymouth	
Phalanx	St Helens	
Northern DBM Doubles 3rd Round	Derby	
Valhalla	Farnborough	
Q-Con	Belfast	
Cuchulain Trophy	Belfast	
London Toy Soldier Show	London	
HoTT Royal Tournament	Sheffield	
Rampage	Dagenham	
Wartorn	Scarborough	
Gauntlet	Broughton	July
Battlegroup South	Bovington	
Campaign	Milton Keynes	
BroCon	Limerick	
Warboot by the Sea	Morecombe	
Festival of History	Kelmarsh Hall	
Toy Soldier	Stockport	
Attack	Devizes	
Strongbow's Shield	Dublin	
Claymore	Edinburgh	August
Britcon	Manchester	
Present Arms	Romford	
SMS 2mm - 10mm	Bristol	
Pompey Pillage 2011	Horndean	
Eastern Front	Norwich	
Military Odyssey	Detling	

Event	Place	Usual month
Border Reiver	Newcastle	September
Axes & Axis	Rushden	
BHGS Doubles	Oxford	
HoTT Berkeley	Berkeley	
The Other Partizan	Newark	
Oxford 25mm FoG	Oxford	
Colours	Newbury	
Stoke Challenge	Stoke on Trent	
Northern DBM Doubles 4th Round	Halifax	
PAWS 15mm DBA Competition	Portsmouth	
Farnborough Bash	Farnborough	
Iceni DBM Doubles	Hoveton	
International Napoleonic Fair	Dorchester	
UWS Open	Belfast	
Skirmish	Sidcup	
Essex Warriors Open Day	Writtle	
Derby World Wargames	Derby	October
Forest Foray	Lydney	
Macclesfield Manoeuvres	Macclesfield	
Skelp	Forfar	
15mm FoG Competition	Oxford	
Six Nations Team DBA Competition	Portsmouth	
SELWG	Crystal Palace, London	
Vexillum	Frome	
Brian Boru Trophy	Dublin, Eire	
English DBA Open	Portsmouth	
Trafalgar Championship	Alvechurch	
Gaelcon	Dublin, Eire	
1st Co. Veterans Open War	Nottingham	
Roll Call	High Wycombe	
Bristol Brawl part deux	Bristol	
Fiasco	Leeds	
Legion DBA Competition	Bath	November
Anderida	Pevensey	
BayFoG	Robin Hood's Bay	
Targe	Kirriemuir	
Warfare	Reading	
Scottish Open DBM	Perth	
Dragonmeet	London	
Smoggycon	Middlesborough	
Northern DBM Doubles 5th Round	Manchester	
Reveille II	Bristol	

Event	Place	Usual month
London Toy Soldier Show	London	
Recon	Leeds	December
PAWS 15mm DBA Competition	Portsmouth	

EUROPE

Event	Place	Usual month
2ème Tournoi Germanicus FoG	Chaniers, France	
FoG Neujahrsturnier	Braubach, Germany	
DBMM 200 Tournoi	Milan, Italy	
Coupe de France DBA	Pau, France	
Giocacarpi	Carpi, Italy	
Journées Figurines et Jeux	Sartrouville, France	January
La Fédération Francaise Les Aigles Open Day	Villeurbanne, France	
Thanatos Tempus	Vitry sur seine, France	
Swabian Open DBM	Bad Urach, Germany	
Tournoi Warlords International Championship de Bruxelles	Brussels, Belgium	
Torneo Impetus	Milan, Italy	
Torneo di FoG	Turin, Italy	
Tournoi de Survilliers	Survilliers, France	
Open DBA de Zaragoza	Zaragoza, Spain	
Italian DBA League 1st Round	La Spezia, Italy	
Tournoi de Selles	Selles, France	
Tournoi de Belfort	Belfort, France	
Audehistorica	Milan, Italy	February
Tactica	Hamburg, Germany	
Justinian's Wars DBMM	Milan, Italy	
FOW Mid War Tournament	Poznan, Poland	
Modelbo	Bologna, Italy	
Dadification	Lodi, Italy	
Festival de Jeux	Cannes, France	
Italian DBA League 2nd Round	Terni, Italy	

Event	Place	Usual month
GTS Torneio de FoG	Costa de Caparic, Portugal	March
Red Barons Wargames Convention	Gentbrugge, Belgium	
Torneo Operation Squad	Milan, Italy	
German Open	Koblenz, Germany	
Giochi in Centro	Bassano del Grappa, Italy	
5° Anvil Dragon Trophy	Cannes, France	
9th Interclub DBM Challenge	Cannes, France	
Glory or Dishonour	Uden, Holland	
Tournoi par Equipes	Sion, Switzerland	
Convention Henry IV	Pau, France	
Do or Dice	Kiel, Germany	
Tournoi d'Amiens - St Fuscien	Amiens, France	
RAGE	Chenove, France	
Torneo DBMM Milano Primavera	Milan, Italy	
Tournoi NPOW	Seclin, France	
Chaniers Tournoi FOW	Chaniers, France	
Rencontre jeu l'Art de la Guerre	Aubagne, France	
Cry Havoc WAB Tournament	Munich, Germany	
FoG Spring Tournament	Lisbon, Portugal	
Play (hosting Wargames Olympiad)	Modena, Italy	
Action	Mönchengladbach, Germany	
Italian DBA League 3rd Round	Modena, Italy	
Petites Guerres	Paris, France	April
Hellana	Agliana, Italy	
Italian DBA League 4th Round	Agliana, Italy	
DBM Stoertebeker Cup	Baltrum, Germany	
Rencontre De Jeux De Figurines	Troyes, France	
Lattes Tournoi FOW	Lattes, France	
DBMM Italian Team Trophy	Bassano, Italy	
Convention FoW Midi Pyrénées	Rabastens, France	
Mutterstadter Rollenspiel Con	Mutterstadt, Germany	
Gothcon	Gothenburg, Sweden	
WAB in Slovenija	Cernica, Slovenija	
Recco DBMM Tournament	Recco, Italy	
Tournoi Normand de Montivilliers	Montvilliers, France	
Après-Midi DBA d'Asnières	Asnières sur Seines, France	
Fiera Del Gioco	Faenza, Italy	
Trophée de la Garde Nervienne	Moncheaux, France	

Event	Place	Usual month
Convention des Grenadiers de l'Essonne	Courcouronnes, France	May
Torneio Internacional Academia Militar	Lisbon, Portugal	
Leineübung V FOW Tournament	Hannover, Germany	
Tournoi de Nancy	Nancy, France	
Tournoi de Saumur	Saumur, France	
Italian DBA League 5th Round	Cremona, Italy	
Lausanne War Wyrm Tournament	Romanel, Switzerland	
SMC	San Marino	
Tournoi de AJSA d'Aubagne FoW	Aubagne, France	
Dadi.com	Milan, Italy	
Naoniscon	Pordenone, Italy	
Città di Verona	Verona, Italy	
Tournoi de Poitiers	Poitiers, France	
Tournoi FoW de Roquebrune	Roquebrune sur Argens, France	
Convention Day	Lille, France	
Convention des Sénéchaux	Biesles, France	
Convention de Chaumont	Chaumont, France	
Italian DBA League 6th Round	Pavia, Italy	
FoG Italian Teams	Faenza, Italy	
LinKon	Linköping, Sweden	June
AttritiCon DBM International	Ulm, Germany	
Tournoi de Strasbourg	Strasbourg, France	
Convention Nationale FoW	Floriac, France	
Helsinki FoW Doubles	Helsinki, Finland	
Montpellier FoG Tournoi	Montpellier, France	
Tournoi Impetus 'Desperata Ferro'	Barcelona, Spain	
Tournoi de Saumur	Saumur, France	
Avaricum Miniatures	Bourges, France	
Tournoi de Tournefeuille	Tournefeuille, France	
DBA Zürihegel	Zurich, Switzerland	
Cry Havoc WAB	Munich, Germany	
Levée en Masse	Kremlin-Bicêtre, France	
Tabletops United WAB Event	Munich, Germany	July
Amburger Clash	Amberg, Germany	
FOG Summer Tournament	Lisbon, Portugal	
Montmeló 15mm FoG tournament	Montmeló, Spain	
Avangardowe Potyczki FoW	Warsaw, Poland	
Sarissa – DBMM200	Milan, Italy	
Scandinavia in Flames FoW	Stockholm, Sweden	
Woreancon	Wildenburg, Germany	
KoMiCon	Koblenz, Germany	August
Mili-Saona	Savona, Italy	

Event	Place	Usual month
Dynamo FoW	Vejle, Denmark	September
CTSHS FoW Tournament	Seville, Spain	
International Team Challenge	Lisbon, Portugal	
Argentoratum WAB	Strasbourg, France	
Convention Lugdunum	Lyons, France	
Lausgames	Lodivecchio, Italy	
Berliner Spieltreffen	Berlin, Germany	
Giochi In Centro	Bassano, Italy	
Campionato FoG	Modena, Italy	
Tournoi de Clichy	Clichy, France	
Trophée Marc-Aurèle DBM	Colombier, Switzerland	October
Giocare con La Storia	Anzola, Italy	
Domenica Tourneo di Impetus	Como, Italy	
Duzi	Wesel, Germany	
Rhein Main Open Sky	Koblenz, Germany	
FoG Autumn Tournament	Lisbon, Portugal	
DBA Torneo	Arezzo, Italy	
Tournoi d'Aniche	Aniche, France	
The Sword & the Cross DBM200	Milan, Italy	
Lucca Comics & Games	Lucca, Italy	
SydCon	Malmö, Sweden	
Crisis	Antwerp, Belgium	November
DBA Torneo	Milan, Italy	
Convention de Mourmelon	Mourmelon, France	
Strait of Gibraltar Trophee	Algeçiras, Spain	
Stratejeux	Floirac, France	
Tournoi de Bordeaux	Bordeaux, France	
Tournoi La Porte Epique	Aniche, France	
What Tabletop Convention	Walddorfhäslach, Germany	
Fantastique Convention des Jeux	Brussels, Belgium	
Après-Midi DBA de la Horde d'Or	Asnieres, France	December
Tournoi de Rueil Malmaison	Rueil Malmaison, France	
Convention Parisienne du jeu d'histoire	Ballainvilliers, France	

REST OF THE WORLD

Event	Place	Usual month
Spartacon	Lansing, MI, USA	January
Winter Offensive	Temple Terrace, FL, USA	
SnowCon	Orono, ME, USA	
ConQuest NW	Seatlle, WA, USA	
The Siege of Augusta	Augusta, GA, USA	
Barrage	Baltimore, MD, USA	
NOVAG Gameday	Woodbridge, VA, USA	
Winter War	Champaign, IL, USA	
OwlCon	Houston, TX, USA	
Drumbeat	Seattle, WA, USA	
Cancon	Canberra, Australia	
Times of War	Hendra, Australia	
Templecon	Providence, RI, USA	February
Williamsburg Muster	Williamsburg, VA, USA	
Gottacon	Victoria, BC, Canada	
HoTT Wax	Worthington, OH, USA	
Genghis Con	Denver, CO, USA	
Radcon	Pasco, WA, USA	
OrcCon	Los Angeles, CA, USA	
Dundracon	San Ramon, CA, USA	
Battle at the Crossroads	Cambridge, OH, USA	
Dreamation	Morristown, NJ, USA	
TotalCon	Mansfield, MA, USA	
On Target	Fort Dix, NJ, USA	
Spring Maneuvers	Lawrence, KS, USA	
GZG ECC	Owego, NY, USA	
Battlecry	Auckland, New Zealand	
IWF World Individual Championships	Wellington, New Zealand	

Event	Place	Usual month
900 FoG Open San Hose	San Hose, CA, USA	March
Cold Wars	Lancaster, PA, USA	
Coastcon	Biloxi, MS, USA	
MMGA Recon	Coon Rapids, MN, USA	
Who's Yer Con	Indianapolis, IN, USA	
Fields of Honor Spring	Des Moines, IA, USA	
Brimfrost	Anchorage, AK, USA	
CosCon	Butler, PA, USA	
ConQuest SAC	Sacramento, CA, USA	
CincyCon	Cincinnati, OH, USA	
Legends of the Spring	Wauconda, IL, USA	
Conquest Vegas	Las Vegas, NV, USA	
Annual SYW Association Con	South Bend, IN, USA	
Battlefields	Dearborn, MI, USA	
Simcon	Rochester, NY, USA	
Recruits	Lee's Summit, MO, USA	
Hot Lead	Stratford, Ontario, Canada	
Smacdown GCC FoG	Biloxi, MS, USA	
Warband	Reading, OH, USA	
Southern Battle Gamers Australia Historical Competition	Sylvania Heights, Australia	
Canberra Invitational	Canberra, Australia	
Havoc	Shrewsbury, MA, USA	April
Trumpeter Salute	Burnaby, BC, Canada	
SynDCon	Washington, DC, USA	
Chimaeracon	San Antonio, TX, USA	
Mag-Con	New Caney, TX, USA	
Michigan Historical Collectables Show	Livonie, MI, USA	
Spring Fever	Raliegh, NC, USA	
Little Wars	Lincolnshire, IL, USA	
Pointcon	West Point, NY, USA	
Egypt Wars	Carbondale, IL, USA	
New Song BBDBA Tournament	Reynoldsburg, OH, USA	
Call to Arms	Kansas City, KS, USA	
Recon	Orlando, FL, USA	
Tank Shock	Danville, VA, USA	
Stoogecon	Pittsburgh, PA, USA	
HenryBrewer-Gus Sailors Memorial FoG Tournament	Birmingham, AL, USA	
Australian Historical Wargames Convention	McLaren Vale, Australia	
Wollongong Easter Competition	Wollongong, Australia	
Leviathan	Sydney, Australia	
NatCon	Upper Hutt, New Zealand	

Event	Place	Usual month
Great Canadian Baycon	Hamilton, Ontario, Canada	May
Mayday	Edmonton, Alberta, Canada	
FoGgy Spring Tournament	Columbus, OH, USA	
Battle Hymn	Richmond, VA, USA	
Annual Toy Soldier Show	Newport News, VA, USA	
NJCon	Kenilworth, NJ, USA	
Borderwars	Kansas City, KS, USA	
HuzzahCon	Portland, ME, USA	
Cangames	Ottawa, Canada	
Barracks Battles	Jefferson Barracks, MO, USA	
Drums Along the Rapids	Perrysburg, OH	
KingCon	Kingston, Ontario, Canada	
Conquest Denver	Denver, CO, USA	
Texicon	Fort Worth, TX, USA	
Enfilade	Olympia, WA, USA	
Nashcon	Franklin, TN, USA	
Kublacon	Burlingame, CA, USA	
Gamex	Los Angeles, CA, USA	
DBA With a Twist	Mawson, Australia	
Battle above the Brynderwyns	Whangarei, Australia	
Diecon	Collinsville, IL, USA	June
Prariecon	Brandon, Manitoba, Canada	
Novag Gamesday	Chantilly, VA, USA	
Consimworld Expo	Tempe, AZ, USA	
Michicon	Rochester, MI, USA	
Rapier	Jacksonville, FL, USA	
Bayou Wars	Kener, LA, USA	
Conquest Reno	Reno, NV, USA	
Day of Days	Menomonee Falls, WI, USA	
Battle Under the Big Top FoG	Loveland, OH, USA	
Origins	Columbus, OH, USA	
Recon	Cool Rapids, MN, USA	
NICon	Mt Muanganui, New Zealand	
WinterCon	Canberra, Australia	
ACT DBA Titles	Canberra, Australia	
Historicon	Valley Forge, PA, USA	July
Wargamescon	Austin, TX, USA	

Event	Place	Usual month
Gencon	Indianapolis, IN, USA	August
Heat of Battle	New Orleans, LA, USA	
Dragonflight	Seattle, WA, USA	
Guns of August	Williamsburg, VA, USA	
Skirmish	Plano, TX, USA	
Spearhead	Hazelwood, MO, USA	
Tagcon	Timaru, New Zealand	
Southern Battle Gamers Spring Historical Competition	Sylvania Heights, Australia	
Call to Arms	Wellington, New Zealand	
Tascticon	Denver, CO, USA	September
Pacificon	San Fransisco, CA, USA	
Gateway	Los Angeles, CA	
Hubcon	Hattiesburg, MS, USA	
FoWSA	San Antonio, TX, USA	
Wasteland Wars	Lubbock, TX, USA	
Fall Recruits	Lee's Summit, MO, USA	
Advance the Colors	Springfield, OH, USA	
Hurricon	Orlando, FL, USA	
Southern Front	Ralieg, NC, USA	
Fields of Honor	Des Moines, IA, USA	
Texas Broadside	Houston, TX, USA	
NowsCon	Sheffield Lake, OH, USA	
Conquest Oregon	Portland, OR, USA	October
Flatcon	Bloomington, IL, USA	
Council of the Five Nations	Albany, NY, USA	
Tactical Solutions	Spokane Valley, WA, USA	
OshCon	Oshkosh, WI, USA	
Migscon	Hamilton, Ontario, Canada	
Charcon	Charleston, WV, USA	
Fall In	Lancaster, PA, USA	
MOAB	Sydney, Australia	
Tormentus DBA	Hawthorn East, Australia	
Conquest	Christchurch, New Zealand	

Event	Place	Usual month
Rock Con	Rockford, IL, USA	November
Kansas City Games Fair	Kansas City, MO, USA	
Conquest SoCal	Orange County, CA, USA	
PentaCon	Fort Wayne, IN, USA	
Luthercon	Chicago, IL, USA	
Fort Meigs Games Day	Perrysburg, OH, USA	
Command Con	St Louis, MO, USA	
Erie's Day of Gaming	Erie, PA, USA	
Colonial Barracks	New Orleans, LA, USA	
Millennium	Austin, TX, USA	
Ucon	Ann Arbour, MI, USA	
Cold Iron FoG	Birmingham, AL, USA	
Landwaster DBA	Mawson, Australia	
WinterCon	Rochester, MI, USA	December
South African Nationals	Lower Houghton, SA	

SELECT BIBLIOGRAPHY

In a work such as this, a full bibliography is rendered somewhat unnecessary because of the constant references to a wide range of books and magazines dealing with the hobby from the outset. The Index kindly compiled for me by Arthur Harman is also very thorough and provides references to all the works covered in this book.

What I thought might be more useful is a short list of just a few of the useful works that have informed my understanding of military history over the years, in the hope that those new to the hobby, and new to historical wargaming in particular, will be able to use this as a starting point for their own, further research into those periods that interest them. There is a particular emphasis on the horse and musket era because of the inclusion of my *Shot, Steel and Stone* rules in this book. Some of the original editions of these works are now out of print but are well worth hunting down as reprints, on online auction houses and – where they still exist – in public libraries and second-hand bookshops.

This list only includes work in the English language. There are, of course, a plethora of other titles written in other languages, particularly French, German, Italian and Spanish, to which the wargamer can fruitfully turn should he have the language skills, armed with a good dictionary and the many automated translation applications now available.

General Military Histories, Theory etc.

The Art of War, Baron Antoine Henri de Jomini, Greenhill Books, 1992

The Art of War in the Western World, Archer Jones, Harrap, London, 1988

Decisive Battles of the Western World: Volume 1 from the Earliest Times to the Battle of Lepanto, J. F. C. Fuller, Book Club Associates, 2003

Decisive Battles of the Western World: Volume 2 from the Defeat of the Spanish Armada to Waterloo, J. F. C. Fuller, Book Club Associates, 2003

Decisive Battles of the Western World: Volume 3 from the American Civil War to the End of the Second World War, J. F. C. Fuller, Book Club Associates, 2003

Dictionary of Wars, George C. Kohn, Facts on File Publications, Oxford, 1986

The Encyclopedia of Military History from 3,500 B.C. to the Present, R. Ernest Dupuy and Trevor N. Dupuy, Harper & Row, New York, 1986

The Face of Battle, John Keegan, Book Club Associates, London, 1978

A Military History of Germany, Martin Kitchen, Weidenfeld & Nicolson, London, 1975

On War, Carl von Clausewitz, ed. A. Rapoport, Penguin, 1982

Supplying War: Logistics from Wallenstein to Patton, Martin van Creveld, Cambridge University Press, 1977

The Sword and the Pen: Selections from the World's Greatest Military Writings, Sir Basil Liddell Hart, Ed. Adrian Liddell Hart, Cassell, London, 1978

War in European History, Michael Howard, Oxford university Press, 1979

Yours to Reason Why, William Seymour, Book Club Associates, London, 1982

Period-Specific Titles

The American Civil War, John Keegan, Vintage Books, London, 2009

The Annals of Imperial Rome, Tacitus, Penguin Classics, 1996

Armies and Warfare in Europe 1648-1789, John Childs, Manchester University Press, Manchester, 1982

The Art of Warfare in the Age of Marlborough, David Chandler, Spellmount, Staplehurst, 1997

The Austro-Prussian War: Austria's War with Prussia and Italy in 1866, Geoffrey Wawro, Cambridge University Press, 1998

Battles of the American Revolution, Curt Johnson, Sampson Low, Maidenhead, 1975

The Campaigns of Alexander, Arrian, Penguin Classics, 1979

The Campaigns of Napoleon, David Chandler, Weidenfeld, London, 1966

Cromwell Our Chief of Men, Antonia Fraser, Granada Publishing, London, 1977

Dictionary of the Napoleonic Wars, David Chandler, Arms & Armour Press, London, 1979

Edgehill 1642: the Campaign and the Battle, Peter Young, The Roundwood Press, 1967

Firepower: Weapons Effectiveness on the Battlefield, 1630-1850, Major-General B. P. Hughes, Spellmount, 1997

Fire & Stone: the Science of Fortress Warfare 1660-1860, Christopher Duffy, David & Charles, London, 1975

The Fortress in the Age of Marlborough and Frederick the Great, 1660-1789: Siege Warfare Volume II, Christopher Duffy, Routledge & Kegan Paul, London, 1985

Forward Into Battle: Fighting Tactics from Waterloo to Vietnam, Paddy Griffith, Antony Bird Publications, Chichester, 1981

The Franco-Prussian War, Michael Howard, Methuen, 1981

Frederick the Great, A Military Life, Christopher Duffy, Routledge & Kegan Paul, London, 1985

The Histories, Herodotus, Penguin Classics, 1996

Liddell Hart's History of the Second World War, B. H. Liddell Hart, Book CLub Associates, London, 1973

Marlborough as Military Commander, David Chandler, Spellmount, Tunbridge Wells, 1989

The Military Experience in the Age of Reason, Christopher Duffy, Routledge & Kegan Paul, London, 1987

Napoleon's Cavalry and its Leaders, David Johnson, B.T. Batsford, London, 1978

Napoleon's Great Adversaries: the Archduke Charles and the Austrian Army 1792-1814, Gunther E. Rothenberg, B. T. Batsford Ltd, London, 1982

The Persian Expedition, Xenophon, Penguin Classics, 1972

The Recollections of Rifleman Harris (as Told to Henry Curling), Ed. Christopher Hibbert, Century, London, 1970

Roots of Strategy: the 5 Greatest Military Classics of All Time, Ed. Brig. Gen. T. R. Phillips, Stackpole Books, Harrisburg, 1985

The Sharp End of War: the Fighting Man of World War II, John Ellis, Corgi Books, 1980

The Thirty Years' War, Geoffrey Parker, Routledge, London, 1987

Weapons and Equipment of the Marlborough Wars, Anthony Kemp, Blandford Press, Poole, 1980

Weapons & Equipment of the Napoleonic Wars, Philip Haythornthwaite, Blandford, Poole, 1979

Wellington Commander: the Iron Duke's Generalship, Ed. Paddy Griffith, Antony Bird Publications, 1985

INDEX

Wargame Figures, Painting, Manufacture etc.

Wargame Genres & Periods

Wargame Rules

Wargames in general

Websites

Pictures

Charts & Diagrams

Historical Artifacts

Illustrations Of Uniforms etc.

Wargame Books, Rules & Magazines [Alpha Order by Title]

Wargame Figures

Wargame Figures: Manufacture, Painting etc.

Wargames [Arranged by Historical Period]

Wargame Tables & Scenery

Wargames Miscellanea

AFTERWORD

It was perhaps inevitable that events would overtake the writing of this book, given that I was first commissioned to write it in 2009 and finally delivered it in 2013! During this time, the fortunes of my bi-monthly magazine *Battlegames* rose, fell, then rose again and finally, in February 2013, came to a close, when Atlantic Publishers asked me to completely redesign and take over the reins of the monthly *Miniature Wargames*, which has been given more pages and re-branded *Miniature Wargames* with *Battlegames*.

After what has been a long and challenging journey, this turn of events seems extraordinary to me, but I look forward to sailing this grand three-decker, a veteran of 30 years covering the hobby, which will seem very odd after captaining my cheeky little frigate for so long.

The new *Miniature Wargames* will have all the flavour of *Battlegames* plus a great deal more besides, so by the time you read this, I hope that you will already be aware of, and indeed enjoying, my new command.

Henry Hyde,
Hove, February 2013

**FORTHCOMING BOOKS FOR WARGAMERS
FROM PEN & SWORD**

Painting Wargaming Miniatures by Javier Gomez Valero

Battlefields in Miniature: Modelling Effective Terrain for Wargames by Paul Davies

Kevin Dallimore's Guide to Painting WW2 Miniatures by Kevin Dallimore

Kevin Dallimore's Guide to Painting Renaissance Miniatures by Kevin Dallimore